To
Wishing you
happy travels!
Jeannette
Belliveau

An Amateur's Guide to the Planet

12 ADVENTURE JOURNEYS AND LESSONS FOR THE CONTEMPORARY UNITED STATES:

MADAGASCAR
The Earth's Fragility

CHINA
Emigration

BORNEO
Modern Missionaries

KENYA AND TANZANIA
Our Love-Hate
Relationship to Africa

JAPAN
Formal Societies

POLYNESIA
Why Culture Survives

THAILAND
Ultimate Sailing

GREECE
National Greatness and Decline

THE YUCATAN
Parallel Evolution

JAVA AND BALI
How We View Heaven

BURMA
Poverty

BRAZIL
Racial Democracy

PUBLISHED BY BEAU MONDE PRESS

Beau Monde Press
P.O. Box 6149
Baltimore, MD   21231-6149

A portion of this work appeared in different form in
The Washington Post and the *Baltimore Sun*.

Front cover photographs
Sky over Phuket island, Thailand
Ngorongoro Crater, Tanzania
Ko Racha Yai, Thailand

Back cover photograph
Long Ampung, Borneo

Title page photograph
Mahakam River, Borneo

Publisher's Cataloging-in-Publication Data
(Prepared by Quality Books Inc.)
Belliveau, Jeannette.
  An amateur's guide to the planet: 12 adventure jour-
neys and lessons for the contemporary United States /
Jeannette Belliveau.
p.cm.
Includes bibliographical references and index.
Preassigned LCCN: 96-96767
ISBN 0-9652344-4-4
  1. Belliveau, Jeannette--Journeys. 2. Voyages and
travels.
I. Title.
G465.B45 1996 910.4
    QBI96-40210

Manufactured in the United States of America by the
John D. Lucas Printing Co. of Baltimore, Md, using the
Screen Taiga Computer-to-Plate System.

Grateful acknowledgement is made to the following for permission to reprint previously published material:

Paul Simon Music: Excerpt from the song lyrics
to "Cecilia," © 1969 Paul Simon/Paul Simon
Music (BMI).

Excerpts from the English translation of the
Catechism of the Catholic Church for use in the
United States of America © 1994 United States
Catholic Conference—Libreria Editrice Vaticana.
Used with permission.

Excerpts from *Japan: A Travel Survival Kit* 3rd ed.
© 1989 Lonely Planet. Used with permission.

Excerpt from "Dr. Seuss and Dr. Einstein:
Children's Books and Scientific Imagination," by
Chet Raymo, *The Horn Book Magazine*, Sept./Oct.
1992, reprinted by permission of the Horn Book
Inc., 11 Beacon St., Suite 1000, Boston, MA 02108.

Excerpt from *The Geography Behind History* by W.
Gordon East. Copyright © 1965 by W. W. Norton
& Company Inc. Reprinted by permission of W.
W. Norton & Company Inc.

Excerpt from *The Serengeti Lion: A Study of
Predator-Prey Relations* by George B. Schaller.
Copyright © 1972 by the University of Chicago
Press. Used with permission.

Excerpt from the *American Journal of Clinical
Nutrition*, 1991; 53:1586S-94S © 1991 The
American Society for Clinical Nutrition.

Excerpt from the *New York Times*, "Tokyo Journal:
Why a Nation of Apologizers Makes One Large
Exception." © 1995. The New York Times Co.
Reprinted by permission.

Excerpt from *Civilization: Past and Present,* by
Wallbank, T. Walter et al, © 1971, Scott Foresman
and Co.   Reprinted by permission of
HarperCollins College Publishers.

Excerpt from "In Praise of the Natural Dog" ©
1993, *HSUS News*, The Humane Society of the
United States (Washington, DC 20037).

Excerpt from *Oceania and Beyond: Essays on the
Pacific since 1945* © 1976, reprinted with permis-
sion of Greenwood Publishing Group Inc.,
Westport, Conn.

Excerpt from *Funny Business: An Outsider's Year
in Japan* © 1989 reprinted by permission of Soho
Press, New York.

Excerpts from *The Odyssey* by Homer, translated
by E.V. Rieu (Penguin Classics, 1946) copyright ©
the Estate of E.V. Rieu, 1946. Reproduced by permission of Penguin Books Ltd.

10   9   8   7   6   5   4   3   2   1

An Amateur's Guide to the Planet

TWELVE ADVENTURE JOURNEYS AND LESSONS
FOR THE CONTEMPORARY UNITED STATES

BY JEANNETTE BELLIVEAU

BEAU MONDE

To my parents, Louis and Mary Belliveau, my husband, Lamont W.

Harvey, and my sisters and brothers and their families, who always lent

a hand: Maureen, Glenn, Matt and Julia Gardner, Sharon Belliveau

and Rob Pavesovich and Sarah Rapalus, Carol and Bill Alderson, Jim

and Judy Belliveau and Paul Belliveau. And to Beau for listening

with doggy patience to absurd rhetorical questions as I wrote.

A portion of the proceeds of this book have been

donated to support the care of a black lemur named

Polydorus as part of the Adopt-A-Lemur program

at the Duke University Primate Center in Durham, North Carolina.

For more information on the program:

- Call 919.489.3364

- Send electronic mail to primate@acpub.duke.edu

- Write to the Duke University Primate Center,
  3705 Erwin Road, Durham, NC 27705

THE AGE OF ADVENTURE TRAVEL

We roam the globe yet lack insight into what we see

Mary G. and Louis J. Belliveau, left, and Lamont Weston Harvey.

A fascinating phenomenon began with the commercial introduction of the jet engine in 1958 and accelerated with the coming to affluence of the Baby Boomers in the 1980s. Exotic travel, once the province of explorers, traders, scholars and pilgrims, became a pastime for average people as well. Frankly written guidebooks detailing how to go places on your own and the opening of China to the West contributed to the trend. Nearly 10 million Americans a year, for example, now visit non-European foreign destinations.

People from Santa Barbara, California, touch the Great Wall of China. Folks from Rockville, Maryland, encounter each other in remote Madagascar. Honeymooning New Yorkers learn about medicinal plants from Amazonian Indians. Norwegians puzzle over Maya pyramids, Parisians visit Burmese temples and Swiss and Quebeçois hike the ridges of Borneo.

And just when more of us are being guided about by tribespeople to gaze at giant mammals, rare forests and historic ruins, the limited focus of the U.S. educational system and the historical insularity of media coverage mean that fewer of us have the background to grasp much of the significance of what we are viewing.

Regular people with typical, provincial U.S. schooling may find that travel stimulates lingering questions about the way the world fits together.

In this book, I attempt to resolve a decade's worth of riddles resulting from my adventure travels and to apply lessons from these journeys, where possible, to understanding the United States. To do so, I consulted top scholars and foreign correspondents in each subject area, and 600 book and periodical references. Two people in particular patiently provided historical and economic perspective useful to understanding the foreign world: my husband, Lamont Weston Harvey, an artist and historian with an extensive private collection of military and African history books, and my father, Louis J. Belliveau, a retired nuclear physicist and Jesuit-educated polymath.

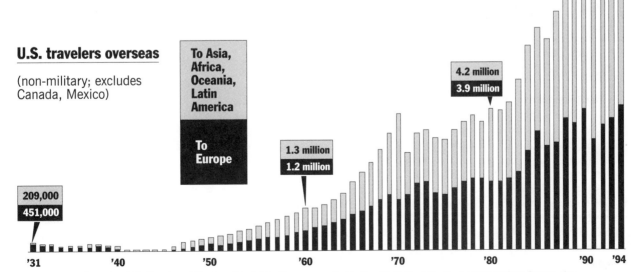

U.S. travelers overseas

(non-military; excludes Canada, Mexico)

To Asia, Africa, Oceania, Latin America

To Europe

9.9 million
8.2 million

4.2 million
3.9 million

1.3 million
1.2 million

209,000
451,000

'31   '40   '50   '60   '70   '80   '90 '94

Based on data from the U.S. Travel and Tourism Administration as reported in the *Statistical Abstract of the United States*; the International Trade Administration, Tourism Industries; and from the Census Bureau's *Historical Statistics of the United States*

Travel makes events in vaguely imagined faraway places as tangible as a pebble caught in your shoe. And nations in the developing world shed enormous light back on Western issues, including poverty, nuclear power, national greatness and decline, immigration and even etiquette. Yet these lessons take ideologically unpredictable directions. The adventure traveler may begin to feel a gap between his or her outlook and others' views. Experiences gleaned around the globe may make one wildly pro-environment, thunderously conservative on the traditional family, and cautiously optimistic about U.S. race relations.

My hope is that anyone who has visited any of these regions in the way I have, as an amateur traveler, will find that this book sheds light on his or her own explorations.

If you have not yet been to the places mentioned, by all means consider going. Many world treasures appear to be more impermanent than you would wish. These include the Maya pyramids, the lemurs of Madagascar, the Buddhist culture of Burma, the pyrotechnic corals of Thailand and the elephants of East Africa.

Please take great care in selecting local transportation and try to avoid ramshackle domestic air connections or bus lines. Make certain that your money gets into the hands of local families who run small lodgings, eateries and guide services. Then your travel will be of

most benefit to all concerned.

Jeannette Belliveau
Baltimore, Maryland,
U.S.A.
August 1996

Acknowledgments

Numerous scholars and foreign correspondents made suggestions of incalculable worth:

Professor Alison Jolly, Princeton University, author of *A World Like Our Own: Man and Nature in Madagascar*, reviewed the text on Madagascar.

Jay Mathews, author with wife Linda of *One Billion: A China Chronicle* and chief of *The Washington Post's* first bureau in Beijing, made suggestions for the China chapter.

Professor Jérôme Rousseau of McGill University and **Professor Allen R. Maxwell** of the University of Alabama reviewed the chapter on Borneo.

University of California at Berkeley **Professor Neil Henry**, former *Washington Post* bureau chief in Nairobi, reviewed the material on Kenya and Tanzania.

Fumiko Mori Halloran, author of six books written in Japanese explaining the United States to her home country's readers and a contributor to *Japan Update*, and her husband, **Richard Halloran**, former Tokyo bureau chief for the *New York Times*, reviewed the Japan chapter.

Professor Yosihiko Sinoto of the Bishop Museum in Honolulu, Hawaii, an authority on comparative Polynesian cultures, and **Professor Lynne Withey** of the University of California at Berkeley, author of *Voyages of Discovery: Captain Cook and the Exploration of the Pacific*, reviewed the chapter on Polynesia.

Tina Sverdrup, a Colorado-based cruising sailor of wide experience, reviewed the chapter on Thailand.

Yoriko Kishimoto, co-author with Joel Kotkin of *The Third Century: America's Resurgence in the Asian Era*, reviewed the chapter on Greece.

Professor Flora S. Clancy of the University of New Mexico, author of *Pyramids, Vision and Revision in Maya Studies* and *Maya: Treasures of an Ancient Civilization* reviewed the chapter on the Yucatan.

Maureen Aung-Thwin, Burma Project director at the Open Society in New York, and **Patrick F. Fagan**, William H.G. FitzGerald Senior Fellow in Family and Cultural Issues at the Heritage Foundation, Washington, D.C., reviewed the chapter on Burma.

Lecturer Tim Behrend of the University of Auckland, New Zealand, an expert on Javanese and Balinese culture, and **Professor Colleen McDannell**, Religious Studies Chair, University of Utah, and author of *Heaven: A History* reviewed the chapter on Java and Bali.

Professor George Reid Andrews of the University of Pittsburgh reviewed the chapter on Brazil, as did **Diana Jean Schemo**, bureau chief, Rio de Janeiro, *The New York Times*; and **Jerry Davila**, Brown University doctoral candidate in Rio de Janeiro.

•••

Keith Sinzinger, Beth Chang and **Tom Kavanagh** of *The Washington Post* and **Ned White** of the Library of Congress edited brilliantly and insightfully. *Washington Post* cartographer **Dave Cook** reviewed the maps. **Sheryl Segal** provided art direction and design consultation. **Curtis Branker** of System Source gave computer advice. **Mike Donnelly, Kate Niemczyk** and other staff of the **Enoch Pratt Free Library** in Baltimore helped find books, periodicals and maps.

Assistance and encouragement were also provided by **David Simon,** author of *Homicide;* **Frank Sietzen,** author of *Apollo 11;* **Jack** and **Marsha Youngblood,** authors of *Positive Involvement: How to Teach Your Child Habits for School Success;* **Graeme Browning**, author of *If Everyone Bought One Shoe;* **Dr. Winston C. Murray** of Morgan State University; **Barbara J. Saffir** of *The Washington Post;* frequent travelers **Marcelo Sánchez, Janet Lottero, Jane Burtnett, Eddie** and **Ginny Earnshaw** and **Audrey Haar**; and most of all travel companions **Jim Belliveau, Sharon Belliveau, Stephany Porter, Michael Kaye, Marci Hartl, Edward Fowler, Steve Wright, Suzanne Loudermilk, Nick** and **Eleanora Dorfman** and **Madeline Leventhol.**

CONTENTS

A lioness studies distant zebra in Kenya's Masai Mara game park.

EDEN UNDER SIEGE

Madagascar … and lessons on the Earth's fragility

Two black lemurs beg from Jim.

G etting to Madagascar has been difficult for, oh, 165 million years. Way back then the island, about the size of California and Oregon, split off and drifted east from the giant parent continent that also calved Africa.

Remoteness made the island one of the last sizable places to be settled by humans and virtually the only place left (aside from the nearby Comoro Islands) where lemurs, an ancient ancestor of humans, still live.

SUNDAY, JULY 16, 1989
The middle of the African night

Even in the 20th century, our shaky air tickets attested to the continuing isolation and lack of flights to the Big Red Island. Our cheap digital watches, selected to be unattractive to thieves, blinked 3:45 a.m. as we stood in deserted Jomo Kenyatta International Airport in Nairobi. Empty darkness surrounded the check-in booth for Air Madagascar. We'd come 7,500 miles from Washington, D.C., without any assurance that we could complete the final 1,400 miles to our goal: the rare creatures of this mysterious island off southern Africa.

We wanted to see lemurs.

Anyone who has happened across a documentary on lemurs, or seen them in a zoo, will perhaps understand the impulse to travel halfway around the world to engage them in the wild. While riotously colored birds soar in Brazil, and Africa displays the most magnificent big creatures anywhere, nothing quite beats lemurs for quirky, almost alien charm. If you crossed a monkey from outer space with a basket of puppies, you might approximate their big bright eyes, foxlike muzzles and gregariousness. No other creature seems so peculiar yet winsome.

Getting to the lemurs' homeland proved especially tricky for us as budget travelers making our own arrangements. Our cut-rate air tickets meant that our names appeared on a waiting list, rather than con-

firmed, to board the three-hour flight from Nairobi to Antananarivo, Madagascar's capital.

Innocent as lambs, with inexplicable optimism, we stood first in our imaginary line, lacking any agents to talk to or other passengers to be in front of. At moments like this, you question everything: Is this the place? Is this the day? Is this the time? Is there even a remote possibility that we're going to Madagascar?

Our intrepid group consisted of my brother, Jim, 28 at the time of our trip, our friend, Stephany, 25, and me, the senior of the group at 35. We all grew up and lived in Maryland, where Jim ran his own company, Steph worked in computer sales, and I at the time edited financial articles at the *Baltimore Sun*. We seemed to have similar tastes in travel and had sailed the storm-tossed seas of Greece, of which more later.

Internal group chemistry worked well. Jim is generous, Steph tends toward frugality, I'm cheap. We found a middle ground. I would read up on a place; they would conveniently agree to go. Physically imposing and personable, Jim would find himself hugely popular with similarly big and friendly Africans in local bars. Observant and cheerful, Steph could out-track most wildlife guides. The two of them tended to be invariably easygoing, I less reliably so. I suspect I have the flaky journalist's talent at being self-centered, judgmental, and prone to episodes of withdrawing and observing the surroundings. Still, I could handle logistics, read between the lines of travel guides to find the hidden gems and learn the first 30 essential words of the local language.

As American budget travelers, we presented a bit of an unusual sight in Africa, more than we anticipated. As backpackers, we differed from package tourists. We tried—successfully, according to several Kenyans—to look like U.S. Peace Corps volunteers: khakis, T-shirts and not a scrap of jewelry. We occupied an unusual niche in the tourist economy, less well off than those circuiting the safari lodges but far better

Reasons to roam the world

Trips such as this one to Africa provide the best and most complete way for us to learn about the world. Our grade school textbooks did discuss foreign countries. But the texts focused on topics that seemed lifeless to me, such as iron ore mining and grapefruit crops. Several patronizing photographs in one showed Africans being supervised by whites in textile mills and health clinics.

Later in our lives, the U.S. evening news slighted foreign countries—to an extent only apparent when I moved to England in the 1980s and watched BBC reports.

And Jim and I, not the best candidates for learning things in a classroom, take to the road as our teacher. When we learn about a place like Belize or Burma, the education takes place through our eyes, the soles of our feet and the words of our boulevard professors: wildlife guides and riverboat mates, market sellers and taverna owners, dhow captains and fellow travelers.

Possibly Acadians operate this way. Our untutored Nova Scotia ancestors seemed to just know, somehow, how to build boats, trap lobster, raise mink and harvest rhubarb. Acadians seem rarely inclined to sit in Georgetown University's foreign relations classes when they could be fixing a tractor or playing hockey. Rather than consult Kissinger's tomes, which we would find both unforgivably amoral and sinfully ponderous, we peruse the "Facts About the Country" chapter in our guidebook, usually one in the Lonely Planet series of Sydney-based backpackers' bibles. Thus we rely heavily on a vagabond writer in the employ of an Australian publisher to place our street observations into a historical framework. We pray that our guidebook has its facts more or less right.

We roam so far partly out of simple curiosity, partly because adventure travel provides us with magic and ritual, commodities lacking in our upbringing in the 1950s and early '60s. Growing up in suburban Washington, D.C., we never experienced the kind of dramatic pageantry that many cultures find essential: Papuans in war paint, Indonesians in demon masks, dancing Masai or weaving Chinese dragons.

funded than many fellow backpackers, especially Australians, who usually had to stretch their budget over a year rather than a month.

As to our fitness to be true citizens of the world, we knew our qualifications to be suspect. Our language abilities lagged those of Europeans, who generally spoke several tongues. So-so at current events and truly feeble at world history, we didn't have the patience to wade through most foreign reportage, with its buzzwords such as—

> military deployment
> bilateral agreement
> a round of talks in Geneva.

Our preferred reading before a trip takes a lighter touch and relies more on street-level experience and unofficial sources of information. We like Dave Barry ("I don't do research") and P.J. O'Rourke ("No interviews with heads of state or major figures on the international scene"). A content analysis of O'Rourke's *Holidays in Hell* finds such reader-friendly phrases as:

> free drinks
> a parrot in the bar
> 25 gin and tonics in a row.

Though more alcohol saturated than ours, his worldview exhibits roughly the same spirit as our blithe, lowbrow excursions in search of good weather, local color and a bit of adventure.

Collectively, we'd seen much of Europe and Asia by the late 1980s. As we grew older, we acquired the time, money and inclination to visit Africa. Jim, Steph and I each arranged a month's vacation. As the core of our trip, we picked the famous game parks of Kenya and Tanzania, allotting 20 days there. Our remaining time permitted one additional destination. We wanted something exotic, with even rarer wildlife than East Africa's rhinos and cheetahs. We debated whether to add Rwanda (gorillas) or Madagascar (lemurs).

"Madagascar is Eden under siege," I said. "I read an article in *The [Washington] Post* saying that it's now or never to see the lemurs."

Of all Madagascar wildlife, the most celebrated are the 40 kinds of lemurs. ... They vary from the mouse lemur, several of which will fit in a teacup when young, to the relatively giant indri, a spectacular animal in thick white-and-black fur, 40 inches tall. It leaps backward, turning in the air to land on another tree 30 feet distant, and its cry, or 'song' as it is always called, can be heard by human ears for a mile and a half.

Henry Mitchell in "180 Million Years Not Enough for Madagascar," *The Washington Post*

In his article, Henry Mitchell had described petting a brown lemur "with fur of softest velvet," letting ring-tailed lemurs jump on him and viewing ermine-white sifaka lemurs. Mitchell made it clear that the Big Red Island should be considered a wonder of the planet, and a disappearing one, like the pyramids in the Yucatan. His unwritten message: Go now or you'll never see it.

We took heed. We would attempt to be among the tiny number of Americans ever to visit Madagascar.

Beyond lemur sightings, we also sought stories,

adventure and good photos. And Madagascar would deliver a full range of road lessons, graduate-level exercises in Adventure Travel 701.

Without telling Jim and Steph, I watched them with pride throughout this trip, especially as we stood patiently in our metaphysical line that morning at Jomo Kenyatta International Airport. I'd gotten to Africa at the age of 35 as part of an orderly progression: first driving around the United States, then living in and bicycle touring through Europe, and later backpacking through Asia. Jim and Steph were learning on a curve far steeper than mine. They had jumped right into the deep end from the high diving board. Remarkably, with any luck from Air Mad, they would see Madagascar before they laid eyes on San Francisco, London or Paris.

LESSON NUMBER 1: IN THE LATTER 20TH CENTURY, KIDS FROM THE MOST ORDINARY AMERICAN SUBURBS WOULD OUTWANDER MARCO POLO.

When the ticket agents eventually showed up, we clung to our positions, first in a (by now) real line. An agent assigned us the only three seats remaining—high fives! Behind us, two unhappy doctors trying to get to the Seychelles via Madagascar argued strenuously for seats. With so few air routes in this part of the world, to miss a flight was to be stranded.

Perhaps they had to rush home to save lives, perhaps they just felt like pulling rank. In either event, no one challenged us to cede our seats, and we didn't dream of offering. We wanted to see lemurs. And we'd done one smart thing, with our precarious tickets, that the doctors had not: gotten there first.

By the slimmest of margins, with a casual confidence that seemed barely warranted in hindsight, we took to the air, on our way to Madagascar. Hundreds of Malagasy (generally pronounced Mal-GASH by those we encountered), some darkly beautiful, some average, also were aboard.

The lone 747 of the Air Madagascar fleet would convey us to the land of lemurs. Air Madagascar had sacrificed a herd of zebu—hardy humpbacked oxen of Asiatic origin—in an offering to the air safety god when the plane entered service. We'd take any edge we could, including superstition, when flying these Third World carriers.

Violá—the stunning sight of Kilimanjaro could be viewed from the right-hand windows. The world's highest freestanding mountain rises straight up out of the plain. Its solo bulk in the middle of the gradually curving Earth made the sight of it from the air much more impressive than the jumbled Alps. After camping at its base for two days earlier, we finally saw it free of clouds.

The attendants served us magnificent croissants,

From our airplane window, we could finally see Mount Kilimanjaro, the world's highest freestanding mountain.

jam and French roast coffee, confirmation that we had joined a flight originating in Paris. At this time, I knew only four people who had traveled or lived in Africa. Their stories focused on how crummy or nonexistent the food had been during hard times in Tanzania and Zimbabwe. Disposed to believe the worst, I had imagined we would be eking out meals of Spam and ground cornmeal broken out of relief agency packages—not buttery, flaky croissants.

8:30 A.M.
Stonewashed jackets in the middle of nowhere

The 747 crossed the Mozambique Channel and flew over the Big Red Island. What a mess it was: nude rust-colored earth, a few lonely trees clinging by muddy rivers. We found it easy to believe that the nation, the most eroded in the world, verged on being nine-tenths deforested. Its level of treelessness was more common to Europe, after millennia of settlement, than a young Third World country.

At 9:30 a.m., we stepped onto the tarmac of the airport outside Antananarivo. Inside, we picked up our bags and cleared with the informally dressed customs agents: two tallish Malagasy youths with long black Indonesian hair, handsome in their stonewashed jean jackets.

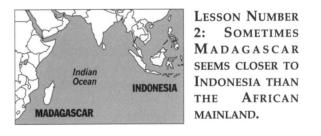

Indian Ocean

INDONESIA

MADAGASCAR

LESSON NUMBER 2: SOMETIMES MADAGASCAR SEEMS CLOSER TO INDONESIA THAN THE AFRICAN MAINLAND.

The trendy jean jackets telegraphed the first dislocating inkling of modernity in this Third World nation. The raven hair offered the first hint of Asia in Africa. One of several competing theories holds that seafaring Indonesians hopscotched along the coasts of India, Arabia and Africa, and 1,500 years ago finally settled in Madagascar.

In the airport proper, we bought tickets from the domestic Air Mad counter to go straight on to the tropical island of Nosy Be, "Big Island" in Malagasy. The agent, unnecessarily mysterious and abrupt, angrily refused my Visa card and demanded Jim's American Express. Ah, the perils of modern travel—where the

Our guide on Nosy Be, Monsieur Abdul, a master of pantomime.

early explorers feared unknown fevers and hostile locals, we confront the unacceptability of certain credit cards.

Finally we boarded the 2:20 p.m. flight. I stretched out and slept, and then forced myself to look out the window at more tortured, gullied red earth 10,000 feet below. The extent of erosion damage was striking even from an airplane's height.

Outside the airport at Nosy Be, a Monsieur Abdul, though we'd never seen him before, picked us up smoothly as if representing a previously booked five-star hotel. A delightful Arab-blooded Malagasy (Nosy Be lies on the northwest side of Madagascar, closest to the Islamic world), he had several points in his favor: energy, hustle and the ability to make himself understood, via carefully enunciated French combined with body English and telepathy.

M. Abdul took us for a tour combined with a reconnaissance for lodgings. As we departed the airport, Nosy Be unrolled beneath our hired wheels: a classical tropical paradise, with palms and balmy scented air and a vibrant quality to the light. Women rolled their hips as they strolled at roadside with baskets on their heads. Steph spotted long-tailed drongo birds and chameleons.

During our hour-long drive, whim inspired Abdul to stop often. He snapped off sweet-smelling ylang-ylang blossoms, used to make perfume, and bought mangoes at a simple wooden stand. He pulled his open, wind-bathed Peugeot to the side of the road to light cigarettes. Baling wire and spit seem to keep the

Skyscapes floated above the main island of Madagascar.

French vehicle together. Ken Kesey's Merry Pranksters would have loved its trippy, neon green color. The car's lack of operating window handles and glass actually proved to be a boon on this perfumed isle.

Abdul took us to the island's main town, the inaptly named Hell-Ville, population 6,000. It takes its name from one Admiral de Hell, of whom we, history impaired as always, knew nothing.

A stunning view of the coast of mainland Madagascar greeted us on the balcony of our room in Hell-Ville's Hotel de la Mer. Across the riffle of a marine-blue channel, 20 miles of pale slate-blue mountains rose on the mainland, under armadas of pink and cerise clouds. Square-rigged dhows, freighters and yachts plied the waters.

Untended poinsettias worthy of a botanical garden flourished just below our balcony, along with banana palms spreading magnificent 10-foot fronds. The foliage supported a spider the size of my hand resting in a six-foot web.

Madagascar seemed incredibly exotic and far lusher than Lamu on Kenya's coast (our previous R&R stop). Beautiful vistas that defied belief formed our first impression. Strange Indian Ocean light bathed the tropical landscape: not the gold of Florence or the yellow of Greece, but violets and reds of startling hue in the sky, clouds and roadside trees.

Meanwhile, back inside our room we enjoyed a less scenic view of ugly burnt-orange walls. In the bathroom, the toilet didn't flush, requiring us to throw buckets of water down it. The light bulb lay on a mirror, and its cord needed to be plugged in for every use. Our room cost $18 a night ($6 each), and we couldn't figure out if that made it a bargain or a ripoff.

Monday, July 17
Insights into videos and child-rearing

Even on the most exotic trip, on some days you see lemurs and some days you wash out your socks in the sink. The latter occurs especially when you're on a budget tour and making your own arrangements, a time-consuming process. We got a lot done on this logistics and errands day, and experienced some intriguing interactions with the local people as well.

Our first order of business involved walking to the bank to cash $300 of traveler's checks. (I wondered: How did the bank clerk view this? For many Malagasy, $300 represented more than a year's income.)

Next we visited the offices of the Bureau d'Eaux et Forets, the government agency in charge of permits to visit lemur parks. The officials there could not help us with permits for Montagne d'Ambre, a national park we planned to visit in a few days on the main island of

Madagascar. They said we must arrange this later, when we reach Diego.

LESSON NUMBER 3: THE ONLY THING RARER IN MADAGASCAR THAN LEMURS ARE THE GOVERNMENT OFFICIALS WHO CONTROL ACCESS TO THEM.

With our errands complete or at least attempted, we ventured to take the pulse of Hell-Ville. At the market, a place of groundcloths and little wooden stands, vendors sold their wares: large bananas, small finger bananas, fish, Chinese buttons and padlocks, tomatoes, cloves, cinnamon, okra, peppercorns and meat. Dark brown vanilla pods, shaped like string beans, lay displayed on white cloths. The smell permeated the place and brought forth a Proustian memory: my 1950s childhood in Rockville, Maryland, when my mother took us to get then-trendy vanilla Cokes at a local soda fountain.

A poster advertised the movie *Action Jackson* at 6 p.m. My previous trip to China, where audiences spat and talked nonstop through awful black-and-white Soviet movies, had taught me the anthropological value of film outings. I decided to ask the others later if they wanted to catch the film—a video version, actually—mainly to watch the audience.

In the afternoon, we took a taxi to Ambatoloaka beach to swim. On the sand lay two triangular masses the size of chair cushions, which looked like oddly shaped fish. When we kicked them over, however, we saw the flat staring eyes of sharks' heads, presumably discarded by fishermen who sold only the flesh.

We'd settle for a stroll instead of a swim.

Back in Hell-Ville at twilight, we were directed by a young woman named Chariffa Rachidi to the show-ing of *Action Jackson*. A 20-cent admission gave us entry to the "theater," a plain one-room building. Rows of folding chairs faced a television set mounted high in the right corner, where Carl Weathers, dubbed in French, shot 'em up.

Everyone quietly watched the violence unfold. We understood "Ak-shawn Jack-sawn" and precious little else of the dubbing. What the gentle Malagasy gleaned from movies such as this, I could only wonder.

Afterward we walked to dinner. Hell-Ville struck me as a pleasant place. Wide wooden steps wrapped around its warmly lit restaurants. The tables overlooked little-trafficked streets where people strolled in the tropical evening. At the Venus Restaurant, we ordered shrimp in tomato sauce and fried rice. Improbably enough, we enjoyed yet more delicious food. While Jim and Steph enjoyed a beer, Chariffa, apparently my unofficial guide for the night, led me to her house in a nearby shantytown of rattan and metal structures connected by flimsy wooden sidewalks.

Chariffa's family crowded into her room, lit by a bare bulb. Dozens of whitish dots of paint makeup marked the faces of Chariffa's mother and sisters, giving them a spooky appearance.

A poster of President Didier Ratsiraka, the man associated with isolating Madagascar from the West and thus worsening its poverty and environmental catastrophe, stared down from the wall. This Orwellian trend in decoration had cropped up throughout Africa. From what we had seen, Kenya especially embraced it, with President Daniel arap Moi gazing over most hotels, shops and buildings.

Chariffa, 22, introduced her son, Claudio, 1½, and a little brother, Ismael, age 2.

Downside of the video revolution

Pico Iyer wrote in his 1988 book, *Video Night in Kathmandu,* of the impact of hole-in-the-wall theaters such as the one in Hell-Ville. Given the portability of videos, cassettes and computer disks, Iyer wrote:

> America could be found uncensored in the world's most closed societies. Remote villagers in rural Burma could now applaud Rambo's larger-than-life heroics only days after they hit the screens of Wisconsin.

Iyer correctly identified the apparent initial good of glimpses of the Western world arriving in remote villages. Later a more negative aspect of the information revolution became apparent: Violent American-made shows travel better than humorous ones. American producers know how to churn out exportable action programs, University of Pennsylvania professor George Gerbner found in 1993, but jokes in U.S. shows may not translate so easily. Gerbner pointed out that action programs, cheap and in need of little translation, could export Western mayhem to the world's children.

Anecdotal evidence of the damage done by videos to traditional ways has crept into a disturbingly wide range of travel literature. One can be reading a richly detailed account of a visit to a village in Ghana, Kenya, the Cook islands or Nepal, and the writer would note parenthetically that the elders there could almost circle their calendars: Between 1984 and 1989, the video came, exposing young people to violence as a means of gaining material goods.

LESSON NUMBER 4: AMERICA DOMINATES WORLDWIDE ENTERTAINMENT WITH VIOLENT MOVIES AND TV SHOWS.

LESSON NUMBER 5: THE OVERLAPPING AGES OF CHARIFFA'S SON AND HER BROTHER ILLUSTRATED HOW WOMEN BEGAN CHILD-BEARING EARLY AND CONTINUED (AS DID CHARIFFA'S MOTHER) FOR YEARS, CONTRIBUTING TO MADAGASCAR'S POPULATION GROWTH.

Little Ismael frolicked with a puckish expression and, despite the coaching of his family, refused to greet me with "*Bon soir*."

"Ismael," said Chariffa's mother with fond exasperation. She reached for his private parts and, to my astonishment, fondled them with a milking motion. Years of reading the guidelines of "Miss Manners" on when to remain poker-faced gave me the presence of mind to suppress displaying my shock. Still, I didn't know what to make of this stroking, more appropriate to extremely skilled adult lovers in private than to a mother and her son in public with a virtual stranger. Maybe in this Eden, people again felt no shame—maybe this constituted extreme behavior even by Malagasy standards.

Andro Linklater wrote in *Wild People: Travels with Borneo's Head-Hunters* that he encountered similar behavior among the Iban people:

> Until they were about five, the children were treated much the same regardless of sex. It was true that the women loved to fondle the penises of baby boys, either nuzzling the little commas of flesh or caressing them gently between thumb and forefinger, but with that exception, boys and girls were left more or less to their own devices.

LESSON NUMBER 6, FROM MISS MANNERS: "WHEN TRAVELING ABROAD, ONE IS GIVEN LEEWAY IN RETAINING AMERICAN HABITS IN NON-CRUCIAL MATTERS. INDEED, IT IS SOMETIMES MORE POLITE TO APPEAR AS A BEWILDERED AMERICAN THAN TO RISK BOTCHING COURTESIES BECAUSE ONE DOESN'T UNDERSTAND IMPORTANT NUANCES."

Only much later did I find a brief mention in an anthropology text about a tribe in Borneo that fondled children to pacify them. This may explain both what Linklater saw in Borneo and what I saw in Madagascar.

The fondling of children, along with similarities in language and rice-growing practices, adds another cultural link in the chain between Madagascar and Indonesia, particularly Borneo. Two years later in Borneo, I would photograph still another connection: elaborate wooden gravesite markers, similar to those in Madagascar. All these similarities suggest that restless seafarers from the world's third-biggest island (Borneo) had circled the globe and did not settle until finding

the fourth largest (Madagascar), which sufficiently reminded them of home. In fact, Professor Jérôme Rousseau of McGill University pinpoints the Borneo hinterland near Banjarmasin as the source of the ancestors of the Malagasy.

As Chariffa and I returned to the restaurant, she told me Malagasy women marry at 14 and live to be 50. When I asked what religion she practiced, she named her parents' tribes.

Chariffa and Abdul, friendly yet not subservient, seemed to be more outgoing than many Malagasy, probably because of their roles as our local "fixers," the people who frequently come out of the non-Western woodwork to help you and to make a bit of money.

We did not expect the instant camaraderie of the United States, with confessionals between strangers in supermarket checkout lines. The Malagasy, like 99 percent of the world's people, behave more formally than that. Still, as we walked through Hell-Ville and other Malagasy towns, some local people wouldn't talk to us. None initiated a greeting. Perhaps half responded to "*bonjour*" and a smile with a radiant smile themselves. No one seemed to have heard of Americans, so conversations with the hotel keeper and market sellers ground to a baffled halt whenever we said we hailed from *les États-Unis* or America.

In all my travels, Chariffa was the only person who had ever asked me, with a curiosity that suggested utter lack of knowledge, "*America, c'est bon?*"

TUESDAY, JULY 18
Our first small lemurs

Abdul took us on a tour of the island. During our tour, all of Nosy Be—the markets, the roadsides, the air—smelled like vanilla. Or so I thought until Abdul showed me the side of his dashboard, where he had inserted the local version of Glade air freshener for taxis: a vanilla pod.

At a little village called Lokobe, he steered us to a man named Remy. For 5,000 Malagasy francs, or FMG, each (the equivalent of $3.30), Remy led us on a nature tour of sorts in a wood V-hulled canoe, which he called by its French name, *pirogue*.

As we slopped through acres of gooey mud flats hot from the sun, the canoe functioned less as a vessel and more as a platform to hang on to. After extensive mud hiking and a fleeting moment of actual canoeing, we beached under a promontory. A path carried us up past coffee plants, pepper, breadfruit, papaya, orchids and ferns that closed at the touch.

And finally, we saw our first lemurs.

Probably the grey-backed sportive lemur, they resembled eight-inch-tall koala bears. As wild creatures go, the pair lacked the dynamism of, say, galloping zebra. In fact, their acrobatic repertoire consisted of clinging to the cleft of a tree, as stationary as rocks and the same dull gray color.

If we weren't such goofy, amateur travelers, we'd have been disappointed with the little guys. But when one is telling adventure travel tales, the worse the experience, the better.

For another reason, we did well not to feel disappointed. *Madagascar Wildlife: A Visitor's Guide* states that this lemur, while admittedly not very sportive, is related to giant megalemurs, now extinct.

On Day 3 in Madagascar, we not only saw our first lemurs, we also encountered another distinguishing characteristic of this country: the *fady*, or taboo. *Fadys* govern what the Malagasy—perhaps the world's most superstitious people outside of U.S. professional baseball players—can eat, where they can walk and what farm animals they can raise.

LESSON NUMBER 7: THE ELABORATE BLEND OF ANIMISM, ISLAM AND HINDUISM OF MADAGASCAR'S CULTURAL PARENT, INDONESIA, HAD SOMEHOW TAKEN A DARKER, EVEN MORE SUPERSTITIOUS TURN HERE.

A village displayed a sign reading, *Les chausseurs interdit* (shoes forbidden). This particular *fady* might be inconvenient, yet it was relatively innocent compared with others that keep the Malagasy peasant from adopting any innovations. Some villages prohibit the use of modern wells for water. A widespread *fady* against plowing, based on a belief that it turns the earth's back on God, maintains a reliance on slash-and-burn agriculture.

Abdul left us at a restaurant for lunch and repaired to his home nearby. He returned with a cassette tape of music from diverse sources: Madagascar; its somewhat distant Indian Ocean neighbor, Réunion; and continental Africa. I had admired the music, having enjoyed African pop first at a wonderful dive in rural Kenya and then on the stereo in Abdul's taxi. Many features ensured its allure: rolling guitars, joyous call-and-response harmonies, evolving percussion so rich it sounded like horn sections, a music of pure joy.

"Abdul," I said, asking in French, "I want to buy this music, is there a store with these cassettes?"

"It's not possible to buy this music," he responded, followed by a lengthy and baffling footnote in French. What did he mean? Then where did he get it?

A standard line from junior high school language-class French proved useful. "Repeat if you please."

Abdul held up his thumb and index fingers about four inches apart—the distance apart of the two cassette ports of a dubbing deck. He fiercely enunciated: If I would buy a blank cassette, he would "en-reg-ee-stray" the music for me. Eureka! *"Enregistrer,"* I repeated delightedly, the light bulb finally switched on, "that means to say 'dubbing' in English."

Now I realize the naïveté of expecting to find a music store in Hell-Ville. Africans and Brazilians and Thais buy counterfeits or tape their own umpteenth-generation cassettes.

LESSON NUMBER 8: SOMETIMES YOU CAN FIND PRERECORDED WORLD MUSIC FROM STREET VENDORS AND LITTLE SHOPS, BUT AT OTHER TIMES IT MAY BE EASIER GO TO A WELL-STOCKED MUSIC STORE STATESIDE.

That tape sparked my long-running love affair with the ebullience of African music. Superb distribution systems, a hallmark of the United States, meant that upon my return Stateside I could purchase dozens of compact discs featuring African-influenced pop. The rapid, melodic guitar on Abdul's cassette, a signature of Zaire's *soukous* style, led to the haunting melodies of Mali, the metamorphosed reggae of Nigeria, and the slyly revolutionary pop that offers hope and fights repression in Algeria (*rai*) and Haiti (*rara*) and Brazil (*tropicalismo*). It's a mystery why more Americans don't love world music; maybe they lack the evocative memories we have of discovering it while driving through Africa itself.

After our return to the Hotel de la Mer, Chariffa showed up, and I exchanged a pair of Reeboks, two T-shirts and 28,000 FMG ($19) for a homemade tablecloth and a pareu (printed cloth) showing a village scene. I told her I would love an embroidered blouse, but we were probably leaving too early the next morning to effect a transaction. She would see if she could bring one at dawn.

WEDNESDAY, JULY 19
Off to a hidden paradise
At 6:45 a.m., Chariffa brought me a handmade embroidered blouse for 17,000 FMG ($11). Each of its 38 inch-square panels showed a scene of peasants farming, canoeing or spinning wooden hoops on their arms. With perseverance and entrepreneurial zeal, she had canvassed poky Hell-Ville's boutiques overnight and managed to obtain what I wanted at a good price.

LESSON NUMBER 9: PARADOXICALLY, MARKET ECONOMICS OFTEN WORKS BETTER IN THE THIRD WORLD, WHERE SELLERS BRING ENORMOUS FLEXIBILITY TO SUCH MATTERS AS PRICE, SHOP HOURS AND DELIVERY TIMES.

The whole exchange brought to mind David Lamb's assertion in *The Africans* of a natural affinity for some aspects of capitalism, that "given an economic incentive and an obtainable goal, [the African] is a tireless worker willing to accept great hardships."

Down at the harbor a half-hour later, we met a tourist boat. The Pirate would motor us to nearby Nosy Tanikely and Nosy Komba.

We anchored off Nosy Tanikely, known for its fine

reef. The crew had managed to bring one set of fins for three people. I got irritated. Why? Why one set of fins for three people, on surely the only visit we would pay in our lives to Nosy Tanikely. We survived; we took turns snorkeling. Nosy Tanikely's waters revealed huge sergeant majors, barracuda, a school of 1,000 silvery fish moving slowly as one, sea slugs, healthy and colorful coral and lots of shells.

Escorted by dolphins, we proceeded to Nosy Komba, a simple tropical island without cars. At first we wandered around confused. We had encountered a traveler who recommended an establishment run by a Madame Madio. The lone village, Ampangorinana, showed no sign of her.

We walked 10 minutes south out of the village. A tidy footpath through waterside palms led through a hamlet of tin-roofed bungalows to three picnic tables, covered with bright red tablecloths showing peacocks. There stood Madame Madio, a thin woman with braided hair and *café au lait* skin.

She offered us accommodation, single-room bungalows on stilts, at $3 and $2. These featured thatched roofs, mosquito nets, no light but a candle and creaky wood-slat floors with a bit of trampoline-style play. The bungalows had a communal rattan shower but no bathroom. *"Toilet natur,"* Madame explained in two words—the world is your toilet.

Parrots gnawed sugar cane on her picnic tables, set on a floor of beach sand. A goat stole Jim's towel. Kids in the hamlet stayed outdoors all day: running after each other, tossing a ball, grinding coconut. Older sisters washed little brothers under a hand pump.

After showers, we walked a few steps to a clearing, to see what we had journeyed so far to see.

Incredible! About 30 black lemurs, about the size of raccoons, grunted in the trees. The all-black males scarcely resembled the larger, tawny females with white-fringed muttonchops in a halo around their faces. These lemurs fluffed their halo of fur in curiosity or fear, as Yoda perked his ears in *Return of the Jedi*. Both sexes stared with huge, unearthly amber eyes, like creatures from a UFO. They seemed to have brightest eyes in the animal kingdom, and oddly reptilian, like David Bowie's lizard eyes in *The Man Who Fell to Earth*.

In the pose of Russian folk dancers, the lemurs made eight-foot leaps, from tree to tree and from tree to tourist. When a male leapt on my shoulder, my knees buckled. His velvety soft fur brushed my neck and face. He smelled like a dog with a wet coat from the rain—musky but natural.

'Like the Third World'

We almost never had any cause to flare up in our Third World travels due to incidents like the forgotten equipment at Nosy Tanikely. I am usually impressed by how well things go despite language barriers and the difficulties of transportation and infrastructure.

LESSON NUMBER 10: THE PHRASE "LIKE THE THIRD WORLD" MUST BE ONE OF THE MOST MISUSED IN THE ENGLISH LANGUAGE.

War, riots and natural disasters, to my eye, look like pure chaos. Yet reporters apply the Third World metaphor. Why? Shabby Third World villages almost always have water, food, transportation and local order and leadership in greater abundance than, for example, South Florida after Hurricane Andrew—which of course had the Third World label slapped on it.

Meanwhile some First World institutions, such as the some of America's subway systems, seem rife with malfunctioning equipment, fetid platforms, surly service and rule-bound bureaucracy.

A decade's worth of news articles in *The Washington Post's* electronic library shows that, with considerable hyperbole, quite a few phenomena have been described as "like the Third World:"

School budget cuts in Montgomery County, Maryland, Motown Records' treatment by MCA, an effort to recall the District's mayor, some shacks in Maryland's Charles County, the economy of West Virginia, sidewalk vendors on the District's Columbia Road and trash in Dupont Circle, roads in Queens, the flies outside a barn at a Florida racing stable, and Moscow itself.

For good measure, Ukraine rated as "worse than Third World; it is like Fourth World."

Yet places such as Brazil and Thailand, at the highest end of the "Third World" category, boast impressive numbers of educated, healthy people with jobs and prospects, making the simile even more dubious. Economist Thomas Sowell noted in *The Economics and Politics of Race* that

poverty is supposed to be the defining characteristic of the Third World, but substantial geographic regions and social classes in the Third World are far from poor, and some whole countries in the Third World are closer to the living standards of Western Europe than to those of other Third World nations.

Even the poorest of nations, such as Madagascar and Burma, possess surpassing beauty, clean yards, friendly, patient and aware people and surprising efficiencies (such as, for example, Chariffa and her initiative).

Above, Jim meets a male black lemur living in a grove near Madame Madio's inexpensive huts, right, which offer a look at village life.

The creature made a throaty noise that could best be transcribed as "Umfr umfr umfr." Jim and Steph instantly mastered Lemurtalk, which comes from low in the throat, almost in the chest, and eventually all three of us uninhibitedly executed the odd noise.

The lemurs sought more than just idle chatter. They focused their extraterrestrial eyes on us with the intensity of a dog waiting for a treat. When we offered a banana, the well-mannered creatures gently unpeeled our fingers to take it. We observed that, in addition to sharing the human characteristic of opposable thumbs, lemurs also had opposable big toes, which must be doubly useful.

The grove of black lemurs gave Madame Madio location, location and location, the equivalent of having the Ahwanee Lodge concession in Yosemite National Park.

LESSON NUMBER 11: WITHOUT A BIT OF INTERVENTION FROM WESTERN WILDLIFE AGENCIES, SHE SEEMED THE EMBODIMENT OF A LOCAL PERSON WHOSE LIVELIHOOD NOW DEPENDED ON THE SURVIVAL OF A RARE SPECIES.

Her culinary arts certainly found favor with us, beginning with our first dinner: chicken in coconut sauce with sticky rice and bread, and split bananas for dessert. We demolished it all, even mopping up the sauce in the serving dishes. Afterward Madame lit kerosene lamps for us to read and play cards by.

Americans who had stayed at Madame Madio's, according to her guestbook: two women in 1986; in 1988, four people, including a scientist (specializing in malarial diseases) and his wife; and our group in 1989. That's all.

More Americans (12) had walked on the moon than had stayed at her guesthouse (9). When doing my pre-trip research, I had read a *Newsday* article saying that fewer than 100 Americans visited all of Madagascar in 1988.

The average American has an equal chance of serving as a member of the U.S. Senate or getting hit by lightning as going to Madagascar. Looked at another way, 99.999999999 percent of all Americans do not visit Madagascar each year; one in 2.5 million do go there. We knew we had picked an unusual destination—but not unusual to that degree. Few of the 800,000 *Washington Post* subscribers who may have read Henry Mitchell's article—enthralling as it was—could be expected to book immediate passage to Madagascar. But even Antarctica gets more than 7,000 visitors annually.

Though Madagascar was not at the time a hotbed for American tourists, by the 1993 tourism arrivals had trebled from the level of 1985. Europeans, particularly French and Germans, represented three-quarters of the 55,000 visitors in 1993, while only 5,300 visitors arrived from the whole of the Americas.

At this stage of our African trip, we performed some fluid revisionism. We downgraded the Kenyan

Stephany discovers that black lemurs are not shy creatures.

coastal resort of Lamu, previously our favorite beautiful hideaway. Nosy Komba moved into the No. 1 attraction spot. We had all the essentials of comfort, none of the extras, rock-bottom prices, a window on the ongoing lives of the people, and peaceable, exotic and entertaining animals. In sum, we enjoyed a Utopian idyll. Wish we had a week here, I thought, instead of just two days.

One night, Madame Madio told us her story. After a divorce she had started selling Cokes out of crates to visitors to the nearby lemur grove. A classic entrepreneur, she scrimped and saved and built the restaurant … then one bungalow, two and three. We wished her all success.

Beau and a lemur: similar ruffs and muzzles.

Combining cuteness and clues to our past

Years after our trip, as I looked at photographs of the black lemurs, a sudden realization explained why I found them so precious. Their little muttonchops and begging eyes recalled our various family Shetland sheepdogs: Rogue, Conan, Beau and Skipper.

Let's play analyst: A 1950s childhood spent watching Lassie led to picking out a string of shelties for pets. Still later we visited Madagascar's lemurs, not for high-minded scientific reasons but because they resemble a "cute" television dog.

At least we do not stand alone in an almost visceral fondness for lemurs. My friend Rose called me after seeing a documentary on these whimsical innocents under threat to exclaim, "Now I understand why you went to Madagascar." The creatures also enjoy cult status among some college students, including a group of Virginia Tech students and others who operate an Internet chat page (at http://www.wam.umd.edu/~ixian/frink7, or search for Usenet alt.fan.lemurs) describing their support of Leonidas, Nigel, Bebop, Nosferatu and others in the Duke University Primate Center's Adopt-A-Lemur program.

The Latin phrase *res ipsit loquitor*—"the thing speaks for itself"—offers a preliminary explanation for why we wanted to see lemurs and why we desperately want them to survive. Yet lemurs offer more: insight to researchers seeking to understand human nature.

For example, lemurs, even more adaptable and diverse creatures than monkeys or apes, live in every Malagasy habitat from rain forest to desert. Some are active in daytime, others at night, and some at either time. This flexibility may be the most crucial lemur heritage to humans, according to Ian Tattersall in "Madagascar's Lemurs."

Despite having smaller brains than higher primates, some lemurs display "complex sociality," according to Tattersall:

> By studying the lives of lemurs we can glimpse something of the Eocene behavioral potential from which our vaunted human capacities ultimately arose. ... It is tragic to see any part of the world's biodiversity disappear, but the tragedy is particularly acute in the case of Madagascar's lemurs, which still have so much to teach us about our own past.

Just another day playing with lemurs

In this hamlet without electricity, we lived with the sun. In our cots at 8:30 p.m., we awakened at 6 a.m. as the place came to life. Our ears became our alarm clocks. On the other side of the bungalow wall, kids banged around. The noise joined the sounds of surf and chickens. Observing everyday routines in Madagascar required no art or stealth. Village life found us.

I read John Cheever's *The Wapshot Chronicle*, breaking for our lunch of fish. We played with the lemurs some more. Just before dinnertime, we watched Madame Madio unsentimentally carry a squawking duck earmarked for our repast to its slaughter.

Afterward she arranged for a man named Joseph to sail us to the mainland next day. I imagined a nice motorboat, such as that which took us snorkeling the previous day, to zip us across.

Local means of travel

Up at 5 a.m., I lay on my back on the beach to photograph the dark palms against a lightening metallic gold sky. A man dragged a little V-sided dugout canoe up the beach and scooped water out of it. I photographed the moment, then returned to scanning the horizon for our motor cruiser to the mainland.

A suspicion nagged at me, but I pushed it out of my mind. Gradually it became impossible to dismiss the truth. The man that I'd been photographing must be none other than Joseph, our captain. That leaky and unstable dugout somehow had to cross more than five miles of water to the mainland.

I had no idea how significant the canoe would become to our travel plans.

The vessel barely contained room for the four of us plus our backpacks, stacked high amidships. The wind blew steadily, straight on our nose. Jim and Steph stroked with almost bladeless implements, more sticks than paddles. "This is a toothpick," Jim said, accurately. The travesty, which would have disgusted a less laid-back traveler, merely amused him. From the tiny prow, I constantly bailed out water using the omnipresent margarine can. We had seen such cans—adaptable as a kid's toy, storage container, water bowl or a thousand other things—everywhere in Africa.

For the privilege of paddling ourselves for three hours, we had each paid 5,000 FMG ($3.30, the apparent price of almost everything in Madagascar). At a crawl, we approached the mainland and eventually reached the shore, where we found a deserted roadhead.

We had only one course of action: to sit by the side of the road and wait, like Vladimir and Estragon, in absurd hopefulness to see if anyone arrived.

Within a half-hour a Mercedes bus showed up. (Question in retrospect: Why did it stop there? To find the occasional group of canoeing backpackers from Maryland?)

We clambered aboard, enjoying Western levels of personal space: a big vehicle bearing just five people, including the driver and his assistant, who wore a fez, another reminder of our proximity to Islam. A burst of optimism and good cheer suffused our ride. It lasted for one mile. Around a point from our canoe's landing spot, giant ferries from Nosy Be disembarked. At the dock, Mr. Fez stage-managed the loading of 50 people in the bus's space for 20.

Everyone's personal space shrank from the Western notion (unlimited) to the Third World definition (less space than your body physically occupies). Three women sat against the windshield facing the back of the bus. Despite there seeming to be no space for him, a boy sat between the driver and his door. My knees dug into the row of seats in front of me. My legs became numb, so I stood hunched under the roof.

Out the windows, we saw our first carts pulled by zebu, the type of humpbacked oxen that had given its life for our airplane's safety. Children in the villages smiled delightedly to see the faces of *vazaha* (foreigners) as we rolled past.

Instead of taking a leaky canoe and a crowded bus, we could have flown to our destination, Diego Suarez. But I had suggested that at least once, Jim and Steph should sample local means of travel. In China and other countries, I had taken train and boat rides that, while arduous, provided an indelible picture of how the people lived.

By 11:30 a.m., we rolled into a weathered little crossroads town, Ambanja. A crew of young touts frantically loaded us on a *taxi-brousse* for Diego as though it were pulling out at any second.

The driver drove off promptly and at speed,

Madagascar trip map

COMORO ISLANDS

Nosy Komba

Nosy Be

Diego Saurez

1 **3**
2

● Ambilobe
● Ambanja

Mozambique Channel

Antananarivo

4 **5**

Perinet

Indian Ocean

MADAGASCAR

0   200
MILES

A jammed Mercedes bus held 50 passengers.

but not for Diego. He whizzed around the undistinguished shacks of Ambanja itself. As though gas prices, air pollution, time and productivity mattered not a whit, for 90 minutes we jounced around town. As if in some slow-motion banana republic version of the middle laps of the Indy 500, the *taxi-brousse* circuited a gas station, a market and a blackboard for the video *Conan Le Destructeur* a mind-numbing 15 times. The driver crushed a duck and passed a shack, apparently an official building, bearing a cryptic sign: Hall of Information.

Every woman that we drove past in Ambanja appeared to be pregnant. One could see how the Malagasy population was projected to double in size every 22 years. World population grows more slowly, projected to double every 45 years. (After our trip, the birthrate in Madagascar and the rest of Africa fell slightly.)

Finally, the requisite number of passengers needed to really depart, 23, packed the Toyota pickup's cab and the benches in the back, some sitting atop each other. We headed out Route National 6.

In the cab, we sat four across: the driver, me, Steph and Jim. There was no room for my left arm to hang at its usual place at the side of my torso. Instead it was wrapped around the driver as though we were great chums, and it quickly became numb. Steph's left elbow dented my ribs, my shoulder crushed her back, my feet crowded the accelerator (!) and Jim barely wedged in his shoulders.

And we occupied the place of honor. The 19 other passengers squashed themselves into the back of the *taxi-brousse*, where wooden benches and stools ran the length of the covered truckbed.

The bush taxi functioned as a stop-and-go discothèque. It appeared incapable of moving more than three kilometers at a stretch without the fuel pump or gas filter malfunctioning. Yet no expense had been spared for a top-of-the-line cassette player with equalizer, and disco lights blinked brightly around the windshield.

Remarkably, the music playing on the

sound system happened to be one of my favorite Caribbean groups, Kassav'. How curious it seemed to be riding through Madagascar to a lively Caribbean sound, with its muscular horns, strong melodies and pretty French Creole singing. Although it first seemed unlikely that an obscure recording by artists from Guadeloupe and Martinique would find its way to rural Madagascar, a simple explanation became apparent. Musicians from the Caribbean and Africa record in Paris, the capital of world music, and the recordings must stream right out again to the former French possessions, even in the remote Indian Ocean.

The Toyota's ailments forced the driver and his aide at each sputtering stop to remove one fuel pump and replace it with its equally shot alternate, without really repairing the units themselves. Whichever pump was not in use lay under Jim's feet, rolling around the footwell along with a wrench, screwdriver and an abrasive cloth.

At one breakdown the ad hoc pit crew actually retimed the engine, using the cloth to clean the point and drawing a little line in the dirt to create a timing stripe. All the men rocked the *taxi-brousse* forward to make the adjustment. The pervasiveness of advertising also became apparent, reaching even the remote Malagasy bush. One of the ad hoc mechanics muttered philosophically as he tinkered, *"Choses fait plus bon avec Coke"* ("Things go better with Coke").

These Malagasy breakdowns, like others in Africa, presented a guy-bonding opportunity. Jim and a cluster of dark men peered under the hood. The women read or talked or stared off in infinite patience.

The repairs also allowed us to visit little roadside "food" stands. We envisioned goodies like the divine homemade samosas we had devoured on the beach at Lamu. But we could buy only stale peanut brittle and tasteless biscuits as hard as rocks. Disappointment and hunger began to gnaw at us.

After four hours we reached our halfway point, Ambilobe, a thriving transit area of 9,000. Once again the taxi touts fought over our bags, though their empty vehicles would not be racing out anytime soon.

In no hurry to endlessly circle wherever it was we waited now (Ambilobe), a sort of more decrepit version of the unpainted market stalls and beaten earth of wherever it was we just left (Ambanja, whose name we had already forgotten), I took a stroll. My comrades waved for me to hurry back.

Jim had reached the outer limits of his endurance. For 55,000 FMG ($38), he'd essentially bought all the empty seats on a *taxi-brousse* so that we could leave immediately. Four lucky Malagasy, winners of the Jim Belliveau Lottery, had already boarded. They lounged around the back of the taxi with more personal transportation space than they'd known in their lives.

The driver bought gas for The Taxi that Jim Bought and rolled out. As usual in Mad, we couldn't really win.

The taxi Jim 'bought' fuels up for Route National 6.

Road tales

Two years after experiencing Route National 6, I drove to a wedding in North Dakota with acquaintance. Construction on a section of Interstate 90 slowed us to 50 mph, a rate of speed probably unheard of on any thoroughfare in Madagascar. My passenger complained. I thought, if only you knew.

LESSON NUMBER 12: MADAGASCAR ILLUMINATES THE UNSUNG MIRACLES OF U.S. LIFE, SUCH AS INTERSTATE HIGHWAYS.

Even Africa hands find Madagascar's roads shocking. "Worse than Zambia," said one in a tone that suggested Malagasy roads surpassed the unspeakable. More than even Guatemala, the Big Red Island left us with a keen appreciation for decent roads. Though these insights and others we sometimes keep to ourselves, as they could be conversation killers with some our Stateside friends and neighbors who don't share our interest in exotic travel.

At times adventure travelers cannot help reminiscing, and family and friends listen patiently. Yet what would the 99.99-plus percent of Americans who haven't visited Madagascar ("where?") and face no familial duty to listen to us ever make of our tales of the horrid roads, the spring-loaded lemurs, the giant plants? Did Marco Polo face the same disbelieving, heavy-lidded looks when he dictated his stories to his scrivener in Genoa ... "Did I mention the giant gryphon bird of Madagascar, the roc, which could carry elephants in its talons?"

Route National 6 worsened markedly outside of town. To avoid smaller potholes, the driver scraped the vehicle against the thick underbrush edging the road. In low gear, he drove down into the biggest craters and clambered out again, the taxi rocking from side to side as its wheels clawed over the lip of each crater. Any idea of making great time on this leg dissolved.

A book called *Languages and Their Speakers* indicates a possible reason for the halts and hitches in our conversations with the Malagasy.

In a chapter called "Becoming a Competent Speaker of Malagasy," Edward Louis Keenan and Elinor Ochs describe a typical sentence:

Manasa ny lamba amin'ity savony ity Rasoa

This translates word by word to:

Wash the clothes with this soap this Rasoa

And the everyday English translation:

Rasoa is washing the clothes with this soap.

"This is already unusual," the authors state. "Probably not more than 10 percent of the world's languages place the verb in the initial position in simple (unemphatic) sentences."

Apparently, as we suspected, the Malagasy language was quite different from French. Also, the authors describe Malagasy villages as being about as opposite as one can get from the information-drenched American existence. With village life centered on the rice harvest, and no great specialization of labor, everyone more or less does the same thing as everyone else year in and year out. Any deviation makes the bearer of news the center of great attention.

To remain the center of interest, one imparts information only a bit at a time. Thus information, generally spread by word of mouth, can be described as a "scarce good." Maybe this further explained our drawn-out arrangements for hotels and transportation. Information did not clatter back and forth, tickety-boom, as it does in many Western transactions.

The sun set at 6. Jim and I sat in the windowless cab as the air turned chill, while Steph actively shivered on a bench in the back. Being uncrowded meant less body warmth. One of the Malagasy women gave Steph an Indian-style kerchief. That the filmy cloth was utterly ineffectual did not detract from the thoughtfulness of the gesture.

At 10:30 p.m., after several eternities on Route National 6, we reached Diego (pronounced Dee-aye-GO). For budgetary reasons, we looked for rooms at the Hotel Fiadanana, with its *chambres de passage,* a French euphemism for a hot-sheets, hourly rate room.

A brothel had to meet certain exacting criteria for us to stay there: It had to be the cheapest place in town that would also admit travelers not seeking paid sex.

LESSON NUMBER 13: IN MUCH OF THE WORLD, DEMAND FOR QUICKIE RENTED ROOMS OUTSTRIPS THAT FOR HOTEL ROOMS, SO AN OVERLAPPING STRUCTURE HANDLES BOTH.

Because this dual function exists widely, the Hotel Fiadanana would not be the last whorehouse I would stay in.

In the United States, the utilitarian lines of the Hotel Fiadanana would probably be found at tire discounter in a town with lax zoning. In the Third World, the hotel's low-slung, cinder-block exterior proclaimed it as one of the anonymous, no-frills structures that could be anything: university, hospital, ruin, bus station, expatriate housing or government ministry.

Our brothel in Diego did not fulfill any fantasy notions of a cathouse from the American West. No saloon doors à la *McCabe and Mrs. Miller* swung onto a red-velour parlor. No big-haired women in teddies lounged about.

Instead of Julie Christie as the heart-of-gold madam, two men, dark-skinned with fluffy Afros, staffed the brothel from behind an oddly proper wooden schoolteachers' desk in a bare hallway. They avoided meeting my eyes, staring slightly down and to my left as they puzzled: *Who are these people and why do they want to stay here?*

I told them we wanted rooms. The statement met with a profound silence. I waited. For all, French took second place—to Malagasy for the staff and English for us. My French, learned in Maryland schools rather than at home as my father had learned his, could it not be understood? But Abdul on Nosy Be seemed to *me comprendre.* And somehow when I traveled in France itself and Francophone Tahiti, communication had proceeded smoothly.

In Madagascar, we got the impression that Malagasy sentence construction differed from European languages so much that the French overlay hadn't taken too well.

Our stalled room arrangements became further fraught with uncertainty when Jim and Steph yelled and galloped inexplicably out of the lobby. What the problem was, I knew not. But to avoid permanent derailment of the room check-in, I tried to bluff unconcern before the brothel-keepers at this insignificance—the hysterical departure of my entire traveling party, including a blood relative, 9,000 miles from home.

Trusting that time would return Jim and Steph intact and with an explanation, I checked into my room, a floor with thick marine-grade paint the color of livid molten lava, puce walls with holes, tile bathroom, battered gray metal table and metal clothes locker. The appointments, however worn, appeared to be clean.

Seeking food, I wandered out on my own. Down the dark road on the right stood a tiny wooden shack with a cloth curtain serving as a doorway, lit by a naked bulb. Famished, I bought what few items lay on the ill-stocked shelves: a stale baguette stranded from the day before, a dusty bottle of Coca-Cola and a can of sardines.

The shopkeeper wrapped the bread in a page torn

The Cascade Grande tumbles at Montagne d'Ambre National Park.

Trying to help Madagascar: The World Wildlife Fund

The World Wildlife Fund has targeted Madagascar as a "priority country" in Africa, along with Cameroon, Gabon, Tanzania, Zaire and Zambia.

In Madagascar, the fund sponsors an educational center at Tsimbazaza Park in Antananarivo, the capital, and two integrated conservation projects, at Montagne d'Ambre and Andohahela in the south. The Montagne d'Ambre project, which receives $1 million a year, educates people in four nearby villages about conservation and guards against illegal cultivation in the park.

Park officials have opened a simple campsite at the park and created a basic map for visitors. It may not sound like much. But it's a significant step forward for Madagascar, whose parks provided nothing along the lines of the standard pamphlets and ranger talks that make a visit to national parks in the United States such as Yellowstone so educational.

The World Wildlife Fund also has planned a nationwide conservation program for all primary and secondary schools in Madagascar.

from a math text in Malagasy. Somehow it didn't augur well for the nation's technological development that math texts doubled as grocery wrap. Back in my room, I made an unwelcome discovery. Sardine tins in Madagascar lacked a turnkey. In the despair of my fatigue and hunger, I dragged out my Swiss Army knife, too tired to do much but poke a hole in the tin and shake oil and a few pitiful fish fragments on the stale bread.

My compatriots returned from their abrupt foray, explaining that Jim had left his fancy new camera on our *taxi-brousse*. They had commandeered a regular taxi, whose driver apparently thought that they wanted to go to Ambilobe (hardly). Shouting and ridiculous pantomime had gotten them turned around to the town's central *taxi-brousse* stand, and they returned triumphant, camera in hand.

Jim and Steph then conducted a quest for open restaurants, apparently an unknown in midnight Diego, and ended up unfed even by sardine oil. They drifted into fantasy. In a Third World brothel, they visualized food rather than sex. First, they imagined eating at the Chart House in Annapolis. Then Phillip's Seafood, Pizza Hut and even Wendy's.

I found our day of hard travel arduous and tiresome. With the benefit of being four years younger, I had done this stuff in Burma. There I would crank up a personal stereo, parachute out of the here and now and recuperate after a night's rest. In Madagascar, I couldn't blame Jim for finding a day of local travel sufficient.

SATURDAY, JULY 22
Bribes and banquets

The morning after our experience with local travel, I awoke with puffy eyes and a headache, feeling fairly wiped out. Trips have cadences of many colors: days of logistics, days of local travel, days of results, days of difficulty or ease. Maybe our rough roads would be smoothed. We would welcome a day of reward.

We wandered into sunny Diego, population 80,000. At Restaurant Yachy on Rue Lally, breakfast provided the first upbeat note of the day. After scarfing down five croissants, bread, sweet butter, coffee and tea, I began to feel human again.

Diego lately rates as a stop on Madagascar's modest tourist circuit because of a nearby lemur park, Montagne d'Ambre. A permit for the park, a travel agent told us, would cost the equivalent of $33, and a tour $20. That looks cheap to me now but it seemed like a fortune to us then.

The agent added that the source of permits, the Forest Bureau, would (big surprise) not be open on Saturdays. However, she gave us an idea. We could proceed without a permit if we offered a *cadeau* (gift) to the guardian.

"We have to give the park officials a 'gift,' " I translated to my compadres. "That means a bribe."

Jim and Steph adored the connotation of a *cadeau*. The word suggested that we could cruise by the nearest mall and pick up some crystal and china for the park officials. In fact, the word actually means something closer to "tip" and reflects a Malagasy attitude that the cash constitutes more of a nice gesture than a purchased service, for which they would reciprocate with a proud tour of the reserve.

A taxi driver agreed to take us to the park. He headed southwest past Joffreville to the park entrance, where stood the guardian's wife. As the woman walked away from us, her face a cipher, our driver augmented an earnest conversation with subtle body language. He

To see lemurs in our few days in Madagascar, we set aside our scruples and subscribed to the religion of Whatever Works. With great reluctance, we embraced situation ethics, which holds that one cannot apply universal laws or principles to a situation. Tips to park personnel helped us unravel logistical snags stemming from our low budget and limited time and, most of all, the fact that permits were not available at park gates and had to be obtained at offices in cities some distance from the parks.

We tried repeatedly to get lemur park permits and found ourselves thwarted mostly by the simple fact that the Forest Bureau was closed on weekends.

We had every national park and reserve we visited completely to ourselves, further indicating a troubling snag in access for both the Malagasy and tourists. Although in a way, we enjoyed our aloneness, feeling like Teddy Roosevelt on safari.

Princeton University Professor Alison Jolly—author of a book and pivotal articles in *National Geographic* in the 1980s that shocked numerous world bodies into addressing the ecological collapse in Madagascar— wrote to me in 1996 pointing out that only recently had the Malagasy government begun to charge entrance fees at the national parks.

Before that, tourism enriched airlines and modern hotels but not the parks or the small hotels in nearby countryside. She wrote that

> There was absolutely nothing from tourism directed to the conservation itself. In other words, people who had spent between $2,000 and $5,000 to reach Madagascar would balk as you did at $33 to preserve the treasures they had come to see.

Later I attempted to repent for our lapse via donations to the World Wildlife Fund's Africa and Madagascar Program.

touched his hand gently to her back, apparently the right move. The guardian's wife, he returned to say, would require a *cadeau* of 10,000 FMG ($6.60), quite a discount from the official price.

We paid up and entered Amber Mountain park. The air smelled of the pine trees. In this exaggerated version of an Eastern U.S. forest, plants climbed trees and Tarzan vines dropped to a floor of ferns. Birds and butterflies flitted about. After we walked two miles, the pretty Cascade Grande came into view. As we made our way back, shy gray Sanford's lemurs played along the branches arching above. Steph wrote in her notes, "They were adorable but not tame like those of Nosy Komba so it was hard to get a good look at them."

She also spotted a chestnut-brown creature, a bit lemurish, a bit ferrety, with a striped tail—most likely the Madagascar ring-tailed mongoose. *Grzimek's Animal Encyclopedia* says these creatures belong to the family "viverrids" and calls them "a very primitive species that forms a bridge between civets and true mongooses."

Our driver dropped us all back in Diego. We walked past the town center's heroic statuary and monolithic buildings—relics of the nation's brief flirtation in the 1970s with the aesthetically deprived Eastern bloc. We continued to a street of shops, turning our attention to fulfilling the request of a sweet, true, utterly loyal but breathtakingly naïve friend from Michigan. She had packed us a food basket for our drive to Kennedy airport in New York to kick off our trip. She asked one thing in return:

A refrigerator magnet from Africa.

"Kathleen," I had said, "I don't think they have many refrigerators in rural Africa, let alone refrigerator magnets. I mean, I don't think they even go for refrigerator magnets in Europe. It's sort of an American thing."

Whereas we had harbored paranoid fears of widespread famine and disease in Africa, her misreading ran in the opposite direction, to imagining a virtual American suburbia. But perversely we decided to throw ourselves into the pursuit of the rare African refrigerator magnet. Like Matthiessen seeking the snow leopard, like O'Hanlon tracking the Borneo rhinoceros, we would catapult our trip into the realm of a true expedition.

The impossibility of our task only increased our determination to magnet reflecting the island's footprint shape, perhaps labeled, "Madagascar: Last of the Lemurs." Purposefully we entered Diego's lone appliance shop, with its stock of rebuilt, outdated, tiny washing machines and refrigerators. The Sri Lankan proprietor, his mouth blazing red from chewing betel nuts, gave away nothing whatsoever in his expression when I asked, "*Avez-vous quelque chose de magnétique pour le frigidaire?*" He wordlessly shook his head no.

The escapade felt like a prank for *Spy* magazine: "Our Third World Village Shopping Survey: Do you have any oven mitts? Any coffee mugs with 'World's Greatest Golfer' in Malagasy?"

So much for our impossible Holy Grail. We wandered along to dinner at Yachy, our breakfast place, a few blocks gently uphill. We sat at our by-now usual table, beside lacquered Chinese doors and a vibrant red painting of swirling six-foot-tall peacocks and dragons with talons. Two terriers and one cat wandered around under our chairs.

We harbored hopes of being fed well after our croissant binge earlier. Yet nothing prepared us for one of the best meals of our lives. In the far back country of the Malagasy republic, we feasted on nouvelle world cuisine, a blend of French, Chinese and Italian. Our menu in Diego, Madagascar, consisted of:

Rice with caramelized pork, spinach linguine with fish, shrimp on romaine with mint, fish deep-fried with apricot (a sweet-and-sour effect), profiteroles (eclairs with whipped cream centers and chocolate sauce) and coffee ice cream. The tab, with a 20 percent tip, totaled $7.20 each.

LESSON NUMBER 14: THE DELIGHTS OF TRAVEL CAN BE AS UNEXPECTED AS THE TRAVAILS.

Later I found a CIA publication noting that the high development of small-scale agriculture on Madagascar had led to a surprising lack of hunger for such a poor nation. We noticed more: a real talent for cooking in this economic basket case.

SUNDAY, JULY 23
Viewing the dusty coelacanth
We flew back to the capital, Antananarivo, nickname Tana. This time we taxied into the city of 2 million, getting our first proper look. In some respects, with its horse carts and political posters plastered everywhere, it felt like Naples, Athens or Iraklion in Crete. But between the standard piles of cinder blocks impersonating buildings, Tana tolerated an exuberant grab-bag of land uses: rice paddies, hilltop Gothic-style churches, tumbledown red brick houses with New Orleans-style balconies and spanking new Renault dealerships.

Piteous beggar children abounded. One boy failed utterly in an unsolicited attempt to translate for a cab driver and then requested a *cadeau*. Others looked like extras from *Les Misérables* or *Great Expectations*. They wore far more ragged clothes than any truly poor children we had seen in our travels, and adults nearby watched them closely. One ostensible waif held out his hand for a *cadeau*. "*Étudiez et travaillez dur à l'école et vous serez riches, vous reússirez dans la vie,*" I lectured the children in my stern, politically incorrect Margaret Thatcher style. Study and work hard and you will do well.

They stared back in utter bafflement, probably at everything: my shaky pronunciation, brisk tone and possibly even the content of my suggestion.

We visited Parc Tsimbazaza, where ringtailed lemurs, as perky as Mary Tyler Moore, played around a lake. Because we were perceived as well-off *vazaha*, several caretakers soon came to spring us from a long line for the reptile house. For yet another *cadeau*, they

A sifaka studies the humans visiting Parc Tsimbazaza.

took us backstage of the cages—while the locals continued to wait.

The rare aye-aye, a lemur filling the niche occupied elsewhere by woodpeckers, displayed a skeletal middle finger designed to fish ants out of their hiding places. A handsome sifaka peered bright-eyed from its cage.

A museum on the grounds exhibited the skeleton of Aepyornis, the extinct elephant bird that resembled a monstrous ostrich, and the coelacanth, a dinosaur-age fish once believed to be extinct.

Covered with dust, the four-foot-long coelacanth looked like a neglected and poorly freeze-dried angler's trophy of a trash fish. The decrepit exhibit took me back to a memory of being about 10 years old in a Catholic elementary school. A story in our *Weekly Reader* told of the 1938 discovery of a coelacanth by fishermen in the seas between Madagascar and the Comoros, probably a promising area to hide if you are an overlooked fish. As a child I never dreamed that one day I'd be looking at a coelacanth in a museum in Madagascar.

We ventured along to the train station for tickets to the reserve at Perinet the next day. There we planned to track the giant indri. We had to pay for our train tickets in hard currency, that is, U.S. dollars, which at the time irked me to no end. Jim happened to have some tens and fives. What if he hadn't? Why couldn't Madagascar take its own money for its own trains? In hindsight, however, I've decided that it's convenient for Americans that U.S. dollars, rather than, say, pesos, are welcome in surprising places (such as smuggling zones like Burma and economic basket cases like Madagascar).

LESSON NUMBER 15: TAKE EXTRA DOLLARS ON TRIPS. AMERICANS MIGHT JUST AS WELL BE FLATTERED AT THE GREENBACK'S WORLDWIDE ACCEPTANCE.

Tickets in hand, we headed to dinner at the Muraille de Chine, deliberately picking Tana's most expensive Chinese restaurant. Our goal: to burn off excess Malagasy francs. We had discovered too late a fact buried almost unnoticed in our guidebook: We could not convert back our remaining FMGs to hard currency. And we had large stacks of the soon-to-be-useless currency. Nothing cost much, except for the air and train tickets, which required Amex cards and U.S. dollars, not FMGs.

So we ordered lobster, giant tiger prawns, duck, wine and beer, and for dessert, crêpes in Grand Marnier sauce. That lightened our cash mountain by $7 each. What to do next: Buy up all the mahogany furniture available? Endow a natural park? Make a poor Malagasy temporarily wealthy? Still rich in a soft currency, we headed off to bed.

MONDAY, JULY 24
In search of the great indri lemur

Our last day in this Dr. Seuss-designed country—with its gold and lilac sunsets, idiosyncratic animals, mildly sinister people and pervasive oddity—began at 4:20 a.m. At 5:15 we arrived at the train station after a fare disagreement, not our first, with a Tana cab driver. My notes indicate, to my chagrin, that we wrangled over preposterously low fares like $3 to $5 with local hackers, not exactly rich men. Mea culpa.

An odd hunch had come to me the second I awoke. I felt compelled to examine our tickets and the guidebook map. Sure enough, my subconscious had suspected a problem and worked on it as I slept. The problem: Our tickets read "Antsirabe." I had carefully asked for "Andasibe," the station adjacent to Perinet, the night before at the station. It figured that

Madagascar would have two place names that resembled anagrams of each other, equidistant from the capital and with similar fares, despite just 660 miles of rail trackage.

Furthermore, Andasibe serves as the post-colonial, politically correct, but unused name for Perinet, home of the indri lemurs. I felt convinced that if I had been retro and used the colonial name, I would have gotten the correct tickets right off the bat.

I felt mentally gone. The country that everyone deliberately nicknamed "Mad" had drained me physically and mentally. Many things defied easy explanation. WHAT AM I LOOKING AT: An airport? The president's palace? A kid dressed up as Fagin to beg? Soviet-style monoliths? Asian oxen? A monkey cousin that sings like a whale?

We all concluded that a group in which no one spoke French of at least high school level, would never get out of the airport. Translating usually wore me out mentally, except in Tahiti, where languid Kiddiefrench did nicely. Not many people miss English as keenly as a professional journalist, used to reasonable command of expression via its nuance and shadings. And Madagascar required translating on two tiers: language and culture.

At the station, the clerk, alert despite the predawn hour, straightened out our immediate source of confusion. She sold us the last three first-class tickets for the 6 a.m. train, the only one that day to Perinet (echoes of our flight to Madagascar).

As we viewed the scenery, the oddity of Madagascar reasserted itself. Like most writers on the Great Red Island, Alex Shoumatoff, in *African Madness*, described its "pantropical" appearance, with clues of French influence and disorienting echoes of many other places.

All these elements could be seen from our window as our train wound through a brilliant green valley. A red farmhouse sat amid fields. If we pretended that we didn't know where we were, the lushness would suggest Asia, while the color intensity—the red of the farmhouse approached a riotous shade of burgundy—would hint specifically at Indonesia. The home's pitched roof called to mind a building in a market town in Normandy. The people working the fields and riding the train looked neither purely African nor Asian, though they had Picasso-like high foreheads and the slender frames of the Balinese.

When the train stopped at stations in the valley, women sold bananas, pineapple and corn fritters from baskets on their heads. Signs read Ambolampy and Andasibe. The very place names reflected chaotic aspects of the evolution of a written language on Madagascar. What would happen if a land were settled by speakers of a simple proto-Malay tongue, but their colonial overlords were French, their workaday names for cattle and the like came from Africa and the missionaries who wrote their first dictionaries were English? And the ship bringing over boxes of type for printing the language lost several letters, including "c"?

Welcome to the Malagasy language. It's probably learnable eventually for a foreigner who can break the Germanically endless words down into their Indonesian components, thought it's daunting at first glance. I was nonplused that my smattering of Indonesian proved of no use in puzzling out the words, until I later learned that Malagasy descends more from a south Borneo dialect called Ma'anyan than from modern Indonesian.

A vendor, above, sells food at a station. The train to Perinet winds through scenery, right, that echoes rural France, Asia and Africa.

Welcome to Madagascar, a place where airports painted lime green, humpbacked oxen and backward-leaping prosimians seems like a book by Dr. Seuss recalled in an unsettled dream devoid of logic. In another sense, though, Madagascar illustrates the wonder of a world where the fantastic exists, where the imagined can be real, on an island in the Indian Ocean.

> **Pick any Seussian invention, and nature will equal it. ... What about the Moth-Watching Sneth? Well the extinct elephant bird of Madagascar stood eight feet tall and weighed a thousand pounds. In its heyday ... the elephant bird, or Aepyornis, probably scared many a Madagascan half to death.**
>
> Physics professor Chet Raymo in "Dr. Seuss and Dr. Einstein: Children's Books and Scientific Imagination"

Many travelers rave about the friendly people and exotica of Madagascar. We found something odd about the place. In my case, a previous trip to Java and Bali overshadowed my perceptions. The people of Madagascar struck me as substantially warier, even more superstitious and less friendly than their Indonesian forebears.

LESSON NUMBER 16: THE ORDER IN WHICH YOU VISIT COUNTRIES WILL BEAR ON YOUR IMPRESSIONS. SEQUENCE MAY DETERMINE PERCEPTION.

On the train, two tourists chatted in seats behind ours. Their language sounded like a blend of Italian, French and German. In English, they told me they were Swiss and would be staying for another month.

Eureka! Jim and Steph, staring out the window at the scenery, came over to strike a deal. We wanted

only the black market rate for our remaining Malagasy francs, but the Swiss, bankers to the bone, insisted that they give us the much higher official rate. They carefully calculated the precise amount of the exchange to two decimal places, rounded to the nearest whole note and handed over 70 or so Swiss francs.

At 10:45 a.m., we arrived at Andasibe with, as was our wont, no exact plan to handle several pressing logistical problems. No trains returned to Tana later that day. No other public transport existed. Once again, we hadn't been able to obtain a lemur reserve permit over the weekend.

Situation normal. Things worked out.

The moment we left the station and walked up the hill to the nature reserve, the wail of the indris carried to our ears, sounding like the forest equivalent of a humpback whale: low and modulated, with immense carrying power. (The sound features in "Lemur Rap," a track on the recording *A World Out of Time*, Vol. 2, by Henry Kaiser and David Lindley.)

An observant man on a motorbike stopped to ask if we tourists, obviously walking to the reserve, needed a guide. Yes, I said simply.

"We don't have a permit," I said in French. I tried to exhibit my lost waif look, innocent and pleading, which had been so effective in China at getting taxis and riverboats and help from English translators.

"We wonder," I added, "if ... something can be arranged." There. The most magic words in all the Third World. (In Brazil, the phrase is "*Tem jeito*?" The answer: "*Sempre tem jeito.*" There's always a way. Most languages have an equivalent.)

LESSON NUMBER 17: PEOPLE LOVE TO MAKE ARRANGEMENTS, TO SERVE AS FIXERS AND GO-BETWEENS, WITH LITTLE SPELLED OUT EXPLICITLY AND MUCH LEFT IN A GRAY AREA TO PERMIT WORKING ROOM.

The motorbike man thought it over and nodded.

There's always a way. He said he would go ahead to the guardian.

At the reserve gate, the motorbiker and the guardian awaited us. The guardian lectured us on how we should have gotten a permit in Tana. On one level, he could fairly berate us. With about 4,000 visitors a year now showing up at Perinet, some management of tourists would be required to prevent them from trampling the vegetation and disturbing the wildlife.

Our entire 9,000-mile journey to see indri lemurs hung in the balance. I knew that our lack of foresight made us unworthy of seeing the magical creatures.

I listened with knitted brow and especially hypocritical delivery of the Waif Expression, but no sympathy. Why didn't these reserves just write admission tickets at the gate? Aided by another *cadeau*, we eventually arrived at a little *entre nous* understanding.

Off we strolled expectantly into a hilly forest. A little boy showed us his chameleon, and the guardian gave us a tour of aquaculture ponds in which fish were raised for human consumption. The sight reassured me. Shoumatoff wrote an alarming passage in *African Madness* about indri being shot for protein by locals, indicating that population pressure had weakened the local *fady* against killing them. Pond-raised fish providing protein for human stomachs could only help the giant lemurs.

An eerie cry rose from a distant group of indri. The guardian and an assistant led us up a muddy hill and told us to wait. They searched for the one group, of the 62 in the reserve, that was accustomed to visitors.

After they departed, Stephany found the indris right beside the muddy path where we stood (and not off where our guides tramped about). We looked up. Clinging 20 feet up the tree trunks, five indris stared at us as fixedly as we gazed at them. There they must have been all along, slightly off the trail.

For 20 minutes, as the guardian chased around elsewhere, we photographed the family of five. The group we saw comprised two pairs and a five-month-old male infant. They displayed no desire to leave or, after they initially looked us over, any additional indication that our arrival had disrupted their activities. They ate leaves in the treetops, bounding effortlessly backward from trunk to trunk in the weightless manner of a shuttle crew.

The biggest non-extinct lemurs, they stood about 3 1/2 feet tall and resembled black-and-white dog-faced pandas. The biggest indri's huge back legs seemed longer than his torso and head combined. The flanks of the males bore cinnamon markings.

The rare indri lemur poses agreeably in the treetops at Perinet.

They gazed at us with apparent curiosity. They made fluid floating jumps—ricocheting forward or backward from tree to tree like steel balls in a pinball machine—and rolled their heads as though on a spring. They finally thrust their muzzles forward to lock their gaze on us. The routine looked like something from a jazz dancing exercise emphasizing head rotation.

Our guardian returned and proved little more adept at reciting lemur facts than in locating the animals. He said they live to be 75 to 80 years old, a figure Professor Jolly of Princeton later revised down to a ballpark of 15 to 20 years, though no one knows exactly.

A boy at Perinet shows us a Parson's chameleon.

Indris form monogamous pairs, the guardian said. This may well be true. Yet many of the assumptions about primate behavior seem in dispute in the wake of a 1994 *Time* magazine cover story, "Infidelity: It May Be in Our Genes." The article related how often supposedly monogamous female primates (human and otherwise) sneak off and secretly manage to have offspring not their mate's.

The word *indri* might actually mean "look at that" in Malagasy. Shoumatoff wrote that a French explorer in the 1700s mistook the exhortation to be the creature's name. Professor Jolly says, however, the term may derive from a local word, *endrina*. The true name for the indri in Malagasy is the more reverent address *babakoto*, or grandfather.

An indri encounter somehow manages to be both magical and surprisingly ordinary, as Henry Mitchell wrote in *The Washington Post*:

The only place you can reasonably hope to see [indri] is at Perinet, and the best we hoped for was a black-

Trying to help Madagascar: The Duke University Primate Center

In October 1993, Dr. Kenneth Glander, administrative director of the Duke University Primate Center, visited the indris.

"Things have not improved since you went there," he said. "In fact, it's gotten worse—more habitat has been destroyed. If you remember at Perinet, the large chunk of forest across the road is being cleared. The indri and other lemurs are being eliminated, essentially. They can't share the forest."

Glander's words echo *Grzimek's Animal Encyclopedia*:

> The indris is not able to cope with conditions that were created by the settlement of people and the resulting deforestation. The number of indris decreased rapidly and is still on the decline.

The cheerful little ringtailed lemur finds itself in the same boat. Human settlers are chewing up its habitat in southern Madagascar.

Glander's focus is saving the golden-crowned sifaka. The 5,000 in Madagascar are expected to be extinct by the year 2000.

"Gold has been discovered in the area where they live," Glander said. "The miners have moved in and are destroying their habitat."

The Duke center, which solicits contributions via an Adopt-a-Lemur program (its Internet address: http://www.duke.edu-/web/primate/adopt.html) cares for three of these creatures, who may form a nucleus of captively bred lemurs.

The lemur expert's words came a week after I had returned from viewing an identical predicament in Brazil, where mercury from open-air gold mining threatened the wildlife of a vast area called the Pantanal.

The Malagasy continue not only to take over lemur habitat but to hunt and eat the creatures outright, given a lack of ready alternative sources of protein. In some respects the lemur, poached for its meat, may be worse off than the elephant, poached for its tusks and thus susceptible to pressure against ivory sales.

Not all the news is bad. "Some of the changes in the past five years you'd like," Glander said. "It's easier to get in the country. There are more flights. They've modernized the airport. This allows more people to see the country and will help the animals." Indeed, American visitors had climbed to about 1,000 a year by 1994, according to an official at the Madagascar Embassy.

and-white blur as they raced and leaped through the branches high above. But the rain forest here is nothing like that of Brazil or New Guinea. It is much like a nice woods in Virginia, except that virtually every plant is unique to the island. ... They are as easily seen (once you locate them in the vast forest) as a mockingbird in a Washington garden.

We took our leave of our distant grandfathers, not overstaying a 30-minute encounter.

Mission accomplished, we reached the point of a trip where all travel begins to take one homeward. After taking a taxi-brousse to Moromanga, we found ourselves more or less stuck. Walking along on a country road west of town with a vague idea to hitchhike, we endured lengthy stares. We must have appeared about as remarkable to the locals as three barefoot Malagasy in print wraps would be herding zebu down Interstate 95 outside Baltimore.

A couple with a utility vehicle stopped to pick us up. Despite there being little traffic, finding transportation did not pose a problem for us; surviving the ongoing construction on Route National 2 did. We jounced for hours. My neck felt like I'd gotten vertebrae damage from the crumbling road. (Reports indicate that the road has since been upgraded.) But a beautiful sunset lit up the valleys.

After arriving in Tana after dark, we gave our rescuers 10,000 FMG ($6.60). They appeared angry. Apparently, not knowing the going rate for a lift, we had made a grave miscalculation. But following our swap of spare FMG with the Bank of Switzerland, we had reset our dials from "money to burn" to "careful cash management."

Later I thought about our encounter with the indris. North American Indians apologized to their prey before killing them. Our pilgrimage to stand looking upward at the little indri family felt like a helpless parallel. Sorry chaps, but 5.7 billion humans aren't enough; we need your patch of forest too.

TUESDAY, JULY 26
Where are you from?

Our time had come to leave Madagascar, but not without one last unanticipated development. At the airport lounge for international departures, we met a young woman, one of the few Westerners in the country.

"Where are you from?" I asked.

"America."

"What area?"

"Washington."

"We're from there. What part?"

"Rockville."

"We're from Twinbrook! What neighborhood are you from?"

"Cinnamon Woods."

So much for the 100 Americans per year who then visited Madagascar. Four from Maryland sat in the airport simultaneously. Three of us hailed from Rockville, an All-American city and probably not the first place you'd think of as a hotbed of globe-trotters.

LESSON NUMBER 18: EITHER THE WORLD TRULY IS A SMALL PLACE, OR PEOPLE FROM ROCKVILLE LURK EVERYWHERE.

For whatever reason, our neighbor did not seem too delighted to encounter more Rockvillians. Mood of the moment? Was it the way meeting others from Rockville undercuts the conspicuous leisure, the travelers' one-upmanship, of going to Madagascar in the first place? Maybe she worked with grave seriousness on an international aid project, and we struck her, with some justification, as particularly naïve and frivolous tourists, bopping around difficult Madagascar on our own.

Nevertheless she informed us of the latest news: an attempted coup involving a takeover of the Tana radio station. This standard revolutionary tactic conjured up an image of a Third World Howard Stern with especially rabid fans. Oh, she added, airline workers had threatened to strike.

Once airborne, feeling as lucky to depart the threatened political and labor unrest of Madagascar as to have arrived despite the scarcity of air connections, we viewed one last time the erosion that human agriculture had set in motion. As we headed away from the island over Mahajanga, red earth appeared horribly visible below, as rivers carried the rust-colored ribbons for miles out to sea.

The flight crossed the straits where the coelacanth still lurks. According to a *National Geographic* article, these living fossils do odd things as they prowl the sea bottom, such as perform headstands. Our jet landed on a volcanic black rock island, set under an overcast sky with dark gold light escaping. We didn't have the foggiest notion where we had landed. The flight attendant clued us in. We sat on the Comoros, northwest of Madagascar in the Indian Ocean. The Comoros looked too remote to attract even the swarms of adventure travelers from Rockville that roam the globe.

Madagascar and the big lesson: the Earth's fragility

We traveled in Madagascar as pure amateurs, kids from Rockville with spare time who wanted to see something different. Home years later, I worked at *The Washington Post*, doing graphics at the newspaper that had inspired our trip. Every day I filled out spreadsheets to chart the graft in Congress, the numbers games in the White House budget and size of the Pentagon arsenal.

My trips to 30 foreign countries also seemed to have facets that could be roughly compared. I began to mentally plot these on an imaginary giant grid, comparing each country in terms of its people, scenery, wildlife, adventure and costs. Certain patterns seemed to emerge. Some widely separated nations epitomize tropical sensuality (Brazil, Thailand) or formal manners (Britain, Japan), navigational prowess (Britain, Polynesia) or shipping talents (Greece, Norway).

The places to which I'd traveled, unburdened by extensive knowledge, attracted me back for return visits, this time via research and data analysis. The moment came to read beyond the Lonely Planet guidebook's chapter containing "Facts About the Country" and to look at weightier tomes. Then the world could be examined in my father's Jesuit-trained fashion, by asking: What is the central lesson of every place I've been?

For Madagascar, the central lesson seemed to be how extinctions on islands, our most fragile ecosystems, provide an early warning of what can happen on continents when wilderness becomes fragmented. Ever since Charles Darwin's 1835 visit to the Galápagos, a discipline called island biogeography has focused on the knowledge to be gained from isolated areas.

By the 1960s, scientists had begun to study the links between habitat size and numbers of species. Preserving species on continents, they found, may require giant reserves, far bigger than previously thought and connected to each other by land bridges. Congress heeded this lesson with the California Desert Protection Act of 1994, which protected additional giant tracts of wilderness to connect existing national parks and monuments east of San Diego. British Columbia in 1993 similarly moved toward protecting the Tatshenshini and Alsek river valleys, creating the world's largest protected wilderness area, adjacent to Wrangel-St. Elias and Glacier Bay national parks in Alaska and the Yukon's Kluane National Park Reserve.

Habitats, threatened species compared

	MADAGASCAR	UNITED STATES
Protected areas	1.9%	13.3%
Threatened mammals	33	22
Threatened birds	28	46
Threatened plants	189	1,845

Based on data in *World Resources 1995-96*

Madagascar seemed to illustrate the worst case of what can happen when contiguous forests are eliminated, leaving only tiny parcels. Habitat loss began to threaten human life as well as the indri, the golden-crowned sifaka and the ring-tailed lemur. A wave of negative publicity beginning in the mid-1980s apparently shocked the government of Madagascar into attempts to help peasants realize that burning the forest, now 90 percent gone, and shooting lemurs translates into cutting their own throats.

A *National Geographic* article by Professor Jolly entitled "Madagascar: A World Apart" quoted a Malagasy minister, Joseph Randrianasolo, addressing villagers at the dedication of a nature reserve: "If there is no more forest, then no more water, and no more rice!"

Jolly wrote that "Madagascar's first wave of extinction eliminated a relative handful of species. Today's extinctions are far more drastic, undercutting the survival of the Malagasy themselves."

The skeleton of Aepyornis standing in the Antananarivo zoo attests to how, over the past 2,000 years, birds on islands have been the creatures most vulnerable to extinction. Aepyornis links Madagascar to the moa on New Zealand, the dodo of Mauritius and 35 types of birds now lost on Hawaii—all of which disappeared after the arrival of man, as did many lemurs.

Peter Ward notes in *The End of Evolution* a "tremendous lesson" taught by Hawaii, which also applies to Madagascar: "People arrived, and species died. … It shows that many species on the Earth cannot tolerate the least human disturbance, so delicately are they balanced on the precarious tightrope of nature."

Madagascar's lessons on the environment provided a framework for many of my later travels. In Tibet and Burma, totalitarian dictatorships like Madagascar's spelled catastrophe for forests, which have been extracted at a fierce pace. A struggle to survive in habitat diminished by logging, agriculture and human population pressures link the lemurs of Madagascar to the hornbills of Borneo, the lions and elephants of Africa (see page 92), the tigers of Asia, and owls, condors, panthers and jaguars of the Americas. Soil problems link Madagascar to Borneo and Central America.

Several factors make the island of Madagascar one of the most dramatic examples of the Earth's fragility.

LESSON NUMBER 19: OF THE 20 PLACES DISCOVERED AFTER CHRIST, MADAGASCAR IS:
- **THE LARGEST GEOGRAPHICALLY AND MOST POPULATED.**
- **THE PLACE WITH THE MOST FRAGILE SOIL.**
- **ONE OF THE MOST UNIQUE IN ITS ANIMAL AND PLANT FORMS.**
- **THE POOREST.**

Twenty places in the world, all islands except Antarctica, did not experience any human settlement until after the birth of Christ. Undisturbed by humans for eons, these island ecosystems have the world's most unusual and fragile wildlife and plants. Island ecologies can tailspin rapidly, as the first extinctions destabilize relationships and lead to further extinctions.

On paper, Madagascar, a huge island, should be able to support its 10,000

unique life forms and humans as well. California supports 30 million people, while Madagascar, which is more than a third larger in land area, has only 15 million people. The problem is that tropical soils make magnificent incubators of genetic diversity—and terrible areas for human agriculture. Soils such as those in Madagascar, unlike fertile California's San Joaquin Valley, bake to brick after only a handful of crop-growing seasons. On the most eroded place on earth, cliffs of treeless red dirt crumble into streams and rivers.

Now 80 percent of the island lies sterile and barren. From the air, the central highlands look like one big series of basement excavation pits for midtown construction projects—an aerial advertisement of the ugliness of habitat loss.

LESSON NUMBER 20: FRAGILE MADAGASCAR TEACHES US, MOST OF ALL, CAUTION IN ESTIMATING EARTH'S CARRYING CAPACITY FOR HUMANS AND RARE CREATURES.

Given its soil problems, Madagascar is one of the world's places least able to cope with a growing population. Yet in the six years following our trip in 1989, an amazing 3.4 million more Malagasy had been born, bringing the 1995 population to 14.8 million. That's more than 10,000 babies daily, or roughly two towns the size of Hell-Ville.

Somehow the island must support a staggering 34 million souls by the year 2025, if current birthrates hold. That's 24 million more people needing living space on an island dissolving into the sea than the number living there when Henry Mitchell visited in 1986. One wonders, where can they go?

Yet numbers of people may not be the entire problem. The Malagasy, even in booming numbers, are so poor that they use comparatively few resources, perhaps $1/70$ as much as an American. Still, poor people, in rocketing numbers, need land. Poverty gives them few alternatives to chopping down a tree to get wood for fuel and land for rice growing. This means less habitat for the lemurs, an odd and defenseless life form that has already flunked out in head-to-head competition with monkeys, let alone humans, in the Americas, Europe and mainland Africa. The lemurs make their last stand on Madagascar.

Madagascar reveals flaws in universally applying arguments presented by advocates of continuing human population growth. Even in prehistoric times, Madagascar's disintegrating soils could not support

Population in Madagascar

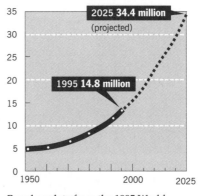

MILLIONS

2025 34.4 million (projected)

1995 14.8 million

Based on data from the 1995 World Population Data Sheet

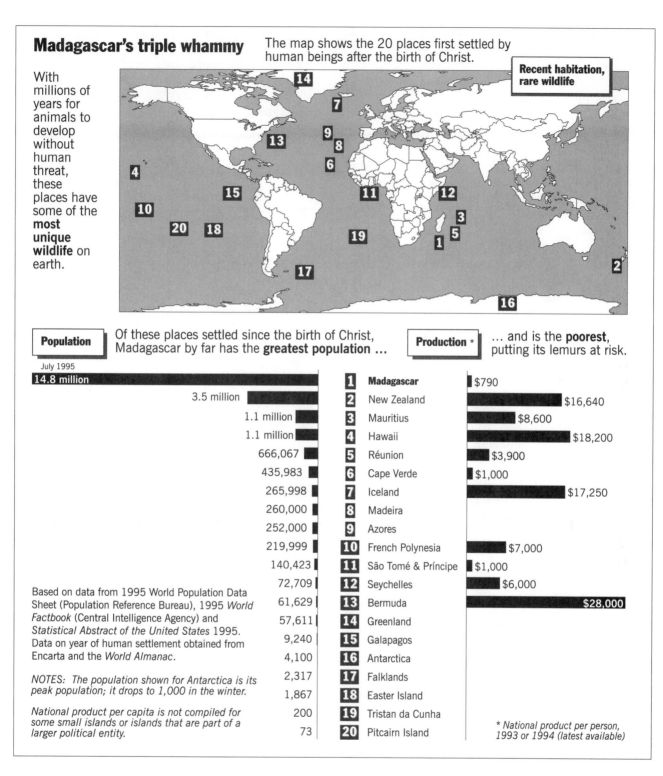

Madagascar's triple whammy

The map shows the 20 places first settled by human beings after the birth of Christ.

Recent habitation, rare wildlife

With millions of years for animals to develop without human threat, these places have some of the **most unique wildlife** on earth.

Population

Of these places settled since the birth of Christ, Madagascar by far has the **greatest population** ...

Production *

... and is the **poorest**, putting its lemurs at risk.

July 1995

Population	#	Place	Production
14.8 million	1	**Madagascar**	$790
3.5 million	2	New Zealand	$16,640
1.1 million	3	Mauritius	$8,600
1.1 million	4	Hawaii	$18,200
666,067	5	Réunion	$3,900
435,983	6	Cape Verde	$1,000
265,998	7	Iceland	$17,250
260,000	8	Madeira	
252,000	9	Azores	
219,999	10	French Polynesia	$7,000
140,423	11	São Tomé & Príncipe	$1,000
72,709	12	Seychelles	$6,000
61,629	13	Bermuda	$28,000
57,611	14	Greenland	
9,240	15	Galapagos	
4,100	16	Antarctica	
2,317	17	Falklands	
1,867	18	Easter Island	
200	19	Tristan da Cunha	
73	20	Pitcairn Island	

Based on data from 1995 World Population Data Sheet (Population Reference Bureau), 1995 *World Factbook* (Central Intelligence Agency) and *Statistical Abstract of the United States* 1995. Data on year of human settlement obtained from Encarta and the *World Almanac*.

NOTES: *The population shown for Antarctica is its peak population; it drops to 1,000 in the winter.*

National product per capita is not compiled for some small islands or islands that are part of a larger political entity.

* *National product per person, 1993 or 1994 (latest available)*

both a tiny number of settlers and certain creatures. Fifteen species of lemurs, all larger than surviving species, as well as tortoises, crocodiles, eagles, pygmy hippos and monstrous ostriches became extinct within 500 years of human settlement, a situation echoed on a smaller scale as species vanished following the Polynesian settlements of New Zealand and Hawaii. The biggest animals became extinct with a swiftness that announced the precarious ecology of Madagascar and foretold the struggle of its modern population to feed itself.

Critics of environmentalism cling to a view that humans hold a right to manage nature, to exploit it to provide people with better lives. At its most extreme, this argument runs that if the spotted owl or indri lemur isn't tough enough to adapt to a habitat altered by human activity, tough luck.

Alarmed scientists and naturalists have pointed out that we may end up needing a wide variety of creatures, even the less hardy ones. Mass exterminations may destabilize the planet. Biodiversity exists for a good reason: Earth needs a vast gene pool to permit the evolution and survival of species that will provide oxygen, medicine, food, stable soil and clean water on which humankind depends. Scientists believe it is quite possible that a cure for AIDS will be found in an obscure plant growing in a tropical forest.

Environmental concerns may eventually split conservatism into factions pro- and anti-. Like many Baby Boomers, I find myself rejecting most tenets of the Sixties canon—drug experimentation, the welfare state, high taxes and alternatives to traditional families. Yet more than ever, I support environmentalism. Conservative guru Margaret Thatcher, the former British prime minister who once viewed pollution controls as economic barriers, typifies the ecologically conscious Tory.

Reflecting her background as a chemist, she espouses a hardheaded environmentalism based on science rather than emotion. She concluded in a landmark speech to the Royal Society (the United Kingdom's academy of science) in September 1988 that protecting "the balance of nature" is "one of the great challenges of the late 20th century." She could have been describing Madagascar when she observed that

> the health of the economy and the health of our environment are totally dependent upon each other. ... But it is possible that with all these enormous changes (population, agricultural, use of fossil fuels) concentrated into such a short period of time, we have unwittingly begun a massive experiment with the system of this planet itself.

Humans benefit profoundly from biodiversity, noted Thomas J. Lovejoy of the Smithsonian Institution in a 1994 speech, "Biodiversity: The Most Fundamental Issue." Strep throat diagnosis has been speeded by the discovery of a useful micro-organism in the slime of Yellowstone National Park's hot springs. Oysters in the Chesapeake Bay clean the water of pollutants, as do the soils of the Pantanal of Brazil.

People with high blood pressure benefit from biological processes discovered in the venom of the Amazon's bushmaster snake. "So it is literally possible to say that millions of people are living longer and healthier lives because of the biology of some nasty snake in a faraway rainforest," Lovejoy noted. "These kinds of connections are very real and are rarely appreciated by people going about their daily lives."

The fragile soil of Madagascar illustrates that in the long term, land managed at the expense of animals also imposes a cost on humans. Though elsewhere, humans have survived so far despite exploiting animals and sometimes exterminating species, Madagascar may be the planet's starkest warning of a need to manage farms and forests for humans and animals alike.

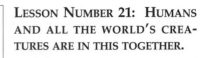

An indri peers about the forest.

LESSON NUMBER 21: HUMANS AND ALL THE WORLD'S CREATURES ARE IN THIS TOGETHER.

Malagasy peasants need to plow, enrich the soil and rotate crops, not take the last remnants of forest. Political isolation during the Ratsiraka dictatorship kept the Green Revolution in agriculture from reaching them. Now United Nations experts have begun to teach new farming methods to the superstitious Malagasy.

Thatcher neatly wrapped up the crucial triangle needed to nurture the environment: science, wealth and political freedom. All are lacking in superstitious, poor and (until recently) dictator-saddled Madagascar. She wrote in *The Downing Street Years* that

> For me, the economic progress, scientific advance and public debate which occur in free societies themselves offered the means to overcome threats to individual and collective wellbeing. The scarred landscape, dying forests, poisoned rivers and sick children of the former communist states bear tragic testimony to which system worked better, both for people and the environment.

Fortunately the international community, including the United Nations, the World Wildlife Fund, the MacArthur Foundation, National Geographic, the National Science Foundation, the Fulbright Fellowship and others now fund programs in Madagascar providing education, conservation and agricultural assistance.

LESSON NUMBER 22: MADAGASCAR TEACHES US THAT GETTING INVOLVED MAKES A DIFFERENCE.

Wherever an endangered species has begun to make a comeback, one finds a person like Alison Jolly, Kenneth Glander or David Anderson who has fought energetically to change matters. Madagascans such as Madame Madio and the staff of Parc Tsimbazaza also play a growing role. Americans can help as well on the home front, by recycling and supporting land use that invests in existing infrastructure in cities and other forms of dense developments and avoids chopping our open land into tiny, Madagascar-like parcels.

Meanwhile the lemurs struggle on. And Henry Mitchell himself departed this Earth in November 1993, leaving us his words in the newspaper morgue:

> Time has almost run out, after 180 million years of evolution, for the unique life of this Indian Ocean island. ... Almost every native thing seen here is found nowhere else.

And let us hope Madagascar's native creatures somehow avoid a fate of being found nowhere at all.

SPITTING, STARING AND A SQUARE CALLED TIANANMEN

China … and lessons on emigration

A woman carries a tray of raw dumplings at a little eatery in Beijing.

In 1985, 600,000 Westerners visited China. I and at least one other person, the writer Pico Iyer, did it the hardest way possible.

"Traveling in China alone, especially without any Chinese language, was still in 1985 an act of folly," Pico Iyer wrote in *Video Night in Kathmandu*. He had decided, however, that he could stomach

> any amount of inconvenience in order to be spared the red-carpet rituals of the guided tour—the picture-perfect vistas, the routine exchange of pleasantries with well-trained hosts and, above all, the infamous climax of every New China visit, the group of adorable schoolchildren welcoming Westerners with an impromptu chorus of "Jingle Bells."

Exactly right, Pico. I too committed this senseless act:

- Going to China in 1985
- on my own
- not speaking the language.

This proved to be a leap of unjustifiable optimism approximately on par with entering the Marine Corps marathon based on a training regimen of watching a few Washington Redskins games on television.

My dream to go to China grew out of several experiences. While many of the elite China watchers in the United States get their start at Harvard's East Asian studies department, my first encounter with Chinese culture was that of the typical American: eating at Chinese restaurants.

During a 1976 working vacation in San Francisco, I grew to love Chinese food, bought for $3 or less at luncheonettes with formica tabletops—places where all one's money went into tastiness rather than decor. Back in suburban Maryland, I studied Chinese cooking for a year. The teacher, Esther Ma, made off-the-cuff remarks that revealed much of how Chinese food and culture intertwine. At our first class, she apologized to all the older pupils "who know so much more than I

about cooking," though of course she was the only expert on Chinese cooking in the room. Clearly here was a culture with far less emphasis on youth than is the norm in the United States.

In her staccato English, she told us early on, "I am Shanghai girl," describing how that city's cooking conveyed sophistication. She detailed the differences between Shanghai's seafood cuisine and those of Beijing (starchy, with the emphasis on duck, chicken and noodles), Hunan and Szechuan (fiery), and Cantonese (stir fried, the style most Americans first encounter).

Esther, Esther, Esther! From your descriptions, I wanted to go to China and eat at all four compass points. But you never said anything about the low end of provincial fare: fish fins and pig stomach lining and other mysteries topping my bowl of rice. Or how, traveling in a country where I expected to have a gastronomical adventure, I would lose 10 pounds. Or how famine forced waves of emigration, which ultimately transformed the Overseas Chinese, as it had American immigrants, especially the Irish.

Esther, you should have told us: Go to Hong Kong or Taiwan to eat well. Order China's great regional cuisines in San Francisco or New York, anywhere other than on mainland China. Chinese-Americans knew these articles of faith, but I did not.

I knew so little then, about that and so many other things. In my mind's eye, I expected China itself to be Asia Fantastic, resembling the vibrant Kowloon district across from Central Hong Kong or San Francisco's Chinatown: a visual sea of bright red and gold gates, flickering lanterns, pagodas and silk robes.

Thus everything basic about the place came as a surprise: the lack of trees, the lack of birds, the lack (in the north) of street vendors, the lack of color in adults' clothes, the paucity of museums and temples in the world's oldest civilization, the soot and charcoal smoke in the cities.

Lesson Number 1: Visiting China required a process of subtraction from the expectations one would rightly entertain on a visit to anywhere else in the world.

In 1985, China's tourism industry for foreigners stood in roughly the same stage of readiness as did the U.S. Vanguard space program in 1958. Though the United States would eventually succeed in putting a man in space, the first unmanned rockets slowly collapsed on the launch pad and then exploded.

Similarly, China entertained lofty thoughts of encouraging more tourism by big-spending Westerners—to add to 30 million or more annual "neighbor Chinese" who visited from Macau, Hong Kong and Taiwan—yet the efforts backfired. Communist orthodoxy had bequeathed a legacy of anti-Western bias and surly service among many older Chinese employees in government shops and tourist bureaus. Big patches of the country stayed closed to Westerners. Air and train transportation could be far more dangerous than on Western carriers; that is, if one could even get a ticket.

Recent guidebooks suggest that individual travel in China has become much easier since 1985, and visitors stay longer and have more fun. But a different story can be told of the years right after the 1981 opening to individual tourists. Not only did I road-test China before its debugging, I traveled solo, without any mutual aid society.

The thought of a trip to China horrified my parents, for all the wrong reasons. For them a tour of the Vatican or the Holy Land represents the outer limit of adventure travel. They feared for my safety during what would likely be the first visit in family history by anyone to a communist country.

"Don't worry, there's little crime," I assured them, based on what I had read in my Lonely Planet guide to China (tellingly, still in its first edition). "They shoot shoplifters in the head in stadiums, they even sell tickets to it. Thailand's a democracy and it's more dangerous. There you could get drugged on a bus and robbed."

Not knowing how little China can be correctly imagined in advance by Westerners, I decided to visit the Middle Kingdom on my way home to the United States from a 3$^1/_2$-year stint living and working in England. China would kick off a 100-day "Singapore Swing," in which I would also visit Burma, Thailand, Malaysia, Singapore, Indonesia, Australia and French Polynesia.

China, one of the world's most demanding destinations, would be my introduction not only to Asia, but also communism and the Third World, all at once. For me there would be no easy starter countries, like Thailand or Malaysia.

Yet as woeful as modern China could be in the areas of cuisine, museums, comfort and scenery, no place on the planet would equal it then for strangeness, for otherness, for unpredictability and for unintended comedy, and thus for distraction from all things mundane.

However grim it might prove to be at some moments, traveling on my own offered the best way to see how a nation of 1 billion people lived day to day, an experience denied the official visitor and the package tourist. Later in Bangkok, a delightful Canadian couple, Mike and Diane, described an expensive package tour they had taken through China at the same time as my backpacker version. Diane said wistfully, "We didn't really see China." I would learn the truth of these words six years later, when I revisited China, officially sealed in the bubble of a journalist's fellowship.

On my first trip, China felt as alien as Mars. Its rigors and oddities accorded me the thrill of feeling like an Earthling on an interplanetary mission. Had I taken a rocket ship instead of a hovercraft into southern China, setting foot there could not have felt any less like the moment in the movie *Total Recall* when Arnold Schwarzenegger entered the processing chamber of the Mars colony.

China seemed far less alien on my return visit. Of course, bizarreness seems less bizarre on second acquaintance. But China appeared to have genuinely become more conventional in the wake of government campaigns to lessen spitting and staring at foreigners. For this reason too, I was glad I undertook my first difficult journey when I did, soon after the opening to the West.

And in retrospect, seeing China four years before the June 1989 deaths of hundreds of protesters, soldiers and bystanders, following pro-democracy demonstrations in Beijing's Tiananmen Square, allowed a glimpse into a window of optimism that was slammed shut by the time I returned to China two years after the event.

FEBRUARY 1985
Preparing for Asia

In my last days of living and working in England, I studied my Lonely Planet guidebook to China and began to realize the arduous nature of what lay ahead. Colds and flu would be tough for travelers to avoid in the winter and spring, the guide said, given the wet weather, widespread spitting and smoky cities. To be in peak condition, I "trained" for China. I swam and played squash and took vitamins and got lots of sleep.

The guidebook broadly outlined possible circuits, with rough schedules for many intercity trains and airplanes. Not knowing any better, I innocently typed a 21-day itinerary and mailed it to friends and family. What a laugh! As though you could just go where and when you wanted in China! As though Beijing was waiting, arms open to tourists, like Orlando or Las Vegas! Three weeks in the Middle Kingdom would make me an older, wiser and thousandfold more experienced traveler.

I gathered the list of supplies the guidebook suggested: a package of chopsticks (to avoid the reused, splintery and dirty ones in some remote eateries); a basic first aid kit with antibiotics; and phrasebooks, water purifiers and malarial treatments.

Most important, I collected family photos, especially ones showing little nieces and nephews. Caucasians arrive in long-isolated China, a land of 99.9 percent dark eyes and black locks, bearing the look of Chinese demons—odd hair colors such as red, brown or yellow; eerie eye colors such as blue or green. Hair sprouts from our arms as though we wear buffalo pelts. Round eyes, big noses, protruding breasts and jutting buttocks complete our freakish appearance.

LESSON NUMBER 2: FAMILY PHOTOS WOULD ESTABLISH ME NOT AS A FOREIGN DEVIL, BUT IN THE REVERED CONTEXT OF ASIA: AS PART OF A FAMILY.

On the last day of February, my plane departed England. It refueled at Dubai and flew on to Hong Kong, flying south of the airspace of the Soviet Union, Iran and any other places where realpolitik prevented taking the direct route.

After four days in Hong Kong, staying at a luxury apartment overlooking Repulse Bay with hospitable friends from Surrey who had just moved to Hong Kong, I traipsed off to China alone.

WEDNESDAY, MARCH 6
Muddy shades of gray, or China in late winter
One Westerner boarded the *Li Jiang Hu* ("Li River"), a hovercraft that left Tai Kok Tsui Pier at dawn for the 10-hour ride from Hong Kong to Wuzhou. Most travelers entering southern China take a boat or train out of Kowloon to Canton. But the Lonely Planet guide claimed that Guilin, a city surrounded by fabulous mountains shaped like shark's teeth, could be reached more easily from Wuzhou than from Canton, 120 miles to the east. So off I went.

The *Li Jiang Hu* quickly left Hong Kong's skyscrapers behind and entered China, a world that subtracted all the neon brilliance of Hong Kong. Brown shantytowns with dirt-splattered water buffaloes clung to the banks of the muddy Xijiang (of which the Li is a tributary), a wide river winding through Guangxi Province. Peasants in coolie hats rode bicycles or carried buckets on shoulder poles. Our wake forced women washing clothes at the edge of the river to scurry up the banks. Decrepit houseboats bobbed as we passed.

Meanwhile, to doubly hammer home the drabness of modern China, a vivid costume drama, set (I will take a wild guess here) in the Ming Dynasty and beamed from Hong Kong, played on the boat's color television. Four of the 80 or so passengers clicked their mah-jongg tiles as I feverishly studied my copy of *Berlitz Chinese for Travelers*. "Do you speak English" translated as … well, as soon as my eyes lifted from the page, I couldn't recall so much as a syllable of "*ni shuo ying-wen ma.*"

From the morning through the afternoon, the colorless landscape consisted of nothing but more shantytowns. Looking out on the alien world of peasants and water buffaloes on the Xi's banks, the entire trip suddenly seemed quite daunting. How exactly would I manage anything here?

Just because I found the food and glimpses of the culture in my Chinese cooking classes fascinating didn't mean I was prepared to deal with the language barrier or some of the world's toughest logistics, especially on my own. The odds against my successfully buying tickets, arranging rooms and purchasing meals without tools past my phrasebook seemed discouragingly long.

At dusk, the *Li Jiang Hu* arrived at Wuzhou, where immigration formalities took place on a floating dock. As the only foreigner to occupy Wuzhou's immigration apparatus, I delighted in the unexpectedly small-town feel to my first minutes officially in China. It was something unlikely to occur at a frantic border post or airport.

Customs consisted of a woman who confiscated my Hong Kong-bought oranges with an apologetic smile. I filled out immigration forms, then a silent man behind the foreign exchange counter cashed my traveler's checks. This took about 20 minutes, and at last I stood on the soil of the People's Republic.

My first photograph of China: I passed through customs in Wuzhou, in the white building on the left.

Few Westerners go to Wuzhou, an industrial city of 150,000 that, technically speaking, lacks any standard tourist attractions. So crowds of children gathered to stare at this unexpected and different-looking arrival—*moi*—as I explored the town.

My misgivings about taking this trip began to mingle with fascination. Wuzhou might have nothing for tourists, but—to walk around! In another sense, Wuzhou had it all—namely, the everyday wonders of Planet China.

Night had fallen, and waves of bicycles without lights, silent except for their tinkling bells, crossed a bridge. An occasional farm vehicle or army truck rolled past.

LESSON NUMBER 3: I PERFORMED MORE SUBTRACTION TO GET FROM MY UNDERSTANDING OF LIFE IN THE WEST TO LIFE IN CHINA: NO PASSENGER CARS.

Here I was in a sizable city in a continental nation—not one of the world's handful of tiny islands without cars—and for minutes at a time no auto engines broke the silence.

The simplest things about this part of China amazed me. At a big department store, with abacuses instead of cash registers, crowds gathered to watch the novelty of the single television set. Outside, cobblers sat with manual industrial sewing machines, repairing shoes by the light of shop windows. Noodle shops and orange vendors, with their hand-held scales, did business on the streets.

Asian vendors seemed a marvel, trading in the open air on the streets, as in medieval Europe. Such a curiosity: the ease of setting up shop without incorporating, leasing space in a strip mall and mastering payroll, quarterly taxes and insurance.

"So far everyone is most forbearing as I try to order and buy food," I wrote in my diary. "New words: *xie xie* (thanks), *fan* (rice), *cha* (tea, one of the few staples with practically the same name in all languages). Everyone most helpful and patient."

My first night in China was spent in a four-bed dormitory room at Wuzhou's single hotel. Happily, an elderly hotel employee knew enough English to book the room for me. He also left his station after work to walk around to various offices to help me arrange my onward bus ticket, a providence of a sort that would be repeated many times on this trip.

A carefully bound-up mosquito net dangled over my bed of plywood. Sandals and a thermos of hot water for tea, rather than a fax and cable TV, came with the room. Noisy conversations in Cantonese echoed down the corridor the rest of the night.

LESSON NUMBER 4: IN CHINA, FOREIGNNESS WOULD BE A 24-HOUR-A-DAY PROPOSITION.

THURSDAY, MARCH 7
Exploring an exotic village
The ticket collector handed out airplane-style barf bags to passengers on the 7 a.m. bus to Yangshuo, a village near Guilin. The need for these became apparent after we bottomed out on a particularly deep pothole. The bus catapulted those of us in the very back three feet into the air, nearly crowning us. A teenage girl sitting one seat up reacted to the bump by calmly hurling her noodle breakfast into the bag, in the matter-of-fact way I would dispose of some chewing gum.

Limestone mountains—spindle-shaped karst formations seen in only a few other places, including Vietnam and Thailand—rose magically out of the rice paddies as we drove farther north and west.

At about 3 p.m, the bus arrived at Yangshuo. Like the hotel worker in Wuzhou, a Chinese friend soon materialized in Yangshuo. A young man in a blue Mao jacket, Wen Pantian possessed a slightly goofy but earnest quality. We walked down to the docks, and Wen pointed out a little groundhog-like creature on the deck of a riverboat. The rodent bit back when the crew poked a stick at it.

"What is that?" I asked Wen.

"Enema," he said.

"Enema?" Curious as the goings-on on the deck might be, no public enema seemed to be in progress. I finally grinned despite myself. "Animal." Wen's shaky pronunciation provided part of the comedy, the rest came from the fact that any simpleton could see it was an animal.

Here in this little South China village, Wen recited factoids he had picked up about America. "Alaska, the biggest state. And I have heard of Texas, the second biggest …" He rattled off a half-dozen more. I doubted I could name six Chinese provinces. I complimented Wen on his English and his geographical knowledge.

"You speak the best English. Americans have the best accent," he replied.

I was suffused with pride. In England, people made fun of my accent; in Asia, Wen was the first of dozens to say how nice he thought American English sounded. And unlike Europe, this part of the world valued my national kinship to Mike Tyson, Sylvester Stallone and other international sports and Hollywood stars. Michael Jackson's coattails would make me more in demand than the Brits, French, Swiss or Australians.

I showed Wen my carefully packed set of family photos. I hoped they would be my passport to acceptance by the Chinese.

A snapshot stopped Wen cold. Puzzlement palpably gripped him. He frowned at a picture of my brother Paul hugging his collie-sized Shetland sheepdog, Conan.

"What is?" he asked in his clipped English. "Is bear?"

In China, dogs can be classified as small, nondescript things that re raised outdoors and then eaten. They do not have coats as shiny and groomed as Barbra Streisand's hair. They do not wear happy doggie grins as their owners hug them. The photograph appeared eccentric to Wen's eyes, as off-kilter as a photo of a Chinese affectionately hugging a chicken indoors would appear to me.

To allay some of the confusion attending the photo, Wen wrote in Chinese on the back, "brother and dog at play."

We ambled through a pagoda at a tiny village park. Two little girls came over to see the photos. They squealed when shown a baby photo of my nephew Matt. "He has no hair," one girl said, with Wen translating.

We headed to the Green Lotus Restaurant, an archetypal backpackers' hangout, the sort of place that sprouts up inexplicably in backwaters from Belize to

A little girl in Yangshuo peruses my phrasebook.

Kenya. A placard at the front door said, with mind-reading insight into the weariness and misty damp of late-winter travel, "Tired? Cold? Come in for our delicious food and company." I sat down to my first good meal in China, sweet and sour fish.

At the Green Lotus, I met two Englishwomen who had been backpacking through China for about a month. They asked for news of the outside world. After years of living in England, I was more up on British news than anything out of the States and knew that just a week before, Margaret Thatcher had broken the coal strike. Starved for information, they exclaimed at what was to them big news.

Wen took us all to the hot night spot, the Yangshuo movie house. On the walk over, I saw many Chinese hawking up phlegm with ear-splitting preliminaries and blowing their noses by leaning over with a finger to one nostril and shooting snot onto the street.

Mars, I thought. I might as well be on Mars. (The Chinese, for their part, reportedly consider Westerners utterly bizarre for blowing their noses and returning dirty handkerchiefs to their pockets.)

The feature that practically nobody paid attention to that night, a 1959 black-and-white Soviet spy film dubbed into Cantonese, memorably demonstrated that aged Russian movies somehow managed the feat of being more primitive, in all possible measures—from plot and characterization to cinematography— than Thomas Edison's 1891 Kinetoscope.

The audience, however, rated a "Most Rowdy" Oscar. A constant hubbub drowned out the nonsensical film. Everyone barked in rat-a-tat Cantonese and stomped around and scraped their folding chairs on the concrete floor. The tumult reached astounding levels for an ostensible place of entertainment, as though a waterfront beer joint had inexplicably decided to show a movie during a bar fight on St. Patrick's Day.

Afterward, we all walked back to the Green Lotus. Wen said I "made his heart feel warm." "Although I haven't had dinner," he added, "my stomach is full." (Food as love, love as food—the great common emphasis of China and Judaism.) Stifling a smirk but also touched by his innocence and sincerity, I thanked Wen for his company.

At this point in my first real day in China, with hours of unusual sights already to digest, a costumed New Year's dragon came down the darkened main street of little Yangshuo. The dragon twisted and turned and elevated its head to receive presents from people leaning out of second-story balconies. Revelers set off firecrackers. The thick smell of gunpower enveloped the Green Lotus.

For a moment, backpackers could pretend to be wheeler-dealers in the decadent Asia of the 1930s. At that instant, China felt exotic and ageless, with the mystery of an opium den in Shanghai, a polyglot "community of occasion" wreathed in smoke, the dragon still dancing in the New Year.

FRIDAY, MARCH 8
Otherworldly beauty on a bike ride

On the one-lane road outside Yangshuo, streams of people walked. Others rode bicycles with heavy loads. A man pedaled along with a woman on the carrier in back; she pulled a large wooden cart.

By rented bicycle, I rode an hour to Moon Hill, a pinnacle shaped like a wizard's hat. A crescent-shaped hole appears near the top of the peak The narrow asphalt ribbon ran alongside rice paddies, where peasants plowed with water buffaloes. The ponderous beasts turned automatically at the end of each furrow—quite a feat with gooey mud up to their knees.

The road continued through a narrow gap with more spires on either side. I pedalled on a bridge over a wide green river. Below the bridge, a man poled a sampan made of only four large pieces of bamboo lashed together. It seemed to float perfectly well.

The landscape outside Yangshuo looks like a classical Chinese painting.

On that misty day—my fleeting brush with roman-tic China—the scenery belonged to another world. The beauty of the ride made me giddy. Vapor swirled around the mountaintops. It felt like riding into a clas-sical scroll painting of jade-colored mountains shaped like shark's teeth.

LESSON NUMBER 5: BICYCLING, LIKE WALK-ING AND SAILING, INTIMATELY CONNECTS THE TRAVELER TO THE COUNTRY. THIS PROXIMITY TO THE EARLY SPRING PLANTING IN THE COUN-TRYSIDE WOULD HAVE BEEN UNATTAINABLE BY AUTO, BUS OR EVEN TRAIN.

I had a mere taste of the delights around Yangshuo, yet was able to say I'd bicycled in China. The time came to try to move on to Guilin.

Each year thousands of tourists float down 50 miles of the Li River, from Guilin to Yangshuo, through some of the world's most eerily beautiful scenery. I intended to reverse the journey, hitchhiking a ride upstream to Guilin on one of the dozens of boats returning empty. (The tourists go back by bus.)

This posed one of the trickier travel arrangements suggested in the Lonely Planet guidebook. Why I felt ready to try it on Day 3 in China, still overwhelmed by the novelty of the place, I don't know. Still, I took my backpack to the wharf.

Flocks of Japanese and American tourists paraded off the flotillas of tour boats for a bit of shopping in Yangshuo before returning to Guilin. I asked five cap-tains, one after the other, my one-word question: "Guilin?"

Five heads shook "no." Then, from Captain Six, came the one nod of assent I needed. I boarded and sat beside him.

Shortly after we left Yangshuo, a dispute broke out between the captain and two crew members. I looked up guardedly from my guidebook, wondering if I should take cover from the imminent fistfight. Shortly it became clear that the crew had been conducting a routine, nonviolent Cantonese conversation. I shrugged off my alarm. *It's just China.*

A tug pulled the small, 60-passenger riverboat upstream through a gorgeous landscape of twisting river and strange spiky mountains.

The crew served lunch with orange soda, *qi shui* in Chinese, and peered over my shoulder as I made notes. I gave them a cassette tape ("disco," the Chinese always demanded) of the Pointer Sisters. Two of the crew happily plugged in to a shared Walkman.

A third crewman played a guitar, bending the notes to make it sound like an Asian instrument. The first mate pulled out another guitar and a songbook, with "Love Me Tender" in both Chinese and English characters. They pressed me into service teaching the Elvis Presley chestnut—my chance to display the

Belliveau singing ability that can render "Happy Birthday" at family get-togethers as a Schoenbergian dirge of multiple atonality.

Despite limited English, the crew attempted a guided tour. They pointed to one spire, slowly wrote "car," and made swimming motions. Then they point-ed to the word "fish" in an English-Chinese dictionary. A light dawned. They wanted to show me Carp Hill. I drew a car and labeled it, then a fish and wrote "carp." Such nimble minds: The Chinese laughed, clearly understanding that they had unintentionally made a pun in English.

Dinner consisted of tripe 'n' rice with what appeared to be weeds. Paging Esther Ma! The Peking duck, the trout in black bean sauce, the eight-treasure soup—where were they? These working Chinese in the provinces certainly couldn't afford it. I picked at the greens and ate all the rice.

In the early evening, we docked at Yangti, more than halfway to Guilin. The crew unrolled thick com-forters on the ship's tables to sleep. The first mate, who struck me as the most handsome Chinese man I had yet seen—serious eyes like an American Indian's, boy-ish face, thick well-cut hair, blue jacket and cap—led me wordlessly into the village.

I found him attractive and fantasized in a most desultory way about a fling with a Chinese first mate, his very silence probably attractive for me, having undergone a bickering divorce in England from my first husband. But China, with its muddy gray ebbing winter and dankness and overcrowding, made me feel dirty and tired and completely lacking in libido.

We stopped before a nondescript door set in a row of attached houses. The first mate knocked and fixed his onyx eyes on the man who opened the door, who seemed to be the lodgekeeper. We walked across a dirt path to a door in a village wall. The man opened what would be my room in Yangti's equivalent of a Red Roof Inn, except that it lacked heat, outlets and cur-tains. Loud music blared from speakers on the village square, which consisted of several pool tables under a roof. A competing amplified tape blared from some-where.

Surveying my quarters, lit by a bare bulb, I mused: *How can it be that the Chinese don't all go mad?*

SATURDAY, MARCH 9
An itinerary in China? Not for long

At about 1 p.m., we arrived at Guilin and moored mid-river, lashed to the side of a boat that was, in turn, lashed to another and another, creating what on the Chesapeake Bay would be called a giant raft-up of at least 30 boats. Open-air woks a yard across steamed on the transoms of several boats. I clambered across decks and sterns of this floating village, across a rope bridge and onto the dock.

Unlike Yangshuo, Guilin appeared full of tourists.

There was nobody like Wen to talk to, just Chinese scalpers wanting to "change-ah mon-ee."

LESSON NUMBER 6: NATIONS WITH SOCIALIST GOVERNMENTS OR HYPERINFLATION INVARIABLY SEEM TO HAVE BLACK OR PARALLEL MARKETS FOR CURRENCY AND GOODS, A TELLING SIGN THAT MARKETS HAVE A DIRECTION OF THEIR OWN, LIKE WATER FINDING ITS OWN LEVEL.

In China, money-changing took an unusual twist. Alone among nations I have visited, China required tourists to use a separate currency for most transactions (although Burma, by 1996, had also taken the dreadful step of instituting a tourist currency). Many stores selling imported goods accepted only Foreign Exchange Certificates. Tourists could sell their FECs under the table to Chinese who wanted Western goods and get triple the official rate for the people's money they received in return.

The Chinese could use FECs to buy furniture and electronics. Tourists could turn around and use this cheaply purchased people's money for many restaurant meals and boat tickets.

> **Under the impact of increased repression, the Chinese people will try to circumvent the political system and the demands of the ruling elite to an even greater extent than they have during the last five years. They will increasingly move away from the socialist economic system toward an ever expanding parallel or second economy of moonlighting, black marketeering, illegal exchange of foreign currency, and underground banking and production. This trend is bound to weaken the structures of social control.**
>
> Jorgen Domes in "China's Internal Dynamics in the 1990s"

Similarly, given China's controlled economy, a parallel market for selling train tickets had sprung up. At a backpackers' cafe, a more likely outlet in a tourist town for a train ticket than the station itself, I made my first attempt to get a ticket for Chongqing, where I planned to take a Yangtze River boat trip.

Impossible! For three days, everything going west was booked solid, due to a convention and Japanese students being on vacation. The same story prevailed at the tourist and the domestic airline offices.

LESSON NUMBER 7: FOUR DAYS INTO MY TRIP, I WAS LEARNING WHAT A BILLION PEOPLE CAN DO TO THE AVAILABILITY OF TRANSPORTATION.

Unable to find a ticket for a plane, train, boat, bus or pony cart, I junked my original, minutely detailed itinerary, designed to provide as many water journeys as possible in China.

Plan B emerged: Grab anything that's leaving town.

Only under these conditions would a third-class ticket for the 32-hour trip to Beijing begin to look good. I paid a nasty little tout at the second place I tried, the La La Cafe across from the station, 36 yuan (the equivalent of $12.50).

Clutching my cardboard ticket, my passport to the unknown, I headed in midafternoon to the Osmanthus Hotel to rest in its dormitory for Westerners until departure. Around sunset, a hint of what lay in store came from four pale blond Danes. They entered the dormitory room greatly amused by their entertainment for the evening: a visit to the train station.

"We just saw *The Rocky Horror Picture Show*," said the tall one with a handsome drooping mustache and thinning hair.

I looked up from my tattered guidebook and shook my head, puzzled as to what he meant.

He referred to the spectacle of the 21:20 Shanghai-to-Kunming train pulling in, already packed to the gills.

The Danes had confirmed seats the following night. They had gone to watch a preview of the spectacle of Western backpackers, Japanese students on spring break and Chinese with unreserved tickets trying to squeeze on to the bursting train.

"First they let the tourists out of the waiting room," the Dane continued. "They ran up the platform, but hard-seat [third class] was already packed, with people on top of each other. One German guy got on somehow and then got off again—he couldn't stand the thought of staying on for 40 hours like that. He had held his hands in front of his balls to keep them from being crushed.

"Then they let the Chinese board. They raced out of the waiting room—there must have been several hundred of them—and they started shoving to get on.

"Some of them stopped to help two girls from Alaska get on. They lifted them over their heads and passed them in through the window, packs and all."

The whole thing sounded as fantastic as if they had reported finding caves with dragons in the limestone peaks above the Li River. But I was to learn it was a rather straightforward assessment of Chinese train travel.

"I wonder if it will be that bad, heading to Beijing," I said. "If so, you may see me back here later tonight."

My simple camp bed seemed unusually luxurious as I lay back for an hour's nap before the ordeal ahead. I had only a third-class ticket, or hard-seat ticket in Chinese parlance, for the 32-hour run to the capital.

At 11 p.m., I walked to Guilin station with a woman I'll call Sadie, a short, brown-haired, 25-year-old waitress from Banff in the Canadian Rockies. She also had a hard-seat ticket on the 1:05. Unknown to me at the time, a legend taking shape on the 1985 China backpacker circuit had latched onto me.

Sadie lugged a rucksack full of canned meat, peanut butter and Western cutlery up the road to the station. Even among the poorer backpackers, few would buy a 40-cent can of meat simply because it cost less than a $3 meal in a local eatery. For those few subscribers to the eat-badly-and-save-money school of thought, Sadie qualified as the Descartes.

I may be one cheap Cajun—I nearly got hit by a car while picking up a penny in downtown Baltimore one day. But while French Canadians tend to be cheap, we still ultimately remain French enough to be perpetually fascinated with various cuisines. Thus Sadie's line of reasoning struck me as mad. Local meals would be inexpensive and might also be good. You would never know unless you tried them.

The huge waiting room at Guilin South glowed brightly, packed despite the hour. That was China for you: no nightlife except for the 24-hour theater of train travel. I took out my two phrasebooks and cardboard ticket, to seek help so that we would end up in the correct line.

We made our way self-consciously to two Red Army officers with red insignia on their green overcoats, surrounded by a sea of string-tied parcels. They rearranged themselves and their belongings to make room for us before we could even ask, "Beijing?" They nodded and gestured to the bench beside them.

Time passed slowly. The 23:30 to Shanghai skimmed off several hundred in the crowd. We moved around the benches, in the shape of a giant letter C, and found ourselves near the front of the queue.

The officers craned their necks to read our luggage tags. I pointed to the "USA" in my address and then showed them the Chinese characters for United States in my Berlitz. They nodded and smiled.

Sadie leaned over to them and said, "I'm from Canada?" with her rising inflection that of a Valley Girl, North of the Border division. "Show them Canada in the book," she ordered flatly. I gave her a look.

She opened a flap on her battered gray rucksack with its Maple Leaf patch and pulled out some tissues. She had been spluttering and blowing noisily all evening.

She coughed right into my face, spittle peppering me.

"Sadie, don't cough on me again," I raged, thinking how much I had swum and worked out to be reasonably health in China. And now I would probably get sick, not from a Chinese crowd but a Canadian waitress.

"Everyone is sick here, you're gonna get it," she shot back without missing a beat.

I could no longer deny that Sadie struck me as lazy, clueless, an idiot and a pest. She would vastly

outshine me, however, in stamina and equanimity on this trip.

At 1 a.m. the crowd stirred. Those at the front got to their feet. We stood and strapped on our backpacks. Sadie in front, I behind gripping her shoulder strap like grim death, we assumed battle stations. "You just run, I'll be pushing," I said.

The train pulled in a few minutes late. An electrifying atmosphere attended the struggle to reach the third-class carriages, a sensation perhaps like being in a Latin American soccer riot.

Everyone stampeded, eight abreast, through the door up a ramp to the loading platform. "Go! Go! Go!" we yelled, shoving our way forward. I managed to keep hold of Sadie's rucksack despite being jostled from side to side. We two small women executed our Far East version of Washington Redskins' fullback John Riggins grinding it out behind the Hogs' blocking.

We pushed our onto the steps leading to Carriage 9, waved on by a ticket collector.

The 1:05 a.m. to Beijing

A solid mass of standing, crouching and hunched figures occupied the landing connecting Carriages 8 and 9. For a few seconds, it didn't appear we could get into the car proper, but shortly the masses behind pressed against our backs and bodily swept us into the aisle of Carriage 9.

On my left, 20 people camped in facing seats designed for six. They perched on the backs of the seats; or placed one buttock on the seat, the other in the aisle; or slept across each others' laps. Our rucksacks bounced off the banged-up yet unruffled Chinese as we clumsily threaded our way through the jumble in the aisle. Sadie found a space where she could at least stand with her feet together.

> **How can an American or European grasp the crowding? Imagine your own office or factory with two or three times as many employees as it has now, working in the same space.**
>
> Jay and Linda Mathews in *One Billion: A China Chronicle*

Just enough space remained in the filthy aisle to lay down my rucksack. I sat myself on it. A ticket collector, hand extended, approached immediately.

He muttered something, which I took to be a request for my ticket. He examined it at great length, disbelieving that two Western girls could rightfully belong here, shoehorned into Carriage 9. He handed the cardboard back reluctantly, evidently wanting to take us to first class (soft sleeper), where we belonged by virtue of our foreign faces if not our printed tickets.

He pointed to Sadie and, in another burst of

Chinese, apparently asked if she had the same ticket. I nodded.

We pulled out and, after a brief stop at Guilin North, began moving toward Beijing at a snail's pace, considering the distance we had to cover. I guessed we were going about 30 miles an hour by the rate the station lights went past. I was roughly correct; the trip averaged about 40 miles per hour, according to my later calculations.

Perched on my rucksack, I pondered how to survive 32 hours sitting up with only a minimum of space, perhaps two square feet, to call my own. Already two men in the aisle leaned up against the rucksack. I hugged my knees and soberly contemplated the floor around my feet. My running shoes stuck to a mixture of spittle, mucus, cigarette butts, orange peel and peanut shells, illuminated in clinical detail by all-night fluorescent tubes. Spirited Cantonese filled the air, competing with a loudspeaker alternating what sounded like political harangues with song and music.

Sadie stood calmly with her paperback, reading. She won't last long, I thought smugly. A man standing beside her cleared his throat and spit on her rucksack. A mother sitting nearby lowered a quiet toddler from her lap to the aisle, where it squatted and defecated through its split trousers. The mother placed a single square of toilet paper over the turd.

At the time, the alienness of it all had me agog. Had I been standing in an ancient crater on Mars, in a sandstorm of yellow dust, it would have felt only a tad more unfamiliar than third class on the Guilin-to-Beijing train.

Yet if I went back this day, far more experienced with Asia, and had to ride the 1:05, I'm sure I would be far more aware that the Chinese live as they must. Really I'm the anomaly in this picture, used to my American money buying me a big house and roomy transportation, not a handkerchief of train aisle.

LESSON NUMBER 8: MOST OF THE WORLD LIVES LIKE CHINA, NOT LIKE THE UNITED STATES, JAPAN, WESTERN EUROPE AND NEW ZEALAND.

No one else seemed tired or uncomfortable, and conversation and smoking continued happily. With my knees drawn up sharply under my chin, my ankles and feet became numb. My watch read 1:45 a.m., and the elation at getting on the train in the first place began to wear thin.

I decided that it was time to see the conductor about first or second class. People got on and off all the time on this marathon train ride, and seats might come open.

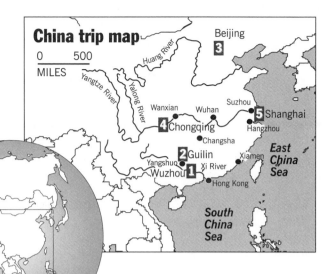

First class (soft sleeper, in Chinese train parlance) would provide a four-berth, luxurious sleeping car. Second class (hard sleeper) consisted of Spartan rows of bunks. Either would seem like Paradise, either squared or cubed, compared with third class.

I struggled to my feet and fought my way to the conductor's cubicle, between Carriage 9 and Carriage 8. I pointed in my phrasebook to, "I would like a hard sleeper please." The conductor took the book from me and slowly read the ideographs. He looked up with a broad grin and handed the Berlitz back.

I'll take that as a no, I thought. I shrugged and weaved back to my rucksack. I'd have to try to sleep a bit. I sat on my rucksack and slowly slid my rump down to the floor, facing the front of the carriage.

Leaning back on my elbows, I carefully arranged a leg on either side of a briefcase, standing up the long way in the middle of the aisle, and serving as a wobbly pillow for a young man with a wispy moustache. Briefcase Man's body was stretched out on the bench seat, his legs curled up, feet in his girlfriend's lap. I had to grasp my thighs firmly and lay each leg in place to avoid jostling his briefcase. My right leg encountered the hips of a squatting Red Army soldier on the far side of the briefcase, so I had to flex my knee and turn out my ankle to avoid him.

After plotting the safest place to lean back, which required a survey of the little area I had to maneuver in for a spot least covered in spit, I gingerly leaned back and let my back touch the floor, and used the edge of the rucksack as a pillow.

One could only imagine what variety of germs had now rubbed from the black blistery floor to my parka. Gob and refuse spread in lavalike rivers, lazily fanned by the motion of the train.

I marveled at the floor. This must be what it's like to wallow in a laboratory Petri dish, in a veritable cornucopia of microbes. I'd better burn my jacket in Beijing, I thought.

I closed my eyes against the glare of the fluorescent dazzlers in the ceiling. I couldn't close my ears against the hubbub. The loudspeaker droned on, punctuated by Sadie's coughing. The cold began to seep up from the floor, into my back. Despite the difficulty in navigating, a constant stream of passengers walked to a giant thermos of hot water at the front of the carriage. They refilled their outsized, lidded metal tea mugs, which kept the tea warm as the loose green leaves brewed.

Terrified of being scalded head to foot by jasmine tea should someone stumble, I opened one eye each time a passerby came along. A brief shadow, blotting out what seemed to my ever-shakier nerves to be blinding prison-ramparts klieg lights, alerted me to each participant in the tea parade.

The foot traffic prevented prolonged stretches of repose, so I attempted to nap in five-second bursts.

Male passengers chain-smoked unfiltered cigarettes, aggravating my allergies heightened by the coal braziers of Guilin. Everyone in China would suffer lung ailments in 30 years, I was certain. Occasionally a draft wiggled into Carriage 9, clearing the smoke but making me shiver. The cold of the floor continued to rise in my back, and my awkwardly arranged feet began to get icy.

I tried to flip onto my left side, but forgot the briefcase between my knees and accidentally toppled it. Briefcase Man, in his sleep, froze his head in midair as his "pillow" capsized. Without opening his eyes he grabbed it in midair and put it back into place. "Sorry," I said automatically in English.

By picking up my right leg and swinging it around the briefcase and on top of the left leg, I managed to get on my left side. There was no way to extend both legs without kicking the Red Army soldier again. So instead I extended my legs at 45 degrees to my waist, arranged underneath the bench of Briefcase Man. My jeans lay on a gobby river of spit.

Several minutes of troubled sleep ensued. Then the stream of people resumed, this time not for hot water, but to go to the lavatory. The door handle squeaked each time someone turned the handle. Seconds later a fetid wave washed over our noses.

I tried to ignore both the smell and my numb left shoulder. Given the tendency of greater miseries to overshadow lesser ones, the lavatory smell did have the relative advantage of momentarily blotting out the cold draft and the cigarette stink.

To allay the pains in my shoulder, I laboriously reversed the previous arrangement of limbs. I lay on my back again, knees wrapped around the briefcase. By repeating the cycle each time either my back or shoulder position got too agonizing, I could maintain the fiction that, by virtue of being horizontal and having my eyes shut, I was resting.

Through the night, members of a family chattered indefatigably in the seats to my left, where they'd staked out territory by tying a string bag of oranges to the window latch. Hawking and spitting on the floor punctuated their half-shouted conversation. At the time the Chinese held the world stage as the grand divas of hawking, collecting their phlegm with a great rattling sound and explosively discharging it.

The practice always seemed to horrify Westerners. In 1941, it drew the attention of wartime journalist Martha Gellhorn. By sampan and pony, she visited central and southern China with Ernest Hemingway, later to be her husband and wittily listed as "U.C." (Unwilling Companion) in her recollections in *Travels with Myself and Another*:

> Everybody has idiosyncrasies. One of mine, involuntary and unfortunate, is a reaction to the sound of hawking up phlegm, collecting it in the mouth and spitting it out. My reaction is to retch. Nothing violent, no carrythrough, but an instant sudden spasm. This hawking was background music from the sampan.

On the 1:05 to Beijing, I did not allow myself to look at my watch until I was confident it would show a sufficient passage of time to boost morale. It seemed nearly dawn when I finally allowed myself the luxury.

2:20 a.m. No way! Bizarre Middle Kingdom force fields had played tricks with my liquid crystal display. I stared glumly into the middle distance. A man in a blue jacket stood, cigarette in hand, not really staring but looking my way. I rolled my eyes heavenward. After a second's hesitation, he broke into a wide grin. It was remarkable, really, that we could nonverbally acknowledge the discomfort of this journey.

I performed several calculations of the ratio of time elapsed and that remaining, and of my remaining patience and fortitude vs. the sentiment I increasingly felt, best described as abject misery.

The situation called for some mental discipline.

"One day," I told myself, "you will sleep again in a comfortable bed." I imagined a carpeted room, dark and quiet, with a wide bed, sheets and a comforter. No concentration-camp lighting, no static-filled renditions of "The East is Red," no wafting lavatory smells would invade this haven.

I managed to keep hysteria at bay until it finally seemed safe to look at my watch again.

3:06 a.m. Only two hours into the trip. Time to dig deep, to find some mental imaging, some positive visualization for next 30 hours.

All right: I would emulate the 53 American hostages held in Iran from 1979 to 1981. If they could keep cool for 444 days under an infinitely worse situation, I could steel myself for a little train journey in China. For some reason, my mind latched onto the fact

Why China feels crowded

China had 1.2 billion people in 1995, and the lower 48 United States, 262 million, in roughly the same overall amount of land area. Thus the population density is much greater in China.

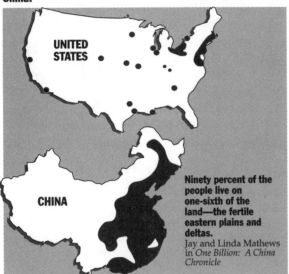

UNITED STATES

CHINA

Ninety percent of the people live on one-sixth of the land—the fertile eastern plains and deltas.
Jay and Linda Mathews in One Billion: A China Chronicle

Why China's trains are 50 times more crowded than those in the United States

UNITED STATES

184,235 miles of rail tracks

15.6 billion passenger miles per year

CHINA

35,200 miles of rail tracks

160.4 billion passenger miles per year

Based on data from the *Hammond Citation World Atlas* and *The New Book of World Rankings*

that one of the Hispanic Marines kept hostage had defiantly written on his cell wall, "Viva el Rosa, Azur y Blanco."

Somehow I doubted that graffiti extolling the American flag would help in my particular case. But I had to find some motto, some war cry. Maybe I should just tell myself: *You're being a baby. Have the will to ignore the unpleasant aspects of the situation.*

Further watch checks revealed 4:22, 4:51 and 5:28. I composed a paperback title: *Hard Seat, The Place Where Time Almost Stood Still.*

First light arrived. I struggled up, perched again on the edge of the rucksack, which now bore two other sleeping heads. Gingerly I stretched my arms.

Sadie was still standing, reading her book and coughing. She looked up.

"Fun, ain't it?" I said.

She nodded. "Yep." I had to admit, she was an iron lady.

Rows of young Red Army soldiers squatted in the aisle, their bodies bobbing and swaying as they slept with their heads on their knees encircled by their arms.

At 6:30 a.m., the family to my left, as though attempting a Guinness Book record for world's longest-running mobile picnic, peeled more oranges. A woman's voice droned over the carriage's public address system. The loudspeaker, one of more than 100 million in the People's Republic's trains and buildings, broadcast news and propaganda.

For all we knew, she was exhorting us to hit the restrooms. In his 1983 book, *China: Alive in the Bitter Sea*, Fox Butterfield reported "a bright, soothing woman's voice from the black round box just above my head" enjoining travelers to get a move on: "Everyone should go to the toilet, brush your teeth and fold your blankets."

A noodle cart battled down the aisle with breakfast fare, nearly removing my toes. Its passage squished all of us even more cozily together, like garbage being compacted by a trash truck.

At 7 a.m., I said brightly to Sadie, "Just 26 hours to go!" Surely the daytime wouldn't be so nightmarish. But another night rolling in the slime was out. I would have a nervous breakdown, right in the middle of China.

"I'm going to check out the rest of the train," I called to Sadie, as an audience of 200 watched with interest. "Could you keep an eye on my rucksack?"

I made my slow way to the back of the carriage. After negotiating the human obstacle course, I passed unchallenged into the dining car, and then into the next car, a hard-sleeper carriage.

This carriage was smoky and full of Chinese passengers in pajamas on rumpled bunk beds. The bunks were arranged in clusters of four, with perhaps 10 clusters, all open to the passageway. Though crowded, it was nowhere near as bad as Carriage 9. In fact, I found a single unoccupied seat by the window to watch the mud-brown world of Hunan province slide by. My human dignity began to return. I was able to tolerate and almost enjoy the journey for the first time.

After calming down for a few hours, I sought out another ticket collector. This time I aimed high, asking the tiny man via the phrasebook not for hard sleeper, but for soft sleeper. He shook his head. I mulled over what to do next.

Awful as it seemed, I had to return to hard seat, Dante's third cornice of Purgatorio—his descent into a realm where "no gloom of Hell ever ... rasped my senses so." Ticket or no, I had to relocate my pack and Sadie, in that order, to hard sleeper.

At Changsha station, I returned to Carriage 9. I needn't have worried about Sadie. She stood, happily staring into space. I described a plan to exit Carriage 9 at the next station, Yueyang, get past any guards, and crash the party in second class. She agreed.

Just as we were fairly close to our planned escape from Hades on rails, the noise, the crush of humanity, the smoke and everything else overwhelmed me. I started to whimper. Tears began to well up in my eyes. My mood darkened with self-pity, and I wimpily thought of romantic turmoil I'd left in my wake in England—both a divorce from my first husband, an Englishman, and after that, a ridiculous affair. I started to cry, just a little. Steel yourself, I thought, and I managed to stop short of bawling.

Sadie—serene, unperturbed but not at all well—hacked constantly, rife with some amalgam of unfamiliar Asian infections of the deep respiratory tract. Unaware that the sight would be among our last in hard seat, we watched parents hold their children out the window to relieve themselves. In retrospect, I decided a system that avoided diapers if anything demonstrated genius.

At that juncture, 10:30 a.m., the travel gods commuted our sentence.

The tiny ticket taker whom I had asked about soft sleeper appeared at the back of our carriage. He methodically scanned the faces in the carriage and then fought his way up the aisle. He gestured for my phrasebook, flipped through the pages and finally pointed to the ideogram:

"Soft sleeper."

Some first-class passengers must have left the train at Changsha. I smiled stupidly at the little ticket taker. My spirits soared. Dippily I pointed out a series of remarks in my the phrasebook section on visiting natural wonders:

It's …	
	zhe
amazing	ling-ren chi-jin
magnificent	hen gao-shang
monumental	yong-yuan bu-xiu
overwhelming	bu-ke di-dang

As he led Sadie and me toward the back of the train, our loaded rucksacks tumbled the Chinese like tenpins. Once in the dining car I looked back one last time at a dozen faces pressed wordlessly, cheek to jowl, against the glass of Carriage 9. I almost shivered. We left the Chinese to their fates, across a divide in a world we would know no more.

The first-class compartment, capable of sleeping four, seemed palatial. A potted plant and a lamp stood on a small table covered with a lace doily. Antimacassars protected the tops of the seats from hair oils. As if on a lazy Sunday morning at home, we could pour hot water from a thermos to make tea and pad about in sandals provided with the compartment.

A Chinese couple in their fifties welcomed me to

A vendor at Changsha passes noodles into third class.

A different perspective on third-class travel

Two weeks after my experience in hard seat, a chance encounter in Shanghai provided some perspective. A trio of businessmen, somewhat bored after weeks of only each other's company, asked me to join them for dinner in the elegant Park Hotel. Ted Chun and his two American colleagues flew first class everywhere in Asia, so they asked me to give my impressions of backpacking through China.

I described the 1:05 to Beijing, and they listened with interest. Had they experienced this sort of travel? Not at all, they said.

Suddenly I worried that Mr. Chun, a dignified 78-year-old, might take affront at my description.

"Maybe third class just offends our Western notions of personal space," I backtracked. "But how do the Chinese tolerate it?"

"They feel lucky to have a ticket," he said.

the compartment. The husband pointed to the ideogram for "factory manager" in my phrasebook. I showed him "American" and "journalist." Thus we conversed after a fashion. They bought four large steamed dumplings at the platform in Yueyang and with a smile gave me two.

This peace and sanity came at the price of a $20.88 upgrade. When I had paid, the ticket collector turned to Sadie. She waved him off, to his mystification and mine.

"Sadie, it's only $20," I said. "It's worth the money."

Sadie wasn't going to pay any $20. She would freeload part of the time in first class with me, without paying an upgrade. The rest of the time she would hang out in hard sleeper, playing cards with the Chinese passengers and scrounging a place to sleep.

I hopped into one of the top berths. There I slept many of the remaining 24 hours to Beijing, awakening when a waiter came around to take lunch and dinner orders. The dining car catered to Japanese students on vacation, Red Army generals in tailored greatcoats and other privileged castes in ostensibly egalitarian China.

A little reverse bargaining

Beijing could be fun, once you got over its sterility, its un-Asian lack of markets, its wide empty boulevards, its dry air that made for nosebleeds, and the vast, Houston-scale distances between buildings. For two days, I enjoyed the tourist aspects of the Beijing circuit. Plenty of Americans, hailing from Virginia, California and elsewhere, could be found riding the bus to the Great Wall, partaking of divine Peking duck at Qianmen Roast Duck, and for a few pennies watching thrilling acrobatics shows.

On a more practical mission, I headed east from Tiananmen Square to Wangfujing Street, Beijing's main drag for department stores. My purchase of a new down parka ($18) and a watch ($7) created a dilemma. What to do with my old jacket?

As much as the jacket reminded me of the filth of my train trip, I did not want to just throw it away in a country like this, where someone could still use it. And you couldn't simply discard old clothes. The Chinese would try forever to reunite even deliberately forgotten items with their owners. Nor could I give it away. The Chinese possessed too much pride for handouts.

Along came Bao Shaokui to see if I needed help. He was sort of a big-city version of Wen: a guy who spoke English well enough to be a valuable day guide. I had bought a new parka, I explained, and wanted to sell the old one. He offered to take me to a secondhand store a 20-minute walk away.

"I'm in a hurry to see the Forbidden City on my last day," I said. "Do you have any friends who might want it?"

"How much?" Bao asked.

"Five jiao," I said. Two cents.

"Two yuan," he countered, upping the bid to 70 cents. He was trying to be hospitable to a foreigner, I was trying to be grateful to a host, and we conducted a reverse bidding war. We settled on one yuan, 35 cents then.

Bao took me on a tour of the Forbidden City, the giant palace of the Ming and Qing emperors. No gold braid à la Versailles surrounded its shabby wooden structures, only grubby green string netting.

The condition of the Forbidden City spoke volumes about how few historic sights and museums had survived Communist Liberation and the Cultural Revolution and how those that did were poorly maintained. In fact, many historic buildings had been torn down in the 1950s to make Tiananmen Square itself.

Bao's story struck me as more interesting than the Forbidden City. In fairly good English learned from language tapes, he told me how he earned 40 yuan a month ($13.80) at the Beijing Arts and Crafts Center,

Bao poses formally at the Forbidden City.

working nine hours a day, six days a week. With those wages, he couldn't afford to get married, even though he was 29.

That night, Don, a traveler from Arlington, Virginia, and I shared a taxi to the Beijing Hotel. We discussed what a pain Sadie, still trailing in our wake, was. Her China guidebook remained pristine, while mine was in tatters from doing all the map reading and trip planning. She depended on us to take her everywhere but wouldn't eat what we ate, invariably relying on her stash of peanut butter.

An international crossroads crowd, along the lines of the Star Wars Cantina, gathered in the Beijing Hotel's bar. We plopped down on a vast U-shaped sofa around our beers and groundnuts, joining an ad hoc group from Hong Kong, Taiwan, Africa, Australia and Alaska.

Two women from Seward, Alaska, described surviving the famous Good Friday earthquake in 1964, when boats and fish lay briefly on a dry seafloor before a monstrous tidal wave roared in.

Wait a minute … two Alaskan women?

"Yup, that was us," confirmed one. Indeed, as the Danes had told me four days before, they had been lifted, backpacks and all, onto the train at Guilin.

A tall African, a foreign student at a Chinese university, sat on my immediate right.

"Where are you from?"

"Burundi."

"Ah yes!"

"You've heard of it?" he asked, disbelieving. (It must be tough to go through life telling people you're from a minor country.)

"Oh yes. Burundi drummers!"

He beamed. My exposure to world music, in the early 1980s while living in England, paid off in a small way. How did he like Beijing?

"Terrible. None of us have girlfriends."

Africans in China lived a lonely life. They particularly bore the brunt of Chinese feelings of cultural and even racial superiority. China had enjoyed the highest standard of living in the world until the 16th century.

It might once again enjoy status as the world's richest nation, in gross terms, replacing the United States in that by the year 2020, if the World Bank's projections are correct. The Chinese bask in their special place in history, even if this was big news to we history-deficient Americans. As Fox Butterfield wrote in *China: Alive in the Bitter Sea*:

> China was the only survivor of the world's great early civilizations: Egypt, Mesopotamia, Greece and Rome. That gives China a language, culture, and state structure that date back over two thousand years.

If the Chinese attitude belittled Africans, it certainly baffled Americans. To us, the Chinese seemed to be resting on some rather old laurels. In keeping with U.S. beliefs in advanced technology as the yardstick for civilization, the American visitor to China tended to find the Chinese arrogance faintly preposterous and to wonder: *What have you done lately*? A California man I ran into at the Great Wall put it crisply: "Every time I ran into their superiority complex, I wanted to say, 'And where's your space shuttle?' "

Apparently the magnitude of the Chinese sense of superiority increased when it came to black people. Socially, male students from Marxist African nations who fetched up in Beijing for their university studies endured a long, cold winter.

Dating Chinese women drew the wrath of Chinese men, as African students at Hehai University in Nanjing discovered in December 1988. When they tried to take their dates to a Christmas Eve dance, a brawl broke out. Word of the incident made its way to other cities. Posters decrying "black devils" sprouted at a Wuhan polytechnic institute, and Beijing students staged a demonstration that Africans perceived as against them.

The Chinese are among the world's most racist people, sneering at and manipulating foreigners behind their backs, fiercely opposed to interracial marriage and inclined to push around the minority people living on their borders.

Jay and Linda Mathews in *One Billion: A China Chronicle*

At least in the bar of the Beijing Hotel, with non-Chinese, the Africans could momentarily enjoy themselves. We toasted each other in a dozen languages.

SATURDAY, MARCH 16
Back on the river again
After the Beijing interlude, I made my way to the airport alone, with no farewells to tip off Sadie to my plans. She would have to attach herself to some other traveler.

I revived my sidetracked plan to explore China by "slow boat." My goal in China, logistics permitting, was to take as many water journeys as possible. I lifted the idea for my 21-day, solo circuit of 2,000 miles by river, lake and ocean from a travel brochure listing an expensive tour. My $400 backpackers' version had so far taken me on the Xi by hovercraft and the Li by riverboat, hitchhiking.

LESSON NUMBER 9: MY WATER JOURNEYS SENT ME FLOATING ALONG THE NATURAL FEATURE THAT HELPED THE CHINESE TO DEVELOP CIVILIZATION: RIVER NETWORKS.

Chinese civilization, which extended over a greater land area than any other homogeneous culture, developed along three main river systems, which provided water for irrigation and transportation. Governing bodies constructed and oversaw irrigation and flood-control systems. "As in Egypt, the beginning of political organization was linked with geography," noted T. Walter Wallbank in *Civilization: Past and Present*.

To continue exploring China's rivers, on March 14 I flew to Chongqing (pronounced Chawn-CHING), in effect retracing most of my way back to Guilin. My goal would be to find a boat to sail down the Yangtze River. To this end I bought a fourth-class ticket for the 60-hour journey to Wuhan on *East is Red No. 5*.

The riverboat booking office listed no first class, China being after all an egalitarian, Communist country. This I had already seen on the train to Beijing, which also had no first class, only "soft sleeper."

On this riverboat, the classes began with "second" and ran through fifth (outside on the deck). Second provided a two-bed cabin, third meant four to eight beds in a room.

Fourth, for which my ticket had cost $12.68, consisted of a 16-bunk cabin. Because of the endless demand for tickets anywhere and everywhere in China, I had a two-day wait before leaving Chongqing, at 14 million people one of the world's largest metropolitan areas.

To my surprise, right away I liked unheralded Chongqing. Located in southern China, well off the most popular tourist circuit of Beijing-Xian-Shanghai-Guilin-Canton, Chongqing resembled Wuzhou, where I'd had my first taste of China. For me, both cities initially functioned strictly as trailheads for water journeys.

LESSON NUMBER 10: THE LACK OF "SIGHTS" TO EXPLORE IN CHONGQING AND WUZHOU MEANT THAT EACH OPENED A PERFECT WINDOW ON EVERYDAY, AS OPPOSED TO TOURIST, CHINA.

Chongqing's lively sidewalks lent it a vastly more

A monkey performs on the streets of Chongqing.

A man hauls a heavy cart up a Chongqing avenue.

simple act drew a crowd of 80 to stare at this freak, a Westerner. A 26-year-old mining engineer's assistant joined me to practice his English. He earned 54 yuan a month ($19 at the then-official rate).

I took out my calculator. "If you worked in the United States, " I said, thinking he would make—at the very, very least—$16,000 a year, "conservatively you would earn more than 4,000 yuan a month."

An expression between sorrowful envy and disbelief crossed his face. I assured him that housing, transportation and food cost more, too.

Thereafter I learned to underplay American affluence to the Chinese, who seemed unready for full awareness of how far they lagged the West.

The engineer's assistant said his institute had a calculator that he could borrow. He imagined everyone in the United States had a calculator. I said that was true, but an engineer would also have access to a computer.

The time came to board the boat for the three-day trip to Wuhan. I took my bunk in the crowded room of 16. Two foreigners in addition to myself, West German students named Anton and Kirsten, joined 350 or so other passengers.

A group of young Chinese trendies, identifiable by their slightly long hair and comically dated hipness—an attempt at a sort of *Brady Bunch* groovy dude and dudette look—corralled me.

"*Meiguo*?" They had asked if I was American. *Meiguo* translates literally as "beautiful country."

I nodded. "Disco!" they yelled. I dug through my backpack for my cassettes and found the Pointer Sisters. We made for the passenger lounge, where my tape went into the cassette player. They politely tried dancing, and I showed them my best shot at break-dancing. Soon enough they switched back to the saccharine Hong Kong pop they preferred.

The days passed with sightings of a sailing junk, terraced fields and a few nondescript hamlets. *East Is Red No. 5* stopped at the riverside town of Wanxian, which kept its market open late so that travelers could spend a few hours browsing for wickerware, meals

Asian feel than Beijing. Monkeys in green bellhop suits and caps performed somersaults for a few coins. A freak show displayed human fetuses in bottles. Eels wriggled in dishpans, awaiting the moment they would become someone's grocery shopping, as did chickens, ducks and geese kept in wicker baskets. Right on the pavement, vendors slit the chickens' throats and gathered their blood in bowls. They stopped kicking after half a minute. After boiling their feathers off and gutting them, the vendors handed the freshly killed birds to afternoon commuters walking home.

Two laborers carried giant building stones on a shared shoulder pole. A man in a harness hauled a cart up the steep streets from the docks.

LESSON NUMBER 11: AS IN EAST AFRICA, WHERE HUMAN MUSCLE INSTEAD OF A WINCH TRIMS DHOW SAILS, CHONGQING'S MEN LABORED TO DO JOBS THAT IN THE WEST BELONG TO THE INTERNAL COMBUSTION ENGINE.

I took a bus, as crowded and rib-crushing as a third-class train, part way to the city zoo. There a bleak cement enclosure featured six scruffy pandas, sharing their cage with two rats. At the zoo's teahouse, a broadly smiling woman sold me jasmine tea with floating white flowers. As I sipped it, a tiny girl tapped my elbow. To smiles of approval from a nearby table of adults, she handed me a cookie.

Walking from the zoo, I stopped on a sidewalk for a bowl of tofu with red Szechuan peppercorns. This

Life imitates art—real and painted hippos yawn at Chongqing Zoo.

and provisions. As I got ready to go explore, a man in our dorm tapped my arm.

"Eh," he said, tapping his watch. I nodded. "Eh," he added, holding up 10 fingers, then two more. "Umm," he said, with utmost gravity holding up his cardboard ferry ticket.

I smiled and said, "*Xie xie*" (thank you). He'd told me, as clearly as a fellow English speaker could have, to be back on the boat by midnight, and to be certain to present my ticket to reboard.

A crowd boards the *East is Red* at Wanxian, bearing motorbikes and smaller parcels.

LESSON NUMBER 12: THE CHINESE CONTINUALLY SHOWED GREAT NIMBLENESS IN GETTING AROUND THE LANGUAGE BARRIER.

I wandered around Wanxian and bought oranges. A vendor weighed a bagful on his hand-held scales and said, "*wu-shi wu*." I looked in my phrasebook: 55. Ah ha, 55 fen. For the first time, I had understood a number in Chinese, marking more progress in language and communication.

I kept strolling and saw, through an open door, a family getting ready for bed. A big wooden platform filled the front room, and five people of various ages were getting ready to lie under their thick comforters. Both the sleeping arrangement and the earliness of the hour, about 8 p.m., struck me as noteworthy.

> **When a worker gets home, the crush is worse. Parents or grandparents must share beds with their children or grandchildren. The rooms are usually so small that the sleeping platforms or beds half fill them.**
>
> Jay and Linda Mathews in *One Billion: A China Chronicle*

No. 5 passed through the famous Yangtze River gorges. Gray luminous clouds floated over gray bluffs 1,000 feet high. Gray and clay-colored villages lay amid soft red earth and subdued green in the terraced fields.

LESSON NUMBER 13: THE SCENE CONFIRMED THAT AS USUAL, NATIVE ART FAITHFULLY RECORDS THE LOOK OF A REGION.

Early Chinese artists believed that brushstrokes of black and white sufficed to illustrate a landscape. Indeed, an artist needed little more than grays to depict this river in late winter; with perhaps a smudge of ocher for the cliffs. Much as Constable looks overly muted until one sees Suffolk, and de Chirico too enigmatic until one visits Siena in Italy or Cape Soúnion in Greece or an abandoned South American town, Chinese art seems rather flat and monochromatic until you see the landscape for yourself.

Somehow we three foreigners found ourselves underwhelmed by the gorges. They seemed only a bit grander than those along the Potomac River near Harper's Ferry.

Perhaps we expected too much, a Grand Canyon-class experience rather than a modestly picturesque one. Or perhaps the Yangtze merely paled compared with the Li River, where my reaction had been wonderment.

Our riverboat soundtrack included a hearty number of Western pop standards, especially for a Communist country. Incongruously, "Beautiful Dreamer," "Raindrops Keep Fallin' on My Head" and "Jingle Bells" were piped over *No. 5's* sound system.

The spectacle of mealtimes broke the low-grade tedium. The Chinese refused to let me wait in the long lines, forcing me to make a grand entrance at the eating hall. As though an irresistible feast awaited, my fellow passengers smiled and gently nudged me toward metal tables where kitchen staff slapped down bowls of rice, topped by mysterious entrées.

I studied the various substances heaped on the rice. One day it appeared to be salted fish fins. At other times we tried to identify grayish meat (pork? water buffalo?) and greasy vegetables. The menu once included "spiny exterior of starfish," as best I could tell. (Solving this mystery took six years. In 1991, at a banquet in Beijing, the same "starfish skin" appeared. "What's this?" I asked, with absurd excitement at the chance to finally name that entrée. "Pig stomach lining," a Beijing official answered.)

On day three, we landed in Wuhan. A perfect bookend for Chongqing, Wuhan offered another example of a heartland giant, an industrial city of Dickensian griminess, but without the dramatic vistas afforded by Chongqing's bluffs over the Yangtze and Jialing rivers.

Today, travel brochures for China depict luxury liners that ply the Yangtze gorges. The photos taken in bright sunshine show a world almost unrecognizably

A sister ship in the East is Red line sails up the Yangtze (top, right), and one day a junk appeared.

third class. After the rib-crushing experience of Chinese buses, riverboats and trains, this rated as paradise: I had it to myself!

After traveling hard, each of us foreign passengers weighed about 10 pounds less. So we swapped jeans, ate, rested and tried to recover from our multiple respiratory ailments. Our bodies wasted, our minds reeling but lively, we huddled like patients at an Albuquerque tuberculosis sanitarium in the 1930s.

Our feet might be leaving the soil of China, but our minds stayed in the Middle Kingdom, obsessing over our experiences. As we left the shore, heading out on our 2½-day trip through the South China Sea to Hong Kong, we sipped Tsingtao beer in the *Haixing's* lounge and played Bruce Springsteen and the Pretenders on the stereo as we tried to fathom all we had seen.

Mike of Ontario, Canada, and Rodney of Perth, Australia, reported on their trip to Xian to see the terracotta warriors, 6,000 figures in battle array at the necropolis of Emperor Qin Shihuang. They had also climbed Tai Shan, one of the five sacred mountains.

Great hilarity erupted when Mike and Rodney discovered that Sadie had latched onto me after they ditched her in Guilin! They said they'd first encountered her in Australia. She had brought five rolls of toilet paper from Perth to China because she was allergic to some brands.

We speculated that Sadie would return to Canada and issue authoritative proclamations on "what China is like" without having really eaten its food or read so much as the guidebook summary of the significance of its sights. If the rest of us were Amateur Travelers, Sadie qualified at an even less enlightened level, as a Sub-Amateur.

Our mutual encounters with a legendary backpacker were not such a great surprise. In China, the people you met from Alaska or California, at the Great Wall or the Jazz Bar in Shanghai, cropped up again a few days or weeks later.

LESSON NUMBER 14: THE BACKPACKER CIRCUIT ANYWHERE, AND CERTAINLY IN CHINA, LOOPED AND INTERSECTED. IN 1985, TRAVELERS IN THE MIDDLE KINGDOM ENJOYED ONGOING REUNIONS.

different from the one I viewed. The river seems a deeper green; the gorges miraculously look bigger and more interesting by their very juxtaposition to a luxury liner, instead of *East is Red No. 5.*

I would think my memory unreliable, if updated editions of the Lonely Planet guidebook did not continue to note that travelers may find the Yangtze gorges trip "quite boring, possibly due to overanticipation."

One footnote: in 1996, a longstanding plan to create a mammoth dam below this stretch of the Yangtze and to relocate the 175,000 residents of Wanxian, as well as 1 million other people, drew an outcry from foreign engineers and environmentalists and even defiant delegates to the National People's Congress in Beijing. The plan seemed unfortunate, I thought; though not so dazzling as the sights along the Li, the Yangtze gorges certainly seemed to be worthy preserving. And an article in *Condé Nast Traveler* cited fears of terrorism or a naturally occurring dam break and pollutants collecting behind the barrier.

SUNDAY, MARCH 24
Floating back to Hong Kong

After the Yangtze river trip, I explored by boat the sublimely beautiful West Lake in Hangzhou and the Huangpu River in Shanghai. The therapeutic effects of these vessels and one called the *Haixing* countered the earlier ordeal of the 1:05 train to Beijing.

At a berth in Shanghai, about 15 Westerners traipsed up the steps of the *Haixing,* a clean and modern cargo-passenger liner. The ticket for my comfortable cabin, its blankets folded into fan shapes, read

On our boat to Hong Kong, Mike, Rodney, a Chinese-American woman on a *Roots* trip and the rest of us tried to make sense of what we had seen:

• A lost generation of uneducated, middle-aged Chinese, victims of the school shutdowns of the Cultural Revolution.

• The younger Chinese, with their efforts at self-improvement and intense curiosity about the United States.

• And the face of Communism, seemingly less oppressive than what we had heard of the Soviet variety, yet destined to outlive the Soviet Union.

Hotel, transportation and tourist staff had treated us rudely, but all others approached us kindly. Only the regular people—and certainly not the "sights"—redeemed this boggling and absurd country. My trip photos appeared to confirm this observation. I ended up with few good scenics and many decent portraits.

My notebook contained the names of three Chinese I'd encountered. They wanted various things: guitar songbooks, copies of *Time* magazine, names and entrance procedures for U.S. colleges.

Lesson Number 15: The Chinese invariably gave a work unit address rather than a residence, an indicator of the extent to which the Communist Party controlled many aspects of their lives.

I had followed a guidebook recommendation to buy lots of extra Chinese stamps before leaving the country. I could enclose these when writing to my pen pals, given that they earned so very little and could barely afford stamps. To salve their pride, I would write that I just happened to have extra stamps.

Getting to meet regular people had been one achievement. More amazing was that, on my own, I had completed most of my itinerary, though as a figure 8 rather than a circuit. Despite no previous skills in communicating in Chinese, I had purchased tickets myself for the water journeys, given patience from ticket sellers and assistance from fellow passengers.

How much could people really enjoy package tours to China, with little chance to meet characters like Wen and Bao? I wondered. Reading between the lines of several marketing brochures provided by travel agencies, I concluded that this vast country possessed only a handful of surefire sights:

• In and around sterile Beijing: the Great Wall, Tiananmen Square and the Temple of Heaven.

• The terracotta warriors at Xian.

• The countryside around Guilin.

• In and around lively Shanghai: the jazz bar at the Peace Hotel and the *tai chi* and dancing at the Bund; the canal cities of Suzhou and Hangzhou.

Lesson Number 16: China seemed to function mainly as a "for the record" trip. Visitors would experience an important nation, in terms of population, land area and future potential, rather than enjoyable sights.

Travel companies have to scrounge a bit to market China to well-off package tourists, because this destination offers more of an education than a vacation. In a revealing focus, the squibs in a sampling of agency brochures keyed on Tang Dynasty dinner theater, Friendship store bargains in porcelain and ceramics, and satellite television and karaoke on the luxury Yangtze River cruises, rather than China itself.

Our discussions aboard the *Haixing* gradually helped us share a realization: We could be proud of our achievement, having survived China independently. We had slogged through a dull-looking yet oddly fascinating nation, and at a particularly happy juncture, as subsequent events would show.

China gripped our attention. China made us obsessive. Even with perhaps only four world-class sights, all likely to look better in the tour brochures than up close, China riveted us with its daily dramas.

Furious notekeeping by fellow backpackers attested to China's sway over its visitors. Each evening at 9, every dormitory I stayed in resembled study hall at a Swiss college: rows of blond female heads bent over notebooks, the Europeans and Americans trying to preserve each of the day's bizarre and touching incidents.

Somehow you just couldn't visit a country that served not just dog meat, but also cat and armadillo and owl and snake and monkey brains, and be content with just scribbling a few postcards home. Some restaurants reportedly serve live rat embryos. The safety posters of mangled bicyclists, the erudite conversations in Shanghai with elderly Chinese educated in Christian schools, the tour of Chairman Mao Zedong's Tomb in Beijing taken at a dead run—in China you never knew what was next.

We were obsessed. With a place simultaneously so dull and so engrossing, so powerful and so backward.

"We should get medals," I said, to group assent. Surviving China would rate high on any list of the world's most arduous journeys.

My Chinese-American friends, of whom several are close, may resent or find naive the more critical portions of my account of their homeland. I know they do not appreciate having the loud and rat-a-tat-tat nature of Cantonese commented upon endlessly.

One friend, Ted, enthralled by his first trip to his ancestral homeland in 1978, eventually worked as a foreign correspondent in Hong Kong and Beijing. "Any American who visits China, as an American they are going to be struck by how uncivil it is," he said.

"Then you come to realize, it's such a dog-eat-dog world there, they are just trying to survive."

But in a way, China surprised me both for being grueling—and for being easy. The Chinese and English languages share few similarities, but the Chinese people brilliantly succeeded at communicating through creative pantomime, or sharing a phrasebook, or just using simple logic to determine, "This Westerner probably needs to return from this temple to the center of town and should board the Number 8 bus."

For all its inadvertent humor, China grabbed my attention far more than Japan did six years later. Shared experience of, say, a meal of *sashimi* or a Japanese public bath carries none of the sensation of comrades in wartime that riding a Chinese train together does.

LESSON NUMBER 17: AMERICANS AND CHINESE APPEARED TO SHARE A CERTAIN DIRECTNESS, INFORMALITY AND BROAD HUMOR.

The all-night commotion on the 1:05 to Beijing could conceivably be found at some U.S. equivalent, say, a fraternity party at the University of Virginia, but probably nowhere in reserved Japan, the Britain of Asia.

Certainly the Japanese always leapt to help the befuddled *gaijin* (foreigners) in the train stations, as the Chinese helped the *guilos*. And when the chips are down, the Japanese, like the Brits, will always come through if they respect you. We saw proof on a 1991 trip to Japan when the staff of Hiroshima TV made numerous hospital visits to help an ailing member of our traveling contingent.

But no Japanese child asked to see my family photos. No Japanese girl brought me a cookie as I lingered at the zoo. In many little ways, Chinese people seemed more open, friendly, curious and unrestrained.

Rosemary Mahoney, who taught English in China, noted the same comparison. "I was relieved to be back in China after the rigidity and coldness of Japan," she wrote in *The Early Arrival of Dreams*.

> Try though they might, the Chinese could not hide that they were human. Their struggles were always right out here on the street for everyone to see, and I felt grateful for that, and for their vitality, and was remorseful for whatever criticisms I had had of them.

And something about my train journey suggested that a people this sturdy and resourceful will ultimately lap the more regimented Japanese when freedom comes to China.

MAY 1991
Revisiting post-Tiananmen

Six years later, I returned to China as a Jefferson Fellow, one of six American journalists selected for a program of Asian-Pacific study by the East-West Center in Honolulu.

Several differences stood out from my 1985 trip:

• Government campaigns had curtailed odd yet intriguing aspects of Chinese life, particularly the incessant hawking and spitting, and the staring squads that gathered to gawk at foreign devils.

• On an official visit, transported everywhere by airplane and minivan and escorted by minders, we journalists would be sealed off from the Chinese people in a way that had not occurred when I traveled as a backpacker.

The extent of foreigner apartheid in China became more apparent when, after 11 days, I left China for Jakarta in Indonesia. With a jolt, I noticed my first morning that local Javanese people were also eating in the restaurant where I was having breakfast. Chinese people had been banned from the hotels where we stayed as official Western "guests."

• Two years after the crushing of the Tiananmen Square revolt, where hundreds had died in clashes with armored troops, the Chinese clearly remained demoralized. Post-Tiananmen wariness kept most Chinese at a distance when I broke away from group activities for occasional solo explorations.

One got a sense, however, that the Chinese excelled at sensing the wind. They adjusted to their periodic convulsions and reversals and did not indulge in feeling sorry for themselves.

In Beijing, we made the rounds of various Communist officials, where all parties sat stiffly and exchanged predictable questions and answers.

We did not build bridges. John Schidlovsky, who had covered Tiananmen for the *Baltimore Sun*, Janet Fix of the *Philadelphia Inquirer*, and Terrence McDermott, a reporter for the *Seattle Times*, barraged the officials with blunt questions. Outrage united our group, with Schidlovsky still clearly finding the actions of China's government unconscionable. Our anger extended beyond its original catalyst, the massacre in Beijing, to the way this government maltreated its own people, people we knew to be likable, patient and industrious.

I questioned the 1987-89 crackdown on Tibet. I had been studying Buddhism since my 1985 trip through Asia and felt the Han Chinese majority practiced something akin to cultural genocide against Tibet's Buddhists. Those who have not fled abroad endured a variety of horrors: arrests, torture, execution, Nazilike sexual depravation, blood removal and infanticide. The Han Chinese had razed temples, clearcut the forest and machinegunned wild animals, according to Alex Shoumatoff in "The Silent Killing of Tibet."

The resonance of Tiananmen for Americans

The symbolism of the 30-foot Goddess of Democracy statue erected in Tiananmen by the students struck a mighty chord with Americans. The resemblance to the Statue of Liberty may have been accidental—the students apparently intended to depict a Chinese peasant—but nonetheless she gripped a torch in the manner of the 300-foot colossus in New York Harbor.

After America's troubled era of racial discord, Vietnam and the Cold War, finally the young students of Beijing reaffirmed America's shaken sense of being history's landmark civilization in assuring human rights and freedom. When it came time for China's collegians to symbolize their dreams, they did not construct a Parthenon or a Parliament but a goddess echoing the most American of icons (though historians will point out that France donated the statue to the United States).

U.S. tourism to China languished markedly after Tiananmen occurred in 1989 (as did tourism from Japan), suggesting a high-minded objection on the part of the average American to handing dollars to the Chinese. Don Keyser of the U.S. Embassy staff in Beijing told us during our 1991 trip that the new hotels transforming the Beijing skyline, needed but nonexistent on my first trip in 1985, languished "tomblike," emptied by widespread trip cancellations.

From 348,000 in 1986, U.S. tourism fell to 128,000 in 1990. A report in *Focus* indicated that China was "making an all-out effort to bring back these well-paying tourists," and numbers rebounded to 399,000 in 1994.

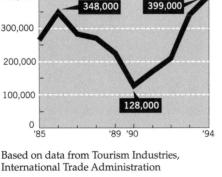

Based on data from Tourism Industries, International Trade Administration

Unreality pervaded the briefings. In a minuet, we asked edgy questions, the officials parried with little spiels. They recited lines about "adjustments to the planned economy" and how the United States "had no right to interfere with China's internal politics." They either denied by rote that corruption existed or maintained the opposite, that rampant corruption showed the need to stick with a planned economy.

Officials, even those who had traveled or lived overseas and had ample cause to know better, hewed to the party line. As soon as the meetings ended and we got out the door, we sputtered in our indignation at the bland insistence that everything in Communist China continued to be just peachy. I felt as though we had been forced to listen to the patter of living, breathing apologists for a latter-day equivalent of Stalin or Hitler—a comparison less exaggerated than it sounds, given the huge death toll that has lately been ascribed to Maoist excess.

The party honchos projected various faces of orthodoxy. Some seemed almost decent and humane, bordering on avuncular. They relied on fancy Diplospeak to tell the United States to lay off its Tiananmen protests, my favorite being "all countries have the right to self-determination."

Others, such as a man we nicknamed Mr. Foreign Ministry, resembled a caricature of a James Bond villain, Cold War Communist evil personified. He slicked his hair with brilliantine and wore stacked heels to disguise his physical tininess. A young woman translated his remarks for us. Like many party officials, he spoke English acceptably, and he repeatedly and brutally corrected the woman's interpretations.

The darkness cast on China by the Tiananmen crackdown colored our meetings. Though as journalists we professed not to be swayed by personal feelings, in our role as American China-watchers we felt particularly sickened by the massacre.

The bureaucrats' spin that "everything's just grand here in China" had fooled nobody at the U.S. Embassy in Beijing. Most of the officials we met there still displayed visible anger with the government's conduct at Tiananmen.

We listened to the cold, clipped tones of Ambassador James R. Lilley, a veteran Asia hand born in China and the top U.S. envoy in Beijing for about six months by the time Tiananmen erupted. He said he found the government's "cruelties hard to accept."

"They're beating up on the Tibetans. They're settling scores on Tiananmen Square by putting demonstrators on trial. ... One has to judge whether these are worthwhile actors to do business with. In China, you're always disappointed."

The dichotomy of China came up in the conversation. "The peasants are off on their own doing fine," an embassy official told us, as were residents of southern cities. Many observers have noted the unevenness—comparable to that in the United States of Silicon Valley versus Appalachia—of Chinese income, despite the obvious Communist manifesto of a level society. By 1993, statistics showed that the per capita GNP of Shanghai residents, at $1,202, had climbed to sixfold that of the $196 in nearby Anhui province.

LESSON NUMBER 18: PEASANTS AND THE PEOPLE IN A COASTAL BELT RUNNING FROM SHANGHAI THROUGH XIAMEN AND ALMOST AS FAR SOUTH AS VIETNAM ENJOYED RELATIVE FREEDOM AND COMFORT EVEN AFTER TIANANMEN, WHILE THE NORTHERN CITIES REMAINED UNDER THE FIRM HAND OF THE PARTY OFFICIALS IN THE CAPITAL.

China's geriatric leaders, Lilley said, still lived in another world. When did the ambassador think overall freedom would come? I asked.

"Five years until they have a humane government, the optimists say. Fifty, say the pessimists," Lilley replied. "It could take two generations to get this out of their system. Fifty million people are still in the Communist Party.

"There are no liberals in the generation now in their sixties," he added. "Those in their seventies and eighties were revolutionary fighters, those in their sixties, Korean fighters. All are orthodox Communists."

From what the American officials told us, my earlier visit in 1985 apparently offered a window on an unusually upbeat China. The trip occurred six years after market reform in agriculture, four years after a more liberal tourism policy allowing individual travel and six months after industry received a greater level of autonomy. So I had managed to see an optimistic China, a nation experimenting in many ways. Those days were gone, at least for a while.

The United States is "so far ahead of the world" in its concern for human rights, Lilley said passionately. I liked his animation and conviction. Corny as it sounds, the United States really led the world in attempts at codifying fairness.

Once we left Beijing and our sobering round of appointments on the theme of, "The Coming Half-Century of Continued Tyranny in China," we faced still another grave problem: Banquet Overload. In Beijing and our later stops in Shanghai and Xiamen, we found ourselves attending one feast after another.

This seemed such a cruel hoax for one who had studied Chinese cooking. Instead of having one or two of these divine gourmet courses every day for the rest of our lives, we were obliged nightly by our hosts to wallow like pigs at a trough of food glut.

But we had to attend every banquet, for our arrival gave the civil servants of Beijing and Shanghai and Xiamen an excuse to dip into their entertainment budgets and throw a food extravaganza. We realized the

banquets took place more for them than for us. The Chinese petty officials sprinkled between us journalists often abandoned any pretext of conversing and wolfed down course after course. Even so, they would pick bits of fish or meat off a platter and lay them in our bowls, good hosts in the etiquette of sharing food if not talk.

We did not begrudge them. In China, the flavor and presentation of the food provides the focus of a meal, not conversation (as in Europe) or raw caloric energy (as in the United States).

In Shanghai, as well as having to find room for another banquet, the Jefferson Fellows got a look at an example of Chinese plans for modernization. We visited the Pudong New Area, an ambitious economic zone planned for the east side of the city.

In 1991, Pudong New Area looked like a sort of post-tornado Arkansas. Low-slung cinderblock structures resembled your basic combination liquor, fireworks and fishbait store on a southern backroad. Between the scattered, nondescript buildings were ample amounts of unlandscaped dirt.

It seemed arbitrary for the party hacks to designate this wasteland and say, "Here's Pudong New Area!" And we had to stifle giggles at the very name Pudong, which sounded vaguely like a word that 5-year-olds enjoying potty humor would make up.

But the Chinese government appeared serious about Pudong. We were handed embossed booklets with raised gilt lettering, on various aspects of the project. Pudong would become a magnificent economic zone with all sorts of tax breaks for foreign investors, officials indicated.

Ultimate proof arrived that the officials were not kidding about Pudong. A videotape extolling the merits of the project unreeled before our exquisitely bored eyes. The Chinese government wouldn't waste money on a video in English unless it really wanted this thing to fly.

The introduction of the video featured an instrumental version of Paul Simon's "Cecilia" accompanying aerial views of the block structures. I mentally filled in the lyrics:

> Making love in the afternoon to Cecilia,
> up in my bedroom

I laughed a bit punchily to myself. China had an unerring tendency to appropriate Western music out of all context. "Jingle Bells" got big air play, though historically China was not known for its one-horse open sleighs. The Ming Tombs had blasted pop standards and chestnuts. Bemused Western visitors would halt in front of its loudspeakers, trying to remember titles of tunes not heard for decades back home.

Even in 1994, 13 years after the opening to the

West, George Kalogerakis and Rachel Urquhart reported for *GQ* magazine on taking the Marco Polo Express from Beijing to Urumqi, listening incredulously as the public address system pumped out such stalwarts as "La Vie en Rose," "Wild Thing," "The Shoop Shoop Song" and "Everybody Likes to Cha Cha Cha." In China, what would be mutually exclusive in the West must be merely eclectic, perhaps not surprising for a nation with 20-course banquets.

After fighting ennui at the briefing—a photograph of the Jefferson Fellows taken reveals the frozen postures and staring of catatonia—I examined our packet of pamphlets. According to Article 4 of a policies booklet, the Shanghai Branch of the People's Bank of China would supervise financial institutions operated with foreign or joint domestic and foreign capital, presumably from behind an unmarked window.

I had come directly to the briefing from a frustrating encounter at the Bank of China (see sidebar below), where a bank clerk slept open-mouthed on a cat-shaped pillow throughout my transactions.

By 1995, entrepreneurs had launched or planned nearly 2,000 foreign-funded ventures in Pudong, and skeptics no longer derided the scheme. But if I personally had millions to invest, I would wonder about China's napping workers.

Aside from sleeping bank clerks—the exception that proves the rule—the Chinese when left unimpeded work and work and work, using their mercantilist and agricultural talents to the fullest.

LESSON NUMBER 19: THE CHINESE SEEMED, LIKE INTRINSICALLY CAPITALIST AND HARD-WORKING AFRICANS, ILL-SUITED TO ENDING UP WITH A COMMUNIST GOVERNMENT.

I wanted to meet regular Chinese people, as I had on my first visit, so on our final day in Shanghai, I went on my own to visit the nearby canal city of Suzhou. The other Jefferson Fellows had fallen to "China-itis"— the combination of aggravation and exhaustion that fells visitors after a week in this unimaginably crowded mega-nation.

At a hidden and little-used ticket office for foreigners on Nanjing Road, an agent briskly sold me a one-way ticket to Suzhou. In more typical fashion, Chinese inefficiency awaited once again in Suzhou station. Before venturing out to the city, I had to buy a return ticket, as rail and air tickets usually were not be sold round trip in China.

Standing in random lines leading to unmarked windows wasted an entire hour. I commiserated with a young woman from New Zealand.

"It's not the language barrier," she said. "It's just simple confusion that sent us from one line to another." And as with the day before at the Bank of China, managers never made the slightest effort to improve the efficiency of their operations. We had an idea—to write to someone offering to do simple signs in English.

I walked through Suzhou, visiting its famed gardens set up by scholars and officials over the centuries.

China's eons of wasted time

In Shanghai, an incident involving banking provided additional insight into China, as I attempted to get reimbursed for $500 in American Express travelers' checks. These must have tumbled from my money belt when I reached for my passport at immigration in the Beijing airport.

For three days, in visits that acquired a ceremonial flavor, I visited the unmarked American Express window of the Bank of China's Shanghai branch on Nanjing Road. The one English-speaking manager, young and chubby, began to seem like an old friend. He heartily informed me each day that he had made no progress in getting authorization for reimbursement from Beijing and Hong Kong.

I waited to grandstand until the afternoon of my third day, when I really did have to end this runaround

before our group headed for the weekend to remote Xiamen. Time for secret weapons: my business card and my notebook. An inherently bureaucratic nation like China or Napoleonic France (the Chinese name for France means "law country") deeply respects bits of paper, especially those with chops, seals or insignia. I passed my *Baltimore Sun* business card to Mr. Manager. Then I stood in front of his window and openly wrote out a timeline of my repeated attempts to get reimbursement.

And then I closed in for the kill. I assumed a tone of sorrowful reproach. My words struck as a knife at the heart of a proud and ancient civilization.

"This," I said to Mr. Manager, "does not reflect well on China."

The words galvanized the staff of the Bank of China. They could not

have moved more quickly had I yelled, "This is a stickup."

Mr. Manager's entire department leapt into action. One clerk finally leafed through a book of procedures. Another telexed Beijing and Hong Kong. After 30 minutes, an instant hereabouts, a clerk brought papers for me to sign. Mr. Manager, chest heaving with exertion, said that he had run twice to the telephone office, whatever that was.

A young female clerk missed the minor drama, sleeping through it all at her desk. The bank had reopened after a 90-minute midday break. Though the lengthy closing would appear to permit sufficient time both to eat and to rest, she zzz'ed, mouth wide open, head propped on a pillow sewn in the shape of a cat.

Once upon a time this would merely have been the siesta guaran-

These focus more on arrangements of rocks and water rather than plantings. A man of about 25 years, cute in a white jacket and stonewashed jeans, greeted me as I strolled around the Surging Wave Pavilion. Yutong's name meant "Red Universe," attesting to his birth during the Cultural Revolution.

Yutong said the Communists sent his parents, both chemistry professors, to the countryside during the upheaval. He had attended Beijing University, where he knew two students killed at Tiananmen.

"China needs reform," he said. "It has reformed agriculture and politics and now it needs to reform the economy."

He presented a balanced and calm assessment of Mao. The Chinese seemed so capable of discussing horrible events in their past rationally and without bitterness.

Yutong treated me to a 2.5 yuan Coke, representing a hefty chunk of his monthly student allowance of 17 yuan ($6). The street vendor misunderstood his request for two bottles, handing us one bottle and two cans. Seeing such a misunderstanding between native speakers reassured me.

LESSON NUMBER 20: CHINA COULD BAFFLE EVEN ITS OWN.

My benefactor escorted me to the bus stop. Because I had little in the way of small change, he carefully gave me 30 fen for the fare. I knew that he couldn't afford these helpful gestures, yet sensed he felt bound to be generous for whatever reason. I thanked him and we shook hands.

"God bless you," Yutong said. The Chinese could express themselves in a very few words, as their love for Confucian and Maoist aphorisms demonstrated. His farewell spoke volumes in the symbolic Chinese way.

Much as students wore pro-Mao buttons to indirectly protest Deng Xiaoping's role in the Beijing massacre, Yutong's mention of "God" in this officially atheistic nation contained a secret code. Had he stood with his palm out, signaling a government tank to stop, his longing for freedom would have been no less clear.

Touched by Yutong's courtesy, I took time five days later, while flying over Borneo, to write a simple hello to his work-unit address. I enclosed some stamps that I'd purchased specifically for new Chinese friends of limited means.

In 1995, after four years of corresponding, he visited me in Baltimore on his first U.S. sales trip for his Chinese company. He had only a quick hour to spare. With a lively and funny colleague from a West Coast office of his company, we chatted and ate crab cakes on the roof deck of my home.

"I can't believe I'm here," he said, looking out on the dark summer night over the Northwest Harbor and Fort McHenry. He stroked my sheltie Beau and presented me with gifts of silk and brocade and wool, presumably a stretch on his income, but perhaps not as much as that Coke in Suzhou had been four years before.

teed in China's constitution, article 49: "The working people have the right to rest." By the mid-1980s, constitutional resting looked more and more like sleeping on the job. Western managers at joint ventures in China went nuts trying to deal with the practice.

The Chinese hold that naps foster digestion and restore spirits, a viewpoint shared by Mozart, Napoleon, Churchill, Salvador Dalí and John D. Rockefeller. Many researchers agree that a midday nap is a natural part of the human daily rhythm. The problem in China seems to be that, unlike with the Latin American and Mediterranean siestas, shops and offices do not stay open later into the evening to compensate.

My journalist friend Graeme Browning noted in her book *If Everybody Bought One Shoe* that the *New York Times* business page ran a photo in 1986 showing a Beijing Jeep worker taking a nap on a bench next to the assembly line. Workers and management at the plant wrote self-criticisms and paid fines but did not lose their jobs.

At the Bank of China, a tiny, English-speaking man with a kind face stood behind me in line. His liveliness and sparkle, rather absent in the Beijingese, seemed typical of Shanghai, a city of 11 million pistols.

I described the way the bank layout confused me. Two long rows of tellers' windows stretched on either side of the huge ground floor. None of the windows bore labels in any language. Customers found out where to go by first standing in several randomly picked wrong lines.

"It's always terrible," he said. "I've been here three times today." He too shook his head, saying he wasted hours on the simplest matters. "It is like this every day for people."

At first, I had seen Asia's inefficiencies in an ironically positive light: as providing useful training in patience for fidgety Westerners. I'd assumed that I had been seeing an impregnable language barrier, rather than a devastating bureaucracy.

LESSON NUMBER 21: OBSTACLES OF DAILY LIFE CREATE A COLOSSAL DRAIN ON THE CHINESE THEMSELVES.

The Bank of China's lack of signs, desk telephones and a fully awake staff, writ on a national scale in every office and ticket widow and government shop, told of vast weeks and years and centuries wasted.

I asked him about China. Being discreet, he ventured less than he had at our first meeting. "People don't try to fight politically," he said before changing the subject. "They just work hard and keep an eye to the future."

He seemed to be a prosperous young man on the way up, who'd lost two friends during Tiananmen but in the classic Chinese manner displayed resiliency. We hugged tightly when he left my home to return to China, where he seemed to have found a niche in a growingly market-oriented economy.

China and the big lesson: emigration

What to make of Yutong's homeland? The World Bank projects China will be the world's richest nation in gross terms by the year 2020, with the United States second and Japan third. Already China leads the world in having the most people, the most workers and the largest land border. It has the third largest area, and one of the fastest-growing economies. Vast China leads in grain, vegetable and chicken production, and even has the most horses (11 million) in the world.

For all that, its people lag grievously in per capita consumption spending, which measures spending by households on goods and services—such as food, housing and clothing. In 1992, the average Chinese spent $170 per year, a Bangladeshi level that attests to a lack of creature comforts. U.S. households spent $15,530, about 90 times more. Many analysts have noted how perhaps in no other nation do expectations, both political and material, lag reality to such as degree.

China's position as world leader or heir apparent in so many areas invites comparison to its fellow global behemoths: Russia, the United States, India, Brazil, perhaps Nigeria.

But much as Japan would remind me unexpectedly of England in the formality of its society, China created a surprising connection in my mind—not just to other world giants, but to Ireland, another famine-wracked nation whose primary export for 150 years has been people.

China exhibited a number of parallels to my mother's ancestral home. In both places, hunger prompted many to leave. The Irish famine had driven perhaps 6 million people to the eastern United States and Canada. The Chinese diaspora scattered perhaps 55 million people to Thailand, Java, Malaysia, Singapore, Indonesia, the Philippines, Australia, the South Pacific, Hawaii, British Columbia and California.

Country of last residence for immigrants to United States

Top 12, 1820 to 1991

		Millions
1	Germany	7.1
2	Italy	5.4
3	United Kingdom	5.1
4	Mexico	4.8
5	**Ireland**	**4.7**
6	Canada	4.3
7	USSR	3.5
8	Austria	1.8
9	Hungary	1.7
10	Sweden	1.3
11	Philippines	1.1
12	**China**	**0.9**
	All nations	58.8

Data compiled by Immigration and Naturalization Service, Department of Justice, 1996

As in the Somalian and Sudanese famines in the 1990s, the Irish potato famines of 1845-47 arose more from government missteps than agricultural disaster. A digression on the most pitiful chapter of Irish history will bear on similar genocide-by-government in China.

In the mid-1840s, Britain refused to assist the starving Irish people. Cecil Woodham-Smith wrote in *The Great Hunger*, perhaps one of the definitive works on Irish history, that

> Much of this obtuseness sprang from the fanatical faith of mid-nineteenth century British politicians in the economic doctrine of laissez-faire, no interference by government, no meddling with the operation of natural causes.

As a result of British neglect, Ireland's population of 8.2 million in 1841 had dropped to 6.5 million by 1851. Between 1846 and 1851, nearly a million people emigrated. Perhaps 1.5 million died in the famine.

Ireland's population continued to flutter downward, declining by 1911 to 4.4 million. This halving of Ireland's population occurred as the overall population in Europe doubled. Numbers increased fivefold in Germany and the United Kingdom.

Populations of Ireland and Britain
1760-1995, MILLIONS

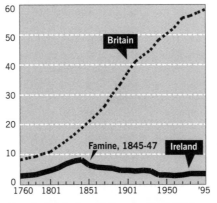

Based on data from Britannica World Data; *Modern Ireland 1600-1972*; *The World Almanac and Book of Facts*; and *Encyclopædia Britannica*

NOTE: Data from 1940 on reflect the switch of Northern Ireland's 3 million people to the United Kingdom census (shown for purposes of this chart in the Britain line) instead of the Republic of Ireland census

Emigration and transformation

Visiting the motherland had staggered one Chinese-American woman on the *Haixing*, a ship connecting Shanghai to Hong Kong where about 15 of us Westerners tried to sort out our impressions of China.

She related how certain aspects of her visit disappointed or embarrassed her: the lack of a concept of public courtesy, the pushing on the buses, a public fistfight she had observed, the decrepit museums and sights.

Her open criticism of China intrigued me. I thought how, by and large, I was proud of my varied heritage. My own *Roots* trips had revealed many things: in Nova Scotia, the self-reliance of the Acadians; in France, Parisian architecture, the glorious art at the Louvre, the stylish food and clothes, the romanticism; and in Ireland (my mother is a Williams-McLaughlin in heritage), the shimmering Celtic way with words, faster and even more creative than that of the facile Anglo-Saxons.

That managed to overlook the embarrassments of Vichy France and the village idiots and alcoholics wandering the roads in rural Cork and Kerry in Ireland. I guess every nationality has a skeleton or two in its closet.

In a way, my Chinese-American shipmate's dismay reminded me of my own visit to Ireland. While most of the people I met there impressed me, others seemed like a shadow rather than a mirror of my towering and professionally accomplished Irish-American uncles and aunts.

Ireland's best and brightest had departed, gone, gone to America, I had thought without censoring myself. China seemed similar. You can't have thousands of physics students headed to the United States and millions of merchants decamping to every cove from Southeast Asia to Hawaii without some consequence.

But was something else at work? Perhaps the phenomenon on view was not that "the best have left."

LESSON NUMBER 22: SOME ANALYSTS BELIEVE THAT THE IMMIGRANT EXPERIENCE ITSELF TRANSFORMS THOSE WHO DEPART INTO NIMBLE COMPETITORS.

The Chinese and the Irish, two groups who fled famine, attained major success in the United States and (speaking only of the Chinese) Southeast Asia. Louis Kraar wrote in "The Overseas Chinese: Lessons from the World's Most Dynamic Capitalists" that

> Like yeast mixed with warm water and flour, the Overseas Chinese rose only when they reached alien lands that provided them with stability and the freedom to flourish.

And my Chinese-American friend Judy noted an ethical transformation as well arising from emigration. During a visit to her ancestral homeland in 1993, she detected that the drive to make money had seriously eroded the Confucian mentality. She also was horrified by China's record of female infanticide and neglect of baby girls in orphanages. As she stood in China, she turned to her mother and said, "Thanks for raising us in the U.S."

"I want to be the best at what I do, but not run over other people on the way," she remarked after her trip, noting disapproval of increasing signs of Chinese selfishness and avarice.

Her criticism reminded me of that of the Chinese-American woman on the *Haixing* and of the dismay of some black Americans who visit Africa and note its inefficiencies.

Though Russia, China and India, population giants that continued to grow, also suffered 19th century famines, relatively advanced Western Europe did not—except for Ireland, victim of a political theory.

Scholars believe that only one European nation, Ireland, tallies a smaller population today than in pre-Napoleonic times.

How does this tie in with China? It illustrates two things: how famines (include the 1992 tragedy in Somalia) result from political rivalries or anarchy rather than crop failures, and how extremism on both sides of the political spectrum can lead to such folly. While pure rightism in Britain cost 1.5 million Irish lives, pure leftism led to a toll of greater numbers in the Middle Kingdom (though one that did not halve China's gargantuan populace).

From 1959 to 1961, at least 20 million Chinese died in a great famine wrought by the misguided policies of the Great Leap Forward. Some scholars place the figure even higher, at 43 million. Want even created a cuisine in China, "famine cooking," where duck's feet and pig stomach lining became entrées.

Perhaps 1 million died in the late 1960s when intellectuals, bureaucrats and urban workers were humiliated, imprisoned and targeted for death during the Cultural Revolution.

Add another 1 million or more dead in China's occupation of Tibet, and perhaps 1 million to 4 million in slayings of landlords during land reform in the 1950s. You end up with estimates of, at bare minimum, 23 million dead due to direct and indirect effects of the leadership of Chairman Mao. Estimates of 45 million to even 80 million, cited in a 1994 report in *The Washington Post*, place Mao in a category that equals or surpasses Adolf Hitler and Joseph Stalin.

The relationship of the modern Chinese to their autocratic and remote government seems at least as distant as that of the 19th century Irish to their British landlords, with good reason. Geographically, a Fujian province peasant today lives six times farther from the

Communist mandarins in Beijing than an Irish potato farmer 150 years ago from his London landlord. And mountain chains and rivers that flood periodically separate the Fujian farmer as wholly from the Chinese capital as the Irish Sea partitioned the Cork tenant from London.

The two nationalities evolved mechanisms of coping with the hardships of hunger and persecution, according to at least one expert—Louis J. Belliveau, my father, the Jesuit-trained expert on all and sundry.

"I suppose the Irish cling to religion, and the Chinese to their ancestors," my father said. "Either would help them ignore adversity. From what you've told me, the Chinese are uncowed by the problems of living there.

"The Irish and Chinese seem to realize that oppression doesn't always have to mean defeat—that oppression can be something you work around."

"Yeah, that's right," I said. "The Chinese use what they call the 'back door' to make arrangements. It's great if you're a Westerner—you can usually make an arrangement to get places and do things."

The Irish turned to "clandestine, grass-roots organizations of all sorts" and "developed skills in circumventing governmental institutions that they regarded as illegitimate oppressions," wrote Thomas Sowell in *Ethnic America*.

The Chinese also took the indirect approach of exploiting personal connections (*guanxi*) to work around the system. Fox Butterfield described the "myriad ways Chinese had invented to ignore, evade, resist or confound the revolution that Mao had thrust on them." Jay and Linda Mathews told how the Chinese

> resent—some actively, the majority almost unconsciously—the oppression and inconvenience of their form of government, but prefer to finesse it rather than challenge it outright.

Many young Chinese men and women I met in 1985 thought that cultivating a relationship, however briefly, with a Westerner such as myself would enable them to enter a U.S. university using my *guanxi*. Connections do indeed become essential in the United States after college, when one seeks a job or promotions. But I had to explain to the Chinese that they would first have to write directly to small colleges, fill out applications and take entry exams.

As well as effective methods for coping with repression, the Irish and the Chinese seem to share an oft-noted trait of having an intimate relationship to their respective histories.

In *One Billion: A China Chronicle*, Jay and Linda

Mathews described an encounter between an American education official and elders in a remote provincial town.

The official asked, "Am I the first foreigner ever to visit your village?" No, the elder replied.

The American thought he had been preceded by Russians, or Japanese, or perhaps missionaries. The elder said, "Part of the Mongol army passed right through here during the great invasion, on the way to the capital."

And that had occurred in the 13th century, 700 years before.

In Ireland there is no past; it is all present.

David Lloyd George, British prime minister, in 1921

The incident bears a striking resemblance to one described by British historian Arnold J. Toynbee in *A Study of History*. An English friend told Toynbee how he had visited Eire in 1921 and heard a harrowing report of

> a particularly ghastly atrocity which had been committed upon so-and-so, at such-and-such a place, by English hands—only to find out that the act had not been done the week before … but in the seventeenth century by the soldiers of Cromwell's army.

When they emigrated, the Irish and the Chinese seemed to take identical values abroad: beliefs in hard work, education, family and frugality.

But once overseas, these two immigrant groups took somewhat different paths. Both succeeded, but one group tilted to academics and politics, the other to making money.

The Irish rose, but not in material terms alone. As Andrew M. Greeley wrote in *The Irish Americans: the Rise to Money & Power*:

> The most interesting phenomenon is not the rise to affluence but rather the emergence of a substantial Ph.D./intellectual class whose members use ideas as a means for rising to (moderate) wealth and (considerable) power.

Meanwhile, the Chinese became "the world's most vigorous capitalists," according to *Fortune* magazine.

Chinese food spurred my original interest in China. Only later did I realize that hunger and famine played a role in lives of the ancestors of both my Chinese-American friends and my mother, forced to come to the United States to avoid hunger—and transformed by the experience of emigration.

HIKING WITH CHILDREN IN THE RAIN FOREST

Borneo … and lessons on modern missionaries

Life in Borneo centers around mighty rivers such as the Mahakam.

We need to travel because, even with considerable information, we cannot perfectly imagine a place without going there. We journey because we must ultimately answer for ourselves questions such as: What is Borneo really like?

How does it look? What does it smell like? Are its people still fierce fighters, or are they largely Westernized?

Writers invariably note how the name Borneo sounds exactly like what one of the world's wildest exotic places would surely be called. Certainly the planet's third-largest island tops the list of destinations for many adventure travelers. Borneo's mystique inspires visions of descendants of head hunters living in longhouses, women with their ear lobes stretched to their shoulders and rhinoceri, orangutans and hornbills roaming thick rain forest.

A trip to this remote island led to Redmond O'Hanlon's amusing book, *Into the Heart of Borneo*. O'Hanlon described how the robust local people, the original inhabitants of the interior, engaged in tireless dancing, drinking and oratory. Parties raged until dawn in the longhouses, communal dwellings that stretched to lengths of one-half mile in cloudy valleys as lost and mysterious as those in *Brigadoon*. The people were known as the Dayaks, a term anthropologists consider unspecific but which is used popularly to include numerous individual tribes, such as the Iban, Kenyah and Kayan. The book told how Dayak men wore penis adornments to pleasure Dayak women, how flesh rotted and death came swiftly in the jungle— the extremes of love and decay in the rain forest.

So there I went, expecting to find the heart, the hypocenter of wild, primitive Asia. In verdant Borneo, rolling thunder would rock the nights in secluded upland paradises. Planet Earth operated the world's most extensive factory for trees and plants apart from the Amazon. Borneo was known for giant lizards, swarms of leeches and sweat-drinking bees.

But for me its primary sensation was not any of these unusual sights, but the feel of warm moist air on the skin and its comforting familiarity. One thing would stand out above all others for me: The humidity. Borneo *felt* like—Maryland in July! In my mind, the humidity of Borneo brought forth a Proustian memory of summer and its childhood associations: easy living, school vacations and the hum of insects.

I, hailing from a typical suburb in Maryland called Rockville, did not expect to feel at ease in Borneo. I had wanted to experience for myself the adventurous sense of dislocation and astonishment described by O'Hanlon and numerous other writers. But this was not to be. Borneo scholars later directed my attention to monographs noting that the jungle island had often been written with excessive breathlessness. In the modern day, its interior remains uniquely interesting, but daily life seems to have quieted down considerably from the wildly costumed exoticness portrayed in turn-of-the-century illustrated books.

My journey, inspired by O'Hanlon's book, would also be memorable for how it brought me in contact with U.S. missionaries, seemingly as opposite to the Dayaks as a group could be. I flew with a pilot whose flight service to the interior represented a way in which missionaries have attempted to be less destructive of culture.

An opportunity to visit Borneo came as part of a Jefferson Fellowship, sponsored by the East-West Center in Honolulu to allow journalists to study the Asia-Pacific nations. Each of the six American fellows in our program could break away for eight days between stops in China and Japan to visit anywhere we liked in Asia. I placed a telephone call to the center's travel director, telling her with dreamlike ease that I wanted to fly to Borneo for a few days. She arranged a flight to one of its major cities, Balikpapan, a Southeast Asian version of Beaumont, Texas, with gleaming shoreside refineries and mini-malls.

I would figure out for myself the details of my itinerary. Westerners seeking Dayak culture typically take a river trip up the Baram River in Sarawak or the Mahakam River in Kalimantan.

If I was traveling all the way to Borneo, however, I wanted to go to one of its most remote areas. Kal Muller's *Borneo: Journey into the Tropical Rainforest* recommended the Apau Kayan, an isolated, roadless highland in the northern mountains of Kalimantan. The area is not directly accessible by water. On foot, it takes two to three weeks to get there. But by air with a local missionary pilot, I could reach the Apau Kayan in 90 minutes.

The Apau Kayan (literally the plateau of the Kayan River) harbored the most traditional Dayak people, Muller believed. To meet them, I flew from Hong Kong to Jakarta and on to Balikpapan, flying over oil wells dotting the water off Borneo's steaming southeastern rim.

Borneo trip map

Village and river positions are approximate, given that maps of central Borneo do not fully agree.

MONDAY, MAY 13, 1991
Arriving in Borneo

A first glimpse of Borneo as we approached Balikpapan from the air revealed fat indigo rivers with midstream islands, wending their serpentine way through green trees. Shadows of clouds fell on the forest, which looked like an endless knobby sweater covered by knots and fuzz balls. Logging roads below resembled whitish scars.

Unlike more touristed Java and Bali, which have a lush and vivid look molded by volcanos and beaches, Borneo is a low giant, a land mass born of a folding in the earth's crust. Erosion and sediment deposits created Borneo's coasts, pancake-flat and low as Florida. Not one road exists in its interior.

I took a taxi out of Balikpapan. We drove through a stretch of land that looked to me like Little Java. Shacks, signs and banana palms lined the road. Scrub grew on areas burned out, I later learned, by forest fires. After an hour, the cabbie left me in Samarinda, a logging city 35 miles upstream of where the wide

Mahakam River empties into the Makassar Strait.

I arrived with a notebook containing a quarter-page of phrases in Indonesian, provided by one of our six Asian Jefferson Fellows, James Luhulima of Jakarta's *Kompas Daily*. A sampling:

"I would like to see the village headman."

"I need two guides to Long Ampung."

"How many days if I walk by foot to -----"

To prepare for my flight the next day into the interior, I made the rounds of a number of tiny *tokos* (stores) in Samarinda. I purchased salt, rice, coffee, tea, cheese, chocolate, water and sardines, in case the highlands lacked provisions.

I cashed travelers' checks at the desk of the Hotel Mesra, where I was staying. Taking heed of a guidebook warning that there was no such thing as a First National Bank of the Apau Kayan, I cashed more in a second round. Better too much than too little, I reasoned.

TUESDAY, MAY 14, 7 A.M.
The movie begins

Captain Emile Borne roared up on a motorcycle to the small hangar at Samarinda's airport. Borne, a handsome 44-year-old, introduced himself to me as "a Cajun who grew up in Fort Worth, Texas." Then he pattered in Indonesian to a clerk. A crisp white shirt lent the bush pilot authority. The motorcycle and a stylish silver bracelet gleaming on his tan right wrist hinted a bit of past wildness in this missionary.

Borne seemed a bit wary of journalists. He suspected he had appeared pseudonymously in a book by Eric Hansen called *Stranger in the Forest*. The book described a Mission Aviation Fellowship pilot renamed "Ian of Long Bia."

Hansen apparently turned up in Long Bia looking half-wild after a trans-Borneo trek and received a less-than-warm welcome from the local MAF pilot. This could well have been Borne, who began his 10-year stint in Indonesia in Long Bia, in eastern Borneo, before being stationed in Sulawesi, the next island to the east, and ultimately in Samarinda.

I wanted to establish a rapport with Borne despite the fact I too was a journalist. "My grandfather was named Emile," I said. "He was an original Cajun, an

Our lives would depend on the reliability of the lone engine in MAF's Cessna.

Acadian from Nova Scotia." Borne smiled and relaxed a bit. We shared a distant cultural kinship. Louisiana's and Texas's Cajuns descended from Acadians expelled in 1755 from Nova Scotia.

The headman of Mahak Baru, an Apau Kayan village, waited outside the MAF hangar at Samarinda's tiny palm-fringed airport. The chief, the first Dayak I'd seen, wore a powder-blue tropical leisure suit. He slung a rattan basket with a beautiful black-on-cane geometric pattern over his shoulder. His ear lobes stretched nearly to his shoulders.

Borne began loading the other passengers' bags and boxes. My own backpack contained a phrase book and a dictionary in Indonesian, malaria pills, and beads and cigarettes as gifts. I had also brought a tarp, sleeping bag and mosquito net, purchased in Hawaii and lugged through China, for roughing it on the village-less trails on a mountain divide I hoped to traverse in the Apau Kayan.

Borne examined his trip manifest, trying to devise an itinerary for various errands to a number of villages. He studied a yellow slip listing our weights and luggage. The day's passengers comprised two Dayak women with infants, a young Dayak man, and myself. I weighed much more than the Dayak passengers. As I would soon discover, they possessed greater strength and endurance than I.

With an expression of intensity, Borne next meticulously checked over his Cessna Stationair 6 single-engine plane. He checked the oil, gently tugged on the ailerons and examined the tires and hubcaps. Huge Indonesia, the world's fourth-largest country, strictly limits missionary visas. So each missionary pilot had to be his own master mechanic.

The preparations for our flight were just another day at the office for the matter-of-fact Borne. To me, however, the whole experience felt strange and thrilling, as though I were Rosie Sayer, Katharine Hepburn's character in *The African Queen*, heading off on the airborne equivalent of a river trip.

The little red-and-white plane with PK-MAJ on the side in huge letters, the motorcycle-riding pilot, the long-eared headman, the village names on Borne's manifest—Data Dian, Long Lebusan, Mahak Baru—these formed the first sights and sounds of the Borneo that I had come so far to experience. If I stood back

from the moment, it seemed incredible that I was about to go upcountry.

As we boarded the plane, a scent like Pinesol hung heavily in the air, some sort of air freshener effect. Borne directed me to the copilot's seat. We all donned elaborate harnesses, far closer in complexity to those worn by military pilots than the simple seat belts on commercial jetliners.

Borne showed me, in an utterly matter-of-fact way, the first-aid kit and how to switch on the emergency locator "if we crash."

I pondered the implications of this remark. Instead of yelling, "What do you mean, 'if we crash'?" I said calmly, "So I'm an ad hoc copilot."

"What's ad hoc mean?" Borne asked.

"A copilot for the moment, for the time being," I said.

"I always come across words and don't know what they mean," he acknowledged frankly. If he did not possess a fancy vocabulary, his practical intelligence manifested itself in other ways—his fluencies in Indonesian, airplane mechanics and navigating a tropical wilderness.

He ran his finger down the preflight checklist, no less careful after 10 years and thousands of takeoffs. Then the Cessna took to the air, its lone engine pulling true over the rooftops of Samarinda. Northwest of the city, we passed over the Hotel Mesra, identifiable from the air by its outdoor pool. Moments later, the intrigued Dayaks peered out at the gleaming silver mosque of the inland city of Tenggarong and the mighty brown oxbows of the Mahakam River.

Flying in a small plane scared me. My life depended on the mechanical worthiness of a single engine. But I couldn't reach the Valium, brought specifically to quell flying anxiety, stashed in my backpack in an inaccessible baggage compartment. I would just have to control or live with my fear. The engine roared loudly but with reassuring constancy.

The plane headed over Borneo's butchered rain forest, bald logged-out ground. Felled trees lay scattered about like match sticks tossed by a giant's hand. "The forest is gone," Borne said over the racket.

He pointed to rice paddies below. "These are all Javanese *transmigrasi*," he shouted—settlers relocated from Indonesia's most populous island.

Few white people book MAF flights ahead, he said: "They show up and have to be turned away." Federal Express had rushed my original flight request from Baltimore to Balikpapan, and I had reconfirmed my plans by fax from Honolulu.

When not directing my attention to a point of interest, Borne leaned a copy of *Newsweek* against his control wheel and passed the time reading an article on a cyclone in Bangladesh.

During our time aloft I wondered about the missionaries' local impact. By their presence, did they change Dayak customs yet provide the region with essential transportation? I would have to see.

We reached the Apau Kayan, an area of tall round-topped mountains that at first looked uninhabited. Solid cloud cover wreathed a ridge that the Cessna had to negotiate to land in Long Sule or Mahak Baru. Borne studied the clouds for a fissure, needing a clear sight line to land since he navigated by visual references rather than radio signal. Eventually we had to turn back. We repeated the same two-hour process that afternoon, with the same result. We spent four hours in the air, yet as often happens, the clouds forced our pilot to try again later.

This delay whittled down my maximum total time upcountry, assuming we could get through the next day, to an impossibly short four days. But even a brief visit to the Apau Kayan would be packed with impressions.

From the air, upcountry Borneo looks less ravaged by logging than the lowlands.

WEDNESDAY, MAY 15, 8 A.M.

Seeing the sights of the Apau Kayan

The weather cleared the next morning for the 90-minute flight to the villages of Long Sule and Long Nawang, 190 nautical miles from Samarinda.

After 50 minutes, the frothing Brem-Brem rapids of the Kayan River, the most northerly and treacherous of Kalimantan's major river systems, appeared below.

This 40-mile stretch of whitewater has never been attempted, let alone successfully navigated, according to all reports. The rapids also isolate the Apau Kayan, reachable by water only via extensive detours and portaging.

Here the forest stood vast and thick, a magnificent tree factory unreachable to lumber companies. The mountain spine of Borneo rose beyond, ridges that marked the cloud-wreathed border between Kalimantan and Sarawak.

The Cessna threaded through the clouds, so close to the treetops that twice we saw the indelible sight of Borneo's signature bird, the hornbill, a cousin of the African banana beak portrayed by Zazu in *The Lion King*. A first group of four looked like white blades followed by huge black bodies. We flew lower and closer to the next three birds, and I could roughly identify them, though I could not be certain whether they were helmeted or rhinoceros hornbills.

Borneo's giant hornbills resemble a four-foot-long toucan with a beak like a double-decker bus, one atop the other. The top beak, actually called a casque (from a French word for helmet), gives them a distinctive appearance. The giants glide above the forest, issuing a barking call.

The maw of logging operations threatens the Dayaks' homeland and also destroys hornbill habitat. Without the large trees providing the holes they need to build nests, the birds have become increasingly rare. Hunting also claims some birds, as I discovered later upon coming upon the drying remains of one giant decorating a Dayak longhouse verandah.

Borne had encountered the effects of logging even at 8,000 feet in the air. Fires had spread through the overburdened rain forest in the 1980s, he said as we flew along, and charred banana leaves floated far above the flames, up to MAF's Cessna in the sky. In fact, a forest fire in 1983, believed to be the largest one of the 20th century, destroyed about 13,500 square miles of forest, greater than the area of Maryland.

Chin cupped in hand, Borne scanned the clouds, hunting, hunting, hunting for a way through to the Dayak villages. "Tell me if you see anything you recognize," he said wryly.

Puffs of clouds eased in stately procession past the winding little plane, passing much more slowly than they would by a jet. They looked like a child's picture-book illustration of heaven. The captain climbed, banked and knifed down through a break to get under the clouds. We continued in a thin sandwich of clear air between the near-solid cloud bank and the ground.

Borne sighted the airstrip for the village of Long Sule 10 miles of serpentine flying later. Dayaks had cleared a narrow patch of trimmed grass the size of an aircraft carrier deck on a mountaintop. They had gotten down on their knees to subject a bit of wild Borneo to golf-course-quality landscaping.

In a swift ballet of the hands on controls, the ex-Navy pilot cut speed and adjusted the throttle. The Cessna hung slowly over a deep valley and then glided onto the lip of the airstrip. He made a perfect touchdown in front of 85 villagers, including a boy wearing a "Batman" T-shirt.

"Mike Alpha Juliet, on the ground in Long Sule," Captain Borne radioed back to Samarinda.

Our passengers disembarked. A group of 10 bearers, one holding an umbrella, carried a sick man on a litter so he could be loaded on the plane.

"Emile of MAF" was the most famous Westerner in the Apau Kayan. Borne served as their lifeline to the

outside world: the big cities of the coast that transship Borneo's oil and lumber riches to Japan, and offer the Dayaks commodities, health care, education and jobs.

We flew along to Long Lebusan. On our descent to its waterside airstrip, the Cessna's wheels practically skimmed the surface of a river, a tributary of the Boh.

Here "Bon Jovi" ballcaps replaced the "Batman" T-shirts. The sight reminded me of reports that former Van Halen singer David Lee Roth has frequented the backwaters of Borneo; adventurous rock stars may be one source of the readily apparent Western gear.

We touched down at my final stop, Long Nawang, another musical-sounding airstrip on this MAF circuit ride. Landing culminated months of mingled excitement and anxiety over visiting the Dayaks. So far so good: our tiny single-engine plane had made it safely into this misty village.

But many logistical unknowns remained. I wondered, what do I do now?

My language ability in Indonesian (10 words) and Dayak tongues (zero words) meant that I would be unable to procure food and lodging other than via pantomime. And how much lodging might there be in a depopulated area with scattered longhouses?

Before I had more than two minutes to weigh these concerns, a young Kenyah man materialized at Long

Nawang's airstrip. Onas (pronounced OH-nass) was in his mid-20s. Inky hair in a Rod Stewart shag topped his glossy dark eyes.

Onas spoke a bit of English learned from tourists. He was exactly what a traveler needed to find on arriving in Borneo.

LESSON NUMBER 1: TRAVELERS SHOULD NOT BE DETERRED BY SKETCHY INFORMATION ABOUT A DESTINATION; THINGS WILL WORK OUT ON ARRIVAL. AS I SAW ON A BASKETBALL PLAYER'S T-SHIRT: "JUST ELEVATE AND THEN DECIDE."

With Onas around, I didn't need my sheet of Indonesian phrases asking the whereabouts of the village headman. In fact, Long Nawang, with nearly 800 people, seemed just big enough that such a request might have brought puzzlement or stifled giggles.

In fact, Onas proved to be Your One-Stop Travel Agency for upcountry Borneo. He and his sister Rosmina ran a *losmen* (in Indonesian, a family-run inn) in Long Nawang. Since I no longer had the four to five days needed for my original plan—to hike the divide to Mahak Baru—Onas told me via Emile that he would arrange a shorter canoe charter up the Kayan River to the village of Long Ampung, where he had relatives,

A hero praises highly skilled pilots

Captain John Testrake survived a 17-day terrorist siege of his TWA plane at Athens airport in 1985, turning to the Bible and prayer for solace. The captain was able to keep his composure while giving interviews out of his cockpit window even as a terrorist held a pistol to his head.

Three years later, Testrake reached the age of 60 and mandatory retirement as a TWA pilot. He became head of MAF's fund-raising campaign for new planes. In 1990, while visiting most of MAF's bases in Africa and Indonesia, he met Emile Borne and his family for lunch in Samarinda.

"These are probably among the most highly skilled and competent pilots I've seen anywhere," said Captain Testrake in a 1991 telephone interview from his Gallatin, Missouri, home. "Things I am used to seeing being done by a whole corps in the airline business would be accomplished by one man working by himself.

"These people go to places TWA never heard of," he added. "The arrival of the MAF plane is the social event of the week. The whole region turns out. People have a great time bantering and laughing and joking with the pilots."

Testrake said he had to shake his head at some of the flying conditions MAF pilots encounter. "It's challenging and interesting, when you fly to a squirrely little mountain airstrip, as little as a fly on a wall. I think to myself, man, O'Hare Field was never like this."

On Feb. 6, 1996, Testrake, 68, died in Missouri of cancer. Max Meyers, MAF's chief executive officer, noted in a farewell article in *Flight Log* that Testrake "believed all of his preceding career in aviation" prepared him to offer his skills and public platform to benefit MAF.

"people of my tribe," that I was to stay with. Emile Borne agreed to pick me up in Long Ampung four days hence. That settled arrangements.

Onas and I walked from the airstrip to the village, passing under a giant wooden archway with two Dayak motifs—hornbills and human figures—and "Welcome to Long Nawang" in Indonesian.

Onas checked me into his *losmen*. This procedure involved, in its entirety, stepping out of my mud-encrusted running shoes, leaving them on the steps of the *losmen*'s verandah and sticking my backpack in a Spartan bedroom. As I did so, children walked up to chat with Onas—most likely in the Kenyah language—and one child began to sing.

Pieces of linoleum covered the floorboards of a little square living room. The Kalimantan Tourist Board seemed to be the interior decorator. A giant travel poster displayed a Kenyah tribesman in a feathery, vaguely Apache-style headdress performing the Hodo' dance. The Mahakam River's freshwater dolphins gamboled on a second poster. Giant round rattan sun hats hung from pegs, and a map of Kalimantan hung on the wall.

It began to rain, as happens in rain forests. As the drops fell, I sat on the verandah with my copy of *Shogun* (the next stop on my itinerary was Japan, where trees felled from Borneo's forest became forms for concrete). I was not really reading so much as using the book as a prop as I looked around Long Nawang.

Chickens squawked, raindrops hammered, but cars made no noise here. A lack of engines, the signature sound of the West, promoted tranquility. Motors could be heard only now and then: on the rivers, where Johnson outboards propelled canoes, and when the missionary pilot's Cessna, the link to the outside world, buzzed a soft approach once a week.

Bougainvillea blossomed, a bright red in front of the *losmen*. A black, white and gold rooster strutted about, as well as a white-footed dog.

At last I could see the "real" Borneo, the head-hunters with blowguns, their canoes probing seamless rain forest along uncharted rivers.

Children play naked in the water below Long Nawang's footbridge.

Onas poses on a bridge at the start of our walk.

The real Borneo, truth be told, was not quite so glamorous. The village of Long Nawang itself, based on the initial view from Onas' and Rosmina's *losmen*, seemed to enjoy long periods of soporific nothingness, a banana republic ennui. The rolling nighttime thunder produced mud, the sun dried it back to dirt, and the unvarying cycle repeated itself.

Dogs slept on longhouse steps.

Rice dried in the sun on mats.

Geckos scampered.

Flies buzzed.

The dogs, unwilling to tamper with a winning formula, slept some more.

A woman almost imperceptibly waved a 15-foot pole with a kerchief at one end over the drying rice to shoo chickens away. In Long Nawang, this constituted a burst of frenzied activity.

Long Nawang did not immediately conjure the wild and dangerous Borneo of colonial days. But even expecting it to be so would be akin to flying to Rapid City expecting to find Lakota Sioux living downtown in tepees.

For example, even in Long Nawang, the capital of the Apau Kayan, not everyone still lived in traditional longhouses. Some people, such as Onas and Rosmina, lived in single-family dwellings.

The rain stopped. At 1 p.m., Onas indicated it was time, insofar as I had come all the way to the Apau Kayan, to put down my book and go for a stroll. I pulled on my mud-caked shoes. Onas stood ready, there being no competing demands on his time, to show me some of the sights.

We walked over a footbridge. Children splashed in the Kayan River below. We turned left after crossing the river and strolled along a 10-foot-wide clay path, eventually walking beside the Nawang River, a tributary of the Kayan.

Black-and-white butterflies flapped along the trail. "*Kupu kupu*," Onas instructed. I repeated the Indonesian word for butterfly. *Indah kupu kupu.* Beautiful butterfly.

Vocabulary drill at the Onas Academy for Tourists had barely begun. By the end of the day I wrote down

Dayak culture faces assaults from many fronts

As Emile Borne pointed out during our flight, an Indonesian resettlement policy called *transmigrasi* relocates Javanese and Balinese from their crowded home islands to sparsely settled Kalimantan, diluting the Dayak character of the island.

(Indonesia controls Kalimantan, the southern two-thirds of Borneo. Malaysia and Brunei govern the top strip of world's third-largest island, the size of Texas and Oklahoma.)

The government of Indonesia has also compelled Dayaks to convert to Christianity or Islam and to live in single-family dwellings, as I saw in Long Nawang and Long Ampung, rather than traditional longhouses.

A Javanese journalist I met, reflecting government policy, criticized Borneo's longhouses as being strictly tourist bait. And he said that visiting the Dayaks was "no better than going to see animals in a zoo."

His sentiments seemed ironic on many levels. The trickle of tourists brought a bit of cash to the Dayaks. And Javanese notions of cultural superiority (as reflected by the lack of support for longhouses) seemed to be more of a threat to the Dayaks than tourism. Finally, he seemed prone to notions of cultural superiority in a way oft-criticized in Westerners.

Professor Jérôme Rousseau of McGill University wrote to me that

> Both in Malaysian and Indonesian Borneo, the main threat to local cultures is the intolerance of the dominant groups, who are prejudiced against the local populations. … *Transmigrasi* is part of a process of homogenisation. Authorities also attack local cultures in various ways, e.g. by subverting local rituals for the purpose of entertaining tourists. Some communities are compelled to stage rituals at the wrong time for the benefit of the tourist industry.

The Javanese prejudice toward the Dayaks seemed comparable to that of Kenya's dominant Kikuyu toward the Masai. Both seemed to prejudiced toward minority groups and perhaps

A longhouse at Long Ampung, featuring wood carvings, is typical of the Apau Kayan.

envious that the tourists clamored to see them.

As for foreign threats, America's worldwide pop culture certainly plays a minor role in eroding traditional Dayak ways, evidenced by the rock groups and U.S. universities on many a ballcap and T-shirt in Borneo.

But systematic extraction of Borneo's resources by domestic companies appears to be the bigger culprit. These companies now trade on stock exchanges and are thus linked to many individual and corporate investors worldwide, particularly via Asia-focused mutual funds.

Japanese demand for Borneo's resources (it is the world's largest importer of tropical woods) created an impetus for urban migration, by ruining interior forests and rivers and creating a cash economy that forced one-time rice growers to migrate to jobs in an arc of booming coastal cities from Pontianak to Tarakan. These centers for oil and lumber jobs have lured many of the 3 million Dayaks, a fourth of Borneo's population, away from the simple but cash-strapped life of the interior.

The logging and huge dam projects also force Dayaks to resettle elsewhere, leading Professor Rousseau to conclude, "There seems to be a conscious desire to break down the society."

Dayaks who want to follow traditional ways have fled far inland. Even dietary differences come between indigenous people, who love to eat wild pig, and the Islamic, and pork-shunning, Indonesians. The Dayaks get by living primarily on rice, easily grown in their rainy climate. But kerosene, salt and other basics are flown in from the coast.

The interior provides Dayaks with few means of producing cash income. Some find a little gold, others sell baskets or necklaces to tourists. Higher education and hospital care, as well as jobs, can only be found by journeying to the coast.

The extent to which the culture of traditional Dayaks has been eroded becomes apparent through a study of Dutch books published 70 years or more ago.

Quer Durch Borneo (1904) and *De Kenja-Dajaks uit hep Apo-Kajangebied* (1926) show photographs and sketches of villagers wearing far more elaborate ceremonial dress than can typically be found today, including beak or horn chestpieces with intricate vine patterns, frond cloaks touching the ground, yard-square face masks and metal loops stretching the ear lobes down to the upper arm.

Fancy towers rose in Long Nawang, with carved hornbill or warrior sentries affixed to the top. A main longhouse, bigger than any I recall seeing, stretched for what appeared to be a half-mile along the river. Four other longhouses branched off the principal structure or ran along the opposite bank.

Some aspects of Dayak country seemed unchanged, however. Old books depict shoulder bags with rattan straps no different from ones I purchased upcountry. Shots of the interiors of longhouses showed the same arrangement of cooking areas as can be found today. And the Nawang River looks as sylvan and rocky as ever.

the words and phrases he had smilingly but relentlessly taught me, from *anjing* (dog) to *silakan duduk* (please sit down).

More than 20 new words and phrases now augmented the mere 10 words of greeting I'd known that morning. Truly necessity was the mother of invention, and immersion the key to learning a language. Onas also insisted also that I roll my "r's" correctly. I struggled at first, but as if by magic, suddenly my pronunciation improved.

After 30 minutes, we walked under a village archway. Instead of shamans, hornbills or tigers, two soccer players acted as support posts. Sports seems to be the universal religion of the late 20th century.

Residents of the first longhouse we encountered invited us in. Chest-high dividers separated the spaces into family areas. We ate fried bread and water as we sat cross-legged on a bare floor. A woman wearing a cap with hornbill feathers arrived. She stood a few yards away, partly screened by a divider, and changed into a sequined tunic and skirt. Later we would see why.

The longhouse children wore "Batman" and "Janet Jackson's Nasty Tour" T-shirts. They surrounded us in a circle as I displayed family pictures. Onas gave me a crash course on Indonesian terms for various relatives.

We continued past a cluster of beached canoes and arrived in Nawang Baru, or "new Nawang." Traditional Dayaks founded this collection of longhouses in 1952, breaking away from the (relatively) modern and Christian ways of Long Nawang.

At Nawang Baru's biggest longhouse, we walked up the steps to the enormous verandah. Hundreds of people had arrived for a gathering of some sort. The assemblage watched a group of 70 local men arrayed on the outer bench of the verandah and 30 district officials, with elaborate shoulder patches like U.S. park rangers, behind tables under the eaves. As soon as my Western visage appeared at the meeting, the Dayaks led me, as though I was expected, to a place of honor, front and center. A woman handed me a glass plate of rice sweetened with oranges and fried bread wrapped in banana leaves.

The village men sat cross-legged on the verandah. With their piercing deep-set eyes, plucked eyebrows, high cheekbones, long ear lobes and shallow noses, they looked like pan-Asian wizards.

A remarkable object captured the men's attention: an eight-foot long hornbill replica with a curlicue wooden beak and head and genuine tail feathers. Black, yellow, white and orange beads covering its body depicted tigers, human heads, birds and jungle trees in a baroque, interlocking design.

A more mysterious object as colorful as a piñata or a holiday decoration hung from the rafters. A beadwork tube hung from a string, with a fan of hornbill feathers and some paper and cloth bands below. A collection of huge rolled cigarettes splayed out, creating an object the size of a pineapple. Men periodically grabbed a cigarette to smoke.

For two hours, village headmen and district officials in khaki uniforms made speeches over the battery-powered sound system. I understood little of the speeches other than the ubiquitous *"terima kasih"* (thank you).

After each speech, a lone cantor sang a verse. Eight of the seated men then chanted "Mal-oooooo" again and again, repeating and modulating the "ooooo" like a Gregorian chant, with a deep silence following each haunting chorus.

Midway through, about 40 women bedecked in sequined tunics and traditional earlobe weights arrived to circle the hornbill figure. In a slow conga-style line, they shuffled their feet and stomped in 4/4 time to tinny Indonesian recorded music. One woman's huge earrings resembled a carpenters' plumb weights. Another wore a dozen narrow wire rings through her shoulder-length ear lobes.

A boombox provided the music. The government officials, apparently as taken with the Dayaks as any tourist, recorded the dancing with disposable cameras. As the century closes, anthropology texts debate whether field workers will run out of isolated societies to study, given the impact of commercialization (such as the boombox and cameras) virtually everywhere outside of the New Guinea interior and the far reaches of Brazil, Peru and Venezuela.

At 4:30 p.m., our return stroll was greeted with local stares. *"Selamat pagi,"* I said to people on the path, and they looked at me curiously, probably (I later learned) because I was wishing them "good morning" in the afternoon. Two little girls walked with us for a bit. *"Saya nama Jeannette,"* I said. They replied with their names, Marta and Sara.

Back at Rosmina's *losmen*, I bathed in a *kamar mandi*. An outbuilding connected to the *losmen* by a gangplank contained a barrel with a scoop to toss water over one's head. I studied the details of the *mandi's* and the *losmen's* uneven planks, popped nailheads and roughhewn wooden latches. These touches reminded me of a rural Nova Scotia campground near the Belliveau family homestead. I wondered whether I gravitate to simple societies because they resemble Acadia.

At dusk, from the verandah, I watched as the sun set pink and gray over the ridge of the Iran Mountains. Everyone in Long Nawang seemed to perk up. Children ran along village paths, looking hopefully back over their shoulders, as homemade kites struggled to become airborne. Wild coleus and caladium thrived beside village paths.

An old woman—Onas had taught me the word *nenek* for grandmother, much like our own "Nanna"—shuffled along with a walking stick. Crickets raised a deafening cacophony, and the heat lightning flashed. Through it all, the dogs on the longhouse steps lazed about.

Inside the *losmen*, a giant spider the size of my palm crawled up the living room wall, between the travel agent posters.

"My friend," Onas said, making no move to interfere with its freedom or happiness. Presumably this spider made Onas's life easier by eating mosquitoes. Since dusk, Onas had been killing the pests, clapping his hands to crush them.

In the flourishing insectarium that was the *losmen*, Onas then spotted a wasp. He squashed it quite thoroughly with his thumb, grinding wasp juice over the wall. "Not my friend," he announced.

With a sort of Sicilian Mafia simplicity, Onas knew his allies and enemies in the declared war on mosquitoes. "My friend," he continued, gesturing to a gecko climbing the walls of our living interior jungle.

We flipped through the guest book, listing 28 people who had stayed from the *losmen*'s December 1990 opening through my visit in May 1991—an average of about one guest per week. Not bad given the location, I thought. The steady trickle of tourists explained why Onas wore a University of Hawaii T-shirt 6,000 miles from the source.

To pass the time, we studied the living room map of Borneo. What did *Long* mean, the word that kicked off most of the place names in Kalimantan? A river junction, Onas indicated, using the word *sungai* for river. The name *Tanjung* also appeared frequently.

What did that mean? Onas stood still, thinking furiously, and then grabbed a little geography text full of world maps off a bookshelf. On the page showing South Africa, he ran his finger in repeated arcs below its coastline. Aha! *Tanjung* meant "cape," as in Cape of Good Hope.

LESSON NUMBER 2: ONAS PRESENTED A CLASSIC EXAMPLE OF THE CREATIVITY MANY PEOPLE IN THE DEVELOPING WORLD DISPLAY IN COMMUNICATING WITH ENGLISH SPEAKERS.

My head swam with new Indonesian words when I retired for the night. In the middle of the night, rain drummed on the *losmen* roof as thunderstorms rolled over the Apau Kayan.

THURSDAY, MAY 16
A plan for modern villages

The following day, Onas took me to see I. Mundi Raharjo, administrator of the Long Nawang clinic. Raharjo explained the goings-on we had seen at Nawang Baru's longhouse.

The *kepala adat* (chief) of the Kenyah tribe, a man named Pare Laing, had convened a meeting of all the villages of the Apau Kayan. "He opened the meeting yesterday," Raharjo said. "Today he will decide on a plan on how to develop the villages. Pare Laing wants modern villages."

Raharjo spoke of the limited government facilities at Long Nawang. "There's just an elementary school

---

Health problems in the rain forest

Given the Western overlay already affecting Dayak ways, the prospect of a program of further modernization in upcountry villages would be alarming were it not for certain troubling aspects of the Apau Kayan's isolation.

Surprising for such as strong people—and most visitors immediately notice that the Dayaks inhabit a living laboratory of survival of the fittest—sickness appeared everywhere. Children sniffled on the longhouse verandas, and a number of women had an eye missing. Pus-filled wounds marred babies' ankles.

Many villagers begged us tourists for medicines. Older women pointed to the throat and described their problem in one word: *sakit* (sick). I myself suffered infected mosquito bites that refused to heal before I returned to Honolulu. A doctor at a Waikiki clinic shook his head at the huge boils and said he had never seen such a serious infection apart from travelers returning from Fiji.

Bare patches on the village dogs indicated mange. Some of the baldest puppies looked not long for this world.

Professor Rousseau said that epidemiologists report that forest fires have led to increased respiratory illness, which now affects 25 percent of the Malaysian population of Borneo, sometimes with fatal results. During his two-year stay doing field work, he recalled being stricken with illness and sidelined cumulatively for more than a month.

Health care is deeply needed here, more than anywhere I have visited. Ample food and water prevents Borneo from seeming "poor" in the sense of imminent starvation. But illness seems unusually rampant given the fertile landscape.

In the rain forest, mosquito bites and cuts infect easily and persistently with staphylococcus. Here, at least two weeks' walk from a hospital, a septic cut can kill. Only airplanes to outside medical care offered hope for the seriously ill.

Pilot Borne had said how MAF had been charging the commercial rate for local sick people, "but people were dying, they just didn't have the money. They didn't have the money for church rate either. Only gold or basket sales provide a little cash."

The human illness seemed incongruous given the luxuriant tree growth all around. But in their lush yet isolated environment, the Dayaks had to cope with opportunistic infections, the risk of accidents and skies besmirched by smoke.

here," he said. "Students go to Tanjung Selor or Samarinda for high school." For hospital care, sick people must fly to Tarakan. The MAF flight costs 95,000 rupiah, about $48. People tried to raise money for the trip from rice farming, he said.

We walked back through a lush pineapple grove, the trees only three feet high. Onas bought one of the fruits for 500 rupiah, the equivalent of a quarter. The pineapple seemed even sweeter than those of Bali or Tahiti.

Onas continued the language lessons. We moved from Vocabulary right into Sentences. "*Saya mau pisang*," he coached. I want bananas. "*Saya mau nanas.*" I want a pineapple. Anyone thrown into Onas' orbit would soon be fluent in Indonesian.

Back at the *losmen*, I turned my bag of rice, as well as salt and cheese and other oddments I'd bought in Samarinda, over to Onas' sister, Rosmina. Because time constraints prevented me from crossing the wild mountain divide to the east of Long Nawang, between Sungai Barang and Mahak Baru, I no longer needed my provisions.

She stifled her laughter. These upcountry villages raised plenty of chickens and grew ample rice and greens. Onas explained that she found it especially hilarious that I had brought rice into a rice-growing area. Rosmina's teasing smile said, *Westerners ... don't they know anything?*

Friday, May 17
Upriver by canoe

On the morning of my third day upcountry, Onas led me to a dirt landing. He loaded my pack into a canoe and entrusted my care to Dessin, the captain, and Iro, his steersman. Their Kenyah monikers echoed the musicality of village names.

From Long Nawang, we headed upriver to Long Ampung, a two-hour charter costing the equivalent of $38. The canoe represented my only major expense in the Apau Kayan. Food and lodging cost little, perhaps only $3 or so a day. Tips for a day guide might run $5. Dayak basketry and jewelry could be a bit more expensive, in the $10 to $30 range depending on bargaining skills. (A side note: Costs can be much higher in the interior of Sarawak, according to Professor Allen Maxwell of the University of Alabama.)

Onas loads my backpack in a canoe.

At first, the brown Kayan flowed swiftly, clear of obstacles. Behemoth trees leaned almost horizontally over the river, and butterflies covered banks of pol-

Iro raises his paddle and eyes the roiling waters of the Kayan.

ished gravel. Huge bromeliads and royal palms lined the Kayan. Giant vines looped out of trees and hung over the water. Borneo smelled of silted water and moist earth, like a giant garden center.

As we rounded a turn, a remarkable sight greeted our eyes. A seven-foot-long monitor lizard basked on a bank of boulders. It crouched and raised its head, eyeing us for a split second.

To my horror, Iro raised his wooden paddle, with its diamond-shaped, sharp-edged blade. He would kill the dinosaur-age giant if it came in range.

At the same moment, a dun-colored hawk began circling overhead, creating an embarrassment of wildlife viewing riches. Consumed with worry, however, for the monitor's fate, I barely glanced at the hawk.

Before I could react in any way except for an instantly conceptualized dread, a flashing thought that, "Oh no, I've come thousands of miles to see rare wildlife and now my chartering this canoe is going to lead to a lizard death," the monitor bolted into the dark racing water under our bow and dove to safety.

After the monitor's escape, we passed stands of giant bamboo five inches in diameter. A kingfisher with an electric-blue body and bright head the color of goldenrod flitted by. Three times, Dayaks in sun hats canoed past, usually hugging channels near the bank.

About a third of the time, the canoe fought against rapids. Dessin artfully controlled the canoe outboard, called a *ketinting*. It was cleverly connected by a long drive shaft to the propeller so that its blades could enter the boulder-filled water at a shallow angle less likely to lead to damage.

On several occasions the current nearly pushed us sideways to the current. At these times Dessin gunned the engine, so we always maintained at least a bit of forward progress. Whenever muscular Iro dug in the paddle, however, the canoe leapt forward mightily, as though being propelled by a crew of 20 paddlers. Thanks to the skill of Iro and Dessin, and against all odds, the interior of our craft remained dry.

After two hours, the outskirts of Long Ampung appear.

At length, the wildness of the forest gave way to structures built by human hands.

Weathered rice barns on stilts appeared on the banks, heralding the outskirts of our destination, Long Ampung. A painting on the side of one depicted a creature midway between man and monkey. The creature's arms and legs grew into baroque, repeating twirls, an echo both of ancient Vietnamese and Chinese art and the look of tangled jungle vines.

Across the river from the rice barns stood curlicue wooden grave markers. My pretrip reading had revealed that spirit worship and appeasement inspired woodcarvers to decorate gravesites and rice barns using flamboyant motifs.

The boulder-ringed landing for Long Ampung appeared around a river bend, looking like a fabled place, a tiny tropical Eden. Red bird-of-paradise flowers lent a sense of careful, almost Amish agricultural husbandry mixed with a wildly equatorial landscape resembling many of Henri Rousseau's paintings, such as *Tropical Forest with Monkeys*, depicting outsized flora in saturated colors.

I tipped Dessin and Iro with packs of cigarettes bought in Samarinda. Though this was not the most healthful gift, the alternative for Dayak guides, according to books I'd read, was shotgun cartridges.

A dozen youngsters watched our approach to the landing. They scrambled to carry my backpack, a smaller daypack and a mosquito net from the canoe to the *toko* (store) belonging to the couple Onas had recommended, Dorothe and Andreas. I paid my small porters with pieces of chocolate bars, carefully breaking two bars into 12 equal pieces. If this was Eden, it was peopled by coal-eyed children well practiced in the art of the sunny and uplifting Indonesian smile.

A front room of the house served as the *toko*, where Dorothe (pronounced Dor-ty) sold batteries and cans of soda at air temperature. Behind this stood the other three rooms: a parents' bedroom, a children's bedroom, and a cooking and eating area. The couple relocated their children, whose room was given to me.

In the kitchen, a low fire burned most of the day. Dorothe was constantly working. She fixed a lunch of rice, mountain greens (spinachlike) and boiled squash. Cans sat in the embers, boiling water to make it safe for drinking.

My friend Mike at *The Washington Post* stayed in a similar house in Sumatra. The simple dwelling at first struck him as belonging to impoverished people. Over time, however, one realizes that while such houses may not look like Western split-levels, they serve their functions quite well. Garbage disposals, for example, become less necessary where dogs, chickens and goats scavenge.

Dorothe and Andreas possessed far fewer amenities than a typical American family, yet they had land, a house and a small business. Their children enjoyed the security of two firmly committed parents.

In remote Long Ampung, I finally encountered fellow tourists. Genevieve, an effervescent woman from Quebec, and her Swiss friend Boris arrived. We all shared the same room in the *toko*. The three of us spoke enough English and French to communicate, and Genevieve had rapidly acquired a grasp of Indonesian. Dorothe might say something in Indonesian, and provide the Kenyah word for an object

Long Ampung's cheery welcoming committee.

as well, with Genevieve translating into English, or French if she didn't know the English word. Our quadrilingual conversations moved along, much aided by Genevieve's technical virtuosity.

In the late afternoon, we three Westerners strolled down to the Kayan, which served a broader purpose than just floating canoes from village to village. Rivers in Borneo serve as showers (upstream of a village) and toilets (downstream).

For our daily wash, I brought a cloth wrap and a biodegradable liquid soap and shampoo. The trick was to somehow stay modestly covered by the wrap, wash, and then manage the way back over the muddy paths to the *toko*, attempting to avoid returning grimier than before.

Beginning at sunset, the children helped their parents fix dinner. Flickering light filled the cooking area, from the fire crackling in the corner and from Coke cans with wicks, filled with kerosene. Andreas and Dorothe were quite close to their children. They conversed and sang softly as we three travelers sat on a rattan mat during their preparations. I hadn't heard a loud voice or seen a child struck since I'd arrived.

Our dinners consisted of chicken or wild pig done in a wok on charcoal, and sweet potatoes or porridgy rice in a banana leaf.

After one dinner, an old woman selling bead bracelets arrived. I bought two, mindful of Captain Borne's comment that the sale of handicrafts provided one of the few cash sources for the Dayaks.

SATURDAY, MAY 18
Hiking through the rain forest

There's nothing quite like a pack of dogs in full cry, baying inches from your ears, to rouse you in the morning.

Borneo's preferred architectural design, with open areas under stilt houses, offered the canines a suitable sound stage for their ruckus. Imperfectly fitted floorboards allowed the caterwauling to reach us with undiminished volume. My sheltie Beau, a howler of operatic range, would have loved to join in.

The dogs were present everywhere in upland Borneo, reflected in the fact that *anjing* was one of the early words in Onas's lessons. They seemed to be scavengers rather than pets or a food source.

Village dogs in the Andes, East Africa, Southeast Asia, and elsewhere show the natural dog's typical form: body weight of forty to seventy pounds; short, smooth coat varying in color from grayish brown, tan, or red to piebald, brindled, or entirely white; long, strong and graceful limbs; deep chest and narrow waist; almond-shaped eyes ranging from gold to deep copper; ears either erect and pointed or slightly folded (never heavily pendulous like a cocker spaniel's); and long tail, curled slightly upward.

Michael W. Fox in "In Praise of the Natural Dog"

A family of dogs hangs out on the steps of the *toko*.

The serenade kicked off my fourth and last full day in Borneo. Dorothe appointed her oldest son, Ampung, as guide on a six-hour, round-trip hike to

Genevieve, Andreas, Dorothe, Boris, Ampung's little brother and Ampung himself pose for a group shot in front of the *toko*.

Lidung Payau, farther up the Kayan.

As we all left Long Ampung, Boris and Genevieve took their backpacks, admirably small and light considering they planned a trans-Borneo trek. While I would only walk to Lidung Payau and return, they would continue on the same path to a village called Long Sungai Barang. From there they would hike and raft across the divide to Mahak Baru. They had enough time to complete the trip I had originally envisioned for myself.

Ampung, Boris and Genevieve walk under the archway for Long Ampung, with its hornbill motif.

The path led north to the outskirts of Long Ampung, where one of the largest footbridges in the area crossed the Kayan. Just before the bridge, a thicket of spears rose in the air. Thirty men gathered to hunt wild pig on foot in the hills, eyeing us as we passed.

Village dogs slept seven deep on the footbridge. Boris, Genevieve, Ampung and I found toeholds around the slumbering canines.

Our hike combined the best of an Indiana Jones adventure and boot camp obstacle course. On the narrow path between Long Ampung and Lidung Payau, I counted 50 bridges. They ranged from swaying rattan contraptions to single strategic logs, each notch just where a foot could best find it, over small watercourses. Though the setting allowed us to imagine ourselves in pith helmets wielding machetes, in reality the walk presented less challenge than a school playground's jungle gym.

Ampung, the most solemn child I'd met in all Asia, showcased the strength of even a 12-year-old Dayak. Stories abound of Westerners taking a week to cover

The look of Borneo: The path north out of Long Ampung toward Lidung Payau runs along a verdant riverbank.

what is a two-day walk for the Dayaks. I can certify that this also applies for younger representatives of the group. The small boy steamed well ahead of me. After he insisted on carrying all my gear, he still had to wait at the top of every little hill for me to catch up.

Something about the fact that a 12-year-old could safely lead tourists around Borneo demonstrated to my mind that getting around one of the world's most exotic destinations could be a cinch. Our wilderness hike, it appeared, more resembled going with my nephew to the Smithsonian Institution in Washington than Stanley's 2,000-man expedition to Ujiji seeking Livingstone.

Although looked at another way, Borneo certainly deserved its exotic reputation if it produced youngsters like Ampung, a preteen who knew the ways of the forest. During a brief shower, Ampung demonstrated that he was resourceful as well as strong, ripping a banana leaf off a tree and using it as an umbrella. He expended no energy on idle talk. A set look to his eyes and mouth revealed a total focus on direction, speed and weather, like the concentration of a sailboat captain scanning the horizon.

The boy was considerably younger than any other guide I'd ever had (including, for example, an Amazonian Indian who was 28 years old). Ampung clearly knew the terrain and village locations, things on which maps of central Borneo rarely agree. Though our way was mostly straightforward, following the north bank of the Kayan, he had to lead us across some

Ampung strikes a typical, no-nonsense expression on our hike.

slippery bridges and underneath a cliff that seeped water.

Butterflies, some tiny blue ones and other big orange ones, bounced off our chests as we followed the path. Coleus, which so often I had planted in Maryland from market packs, grew wild by the paths.

Women with long ear lobes hoed manioc, a root crop, in swampy areas. When they spotted me, they grinned in welcome. On foot, we passed Dayak totems and gravesites, topped by intricate woodwork patterns, as were the longhouses.

At a longhouse in Long Uro, women eager to sell their basketry and beadwork waved for us to stop and buy, as though we were at a suburban American craft fair. Others sold us luscious pineapples.

The hike gave me a chance to begin categorizing my overall impressions:

Civil Engineering in Borneo: We had crossed excellent suspension bridges and hewn logs with foot-sized indentations or crosshatching in the wood to provide traction. Beside one slippery inclined log, a single pole perfectly placed at 45 degrees ingeniously provided a crucial handhold.

A Gourmet Guide to Borneo: Pineapples garnered a rating of "splendid." Otherwise, we ate Asia's least interesting cuisine two times a day: rice and mountain greens (probably cassava) with bony chicken or wild pig added for dinner. But Ampung's powerful hiking suggested that Dayak food was nutritious if not exciting.

Answer to the Big Question: What is Borneo really like? The humidity reminded me of my home state. The people, such as Onas and the Nawang Baru longhouse residents, were tremendously kind to outsiders. Couples such as Dorothe and Andreas raised their children much like people the world over.

LESSON NUMBER 3: PERHAPS THE LENGTHENING LOG OF MY TRAVELS TO EXOTIC PLACES MUTED MY RESPONSE TO A PLACE THAT EARLIER MIGHT HAVE LEFT ME SPEECHLESS.

Yet even to my eyes, Borneo's longhouse dancers and pig hunters, its fancily decorated rice barns and intricate beadwork, seemed to define it as more exotic than places like Java and Thailand.

Ampung announces our arrival at Lidung Payau. An elaborate archway features a tiger.

Given the ease of getting around if you charter canoes or traipse from village to village on wide paths and if you can handle the Maryland- or Louisiana-grade humidity, I composed an overall title for the trek that might capture its feasibility: "Borneo without the Leeches." This working title would not last the afternoon, as events would show.

Ampung led us to our midday destination. A collection of longhouses stood in a sylvan clearing. He halted at a village archway and uttered the only two words he would speak to me all day.

"Lidung Payau," he announced crisply.

"*Terima kasih* (thanks)," I said. I regarded Lidung Payau. "Bright lights, big city," I added in English, just amusing myself really, as Ampung couldn't understand and didn't seem the chatty type, even in Indonesian.

At the first longhouse, a woman beckoned our mud-splattered group up the steps for rice and oranges. We addressed her as *ibu* (mother).

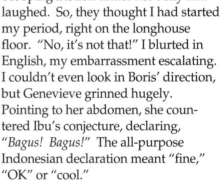
My foot bleeds from a leech bite.

I had carted a box of beads halfway around the world for the occasion. Our guidebooks said to pay cash for actual meals and to offer little gifts for snacks. As a gesture of thanks for the food, I presented the box to Ibu, and she seemed quietly pleased.

Beads play a huge role in Borneo's handicrafts. Women decorate baby carriers and bracelets with individually named beads that had made their way to the rain forest along trade routes from Europe, Africa, China and India—and now, from Baltimore. Ibu and another woman with ear lobes stretching to her shoulder taught us some bead names.

Yet again I dragged out family photos. I drew a

flow chart— the Dayaks seemed to readily comprehend my little graphic—to explain the relationships among my parents, sibling and nephew.

Midway through the visit, I discovered a pool of blood spreading below me on the floorboards. My left foot bled like a spigot, without any signals of pain. An unnoticed hitchhiker had literally leeched on to me during our trek. Leech bites contain an anticoagulant, hence the amount of blood.

Ibu made a scooping motion under her belly and laughed. So, they thought I had started my period, right on the longhouse floor. "No, it's not that!" I blurted in English, my embarrassment escalating. I couldn't even look in Boris' direction, but Genevieve grinned hugely. Pointing to her abdomen, she countered Ibu's conjecture, declaring, *Bagus! Bagus!* The all-purpose Indonesian declaration meant "fine," "OK" or "cool."

Everyone roared with laughter. Dayak women tossed off menstruation jokes as uninhibitedly as if discussing wild pig recipes.

Family members watched with mild curiosity as the culprit leech, the color of a garden slug, departed the scene, walking end over end like a Slinky. Apparently bleeding over the floor of complete strangers constituted no lapse in Dayak etiquette. The family airily indicated not to trouble myself as I dutifully gathered water and tissues to mop up the mess.

LESSON NUMBER 4: ONE LEECH BITE CONSTITUTES THE IDEAL MAXIMUM NUMBER.

One bite satisfied a traveler's curiosity without the

tedium of having hundreds burrowing into the feet and ankles, as many Borneo hikers have described. Yet the relative lack of leeches also reflected something more sinister: a change in Borneo's climate wrought by logging. As humid as I found Borneo, the island had become much drier over time. Logging had set up a vicious chain reaction of deforestation, dryness, forest fires (including the giant 1983 conflagration) and additional treelessness.

After lunch, Genevieve and Boris continued to Sungai Barang, and Ampung guided me on riverside paths back to his home.

After our hike, I gave Ampung the equivalent of a $5 tip. "*Bagus* [good] guide," I complimented him.

The strong little Dayak, a descendent a half-century removed of Borneo's feared headhunters, wordlessly took the cash and handed it to his mother.

Borneo and the big lesson: the role of modern missionaries

Missionaries have reinvented themselves several times in this century. Many historians have described the historical relationship between missionaries and colonialism that prevailed until the early 1900s. By the 1960s, missionary work had changed considerably, with missionaries accepting limits set by local governments and Christian churches.

By the 1990s, the role of the world's 200,000 missionaries (about 67,000 are from the United States) had further evolved. Many adopted lives of Christlike simplicity, living with the poor in Calcutta and Cairo. Significant numbers of U.S. minorities and Asian and African nationals now participate in mission work. There are 15,000 Protestant missionaries from Africa, 11,000 from Asia, and 3,000 from Latin America, according to a report in *Christianity Today*.

At the time of my journey to Borneo, I was familiar with some of these trends after reading a *Time* magazine cover story in 1982 called "The New Missionaries." The piece described missionaries who taught children and tended to the sick. Today, missionaries create jobs in Bolivia using computer technology and marketing techniques, distribute the Bible in Los Angeles and run little cultural museums in Brazil and Papua New Guinea.

Language skills picked up by many of the 67,000 U.S. missionaries may potentially increase our economic competitiveness. Many Utah residents, for example, are Mormons who speak foreign languages learned during mission work abroad. Not only do they speak Mandarin, Hebrew and other languages, they know how other cultures value the role of personal relationships in business transactions. An estimated 30 percent of the population of Utah is bilingual, according to a report in *The Wall Street Journal*, and this has sparked an explosive growth in Utah's international trade.

Numbers of North American missionaries overseas

CAREER PERSONNEL, LATEST 1990s DATA AVAILABLE

Mormons *	25,000
Evangelical Protestant	20,418
Fundamentalist	10,353
Roman Catholic	5,881
Mainline Protestant	3,235
Pentacostal	2,054
TOTAL	**66,941**

* The Church of Jesus Christ of Latter-Day Saints had 51,000 missionaries worldwide in 1996, according to its missionaries office. Nearly half are estimated to be serving overseas.

Based on data in the *International Bulletin of Missionary Research* and published reports

Pope John Paul II, the modern world's champion missionary (and perhaps even its foremost traveler at 625,000 miles), issued an encyclical in 1990 calling for increased missionary zeal. He wrote that "faith demands a free adherence on the part of a person, but at the same time faith must also be offered to that person." Even so, he acknowledged that simply preaching at people would have little success in the modern world:

People today put more trust in witnesses than in teachers, in experience than in teaching and in life action than in theories.

The scholars I contacted credited Roman Catholic missionaries, one of the smaller groups with less than 6,000, as most receptive to local culture, especially in Borneo.

"In my experience, the role of missionaries in preserving local cultures depends in part on institutional factors," McGill University Professor Jérôme Rousseau wrote to me. "In many, but not all, parts of the world, Roman Catholic missionaries have been more positive toward local cultures; at the other extreme, fundamentalists have been more negative."

Rousseau noted that Catholic missionaries integrated "the local iconography and melodies in church decorations and rituals." Roman Catholic missionaries "actually attempt to preserve as much of native values as they can," agreed Professor Allen R. Maxwell of the University of Alabama.

I asked my father, Louis J. Belliveau, why Roman Catholic missionaries might be the most receptive to local cultures. "In the late 19th and early 20th centuries," he said, "the Church issued a number of encyclicals promoting the sanctity of the family, in part to counter Marxism." Because the family is the initial building block of cultural transmission, the Roman Catholic Church tread more lightly on customs, "while the fundamental Christian relies strictly on the literal instructions of the New Testament," he said.

Scholars believe that evangelical Protestants have

done the greatest damage to traditional ways in Borneo, especially by attacking dancing and drinking, closely allied to traditions of hospitality (and not just in the Apau Kayan). In some cases, native art, dependent on spirit worship and appeasement, lost its vitality. The beautiful beadwork on Kenyah baby carriers, for example, depicts a creature originally designed to scare away evil spirits.

A baby carrier that our longhouse hosts in Lidung Payau displayed.

In Borneo, the missionary pilots, though born-again Protestants, illustrated the overall shift to a modern role of being useful. "When I was flying with MAF in the '60s," wrote Max Meyers, MAF's chief executive officer, in a retrospective on the fellowship, "80 percent of my passengers were white missionaries. Today, the majority are nationals."

Perhaps missionaries had originally set in motion some of the changes in Dayak life. Yet today, without MAF flights, the Borneo interior might become completely depopulated.

Since the turn of the century, the Apau Kayan lost thousands of people, and only about 5,200 remain today. In *Borneo: Journey Into the Tropical Rainforest*, Kal Muller credited the "skilled pilots of the Missionary Aviation Fellowship" for beginning to stem the tide in the 1970s. More recently, the Indonesian government began subsidizing flights on Merpati and Asahi airways into Long Ampung, the largest of six MAF airstrips in the Apau Kayan. Muller wrote that "now that there is plenty of land, regular air service, and government-built schools, the exodus from the Apau Kayan seems to have ended."

Indeed, at the time of my 1991 visit, district officials counted more than 5,200 people in the region's Dayak villages.

Apau Kayan population

1903-04	19,600
1930	16,656-16,870
1948	16,013
1970	12,521
1991	5,200

Based on *Central Borneo: Ethnic Identity and Social Life in a Stratified Society* and Apau Kayan officials

It seemed to me that the work of the Mission Aviation Fellowship in the Apau Kayan demonstrated an intriguing benefit of missionary work, albeit an unstated and unintended one—preserving the access of isolated people to medical care and education.

Profile: The Mission Aviation Fellowship

Every four minutes, a Mission Aviation Fellowship plane takes off or lands somewhere in the world. Many operate in remote areas of Central and South America, Africa and Indonesia.

The cost of keeping one plane going runs about $8,000 a month. Fees charged to users cover one-third of MAF's $21 million annual operating costs. Individuals and churches, who may pledge $8 to $15 a month, cover the rest. In Maryland, for example, nearly 100 churches, 1,500 individuals and 30 other organizations support MAF work.

World War II combat pilots, from the United States, the United Kingdom, Australia and New Zealand, sought to unite their Christian faith and their flying skills by founding the group. MAF's first pilot, Betty Greene, began flying a biplane in Mexico in 1946 to aid mission work. In 1996 the world's largest Cessna air service comprised 115 pilots in 18 countries flying 82 single-engine planes, according to the organization's web site at http://www.maf.org.

My hypothesis that missionaries helped to preserve culture by maintaining transportation links to the Apau Kayan won no support, however, from scholars who have lived and worked in central Borneo. Professor Rousseau wrote to me that

By providing transportation services, MAF has an effect on the economy. However, I don't think this role is crucial. Although the Apau Kayan is remote, it is not inaccessible, and it has traditionally been part of many trading circles. Before the MAF, there were already outboard motors, but of course, petrol was more expensive. The migration from the Apau Kayan to the lower Kayan as well as tributaries of the Mahakam occurred at the instigation of Indonesian authorities, which wanted to depopulate the Apau Kayan. I suspect that they have allowed the remaining 5,000 people to remain because of geopolitical reasons related to the relationship with Malaysia.

I learned about Emile Borne's views about his work when he invited me to visit his family the evening after he flew me back to Samarinda. I met Borne's family: his wife, Christy, and their children, Glory, Andrew, Grace and Charity. They lived in a comfortable house, full of traditional Dayak basketry and beadwork.

The attractive pilot described his relationships with women before he was "saved" in the spring of 1976. "For six months I prayed that if He [God] gave me a wife, that I would have none of this turmoil because of the flesh, of being involved with sex." He and Christy met six months after his conversion.

He came to view the world through the prism of the born again. Life events came in two categories,

Emile Borne chats in Indonesian with a Dayak at Long Lebusan.

"burdens" and "blessings." Blessings included good turns of events, such as safe flying. Burdens comprised setbacks, such as the aggravation of dealing with corrupt Indonesian officialdom.

He'd had sick people die in his plane. He'd watched villagers pull out their wallets to raise money for a comrade's journey. Despite the crucial link he provided in getting Dayaks to health care, Borne expressed mixed feelings about the role MAF play in the Apau Kayan. He said he wished his work was more obviously gospel related. I found his actions laudable, in part because I'd observed no obvious proselytizing, yet Borne took no particular satisfaction from providing transportation per se.

"MAF in East Kal [Kalimantan] is not so much church work, so donations aren't as readily given," he said. "Donors want to see their money go for Bibles, not to enable people to live where salt will cost only half as much. Every day I'm on cloud 9," he said of his work, "but then I have to explain that we carry kerosene and tourists." Still, he concluded, "Jesus also meets people's physical needs."

Of his work, he said, "I love it. I love it. It is glamorous." His work *was* glamorous—and it carried genuine risks. MAF bush pilots began a formal safety program in 1979. Despite undertaking some of the world's most difficult flying, MAF's recent records show an average of only one accident per year.

Emile and Christy Borne told the story of fellow pilot Terry Wohlgemuth, stationed in Tarakan, East Kalimantan. The pilot had survived a crash landing in the jungle, helped to safety by villagers he'd assisted in the past. The story stayed on Borne's mind.

"Sometimes I look at that one propeller and wonder what I'm doing," Borne said. Should anything ever happen to those whirring blades, "Either the Lord will protect me and I'll be like Terry," the pilot said, "or I'll be in the presence of the Lord."

I liked the pilot and his family. Years later I would understand why. It was not because they accepted the hardships of similar Latin American missionaries who live in dirt-floored huts, for they did not. Their house was large, and they could afford three household helpers. (A report by Andrés Tapia in *Christianity*

Today noted that 50 Third World missionaries can be funded for the same amount required to support one North American missionary family.)

The Bornes also did not seem especially ecumenical. Christy was a true believer who did not hesitate to press her faith on others. She wrote in newsletters MAF distributed to the churches that backed them financially of how their Muslim cook, Ibn Atun, listened to her stories about the Lord and how one of their helpers, a woman named Maren, "had repented of her sins."

Clues as to why I respected the Bornes' work only became apparent when I later found an article in an anthropological journal called *Man*. "Anthropologists and Missionaries: Brothers under the Skin," by a Dutch professor and former missionary, noted a crucial point: the lengthy time commitment of a missionary to an area.

Sjaak van der Geest of the University of Amsterdam wrote that

> There can be no doubt that, through their prolonged stays in a community, missionaries often acquire a vast and detailed knowledge. ... A stay of 10 years or more in the same area is (and certainly used to be) quite normal. Language study is therefore a logical investment. Many missionaries begin their work with language training which may take six months or longer.

Van der Geest also noted that the "missionaries' greater openness to transcendental experiences can make them receptive to local religious opinions." Further, he felt that the zeal of missionaries showed an interest in others not so terribly different to that of anthropologists or explorers. And their concern for the souls of those they lived with affirmed their belief in the humanity of men and women who lived in premodern societies.

Reading the professor's article, I recalled how Borne pattered in effortless Indonesian to members of the MAF ground crew in Samarinda and the villagers in Long Lebusan and Long Ampung. He had interviewed the Mahak Baru chief and Onas on my behalf to set up my itinerary. No English words or slang crept into his sentences. Speaking Indonesian, the national language (Dayaks also have their own languages, including Kenyah and Kayan), he met the villagers on their own ground, displaying a businesslike and unpatronizing manner.

That Emile Borne could readily communicate with Dayaks impressed me, as did the fact that he and his family had lived in Indonesia for a decade. The "anthropologist is non-committed and free to leave," van der Geest pointed out. The same applied to me as a traveler.

Emile Borne exemplified the way U.S. fundamentalists seemed the most provincial of all Americans, unquestioning of the Bible and simplistic in their approach to foreign cultures. Yet from this group came those most willing to leave the familiarity of places like Fort Worth, Texas, to help the people of Long Sule and Data Dian, hidden hamlets almost no one back home would be able to place on the map.

Though not as intrigued by foreign cultures as Peace Corps volunteers, missionaries opt for longer stays in equally rough places. Their fixed views revolving around the Bible might give missionaries more grounding in dealing with an unfamiliar environment.

Missionaries have written the scriptures in Ixil, Dani, Ainu, Micmac and Tahitian. Wycliff Bible Translators of Huntington Beach, Calif., has translated the Old Testament into 1,200 languages, including some that do not exist in written form.

Because language is the signpost of culture, someone truly in the business of promoting Western cultural superiority would be teaching the Bible in a language such as English.

At first glance, it seemed to me that Bible translating, in a way, shows an impressive respect for local ways. Professor Maxwell pointed out, however, that "making Bible translations available hastens the loss of local ways and in some cases, creates a marked disrespect for them, which in turn accelerates their loss." He added that

> missionization paves the way for Englishification, which in turn, speeds pop-culturification. Net result: loss of local culture! No matter how you slice it, a net effect of (Christian) missionization is the proliferation of an Amero-European culture, value system and social system. It is just another example, as is the "Coca-Colaization" of the planet.

Language, transmitted today by a world pop and computer culture dominated by English, ultimately exerts a much bigger influence than religion on a cultures such as that of the Dayaks.

LESSON NUMBER 5: LANGUAGE MAY BE A MORE IRREVERSIBLE RE-DIRECTOR OF THOUGHT PATTERNS THAN THE DISCARDING OF ANIMISM FOR CHRISTIAN BELIEFS.

For example, Afro-Brazilians, despite adopting Portuguese and nominally Catholicism, fused tribal gods to saints to create the religion called *candomblé*. They use the Yoruba language for ceremonies to the present day, and thus preserve an important aspect of African culture.

Professor Rousseau put it this way:

Dayaks wearing sunhats canoe along the Kayan River.

The main threat to local cultures, in Borneo as in Canada, France, the United States, or what have you, is probably television. It, not religion, is the opiate of the masses. [And] the the most significant re-director of thought patterns is the socio-economic changes of a society, e.g., moving from subsistence to commodity production, moving from the country to the city and changing educational patterns and media of communication.

Change wrought by missionaries, logging and emigration had already come to the Dayaks. Perhaps it had weakened their art, perhaps it had created a need for kerosene and 90-minute air transport to the coast that people had previously managed to cope without. Possibly this was bad. But as van der Geest pointed out, if one accepts change as a normal part of life, "it will be agreed that the prevention of change is indeed 'change' in another more complex sense of the term."

The modern world was bound to reach the remote Apau Kayan, in the same way that Chinese bead traders, Javanese *transmigrasi* and people who enjoyed Redmond O'Hanlon's book have also turned up.

LESSON NUMBER 6: EXPLORERS, ADVENTURER TRAVELERS, ANTHROPOLOGISTS AND MISSIONARIES ALIKE BRING CHANGE NO MATTER HOW MUCH LIP SERVICE THEY PAY TO CULTURAL PRESERVATION.

Van der Geest wrote of anthropologists and missionaries (he could have included travelers as well) that

> Their mere presence is in itself a formidable factor of change. The culture which missionaries and anthropologists carry with them is "contagious."

At least Emile Borne helped to allow the people of the Apau Kayan make a new way while living in their old valleys, so that the last Dayaks were not forced to become shop clerks in Balikpapan and Samarinda.

GIRAFFES BY THE ROADSIDE

Kenya and Tanzania … and lessons on our love-hate relationship to Africa

A giraffe at Masai Mara looks over our safari van.

In Africa, we dressed like scruffs. Before going, I bought lots of used clothing—T-shirts at Goodwill that I could wear for a few days and discard and two pairs of comfortable green U.S. Army pants for $5 apiece from a surplus store.

Our purchases of simple clothes took heed of our guide book's warnings about street crime and countryside bandits. We also wore no jewelry and did not leave our photo equipment in plain view. The need to take security precautions would be demonstrated by events in Kenya that summer that drew worldwide attention.

We prepared for another reality of travel in the developing world—inevitable delays—by buying pulp paperbacks at a used bookstore.

Our trip was an encore for part of a group that sailed together the previous autumn in Greece: my brother Jim; our friend Stephany; a friend from London, Steve Wright; and myself. We planned a budget safari to Kenya's game parks and a beach trip to its Indian Ocean coast.

Making arrangements on our own to save money, I had awakened one morning at 3 a.m. to call the Nairobi offices of a travel agency. The agency booked us on a week-long camping safari for $231 apiece. A guide would drive us around Kenya and locate wildlife, and a cook would prepare our meals outdoors. By sleeping in little tents that we set up ourselves, we would save anywhere from $1,000 to $3,000 compared to the cost of staying at the same parks in fancy lodges.

So with backpacks full of old clothes, used books and fresh film, we flew to Africa, which means first flying to Europe, given the paucity of direct flights between North America and anywhere south of Madrid.

LESSON NUMBER 1: WE WILL KNOW AFRICA'S ECONOMIC STATUS HAS IMPROVED WHEN MORE PEOPLE CAN FLY THERE DIRECTLY.

After traveling for an evening, the following full day, and part of the next, we finally found ourselves waiting for our luggage at Jomo Kenyatta International Airport in Nairobi. We stared, stupefied, at a little clock above the luggage carousel. Very slowly, because we were shattered with fatigue, we calculated the time difference and realized that getting to Africa had taken us 32 hours.

Our travel time

Baltimore-JFK airport, driving	5 hours
Waiting around airport for flight	7 hours
JFK-Frankfurt	6 hours 50 minutes
Delay in Frankfurt	5 hours
Frankfurt-Nairobi	8 hours 8 minutes
TOTAL	32 HOURS

During our dead-of-night taxi ride to the Hotel Boulevard, we could detect the Britishness of Kenya in the roundabouts and the road signs. The staff of the hotel spoke English with not only a British lilt but the diction of Shakespearean actors. We got to our hotel room at 5:30 a.m. and slept until 3:30 p.m.

Getting to Africa had been grueling. Our preparations—buying old clothes and reading matter—focused on its more negative aspects. Yet traveling around it, we would soon discover, was enchanting. We came to understand the euphoria the continent inspired in many writers.

Some African-American soldiers, diplomats, journalists and others, however, feel more dismay than ecstasy about their motherland. And each time they publicly express their frustration, particularly in newspaper articles, supporters and critics reveal the divided feelings that Americans hold toward Africa.

LESSON NUMBER 2: AFRICA, SO MUCH BIGGER THAN ALL OF NORTH AMERICA, PRESENTS A DIZZYING RANGE OF POSSIBILITIES FOR THE VISITOR. ONE CAN EXPERIENCE EITHER A HORROR SUCH AS RWANDA OR DELIGHT IN COUNTLESS OTHER PLACES.

MONDAY, JULY 3, 1989
Off to see elephants

At 9 a.m., we arrived at the offices of Let's Go Travel on Standard Street in Nairobi. Within the hour, we departed in a minivan with the driver, Joel M. Mbugua, and the cook, Hardson Omuaro, both members of Kenya's largest tribe, the Kikuyus. Four English girls made up the rest of our traveling party.

Joel drove south out of Nairobi towards Amboseli National Park. Fifty minutes out of Nairobi, an impossibly tall apparition loomed on the left side of the road. A giraffe, perhaps 16 feet high, regarded our approach.

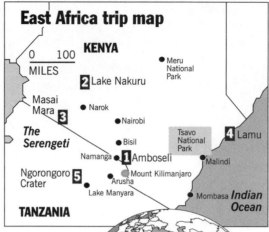

LESSON NUMBER 3: THE SPLENDOR OF AFRICA BECAME MANIFEST, MAKING OUR AIR-TRAVEL ORDEAL WORTHWHILE ON THE FIRST MORNING.

We were not an hour out of the city and we had experienced our first gasp of astonishment, before even reaching a game park.

The giraffe watched us. It then loped off with a surreal floating gait, neck bobbing gracefully to balance its NBA-star forelegs. Giraffes move with a rolling motion, comparable to that of a pitching ship or a rocking horse.

Ninety minutes out of Nairobi, we drove through a Masai village, Bisil. The famed Masai wore their trademark bright red cloth wraps. The women accessorized with shoulder-length earrings and the men with spears. About 200 people shopped and visited in its jumble of wooden bars and stands.

The straggle of village buildings yielded again to the bush, brown-green grass with flat-topped trees and low mountains in the distance. Wild ostriches, donkeys, cattle and goats dotted the landscape. Termite hills as big as a man rose from the ground.

The cloudy morning gave way to sun and perfect weather, perhaps 72 degrees with negligible humidity. So far traveling in East Africa seemed more comfortable than in Asia. The heat of Kenya oppressed less, many people spoke English, and both the cities and the

countryside felt far less crowded. (By 1995, each square mile of China contained an average of 338 people; Kenya, 128; and Tanzania, 83).

Joel parked the minivan under a tree on the dusty flat plain of Amboseli National Park, at 150 square miles more than twice the size of the District of Columbia.

Using badly twisted pegs, we managed somehow to set up our tents, primitive affairs of heavy canvas with little ventilation. With a bit of free time, we entertained ourselves on our first afternoon in the African bush with a little walk. Not far from our tents, we climbed a huge tree with limbs that spread like arms to get a good look around. Rocky outcroppings called *kopis* rose from the flat plain. In the far distance, one of the *kopis* appeared to move. A faraway elephant, dwarfed by the immensity of the plain yet still immense itself, appeared as big and square as a pile of boulders until it began to move.

Aviatrix Beryl Markham, a bush pilot who flew above East Africa in the 1930s to spot game, wrote in her book *West with the Night* that surprisingly,

> elephant are seldom conspicuous from the air. If they were smaller, they might be. Big as they are and coloured as they are, they blend with everything until the moment they catch your eye.

At dusk, we returned to our van for our first game drive. Our Nissan minivan, a diesel, seemed exceptionally rugged for a vehicle from a largely urban nation like Japan. It handled the ruts and jolts of Amboseli's dirt tracks as easily as it had the main road from Nairobi. A pop-top enabled tourists to stand and take photos safe from passing wild creatures.

We saw just about everything one dreams about sighting on a trip to Africa: dozens of elephants, zebra, wildebeest, hippos (at a watering hole, nostrils visible only), kudu, Thompson's gazelles, impala, ostriches and crested cranes, as well as hordes of fellow tourists in minivans.

Having Joel as our guide paid off. He stopped the Nissan and chatted to other guides, comparing notes in Swahili about something called *duma*. These turned out to be cheetahs. Joel drove up a hill, and we became the first of a half-dozen vehicles to surround a pair of

We set up camp at Amboseli.

We had no trouble seeing relaxed cheetahs, left, and zebra, below.

the lithe spotted cats, two of only 20,000 worldwide. One cheetah slept while the other posed sitting. Then the poser flopped on his back and, as though the duo enjoyed complete solitude miles from observation, he stretched luxuriantly and fell asleep.

Dazzled by such a remarkable sampling of African wildlife on our first drive, Jim announced, "We can go home now." Already our cheap camping tour had produced excellent results, and we had two more parks yet to visit. Even our guide was impressed. Joel said he hadn't seen cheetahs in 20 previous trips to Amboseli.

When we got back to the campsite to Hardson's beverage selections, the English girls in our group zeroed in on the teapot. "This is *pukkah* [first-rate] tea," they said in the languid manner of the Sloane Ranger, the set typified by Princess Diana. The world of the unambitious Sloane revolves around one's clique (preferably based near London's Sloane Square), shopping at the upscale Harvey Nichols department store and motoring in one's Jeep to the country at weekend. Pippa, Fiona and the two others had the required first name ending in a sounded vowel of an official Sloane, though actually they were from Tunbridge Wells in Kent, a suburban equivalent.

Despite the fact that Steve hailed from London and I had lived in England for $3^1/_2$ years, apartheid reigned almost from the beginning between the Sloanes and our foursome. Perhaps they viewed all of us (even Steve on an honorary basis) as lumpen Americans, possibly a redundancy in their minds.

We viewed the girls as aloof or worse, spoiled brats. Some evidence points to the "spoiled" hypothesis. They were last-minute additions to our group, having been more or less found on the street by our travel agency the morning of our departure. We had

booked the safari months in advance. Yet they hogged the minivan's more comfortable middle seats as though by birthright. They airily announced they would get sick occupying the lurching rear bench. Left hanging was the implication that Yanks were either too crude to mind or beneath notice. Typically, Jim, Steph and Steve took the Sloanes in stride while I fumed and complained out of their earshot.

On a comfortably cool night, before the incipient gulf between our two groups hardened to stone, we all sat around on our camp chairs talking. The stars above shone brilliantly, the Southern Cross rising over the overcast shape of Kilimanjaro, which we still hadn't really seen, given its perpetual cloud cover. Africa's biggest mountain lay just across the border in Tanzania, a now-silent giant whose mammoth volcanic eruptions eons ago deposited a rich layer of ash that became the grasslands of the Serengeti.

This had been my mental image of a trip to Africa: under the stars, around the campfire, with a guide telling us stories.

Joel described how hyenas, the most dangerous wild creatures, could sneak into a tent and rip a person's face off. Next most dangerous, he claimed, were elephants, who without malice could step on sleeping campers as they made their heedless way through the bush. Food also attracted the giants. One time a cook left some food in his tent, and an elephant tossed him into the bush.

Hyenas' strong jaws make them dangerous.

In the morning, he said, the elephants might be all around our tents. We wondered if such a magical possibility truly existed.

A scorpion walked around the campfire, tail curved up menacingly back over its four-inch-long body, as gray and dusty as the Amboseli ground on which it walked. We incinerated it in the campfire. Thenceforth we all exhibited scorpion paranoia, checking all over the tent for them. And like old Africa hands, we learned to carefully shake out our dusty boots each morning.

The dust illustrated the aptness of the name Amboseli itself, coming from a Masai word that means "salty dust," "open plain" or "barren place." While Amboseli seemed an intrinsically dry place, especially outside of the wet season, we wondered to what extent elephants affected the ecosystem. The giants can destroy trees by leaning on them and by eating young plants.

While historically this has led to a desirable mosaic of forest and savannah, animal behaviorists debate whether today elephants accelerate desertification when crowded into parks and reserves smaller than their optimal range.

On our first night in Amboseli, we heard via our

campers that bandits had killed some tourists at nearby Tsavo National Park. We pondered what risks the incident posed to ourselves. We hoped our van, our clothes and our meager backpacks appeared sufficiently shabby to render us less of a target.

Our "camp elephant" makes an early morning appearance.

TUESDAY, JULY 4
An elephant comes to us

At 6:15 a.m., we woke to what sounded like an earthquake: the pounding hooves of a wildebeest stampede. I peered out of my tent toward a copse of trees on my left, where an elephant eyed Jim and Steph and a French couple. In the dim light, his tusk shone brightly as he took a step or two toward them and flapped his ears aggressively. Not being fully awake, it took me a moment to re-establish that I was in Africa. Even acknowledging this fact, the sight still seemed remarkable. One could regard a real elephant as one's first waking act.

This particular elephant, a lone male, possessed an impressive sex organ resembling a fifth leg in size and a trunk in agility. My husband Lamont later assured me that a group of guys would have been joking, "wish I were hung like that." An all-women group might have mused about the thrill of being a female elephant. In mixed company, however, all stood in prim silence, though mental gears could be sensed turning.

> Dear Miss Manners: When enjoying mixed company in Africa, what is the proper response to likely scenes of rhino sex, duck sex, and elephant self-love?

The elephant sighting kicked off America's 213th anniversary of independence. Later over breakfast, I mentioned how unusual it had felt, when I worked for newspapers in England during the early 1980s, to be expected to work on the Fourth of July.

Our morning and evening drives located warthogs, a big favorite of the Sloane Rangers, who found them precious grotesques, as would audiences for *The Lion King* five years later. At dusk we watched a column of giraffes, necks bobbing as they ambled across the grasslands. We added rhinos, waterbuck, maribu storks and vultures to our lengthening list of creatures spotted.

Joel parked to the side of a column of 20 elephants, bought up in the rear by a creature significantly more gargantuan than the others. Joel slammed his door a few times, provoking a snort and ear-flapping from "Big Daddy," as Joel called him.

LESSON NUMBER 4: WITH ITS EXTRAORDINARY NUMBERS AND SIZES OF CREATURES, KENYA OVERSHADOWED ANY OTHER PLACE WE HAD VISITED.

Kenya recalled descriptions of the vanished American West, when the earliest trains cut through a seemingly infinite sea of bison. And we hadn't yet visited the giant wildebeest herds to the northwest, in Masai Mara.

Later we heard of unfortunate visitors who had missed out on seeing lions, rhino, elephants, cheetahs or giraffes in Africa. This perplexed us, as we were treated to the sight of these creatures, often at very close range. Save for the elusive leopard, our party witnessed a variety of species that impressed even our guides.

TUESDAY, JULY 5
The Florida Day and Night Club

Our familiar camp elephant stood at the edge of our site again that morning. We captured the

"Big Daddy" trails the other elephants heading along at dusk at Amboseli.

Kenya's summer of growing discontent

The news of slayings in a nearby park illustrated the efficiency if not the accuracy of the bush telegraph.

My later research showed that indeed, deaths had occurred at Tsavo on the day we arrived in Nairobi—but not of tourists. Kenyan security forces had shot five elephant poachers.

Soon enough, however, our rumor would be presciently correct. On the Wednesday of our week-long safari, the bodies of two French tourists were discovered in Meru National Park, 100 miles northeast of Nairobi. They had happened upon poachers eating a zebra they'd killed.

In many ways the summer of our visit in 1989 was highly eventful for Kenya. Interlocking regional problems came to a head: instability in Somalia, highly armed poachers, the loss since 1973 of 90 percent of Kenya's elephants, and tourist attacks.

• On **July 18**, two weeks after our first glimpse of wild elephants, Kenyan President Daniel arap Moi burned a 15-foot-high heap of confiscated ivory valued at $3 million. At the event, Dr. Richard Leakey, director of Kenya's wildlife conservation agency, said that in June, 22 poachers had been killed as part of a shoot-on-sight policy and "not one elephant" had been poached in that time. The intensity of the poaching—as many as two elephants daily at Tsavo National Park, a slaughter observable by visiting Western tourists—prompted the action.

• Ironically, the success of the rangers led poachers to turn their gun sights on tourists instead of tuskers. On **July 27**, on the road from Amboseli to Tsavo, a gunman in military-style garb confronted an Audubon Society group from Connecticut. He shot from the hip into the first of three vans that had slowed on a rutted part of the road. Marie Ferraro, 49, of Bethany, Conn., died. By the end of the year, four other tourists had also returned from their trips to Kenya in coffins.

The fact that a bird-watcher from Connecticut had died on a Kenyan safari soon after our own haunted me for a long time after the trip. I wondered if our deliberate attempts to appear of limited means had paid off

or if we had just been lucky. I talked to Milan Bull of Fairfield, Conn., leader of the ill-fated Audubon safari. He described the attackers as "totally arbitrary" in selecting their targets. He cited the fact that eight vans had passed before and after his group's and that the attack had occurred four miles from a police station.

"They were roaming the country, hanging out on the main tourist roads," he said. "They just looked for whatever tourist came down that day. They weren't scoping a particular group. They looked for opportunity—brush and hinterland to escape into.

"These guys had run out of elephant ivory and rhino [horn] and were going for tourists," Bull said. "The guy I saw was in military garb. They had joined the [Somali] Army to get equipment and deserted and came around northeastern Kenya."

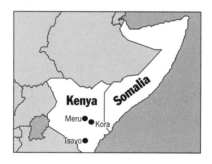

The first notorious killing occurred in **September 1988**, when English tourist Julie Ward, 28, was murdered in a remote corner of Masai Mara. In *A Death in Kenya*, Michael Hiltzik describes testimony that at the time she was wearing a pullover and jeans—and carrying an expensive camera. We had not looked so very different. So we had just been lucky to escape bandits or rogue rangers, who might have randomly attacked despite our impoverished appearance.

Despite everything, Bull said that he was considering a return trip to Kenya. "You have a greater chance of something happening visiting the Bronx Zoo," he said.

Banditry continues to be a problem in several Kenyan parks. The U.S. State Department advises tourists to stick with reputable tour outfits and to travel in convoys.

• On **Aug. 20**, poachers bearing

assault rifles murdered conservationist George Adamson at his camp in Kora National Reserve, 150 miles northeast of Nairobi. Adamson's wife Joy had written *Born Free: A Lioness of Two Worlds*, the 1961 best-seller about Elsa the lioness.

LESSON NUMBER 5: THE SLAYINGS PRESAGED THE ROGUISHNESS AND GROWING DISINTEGRATION OF NEIGHBORING SOMALIA.

In March 1987, Somali President Siad Barre authorized his ministers and police to bring elephant tusks in the country from Ethiopia and Kenya. By 1989, heavily armed Somali gangs of poachers, including some army deserters, roved Kenya's empty northeastern quarter.

Three years later, the Somalis would play on world sympathy, and U.S. forces acting under a U.N. mandate invaded Mogadishu to ensure orderly food distribution to avert starvation.

For its $4 billion effort, U.S. troops suffered taunting, black-on-black racism and even death and desecration. A mob beat soldiers from a downed helicopter, and videotapes showed their naked bodies being dragged through the streets. One could aim for sympathy for Somalia's women and children—except for the fact that they joined in the savagery.

We observed—but did not fully grasp the significance of—signs of how the Somalis, once a proud collection of clans as respected as the Masai, preyed on their own starving women and children, U.S. soldiers, Western tourists and wise elephants.

LESSON NUMBER 6: AMERICANS PROCEEDED SWIFTLY FROM IGNORANCE OF SOMALIA TO SYMPATHY AND FINALLY DISGUST. YET KENYANS AND OTHER AFRICANS MUST LIVE WITH UNSTABLE REGIMES LIKE SOMALIA'S LONG AFTER U.S. INTEREST WANES.

Profile: The elephants of Kenya

Our guidebooks noted that it was easy to see elephants clearly at Amboseli, due to the lack of forest. We did not realize at the time that it was more: perhaps the world's premier elephant park, home to 650 of Kenya's 17,000 elephants.

Cynthia Moss describes in *Elephant Memories: Thirteen Years in the Life of an Elephant Family* how at Amboseli, the intricate social fabric of elephants had not been sundered by poaching and alien elephants migrating from outside the park.

The Masai extended protection to the elephants, who shared the area's watering holes with Masai cattle. Although the Masai might kill the occasional elephant or lion to show bravery, on a larger scale, Moss wrote, they

did not not hunt wild animals for meat or trophies, and they were intolerant of other tribes hunting in their area. Throughout East Africa the areas noted for wildlife today are those that are held by the Masai or other pastoralists.

Culling and the poaching frenzy that peaked circa 1989 obliterate the literal "elephants' memory" of older females in these matriarchal societies. Moss observed strong bonds between immediate families and extended "bond groups," as evidenced by ecstatic greetings and assisting sick and wounded relatives. The oldest females, those from 40 to 60, demonstrate to younger females and babies where to find water and leafy trees in a drought and how to suckle a first-born infant.

Older elephants transmit knowledge of the locations of water holes to younger ones.

Elephant population of Africa

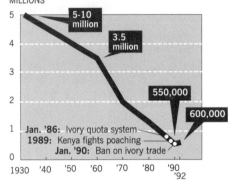

MILLIONS

5-10 million
3.5 million
550,000
600,000

Jan. '86: Ivory quota system
1989: Kenya fights poaching
Jan. '90: Ban on ivory trade

1930 '40 '50 '60 '70 '80 '90 '92

Based on data from *National Geographic* and published reports

NOTE: Some estimates of the 1930 elephant population run as high as 10 million.

Another writer, Elizabeth Marshall Thomas, noted that given the way elephants acquire wisdom through experience, culling equates to killing a society's professional class. She wrote

If the aging animals in question were chickens or pigs, a frugal farmer would certainly cull them—old animals eat more and produce less. But a policy that makes economic sense for a farm cannot be automatically translated into good wildlife management. ... Analogous in human beings would be to slaughter all CEOs and managers, all teachers, coaches, librarians, and all elected political leaders.

"Far from being expendable," Thomas concluded, "the older elephants possess a lifetime of acquired information that can be indispensable to the survival of those in their care."

Given the abhorrence of killing such an intelligent creature and the conflicts between the giants and human agriculture, experts are exploring the option of birth control instead.

Some Masai have begun to grow crops, a target of elephants. And with animals on the rebound after strong poaching curbs began in 1990, lions have begun to prey on Masai cattle and goats. In 1996, Kenya responded by opening its first "community wildlife reserve" near Amboseli, allowing the Masai to benefit directly from entrance fee revenue.

moment in photographs before striking camp at 7:30 a.m. Joel backtracked to Nairobi and continued northwest across the Great Rift Valley to Lake Nakuru National Park.

Most parks required visitors to stay in a vehicle. The necessity of this becomes apparent when the occasional tourist—this happened to at least one Australian—hops to the ground and becomes a lion snack. At Nakuru, one of a handful of parks in Africa where you can walk around, we trekked along vast soda flats to approach the lake and its 2 million flamingos.

We beheld a wonderful sight: a Creation vista of constant balletic motion along the lake. Entire flocks of

the vivid pink flamingos glided from left to right in my camera lens, while farther away uncountable numbers flew in the contrary direction. Some of the heavy-billed birds stood still, heads bent to feed. So many individual flocks of flamingos soared that it looked like a duck shoot at a carnival, with rows of crosscutting creatures. A shot in the 1985 film *Out of Africa* captured this shimmering and impressive sight from an aerial perspective.

Journalist Martha Gellhorn similarly raved about her visit to Lake Nakuru in *Travels With Myself and Another*: "At the shore, thousands of flamingoes lifted off and spread a coral pink streamer against the sky. The sound was like tearing silk."

A waterbuck, pelicans and flamingos at Lake Nakuru.

She saw a herd of zebra

now joined by visiting friends, small antelopes with a black stripe along their tan sides and neat black horns spiralled to a point, and a short black tufted flicking tail. I disturbed them and they ran, bouncing as if the earth was a trampoline.

As Joel drove us through a forest back to our campsite near the park entrance, we spotted a hyrax (like a little groundhog, yet oddly enough related to the elephant), tortoises, and a lone baboon. And then, three yards from our minivan's tires, Joel's sharp eyes detected something quite big under a canopy of bushes. A lioness was eating the torso of a water-buck she had caught. She was the first wild big cat we'd seen in our lives—and we'd seen her in a park known for not having lions.

A solitary baboon regards our group.

As night fell, a light drizzle dampened our camp-site. We debated whether to sleep or to accompany Joel and Hardson to a roadhouse just outside the park. Steve opted to turn in for the night. Jim, Steph and I caught our second wind and joined our guides.

We pulled up to the Florida Day and Night Club, a bunker-like, electric-blue building. The roadhouse's beguiling name itself seemed a sly plea for customers at all hours: "We're a day AND a night club, with a subtropical American name."

Inside, the low-slung chairs with huge wooden arms recalled furniture from a 1950s college dormitory. Fluorescent lights shone on portraits of President Daniel arap Moi and nationalist hero Jomo Kenyatta. The walls were a robin's-egg blue. A green door led to a privy that contributed to the atmosphere.

A woman sold Tusker beer and soft drinks from behind a blue metal cage. I drank room-temperature Cokes and contentedly read a tattered copy of Kitty Kelley's *Jackie Oh!*

LESSON NUMBER 7: SIMPLE THINGS BRING PLEASURE ON TRIPS: BEING IN FROM THE RAIN, WITH A SOFT DRINK, A DECENT LIGHT TO READ BY AND A HIGH POP GOSSIP PAPERBACK THAT DOESN'T TAX THE BRAIN.

The jukebox poured out beguiling Afropop music, interrupted by the odd disco or Kenny Rogers number, as the local men shuffled around in a scuffling dance.

Two of the club's apparent regulars, Bwana Sam and Miss Gladys, took an enormous shine to Jim. I guessed that his big, friendly self, prepared to laugh uproariously at their banter, offered a white counter-part to themselves. And possibly their intense interest was bestowed to honor a traveler who had come 7,500 miles for a neighborly drink.

Africans are outwardly (the only way I knew them) the best-humoured people I have lived with.

Martha Gellhorn in *Travels With Myself and Another*

Sam taught Jim some Swahili, including *bwana* for mister. "*Bwana Jeemmm*," Sam pronounced it. Stephany asked the form of address for women.

"Be Be," Sam said.

"Be Be Stephany," Steph said.

"No," said Sam. "Be Be Jeemmm's."

We collapsed with laughter. The sobriquet "Be Be Jeemmm's" lasted the entire trip.

"That ought to tell you something," I said. "But it isn't that different from a time I saw Chris Evert play at Wimbledon, and she was listed as 'Mrs. J. Lloyd.' "

Hardson had hooked up with some new buddies and, wearing a gentle grin, sat drinking beer at the next table. At that moment our cook seemed to be a man with no concerns whatever.

I felt approximately the same. Relaxed, I drank more Coke, relished *Jackie Oh!*, and thumbed our East Africa guide to learn about upcoming destinations. The Afropop music thumped and rang out, and we counted the Florida Day and Night Club as a must des-tination unlikely to appear in a guidebook.

The Florida Day and Night Club, seen in the light of day.

Meeting the Masai people

A Masai chief bends down to enter the *boma*. He watches as Bopol plays with my camera.

As we prepared to leave Nakuru and visit a Masai village, vervet monkeys took over our campsite. They hung from several trees and observed us, as though on a safari to view humans. They clearly would ransack the camp, grabbing every scrap of discarded food the instant Joel put the Nissan in gear. One impatient vervet could not wait and stole a piece of burnt toast from our campfire, tossing it from hand to hand until it cooled.

We drove on to Narok, a regional trading center, and stopped there for lunch at an outdoor table on the edge of a bustling market. An entire herd of cows wearing bells crossed the ground behind where we ate. A Masai wearing a traditional cloak placed a call in a modern red, British Telecom-style telephone kiosk nearby.

On the drive to Masai Mara, we stopped at a Masai village, where we paid 150 Kenyan shillings ($7.50) each to walk around and take photos. The independent Masai have long captured white colonials' imaginations in the way the Great Plains Indians appeal to American schoolchildren. A warrior tribe, rarely enslaved, these romantic figures drew the respect of early Kenyan settlers such as Lord Delamere.

The Masai lived in a circular thorn enclosure, called a *boma*. Doors of thorn lie beside openings that serve as gates during the day. At night the thorns plug up the openings, when boy herders bring the cattle inside for protection from lions. Within the *boma* stood individual huts, smelling strongly of smoke from little cooking fires.

Three women carried water up a path. Others with pates as smooth as Michael Jordan's sat in a big circle on the ground. A woman stood to tell with great animation a story that moved her listeners to fits of hilarity.

The village illustrated the dilemma of male and female roles in Africa. A group of men, superfluous in a modern world not needful of the services of Masai warriors, hung out under a tree chatting. While women raise Africa's children and food, the men occupy themselves with other pastimes, as David Lamb described in *The Africans*:

> The elderly ones are apt to be sitting in the shade of the trees, smoking their pipes, drinking homemade beer, discussing their cattle—or saying nothing at all. The younger ones are either in school, in the city or in the local beer hall.

A chief with an elegant, high-cheekboned face of the type that inspired Picasso's cubist style handled our fees for visiting the boma. He wrapped one long shin around the other in the storklike pose favored by some Nilotic tribes, a grouping that runs across a band of Africa just south of the Sahara.

The chief draped a blanket in a red Scottish-clan plaid around his shoulders. The pattern, which at first seemed incongruous in an African village, in fact showed off his skin beautifully. The Masai believe that red clothes repel lions.

Toddlers asked us for T-shirts, pens, "machine gun" (somehow we figured out that they meant "chewing gum") and, a bad trend, "one shilling." One little boy named Bopol asked not for handouts, only to experiment with my camera. He pressed his eye against the viewfinder and grasped the camera with great concentration.

We continued along to Masai Mara, a Kenyan extension of the abundant wildlife of Tanzania's Serengeti plains. Unlike compact, dusty, elephant-gray Amboseli, this park's wheat-colored grass waved for miles, reaching to far-off escarpments and hills. The Mara appeared gold, pink and green, especially at sun-

Women at the Masai village told stories and carried water. The men sat under a tree.

set. Its grand vistas resemble those of the American West, particularly the Dakota grasslands.

Joel took us for a drive to see hartebeest, jackals and lots of giraffes. We viewed our first topi, another member of the antelope/gazelle clan, this one with a lustrous dark coat.

We returned to the camp, where Hardson had fixed another feast, this one steak and potatoes. A big storm came in, so we ate in the van as the rain drummed on the windshield. The others played a hand of hearts while I continued, by the light of Hardson's kerosene cooking lamp, to be enthralled with *Jackie Oh!*

THURSDAY, JULY 7

Hippos play hippo games

Huge herds of zebra and dozens of giraffes made our longest game drive, five hours, well worthwhile. The giraffes flicked their ears in a comic manner as they nibbled at treetops. Golden light fell on their tawny skins and the gray-green leaves. The zebras rubbed their noses on each others' rumps. Wildebeest raced us for the sheer play of it, cutting across the track in front of the van at the last instant.

The animals' coats shone. They all looked fat and glossy and not like the subdued creatures in zoos. Years ago comedian Richard Pryor performed a skit describing his visit to Africa. He captured the regal aggressiveness of the animals, noting even the rabbits of Africa looked more menacing than those of America.

The greater Mara-Serengeti area serves as Lion Central, with approximately 2,000 of these big cats. Joel drove into a big thicket of bushes to show us three of them, lying in the shade apparently unbothered by our barging in. The stand of eucalyptus smelled lovely, but the branches grew too densely for us to take decent photos of the big cats.

After watching for a while as the lions in the thicket breathed but put on no additional entertainments, we headed to Hippo Point on the Mara River. About 20 hippos stood midriver, some submerged, others emerging with a big blow and flicking their tiny ears dry. I crossed a branch of the river to watch them from

A pair of hippos squabble with much noise and splashing.

a little cliff directly above. Every so often, one must have goosed another underwater. A giant commotion would ensue, the two principals roaring angrily, and the rest up and down the river joining in. Very large animals with huge vocal cords obviously produced the sound, impressively penetrating like a tugboat blast.

Before our trip, I had expected that while we would have a marvelous time in Africa, nothing would compare to the sights and color of Southeast Asia.

LESSON NUMBER 8: YET FOR WILDLIFE, EAST AFRICA SEEMED THE MOST SPECTACULAR PLACE ON EARTH, A COSMOS OF GIANT ANIMALS.

Land mammals compared

LARGEST IN AFRICA	POUNDS
African elephant	15,400
Hippopotamus	8,000
Giraffe	4,000
Rhino	3,500
African buffalo	1,700
Lion	500
LARGEST IN ASIA	
Asian elephants	11,000
Siberian tiger	700
LARGEST IN NORTH AMERICA	
Bison	2,400

Joel drove our minivan a few yards into Tanzanian territory, indicated only by a stone marker in waving grass precisely identical to that on the Kenya side. Unofficially, this became the 29th country I'd visited.

On our way back, three more lions strolled along. Minivans jockeying for position promptly surrounded their stand of bushes. Oh, to be a lion in modern Masai Mara, unable to move a muscle without an audience of minivan drivers yelling at each other in Swahili and tourists frantically poking video cameras and telephoto lenses out of the sunroofs.

One lion glanced up disdainfully when a minivan

got stuck in a rut and gunned its engine. He had huge hazel eyes and gorgeous countenance, this young male not yet possessed of a full mane.

All the others ignored the vans, evidencing a trait researchers had been noting since the mid-1930s: Lions generally pay no attention to people in vehicles, while they usually flee from a person on foot. Joel said he had seen exceptions to this, however, and we believed him. Just before lions attack a van, he said, they gave a signal: "Their eyes change."

Trios of zebra and wildebeest take it easy at Masai Mara.

LESSON NUMBER 9: HERE THE ANIMALS ROAM FREE AND THE PEOPLE STAY CONFINED—EXCEPT THE MASAI, WHO INHABIT AN INCREDIBLE WORLD.

Between the game drives that bracketed our day, we attended to minor tasks or idly passed the time. I washed clothes to the music on my personal stereo of the Bach "Concerto for Four Harpsichords." The Sloane Rangers dragged their sleeping mats from their tents to a sunny patch of ground and played cards. Jim and Steph read and hung socks out to dry.

The Masai strode up, bringing us firewood. They carried massive tied bundles of six-foot branches horizontally on their upper backs. They wore what seemed to be plastic huaraches on their huge feet—perfect for fording streams, as they simply poured out the water after crossing.

A Masai boy came by to ask if I would give him my umbrella. (No.) He picked up the body of my personal stereo and held it to his ear as though it were a transistor radio. I placed the headphones on him. The music of a group from Martinique, Kassav', played for this budding *moran*, or Masai warrior. He smiled with delight at the Caribbean rhythms: African-based music coming home. "Bye bye," he said as he left, and I replied with the Swahili counterpart, *"Wahele."*

After a five-hour morning drive on rough tracks, everyone had stiff necks and mild headaches. Remarkably for people who had come so far to see East Africa, but perhaps understandably given the surfeit of game we had already seen and our crumbling vertebrae, we told Joel we were not interested in the afternoon game drive.

"You make me a happy man," he said, grinning widely. "I'll go for a beer now."

Joel drove off to we-knew-not-where and returned with cases of air-temperature Coke. We drank it to wash down our toast and buttered bread, violating all Western notions of nutritional correctness. But we were on safari. Somehow this meant we could eat, guilt free, the foods of our 1960s childhoods.

That night we ate dinner under the stars. Joel told

of aspects of life in Kenya, such as his arranged marriage.

"Do you like your wife?" we asked.

"Oh yes!" Joel replied. "I like her very much. I am even missing her now during one week away."

Joel talked about his father's coffee farm and his reverence for Jomo Kenyatta. He seemed lukewarm about Moi, the current president. He told us that Kenyans love their game parks and drive to the nearest one to the capital, Nairobi National Park.

Joel said he had gone to college for two years to become a game driver. "I was wanting to do this since I was born," he said. Only about 2,000 Kenyans serve as tour guides, so he enjoyed good fortune in achieving his dream.

His love for animals showed in how he intently watched them when he stopped the van. His hand just touched his mouth, and his curling eyelashes could be seen in profile. His warm-timbered voice lent a rolling cadence to his one-word announcements of wildlife in view:

Hartebeest. "Harrrrt. Beeest."

Wildebeest. "Wild. Beeest," he pronounced it, not WILL-da-beest, as in the U.S. dictionary. We lacked the nerve to correct a Kenyan on how to pronounce one of the animals that comprised his national patrimony or even to ask if Africans used a different pronunciation.

"Waterrrr. Bukk," he said, with a trilling "r" and a rock-hard "k." "Reed. Bukk."

Most inexplicably, zebra he invariably called "zebbla." We never quite figured a way to ask if this was proper Kenyan or merely a Joelism.

Jobs could be hard to come by, Joel continued, "unless you are educated." Hardson had also been to college for two years to learn how to be a cook, he told us. They had both received training—most likely at Kenya Utalii College, which awards an associate diploma for tour guides—on methods of ensuring that even difficult customers enjoy the trip. For example, Joel told us Hardson was willing to make a second type of dinner for people who complained about the fare. "No!" we cried in sympathetic protest. Who could complain about Hardson's delicious pancakes for breakfast and chicken or steaks for lunch and dinner? And we cringed at the thought of arrogant Westerners aggravating dedicated Joel and Hardson.

As Joel talked around the campfire, Masai guards appeared. They plunged their spears into the earth and stood, occasionally talking among themselves or to Joel, wrapped in their red cloaks, with flashlights and razor-sharp machetes under their wraps. Rows of multicolored Swatch watches, the modern equivalent in primary hues and playfulness to traditional beadwork, marched up the forearms of these cattle herders. No doubt vigorous trading occurred between the Masai and any tourists who happened by with the coveted Pop Art timepieces.

LESSON NUMBER 10: THE CONSTANT ARRIVALS AND DEPARTURES OF THE MASAI AT OUR CAMP MADE IT CLEAR THAT THEY LIVED HERE AND WHAT WAS A PARK TO US WAS TO THEM A HOMELAND.

Tourists could come and go, and the Masai would neither avoid them nor pander to them.

A Masai named Philip wore a dear little cap and child's coat over his red plaid tunic. He seemed a bit fey in both his outfit and mannerisms. He asked to borrow my paperback. I would not soon forget the campfire-illuminated sight of him reading, or at least

holding open and scrutinizing many of the pages, of *Jackie Oh!*

These Masai visits made camping, even with no amenities whatsoever, infinitely preferable to staying in the expensive nearby lodge. We had no showers, running water or shops, but we felt no hardship. We washed our clothes in the river and dried them in the bushes on what we came to call the Underwear Tree, and relied on Hardson for provisions.

FRIDAY, JULY 8
Closeups of hunting lionesses

On a 6:30 a.m. game drive, Joel—ever on the mark—found three lionesses prowling in open grassland and drove right up to them. The lionesses ignored us as they passed by our minivan headed to higher ground, their bodies all taut muscle and their expressions full of purpose.

The trio studied some distant zebra and then walked in their direction. We wondered if they had begun to plot an ambush. The huntresses paused outside a broad cluster of bushes. One sat on a mound of earth almost as high as the top of the Nissan's windows. She then lay down, majestically composed.

Joel parked 10 feet away from her so we could take photos. She stayed put. Being so close, we were entirely transfixed. This we had not expected. We could not use the 400-millimeter telephoto lenses we had purchased especially to photograph Africa's wildlife, which would have shown perhaps a closeup of the lioness's ear. Frantically and rather roughly, we took our telephoto lenses off the cameras and put them on the minivan floor, replacing them with more appropriate lenses of 50 to 125 millimeters.

Fiona, Pippa and the other Sloane Rangers watched with bored disdain. "Americans," harumphed Pippa, indicating, *obsessed with snapshots and gadgets.*

In Masai Mara, each riverlet or cluster of trees seemed to harbor something interesting. We encountered a troop of about 18 baboons at play, some walking on their fingertips and soles of their feet, tails arched. They were a species called yellow baboons. Their long smooth muzzles emerged from a head of

We did not need telephoto lenses to photograph this lioness.

fuzzy fur and deep-set eyes, giving them the shaggy topknot look of clipped French poodles.

They resembled unforgettably a primate summer picnic. Adults groomed each other, gave the babies piggyback rides, watched us or sat lost in baboon reveries. Grooming, wrote the authors of *A Field Guide to the Mammals of Africa*, marked "an important feature of troop life as a means of communication, indicating befriending, rewarding, comforting, etc."

Meanings of eight baboon vocalizations

Lip smacking	Enjoyment of grooming
Barking	Warning or excitement
Grunting	Satisfaction or warning
"Wah-wah"	Great pleasure
Ooo-ooo (young only)	When playing or hungry
Chattering	Alarm
Eek-eek	Surprise
Scream or yell	Suffering

Based on descriptions in *A Field Guide to the Mammals of Africa*

After watching the engaging baboons, we returned to our camp, again a midday hive of inactivity. The sight resembled a garage sale. Pots, pans, coffee cups and camp chairs lay scattered everywhere. Towels and sleeping bags aired on the sides of the tents. Unmentionables slowly dried on the Underwear Tree. The Sloanes' card game resumed. Plugged into my personal stereo, I played Mozart's "Requiem" in honor of 1930s aviator and safari guide Denys Finch-Hatton, the big-game hunter depicted by Robert Redford in *Out of Africa*. He had played the West's most inspired composer on a gramophone in the bush, confounding the baboons.

A little Masai boy came by, perching on the edge of the Sloanes' al fresco card mat. I noticed a wound on his left calf. As I dressed it, my fingertips felt his skin, as tough as rough leather. He departed, thanking me.

After dinner, Dutch campers at a nearby site arranged for six of the Masai to come dance. As with gospel music, one singer provided a narrative while the others called responses. They moved with serpentine body movements and issued sharp, deep "hunh" chants from the chest, almost subsonic, like the deep bass harmonies used by the Temptations, Sly and the Family Stone and South African pop groups.

They took turns leaping in the air, higher and higher. They danced so close that we could smell them. They had a distinctive odor like fresh meat in the supermarket—not unpleasant, merely reflecting their diet of cattle blood and milk. Lit only by the moon and stars and a bit of glow from our lantern, I had a feeling of seeing this as the early European explorers did. How the spectacle, clearly warlike and ferocious, must have both stirred and intimidated them.

Different lives for U.S. baboons

Years after watching baboons in the wild, I met a drug researcher at Johns Hopkins Hospital in Baltimore who gave baboons cocaine and recorded their reactions. I remembered the baboon families playing in the wild. Clearly from what we had seen in Masai Mara, baboons could come up with nicer ways to pass the time than to live in wire cages, somehow being the ones to pay the price for an addictive pathology involving *Homo sapiens*.

"Tell me," I had asked the researcher, "do you name or just number the baboons?"

"They have names," he said, in a slow way, as if a light were dawning.

"They are distinct creatures, even to humans," I said. "We saw them interact socially with each other in Kenya."

I had not further belabored the point and hoped the doctor might at least try to order fewer primates for his cocaine studies. A group called the International Primate Protection League points out that demands for research animals by Western medical researchers have stripped endangered species from their homes in the wild.

People say, "How can you tell one baboon from another?" I say, "They are as different as people."

Stuart Altmann, baboon researcher in Kenya

In reality, neither science nor the world will come to a tragic end by attempting to refine, reduce or replace part or all of the use of animals in biomedical research, education and testing. It would be lamentable if being a physician or scientist meant that one could not care deeply about the welfare of sentient beings other than human beings.

David O. Wiebers, Jennifer Leaning and Roger D. White, "Animal Protection and Medical Science"

SUNDAY, JULY 9

A house in Africa, a train to the coast

Just outside Masai Mara, as Joel drove us toward Nairobi, two dik-dik, a type of tiny antelope, darted over a hillock beside the road. A pair of grown hyenas—big, snarly ones, just like the sinister cartoon creatures in *The Lion King*, and not small and cute like pups we had seen at Amboseli, trotted in the bush. One carried a bloody hunk of animal in his huge jaws.

We also saw jackals, their disarmingly cute bobbing steps reminding me of shelties. Could it be that our family pet, unlike other dogs descended from wolves, owed its genetic heritage to foxes or jackals?

A huge white eagle circled over a stretch of several Masai villages. The bomas, low and the color of brush, had been invisible to our eyes when we had first driven to Masai Mara. But as we retraced our steps to

Narok, we knew what to look for and became aware of many.

In Narok, I spotted a bookstore and traded a pair of Reeboks, some army surplus pants and about 40 shillings ($2) for a paperback of East African poems and a copy of *Things Fall Apart*, a 1958 classic about the arrival of missionaries at an Ibo village by Nigerian writer Chinua Achebe. The trade was designed in part to give away, in a way that did not offend Kenyan pride, badly needed shoes.

On the way back to Nairobi, we asked Joel to take us to the house belonging to Karen Blixen, the Danish author of 1937's *Out of Africa*, who wrote under the pseudonym Isak Dinesen.

Fortunately for us, given the difficulty of reaching Blixen's house on our own using public transportation, Joel agreed. He traversed the western suburbs of Nairobi, taking a road lined for a half-mile by little open-fronted huts with weathered wood counters. These rows of small shacks served as the local equivalent of a shopping mall. Signs advertised Premier Auto Repair and Muthaiga Beauty Salon, with hubcaps and bunches of bananas hanging out front.

Karen Blixen's house—simple, cool, comfortable and fabulously sited—contained a library and bedrooms with lion rugs on the floor. Gardens outside offered a view of the low purple Ngong Hills.

"I had a farm in Africa," Jim intoned, mimicking Meryl Streep.

The movie *Out of Africa* made a contribution to the yo-yo nature of African tourism. Two years after the 1985 film with Redford and Streep, U.S. tourism to East Africa peaked at 100,000. It drifted down to 40,000 by 1993 in the wake of AIDS, rising costs and crimes against tourists (which received close to no coverage in Nairobi's papers, controlled by the government). Tour operators said travel began to perk up again after Nelson Mandela's 1994 assumption of the South African presidency.

Our visit to Blixen's house concluded the opening chapter of our Kenya visit. From Nairobi we would proceed to the Swahili coast, an area of East Africa that had experienced enormous influences from Islam in general and Omani, Indian and Portuguese traders in particular.

To get there, we made our way that afternoon to Nairobi's rail station. Our names appeared handwritten on a blackboard alongside the notation "Car 2314, compartment D." Our second-class compartment comprised four wide berths and a washbasin, with bedding included, for $9.

At 7 p.m., the train pulled out. At 8:45 p.m., a white-coated porter strode through the carriage, playing a small xylophone, to signal the start of the "second sitting" for dinner. We moved along to the dining car. Whirring ceiling fans lent a *Casablanca* atmosphere. Our four-course meal included beef curry and Mateus rose wine and cost $5. We conducted a slightly drunken toast to "roughing it in Africa."

We all slept comfortably except when the train stopped. The journey of less than 300 miles, at an average of less than 25 mph, took 14 hours and 15 minutes.

MONDAY, JULY 10

A look around Mombasa

As the sun rose over green and gold eastern Kenya, we stood in the aisle to look out the window. Children waved from beside the tracks. The houses on the coast, surrounded by palm trees, displayed rectangular lines, as opposed to the round huts in the bush of western Kenya.

In Mombasa, we visited a travel agency to arrange air tickets to Lamu. As rain fell determinedly outside, we watched the agent, a young Indian woman, spend three hours on an old-fashioned rotary telephone, unable to get through to Equator Airways or alternate sources of reservations.

Jim, Steph and Steve, each perched on a chair in the little office, calmly read junk paperbacks bought specifically for such delays. Each had adapted smoothly to the unhurried *mañana* culture of the Third World. None of us directed impatience toward the agent, who had not asked that Kenya make her life difficult with an outmoded telephone system.

Eventually, with our tickets arranged, we headed out to explore Mombasa. Our lunch of *thali*, a vegetarian meal of chapatis, curried potatoes, beans and bok choy, reflected India's influence on the Swahili coast.

We walked through Mombasa's Old Town, a maze of streets lined with notions and curios shops and houses with intricately carved wooden doors. Steps descended from the Old Town to the water, where four lonely dhows sat at anchor. Later we learned this quiet site comprised the Old Docks, a shadow of what centuries ago must once have been a lively seaport. We visited a bookstore and bought books by Ernest Hemingway and Beryl Markham.

We rewarded ourselves for our mild exertions with a refreshment stop at the Istanbul Bar, a gloriously seedy place that could have bottled its Graham Greene-style atmosphere alongside the hard liquor. Jolly, laughing Mombasa prostitutes sat on the knees of fat, ruddy-faced white men. Even from 30 feet away, Steph and I found the men hugely repellent.

In finest happy-hour tradition, our conversation meandered to the Washington Redskins and other sports topics. While others in the bar conducted sexual transactions, our more prosaic table discussed computers. Steve told us a bit about the aviation software he works on. We all debated the merits of various word-processing and spreadsheet programs.

"We might as well just check into a Ramada Inn in Rockville," I noted. "We could read and talk about Quicken and drink beer just as well there as here."

LESSON NUMBER 11: MANY OF OUR EXOTIC VACATIONS CONSISTED OF CATCHING UP ON READING AND ENJOYING LEISURELY CONVERSATION, AWAY FROM TELEPHONES AND DAY-TO-DAY MINUTIAE.

Rain leaked through the open sides and leaky *makuti* (palm braid) roof of the Istanbul. Jim, though indoors, unfurled my umbrella to protect himself from a particularly heavy torrent. When the rain slacked off, we continued our Mombasa Drinking Tour, with one round at the Castle Hotel and a nightcap at the bar of our own Mvita Hotel.

"This is the worst hotel I've ever stayed at," said Steph in a tone of awe rather than dismay. Jim and Steve agreed immediately. They chalked the Mvita up as a "travel experience" and certainly rated it as bearable, given that we would spend only one night there. Even at $2.20 a night, however, my travel mates found our metal beds, wobbly ceiling fans, peeling paint and shared toilet and bath less than impressive. My more benign attitude stemmed from a philosophical tenet, formulated after my 1985 trip to Asia, that "everything's worse in China," whose dirt-floor hostelries in remote villages set a lower low than anything in Mombasa.

TUESDAY, JULY 11
Off to Lamu

Awaiting our 8:30 a.m. flight from Mombasa to Lamu (pronounced LAH-mu), we met Davis Gathaara, a handsome and well-dressed Kikuyu in a suede outfit. We chatted about his plans to study accounting in London and about the U.S. Federal Reserve Board.

LESSON NUMBER 12: ENCOUNTERS SUCH AS THE ONE WITH GATHAARA TYPIFIED THE WAY IN WHICH OUR AFRICA TRIP PROVIDED IMPRESSIONS AT VARIANCE WITH THE LATER CHAOS OF RWANDA AND SOMALIA.

And to my mind, as usual in Margaret Thatcher personal-responsibility overdrive, Gathaara would later demonstrate how widely the New York and L.A. gangsta rappers of the 1990s missed the mark with rhymes of destruction that they imagined to reflect Afrocentric consciousness. Gathaara displayed a buoyant yet dignified confidence. He clearly planned to succeed in one of the West's financial centers. This Kenyan seemed like what Malcolm X might have become were he born in the year 2100, presumably able to explore unlimited professional options rather than the urgent priority of helping blacks in America.

We boarded a 10-seat Brittan-Norman Islander. Our pilot, a Kenyan wearing an immaculate starched white shirt, directed Jim to the copilot seat. The white surf line where the Indian Ocean met magnificent beaches served as our aeronautical chart, pointing us northeast up the Swahili coast. After picking up five more passengers in Malindi, we landed at our final destination: an airstrip with no buildings, just a wind sock and trimmed grass.

A leaky dhow, the traditional triangular-sailed Arabic sailing vessel, shuttled us from the islet where the airport was located across a strait to Lamu proper. The town of 7,000 appeared to be as guidebooks described: a palmy oasis in a relaxed time warp. Women wore traditional *boi bois*, long black robes. Braying donkeys roamed loose, part of a U.K.-run sanctuary. Only the district commissioner had a car.

Lamu recapped the scene in Kuta Beach, Bali, I'd visited four years previously: daily lobster for $6, a few hip Westerners unwinding at the beach and cheap plain rooms at little family-run hostelries. For $2.20 a night, we booked a room in the Kisiwani guest house, a sunnier and more spacious version of the Mvita. It had whitewashed rooms with ceiling fans, torn screens on the windows and shared toilet, shower and laundry facilities.

The universal symbol of pan-Africanism, a portrait of Jamaican-born Bob Marley, adorned an upstairs wall of the Kisiwani.

LESSON NUMBER 13: EVERY EQUATORIAL OR TROPICAL PLACE TO WHICH I'D BEEN—THAILAND, INDONESIA, TAHITI, ST. MARTIN AND NOW KENYA—SEEMED TO EMBRACE REGGAE AND MARLEY'S LIBERATION MESSAGE.

We made a beeline for Shela Beach, a one-hour walk south between fantastic dunes and jade-colored Indian Ocean waters. Visitors in more of a hurry could take a dhow or even a camel most of the way to the beach.

At Shela we bought homemade samosas from a tranquil, clear-eyed boy named Ali Hamed, who said his mother had made them. We swam and lounged on the sand and read books by Hemingway and Markham perfectly suited to our moment in time.

Ali Hamed sells samosas.

WEDNESDAY, JULY 12
Exploring a ruin

The nearest of 20 mosque loudspeakers on Lamu woke us each day at 5:30 a.m, one signal that Lamu lay positioned on the cusp of two worlds. The local people resembled dark-skinned Arabs, looking not of Nairobi or Masailand, yet not of Egypt or Saudi Arabia either.

At 9 a.m., we ran into a local fixer named Abdul at the post office. He introduced us to Omar Famau, captain of the *Tak Rimi*, a dhow whose Swahili name referred to a star (which one, we never determined).

Omar, we agreed, would take us exploring ruins that day.

For sailors such as ourselves, Lamu held great interest, for it appeared to have overtaken Mombasa as East Africa's dhow capital—the regional equivalent to Annapolis. The dhow, made of mangrove, cyprus and mahogany by shipwrights at a nearby village, had become Omar's for the equivalent of $1,500.

Every aspect of the *Tak Rimi* became an object of fascination to us. Each working component of the modern yacht has a more ancient counterpart on a dhow. A sandbag approximated the ballast of a keel. A cooking oil can made a primitive bilge pump. A plank served as a trapeze. A slanting peg acted as the jib cleat.

The lateen (triangular) sail pivoted and could be furled, enabling the dhow to tack, run downwind and stop, as a sailboat would. A wooden pole made of four lashed mangrove branches functioned as a forestay, though it was not fixed as on a yacht. A sheet (rope) controlled the forestay's position relative to the mast. Another sheet kept the bottom of the pole near the bow most of the time but could be loosed to allow furling or downwind sailing.

A peg serves as the *Tak Rimi's* cleat.

The arm muscles of Omar's first mate substituted

Good books in Africa: II

Jim and Steph in turns read Beryl Markham's *West with the Night*, a remarkable autobiography. First published in 1942, the book achieved critical acclaim but little commercial success. After its 1983 reissue, it eventually sold a million copies.

Markham grew up outside Nairobi with her father. Men of the Nandi tribe fulfilled the role of her absent mother and taught her the Swahili language and tribal ways. She achieved local fame training racehorses. Then from 1931 to 1936, her book's introduction notes that she carried

mail, passengers, and supplies in her small plane to the remote corners of the Sudan, Tanganyika, Kenya, and Rhodesia.

In September 1936, she became

the first person to fly solo across the Atlantic from east to west, making a forced landing in Nova Scotia, where she announced to two fishermen, "I'm Mrs. Markham. I've just flown from England."

Her looks, adventurousness and unpossessive temperament attracted many loves, including Prince Henry, the Duke of Gloucester; game hunter Denys Finch-Hatton; and a good number of other males in the smart sets in Nairobi and London.

Markham's book lyrically recounts scouting flights for elephant, the skills of African trackers, the birth of colts, and scrapes between pet dogs and leopards. Markham's writing

Steph reads Beryl Markham properly: while on a beach in Kenya.

style astounded Hemingway, who said "she has written so well, and marvelously well, that I was completely ashamed of myself as a writer." She had practical help from fellow aviator, Africologist and writer Antoine Saint-Exupéry, author of *Le Petit Prince*, and her third husband, journalist Raoul Schumacher.

I had enjoyed reading *West with the Night* in Maryland. Jim and Steph enjoyed the good the fortune of reading an East Africa classic on Shela Beach, and by then knowing at first hand its references to Nairobi and the Ngong Hills.

The past glories of the Swahili coast

As shabby subyuppies piggybacking on a hippie paradise, our agenda for Lamu simply listed one item: hang out. Yet Lamu's waterside mansions hinted at a story of onetime wealth and importance, and its narrow winding streets suggested ancient roots.

Our search for sun, relaxation, a good beach and cheap lobster had led us unwittingly to a cog in a historic trading empire that once extended from the inland kingdom of Great Zimbabwe to Asia.

Years after our visit, while consulting my husband's history book collection, I learned that the town harked back nearly a millennium. Lamu and a dozen other trading city-states had strung themselves unevenly, like beads in a rough necklace, on the East African coast.

Beginning in the 10th century, gold, ivory, precious stones and leopard skins from Great Zimbabwe had transited Lamu, which lay between Mombasa and Zanzibar to the south and Brava and Mogadishu to the north. Giant dhows freighted African treasure to Araby, India and China, riding winds that still blow one way six months of the year. The dhows

returned when the winds reversed, bringing back Persian and Chinese porcelain and T'ang and Sung dynasty coins, which have been found in ruins of Swahili cities. The Portuguese couldn't abide the competition and pillaged Lamu in the 16th century.

Historian Basil Davidson noted in *Africa In History* that the people of the Swahili coast, on one level members of the Muslim world,

were none the less African. … They traded with all the peripheral countries of the Indian Ocean, exporting metals, ivory, tortoiseshell, a few slaves, and buying cottons and luxury goods from as far afield as China.

A Lamu boatman reflects the clothing and appearance of Swahili people.

---

for a winch and pulley. He hauled like crazy on the sheets without benefit of these simple machines to multiply his effort. Clearly, single-handing a dhow would be tricky. It did not seem possible that the captain could leave the tiller to adjust the lateen sail, which demanded continual attention from the crewman. Omar confirmed that dhows require two hands on board.

The *Tak Rimi* smelled of tar, wet rope and aging wood. A pungent component of its odor, shark liver oil canned by the people of Malindi, killed some *dudus* (Swahili for insects) and made *Tak Rimi* waterproof. Over time, Omar would haul the dhow ashore and light a smoky fire under the keel to remove boring insects, a procedure we had viewed along the shore during our walks to Shela Beach.

Omar sailed to the neighboring island of Manda. There stood the ruins of Takwa, according to our guidebook a flourishing Swahili city in the 15th to 17th centuries. The dhow anchored in a narrow channel between mangrove trees. Carrying shorts, pants and day packs over our heads, we hopped over the side.

A man on the beach of Lamu singes his boat's hull to kill *dudus* (insects).

Looking like shipwreck survivors, we waded in our underwear to the shore.

Takwa's ruins consisted of a collection of about 100 low buildings made of limestone and crumbling walls. The ruins, while not stunning in themselves, in combination with the surrounding baobabs made for a pleasant visit. The magnificent baobabs are trees with fat trunks that I associated strongly with Saint-Exupéry's *Le Petit Prince,* a children's classic enjoyed for its allegorical wisdom by adults, which we had read in high school French class.

That night we wandered through the bazaar of Lamu. Shoppers jammed the streets. In respect of local Islamic custom, we covered up our legs with *kangas* (cloth wraps) tied over shorts. One stroller, a dhow captain, taught me how to tie my *kanga* properly—I had been fastening it with the knot for men rather than that for women.

THURSDAY, JULY 13
Swahili wedding customs

Lamu boasted a tiny jewel of a museum. Its rooms featured dhow models, a typical local house and samples of door carvings. A display noted that

> Commerce bought the East African coast into contact with China, India, Egypt, Arabia and other cultures as long as 2,000 years ago. Arab and Persian merchants began to settle permanently on the African coast from the 9th century, bringing with them Islam. Lamu town already existed in the 14th century as an independent city-state, exporting ivory, timber, amber, spices and slaves. Manufactured luxury goods from across the Indian Ocean like carpets and porcelain were imported.

Lamu declined when it lost its middleman status to the Portuguese traders who ran things from 1497 to 1698. The town revived under Omani influence in the 18th and 19th century, when the mansions seen today were built, and "fell into oblivion" with the late 19th century abolition of the slave trade. Only traditional maritime activities sustained the remote island town.

An exhibit provided information on Swahili wedding night customs, showing a bed, strewn with jasmine petals, under mosquito netting. Friends and relatives spend days painting the bride's hands and feet with intricate henna designs. The groom, in effect throwing a bachelor party, partakes of a last meal with friends. If I read the exhibit correctly, the bride doesn't attend the actual wedding ceremony. I made a mental note of the exhibit. Not the part about the bride skipping the wedding, but the jasmine. Six years later, for our wedding night, I obtained rose petals from a florist in honor of my American husband's part-African background.

In the afternoon, we took a long walk to a whitewashed, flower-bedecked hotel-bar on Shela Beach, Peponi's, to catch up with postcards, letters and journal entries. Coached by our

An ornate Lamu door.

The little girl on the left greeted us with a cheery *"jambo."*

waiter, I learned to order "*moja* [one] Coca-Cola," my first venture into Swahili numbers. To celebrate Steve's last night—he had less vacation time in Africa than we did—we had a delicious dinner at the Equator Restaurant, a lovely place of warm wood surfaces and soft lighting.

SATURDAY, JULY 15
A village of dhow builders

Omar and his crewman sailed us to Matondoni, a dhow-making village on a mangrove channel that winds north and then west of Lamu. They seemed a bit sloppy tacking up wind. The dhow lay in irons (motionless, bow directly in the wind) a lot and once even went aground on the lee shore.

Upon our arrival at Matondoni, a palm-shaded village with a dozen cradled dhows in various stages of construction, Omar delivered us to an older man named Boré. He explained that the biggest dhows, in Swahili called *jehuzzi*, cost the equivalent of $15,000. Boré said that "special people" found bent ribs of mangrove to lay the keel and ribs. A fibrous length of raw cotton and an application of coconut oil sealed the joints. Historically the nails, the only metal on the entire vessel, came from Bombay, but in the modern era, they arrive of Kenyan and Tanzanian manufacture.

As Boré walked us around, children greeted us in high sweet voices with "*jambo*" (hello). A group of boys pulled a truck on a string, wheels made from scraps of wood and chassis from a Cowboy-brand cooking oil tin.

Why a truck, we asked Boré, when Lamu had none? Donkeys, dhows, camels and your own feet covered the available transportation options. He surmised the children had seen a truck in a book or on a video.

On our last day in Lamu, we tried to collect our impressions. Some visitors (though not us, being fairly accustomed to such sights during out travels) might be bothered by heaps of donkey droppings and trash dumps on the streets. We sensed a bigger problem: that Lamu's residents harbored a quiet but broad and at times justified resentment of tourists. Westerners did not always dress respectfully, for example, going topless or nude on the beach where the Muslim boys sell samosas. And perhaps the locals were not wild about making a living serving at-times demanding tourists.

We covered up to follow the Islamic dress code. We enjoyed sailing with Omar and the children we met at Matondoni. Yet we also encountered the occasional sharp word or mocking offer of a handshake, withdrawn with a devilish grin. If resentment explained part of the equation, Swahili arrogance explained the rest.

LESSON NUMBER 14: AS IN SOMALIA UP THE COAST, WHERE IN THREE YEARS INSOLENT TEENS WOULD PROVOKE U.S. SOLDIERS BY STEALING SUNGLASSES AND HURLING INSULTS, LAMU'S PEOPLE SEEMED TO AGGRESSIVELY AVOID SUCKING UP TO WESTERNERS.

Local men, like those in Southern Europe, could come on strong. "It's easy to get pregnant here, girls come from Germany, America. It's good food and so on," a leering man with many crooked and missing teeth told me when I got briefly separated from the rest of our group during an errand.

Lamu could also be read as yet another variant on the worn theme of the remote $10 a day paradise. Vagabond hippies, Euroyuppies, dropout yachties and American aid workers on leave roamed its seashore and thatched roof restaurants—a scene reminiscent of Kuta Beach in Bali and many other places, but less compatible with this small Islamic town.

Yet Lamu, one of the big hippie hideaways in the 1970s, may have emerged the least spoiled by the love tribe invasion. Its very Islamic character may have made it less vulnerable to tourism.

We concluded that the finest thing about this "beach resort" might be its culture: the sterling museum, the dhow rides to Matondoni and Takwa, the nice children like Ali Hamed and those of Matondoni. We enjoyed the culture, but the culture didn't seem to enjoy the threat of potential conflict and change wrought by tourists.

In the afternoon we sat at Lamu's little airstrip and awaited an endlessly delayed flight to Nairobi. Finally a six-seater plane materialized as well as its British pilot, who seemed to possess little of the polish and self-confidence of our previous Kenyan pilot.

We boarded, and the pilot turned around at one end of the runway and gunned the engines for takeoff. Another propeller plane appeared in our rear window, beginning its landing—right on our tail.

Our pilot muttered angrily and decided reflexively to go hell for leather. The takeoff resembled a James Bond escape, sharp in a 007 movie but absurd in the minimal air traffic of Lamu, Kenya. Through the back window of our plane, we watched pop-eyed with

amazement as the other plane followed right behind as we accelerated down the runway. As though performing an air-show stunt, it landed as we ascended, too close for me to dare look.

Back safely in Nairobi, we paid a visit downtown to the Minar Indian Restaurant. After dinner, a tall, dignified and lively cab driver returned us to the Hotel Boulevard and taught us the meaning of the Swahili words to the current radio hit in Nairobi, "Jambo Bwana" ("Hello Mister"). The encounter contained a similar warmth to an encounter I recalled in China, when a little girl visiting Chongqing zoo spontaneously handed me a cookie. The cabbie's aplomb and self-confidence stayed in my mind, fairly or no, as representative of the people of Kenya.

TUESDAY, JULY 25
Can we squeeze in Tanzania?

After 10 days of looking at lemurs in Madagascar, Jim, Steph and I landed back in Nairobi. The Nairobi papers made much of an event we'd missed hearing about in remote Madagascar: President Moi's burning seven days previously of $3 million worth of ivory. The wider world also took great notice of this event, news seen by an estimated 850 million people worldwide either on television or in newsprint. By the following January, a ban on global ivory sales took effect.

We had just three full days left before flying home Saturday. Conservatively, we only had time for day trips to parks outside Nairobi. But we all thought the same ambitious thought. Jim said it out loud: "Let's jam over to the crater in Tanzania!"

After three weeks, we had a better grasp of distances and logistics in Africa. We realized Tanzania was not impossibly far, even allowing for minor vehicle breakdowns or other delays.

I told Jim and Steph how six years earlier I had heard glowing reports about the Ngorongoro Crater, not far from the Kenyan border. "My friend Jane from Arizona went there and saw a lion kill," I said. "She had a photo of a male lion with blood up to his eyes."

We checked back into the Hotel Boulevard. In the lobby we ran into Carly and Rembeaux, a couple from Santa Fe, New Mexico. Rembeaux resembled James Taylor, appropriately for someone with a woman named Carly. The couple, on a world trip of some years' duration, had already visited the entire length of South America.

They, too, planned to visit Ngorongoro. We agreed to meet the next morning to go together to Arusha, a center for safari outfitters in northern Tanzania.

WEDNESDAY, JULY 26
Onward to the crater rim

At the Nairobi stand for *matatus* (bush taxis) to the border with Tanzania, we bought places on a van at 80

Kenyan shillings ($4) each. After taking our money, the ticket taker tried to raise the price and to charge us additionally for our luggage. He also offered to sell us Tanzanian currency on worse terms, we soon confirmed, than both the official rate, 144 to the dollar, let alone the black market rate of 230.

A ringer, posing as a passenger, loudly agreed. "That's a good rate." (Lie No. 1.) "There are no banks at the border." (Lie No. 2.) Confirming our suspicions, the ringer got off before we departed.

The ticket taker's additional falsehoods included how we would depart immediately (meaning in 45 minutes) as soon as we had 10 passengers (meaning 15).

Recognizing most of his mouth-flapping as Standard Operating Procedure, comparable to but worse than that on Madagascar's bush taxis, we did not get angry until he moved in, piranha-like, on a young Japanese man traveling alone. The poor fellow possessed a face of utter innocence and looked rattled when the ticket seller began to insist that he had not paid. He protested in paltry English that yes, he had. Given the ticket ticker's record with us, we believed the Japanese.

In honor of our imminent visit to Tanzania and its founding leader Julius Nyerere, we decided to pursue one of his favorite concepts, *ujamaa* (Swahili for "unity") with our fellow backpacker.

"LEAVE HIM ALONE. HE'S PAID," Jim roared, fed up with the lack of fair play.

After 2$^1/_2$ hours we arrived at Namanga, a Kenyan border town, and crossed into Tanzania. As we suspected, plenty of banks awaited us.

Tanzania differed from Kenya in marked ways, most obviously by being a socialist nation, the fourth one I had visited (the others being China, Burma and Madagascar). My friend Jane made a valuable observation about socialism's disastrous track record with agriculture. She noted that on her 1983 visit to Tanzania, the British tour company shipped in staples such as sugar and sold some on the black market to subsidize the trip. We would see if markets remained as bereft of supplies and with only the unripe produce—green tomatoes, grapefruit and oranges—that Jane had remembered.

Our group proceeded two more hours by a second *matatu* to the Arusha International Conference Centre, a mid-rise office building full of safari operators. We interviewed a man at Star Tours, a fat Indian chewing betel nut. The Indian suggested a possible three-day itinerary for seeing the Ngorongoro crater.

Rembeaux proved to be a hard-headed bargainer, excellent at asking about details and arriving at a good price for our final arrangement. We got a better rate by paying in U.S. dollars, far more in demand than the inflated Tanzanian shilling. Carly and Rembeaux raid-

The ability to live in the moment

Carly, the experienced world traveler whom we met in Nairobi, told us how she could cope with any deprivation or delay as long as she had something to read. Almost everywhere in the world, she said, she had been able to find English-language bookstores or fellow travelers with books or magazines to swap.

On an isolated estancia in rugged Patagonia that catered to hunting groups, however, she had run out of paperbacks. "Carly went and met an incoming group of duck hunters from Texas," Rembeaux recalled, "and borrowed their hunting magazines and gun catalogs."

That indeed sounded like desperation from this New Age couple, who predated the actual invention of the term. We certainly sympathized. We too could tolerate snags if we had reading matter, as witnessed by our painless three-hour wait for airplane tickets from Mombasa to Lamu. In fact, such hitches seemed almost a blessing, so deprived where we of reading time at home.

Three years after my Kenya trip, a Baltimore friend, Abby, learned how to pass the time without any entertainments at a Buddhist meditation center on an island in Thailand. Two weeks at a time, participants at the *wat* (temple) maintained silence. They had to live in the present, without conversation, books or music.

At first I thought, *impossible*, I would always need a book and a personal stereo to cope with the rigors of travel. Buddhism, with its focus on disciplining mental processes, had showed Abby a different way.

LESSON NUMBER 15: IT TAKES COURAGE TO LIVE AND ENJOY THE PRESENT WITHOUT A BOOK, A MOVIE, AN ALCOHOL DRINK, WORK TAKEN HOME, OR ANY OF OUR OTHER WAYS OF ANESTHETIZING OURSELVES FROM THE MOMENT.

ed a stash of greenbacks sewn into secret compartments in their backpacks. We too had bought dollars for this eventuality.

The Indian sent an assistant out, who returned with Mr. Jeffir, an Arabic-looking man with dreadful teeth and a scraggly Bruce Springsteen-quality beard. He wore the same open-necked white shirt with pointed collar, chain and dark sport coat for three days, sleeping in the outfit without looking better or worse.

Mr. Jeffir met us that afternoon, ferrying us in a Land Rover to the Arusha market to buy basic provisions such as canned margarine, bread, fruit and snacks. We learned first hand that Tanzania had some new free-market policies, as evidenced by plenty of food to buy, including quality fruits and vegetables. Three years after Jane's 1983 visit, Nyerere had stepped down as president, and his successor, Ali Hassan Mwinyi, carried out economic reforms mandated by the International Monetary Fund, the World Bank and others. Private enterprise and peasant farmers had won more freedom. By the third year of these reforms, economic growth seemed evident.

We rolled down the road. The savanna stretched for miles to distant purple ridges, scenery that I recalled later while driving through eastern Montana, with its eroded, pinkish dinosaur-fossil mountains. At a town called Karatu, "Safari Junction" as it is known, Mr. Jeffir pulled up to a roadhouse. We ate rice and meat for dinner and stayed in a simple $2 room, set around a courtyard like a U.S. motel.

The Ngorongoro Crater looks like what it is: an inactive volcano.

Gene pools become gene ponds

All the animals we saw in Africa on our random wanderings seemed to be media stars: a 1988 book featured Amboseli's elephants and a 1992 *National Geographic* article focused on the Ngorongoro lions.

The crater lions, which we found to be quite similar looking to each other, had indeed inbred to an enormous extent, *National Geographic* reported. All 100 or so of these lions descended from 15 animals and had been born on the crater floor.

LESSON NUMBER 16: THE FROZEN GENE POOL OF THE CRATER LIONS SERVED AS A MICROCOSM FOR MOST OF AFRICA'S WILD CREATURES, NOW MAROONED IN GAME PARKS, FRAGMENTED ISLANDS OF HABITAT SURROUNDED BY HUMAN DEVELOPMENT.

These "population bottlenecks" among animals in game parks could lead to weakened creatures with compromised immune systems, scientists fear. A near-extinction disaster 10,000 years ago, for example, means that all of today's cheetahs are almost identical genetically.

THURSDAY, JULY 27
A demonstration of hunting

Mr. Jeffir drove the Land Rover to the edge of Ngorongoro. The crater stretched 12 miles across from rim to rim and descended nearly 2,000 feet to the valley floor. Its size made it one of the world's largest calderas—volcano craters created either by collapse or cataclysmic explosion.

We wound in low gear down the steep road to the valley. Like sections of the Grand Canyon on a clear day, the massive bulk of this natural wonder could be seen edge to edge by the eye yet not absorbed by the mind.

After perhaps an hour, we reached the valley floor. Mr. Jeffir knew the names of none of the animals. But at least he managed to spot a pride of lions, a dozen of the crater's 100 or so, scattered in front of the valley's Lake Magadi.

In Kenya, we had seen many lions relaxing or sitting in the shade. We'd observed one lioness eating her kill. Now we would see a more active facet of lion behavior. We'd happened on the initial stage of a hunt.

Four advance lionesses stalked in a two-pronged attack. About 100 yards in front of our Land Rover, two froze almost hidden in the grass. Every few minutes, they advanced crouching stealthily toward a wildebeest herd and a lone hartebeest. A third and

Tanzania

Kenya

At Ngorongoro, left, I improved on my ears-only shot of rhino taken in Amboseli, right.

A Ngorongoro lioness advances, stalking a herd of wildebeest.

fourth female worked behind and to our left, stalking a larger group of zebra.

From our vantage on the roof of the Land Rover, we could see only the flat tops of their heads and a bit of their haunches. From the lower angle of the wildebeest, the lionesses would have been invisible in the grass.

Mr. Jeffir put the Land Rover into park and switched off the engine. Although our driver seemed for the most part disengaged and verging on somnolent, even he perked up for the drama about to unfold. Rembeaux, Carly, Jim, Steph and myself were electrified by the possibility, squeezed into the waning moments of our visit to Africa, of lionesses demonstrating how they killed their prey.

"I have been here 20 times, and never seen this," said Mr. Jeffir, with relative vigor.

Foot by foot, for 30 minutes, the lionesses advanced. "Exactly how my cats stalk birds," Jim said.

Lionesses, faster and more agile than lions (a fact women seem to love), can reach speeds of up to 35 mph. Still, they lack the upper range of speed of many of their prey, such as wildebeest, which can attain 50 mph. So the lioness must approach closely and lunge before its target can bolt.

We watched a wildebeest, heedless, walk calmly away from the larger group toward the hidden huntresses. "*Uh oh*," I breathed.

The end game unfolded. The lead lioness tore toward the isolated wildebeest. A nearby hartebeest, terrified, bolted for its life. The panicked wildebeest ran two steps and made a desperate, tight U-turn.

The lioness, reversing field swiftly in reaction, caught up in two gallops to her prey and raised a mighty right leg toward its shaggy withers. The attacker, probably weighing 300 pounds, swept her huge right paw towards the wildebeest's middle spine. In a display of might, she dug her spread claws into its back and pulled her giant foreleg to earth, bringing along the entire wildebeest. The victim toppled, its back crashing to the ground. Its four hooves flung once in

the air and then fell. Resistance ended, and the animal lay still. The final chase had lasted perhaps 10 seconds.

We swung our cameras at the commotion in another direction. Just as the wildebeest met its end in front of us, two other lionesses behind our vehicle nearly felled a zebra. The herd stampeded, hundreds of hooves raising a reverberating thunder and a cloud of dust. Jim's photos later revealed the surging head of a lioness above the haunch of the targeted zebra, who somehow barely escaped. Jim and I agreed that the family sheltie, Conan, would last perhaps five minutes out there.

Back at the downed wildebeest, eleven lions and cubs began to eat simultaneously. The killer stood quite near our Land Rover, perhaps three yards away, panting heavily like a struggling train engine. Long scars from past battles ran along her ribs. Too exhausted to eat, she shuffled wearily away.

As we photographed her and the feasting pride, another lioness from the failed zebra maneuver strolled up, unnoticed, inches away from our rear bumper. Had she wanted to jump up, she could have clawed us more easily than the slowest of wildebeest.

A lioness gives up on a diversionary zebra stalk and watches the successful kill.

The huntress, left, pants heavily after downing a wildebeest. Below, the younger lions consume the victim.

The lion sleeps today and tonight

As we drove around the Ngorongoro crater, we came upon three huge male lions. We had just seen sleek lionesses kill a wildebeest. The males, however, brambles matting their manes, slept deeply. They look far less like the sovereign of the jungle than their female counterparts, and more like leonine Al Bundys.

How much lions sleep seems to be in dispute, with some estimates of 20 hours a day. In zoos, they sleep 10 to 15 hours per day. Lion authority Schaller noted long rest periods with eyes shut but ears twitching as though the lion remained aware of its surroundings.

Years later, I heard a statistic that made me feel exceptionally lucky to see the successful hunt. In an IMAX movie called *Africa: The Serengeti*, narrator James Earl Jones related that only one lion hunt in five succeeds.

While that 20 percent figure is broadly true, wildlife researcher George B. Schaller, in *The Serengeti Lion: A Study of Predator-Prey Relations*, broke down the success rates of lion kills in greater detail.

LESSON NUMBER 17: WHEN LIONS STALK IN A GROUP, RATHER THAN SINGLY, AND WHEN THEIR PREY IS WILDEBEEST OR ZEBRA—TWO FACTORS PRESENT IN THE CASE OF THE HUNT WE WATCHED—SCHALLER FOUND TRIPLE THE USUAL RATE OF SUCCESS: ABOUT 60 PERCENT.

The unusual aspect of our good fortune, according to lion statistics, lay in seeing a successful daytime kill, as lions have better luck at night. In other respects, we seemed to have witnessed a classic kill. Females do most of the hunting, with the males often taking over the kill to eat first. Also, most lions hunt communally, as we had seen, and the number of lions we'd seen feeding was apparently typical.

Mr. Jeffir drove us around the rest of the crater to look at its rhinos and other wildlife. For some minutes the solitary, gasping exhausted warrior queen trudged along in front of us.

FRIDAY, JULY 28
The pride rests

Ten lionesses and cubs, recovering from the previous day's excitement, sunned on the valley floor. Sated by their feast, they adopted the classic pose of big cats in repose. They cast their eyes with dignified alertness to distant wildebeest and zebra. All but a few of the lions, tangled together like a box of puppies, swung their heads in unison to follow the herd. Others napped, resting their heads on the shoulders or backs of one another.

The lions displayed a sociable nature, but not in the eternally loyal sense of elephants. Whereas elephants will try to help their sick and dying by keeping them on their feet, protecting them or patting mud on wounds, lions can be so aggressive at kills that they injure each other. And both males and females have been recorded killing cubs, unthinkable behavior among elephants.

After our morning farewell tour of the crater, our blitz of Tanzania continued to Lake Manyara, where we saw a sight almost more incredible than a lion kill: the remarkable noises and swirling in the water of hippo sex. Fortunately for our delicate sensibilities, much of the action occurred underwater.

Crater lions huddle socially as they watch distant zebra.

Mr. Jeffir nursed the Land Rover, which suffered from drive-train difficulty, back to Arusha. Despite the intense supervision of Rembeaux and Jim at numerous pit stops, he failed to repair whatever was wrong. He mumbled that we would have to return the rest of the way in third gear only.

Our driver roared at nearly 40 mph into a parking space at the Miami Beach Guest House (another name indicating, along with the Florida Day and Night Club, incongruous homage to the Sunshine State). Grinning for the first time since we'd met him, perhaps at being home even via a clapped-out vehicle, Mr. Jeffir deposited us and lurched away in high gear.

Though lacking the charm and the knowledge of Joel and Hardson—he had barely spoken to us over three days—Mr. Jeffir possessed at least one virtue as a guide: sturdiness. He spared us the experience that befell two young British tourists, whose guide suffered an attack of acute malaria while at the crater. They had to cut short their visit and ferry their driver back to Arusha for treatment.

At the Miami Beach, which charged us $5 for a triple, the guest book listed headings for name, passport number and "tribe." After some thought, I entered "French Canadian" in the last column.

I washed, taking off the first layer of dirt. I laundered my surplus fatigues and slowly ironed them dry in an open-air courtyard, while talking to a Tanzanian veterinarian who specialized in large animals. That professionals such as the vet stayed in cheap places like the $5-a-night Miami Beach Guest House testified to their paltry salaries.

The vet planned a trip to a conference in the United States. He described the changes in the government, which had led to the hint of prosperity we had noticed.

His friendliness seemed atypical. During our brief stay in Tanzania, we sensed less warmth towards us, either as whites or Westerners, which may be explained by some sort of legacy of President Nyerere's high-profile support of African liberation movements, a difference in national or tribal characters, or our imaginations.

SATURDAY, JULY 29
Leaving Masailand

A series of *matatus* bore us back to Namanga and Nairobi. One last time we watched the elegant (some observers have used the word supercilious) Masai. A warrior cloaked in a shade I thought of as Lion-Scaring Red toted his spear aboard our *matatu*. He took a seat and stared into the infinite distance. He paid no fare. At the border, he didn't even return the gaze of the police who asked to check an ID card. They quickly turned to the next passenger.

Different rules applied for these natural aristocrats with angular Picasso faces. I quietly applauded them. Here was one way to protest national boundaries that split tribal lands. The warrior thumped the side of the *matatu* to get off. He walked away from the road, on a bit of ground with no path or trail, disappearing straight into the bush.

Hours later in Nairobi, we checked in with Pan Am at Jomo Kenyatta International Airport. A neatly bearded security officer of medium height, in a blue sports coat, worked down the line. Seven months previously, just before Christmas vacation, terrorists had bombed a jetliner over Lockerbie, Scotland. Airlines had greatly tightened security.

"How many bags do you have?" asked the security officer, looking from his clipboard to me. I ransacked my brain for the vocabulary word the Lamu waiter had insisted I learn to order a Coca-Cola. *"Moja,"* I said.

A smile as bright as the Serengeti dawn spread on the man's face. "Ah, I see you speak beautiful Swahili," he said, delighted at my lone vocabulary word.

For my part, I basked in the beautiful timber of the African voice. The small exchange warmed me, then and now.

Kenya, Tanzania and the big lesson: our love-hate relationship with Africa

Of the 44 million Americans who traveled overseas in 1995, only about 325,000 (less than 1 percent) visited sub-Saharan Africa, according to the State Department. While we visited Kenya and Tanzania, many black Americans seem to favor the West African nations of Senegal, Togo, Ghana, the Ivory Coast and Gambia for their culture and vibrancy.

Mary Lee of Voyagers International, an Ithaca, N.Y., travel agent, wrote to me on the Internet:

> Our sense of it is that, as you suggest, white Americans go to East Africa while blacks go to West Africa (if they go at all). And our sense of why this is so is that whites go to see the wildlife, of which there is little left in West Africa, while blacks are more interested in their cultural background, which generally comes from the west.

About 80,000 Americans visited Kenya in the year of our visit, compared to 500,000 European visitors. White Americans, particularly Anglophiles, may find the echoes of colonial days, as well as the wildlife, of interest. For 100 years, East Africa has been a playground for well-to-do Europeans and Americans. At Nairobi's Norfolk Hotel or Karen Blixen's house, one can imagine the world of Markham, Finch-Hatton and Lord Delamere.

Black Americans may have little interest in this era. My husband, who is of mixed race, further suggests that many urban blacks may be disinclined to go on a camping safari as our group did.

I claim no special insight into the responses of black Americans to their motherland. But I think it broadly significant that black Americans travel in a different way to Africa.

One day, Africa might be a very important continent (as the artist Salvador Dalí hinted in his work "Geopoliticus Child Watching the Birth of the New Man," which shows the world, with an outsized depiction of Africa, as an egg about to hatch).

I speculate that ties of black Americans to Africa may, down the road, help the United States economically. Travel patterns of black Americans show a developing triangle between the United States, the Caribbean and Brazil, and West Africa. Pleasure trips by black Americans create a cultural triangle to augment the economic and political triangle begun at African-American summits held in Senegal (1995), Gabon (1993) and the Ivory Coast (1991). We will see the influence of this commingling as the triangular relationship matures. As a resident of a majority-black U.S. city, I hope to see evidence of these socioeconomic links in the future.

As for our three-week encounter with Africa's grandeur and magnificence, we could only rave. Nothing, not even the tourist killings during our visit, clouded our outlook at the time. (Though a later reading of *A Death in Kenya* by Michael Hiltzik made me retroactively quite queasy, describing as it did the gruesome slaying of tourist Julie Ward, whose body was dismembered.)

Overall, I agreed with writer Martha Gellhorn's opinion that what we had seen was

> far more beautiful and exciting than anything I had seen in the museums of the civilized world, and music never gave me such joy.

LESSON NUMBER 18: FOR US, AS WHITE AMERICANS, OUR OPINION OF EAST AFRICA WAS SIMPLE: WE LOVED IT.

In fact, when Jim later flew on honeymoon to Hawaii, he reported an unexpected observation: "It's sterile." He meant that Hawaii might be as beautiful as Africa but it lacked the majesty of a continent where lions, elephants, rhinos, hippos and giraffes roam. Hawaii's little red birds and fragrant flowers and sea cliffs also did not compete for Jim with the timeless natural cycle of lions chasing wildebeest.

While black friends were enthralled with our stories of Africa, white friends seemed dubious when we recounted fun times in Kenya and Tanzania, particularly after 1992. The perpetual vacuum in U.S. news coverage of Africa ended as hundreds of stories portrayed negative developments in Somalia and Rwanda.

LESSON NUMBER 19: POSITIVE NEWS OUT OF SOUTH AFRICA'S 1994 SWEARING IN OF NELSON MANDELA AS PRESIDENT COULD NOT OUTWEIGH THE NEGATIVE ON THE U.S. AND WORLD OPINION METERS.

We visited Africa with modest psychological baggage. Jim and I, backpackers to save money and to have the challenge of solving some obstacles using our wits (most likely Acadian traits), probably hold unusually conservative political views compared to those budget travelers who hew to liberal, New Age or hippieish views. So unlike some white liberals, we did not feel it necessary to hold African culture in exaggerated worshipfulness, to prove we were the exact opposite of any racists who hold Africa to be worthless.

Africa could be itself, neither perfect nor horrible. And Africa did not have to meet any expectation of deep genetic resonance. In the same way one might

cringe at one's own rambunctious blood relatives at a wedding reception yet find the noisy in-laws merely comic, as whites we could take Africa's flaws in stride and dispassionately compare them to comparative places in Asia or Latin America.

We never burdened ourselves at the time with a tough hypothetical proposition that faces more introspective black Americans who visit Africa: Is it worse to be a slave descendant alive in the United States? Or to be an African tracing one's genealogy of freedom back to Adam and Eve but floating dead down a river in Rwanda?

For myself, I later wondered how I would answer the question if I were black. I did not envy the back-breaking labor and minuscule opportunities for the average Kenyan woman. Nor would I want the obstacles black Americans face in knowing their roots, especially given the reward of having a thorough Belliveau genealogy, which a Canadian priest traced back to 1644 and recorded in a 940-page book.

The puzzle constitutes a solipsism for those who believe that European colonialism and the aftermath of the slave trade undercut modern African confidence and capability almost as surely as did slavery in the Americas. In the words of German naturalist Alexander von Humboldt, the consequences of the slave trade "have been alike fatal to the old and new world."

Africa, especially in the 1990s, engendered a number of conundrums for some U.S. blacks. Tourists from Detroit, Washington, Los Angeles and other areas, in search of their cultural roots, visited Ghana, Senegal, the Ivory Coast and South Africa. Mothers and daughters flew to West Africa for naming ceremonies and rites of adult passage. While some visitors noted the low status of women, others termed the visit the best trip of their lives, "a vacation from racism," a homecoming and a wondrous encounter with the creativity of African peoples.

Though amateur travelers black and white generally returned with positive impressions, particularly of African generosity and community spiritedness, U.S. journalists, diplomats and soldiers cited disheartening experiences. Black-on-black racism, homegrown African tyranny and a lack of cultural affinities seem to lead the list of problems.

Blacks are not immune to the lethargy, frustrations, inefficiency and ignorance in Africa, and no small number merely throw up their hands in disillusionment.

David Lamb in *The Africans*

Three *Washington Post* correspondents have written searingly of the complex reactions Africa stirs in black Americans.

In a 1995 piece entitled "Continental Divide," Keith B. Richburg described the experiences of a black

American woman assigned to the U.S. Embassy in Nairobi. She had born the brunt of "the Kenyans' own perverse form of racism, under which whites are granted preferential treatment over blacks."

For example, restaurant waiters would serve whites before her, as the waiters thought she was Kenyan. Americans of Jamaican descent report comparable slights on returning to the Caribbean.

Mary Ann French wrote in *The Washington Post* in 1993 of the difficulties African-American soldiers experienced during the "dramatic visit to motherland" of the U.N. mission to Somalia. She told how one soldier met the eye of a beautiful, delicate-featured Somali woman. She wrote that the Somali woman "put two fingers up to the middle of her face, spread them wide, smirked and laughed." A black woman had called the U.S. soldier "a nigger," mocking his broad nose and generous lips, common to many sub-Saharan Africans and American blacks.

Africa's political disasters soured other descendants of native sons. Richburg's predecessor as *Washington Post* Nairobi correspondent, Neil Henry, underlined that Africa is not "the mythical land of goodwill and racial togetherness that some idealistic black Americans in search of illusive 'roots' imagine or wish it to be."

LESSON NUMBER 20: AS MY AMERICAN HUSBAND POINTS OUT, NEATLY ILLUSTRATING A GIANT BARRIER WITH AFRICANS, "WE'RE HERE BECAUSE THEY SOLD US, SO THAT TELLS YOU SOMETHING."

Unlike black Americans, we felt no need to have Africans welcome us as distant kin. If anything, we may have tiptoed into Kenya, wondering how we would fare as a tiny minority, curious if we would be "mau-mau'd" by militants. Instead, nothing untoward happened and we had a terrific time.

Richburg's report of anti-black prejudice by Kenyans suggests that as whites we may have gotten a rosy picture based on a lingering vestige of colonialism leading to favoritism toward whites. Quite possible, yet we sensed no particular obsequiousness.

Behind our relaxed dealings with Joel, Hardson, Sam, Gladys, Omar, Ali Hamed, Bopol and others lay the simple fact none of them suffered any residual head trips from slavery. You could just about put your finger on the distinction: most East Africans neither wore "the mask" to conceal their true feelings, a tradition that evolved during U.S. slavery, nor projected "attitude," its modern variant used to "mau-mau," in Tom Wolfe's memorable term, whites.

The geniality of East Africans provided a gauge to measure the disquiet of their distant American cousins, a disorientation that appeared to have no antecedent in the motherland.

Richburg wrote that while black Americans on two-week visits can enjoy "touchy feely *Roots* stuff," three years as a Nairobi correspondent forged a different impression:

> I want to love the place, love the people. I can tell you I see hope amid the chaos, and I do, in places like Malawi, even Mozambique. But the Rwandas and Somalias and Liberias and Zaires keep intruding into my mind. Three years—three long years—have left me cold and heartless. Africa is a killing field of good intentions, as Somalia alone is enough to prove.

Four years earlier, Henry had written a piece entitled, "A Stranger in Africa." It described how Africans admired many U.S. figures, at the time including musician M.C. Hammer and fighter Mike Tyson, yet frowned "upon what they perceive as a melancholy lack of substantive social or cultural identity" among American blacks.

> Often African-Americans are recognized simply as woefully disconnected descendants of the millions who were sold away in chains. We may have more money and material goods than Africans, but at least Africans know where their ancestral village is and where their bodies should be buried when they die. And few things are more important to Africans than that.

Observers more qualified than ourselves, such as the authors of the *Cultural Atlas of Africa*, cite at least some African traits that have survived in African-American culture: obligations to share material advancement and to help the extended family, fatalism, forgiveness and a belief in redemption, improvisational thinking talent, abilities to compose polyrhythmic music and an ability in dance movements to split the body into seemingly independent areas.

Yet other fundamental differences in attitude and behavior divide Africans and black Americans. Writer Eddy Harris wrote in 1992 in *Native Stranger* about his largely overland trip, an S-curved traversal of two dozen countries.

Ultimately, too many instances of corruption and incompetence laid to rest any expectations of solidarity he originally held. After the best part of a year in Africa, he concluded that African-Americans must accept the fact that they are not Africans and that they long for an image of a continent that exists "only in dreams and prayers."

Some ethnic groups, for example, Chinese Americans, feel relatively free to criticize negative aspects of their homelands. African-Americans, perhaps more than any other U.S. ethnic group except the landless and languageless Hawaiians, may feel great pressure to discover and treasure a perfect Africa that exists only in the imagination.

Africans especially treasure knowing the place of their ancestors. Thus their U.S. descendants possess a poignant "deep memory" of the importance of knowing one's ancestors—and have had that need for connection severed by slavery in the New World.

For black Americans, the Motherland had become an ever-more receding memory of the kingdoms of Songhai, Dahomey, Ghana, Mali, Aksum and Great Zimbabwe, and the empires of Kanem-Bornu and Tukolor.

Giraffes amble across Amboseli National Park in Kenya at dusk.

LESSON NUMBER 21: MANY AMERICAN RACIAL AND ETHNIC GROUPS, NOT JUST BLACKS, HAVE EXPERIENCED SIGNIFICANT DRIFT FROM THEIR PARENT CULTURES AND WOULD DO WELL NOT TO EXPECT TOO MUCH OF "ROOTS" TRIPS.

Probably no member of any assimilated American ethnic group returns to his or her homeland to discover epiphanies of a perfect kinship with the parent culture, only subtle shared echoes or "deep memory." This does not seem surprising to me, of mixed Acadian (maritime French Canada) and Irish descent. I could list ways the Americas have made the French immigrant steelier and the Irish one healthier and more accomplished.

Thomas Sowell of the Hoover Foundation at Stanford University noted in *Race and Culture: A World View* how the Irish, Jews and blacks of the United States weakly preserve their ancestral cultures, meanwhile maintaining political ties with their homeland.

Though black American voters have been "a factor in American foreign policy toward African nations in general and South Africa in particular," he noted that "cultural affinities between Afro-Americans and Africans are tenuous at best."

Historian Carl N. Degler described in his 1971 book *Neither Black Nor White* how Brazil's blacks maintained an African consciousness as generations of U.S. blacks, until quite recently, displayed little inquisitiveness about their homeland, with some even embarrassed by its one-time image of primitiveness. He wrote that

> There are many reasons for this lack of interest in or even aversion to Africa, but certainly one of them is the closing of the slave trade early in the history of slavery in the United States as compared with Brazil. It has also meant that so-called African survivals [cultural traits outlasting their original function] are com-

monplace in modern Brazil, especially in Bahia, but almost undiscoverable among Negroes in the United States.

Former Peace Corps teacher Teddy Eisenman offered a useful summary of the value to both white and black Americans of holding a balanced view of Africa. Quoted in *The Washington Post* on his experience in Senegal, he cited a largely healthy impression of the continent in line with our own:

> I now better understand a part of the world usually portrayed as in crisis, because most of what we hear about Africa are stories of famine, strife and suffering. This is a narrow view. Sure Senegal and Africa may be poor, financially speaking, but they are incredibly rich in other, possibly more significant ways. I consider myself very fortunate to have experienced this—the family unity, the generous hospitality, and the well-established sense of community.

How to explain the two visions of Africa, one idyllic, one apocalyptic? If one studies, for example, the index topic of "Africa" for the *Los Angeles Times* for the decade from 1985 to 1995, one will discover a catalog of horror, from AIDS to famine to war to debt defaults, with one glaring exception: the 1986 release of Paul Simon's *Graceland* album, inspired by South African music, and his subsequent tour of Africa. If Africa is really so horrible, how does it produce the world's most joyous music?

LESSON NUMBER 22: AFRICA'S MUSIC GIVES A CLUE TO ITS PEOPLE'S CAPACITY FOR HAPPINESS AND THE INSPIRATIONAL POWER OF ITS SPLENDID SCENERY.

On the macro level, the professional abroad—the diplomat, the reporter, the soldier—must grapple with the brutality of a Somalia or a Rwanda. On a micro level, the amateur traveler will encounter Africa's happiness and beauty, via Kikuyu tour guides, patrons of a backwoods night club, the children of Masailand or a Nairobi cabbie.

CIVILITIES, SHEEPDOGS AND BOMB SURVIVORS

Japan ... and lessons on formal societies

A torii arch at Miyajimi serves as a symbol of Japan.

To get ready for budget travel in grimy and arduous China, one packs antibiotics, vitamins, clean chopsticks and a phrasebook. To prepare for an official visit to spotless and formal Japan, one practices the correct manner of handing out business cards.

Our group of seven American journalists, six selected by the East-West Center in Honolulu as Jefferson Fellows to study Pacific Rim issues and one spouse, received coaching on how not to embarrass ourselves during the Japan segment of our travels.

Quite unlike most of my improvised cheapie adventure trips, this trip would be planned, paid for and guided. Three experts would lead our group: Richard Halloran, former *New York Times* Tokyo correspondent; his wife, Fumiko Mori Halloran, who had written six books explaining facets of U.S. life to the Japanese; and John Schidlovsky, a former Beijing correspondent for the *Baltimore Sun*.

Before we left Hawaii in April 1991, where we'd attended a month of seminars on Asia-Pacific issues, Dick Halloran groomed us on how to behave in Japan:

• Address people by their last names (the first name is overly familiar).

• Exchange business cards ceremoniously, using both hands to proffer your card facing out. Do not sling it on the table like you were dealing a hand of poker. Take the card you are given and study it carefully for about a minute, with an expression of respect and attentiveness.

• Do not try to master the intricacies of bowing etiquette. As a non-Japanese, you don't have much hope of bending to the exact degree specified in various situations. A small nod of the head will do.

Such preparations had been conspicuous by their absence before our visit to brusque China, where assertiveness training was more in order. Halloran's suggestions indicated we would be entering an etiquette-driven nation that in some ways would resemble, of all places, England.

Japan might mimic the United States in economic robustness and Germany in a shared past of military aggression. Yet as a formal society of ingrained ritual and indirect discourse, the Land of the Rising Sun exhibited some aspects of the Empire Where the Sun Never Set.

The comparison was not unknown among Asia watchers, who noted additional analogs between Pacific Rim nations and other places. As well as the social dimensions of politeness (Japan and England) and directness (China and the United States), Korea and Ireland shared certain traits, as noted in an insight from P.J. O'Rourke. Koreans, he wrote, were "hardheaded, hard-drinking, tough little bastards, 'the Irish of Asia.'" And a correspondent for an Asian bureau of *Time* magazine compared colorfully religious Indonesia and Mexico, both historically unhurried places and now up-and-coming economically.

To prepare for visiting Japan, I could fall back on my experiences from 1981 to 1985, working on little newspapers south of London.

Time to brush up my skills in:

• Reading between the lines.

• Abandoning literal-mindedness.

• Realizing that the word "no" would sound ringingly rude.

• Speaking more softly.

• Refraining from asking personal questions, being sarcastic, or using slangy or—above all—vulgar language.

Deborah Tannen, a linguist noted for her work unraveling various communication styles, wrote in *Gender and Discourse*, "Many Americans find it self-evident that directness is logical and aligned with power whereas indirectness is akin to dishonesty as well as subservience."

LESSON NUMBER 1: (FROM DEBORAH TANNEN): "FOR SPEAKERS RAISED IN MOST OF THE WORLD'S CULTURES, VARIETIES OF INDIRECTNESS ARE THE NORM IN COMMUNICATION."

England and Japan: Shared interests and facets of life

Royal families and public fascination with them, especially when the princes marry commoners.

Sheepdogs.

Theater.

Poorly heated housing.

A love of formal gardens.

Celebration of tea in literature, the arts and everyday life. *The Book of Tea* describes Japan's ancient rituals, and how-to diagrams on aprons sold at Harrods in London depict proper brewing techniques.

Eating fish (with chips in England, as sushi in Japan).

Food that seems uninteresting or ascetic to outsiders. In Japan: miso soup, sashimi (raw tuna) and tofu; in Britain, Vegemite (a sandwich spread consisting of yeast extract), cucumber sandwiches and bland cheeses.

Tabloid newspapers.

Unconventional sports, televised for hours, such as snooker (England) or sumo wrestling (Japan).

Socializing outside their often humble homes, in pubs (England) or restaurants and karaoke bars (Japan).

Alcohol consumption to loosen their social inhibitions.

Lack of overt religiosity.

Unpuritanical and occasionally kinky attitudes toward sex. For example, the London stage often features full-frontal male and female nudity. And the Japanese hold a tradition of allowing a masked man to sneak at night into the room of a woman, so that he can be accepted or rebuffed without risk of awkwardness.

A self-effacing and stoic attitude.

Honesty.

Modesty.

OTHER AREAS OF COMMONALITY:

A medieval era.

An era of empire.

An era of dominance in manufacturing.

Powerful 20th century navies.

Written languages with many borrowings from the nearest continent.

Homogeneous populations that may rely more on shared assumptions than explicit conversation.

Limited natural resources.

Remnants of a class system.

A major role in world shipping.

Low crime rates and an exceptional level of personal safety.

High levels of male chauvinism.

A complex attitude toward the United States, a contradictory blend of national superiority and envy.

Perverse pride in the incomprehensibility their culture presents to outsiders, who tend to decide "you could live there 20 years and not begin to understand the people."

Geographical similarities in latitude, approximate size and positions as outriders to the Eurasian continent.

BRITISH ISLES

JAPAN

For many thousands of years the [British Isles] stood remote from, and marginal to, the most highly developed civilisations of the time. They formed a veritable cul-de-sac at the western end of the Eurasian land mass, as did the Japanese islands at its eastern end. ... The British Isles, despite their cultural individualities, were actually outliers of cultures which had matured on the continent.

W. Gordon East in *The Geography Behind History*

"In Japanese interaction, for example," Tannen wrote, "it is well known that saying 'no' is considered too face-threatening to risk, so negative responses are phrased as positive ones: one never says 'no,' but listeners understand from the form of the 'yes' whether it is truly a 'yes' or a polite 'no.' "

I had learned the hard way that Tannen was correct. At the small newspaper in Surrey where I worked, the copy chief would ask what only sounded like a question: "Would you like to edit the community news page?" Fortunately even I realized that in Britspeak, this amounted to an order.

One could give offense in the most unforeseen ways. I had once complimented an Englishwoman on her "yard" instead of her "garden," not realizing a "yard" connoted more of an auto junkyard with garbage and parts strewn everywhere.

American expatriates invariable commit various

faux pas in language or behavior, as recounted in the book *Brit-Think, Ameri-Think*. For me, numerous gaffes in England might finally pay off as hardwon experience in negotiating the unwritten rules of formal societies. Six years after leaving England, I felt ready for Japan—ready to watch quietly, to try to hear the unsaid.

TUESDAY, MAY 21
A miniature hotel room

Before I began my visit to Japan, I flew with a missionary pilot over Borneo in a single-engine plane. Under our wings passed the consequence of Japanese needs for cheap plywood furniture and planking to form concrete. Logs from the deforested interior floated down silt-choked rivers.

Forty-eight hours later, a modern Garuda jet deposited me at Tokyo's Narita airport. Borneo's muddy rivers, along with other experiences gathered in the Pacific region, colored my expectations. Traveling to many nations in the penumbra of Japan had provided tales from older Chinese, Burmese, Thais and especially Indonesians. They decried their historical regional bully, in the same way a significant number of Dutch, Britons, French and Greeks old enough to recall World War II openly dislike Germans.

Not quite knowing what to expect, I set foot in Tokyo. I would see up close the nation that was the invisible hand behind so many sights in my earlier travels: Indonesia's raw materials pillage, Shanghai's hotel construction boom, Thailand's sex trade and Hawaii's escalating real-estate prices.

Certainly Japan did not rate my "A-list" of places to visit. Three dollars is what I want to spend for dinner or an all-day bus ride, not a single Coke. Given $100 to spend, I would rather enjoy a week at a Kenyan or Balinese beach than settle a restaurant bill for some raw fish and teriyaki dip.

LESSON NUMBER 2: THOUGH JAPAN MAY NOT RATE AS "MOST LOVABLE" COUNTRY FOR ADVENTURE TRAVELERS, IT FULFILLS (AS DOES BRITAIN) AN IMPORTANT ROLE FOR THOUSANDS OF AMERICAN EXPATRIATES: SERVING AS A DAY-TO-DAY FINISHING SCHOOL.

Japan's global role may be to counterweigh the excesses of American and Australian informality, to be one of a few places where a subtle, understated approach, for everything from speech to rock gardens, is exalted. Otherwise, U.S. civilization and its numerous imitators might devolve even more into what British historian Arnold J. Toynbee described as "vulgarization and barbarization by the proletariat." This is a fancy way of saying that everyone would dress loudly and carry on as depicted in the restaurant scenes in the 1994 Australian film *Muriel's Wedding*. So we may not love Japan, but we need to learn from it.

A new train running from Narita airport to downtown Tokyo ensured that Japan made a stellar first impression. Before passengers boarded, women in white work outfits and spotless gloves meticulously cleaned the cars. Once underway, the train tracked its location and remaining time to arrival on an electronic wall map.

Again, Asia felt like a hyperkinetic, 24-hour Tomorrowland, a Jetsons cartoon. At 2 a.m. welders erected office buildings in Bangkok. Madonna's European tour beamed down from Star TV satellites to the smallest Indonesian greasy spoons. And in this Japanese train, a digital readout above each car door, with words racing along like symbols on a stock ticker, displayed the latest news—in Japanese and English.

After individual travel around often futuristic Asia, the Jefferson Fellows reunited at the Mitsui

Urban Hotel in the Ginza district, Tokyo's retail and office heart. The front-desk staff, unintentionally reminiscent of John Belushi's samurai, shouted *"hai"* ("yes") into telephones that rang constantly.

The hotel's hallways vibrated to the tune of "Love Is a Many Splendoured Thing," played far more loudly than the subliminal level common in U.S. supermarkets. My room, once I found it, felt like a sailboat berth, both in its tininess and clever design.

Not even in jampacked China had I seen such a claustrophobia-inducing design for living. The bed occupied almost the entire floor space. A few coathooks on the wall substituted for a closet. The minute bathroom's tub, deep but not long, reflected both the Japanese stature (relatively short) and love of soaking.

Tokyo also required switching gears mentally from Borneo's Dayaks paddling their canoes to white-gloved drivers piloting taxis with doors that opened automatically when passengers approached. And I had to dress less casually, upgrading from shorts and T-shirts to a dress skirt and stockings.

Our group touring Japan included Janet Fix, then of the *Philadelphia Inquirer;* Dawn Gibeau of the *National Catholic Reporter;* and Terry McDermott, a special projects reporter at the *Seattle Times*.

I felt closest to three members of the group: Barry and Leslie Henderson, a couple who then worked at the *Knoxville Journal* in Tennessee, and Lewis Leader, then an associate editor at the *Monterey Herald* in California. All seemed like spirited and fun people who could see the humor of most situations.

By the end of the trip, circumstances would dictate new groupings among the Jefferson Fellows, as our tale will show.

Whereas Amateur Travel relies upon the serendipity of random street encounters, in Japan, our 10-strong delegation taxied around to appointments at various ministries and organizations. My notes of our meetings buzzed with the hot catch phrases of the 1990s:

• U.S. vs. Japanese savings rates.
• Non-defense research and development.
• Integration with the world economy.
• Difficulties for U.S. companies in trying to compete against *kereitsu* (large groupings of Japanese companies that exercise control through interlocking shareholding and tend to deal with each other, not foreign companies).
• The Structural Impediments Initiative, designed to increase U.S. imports by removing such deeply embedded practices as Japan's exclusionary business policies, poor retail distribution network, and high housing prices, which tend to discourage Japanese consumerism.

As we made our rounds, we discovered that most of Tokyo's officialdom lacked the unintended comedy of Beijing's bureaucrats. I began to look back almost fondly on the badly dressed group of martinets, resembling the broadbrush villains of 1960s James Bond movies, whom we met in China three weeks previously.

The only moment of relief from the competent and machine-like torrent of information came in the office of a Foreign Ministry official. He droned on with the day's umpteenth oblique compliment about a "unipolar world led by the United States." Our brains geared down into the low-frequency delta waves produced during dreamless sleep and government briefings.

At exactly 4 p.m., the minister's office loudspeaker crackled with chimes. The official leapt up in mid-sentence and began doing torso exercises, swinging his arms wildly about, startling us out of our mood of torpor. For such a reserved people, the Japanese didn't mind looking a bit gung-ho to outsiders as they performed office gymnastics or company anthems.

WEDNESDAY, MAY 22
Making more of the rounds
At the U.S. Embassy in Tokyo, we met for breakfast with representatives of the American Chamber of Commerce in Japan.

Top representatives from the Tokyo offices of DuPont, AT&T and Digital grabbed trays of juice and muffins from the embassy cafeteria and sat down to brief us on the "Climate for American Business in Japan." Yet before saying a word, they sent a powerful message. One man in particular was a dead ringer for the character Blake Carrington that John Forsythe played on *Dynasty*. Others might be a shade less like Central Casting's image of a financial titan, but all conveyed a similar well-dressed and successful aura. They might as well have written "charismatic American executive" on their foreheads.

This struck me as a shrewd maneuver by the home offices: Dazzle the Japanese. Make them think all Americans are as tall, tan and manicured, with newsanchor hair streaked with distinguished gray, as the social climbers in our exported television programs.

As for what the Chamber of Commerce folks actually said aloud, it boiled down to: "If you can make it at all, you can make it big." Everything was much better than in the 1980s, they indicated. Japan had been taking down trade barriers, and they had been making profits.

They displayed only a tiny particle of the angst that we might have expected, given the publicity attending U.S. trade disputes, particularly over American automobiles and rice. Blake Carrington and his glossy colleagues gave the sense that the United States had turned a corner. Disneyland, Shakey's, IBM, Coca-Cola and McDonald's had prospered, they said.

A Japanese official at MITI, the Ministry of International Trade and Industry, had complained to us about representatives of the successful conglomerates that "those people from the U.S. keep their mouths shut. They don't tell you how successful they are." Carrington & Co. seemed open in describing how their ventures were prospering, but MITI official correctly perceived that the word was not getting around.

Our raft of appointments included a foreign correspondents' dinner. I had the fortune to be seated alongside T.R. Reid of *The Washington Post*, to be a future colleague. In his own right Reid enjoyed celebrityhood in Japan, appearing on television and commenting on the culture. At our dinner he described his wife's job with a Japanese bank. Peer pressure forced her to stay late, Reid said. Long hours put in for show, he added, did not lead to genuine productivity.

Across the table sat Paul Addison, a British journalist who in 1982 had been a Jefferson Fellow. He worked as a news editor at *Nikkei Weekly* in Tokyo (he later transferred to Bloomberg Business News).

"You must find Japan a lot easier to figure out than Americans do," I said. Addison vigorously agreed that a Briton could well be more adept at deciphering a formal society.

Fumiko Mori Halloran also subscribed to my hypothesis later when I presented it to her. "Both Britons and Japanese try to avoid at any cost saying 'no' or 'I disagree with you' in a blunt way," she said.

"Another common characteristic is sensitivity so as not to hurt other people's pride. In London, for example, civilized people never ask, 'Where do you live?' when they meet a person the first time because an address might reveal social class. In Tokyo, civilized Japanese never ask, 'What university did you attend?' even if they are dying to know because which university you graduated from often determines their image of elite or non-elite."

LESSON NUMBER 3: THE RESPECT IN FORMAL SOCIETIES FOR THE SENSITIVITIES OF OTHERS STANDS IN MARKED CONTRAST TO THE AMERICAN TENDENCY TO PROBE FOR PERSONAL DETAILS ON INCOME, ROMANTIC STATUS, EDUCATION AND POLITICS.

THURSDAY, MAY 23
Downside of an economic superpower
Before our visit, we did not know how unhappy many Japanese felt about their quality of life. Once you begin to look into the matter, however, it seems many authorities have tackled the subject.

Takashi Koyama, a writer for *Sankei Shimbun* in Tokyo, spoke at a luncheon for the Jeffersons held at the Asia Foundation. He candidly addressed drawbacks to Japanese life.

"Figures show that the average salary is higher in Japan than the United States," Koyama began in a matter-of-fact tone. "But our houses are small, our money doesn't go far due to high prices, and our work hours are long.

"I commute three hours a day on a train without a seat," he continued. "Sunday is my only day off, and I often stay home with my family, because it would cost us $80 to go visit an amusement park or go on a similar outing. So although we may appear to have a higher salary, Americans have a higher standard of living— and quality of life."

Crowding has created problems. "The No. 1 complaint the Japanese Metropolitan Police receive annually is noise," he said. Visitors sometimes wonder about the "slums in Tokyo's suburbs" they see from their passing train or subway car, but "this is a typically Japanese living area."

In some respects, he concluded, "Japan is an underdeveloped country."

Koyama correctly intuited a different reality from that indicated by World Bank figures for per capita gross national product. In 1989, this measure showed $23,730 for Japan and $21,100 for the United States. At the time of our visit, commentators in both nations made much of Japan's move past the United States (though technically, per capita GNP measures production and is not the same thing as income per person).

By 1995, the Central Intelligence Agency's *World Factbook* and the U.N.'s International Comparison Programme began to use an accounting method that factored in purchasing power. Japan dropped like a stone to a more realistic level, and the United States rose. The new measure accounted for overvaluation of the yen and accounted for the expensiveness of Japanese life.

National product per capita

1994 ESTIMATED

1	Bermuda	$28,000
2	**United States**	**25,850**
3	Luxembourg	22,830
4	Canada	22,760
5	United Arab Emirates	22,480
6	Norway	22,170
7	Switzerland	22,080
8	Qatar	20,820
9	Australia	20,720
10	**Japan**	**20,200**

Data from *The World Factbook* 1995

Others at the Asia Foundation's round-table discussion complained about problems in the workplace.

Mikio Haruna, deputy foreign news editor at Kyodo News Service, sat at my left. He told me quietly that he had loved an earlier posting as a Washington correspondent and had spent much of his career studying the United States. Much to his dismay, his employer wanted to post him to Germany. "But I feel I can't refuse my boss," he said.

He received 20 days of vacation a year, but he only used about eight of them. "What would happen if you took all your vacation?" I asked. "I'd be demoted," Haruna replied with a drawn smile.

"It's rule by coercion," said Koyama, citing peer pressure as one reason for the long hours and forfeiting of vacation time. (The Japanese work an average of 200 hours more than Americans per year, according to the Japanese Ministry of Labor.)

LESSON NUMBER 4: MUCH DISGRUNTLEMENT LIES BENEATH THE SURFACE GLITZ OF JAPAN'S MULTISTORY MALLS AND NEON NIGHTLIFE.

For example, by day in Tokyo's glamorous Ginza district, young Japanese clotheshorses rivaling Florentines and Parisians for style stride in front of spectacularly stocked department stores. At night, drunk businessmen stagger down the same streets, weeping and vomiting.

An overvalued yen and resulting high prices meant the average Japanese simply didn't have much fun with his earnings. Many could not dream of making the main lifetime investment of a typical U.S. family: a house. Housing prices made enforced yuppies of young professionals who couldn't afford a starter home and instead bought clothes, electronic gadgets and foreign vacations.

In Japan, those who could afford to buy a home typically enjoyed less than half the square footage of U.S. homes, and about a third of these houses lack central heating. Such modest homes mean that high-end restaurants with meals costing $40 to $100 take on the role of family and business entertaining.

The fact that this seemingly enviable techno-paradise fell short of perfection offers reassurance to the American visitor. The United States might have a whopping trade deficit, deteriorating education system and pathetic savings rate. But we spend (relatively) little on housing, food and entertainment and can really take our allotted vacation days.

One trivial example: Since returning from Japan, I have frequently marveled that bagels at U.S. supermarkets cost 60 cents or less. Nothing in Japan seemed to be 60 cents (although the stratospheric exchange rate for the yen somewhat distorts comparisons). The closest thing to a bargain there seemed to be a Shakey's pizza for lunch, at about $5 for a version topped with ginger root and seaweed.

LESSON NUMBER 5: SEEING OUR RIVAL ECONOMIC SUPERPOWER UP CLOSE ACTIVATES A SEISMIC CHANGE IN ATTITUDE, THE SAME REMOVAL OF HERO STATUS THAT OCCURRED WHEN DOROTHY LOOKED BEHIND THE CURTAIN AND EXPOSED THE WIZARD OF OZ. JAPAN IS A HUGELY SUCCESSFUL COUNTRY, BUT IT DOESN'T HAVE 60-CENT BAGELS.

"The Japanese economic miracle seemed to have much more to do with the Zen-like discipline and self-lessness of the work force than any innovations in corporate management," such as reduced inventories, full employment policies and quality circles, wrote Gary Katzenstein in *Funny Business: An Outsider's Year in Japan.* He wrote that relying on these Japanese social traits

> wouldn't ultimately work for Americans, and maybe did not even work so well for the Japanese, judging from their comparatively low standard of living, woefully inadequate social services, civil facilities, housing and retirement systems.

Katzenstein underlined T.R. Reid's observation about middling Japanese productivity. The Japanese generally lack private offices or even partitions between desks, spending workdays in cluttered, noisy rooms.

But despite the outspokenness a handful of Japanese may display to visiting Americans, there seems to be little complaining to bosses and no concerted efforts to improve matters.

Opinion polls reveal a good number of Takashi Koyamas. The Japanese lag Americans in overall personal satisfaction.

Personal satisfaction

18 NATIONS SURVEYED

	TOTAL SATISFIED	RANK IN SURVEY
United States	83%	5th
Japan	**60**	**7th**
For comparison:		
Iceland (highest)	87	1st
Hungary (lowest)	21	18th

Based on a poll reported in June 1995 by *The Gallup Monthly*

Some caveats need to be remembered:

• Any discussion of quality of life must include the fact that Japan has a far, far lower crime rate than the United States. The U.S. rape rate is 24 times higher than Japan's, the homicide rate, 14 times higher.

• The Japanese can and do enjoy themselves. In Japan's baseball stadiums, karaoke bars, rice-growing villages, temples and public baths, we met relaxed and pleasant people who knew how to have fun.

• Perhaps most tellingly, many U.S. expatriates among the 32,000 who live in Japan willingly work for Japanese firms on Japanese terms—long hours, high costs and all.

FRIDAY, MAY 24
Japan and the Sheltie Question

Staying in deluxe accommodations, eating three-figure expense account lunches and running to

A bullet train flies through the Ginza district.

appointments in one skyscraper after another do not epitomize the preferred activities of Amateur Travelers. Amateurs don't care deeply about *kereitsu* or the Structural Impediments Initiative. These areas are best left to the pros. Amateurs really want to know things such as:

• What role do Shetland sheepdogs play in Japanese popular culture?

• Can I get a terrific personal stereo, better than the ones for sale in the States?

• What's it like to go to a baseball game? The public baths? A karaoke bar?

Somehow our leaders, Schidlovsky and the Hallorans, despite being authors and foreign correspondents of major accomplishment, neglected to schedule any sheltie experts during our whirlwind visits to Tokyo, Kyoto, Hiroshima and Nagasaki.

I would have to do some digging on my own. The question of sheltie popularity loomed large. My little dog's breed seemed to occupy an iconographic place in Japanese culture. Witness this virtual haiku, reported in a *Baltimore Sun* article on T-shirt inscriptions in Japan:

SHETLAND SHEEPDOG

Sheltie need strength speed and
intelligence to guard flocks of animal
Sheltie.

In the late 1980s, when shelties peaked in popularity to become the No. 1 breed in Japan, only strains traced to U.S. dogs could be registered with the American Kennel Club. In fact, in the early 1990s the Maryland breeder of my own dog air-freighted 28 of his puppy cousins to Japan.

Multiply this canine shipment severalfold and, as John De Hoog wryly noted on the Internet Shetland sheepdog home page, "In this case the trade imbalance is all in America's favor."

With one day free of official appointments, I could check firsthand on sheltie mania and the latest personal stereo models. Near our Ginza hotel stood one of

Japan's premier toy shops, Ginza Hakuhinkan Toy Park, a huge multistoried affair with electronic gizmos and traditional toys. Just inside the main entrance were dozens of plush toy shelties, in puppy and full-grown sizes.

1992 sheltie rankings

AMONG PEDIGREE DOG REGISTRATIONS

Breed	Number
In Japan	
1. Siberian husky	58,381
2. Shih Tzu	44,322
3. Shetland sheepdogs	**24,230**
In the United States	
1. Labradors	124,899
2. Rottweilers	104,160
3. German shepherds	79,936
...	
9. Shetland sheepdogs	**43,449**

Bingo—the toys gave the first evidence of sheltie love. More proof arrived at my next stop, the Asakusa Kannon Temple (Kannon is the goddess of mercy in a Tantric sect that grew out of Hinduism and Buddhism). At stalls surrounding the giant red temple on the northeast side of Tokyo, Japanese burned incense for special devotions. A young woman in an elegant suit strode swiftly through the temple grounds, a prancing, silky-coated sheltie at her side. The dog, lavishly cared for, made as much of a fashion statement as his mistress's outfit.

Eagerly I walked toward her, already reaching for my wallet photos of Beau **(right)**. With an embarrassed smile, she emphatically shook her hand "no" to deter my approach, and strode away as fast as she could without actually breaking into a dead run.

How her avoidance differed from reactions a week previously in Borneo. There, a chance to peruse a visitor's wallet photos created a sensation, drawing dozens of friendly longhouse residents seeming to be thrilled at a little break in the routine.

The woman's standoffishness averted one problem. I certainly didn't know how to say in Japanese, "Here's a picture of my dog. He has 28 cousins here in Japan. Is your dog related?"

However aloof, the woman nonetheless had bestowed the ultimate compliment, ownership, to a hardy working dog hailing from the seasprayed edge of the British Isles nearest Norway. That shelties found favor with the stylish and fastidious Japanese testified to the breed's cleanliness, intelligence, compact size and striking looks.

From the temple grounds, the subway took me to Akihabara, the 500-store site of my quest for the ultimate personal stereo. The subway excursion demon-

strated the helpfulness of the Japanese, who approached every time I began to squint at the station route maps and my useful booklet, *How to Ride Tokyo Subways*. As the day went on, I eventually relaxed and succeeded in reading the fare charts unassisted, matching the characters on the subway wall with the English names in the booklet.

The subway trip marked progress for me in deciphering languages written with ideograms in the six years since I first visited Asia in 1985.

At first, comprehending Chinese in particular had seemed an ironclad impossibility. Given necessity and gradual acclimatization, I had begun to recognize a paltry few characters: those for "China," "Beijing" and "ladies room." Similarly, after three days, Japanese began to seem slightly less out of the question for me. And if imported shelties could learn their commands in spoken Japanese, I could take a stab at the written form.

At Akihabara, the world's greatest assemblage of electronic products, street vendors hawked cheap calculators and watches along several blocks. Flashing neon and swarms of pedestrians recalled Times Square in New York City or Piccadilly Circus in London. In narrow, six-story department stores, shoppers seeking high-end equipment whizzed up escalators.

Floors aimed at the domestic market displayed that year's rages: cordless telephones, DAT tape recorders and tiny liquid-crystal-display televisions. The top floors of an emporium called Laox featured items with chargers set to foreign voltages for the 20 percent of Akihabara's shoppers who hail from overseas.

Here I hunted for a successor to an old unit that hadn't lasted. A personal stereo and reading material serve as my security blankets, especially during solo travel, allowing me to parachute out of the anxiety of the here and now. My love for travel is not pure. Excitement and fun blend with worry and sensory overload.

After hours of sound comparison, I finally bought an Aiwa personal stereo of polished black metal, the size of a cigarette pack and with terrific range and clarity of sound. Years later I still have not seen one remotely so elegant for sale in the United States.

That evening, Schidlovsky, Leader and I prowled the west side of Tokyo in search of a rumored batting cage in the brightly lit Shinbuyu district. Trendy teenagers strolled the clean streets from snack shop to ice-cream boutique. We asked various Japanese men if they knew of a batting cage anywhere. We chased around various districts following leads that went nowhere. Finally, we found one, on top of a office building in either Shinbuyu, Shibuya or Shinjuku. (Shades of Madagascar: All the place names sounded similar).

At the batting cage, girls in office attire giggled but tagged few of the pitches. Leader connected, and

Schidlovsky positively pounded ball after ball. I kicked off my shoes and batted as best a woman can when wearing a skirt and hosiery.

In obsequious gratitude for being included with the guy jocks, I treated them afterward to ice cream floats and sodas. The tab came to a rather hefty $30.

At our wrought-iron table, Schidlovsky and I, both with Maryland roots, droned on interminably about favorite Washington Redskins football games. Schidlovsky possessed a tranquil baritone voice like that of a late-night disc jockey on a jazz station, appropriate to a devotedly detailed recounting of our favorite team's exploits. The Redskins' five touchdowns in the second quarter of the January 1988 Super Bowl, which had created unequalled pandemonium in my parent's living room and many others in the Washington area, received special mention.

"I watch my video of that about once a year," said Schidlovsky. Silently, knowingly, I nodded.

LESSON NUMBER 6: SOMETIMES TRAVELERS IN STRANGE LANDS NEED THE FAMILIARITY OF SPORTS TALK, CHERISHED CASSETTE TAPES AND REMINDERS OF THEIR DOG BACK HOME.

SATURDAY-MONDAY, MAY 25-27

Our definition of "clean" goes up, up, up

Invariably the sequence of traveling colors impressions. After the dramatic sea-cliff beauty of Hawaii, where our fellowship commenced, the supposed exquisiteness of Kyoto did not seem apparent to the Jefferson Fellows when we arrived on the bullet train from Tokyo.

This city of 1.5 million served as the capital of Japan for more than 1,000 years, until Tokyo took over in 1868. In World War II, Secretary of War Henry L. Stimson vetoed Kyoto as a bombing target, citing its antiquity and how the Japanese might permanently resent America and tilt toward the Soviets if the ancient city were damaged.

Kyoto almost always makes must-destination lists. Pico Iyer wrote in *Video Night in Kathmandu* of its "enraptured stillness," the "ringing, silver purity of the streets," the "smell of woodsmoke, the drift of incense."

The author of *Japan: A Travel Survival Kit* warned against hyped-up expectations, noting that overly enthusiastic writers had called Kyoto one of the world's most beautiful cities. Ian L. McQueen wrote that Kyoto displayed "a full share"

Young women shop in a Kyoto shopping arcade.

of urban ugliness, though this was relieved with "oases of beauty, exemplifying the best of Japan."

In sunny, pleasant weather we traipsed through various temples and palaces, including the large Nijo-jo, about on a par with your high-end English castle in Windsor or Arundel. Ieyasu Tokugawa (the character Toranaga in the 1975 novel *Shogun*) ordered the castle's construction in 1601.

Feudal eras

	JAPAN	BRITAIN
Peak of era	1336	1000
	to 1573 A.D.	to 1300 A.D.
End of era	1860	1660
Comparative terms	Daimyos	Lords
	Samurai	Knights
	Jo	Castle

We also visited gently pretty temples on the outskirts of Kyoto, surrounded by wooded countryside that resembled western Maryland's Catoctin National Park.

The Nijo-jinya house, my favorite among the places we visited, previewed the "Dungeons and Dragons" or "Myst" computer games. With its secret passages and traps and places for ambush, the Nijo-jinya recalled the heyday of the unimaginably clever and disciplined ninja fighter. *Shogun* depicted the ninja secrets: "how to swim vast distances under water and scale almost smooth walls, how to make themselves invisible and stand for a day and a night without moving."

The book also captured a romantic warrior vision of Japan. *Shogun* means generalissimo, or head of the samurai. The book, inspired by the real-life story of shipwrecked Will Adams, told how an English pilot-major renamed John Blackthorne, his Dutch and Portuguese crew and their body odor fetched up on the coast of Japan in 1600.

Blackthorne (Richard Chamberlain in the TV series) learned to bathe better, to speak Japanese, to please his mistress Mariko when she sneaked in to him at night and to negotiate the intricate politics of the daimyos and the shogun.

I had missed the September 1980 TV series and so began a paperback of *Shogun* while traveling around Borneo. At 1,210 pages, it lasted through my 3,600-mile flight from Jakarta to Tokyo and then the

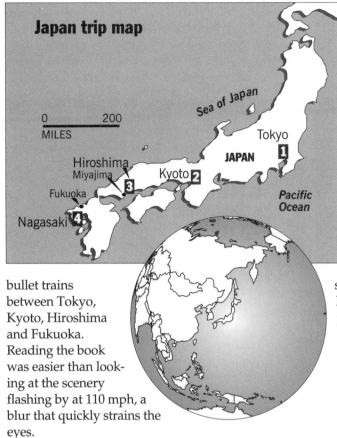

Japan trip map

0   200
MILES

Sea of Japan

Tokyo

JAPAN   **1**

Hiroshima
Miyajima   Kyoto **2**

3

Fukuoka

Nagasaki **4**

Pacific
Ocean

bullet trains between Tokyo, Kyoto, Hiroshima and Fukuoka. Reading the book was easier than looking at the scenery flashing by at 110 mph, a blur that quickly strains the eyes.

Dick Halloran looked skeptical when I asked him of the validity of *Shogun's* observations on Japan. Desperate to learn in some easily accessible way about Japanese history—which seemed weird and far more inward than North American or European history—this Amateur Traveler stayed with the accessible novel.

Much as many acknowledge that James Michener's *Hawaii* faithfully portrays the history of the 50th state, I suspected that James Clavell's *Shogun* captured the general drift of Japanese history. My brother Paul, an East Asian studies major in college, vouched for this. "It's probably like using Captain America comics to teach World War II," he said. "But you've got to start somewhere with American students who don't known any Japanese history."

A 1980 book issued by the University of California at Santa Barbara's Program of Asian Studies, *Learning from Shogun*, contained a wide range of essays affirming the overall value and enormous impact of Clavell's book. The preface noted that

> In sheer quantity, *Shogun* has probably conveyed more information about Japan to more people than all the combined writings of scholars, journalists, and novelists since the Pacific war.

Some scholars wrote in *Learning from Shogun* that the Clavell book contained errors here and there but acknowledged it to be one of the finest accounts of a cross-cultural experience ever written.

As with the novel's Blackthorne four centuries previously, the mundane aspects of daily life in Japan—bathing, eating raw fish, sleeping on tatami mats—confounded us the most.

For example, in Kyoto we stayed in the Coop, a ryokan or traditional Japanese inn. A chambermaid set up a short-legged tea table on the tatami (rice-straw) floor mats, which smelled sweetly of grass. She showed us where to store the tea table at night and how to roll out the stored futons.

The futons felt snug, and the room was fragrant. The appointments appealed to my sailor's eye for efficiency and elegance. The ingenious use of limited space resembled that in cruising sailboats, where a dining salon doubles as a sleeping area.

However, after we turned in, drawbacks of the arrangement became apparent. Dawn, a heavy smoker, rattled a bit as she breathed (a harbinger of a health crisis). The sound became so distracting that I picked up my pillow and curled up in the hallway.

LESSON NUMBER 7: THE FACT THAT THREE AMERICAN WOMEN COULD NOT SHARE A SMALL AREA MAY ILLUSTRATE HOW LITTLE WE ARE ACCUSTOMED TO CROWDING AND ITS ATTENDANT NEED FOR COMPROMISE.

Schidlovsky, Leader and McDermott, meanwhile, happily shared their ryokan room, ordering beer and clearing space for a late-night card game. So perhaps Lesson Number 7 does not apply in many cases to guys.

The next morning each woman moved into a Western-style room. I felt frustrated by the switch, because a ryokan room looked like it could be quite restful.

But on our blitzkrieg pace in a foreign nation, getting enough rest was imperative. In fact, after a month of travel in Asia, many in our weary group would soon fall like so many dominoes.

Our ryokan stay might have been an unfortunate flop. But another traditional facet of Japanese life, the public baths, made up for it. A light-rail train hauled us to an open-air spring in the mountains above Kyoto. Here our travel group first encountered the defining characteristic of Japanese life: bathing for hours, with great completeness.

Further, the Japanese, like their Hawaiian descendants and another group, U.S. construction and landscape workers, bathed at night. Since childhood I too had preferred to go to bed clean, so different from the tendency on the U.S. mainland to bathe before going to work. The Japanese and Hawaiian custom of keeping street shoes by the front door, to avoid tracking dirt through the house, also made eminent sense.

At the Kyoto baths, men and women proceeded to separate areas, a relatively recent segregation dating from Gen. Douglas MacArthur's postwar management of Japan. Leslie, Janet and I left our gear in the ladies locker room and, wrapped in towels, emerged into the bright afternoon sun. We perched on the side of a square polished-stone basin, about 15 feet long on each side. A wooden enclosure provided privacy yet was low enough to allow us to view a pretty ridge of mountains.

A relaxed atmosphere attended our session in the open-air baths. We soaked, lazed, cat-napped and chatted.

Later Janet and I went to an indoor public bath in a downtown building in Nagasaki. We rode up an elevator, paid an attendant about $7 each and found our way to a sizable area with many different whirlpool baths, each labeled with a different temperature. Some tubs appeared as utilitarian as those at an athletic club. Pagoda- or castle-like roofs capped others, evoking the scale and corniness of a miniature golf course. In a separate sauna, we could sit in the low light and watch a color television, set behind a glass window cut into the wood-paneled walls.

Before immersing ourselves, we scrubbed for many minutes at stations set in front of a long vanity, then rinsed off using shower heads on flexible hoses. Racks on wheels held trays of washcloths, ear swabs and other toiletries.

We unwound in one whirlpool after another after washing probably three times as fastidiously as we had ever before in our lives. We rinsed carefully, aware that dirt, soap and suds must not enter the shared water.

A woman in her fifties came in and sat down at a vanity. She began scrubbing every inch of skin and every body crease many, many times. She went on considerably longer than we had, even in our attempt to be correctly Japanese in bathing. She twisted the moisture from her washcloth with a vengeance and repeatedly ministered to a tiny bit of her skin as though sanding a much-painted bookcase down to bare wood.

The nuances of bathing, as with bowing, seemed out of our barbarian reach. Maybe Americans hurry everything, rushing through fast-food meals (where the French would linger) and hopping in and out of the shower. In Japan, Turkey, Persia, Java, Finland, Russia—perhaps in many areas with access to hot-water springs—bathing, dressing, napping and chatting become an drawn-out, ritualized affair, an opportunity for a community to get together and share information.

LESSON NUMBER 8: JAPAN'S BATHS ILLUS-TRATED A NATIONAL FIXATION WITH WATER, BATHING AND OVERALL CLEANLINESS.

Perhaps this reflects the fact that no part of the ragged crescent of Japan lies more than 100 miles from the sea, a peculiarity the island shares with Britain and its less fastidious inhabitants.

How Westerners smell to others

At the baths in Kyoto, I mentioned an item in *The Japanese* by Jack Seward, a book I'd been reading along with my pet *Shogun*. Seward wrote that the Japanese "have grave misgivings about some of our habits of personal cleanliness." He quoted a Japanese ex-diplomat who felt that "Westerners have a strong body odor that is quite nauseating." This smell, Seward reported, came from "our consumption of animal fat which produces butyric acid in our perspiration."

"The Japanese think we smell bad," I remarked, idly kicking my legs in the water. No one was ready to believe this until Fumiko Mori Halloran, a treasure trove of practical information about her homeland, confirmed that the Japanese have an expression to describe Westerners as *bata-kusai* (smell like butter).

An essay from *Learning from Shogun* entitled "Raw Fish and a Hot Bath: Dilemmas of Daily Life" noted how many of the things that surprised Blackthorne have recently crept into American life: California hot tubs and Jacuzzis, futons, sushi bars and the emphasis on lightness in nouvelle French and American cuisines.

Maybe in the future, American visitors to Japan will feel reasonably familiar, if not utterly at home, with some aspects of Japanese life.

TUESDAY-WEDNESDAY, MAY 28-29
Ideological conflicts at a peace museum

The Hiroshima Peace Memorial Museum would be hard to top for morbidly fascinating exhibits.

Photographs testified to the power that an atomic bomb known as Little Boy unleashed on Aug. 6, 1945. With the luminosity of 10 suns, the thermal rays from the bomb created some remarkable natural photographs: silhouetting a valve on a fuel tank, burning a kimono pattern into the back and upper arm of a woman, imprinting the leaves of a *Fatsia japonica* near Meiji Bridge on an electric pole, outlining the last moments of a man and his handcart crossing the Yorozuyo Bridge.

A diorama showed wanderers unlucky enough to survive the initial blast. Unknowingly doomed to die of radiation poisoning, they staggered like zombies with their clothes in tatters and strips of skin hanging off their fingertips.

Museum staffers provided Janet Fix and me with several booklets in English. A photograph in one booklet depicted the mushroom cloud towering to 12,000 feet, taller than Mount Hood in Oregon. The photo showed a black rain of mud, dust, soot from fires and radioactive substances drifting northwest and falling on towns sharing the Hiroshima peninsula.

I wandered through the museum feeling overcome

A diorama at the Hiroshima Peace Memorial Museum shows blast survivors with skin hanging from their fingertips.

with the hideousness of the bombing's aftermath and self-conscious of our American faces—and outraged at the reckless lack of context.

A month earlier we had toured Pearl Harbor, watching a drop of oil float every few seconds to the surface above the USS *Arizona*, 50 years after its sinking. On edge, we had warily watched the Japanese tourists. We had heard they sometimes laughed and smirked during visits to the memorial, sparking fights with U.S. veterans. Young Japanese who did not comprehend the history behind the memorial (shades of my own ignorance and reliance on *Shogun*) had been the offenders. Now travel agencies warn clients to mind their manners. "Americans these days comment on how respectful Japanese visitors are," noted Fumiko Mori Halloran.

At Pearl Harbor, our guide had described how some of the sailors trapped in ships after the Dec. 7, 1941, attack lived past New Year's Day in their half-floating tombs. The men scratched a line in the wall of their chamber to represent each passing day. Divers using blowtorches tried to cut a way to those trapped. But gasoline and oil lingering in the water after the attack blew them up, and rescuers abandoned their attempts.

It seemed to me that at Hiroshima, Japan had paid dearly but predictably for its sneak attack on Pearl Harbor and its wartime atrocities. Malcolm X's infamous line on violence claiming the life of President John F. Kennedy—"the chickens coming home to roost"— seemed applicable to the bombing of Hiroshima.

My father, a nuclear physicist, offered a slightly different slant.

Visitors pose in front of the cenotaph at the Hiroshima Peace Memorial Museum.

Speaking generally of why a practicing Roman Catholic worked to help the U.S. military maintain its nuclear edge, he said, "War is hell for everyone, but the hell is worse for the losers." Several historians have written that Japan, Germany or the Soviet Union would have bombed U.S. forces had any of them won the nuclear arms race, supporting this realpolitik rationale for bombing Hiroshima.

Janet and I got our translator to ask a little schoolgirl how the museum made her feel toward Americans. "I hate them," she said without tone.

Great, we thought. Japan's counterpart in emotional impact to the United States Holocaust Memorial Museum in Washington, D.C., seemed criminally lacking in balance and completeness. In *Dave Barry Does Japan*, the author noted that "the way the museum presents it, the atomic bomb was like a lightning bolt— something nobody could foresee, and nobody could prevent. It was as though one day, for no reason, the Americans came along, literally out of the blue, and did this horrible thing to these innocent people."

> The A-bomb was treated, as it always is here, as some tragic truth of the world that floats in the memory free of history, free of cause and blame, free of politics and power.
>
> T.R. Reid in "Once Again, Life Stops in Hiroshima,"
> *The Washington Post*

In front of the peace museum, at an arch-shaped cenotaph, groups of schoolkids in uniform asked without rancor if we would sign autograph books bought specially for their visit.

I had imagined that Hiroshima (pronounced He-RO-shih-ma) would be a flattened little place, a remnant of its pre-August 1945 population of 340,000. Maybe the site remained dangerous from radioactivity, and a post-apocalyptic guard patrolled a fenced-off epicenter.

This was not so. The city and its environs had flourished, growing to 1 million people who made cars, ships and textiles, grew silk and fermented sake.

Hiroshima, with its unheralded appeal like that of Chongqing and Wuzhou in China, wowed me more than exalted Kyoto. Little things showed that Hiroshima tried harder.

Our "Welcome to Hiroshima" tourist map displayed a clever full-page graphic labeled "Please help me" with a helpful phonetic *"Sumimasen oshiete kudasai"* underneath. Then it listed 14 of the city's attractions, in English and Japanese.

Katsukini Tanaka, another former Jefferson Fellow and an executive for

Hiroshima Home Television, hosted our visit and ensured that we enjoyed his city. Following Dick Halloran's formality lessons to excess, I called him "Mr. Tanaka-San," though literally that meant "Mr. Tanaka Mister."

Tanaka took us first to the Mazda factory, where white-jumpsuited workers flew around the chassis of each car. An unpainted frame at the start of the assembly line became a drivable vehicle in two hours. Our congenial host also exposed us to two less economically threatening aspects of Japanese society: baseball and karaoke.

At a baseball game between the Hiroshima Carp and the Yomiuri Giants, the Carp publicist, a Mr. Ikeda, gave us a background paper. It described how Kohhei Matsuda, then the president of Mazda, constructed the Hiroshima ballpark and managed the team. The briefing paper didn't mince words on the sorrowful history of the Carp's home city:

A crowd cheers on the Hiroshima Carp baseball team.

> THE HIROSHIMA BASEBALL
> BORN IN THE RUINS
>
> Hiroshima baseball was born in 1949 as "the municipal baseball team" by loud cries of the citizens of Hiroshima City which had been totally destroyed by the atomic bomb and that was a year before Japan Professional Baseball was devided [sic] into two leagues.

A second paper, *Brief History of Japanese Baseball*, contained a Zen-like passage on the popularity, dating to 1915, of high school baseball:

> Baseball came to be received among the youth and instructors as the edifying meaning or means rather than the enjoyment of playing it like Martial Arts; therefore, baseball has played a greatly important roll [sic] in building up character of the youth.

Schidlovsky, Leader, Barry Henderson and McDermott certainly seemed to be tuned in to whatever frequency provided the "edifying meaning." They male-bonded in spectacular fashion, abandoning our good seats between home and first to stand at the fence

A Mazda worker tests a door handle.

along the first-base line and watch the game at even closer range.

I was warming up to the Japanese, including several elderly, white-haired gentlemen in our section at the Carp game. Janet, Leslie and I exchanged business cards, our names and organizations printed in both English and Japanese, with the gentlemen.

"Ah. Ah-ha," they said with vigor, smiling as they studied the Japanese characters on the reverse of our special cards.

LESSON NUMBER 9: A FLIP SIDE TO JAPANESE AND BRITISH RESERVE IS INNATE POLITENESS.

We carried our end of the conversation with "Carp, *ichi-ban*!" (Visits to a Maryland restaurant called Ichiban had taught me the phrase meant "number one.") We covered up our lack of finer language skills by teaching the Japanese how to do the wave. The whole thing made the May 29 edition of Hiroshima's *Daily Sports Papers*, under the headline, "Journalists with blue eyes watching Carp-Giants baseball game."

Tanaka next furthered our cultural exchange by escorting us to a karaoke bar. We wandered through a lively pedestrian mall with late-night ice-cream shops and passed through a door and up the stairs. The city Americans know as a bomb site seemed to be Party Town.

I had harbored a mental picture of karaoke bars as small auditoriums where each singer waited in turn to perform before dozens of people. This tastefully appointed and intimate nook dispelled it. Our party sat at one of the two tables, each with a karaoke video jukebox and several lyric books. A female bartender took rounds.

We paid homage to the standards of the karaoke genre. Barry Henderson ripped through a basso profundo version of "Mack the Knife." Leslie and I added backing vocals and choreography for "Barbara Ann" and some Motown numbers.

Mr. Tanaka and Janet Fix share a joke, as the two men on the right prepare to give us their business cards.

Mr. Tanaka-San belted out a forceful rendition of "My Way," delicately holding the microphone with just thumb and two fingers like Ole Blue Eyes himself. He provided the only instance, aside from the drunk salarymen in Tokyo's Ginza, that we saw in 12 days in Japan of a person acting without reserve. He tackled the ironic anthem of the regimented salaryman with panache, demonstrating the oft-noted fervor the Japanese bring to karaoke.

On a side trip to Miyajima, we viewed a classic torii (an arch with double crossbars, the top one upswept), surrounded by water at high tide and swarms of noisy schoolkids at low tide. The island's tame yet pushy deer nosed open tourist backpacks and took apples and other treats. I took a quick walk up the hilly side streets and enjoyed a view back over the rooftops to the mainland.

I meet two of the tame deer on Miyajima.

Miyajima was one of the lovely hilly islands where you can sidestep the bustle of Asia. Cheung Chau, an idyllic island west of Hong Kong, falls into this category, as does Gulangyu, an island off Xiamen in southern China, known for its graceful homes with upright pianos.

Nagasaki, our final stop, beckoned. But Dawn experienced discomfort that blossomed into a burst appendix and a lengthy hospital stay. Tanaka, up to that point a steady and ever-pleasant fellow, showed even finer mettle. He acted as a quiet hero, arranging her care and locating English-speaking colleagues from Hiroshima Home Television to visit and keep Dawn's spirits up.

Barry's stamina also appeared to be affected by cigarettes. He caught a severe cold, and he and Leslie elected to stay behind in Hiroshima.

Leader, whose homesickness was evidenced by a tireless hunt for reports of U.S. baseball scores, telephone calls to his wife and daughter and ever-shorter fuse when paying $110 tabs for *sashimi* (raw tuna) he could barely eat, begged off Nagasaki too.

Schidlovsky stayed behind in Hiroshima to sort everything out. Dick and Fumiko Halloran had a separate circuit of visits to complete, given their extensive family and professional connections to Japan. Only three of our band of 10 remained to carry the banner onward to Nagasaki.

THURSDAY, MAY 30
A bomb victim's viewpoint

Terry McDermott, Janet Fix and I made our way to Nagasaki. Three independent characters, we hadn't spent a huge amount of time together on the trip. But now, as the only remaining participants in our Asia marathon, we shared a common goal: to fulfill our group's last round of appointments.

McDermott, tall, blonde and attractive in a classically American way, received star treatment from awestruck females throughout Japan. "He's a famous baseball player," I said breezily to uncomprehending girls, smiling dreamily at our colleague at the train station in Fukuoka.

Janet truly was "Janet Fix," a name of Dickensian appropriateness. Her aggressiveness and attention to detail helped us get good hotel rooms and train seats. Her logistics savvy served as a good counterweight to my approach, a laid-back combination of fatalism and "going Asian"—that is, avoiding confrontation and a fuss whenever possible. Maybe my role was to be the diplomat, the American whom Asians could relax with.

We boarded a train that was a step or two below the bullet train in quality—it even rattled a bit—presaging the palpable distance between Nagasaki and the rest of Japan.

Tokyo had seemed like the apotheosis of what New York City could be if rendered magically clean, polished and free of crime. Kyoto had no ready American equivalent. It seemed most like Oxford, England: a destination with a full weekend of sights and a sense of a distillation of a nation's identity, but simultaneously a slightly airless, dull aura of refinement.

Hiroshima's baseball team and manufacturing plants lent it a semblance of the Baltimore of Orioles fans and shipbuilders. But at a deeper level, its incineration placed Hiroshima in the grim category of Dresden in Germany, Coventry in England, and Tokyo. Each demonstrated a new aspect of 20th century warfare: burning civilian centers to "send a message" to a nation's rulers.

Nagasaki also enjoys a long history apart from

World War II's finale. If polyglot San Francisco were shrunk in size a bit and situated on a Norwegian fjord, it would feel like Nagasaki. A stunning harbor gives the city instant drama. An arm of the East China Sea slices a mile-long cleft through hills that rise steeply to pretty neighborhoods.

Nagasaki, a city of 450,000, felt less tangibly Japanese, a legacy of staying open while the rest of the country for 200 years hung up a "Closed for Business" sign. When an edict in the early 1600s prohibited foreign travel and even the building of large ships, only a small group of Dutch traders restricted to an island in Nagasaki's harbor continued to operate. A Roman Catholic church and about 100,000 Christians in the area make the effects of Nagasaki's outside contact detectable.

We visited the Church and Museum of the 16 Saints of Japan, with its beautiful old maps and historical exhibits on Christianity in Japan. And at Nagasaki's peace museum, we saw emotionally wrenching rubble and artifacts, similar to those at Hiroshima's museum.

Our main goal in Nagasaki was to meet one of Japan's most controversial scholars, Shigetoshi Iawamatsu. A professor of economics at Nagasaki University, he had called for the nation to take responsibility for its role in World War II.

"Japanese people don't like to use the word 'war crimes,' " Iawamatsu told us at our meeting. "Japanese people think we don't have responsibility. In Japan, they're not telling the history correctly." He said elementary school students did not study much history and high school students learned nothing of what he termed "the newest war."

After World War II, Iawamatsu said, "the Japanese didn't have the idea [that] 'we did something wrong, that's why we were defeated.' " Most Japanese, he said, focused on "the horror of nuclear weapons" rather than the war crimes that contributed to the U.S. decision to bomb.

We had seen this at the Hiroshima Peace Memorial Museum, which at the time had no displays dealing with Japan's war crimes. The best-known atrocity occurred in 1937, in the Chinese city known today as Nanjing. Japanese soldiers killed 20,000 Chinese men, using some for bayonet practice and dousing others with gasoline and setting them afire. The soldiers also raped, killed and mutilated perhaps 20,000 women and girls.

This and other events during the occupation of China and the Philippines, and the death rates in prisoner-of-war camps, placed wartime Japan among history's cruelest societies, according to Western historians. In the ancient world, Assyria and the Mongols wreaked near-destruction of their enemies. In the modern day, Japan and Germany used technology to create cruelty almost beyond comprehension.

Fumiko Mori Halloran, in a letter to me after our trip, described the economic pressures and military paranoia that led Japan to act badly during the era of atrocities, in a way roughly analogous, she felt, to the United States in the Vietnam War era. Other writers also have cited intense idealism, poverty and a lust for power as factors in Japanese civilian support for the military in World War II.

Iawamatsu described the role of groupthink in suppressing this past. "We think that Japan is one family, and the Meiji Emperor is our father. During the Shogun period, people couldn't have their own ideas. You had, in order, soldiers, farmers, craftsmen and artisans, merchants and ewa [untouchables]. People cannot change their position. The common people cannot have their own ideas. We cannot criticize leaders. If you criticize, you might be killed or put in jail."

This applied in the 20th century as well. As long as Emperor Hirohito, a long-lived soul who lasted much of the century (from 1901 to 1989), was alive, Japan could not decry the militarism that occurred during his watch.

The professor cited his bona fides to speak on the matter: "I am atomic bomb survivor." At the age of 17, he lived through the Aug. 9, 1945, attack on Nagasaki, three days after the Hiroshima bombing. But he almost did not outlast the emperor's Aug. 14 surrender.

He had considered himself "a patriotic boy" and, because his efforts had not been enough for the emperor, on Aug. 15 thought about killing himself. "I prepared the blades, but we had information that American occupation army was coming," he said. "I had to go to my relatives to help move things."

As a result of his crusade to have Japan take responsibility, Iawamatsu said, he gets calls at 2 a.m. from angry critics. "I lost all my relatives and friends," he said, but "the war crimes [are] first in my mind."

Though Iawamatsu, a humble, bespectacled man, spoke mildly about the stress of being an outcast for his views, he said acknowledged he had paid a price also in mental health.

"There is great conflict in my mind about atom bomb, loyalty and peace," he said. "I had mental illness from too much thinking of what I should think as a Japanese. I'm not Catholic but I like the idea of 'love thy enemy.' So I try to not have enemies."

The quietly strained life of the professor illustrated Dutch journalist and author Karel van Wolferen's theory that many Japanese, far from being mindless in the face of demands to obey and conform, live in private worlds of the mind, disturbed by social pressures rather than accepting of them.

Japanese society, molded from the cult of the warrior, for hundreds of years defined truth itself as whatever one's emperor, commander or boss said it was. Historically the Chinese revered the scholar, who seeks the ultimate truth. In Japan the soldier, trained to obey, held the top rank.

The professor alluded to Japan's abrupt switch after 1945 from this warrior mentality to equally rabid peaceableness. "Most common people have an idea to love peace," Iawamatsu said. "I don't think we'll go back to militarism. [But] it is not peace-loving born of understanding history."

As Iawamatsu and many Western observers have noted, Japanese society prizes the traits of unquestioning obedience and conformity. Behavior is often determined by one's rank in a situation. With a low crime rate, Japan appears moral in the *petit* sense of following certain rules in certain situations, but some Westerners and Japanese have questioned whether the Japanese practice morality in the grand sense.

"There is no overall idea of doing right on principle," McQueen wrote of Japanese culture. Yet this implication stirred objection from Fumiko Mori Halloran.

"Doesn't the fact that Japan's crimes overall, but particularly such felonies as murder, rape and kidnapping, are far fewer than those in the United States indicate that strong moral codes are at work in Japan?" she wrote in a letter to me. "Christianity teaches 'thou shalt not kill,' yet the murder rate in the U.S. is one of the highest in the world. McQueen's comment that 'there is no overall idea of doing right on principle' can apply to the U.S., too."

She also cited humanitarian measures taken by individual Japanese to help Jews during the Nazi regime as evidence of core principles. The most dramatic act involved a civil servant in Lithuania named Chiune Sugihara (see box at right).

And during the 1990s, Japan began a makeover of the psyche—moving toward becoming a nation of conscience, the first step toward being one of the world's moral as well as economic leaders. Its actions included nearly a dozen public apologies to various nations, revamping its school curriculum, and installing an annex on war atrocities to the Hiroshima Peace Memorial Museum.

Japan says it's sorry

Year	Japan apologizes or "expresses regret" to:
1990	• South Korea, for 1910-45 occupation
1991	• Those harmed by Pearl Harbor
	• Southeast Asia, for World War II
	• North Korea, for 1910-45 occupation
1992	• China, for World War II
	• South Korea (again)
1993	• Everyone, for World War II
	• "Comfort women" (sex slaves kept by Japanese soldiers in World War II)
1994	• Its own people, for failing to warn the United States of Pearl Harbor attack *
	• "Comfort women" again
1995	• Japan's wartime enemies

* This slipup was seen as bringing shame to the Japanese, so the apology is directed to them rather than the United States.

Japan's man of conscience

The reluctance of the Japanese to kill, rape and assault each other at U.S. levels could be ascribed to blind obedience to social codes. But adherence to a morality dictated by conscience might be another explanation. The tale of Chiune (pronounced chee-OO-nee) Sugihara perhaps serves as the strongest illustration of a Japanese taking a noble stance despite great risks.

Sugihara worked at a Japanese consulate in Lithuania. In August 1940 he looked out the window to see dozens of hungry and despondent people. These Jewish refugees from Poland desperately needed transient visas from Japan to ultimately get to Curaçao and Dutch Guiana, Dutch colonies that could serve as safe havens until the end of World War II.

The civil servant looked into the faces of the young yeshiva students among the refugees and then spoke with his own 5-year-old son about their plight. "If we don't help them, won't they die?" the boy asked.

Sugihara signed so many visas, in defiance of orders from Tokyo, that his wife had to massage his hands at night. Solly Ganor, a Holocaust survivor who received a visa, recalled that Sugihara, with sympathy in his eyes, told him, *"Vaya con Dios"* (go with God).

Sugihara's actions stand in profound contrast to U.S. and European temporizing during the butchery of the Nazi death camps. And unlike the more heralded Oskar Schindler's rescue of about 1,000 Jews, Sugihara was not motivated by economic profit. In fact, he ultimately lost his job.

The Holocaust memorial group Yad Vashem has designated Sugihara a "Righteous Gentile" for saving 10,000 lives. In 1994, Israeli officials began to seek funding for a Sugihara Life Science Research Centre at Ben-Gurion University, which would have a bioethics focus.

LESSON NUMBER 10: ANALYSTS OF THE ALTRUISTIC PERSONALITY FIND THAT ACTS OF COURAGE, SUCH AS HELPING THE PERSECUTED JEWS, GENERALLY DO NOT ARISE AS LONE ACTS OF SPONTANEITY BUT FROM STANDARDS OF BEHAVIOR SET BY RELATIVES, FRIENDS AND THE COMMUNITY—ESPECIALLY THOSE SET BY ONE'S PARENTS.

This observation would support a conclusion that the Japanese can act based on overarching moral beliefs imbedded in their culture.

Sugihara himself ascribed his acts to a conviction that despite the Foreign Ministry's objections, his ultimate loyalty was to the emperor. And he was convinced that the emperor, the model for his nation's conduct, would have acted in the same circumstances to save Jewish lives.

One has to be cautious in in assessing Japanese pro-peace attitudes, however, given a certain faddishness in the national character—where everyone seems to all at once take up golf, be a fan of actor Richard Gere or switch from shelties to golden retrievers, as began to happen in the mid-1990s.

In the United States, a controversy in 1994 at the Smithsonian's Air and Space Museum in Washington, D.C., provoked distress in veterans closely comparable to ours upon visiting the Hiroshima museum. Written materials planned for an exhibit of the fuselage of the Enola Gay, the plane that bombed Hiroshima, focused on the suffering of the bomb victims and not Japanese aggression. Protests by veterans and historians ultimately forced the museum's officials to display the fuselage without the disputed additional materials.

As Fumiko Mori Halloran wrote, "Americans and Japanese never seem to be able to discuss World War II on the same psychological level."

Citing the American emphasis on Pearl Harbor and the Japanese feeling of victimhood after Hiroshima, she concluded, "I often feel these kinds of arguments are futile, since both sides are frustrated because the other party seems not to listen or understand."

As the legacy of slavery haunts the modern Americas and Africa, World War II burdens the United States and Japan. Yet perhaps the Enola Gay controversy marked the last paroxysm from the lingering poisons of World War II.

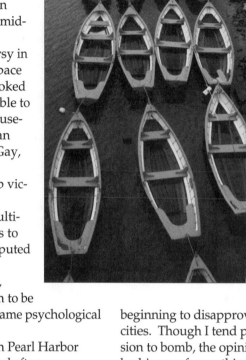

Modern Hiroshima preserves war memories (above, a bank near the bomb epicenter) yet enjoys scenes of great peacefulness (left, boats moored near the ruin).

Earnings for the film *Schindler's List*

SELECTED NATIONS

	GROSS EARNINGS	PER CAPITA EARNINGS
United States	$96.1 million	$.37
Germany	41.2 million	.50
Japan	**40.3 million**	**.32**
Italy	14.2 million	.25
Austria	4.2 million	.52
Poland	2.2 million	.06

Based on data prepared by the Exhibitor Relations Co. in Los Angeles and the 1995 World Population Data Sheet

In 1994 the film *Schindler's List* dominated the box office in Japan, as it had a year earlier in the United States. The sizable audience for *Schindler's List* serves as a cultural signpost to Japan's willingness to explore the pain of World War II.

And an opinion poll showed younger Americans beginning to disapprove of the bombing of Japanese cities. Though I tend personally to agree with the decision to bomb, the opinion shift may serve as an indirect harbinger of something positive: better relations between Americans and Japanese.

U.S. views on bombing of Japanese cities

	APPROVE	DISAPPROVE
July 1995	59%	35%
1945	85	10

1995, BY AGE

	APPROVE	DISAPPROVE
18-29 years	46%	49%
30-49 years	51	43
50-64 years	72	24
65 & older	80	13

Based on a poll reported in August 1995 by *The Gallup Monthly*

Maybe now that the psychic resonance stirred by the 50th anniversaries of Pearl Harbor and Hiroshima has dissipated, both nations can move past acrimony. In 1991, at Pearl Harbor five decades after the Japanese attack, President George Bush said, "I have no rancor in my heart toward Germany or Japan—none at all. I hope you have none in yours. World War II is over. It is history." The words' significance took on added impact coming from a man who had been shot down in 1944 by the Japanese.

For ourselves, we knew firsthand of Japan's humanitarian impulses, from the way Katsukini Tanaka extended himself to assist our colleague Dawn in her distress. And as much as the U.S.-style openness of the Chinese appealed to me, one had to credit the

Japanese with holding higher public standards of courtesy toward strangers, a foreign concept to Chinese people on public transportation.

LESSON NUMBER 11: IF A GOLDEN MEAN EXISTS SOMEWHERE BETWEEN U.S. INDIVIDUALISM AND CREATIVITY AND JAPANESE RESPECT FOR THE LIVES OF OTHERS, PERHAPS TODAY IT LIES FAR CLOSER TO JAPAN.

Japan and the big lesson: formal societies

A small incident during our trip shed light on a facet of most Asian cultures: the distaste for confrontation and the desire for group harmony.

Three members of our group took a Japanese official out to dinner. We went to a traditional restaurant, where we left our shoes at the door and donned slippers. In a private room enclosed by shoji sliding doors, we sat on tatami mats.

The surroundings subtly suggested we turn to light dinnertime conversation. But as though at a White House press conference, my colleagues, wearing sternly critical expressions, doggedly questioned our guest about the question of war crimes. He began to smile edgily, a sure sign in many Asian contexts of discomfort.

His smile illustrated how formal societies communicate indirectly. It was a subtle signal of unease rather than a forceful attempt to change the subject.

My colleagues' faux pas left me, as an American journalist who had lived in Britain, stranded between two worlds. While I appreciated my colleagues' aggressiveness—so apropos to many situations in journalism that demand the asking of tough questions—I equally understood the Japanese official's unease.

Later I explained my awkward feeling to one of the interrogators, a talented journalist. "I learned when living in England that you just can't corner people with a million questions," I said. "You need to spend years discussing pets and daffodils and flower arranging and the weather before you even dream of discussing politics and controversy."

She brushed off my concerns. "We don't have any time," she replied. "We just have these few hours to talk to him."

Her point was obviously valid. Still, I felt that a confrontational style had never borne any fruit in England. Similarly, at our dinner in Japan, the official communicated little except his unease.

In my final days in England, British friends unburdened themselves of many confidences and expressions of fondness, feeling free to reveal themselves only because I was leaving. Actor Richard Chamberlain reported an identical experience on his last day in Japan after filming *Shogun*.

In a formal society, personal views will be volunteered only when friends or acquaintances feel like it. The less information you seek, the more you will gain. And some things will not be spoken of unless you are leaving for good.

The search for an explanation for the customs of formal societies, such as subtle discourse, begins with examining their shared antiquity. Japan and Britain, pupils of the more ancient empires of China and Rome, themselves now number among the oldest nations on Earth.

Both Japan and Britain are also island nations. Most continental nations, including the United States, Canada, Brazil and Australia, are generally:
- younger
- more democratic
- less homogeneous
- and more roughly frontier-like in spirit.

That's four strikes against evolving a sophisticated palace tradition and having its traditions trickle down to courtiers and the merchant and academic classes. And because Japan and Britain are also societies more conscious of rank, etiquette arose to preserve modes of behavior that would enforce class boundaries.

During the eras of Roman and Chinese domination, insular Japan and Britain sat as remote outriders to giant continental powers: dark outposts, "here be dragons" spots on the map. In the 16th century, "Geography gave a prime strategic asset to the Japanese (as it did to the British), for insularity offered a protection from overland invasion which China did not possess," wrote Paul Kennedy in *The Rise and Fall of the Great Powers*.

The settlement and economic ascendance of the Americas, however, thrust Britain and later Japan from backwater to beautifully situated trading crossroads, conveniently located between the United States and each side of the mass of Eurasia.

Tom Wicker compared Britain and the United States in *On Press*. His description of Britain could also apply to Japan:

> a society that derives from monarchy, aristocracy, primogeniture, and class privilege does not have the tradition of bumptious personal liberty that marks a people descended from those who came to a frontier land to escape kings, lords, and caste. And an embattled island long ago came to accept certain government and military exigencies that have been regarded as excessive in a continental and mostly unthreatened land.

You'd need an overwhelming force to be a hostile invader of Topeka, Winnipeg, Manaus, Wuhan or Alice Springs. The secure, "What, me worry?" attitude of continental nations creates loud, direct go-getters, informal to varying degrees.

Lesson Number 12: Geography bestows innate security upon continental nations, which combined with the frontier mentality leads to great casualness of manners.

An island nation needs to watch its step a bit more. So we see code words, indirect phraseology, poor map-making, secrecy laws, a lack of precise data and vague directions. Britain may be a worse offender than Japan in this regard. Upon moving there in 1981, I soon noticed the dearth of charts and statistics accompanying articles in the national press. (Despite Japan being an insular nation, the tables at the Foreign Press Center in Tokyo groaned with stacks of free booklets in English. These explained and measured almost every aspect of Japanese life, from manufacturing trends to the status of women and the increased focus on leisure.)

And Britain's confusing telephone numbers prompted me to complain to my father. In the United States, we always have a seven-digit telephone number and a three-digit area code. In Britain the telephone number could be anywhere from three to seven digits. The "dialing code" prefix could be two to six digits and might vary depending on where the call was placed.

My father observed that any nation that had been bombed by Germany would think twice about having a telephone communications system that a potential invader could figure out.

Britain surely leads the world in misdialed calls. No wonder the Brits answer the phone by reciting their phone number rather than saying "hello." As for the Japanese, they prefer their incomprehensibility in the realm of street names and address numbers.

In Japan, only major avenues have names. Most addresses are based on a district, starting with the smallest, a chome, and graduating upward:

chome	a few blocks
cho, machi	more blocks
ku	ward
hi	city
gun	county
ken	prefecture

Within the chome, buildings have a number that may be based on the age of the building rather than the sequence of structures on a block. The system is particularly confusing in comparison to the quadrants that demarcate U.S. cities such as Washington and Baltimore into northeast, northwest, southeast and southwest, and the street numbers that follow a pattern of 10 blocks to a mile, consistent not just within city boundaries but often for 30 miles into the suburbs. Obviously Baltimore fears a Chinese invasion less than Tokyo does.

Despite improvements in the last 20 years, "visitors to Japan should know from the outset that it is almost impossible to find a place just from the address; even Japanese find it very difficult," McQueen wrote. "So don't get upset and berate [a taxi] driver if he takes a long time and has to stop at one or more police boxes to get you to your destination. This is simply standard operating procedure."

The parallels between Japan and Britain are far from perfect. Britain treasures a tradition of amateurism and muddling through. Its people harbor a suspicion of anything done too well or slickly. Paul Theroux observed in *The Kingdom by the Sea* that the English "would be deeply dismissive and self-critical. "We're awful," they said. "This country is hopeless. We're never prepared for anything. Nothing works properly.""

The Japanese share British humility but, in a country where competence is expected, have less cause for reproaching themselves. Dave Barry described the Japanese

with their booming economy and their high literacy rate and their low crime rate and their tourists showing up all over the world wearing designer clothes that we can't afford and spending bales of money in exclusive stores that we don't even dare walk into.

There remains the most underappreciated link between Britain and Japan, and the United States as well: the popularity among the cognoscenti of the Shetland sheepdog.

When we all tire of squabbling about World War II or trade disputes, maybe we can rally to an agreement on the fun of owning a vocal and energetic dog with a personality adaptable to three wildly divergent national characters.

Lesson Number 13: If shelties can decode both formal and casual societies, perhaps humans can as well.

A sheltie puzzle manufactured in Japan.

WATERWORLDS OF THE GREAT NAVIGATORS

Polynesia ... and lessons on why culture survives

Sea cliffs rise above the Pacific on the Hawaiian island of Kauai's Na Pali coast.

Silvery ocean and clouds stretch for 8,000 miles and nearly 15 flying hours from Sydney to Los Angeles. Saltwater air billows around an airplane's skin during these long hauls. Over time the corrosion of the oceanic atmosphere combined with frequent takeoffs and landings can turn metal to powder, as when the roof peeled off an aging Aloha Airlines jet flying near Maui in April 1988.

Given the size of the Pacific, the Earth's largest single geological feature, it is no wonder airplane skins decay. No wonder world atlases struggle to map the Pacific. Water comprises 98 percent of its area, and islands only 2 percent. The high desert state of Utah contains more water (3 percent) than the Pacific contains land.

Explorers also have confronted the Pacific's vastness. Magellan's transit underlined how scattered and tiny its islands are. After rounding Cape Horn and entering the Pacific on Nov. 28, 1520, his crew encountered only a few reefs before sighting Guam on March 6, 1521, after 99 days of increasing thirst and hunger.

Yet somehow, more than 3,000 years before Magellan, Austronesian seafarers from Borneo or another part of Southeast Asia began to find the Pacific's tiny specks of land. They happened upon virtually every island and settled the habitable ones. In the process, they formed a new culture, evolving into Polynesians, the most dispersed people in the world.

FRIDAY, MAY 24, 1985
An ocean as trackless as the desert

My own marathon trajectory of the Pacific involved flying from Australia to Tahiti. As with my other trips, a simple trip goal—exploring a famed tropical paradise—spurred me to visit French Polynesia, which consists of Tahiti and 129 less famous islands. And as before, my lowbrow search for beautiful beaches would lead to lessons on how navigators from Asia and Europe converged on the Pacific, and to what extent Polynesian culture lived on in Tahiti and Hawaii.

Our approach to Tahiti, after hours of impressively empty oceanscapes, revealed a mountainous island with a cloud cap. Palms grew thickly along the shore. The airplane landed at Faaa (fah-AH-ah) International Airport, south of the capital, Papeete (Pah-pay-AYE-tay). The Tahitian language features the vowel-oriented sound of Austronesian, and the islands themselves relate as easterly cousins to the Indonesian archipelago.

At dusk, I watched the sun set behind the gray French battleships in Papeete's harbor. For 40 minutes, a display of molten gold and crimson lit the sky behind neighbor island Moorea, all but hidden in a mammoth blue-violet cloud. In the incongruous setting of the wharf parking lot, I ate a gourmet dinner costing $6 beside a parked van with an awning over a picnic table for patrons. Out of these vans emerged grilled French and stir-fried Chinese meals and dessert crêpes. My charcoal-broiled steak, with *salade verte*, Coke and French bread, arrived very tender.

This meal assembled in a van kitchen handily surpassed anything from my preceding two weeks in Australia. A nation of macho beer-drinkers, the land its natives call Oz had disrupted the steady procession of feminine Southeast Asian and Pacific cultures of my 100-day regional tour. Australia had seemed the regional anomaly, a crushed beer can strung jarringly in a bracelet of little pink shells.

Buoyed by feeling back in a tropical near-Asia, I took an after-dinner stroll around Papeete, visiting the central market to look at the displays of tuna and parrotfish on ice. The people seemed quite striking. The women still wore flowers in their hair, as depicted in the paintings of Paul Gauguin.

Tahiti felt to me like Bali East, though its darkly handsome people stood taller and often much wider. Perhaps a diet of fish and taro root created more imposing adults than one of rice; perhaps surviving open voyages of thousands of miles required a hefty build.

Unsurpassed aerial views

The most beautiful flights in the world may be those connecting the Tahitian islands. Our propeller plane from Papeete provided fabulous views as dusk fell on the volcanic folds, looking as soft as green pool-table baize, of Huahine and Raiatea, on the way to my destination, Bora Bora.

We landed in the dark on a motu, a sizable coral island on Bora Bora's outer barrier reef. The airstrip had been built in 1942 by the United States to send World War II supplies to the front lines. But this island of former warriors never saw any 20th century military action. Now only a few cruise ships call in each year on the island of 3,700 residents.

A boat ferried us to the main island. The two peaks of Bora Bora rose as dark outlines, magnificent even in silhouette.

Most visitors to Bora Bora stay at the Hotel Bora Bora, Club Med or another luxury place overlooking the lagoon. With a budget closer to $30 than $300 per day, I tromped in the dark from the boat dock south on the main road and landed instead at a pension called Chez Fredo. A path past a depot of parked buses led to initially suspicious stares from the Doom family, odd behavior for a group of pension-keepers.

Mama Doom eventually bestirred herself to show me a room in an adjoining bungalow. My bedroom smelled a bit dank, and a communal kitchen serving several rooms for rent seemed moldy.

But I would get a real taste of life with people who lived on a Pacific island, enveloping humidity and all. And from the first night, through the rear window of the bedroom, I could view the shadowy bulk of Bora Bora's mountain peaks, to be stunning under a full moon a week later.

Beauty worth applauding

Most guidebooks mention the magnificent chorales at church services in Polynesia. Curious to see this, I walked up the main road to a Roman Catholic church in the village of Vaitape. At a 90-minute Mass celebrating Pentecost Sunday, a huge Tahitian choirmaster in an orange floral print shirt led the men and women in call-and-response singing. The congregants in their embroidered white shirts and dresses sang like angels, bringing tears to my eyes.

The church windows opened out on a vision of loveliness, the sun streaming on the steep slopes behind the building. Three Chinese girls made paper hats out of the song sheets.

The priest conducted the Mass in both French and Tahitian, the latter for the Gloria:

Ei hanahana i te Atua i te rai tetei.

A bird takes flight at Poofai Bay.

LESSON NUMBER 1: THE CHURCH SERVICE GAVE THE FIRST INDICATION THAT THE TAHITIAN LANGUAGE, AND THEREFORE ITS CULTURE, LIVED ON THE OUTER ISLANDS.

As in childhood, when I studied the Catholic missalette, a small guide containing readings and responses for each week's Sunday Mass, to compare the Greek and Latin words to the English translations, I read over the one-page program to try to learn a few words of Tahitian.

The sign of peace, the part of the service when Catholics turn to each other and say "peace be with you," took some minutes. People wandered around the church, turning the Mass into a social hour. The priest, the assistant and the altar boys shook hands with everyone.

Back at Chez Fredo, I rented a bike from Mama. As I cycled south past little Poofai Bay, two gray egrets posed like statues. A sunken, gray-metal ship looked more picturesque than derelict. Bora Bora seemed to have the powers of alchemy, transmuting wreckage into beauty.

The south end of Bora Bora sharpens into a tip called Matira Point. Its beach of talcum sand, rated one of the world's best, adjoined a luminous, lime-colored lagoon. At the Matira Hotel, I ate delicious sweet-and-sour duck with the triple influence of French, Chinese and Polynesian cuisines. Afterward, I strolled the powdery sand, marveling at the delicate tints of Tahitian water, as pretty up close as they had been from the air.

That night a half moon lay on its back, reflecting off Bora Bora's 2,300-foot main peak, Mount Otemanu. On viewing the island's beauty, the original inhabitants applauded as a tribute to God's masterwork and named it Pura Pura, which meant "hands clapping." The name gradually evolved to its present form. Writer James Michener seconded the Tahitians' opinion when he called Bora Bora the most beautiful island in the world.

LESSON NUMBER 2: RARELY DO ISLANDS COMBINE SUPERLATIVE BEACHES AND MOUNTAIN SCENERY. BY HAVING THE BEST OF BOTH, BORA BORA SEEMS TO BE A RARE FIND.

Palms wave on Bora Bora, perhaps the world's most beautiful island.

MONDAY, MAY 27-TUESDAY, MAY 28
A parade of friendly lagoon fish

On Monday, Tahitian guide from one of the big hotels introduced a group of us to various lagoon residents on an underwater snorkeling safari.

The guide rapped on the base of a coral head, and a moray eel emerged from its little cave. The moray's fat head, as big as a cat's, a brown color spotted with white, appeared at first utterly menacing and serpent-like. The guide gently stroked the eel under the chin, however, and it appeared to smile and gulp repeatedly.

The guide picked a clam off the lagoon bed, slipped a knife through its hinged base to sever its muscle and opened the shell. He fed the clam meat to the moray.

I had never seen this done before, despite extensive snorkeling in Malaysia and Indonesia. I latched onto the practice and fed the longnose butterfly fish, which arrived in droves. About 100 of the creatures, a sun-gold shade of yellow with pointy black noses like those of tiny swordfish, pecked at my fingers with their sharp teeth.

During the week I spotted most of the varieties, including boxfish, imperators and goatfish, depicted on my *Great Barrier Reef Fishwatcher's Field Guide*, a plastic card also valid for the tropical Pacific that hung from my wrist on a rubber band. One diver said that 3,000 types of fish live in the lagoon.

On Tuesday, I joined a boat trip for a shark rodeo, sponsored by the Club Med. Our boat motored out near Bora Bora's outer reef, and the crew began tossing out pieces of fish. Soon eight sharks, as best I could count them, roiled the water. Our two guides attempted to lasso one to bring on board for photographs but repeatedly missed. The entire encounter was quite

staged for tourists and at odds with the more natural encounters one can have swimming with sharks.

That night I talked with Mama's son, a man of saturnine slowness and size named Fredo Doom, who ran the island bus company. Fredo issued an invitation to a more authentic lagoon experience.

"Saturday," he began. He paused for what felt like a count of 10. "Want to go spearfishing?"

Yes, of course, I replied instantly.

LESSON NUMBER 3: ONE STAYS AT A $7 PER NIGHT PLACE NOT ONLY BECAUSE IT IS CHEAP, BUT BECAUSE FAMILY-RUN ACCOMMODATION OFFERS INSIGHTS INTO LOCAL LIVES.

WEDNESDAY, MAY 29
Views from a bicycle

I cycled the 20-mile coast road counterclockwise. A rolling wave of crabs scuttled noisily into roadside holes as I rode by. Little red-brown birds hopped about.

Rain came and went, minor rivers washed momentarily over the road, and a rainbow formed. Coconuts bobbed in the lagoon.

On the eastern side of the island, away from the hotels, the locals seemed friendlier. Some smiled and greeted me with "*bonjour*." A good number jogged. One man cycled past, wearing a colorful shirt advertising Gitane, the brand of his racing bike.

The paved road became gravel on the eastern edge and northern tip of the island. I noticed the rough wood and corrugated iron construction of many local houses. Dwellers in humid latitudes that endure the occasional stray typhoon clearly do not—and should not bother to—keep Martha Stewart levels of home decor.

LESSON NUMBER 4: THE APPEARANCE OF THE BORA BORANS' HOMES DID NOT NECESSARILY INDICATE POVERTY. THAT THE TAHITIANS, UNLIKE MANY HAWAIIAN POLYNESIANS, EVEN OWNED LAND AND HOUSES (AS WELL AS BUSINESSES AND BOATS) INDICATED ECONOMIC STRENGTH.

With a smile, an old woman sold me some bananas

at a roadside stall. I continued past what looked like unusually long metal mailboxes—actually designed for daily deliveries of baguettes, the long sticks of French bread.

A coconut grove looked out on the beautiful neighboring island of Raiatea. Some scholars believe that Raiatea may be a place called Havaiki, the spiritual motherland of Polynesians and the namesake of Hawaii.

Condos marched up a scarred hillside at the north end of Bora Bora, testament to a Hyatt construction that ultimately foundered. In their own way, the abandoned condos seemed as remarkable archaeologically as the *heiaus* and *marae* (open-air temples constructed on stone platforms, some with upright pillars) of Polynesia. The weathering structures gave the first sign of the impending tourism bust to hit French Polynesia in the late 1980s.

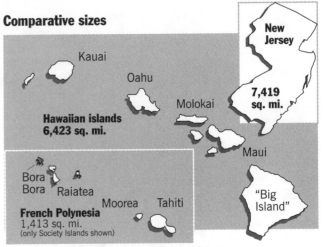

Comparative sizes

New Jersey
7,419 sq. mi.

Kauai
Oahu
Molokai
Maui
"Big Island"

Hawaiian islands
6,423 sq. mi.

Bora Bora
Raiatea
Moorea
Tahiti

French Polynesia
1,413 sq. mi.
(only Society Islands shown)

Based on data from *The World Almanac 1996* and *The World Factbook*

A box permits roadside deliveries of French bread.

Despite the rainy weather, the circuit only took three hours. My pokey bicycle ride around Bora Bora illustrated the cramped scale, compared to Hawaii, of the islands of French Polynesia. (The water between the islands, however, covers an area as great as Europe without Russia.)

How the Tahitian discoverers of the Big Island of Hawaii must have marveled at its relatively vast size. The voyagers had found territory to spread out in: the Pacific equivalent of a Plymouth Rock without the Indians.

That evening, Fredo took me along as he bused a local dance troupe to its engagement at the Hotel Bora Bora. The dancers, from the village of Nunue, performed in the hotel's spacious bar. Some of the little girls, bedecked in flowers, danced uncertainly, while the better dancers could hip-shake with skill.

Clearly those with lesser talents had not been bounced from the group. Presumably they could improve given time, and even if they didn't, their tolerant comrades did not seem concerned.

A man from Hawaii watching the show leaned over to me and said, "You'll see much better shows in Waikiki, but they won't have the charm of this one."

Nunue dancers perform.

FRIDAY, MAY 31
A scrivener's tale

In the morning, Mama enlisted me to respond in English to letters, some several months old, from friends in the United States.

As I wrote, Mama told me about her five children, spread over France, Tahiti and Bora Bora. One daughter, whom she apparently didn't approve of, had had four babies and left them with Mama. "My husband no like because they take too much of my time," she said.

She also talked about herself. She said she was Hakka Chinese and Tahitian, and spoke those languages and French and English as well.

Her son Fredo may have been the South Pacific's most impassive person, his broad face revealing nothing. A family album showed the stolid islander posed between widely grinning Western couples.

Yet, perhaps unintentionally, Fredo still exhibited a certain drollness. He told me one story concerning a pest problem at Chez Fredo:

"Hear something. In bathroom. Me put trap. Five minutes. Crack." (Long pause.) "Five minutes … crack. Eight. Rats."

His tale struck me as a lulu, considering that after all he was a pension keeper addressing a guest.

That afternoon, a fisherman in a station wagon rode along the coast road, calling out that he had fish for sale. In return for my help with the letters, Mama bought me a present, a bonito tuna for $3. In the evening, we grilled it over coconut husks, and it turned out quite well.

We assembled a feast to go with the tuna: a salad, bread, haricots from Mama and white wine provided by Nancy, a Quebeçois who had arrived at Chez Fredo.

SATURDAY, JUNE 1
Fishing with Fredo

Our fishing trip got underway at 10 a.m., after many delays in finding a working engine. Fredo, as round as a planet (many Polynesians run to hugeness after age 30), got in. The small motorboat tipped precariously. Its bow rose in the air at a sharp angle, and the stern seemed in imminent danger of swamping. Fredo directed Nancy, me and Jean, a much smaller man who assisted him in his bus business, to the tip of the bow to act as counterweights.

> Polynesian settlement required long ocean voyages into prevailing trade winds and unknown waters. The sailors on these early voyages of indeterminate length and unclear destinations may have experienced a significant risk of starvation and death when on-board food supplies dwindled and ceased. Overweight individuals and/or those with efficient metabolisms ... may have better survived such voyages because of their large store of energy reserves in the form of adipose tissue.

Stephen T. McGarvey in "Obesity in Samoans and a perspective on its etiology in Polynesians"

Fredo's weight testified to his quality genes, which had helped Polynesians for 3,000 years to withstand the cold and hunger of ocean voyaging and the periodic cyclones that wiped out island crops.

These same genes, in the modern era, mean that Polynesians have recorded the greatest increase in body fat of any of the world's traditional people who have adapted to urban living and a diet of snack foods.

Polynesian NFL players, 1995

SOME MODERN POLYNESIANS HAVE MADE A NAME FOR THEMSELVES AS NATIONAL FOOTBALL LEAGUE PLAYERS.

	TEAM	ANCESTRAL ISLAND
Junior Seau	San Diego Chargers	Samoa
Jesse Sapolu	San Francisco 49ers	Samoa
Dan Saleaumua	Kansas City Chiefs	Samoa
Alfred Popunu	San Diego Chargers	Tonga
Alai Kalaniuvalu	Philadelphia Eagles	Tonga
Siupeli Malamala	New York Jets	Tonga
Vai Sikahema *	Philadelphia Eagles	Tonga
Kurt Gouveia	San Diego Chargers	Hawaii
Mark Tuinei	Dallas Cowboys	Hawaii

* Retired, now a newscaster

Based on published reports and information from individual teams

When big Fredo first jumped in the water, he looked comical. A diving weight cinched deep into his

---

Living on easy street

For dessert one night, Mama picked some bananas hanging from a tree in front of her house. Her effortless contribution to our meal illustrated that Tahiti still manifested some evidence of the easy life—a subject that has stirred controversy for two centuries.

LESSON NUMBER 5: THE MEETING OF THE GREAT EUROPEAN AND PACIFIC NAVIGATORS IN THE LATE 1700S POSED A CHALLENGE TO EUROPEAN BELIEFS IN THE CENTRALITY OF WORK TO EVERYDAY LIFE.

Calvinism and the Protestant work ethic, which hold that moral virtue is to be found in industry and hard work, prevailed in Europe prior to the time of Cook's voyages. A challenge arose to this view from French philosopher Jean Jacques Rousseau. He wrote in 1751 in *Discourse on the Origin of Inequality Among Mankind* that industrialization,

private plots of land and other features of society enslaved man rather than freed him and that the primitive state is morally better.

In *Voyages of Discovery: Captain Cook and the Exploration of the Pacific*, author Lynne Withey described how Cook, with "convenient timing," turned up the Tahitians in 1769 as candidates "to make Rousseau's point about the virtues of a simple life."

For Europeans in general, a society so devoted to pleasure, where work was scarcely necessary, raised profound moral questions. In some ways the fact that the Tahitians could devote most of their time to play and still live comfortably was even more disturbing than their sexual license. As Banks explained, a Tahitian who planted ten breadfruit trees, a task requiring about an hour's labor, did as much for his family's food supply as an English farmer who labored the year round planting and harvesting crops.

Since the time of Rousseau, the people of Polynesia and, to an extent, Bali, have epitomized the appeal of the simple life. Modern economies based on military spending and tourism have radically altered life on Hawaii and Tahiti, and a 10-fold increase in numbers of visitors has also changed Bali considerably.

The people I have seen that most maintain the simple life in the modern day live not in a tropical paradise but in Burma. Its people extol the virtue of a simple and non-material existence, illustrating that the way the human mind views the world—in this case, through the prism of Buddhism—rather than the physical environment is key to attaining the Rousseau ideal.

Today, many Baby Boomers plan for the best of both worlds: subscribing to the work ethic to make money early in the careers, with a view toward retiring early to enjoy family and perhaps the tropics. Perhaps it makes sense to start life as a Calvinist and end up as a Polynesian—or to hold a Buddhist outlook throughout.

jiggly middle almost cut him in half. But he moved with enormous grace.

We snorkeled near Teveiro, a motu northwest of Bora Bora. Some flute-mouths and a pair of huge brown and white angelfish glided about.

On that beautiful day, we looked up from swimming to see the incomparable Mount Otemanu. The toppled pyramid of its angular peak resembled a jungle miniature of the Matterhorn, green and knobby where the Alps would be flinty and snowcapped.

A view of Mount Otemanu from Fredo's boat.

We moved to another spot, where a giant brown coral head, the size of a van, offered over-hangs for dozens of fish to hide under. I came across a moray eel and studied it for a while as Fredo, his huge-ness and ease in water suggesting a manatee, suspend-ed himself about 15 feet underwater. His head moved slowly side to side as he surveyed the coral's little bios-phere.

Next we swam in six to eight feet of water over a sandy-bottomed area to try our hand at spearfishing. Fredo had constructed a homemade spear-gun, sharp-ening a bar to make a harpoon and setting it into a wooden stock with a trigger. The bar bore the rust of hours upon hours in saltwater. It looked like we would keel over, dead of tetanus, were it to nick us.

I stalked a group of black tangs that swam warily about two yards ahead of me. For the first and last time in my life, I felt the adrenaline surge of hunting. With my first shot, I got one of the tangs, right through the center of its body. The second shot scored a second bull's-eye. I preened with pride at this minor accom-plishment and felt myself an honorary Polynesian.

As our foursome swam along, Jean and I dragged 10 or so speared fish strung by the gills on a piece of rope. A little crosspiece of wood acted as a stopper.

Jean and I snorkeled in shallow water. Suddenly he gestured behind us. I looked back to see a small reef shark swimming a discreet distance away. Jean sur-faced, muttering *"requin"* (shark). He chucked a piece of coral at the shark, and it disappeared like a chas-tened stray dog.

Later that night I made certain to clean my two tangs and eat the little scraps of flesh that could be got-ten from them. I could only justify killing the fish if I ate them, though they were barely worth the effort.

SUNDAY, JUNE 2
Goodbyes and moist eyes

June 2 marked Mother's Day in Tahiti, and to cele-brate, Mama made barbecued chicken and delicious *poisson cru*, the Tahitian version of raw fish essentially "cooked" by the acidic action of lime juice.

Chez Fredo had been the longest stay in one place of my 100-day Singapore Swing from Hong Kong to Los Angeles. As I prepared to leave, Fredo carefully wrote his full name, which sounded like it could belong to a protagonist in a bodice ripper …

Alfred Noel Doom

… and his address in my notebook. To repay him for his hospitality, I pledged to send two 90-minute cassette tapes with new reggae or country music. In his slow and implacable way, Fredo requested that I use registered mail and also send a separate letter detailing what the cassettes contained and what day they were sent. He implied that otherwise a postal worker somewhere between the United States and Bora Bora would intercept the rasta vibration.

Nancy, Mama and Fredo gave me a big send-off. For the first time in my travels, attachment to a place outweighed eagerness to see more. I wiped away a tear as I boarded the ferry back to the airstrip.

A domestic flight took me the 250 miles from Bora Bora to Rangiroa. By happenstance, shortly before my trip I had read of Rangiroa at a library in Guildford, England. I picked up a travel book, *Across the South Pacific: Island-hopping from Santiago to Sydney*, in which Iain Finlay and Trish Sheppard told of taking their two children to explore Polynesia, largely by inter-island packets. Their book described Rangiroa as a premier spot to swim safely with sharks.

Ancient Rangiroa, a very different type of island than Bora Bora, is an atoll—a coral necklace 42 miles long and 14 miles in diameter. Its sands rise only a few yards above the open sea and enclose a vast lagoon.

The far side of the lagoon, where the atoll was uninhabited, could not be seen even from our bird's-eye view as we descended to 1,000 feet. You could fit much of Oahu, the Hawaiian island where Honolulu is located, in the lagoon of Rangiroa.

Bombs away on Mururoa

Polynesia has rarely appeared on the modern world stage in the half-century after Pearl Harbor. Examine an index on the region, and sporadic mention will be made of three thoroughly unrelated names: a near-saint (Father Damien, who cared for the lepers of Molokai in Hawaii), a perverted artist (Gauguin) and an eccentric actor and his troubled family (Marlon Brando).

The invisibility of this part of the South Pacific ended in September 1995, when French President Jacques Chirac ordered the resumption of nuclear tests suspended by predecessor François Mitterrand. Three decades of sputtering concern over explosions at Mururoa, an atoll in the Tuamotus 800 miles southeast of Tahiti, achieved critical mass.

Algeria's independence in 1962 deprived France of its nuclear test sites there and set the stage for the testing in Polynesia. The French government constructed Faaa airport in Tahiti not to boost visits by sunseekers, but to prepare for the testing, which began in 1966 on two out-islands: Mururoa and Fangataufa.

William E. Tagupa wrote in "France, French Polynesia, and the South Pacific in the Nuclear Age" that the decision to test in French Polynesia created a debate over three points:

(1) the effects of radioactivity upon the biota and human population of the territory; (2) the political morality of conducting such tests without consulting public officials or conducting a public referendum in the territory; (3) the socio-economic effects resulting from the mass influx of civilian and military personnel and the migration of rural population into the urban area.

With the islands' conversion from agriculture and fishing to military work, prices rose sharply. Many people moved from the already thinly populated outer islands to shantytowns in Papeete. Today 70 percent of the population of French Polynesia lives on Tahiti.

The *British Medical Journal* reported that French scientists conducted 44 atmospheric tests up to 1976, thereafter switching to explosions in underwater shafts for an additional 110 tests. The testing was designed to predict the performance of warheads for submarine missiles.

In symmetry worthy of fiction, the resumption of tests on Sept. 5, 1995, led an anti-French mob to destroy Faaa airport over the next two days. Political protests also exploded worldwide. Demonstrators took to the streets of Britain over perhaps the most colonial act of the contemporary world. The French consulate in Perth, Australia, was firebombed.

Japanese Science Minister Makiko Tanaka suggested that France ought to consider conducting nuclear tests in the Paris suburbs rather than in the South Pacific. Australia, New Zealand, Chile and smaller Pacific island nations also vociferously opposed the tests. They feared that radioactive plutonium, cesium and strontium would leak into the environment, affecting fish and ultimately humans.

Champagne and wine sales plunged. A French restaurant in Auckland, New Zealand, had to change its theme. Even a large majority of the French opposed the blasts.

Finally, on Jan. 29, 1996, the French government announced a permanent end to the program.

I messaged my father to get the view of a nuclear physicist on the testing in Polynesia. He replied via the Internet:

Testing is the lesser or greater of two evils when it comes to weapons. The prizes and honors in science go to the new and unexpected, and an unintended test result can result in a great deal of excitement within the scientific community and some puzzlement in the outside world about a test that apparently did not meet its objectives.

To anybody who might have to use a device, and has to be darn certain it will work as intended, testing is regarded as essential. Engineers think that way. Politicians get testy when military men promise a result that does not compute in actual practice, and they in turn get real nasty with the engineers.

As for the fish, they are usually disturbed negatively initially but in past testing they bounce back even stronger. I shall not comment on the recovery of Japan, even though it is tempting.

Protesting the testing of weapons is not aimed at the engineers or the military, but at the political decision to have such weapons in a usable state in the first place.

My attitude has been and will continue to be that there are no winners in warfare (basically a political activity) but that losers appear to me to have the harder time of it. France has been a loser twice in this century and may feel that is sufficient for a while.

Chew on the above and let me know if you feel otherwise.
Love, Dad

Targets of nuclear bombs can indeed recover over time, as shown by my excursion in 1991 to Hiroshima, a place that marks its tragic past each August yet at the same time displays great vibrancy.

And in 1995, *National Geographic* reported on a return visit to Bikini Atoll, 2,520 miles southwest of Honolulu. In 1954, scientists set off an explosion there 1,000 times more forceful than the bomb dropped on Hiroshima.

The island remains too radioactive for the return of its 167 original residents, but sea life has returned. Experts concluded that the atoll has healed after decades of exchange of lagoon and ocean waters.

On Mururoa, the jury remains out on the health of former site workers and their families. In 1995, visitors from *Médecins Sans Frontières* (Doctors Without Borders) reported encountering a wall of non-information on radiation-related diseases as they made the official rounds in Papeete.

And physicians writing in the *British Medical Journal* noted rumors of handicaps, birth defects and thyroid cancers.

The authors also wrote of a perplexing lack of data and registries, especially for an area administered by France, a nation with an ingrained love of laws, lists and registers.

LESSON NUMBER 6: IN MANY WAYS, RANGIROA WAS THE ANTI-WAIKIKI, WITH AN OPEN LAGOON INSTEAD OF HONKY-TONKY DEVELOPMENT, SOLITARY TRAVELERS INSTEAD OF HONEYMOONERS, AND DIVERS INSTEAD OF SUNBATHERS: PEOPLE CONCERNED WITH WHAT LAY UNDER THE SURFACE OF A PLACE.

Millions of years ago, Rangiroa probably looked like Bora Bora. Rangiroa's peaks gradually fissured and eroded until they disappeared below the sea. The pulverized coral that constitutes an atoll marks the fringing reef that once lay several hundred yards from the shore of the original island. The lagoon represents the area formerly occupied by the bulk of the volcano.

Rangiroa drew "oohs" and "ahhs" from the tourists on our Air Polynesie flight even before we landed. Below our propeller plane we could see a sweeping arc of narrow island, a half-mile wide, separating a midnight-blue ocean from the lagoon, a lighter kaleidoscope of jade, turquoise and aqua denoting various depths. An impossibly delicate lime color indicated the shallows.

The tiny village of Avatoru appeared below. A single road ran through its few dozen houses, red-roofed and looking almost Mediterranean in style. Thick, unbroken stands of coconut palms, breadfruit and banana trees, their emerald shades startling against the bright sands, surrounded the village.

After landing at Rangiroa's airstrip, I approached a Polynesian woman. Maria Belais arranged her hair in a chignon, showing the French influence on Tahiti. Above her shorts and sandals she wore only a Maidenform-style bra with pointed cups and rigidly sewn concentric circles. I asked Maria in French if she could direct me to any of the families shown on a dittoed list I'd obtained in Sydney.

She pointed to the last name on the list, Chez Teina. "C'est moi," she said—that's me.

For $24, she would provide a bungalow and three meals a day. I did not know quite what to expect for the money. Maria drove Roz Marshall, an Australian woman also traveling solo without advance arrangements, and me in her white pickup along a road with overhanging palm fronds. We proceeded to the eastern end of the main islet, a six-mile-long fragment of the atoll, where most of Rangiroa's inhabitants live.

Family dwellings, a separate cooking structure and six tourist bungalows stood surrounded by palms. They nestled beside the lagoon near a deep channel, the Tiputa pass. The Pacific rushed via the pass in and out of the lagoon in cresting swells. The compound stood a minute's walk from the Tiputa pass and five minutes from the ocean proper, where you could stroll for hours without seeing a soul.

Roz and I agreed to share a basic bungalow with two cots, wood floor, woven palm roof. A cloth curtain served as a door. The generator provided electricity only until around 9 p.m.

Chez Teina seemed to epitomize reasons to stay in family-run accommodations. Our bungalows, plainer than those at the nearby $180-a-night hotel, nevertheless felt cozy. Chez Teina enjoyed nearly as good a view of the lagoon as the hotel and a better overlook of the Tiputa pass. And, as at Chez Fredo on Bora Bora, guests could take part in the daily routine.

And a chef from Lyon prepared the meals and served them at a picnic table beside the lagoon.

Lyon—the cuisine capital of France, itself the cuisine capital of the world! Here at a pension at the end of the universe!

François Caramelli, a slender 27-year-old whom the island grapevine reported could out-cook the hotel chef, already listed restaurants in France, Germany and Papeete on his résumé. His

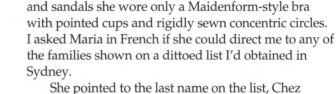

Polynesia trip map

A FRENCH POLYNESIA

3 Rangiroa

2 Bora Bora — Raiatea — Huahine

1 Tahiti — Moorea

B HAWAII

Kauai

Niihau

4 Oahu

U.S.

B Hawaii

5 Molokai

Lanai — Maui

Marquesas ►

Kahoolawe

A Tahiti

AUSTRALIA

NEW ZEALAND

Pacific Ocean

0   50
MILES

6 "Big Island"

0   200
MILES

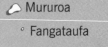

Mururoa

Fangataufa

A black tip reef shark, of the type I saw in Rangiroa, swims in a lagoonarium in Tahiti.

French-Tahitian cuisine verged on the sublime. The half-dozen guests at Chez Teina experienced rapture over his *poulet dijonnais* (chicken in mustard and bread crumbs) with *sauce piquant*; lobster; various silvery and red lagoon fish; Chinese fried fish with soy sauce; asparagus with French-style mayonnaise; lychees; and *choux* pastry with chocolate and cream.

In un-Gallic fashion, François seemed not to mind chatting with us guests despite the atrocities we committed on the French language, perhaps because many of our attempts focused on flattering his cuisine.

Sometimes we ate at a picnic table beside the lagoon, where the noise of the splashing schools of flying fish, *marara* in Tahitian, sporadically drowned out conversation. At other times, meals would be served at a dining bungalow with an open front and a pandanus roof, woven from the dried leaves of the screw pine. Breakfast appeared with a soft rustle on our bungalow porch.

On our second day on Rangiroa, François shooed the chickens out of the kitchen and let me read his classic French cookbooks and watch him prepare meals. Why he had been working at little Chez Teina the past year remained something of a mystery, especially since he told me he hated swimming. The answer seemed to lie in his contented expression as he took the family's boat each afternoon to pick up the mail at Tiputa, a village visible on the far side of the ocean pass.

When I asked how long he was staying, François gave me a Gallic shrug and a noncommittal smile.

MONDAY-FRIDAY, JUNE 3-7
Women who swim with the sharks

My five days on Rangiroa revolved around snorkeling in anticipation of mealtimes and emerging at the waterside table to admire the latest repast. I appreciated the irony of feasting on tasty lagoon fish and then going out to swim with sharks, trying to avoid becoming the next step on the South Pacific food chain.

Hundreds, perhaps thousands, of six-foot Pacific black tip sharks live in the lagoon and the two principal ocean passes. In addition, white tips, grays, bronze whalers, tigers and nurse, lemon and hammerhead sharks frequent these waters. The fish-food-rich Tiputa pass, and another westward near Avatoru village, enjoy fame among divers and marine researchers for both their sharks and some of the world's most dangerous currents.

The day after we arrived, Maria arranged for her cousins, Deborah and Simone, to take Roz and me out in the pass to see the sharks. Our plan was to drift snorkel, swirling with the current into the lagoon while clinging to the tie rope of the empty boat as it drifted along with us.

The young Polynesians expertly guided the boat to the middle of the pass and jumped overboard. Deborah dived gracefully, despite wearing flip-flops instead of fins. Simone entered with a shriek, doing the cannonball more like a kid at a community pool in the suburban USA rather a Polynesian water baby. Third overboard was Roz, and last, me.

"*Requin*" (shark), Simone bellowed over and over, for a half dozen ambled on the bottom of the 80-foot-deep channel. The water clarity reassured me, for it seemed *les requins* could not get close without ample warning.

Another extraordinary sight appeared: a giant manta ray. About 12 feet across, it passed below us, at first seeming to be a strange shadow. The manta gently flapped its wing tips to undulate forward, resembling a living flying carpet.

Dead coral, on a disastrous scale, appeared in parts of the lagoon, legacy of a February 1983 typhoon. The 1981 book *Across the South Pacific* had talked about the beauties of Rangiroa's corals, but that had been before the storm.

A "surface" storm, it appeared, could create an amazing degree of irreparable damage well under the water. Chunks the size of school buses lay tossed about. Dead coral, its neon beauty sapped away, displayed a non-color—a cement-like gray-white. The bottom of Rangiroa's lagoon looked like a parking lot that had been jackhammered by giants, a far cry from a healthy reef, growing for thousands of years.

After drifting perhaps a mile, we climbed back into the boat and steered back up the pass for two more rides. On our third drift snorkel, we passed over a long ledge of coral, and I dove down for a closer look.

Out of nowhere, a muscular black tip appeared, right alongside and swimming parallel. The six-footer gave me a blood-chilling stare, mouth open, his flat eyes pivoting forward and back in their sockets.

I had a split second to decide whether to try to scare him off or to believe a prior assurance from Deborah that the black tips fell into the "perfectly safe" category. Numb with shock, I managed to decide, "When in Rangiroa … ." I quietly swam back up to the boat, and my curious friend wandered off.

Much to Deborah's amusement, I shook with delayed fear for hours afterward. She did not fear the sharks. In fact, she said she liked them (after a few days of meeting Rangiroa's shark, I would share much of her admiration). It seemed that families in Rangiroa and nearby atolls believe a particular shark guards

Playing it safe with sharks

S harks live in salt water everywhere from the Arctic to the tropics. They can also be found in some brackish and even fresh waters. The phrase "shark-infested waters" seems to always appear in articles after ferry sinkings off Puerto Rico or capsizings of boatloads of Cuban refugees. Yet it makes as much sense as saying "bird-infested trees."

"Sharks do not infest, they inhabit," George H. Burgess, director of the International Shark Attack File, wrote to me. "Concentrations occur, with few exceptions, in naturally occurring areas of productivity."

In waters less crystalline than Rangiroa's ocean passes, sharks are just not always as visible. Further, sharks are drawn like magnets by the sound of explosions or the smell of blood. A boat sinking does not occur in shark-infested waters; by its very nature it attracts sharks already nearby and others who notice the commotion.

Sharks have been attended by mass hysteria ever since Steven Spielberg's 1975 movie *Jaws*, based on Peter Benchley's book of the previous year.

Written accounts of attacks rarely lack for gory detail, describing human bodies slashed in half or sharks swimming with victims' feet protruding from their mouths. Yet on the balance, the ledger shows that each year sharks kill an average of 10 humans worldwide, while fishing fleets over time have killed millions of sharks.

As undeniably horrific as a shark attack must be, swimming with them provides a unique type of adventure. These creatures on the move provide one of the most impressive sights in

Shark attacks
WORLDWIDE BY DECADE

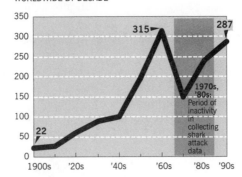

Based on data from the International Shark Attack File

NOTE: 1990s data through June 1996

the natural world and can be observed safely with proper precautions.

Safety guidelines for swimming with sharks:
• Stay in protected lagoon waters, home to the reef sharks rather than the larger pelagic (ocean-going) varieties.
• Swim gently and quietly. Splashing suggests a fish in distress and attracts sharks.
• Get out of the water in good time if you are bleeding from a cut or have harpooned fish.

Although most references counsel menstruating women to stay out of the water, male shark victims outnumber females by a 9.2-to-1 margin, even when only attacks on recreational swimmers (rather than fishing-related attacks) are examined. In fact, attacks on women below depths of five feet numbered exactly zero, from the first records in the 1500s through 1974, according to the book *Shark Attack*.

From 1974 to the present, there are only four cases of attacks on women below depths of 5 feet.
• Swim in clear water, where the shark's behavior can be observed. Leave the area if the shark gives the signs of an impending attack: First, it abandons random swimming to investigate you. Next it may bump you once, to see if you are injured or defenseless, and perhaps a second time. Just before an attack, it may swim in a violently hump-backed and agitated fashion, side fins down, mouth in a near-snarl. The shark may then take a single bite and leave, or attack until it kills.

The number of shark attacks has risen continuously this century, as human populations and recreational use of the water have grown. In 1995, they attacked 44 people in U.S. waters, 29 of them in Florida.

This period coincided with population growth and increased recreational use of the waters in Florida, California and Hawaii. Humans have encroached on the domain of sharks to an extent far higher than two generations ago.

Burgess wrote to me that

Per capita, i.e., per human hour in the sea, the rate of attacks probably has declined, in part because of reduced numbers of sharks attributable to overfishing, but mostly due to human hours "swamping" their half of the human + shark = attack equation.

their welfare and can be called upon to avenge a slight. Thus a fisherman will not go out if he has fought with his wife the night before.

LESSON NUMBER 7: POLYNESIANS EVALUATE EACH SHARK SPECIES RATIONALLY, RATHER THAN SUCCUMBING TO *JAWS* PHOBIA.

"White tip, OK. Black tip, OK," Deborah said simply. "Gray shark, no tip, not OK."
Research I read later bore out her observation, cit-

ing gray reef sharks as a notorious variety that would indeed launch unprovoked attacks.

Without statistics, predator behavioral profiles or a cultural comfort zone to allay my fears of sharks, I walked about 20 steps each mornings from the bungalow to the water and steeled my quaking nerves. Almost at war with myself, torn between fascination and repulsion, I would snorkel straight out into the lagoon.

Even in the shallows, I encountered sharks of all sizes: some, at six feet, larger than my 5-foot-4 self, others juveniles of about two feet long. Startled to see me in their watery living room, they would reverse direction, able to turn around in a space no greater than their own length due to their flexible cartilaginous skeletons, and zoom away. I came to admire the sleekness of the beasts, as wondrous in their way as Olympic athletes, lion huntresses or the sharks' fellow scavenger, wolves.

LESSON NUMBER 8: SHARKS DISPLAY ONE OF NATURE'S MOST ELEGANT DESIGNS. THEY CAN BE CAPTIVATING TO WATCH, AND SWIMMING WITH THEM CAN BE WELL WORTH THE INTERNAL STRUGGLE WITH FEAR.

AND LESSON NUMBER 9: DESPITE THE BEAUTY OF SHARKS, I NEVER AGAIN SNORKELED ANYWHERE WITHOUT CONSTANT CHECKS OVER MY SHOULDER AND 180-DEGREE TURNS TO SEE IF I HAD COMPANY.

The days passed. I caught rides to Maria's general store in Avatoru for ice cream, collected shells and daydreamed. After exploring Avatoru, where most of Rangiroa's 1,430 inhabitants live, I had finished my limited checklist of "must" things to do. Wiggling my toes in the sand became a perfectly pleasant way to pass the time.

I read a book a day, sometimes by flashlight after the generator shut down. These included *So Long, and Thanks for All the Fish* and *The Restaurant at the End of the Universe,* two volumes in a series based on *A Hitchhiker's Guide to the Universe*, the whimsical British radio and television science fiction series.

I zipped through the books and obviously admired their titles, as seen by this book being called *An Amateur's Guide to the Planet.* Despite their setting in Guildford, England (where I had lived until three months previously), and intergalactic space, they seemed to be perfect reading for Rangiroa. This island seemed as far from First World Frenzy as a rocket ship bound for Magrathea, Bwenelli Atoll, Bartledan, Grebulon or any of the other fancifully named *Hitchhiker* destinations.

Rangiroa felt light and uncommon and fantastic. Perhaps other parts of the world suffered through war, famine, genocide, epidemics and blizzards, but not here; only the rare typhoon rippled the waters of paradise.

LESSON NUMBER 10: ATOLLS PROMOTE INTROSPECTION AND PROVIDE A PERFECT SPOT TO SIMPLY SIT AND WATCH THE WORLD GO BY.

Rangiroa means "immense sky" in the local dialect, and above the island a three-ring circus would appear. I saw big black thunderheads miles away and clear blue overhead, along with shifting stripes of pink and gold clouds, all of which would be completely rearranged every few minutes.

The picturesque lagoon, with a yacht or two at anchor, held schools of large blue, green and orange parrotfish, their beaky mouths audibly scraping the coral as they nibbled it and created sand. A buttercup-yellow flutemouth hid shyly on the bottom. Hundreds of transparent pipefish darted about near the surface. A narrow strip of sandy beach appealed to sunbathers, who even from a distance could easily see fish in the clear lagoon.

At night, after the electricity cut off at 9 or 10, guests would sit at the water's edge at Chez Teina. Any amusements that might have relied on power were not missed. A luminous full moon, etching sharp shadows, rose to group admiration.

Sometimes we'd walk to the Kia Ora Village, the expensive hotel just around the lip of the lagoon from Chez Teina. There Taeva, a strapping and outgoing young man of part-Polynesian heritage, gave tips on how to scare off sharks. If bopping them on the nose didn't work, he advised, coil into a tiny ball and throw out your legs and arms explosively.

After five days, I said goodbye to Roz, Maria, François, Deborah and Simone, happy to have met them but relieved not to have met any hungry great whites—an event far more likely in ocean waters than in lagoons. Maria put a flower lei and a shell necklace around my neck. I wore each until they fell apart.

Many serendipitous events made my stays on Bora Bora and Rangiroa fulfilling: Fredo's spearfishing trip, François's cooking, Deborah and Simone's esprit on the shark trips. Someone flying all the way to French Polynesia might not be able to rely upon finding an identical experience, what with François's wanderlust and the lure of jobs in Papeete possibly relocating some of the Tahitians I encountered in the outer islands.

APRIL 1991
Fish ponds on Molokai

By 1200 A.D., Polynesians from the Marquesas had ventured forth in massive sailing canoes and discovered Tahiti and then Hawaii. Captain James Cook followed the same pattern, visiting Tahiti first (1769) and Hawaii second (1778).

Unknowingly following a pattern as old as the Polynesians, I visited Hawaii after Tahiti, arriving in Honolulu to study Asian-Pacific issues at the East-West Center as a Jefferson Fellow.

Based on the advice a journalist friend who disparaged the commercialization of Waikiki and Maui, I held ridiculously low expectations for Hawaii. Yet coming from polluted Baltimore, I immediately loved the perfumed smell of its perfect air.

During our five weeks in Hawaii, my affection for the islands grew as my colleagues and I explored its scenic splendors. We visited the Keaiwa *heiau,* consisting of a giant stone terrace 100 by 160 feet, in the hills above Pearl Harbor.

On weekends, we rode Zodiacs along Kauai's Na Pali coast, visited the observatories on snow-capped Mauna Kea on the Big Island of Hawaii and admired the sea cliffs on the North Shore of Oahu between Waialua and Kaneohe Bay.

At the Bishop Museum in Honolulu, I enjoyed a computer simulation game recreating the voyage of the Marquesan discoverers of Hawaii. Visitors have to tack a cybercanoe skillfully against a dastardly head wind to arrive before perishing of thirst or hunger.

During a lunchtime break in our seminars one day, I watched several dozen students at the University of Hawaii's Manoa campus protest for courses to be taught in Hawaiian. In much of French Polynesia, the Tahitians clearly had preserved their language. They had no need to protest the use of French, as it came in second.

The arts seemed to be the main modern preserve of Hawaiian culture. Hula dancing, once outlawed for its sensuality, had made a giant comeback, particularly at the Merrie Monarch Festival held in Hilo each April. And I heard the most extended use of the Hawaiian language at a concert at a Waikiki hotel featuring the Cazimero Brothers, two gifted singers of Portuguese and Hawaiian descent.

Some Polynesian words still cropped up in everyday use. Locals referred to locations as being toward the ocean or toward the mountains, a construction also found in Indonesian.

Islanders' directions

	HAWAIIAN	TAHITIAN	INDONESIAN
Toward the mountains	Mauka	Uta	Kadja
Toward the sea	Makai	Tatahi	Klod

Hawaiians say mahalo for thank you and aloha for greetings and farewells. They call white people haoles and long-term residents kamaaina. Polynesian place names lived on in the lengthy but melodic monikers on street signs, an explosion of vowels and the "k's" that Hawaiians used to replace some of the glottal stops of Tahitian (manifested in Faaa airport, which sounded like Fa-AH-ah). Yet no one in public areas, on the buses or in the shopping areas, spoke Hawaiian in complete sentences. English dominated the 50th state (as it did the other 49), with Japanese second, reflecting both Japanese tourists and residents of Japanese descent.

On Oahu, I tasted poi, a starchy, whitish-purple dish based on ground taro root, at a traditional Hawaiian restaurant. I wasn't wild about it, but one had to admire its calorie content, essential to adding the bulk needed for long-distance voyaging.

On the Big Island of Hawaii, we visited the Pu'uhonau O Honounau National Historical Park (the

Place of Refuge), the site of a Hawaiian village where breakers of taboos could live in safety. It featured a replica of a house for high chiefs, a canoe landing and a heiau. At Hawaii Volcanoes National Park, a ranger warned us semi-seriously that if we took samples of its pretty volcanic rocks home, the fire goddess Pele would bring us bad luck. He described how the ranger station received a steady stream of parcels returning bits of Pele's volcano from tourists who reported all manner of misfortune.

On Kauai, a group of female Jefferson Fellows hiked the Awaawapuhi and Nualolo trails in Kokee State Park. There we enjoyed profoundly beautiful views of the green-needled peaks of the Na Pali coast and paths that wound through magical groves of huge sun-dappled ferns.

We stayed with a pleasant couple overnight in a bed-and-breakfast place in a modern home in Waimea. They were new transplants from California, however, with little local knowledge, who had just finished fumigating their house for insects under a giant tent. The experience was a universe apart from both the people and the setting of Chez Fredo on Bora Bora.

Near Waikiki, at the Hilton Hawaiian Village, my friend Suzanne and I hooted with merriment at a show by singer Don Ho. Here Polynesian culture had been packaged with a wink and a nudge for military families and honeymooners. Newlywed men were led off-stage by willowy vahines, Polynesian women. Don Ho irritably sang parts of "Tiny Bubbles" in front of a lush backdrop that looked like a painted version of Moorea's mountains and waterfalls.

In daily life in the northern apex of the vast area of Polynesian settlement, a melange of American, Japanese, Polynesian, Chinese and Filipino cultures prevailed. Polynesian culture could be seen in Hawaii, yet in a lamentably packaged way. Hawaiian sovereignty activist Haunani-Kay Trask decried the degraded hotel versions of the hula—when what was sacred and erotic becomes mere sexual athleticism or smuttiness. In From a Native Daughter: Colonialism and Sovereignty in Hawaii, she wrote that "the renowned beauty of our women, especially their sexual beauty, is not considered a commodity … but an attribute of our people."

In search of Hawaii's Polynesian roots, I flew to Molokai, an island lying east of Oahu with the second-highest proportion of ethnic Hawaiians (behind Niihau, 95 percent Hawaiian, whose 230 residents cannot be visited by tourists except by invitation). About half of Molokai's population of 6,700 have some Hawaiian blood.

Only 100,000 people visit Molokai each year, a tiny proportion of Hawaii's overall 7 million yearly tourists. A quiet road winds down from the airport, affording a view across the placid water of the Lahaina Roads. The lavender slopes of neighbor islands Lanai and Maui

Frustration at the history education gap

My friend Suzanne, visiting from Maryland, and I flew to the Big Island of Hawaii in April 1991. We decided to hike down to Kealakekua Bay, following an obscure trail described in my guidebook.

After snorkeling in the choppy bay, we toweled off on the breakwater, watching a mongoose peek out from some rocks. Then Suzanne shot a photo of me in front of a monument to Captain James Cook, who explored the South Pacific and who died on these rocks.

The land around the monument is actually under British rule. Once a year, an Australian ship comes to tend this, one of the more remote and little-visited monuments in the world.

Cook's place in the pantheon of great navigators and explorers rests on several major advances. He brought artists on his explorations, an act that warms me as a graphic journalist. He kept such careful charts that his New Zealand map looks nearly identical to modern versions. He demanded, on penalty of flogging, that his men eat fruits, soups, vegetables and sauerkraut to avoid scurvy, caused by a diet lacking ascorbic acid. While previous explorers had lost up to a man a day to the disease, none died under Cook.

Most scholars conclude that Cook, considering his era, kept violence to a minimum, took responsibility for fair dealings with islanders and showed unusual enlightenment in his interest in Polynesian culture and language.

A shattered foremast on the ship *Resolution* after he left the Big Island of Hawaii would ultimately prove fatal to the great navigator. He returned to the bay where, 212 years later, we snorkeled in ignorance of a tragic history. In the shallows near the monument, Cook went ashore, livid, to investigate the theft of a rowboat. The Hawaiians responded by stabbing Cook and holding him under water. He struggled mightily, but the Hawaiians bludgeoned him to death.

The first modern scientific navigator's charting filled in the great void in European knowledge of the Pacific. Though word of his death in 1779 took a year to reach London, the news was the equivalent of the Kennedy assassination of his era. A media frenzy ensued, manifested by portraits, murals of his slaying, stage plays, medals, books and articles. Yet Cook has become a blank to most American Baby Boomers.

At the time the significance of the place known informally as Captain Cook's Bay largely passed us by. I could barely recall who Captain Cook was ... Captain Hook? Captain Kirk? Captain Crunch? In seventh grade, our class had learned a scrap or two about the great British navigator, an intriguing counterpoint to the Polynesians themselves. But our text contained only few facts, bare in proportion to his achievements. It

Boats rest at anchor near where Captain Cook died.

I stand in ignorance at Captain Cook's monument.

noted how Ferdinand Magellan was later followed by Captain Cook,

who might be called a collector of islands because he discovered or visited so many of these charming places. We have seen how he surveyed the coast of Australia, and brought it and New Zealand to the attention of his countrymen.

As for Cook's murder, the text noted only that he died "on one of the lovely islands." Reviewing this passage 30 years later, I felt it was no wonder that I hadn't recognized Kealakekua Bay for what it was. I later felt fortunate to have visited the remote site, yet frustrated that its significance passed me by.

Lesson Number 11: Students lack knowledge of much basic history—especially about other nations.

"Americans ignore history," Frances FitzGerald wrote in *Fire in the Lake,*

for to them everything has always seemed new under the sun. The national myth is that of creativity and progress, of a steady climbing upward into power and prosperity, both for the individual and for the country as a whole. ... They believe in the future as if it were a religion.

Some adventure travelers find the national disinterest in history no hindrance, for they prefer to make up their own minds about a place anyway and deliberately do not read about it until they return from a trip. While I understand this approach, I still rely on basic knowledge gained in school for my initial appreciation of historical areas—knowledge U.S. students don't seem to be grasping, according to national assessments of U.S. social studies in 1986, 1988, 1991 and 1994. A 1991 report concluded that the social studies achievement of U.S. 11th graders was "dismal." Less than half of high school graduates possessed "in-depth knowledge and understanding of ... history, geography, civics and economics."

Our oblivious hike to the site of Cook's slaying on Hawaii epitomized my frustration at the gaps in my own knowledge. My nephew, Matthew, told of his simple solution. As a sixth-grader who wants to know more than the fixed curriculum, he made a good point: "That's why I read a lot on my own," he said. "I *like* history." That's one reason why I travel, too—to fill the American curriculum gap.

taper to the horizon like the backs of enormous sleeping whales.

After a few minutes, the road drops into Kaunakakai, Molokai's easygoing main town. Its rustic shop fronts lent it the flavor of a movie set for a spaghetti Western. No stop lights slowed the visitor either at Kaunakakai or anywhere else on Molokai. I continued east, hugging the ocean on the King Kamehameha V Highway.

None of the handful of homes, churches and corner stores rose remotely as high as the five-story palms. Molokai seemed as beautiful as the more touristed islands of the Hawaiian chain: Oahu, Maui, Hawaii (the Big Island), Lanai and Kauai.

After a half-hour, I beheld a truly Polynesian scene for the first time in Hawaii. In knee-deep water, families tended fish traps.

Molokai's wooden stake traps echoed the classic Polynesian construction: a stone barrier separating a fish pond from the ocean. A wooden gate with slats completed the enclosure. Fish could enter freely from the ocean as long as they were small enough to pass through the slats. As they grew bigger in the pond, they could no longer wiggle through the gate back to the sea. The Polynesians then plucked the grown fish.

Using this elegant and ingenious scheme, weeks or months of work to establish the fish trap eventually provided a virtually effortless existence, an aspect of Tahitian daily life that Captain Cook noted in his journal.

Past the fish traps, the highway became a cross between a Grand Prix event and a scenic road. I sounded the horn as the road narrowed in places to only one lane, winding sharply and climbing through eroded volcanic rock. The eastern end of the Molokai highway afforded a distant, twinkling view of the Kaanapali coast high rises on Maui, nine miles distant and a world away from Molokai's serenity.

On the car radio, a station broadcast a sunset hour of modern Hawaiian music. The Cazimero Brothers provided the perfect soundtrack for a drive at dusk. Back in Honolulu, I bought some of their music. I know many people who have lived in Hawaii, however briefly, who rely on their Cazimero CDs when "homesick" for Hawaii.

LESSON NUMBER 12: AS THEY HAD IN BRAZIL, THE PORTUGUESE SEEMED TO HAVE INJECTED A MUSICALITY OF ENORMOUS RADIANCE INTO A HAWAIIAN MIX THAT ALSO INCLUDED RELIGIOUS CHORAL MUSIC, AS I'D ALSO SEEN ON TAHITI.

After rounding the last turn of the road, the Moaula Falls appeared, like the realization of a mental picture of Eden. They spumed down the deep V of the garden-like Halawa Valley, its air perfumed by euca-

lyptus. Tents dotted the shoreline, the only remaining habitation after the valley suffered a double-punch in 1946 and 1957 of tsunamis—tidal waves from distant earthquakes.

On the way back from Halawa, 17 miles before Kaunakakai, I noticed a tiny sign for Honomuni House, a bed and breakfast place. A couple answered the door: Jan Newhouse, a wiry, shirtless blond man, and Keaho, his wife, a woman with beautiful, incredibly thick long hair the color of ink and warm brown Polynesian eyes and skin.

Their cottage was booked. It was getting dark on a busy Saturday night, and they knew I would soon run out of affordable places to stay. Jan and Keaho offered to rent me a room in their house full of Polynesiania.

Jan, a historian and mountaineer, grew up on Kauai. Keaho, a native of Molokai, taught school on Oahu during the week, returning home on weekends. This Molokai couple, the only people I encountered in two months in Hawaii with knowledge of Tahitian culture, owned an authentic Polynesian trimaran, a speedy, three-hulled sailboat. They contemplated sailing to French Polynesia with Tahitian friends who could still navigate using the stars and traditional chants.

I flipped through their extensive library. One book on Hawaii contained a drawing of the Polynesian dog, a food source. Captain Cook had taken three of them back to Plymouth. In another month, at a village in the uplands of Borneo, I would see an identical stubby dog, weighing about 30 pounds, with erect triangular ears and a short yellowish coat. The dogs slept on every village step and footbridge.

LESSON 13: THE RESEMBLANCES BETWEEN BORNEO'S VILLAGE DOGS AND THOSE OF HAWAII'S DISCOVERERS SUPPORTED THEORIES THAT INDONESIANS BEGAT THE POLYNESIANS.

Keaho was one of a tiny handful of people I saw in Hawaii who fit the romantic conception most mainlanders have of what a "Hawaiian" looks like (on Tahiti, despite extensive intermarriage, many people appear recognizably Polynesian). A hefty, silver-haired couple on my plane to Honolulu had looked like the royal giants described in Hawaiian history. And some small, brown-skinned cowboys on Molokai—roughnecks

A village dog in Borneo. His appearance links him to the Polynesian dog.

with bad teeth, leering expressions and mono-syllabic English—had looked partly Hawaiian, as well as vaguely Portuguese or Filipino. Otherwise, Hawaiian looks seemed to have left only a trace in the children of white or Asian intermarriages.

The next morning, I drove on the nearly empty road, surrounded by scrub as empty as Nebraska's and similarly used for ranching, to Molokai's west end. I visited Papohako Beach, considered to be perhaps Hawaii's finest and certainly its largest white-sand beach. Perfect curling breakers about five feet high crashed on its 2½ miles of sand, which had a peach-gold tint and nary a footprint.

With a flight to catch to my seminars back in Honolulu, I left Papohako reluctantly. My guidebook told of other lovely hidden beaches on Molokai, as well as on Lanai and the Big Island.

Even in Hawaii, with 70 times the tourist numbers of Tahiti, one could find solitary places to imagine the wonder of the first Tahitian voyagers at discovering these giant, empty islands of surpassing loveliness.

Few footprints mark the beach at Papohako.

Polynesia and the big lesson: why culture survives

Tahiti has held on to considerably more of its Polynesian culture than Hawaii for a simple reason: It has a higher number of Polynesians, despite inter-marriage with Asians, French and Americans, and that has led to the preservation of local dialects.

"The main thing is, language is the identity of the culture," said Professor Yosihiko Sinoto of the Bishop Museum in Honolulu, an expert in comparative Polynesian culture and prehistory. He agreed that Tahiti seemed well ahead in this regard. "You can hear people talking Tahitian," Sinoto noted. "We don't hear Hawaiian being spoken."

I ka 'olelo ke ola; i ka 'olelo ka make
(In language is life, in language is death)

Hawaiian phrase in *From a Native Daughter: Colonialism and Sovereignty in Hawai'i*

Professor Sinoto pointed out that while the original language remains alive and well on the outer islands, on the main island of Tahiti, "they put the Tahitian lan-guage second," he said. "About 10 years ago, they were going to start teaching Tahitian in schools. The language was dying. Especially in Papeete, kids speak only French. So they had to train teachers to teach Tahitian."

In Hawaii, other than on Molokai (and presum-ably Niihau, which I could not visit), you simply don't see many Polynesian scenes. On Bora Bora, I

photographed a young man, a guide on a hotel snorkeling trip, sitting on the prow of a boat, looking for devil rays in a lagoon. The sun had streaked his long black hair blond in places, and he wore only a dyed pareu (cloth wrap) tied around his middle. His beautiful Polynesian parents must have caught each others' eyes before too many French or Chinese partners could intercede.

This man on Bora Bora dresses simply and traditionally.

Take the motor off the boat, and the Bora Boran's life and possessions would be little changed from the time of Cook's visit.

Sinoto credited cultural preservation movements to individual Polynesians, particularly the young, rather than governments. "I'm really frustrated in working in Tahiti," he said in a telephone conversation. "The politicians don't care about culture." It is "the young guys," such as a group now replicating the voy-ages of discovery in ocean-going canoes, "reviving their own culture."

Also, Sinoto said, "you have to preserve the ances-tral structure. I work to preserve the *marae* on many islands. I say to the adults, 'You don't have to worship, but please tell your children to preserve the site, in order to learn what your ancestors thought.' "

I was immediately struck upon my arrival in Hawaii by how, in comparison to Tahiti's outer islands, the 50th state visibly lacked Polynesians who owned houses, land and boats.

I soon posed the question of land ownership to a lecturer on Oceania at the East-West Center, who unfortunately was not familiar with historical reasons for this.

Later a bit of research revealed that Hawaiians became dispossessed of their land beginning with the Kuleana Act of 1850, which authorized land sales to resident aliens. Less than 1 percent of the lands were awarded to 28 percent of the Hawaiians, leaving the remaining 72 percent landless.

Within a generation, most land fell into foreign hands, and much of the acreage was used for sugar-growing. By 1890, fewer than 5,000 of the 90,000 Hawaiians owned land. Despite their small numbers, non-Polynesians owned over 1 million acres in the Hawaiian islands, amounting to 75 percent of the land.

The Hawaiian Homestead Act of 1921, giving land to people with at least 50 percent Hawaiian blood, flopped on Molokai. The land was poor, and many locals subleased it to pineapple growers.

The Hawaiian sovereignty movement lists acquiring "a land base" as one of its goals. How to achieve this given modern Hawaii's high real estate prices, which have frozen out many Hawaiians, Polynesian and otherwise, will pose a quandary. Hawaii has the lowest homeownership rate of any U.S. state, a rate that has been declining since 1991. In fact, I was so enthralled with Hawaii that I talked to a local newspaper about jobs—but could see no way to live on the salary quoted to me, given the costs of buying or renting property.

U.S. homeownership rates

Maine (highest)	77%
U.S. average	65
Hawaii (lowest)	50

Based on 1995 data from the U.S. Census Bureau

Yet on Tahiti's islands, Mama, Fredo and Maria Belais owned their own places and businesses, making Polynesian homestays much more of a possibility. They and their ancestors were lucky to be farther away from colonial powers, on small islands offering less land to grow sugar beets or pineapples. French Polynesians were able to quietly stay on their land, attracting little notice until tourism and nuclear testing arrived in the 1960s, more than a century after the Hawaiian land grab.

Today hotels and foreign interests control much of the flat land on the main island of Tahiti, and land redistribution has become an issue for the Independent Party, or *Ia Mana Te Nunaa*. On the outer islands, however, Polynesians retain their original land, often communally. Yves Courbet, a Los Angeles-based business and investment consultant for persons interested in Tahiti, wrote to me that

> Land has traditionally been owned by families and not by individuals, even though the French tried to

implement the individual concept of ownership. To this day, this can create major problems in the Tuamotus, for example. Even the most remote atoll is owned by many people, with every cousin and uncle laying claim to the ownership of a plot when it goes on sale. Furthermore, in the past the Tahitian government has made it difficult for foreigners (including the French) to buy properties.

Hawaiian sovereignty activist Haunani-Kay Trask, stating that Hawaii is the "most colonized" place in the Pacific, underlined the pivotal role of land and language in *From a Native Daughter: Colonialism and Sovereignty in Hawaii*:

> Unlike the Samoans, we do not control our islands, the bulk of which are held by the State of Hawai'i, the Federal Government, and a dozen or so major multi-national corporations. Unlike the Tahitians, the vast majority of our people do not speak their Native language.

Other factors also seem to play a role in Tahiti's greater preservation of its culture. Hawaii gets 7 million tourists a year to French Polynesia's 100,000 or so. And Hawaii lies 2,700 miles closer to the engulfing cultures of Japan and the United States.

Island demographics

	HAWAII	FRENCH POLYNESIA
Total population	1.1 million	220,000
Polynesians	50,000	172,000
As a percentage	5%	78%

My curiosity to learn more about differences among Polynesians inevitably led to Captain Cook. On his third voyage in 1778, he became the first European to compare Tahitians and Hawaiians. He noted little difference between the language, customs, tools and foods of Hawaiians, living on the islands of Kauai and Niihau, and Tahitians. Hawaiians wore less clothing, and greater exposure to the sun explained their darker hue, Cook surmised.

Cook and his crew apparently found the Tahitians a handsomer group and the Hawaiians more clever. Hawaiians constructed more elaborate houses and showed greater skill at agriculture. They asked intelligent questions of the visiting Europeans and displayed ingenuity in working iron they traded from them.

They shaped their canoes and outriggers with "more judgement," Cook noted. His officers felt that the Hawaiians were the most superior Polynesians.

In the centuries after Cook's explorations, the survival of Hawaiians has been compromised by the unexpected fragility of these hulking people in the face of Western diseases—and their beauty.

Hawaiians—the most numerous Polynesian group at the time of Cook's visit—have vanished in part because outsiders find them attractive. They marry outside their group at perhaps the world's highest rate, almost 100 percent. If a Hawaiian independence movement were not underway and militancy on the rise, I would predict that Hawaii would be the first U.S. state to abandon racial designations, given the prevalence of many sorts of mixed marriages. Yet Polynesian Hawaiians may want more than ever to keep their ethnic designations as a lever in the movement toward reacquiring land, admittance to special schools or access to sacred sites.

> **While politicians and pundits continue to debate who should benefit from race-based programs, the country is entering a new era in which old racial categories are rapidly becoming obsolete. The main reason for this is intermarriage.**
>
> Dinesh D'Souza in *The End of Racism*

Tahitians similarly often have Chinese, French or American blood, but their proportion of Polynesian background seems greater.

How Polynesian groups have fared

POPULATION	PRIOR TO EUROPEAN DISCOVERY	IN 1994
GROUPS DECLINING IN NUMBERS		
Hawaiians	400,000	50,000 [1]
Easter Islanders	7,000	1,000
GROUPS INCREASING IN NUMBERS		
Maoris	200,000	400,000
Samoans	60,000	246,000 [2]
French Polynesians	106,000 [3]	172,000 [4]
Tongans	27,000	104,500

[1] 50,000 people have at least 50 percent Hawaiian blood, and 218,000 have smaller amounts of Hawaiian ancestry. Only 7,000 pureblooded Hawaiians are believed to exist.
[2] 195,000 in Western Samoa, 51,000 in American Samoa.
[3] 71,000 in the Marquesas, 35,000 in the Society Islands (on and near Tahiti).
[4] Many of those officially listed as "Polynesian" in fact have some French, American or Chinese admixture. Estimates of pure-blooded Tahitians run as low as 10 percent (22,000 people) of French Polynesia's population.

Based on data from *The Polynesians: Prehistory of an Island People,* the *World Factbook 1995* and published reports

Some recent signs point to erosion of Tahiti's lead in cultural preservation. Hawaiian traditions have experienced at least a minor renaissance, and threats to the Tahitian culture have arisen.

Hawaiians have begun to revive their culture via voyages reenacting their ancestors' migrations. The Polynesian Voyaging Society sailed a replica of an ocean-going canoe from Hawaii to Tahiti in 1976. During five subsequent voyages, young Polynesians have relearned the ancient art of wayfinding, a navigational system relying on a study of waves, current, wind, weather, birds and cloud reflections, rather than instruments.

An incident aboard the *Hokule'a* during the first reenactment voyage suggested that the cultural loss felt by Hawaiians can attain painful levels. Hawaiians on the crew felt a profound sense of cultural resurgence during the voyage—and discomfort over their white comrades' focus on the voyage as a scientific experiment to learn more about Polynesian navigation. Physical hostilities broke out aboard ship, according to the Polynesian Voyaging Society, and the rawness of the Hawaiians' emotions told a story in itself.

Despite many threats, a "deep memory"of Polynesian culture seems to live on in Hawaii, perhaps best seen in comparison to the U.S. mainland rather than to islands in the South Pacific. Hawaii is famous for its "aloha spirit," defined as making the world a better place through sharing, tolerance and respect for others, tidiness, kindness, extending help without concern about repayment, and enjoyment of nature. Courtesy lives on in drivers' respect for pedestrians, the helpful telephone operators for Oahu's public buses and in many daily transactions large and small. As the weeks of our fellowship passed, I felt the guardedness and suspiciousness that attended my daily life in a big East Coast city drain away.

The tolerance of the original Hawaiians may also be a needed component of America's only majority non-white state. In the same way historians note that *the conquered conquers the conqueror*, observing how Greece, for example, lived on in Rome, some observers feel that Polynesian culture has had an undergirding effect on Hawaii's unique mix—seen in pidgen English, with its many borrowings from Hawaiian, luaus to celebrate a child's first birthday and flower leis given to commemorate weddings and graduations.

Hawaii's demographics

Asian, Pacific islander	63%
White	34
Black	3
Indian	1

Based on 1992 data from the U.S. Census Bureau

Some militant Hawaiians argue that their culture has been packaged and made into a commodity—a reaction in line with my impressions of Hawaii. Militants seem to be putting the "aloha spirit" to the side and struggling to revive their culture. Signs of this included the student language protest I saw at the Manoa campus; the fight for control of Kahoolawe, an island off Maui used for military target practice from 1945 until it was returned to the state of Hawaii in 1994; land-rights activism; and the dis-inviting of tourists to a 1993 ceremony mourning the century mark of the overthrow of Queen Liliuokalani.

Meanwhile Tahiti's culture has been eroded by the

What drove islanders to explore—and stop?

Polynesian explorers were no more able to remain on islands such as the crowded Marquesas than the English, Germans and others could stay in their homelands. Like the settlers of the Americas, Marquesan voyagers also headed into the unknown, finding Hawaii circa 700 A.D.

These is some evidence that a second, fiercer wave of Polynesians, Tahitians perhaps from the area of Raiatea or Bora Bora, arrived in Hawaii circa 1200 A.D., 500 years after the first settlers from the Marquesas, to escape rampant human sacrifice. The Polynesian Voyaging Society notes:

> According to oral traditions, the people who settled the other Society islands, and who migrated to other islands like Hawai'i, had fled Ra'iatea because of the oppressive, tyrannous rule of the priests of 'Oro.

"These later voyagers," wrote O.A. Bushnell in a guide to Hawaii Volcanoes National Park, "arrogant and aggressive, took over the lands and the achievements of their gentler precursors in Hawai'i."

The Polynesians, like America's settlers, fled overcrowding and religious persecution. Yet they never developed beyond their principal feat, exploration and settlement, into long-term commerce. They conducted only limited two-way voyaging.

British historian Arnold J. Toynbee wrote in *A Study of History* of the Polynesians as an "arrested civilization," their frail canoes barely able to briefly conquer the ocean before the challenge overwhelmed them. As the world's climate worsened around 1400 A.D. and the ocean got rougher, the sea marooned the Polynesians in disparate island paradises, in a manner roughly analogous to how the jungle simultaneously swallowed the declining Maya. Had the Polynesians (and for that matter, the Maya) continued to progress as a civilization, they might have discovered Europe, rather than the other way around.

Polynesians also fall short of the Rousseau ideal of enlightened folk living in simple harmony with nature. Wildlife fell at the hands of Polynesians in one of prehistory's greatest wave of extinctions. The Maoris extinguished the giant ostrich-like moa and other birds of New Zealand and overharvested shellfish and sea mammals. The Hawaiians also extinguished at least 35 types of birds. The forests of Hawaii, New Zealand and Easter Island fell to create land for agriculture.

LESSON NUMBER 14: HAWAII CLOSELY PARALLELS MADAGASCAR IN EXPERIENCING AN INITIAL WAVE OF SETTLERS WHO RENDERED MANY SPECIES EXTINCT, FOLLOWED BY A MODERN CRISIS THAT THREATENS ADDITIONAL CREATURES.

economic impact of French nuclear testing. Many observers write how the influx of personnel and money has disrupted French Polynesia's "social harmony" and replaced a diet of fish with one of croissants, baguettes and imported mineral water. As in Hawaii, military activities and tourism have displaced agriculture and fishing as the main sources of income.

In Tahiti, the side-effects of nuclear testing not only include high prices but signs of a demise of the easy South Pacific life, which Mama exemplified on Bora Bora: plucking a banana from the tree, a fish from the lagoon and a flower to wear in the hair. Drawn by jobs and wages, many out-islanders have migrated to slums that have sprung up on the outskirts of Papeete.

LESSON NUMBER 15: TAHITI AND HAWAII DEMONSTRATE A LOSS OF CULTURE, IN A WAVE FROM HAWAII TO SAMOA THAT REVERSES THE POLYNESIANS' DIRECTION OF DISCOVERY—AS WELL AS EFFORTS BY POLYNESIANS TO REVIVE THEIR TRADITIONS.

In 1995, Polynesian independence movements picked up steam in Tahiti and Hawaii. Yet with France injecting a $1.4 billion annual subsidy into French Polynesia, observers note that Tahitian per capita income would probably drop to a third of its current level of $7,000 if France withdrew. Similarly, Hawaii's economy benefits from nearly $1 billion of federal aid and the presence of 57,000 active-duty military personnel.

Though recognition of the French gravy train dampens revolutionary ardor among Tahitians, latter-day Polynesian chiefs continue to debate the merits of the now-linked issues of independence and an end to nuclear testing—on the WorldWide Web. Tahiti, whose outer islands only got telephones in 1988, leapt onto the Internet in 1996.

Tahitians (assuming they can write a bit of English) will be able to contact their Polynesian relatives on the Pacific anti-nuclear chat pages, where the 50th state is known as "the Nation of Hawai'i."

As the ancient Polynesians once charted their watery universe by chanting directions from one star cluster to the next, their modern descendants will look from their computers to Intelsat in the heavens. In the next century electronic mail may augment the navigational chants of commemorative voyages as the means of renewing dormant links between Hawaii and Tahiti, Tonga, Samoa and New Zealand.

The faint heartbeat of Polynesian language and culture, an ethereal WorldWide Web thousands of years old, may enjoy a resurgence across the enormity of the Pacific.

PERFECT SEAS

Thailand … and lessons on ultimate sailing

Boats lie at anchor at the Thai island of Phi Phi Don.

The ad that launched a single ship ran on a gloomy January Sunday in *The Washington Post*. After it appeared, I got only two phone calls, both from non-sailors. By amazing fortune, however, both callers, and one of their spouses, expressed completely genuine interest: It had been their dream to go sailing in Thailand.

That was my dream, too, one of a veritable flotilla of sailing fantasies stretching from Baja California to Tonga in the South Pacific. But other commitments prevented my usual sailing buddies from going to Thailand that spring.

The long shot of placing an ad somehow worked. My farfetched trip idea began to achieve critical mass. I now had three newfound crew members, all residents of Maryland: Nickolas and Eleanora, married scientists originally from Russia and now living comfortably in Montgomery County, and Madeline, owner of an international boutique in Ocean City.

Add my brother, Jim, owner of a service company and an expert sailor and mechanic, and myself, filling the role of navigator and co-captain, and we numbered five, all willing to traipse 12,000 miles around the world on a hunch that Thailand might contain the perfect sailing ground.

We still needed one thing: a sailboat. Calls to the toll-free number of a charter company in Florida led us to *Sweet Robin*, a flawless 39-foot Jeanneau yacht moored on the giant island of Phuket (puhk-GET) in southwestern Thailand.

Forty-eight hours before a gigantic blizzard—a winter hurricane in essence—buried Washington in snowdrifts in March 1993, we soared off to rendezvous with *Sweet Robin*. Our first staggering leg, a numbing 14 hours, took us from New York to Seoul. We looped by air over desolate Alaska—a jaw-dropping Planet Snow, like the remote Ice World of Hoth in *The Empire Strikes Back*. Even at six miles up, Alaska looked unforgettably brutal and alien-looking. Land met the Bering Sea at Nome, identifiable by a cluster of houses appearing as lumps in the snow and the black stripe of a tiny airstrip. Crushing ice pack could be seen, still solid in March. The flight, in the simple process of following the Great Circle route from the East Coast to Asia, felt to be a world tour in itself, descending from the Arctic to the tropics in half a day.

We hopscotched through Seoul and Bangkok and eventually ended up with a few days relaxing on the island of Ko Samui in the Gulf of Thailand. Masseuses plied its pretty beaches, as did food vendors carrying small smoking grills on shoulder poles. The sound of hammering and the whine of circular saws carried onto the beach, as local people built additional $5-a-night bungalows to meet demand generated by the youth of Europe, particularly Germany.

At dawn, young monks bought begging bowls to the seaside restaurants for rice. At dusk, the towering Reggae Bar—as big as a Loire Valley chateau and similarly surrounded by a moat—played party music for the vacationing Euros. Ko Samui seemed to me like a less dramatic Bali—and a place in the process of becoming as cluttered by discos and video rental shops as a U.S. honky-tonk resort.

On our final domestic flight southwest to Phuket, we gaped at the aerial preview of our cruising ground: fantastic limestone peaks like shark's teeth rising out of calm jade water. They looked like the hairpin mountains I'd seen eight years earlier in Guilin in southern China, floating in a shallow sea instead of surrounded by rice fields.

THURSDAY, MARCH 19, 1993
Jade-green sea mountains

We arrived at our departure point, with eight day's worth of provisions, including rice, pasta, tuna fish and cookies. The setting seemed so extraordinary as to be unreal, as did our planned adventure. *Sweet Robin*

Sailing through geological history

The spiky green islands we sailed past in Thailand represent an unusual variety of karst, a limestone formation that covers 17 percent of the Earth's surface. Typical karst, featuring underground streams, caverns and sinkholes, can be found at the Mammoth Cave in Kentucky, in the Yucatan peninsula in Mexico, and in parts of central Florida, Indiana, Cuba, Puerto Rico, Ontario, Italy, Croatia, Slovenia, England and France.

But none of the European and North American karst formations look as dramatic as the odd, spindle-shaped peaks that rise abruptly from paddy fields and shallow seas in a band from south China through to Indonesia. Geologists explain that there, flat layers of limestone (composed mostly of calcium carbonate from shells and coral) were thrust vertically by magma, which hardened to granite. Rain, wind and erosion eventually removed the granite, leaving (surprisingly) the softer limestone, which resisted weathering longer because it was unusually free of impurities. The resulting spires tower above southern Thailand's paddy fields and shallow bays.

The best-known karst monoliths rise at Guilin, China; Halong Bay (or Vinh Ha Long, "Where the Dragon Descends in the Sea"), near Haiphong in Vietnam; and Phangnga Bay near Krabi in Thailand. The Thai formations feature "napes" carved by rising and falling tides. These overhang the shores by as much as 50 feet.

In China, the karst inspired classical landscape painting. In Thailand, the formations have appeared, not in

Jim gestures to karst mountains on our first afternoon.

Thai classical art—which typically features vignettes from the Buddha's life—but rather in Western movies. Tourists now inundate "James Bond" Island, north of Ko Na Khae. (In *To Venture Further*, adventure sailor Tristan Jones called the linking of the "sheer beauty" of the island to a trite film a "blasphemy.")

Ecotour operators take limited numbers of travelers in sea canoes to explore less well-known monoliths. The karst hides secret *hongs* (Thai for rooms): stunning inland lagoons accessible via archways, tunnels and sea caves, surrounded by vertical, vineclad cliffs open to the sky.

Hongs are created when rain water hollows out and eventually collapses the top of a peak, and salt water crumbles the rubbly fill-in, until a peak that once resembled a witch's hat looks more like a hollow cylinder. A monograph containing information on hong structure, *Sea Canoes and Their Importance to Thailand,* by John C. Gray of Sea Canoe Thailand Co., can be found on the Internet at http://www.inet.co.th-/cybermall/seacanoe/tei.html.

These geological formations provided us with sailing that was both aesthetically pleasing and unusually gentle. On our last afternoon we had magnificent conditions: 15-knot breezes that filled the sails, with only tiny waves due to the protection of the scattered karst mountains.

A passage in our sailing guide attested to the kindly seas hereabouts. *Sail Thailand* described how in 1989 a junk-rigged boat named *Suwan Macha* got caught in Typhoon Gay. The freak storm struck suddenly and stripped the sail panels from the masts. Nevertheless, Captain Bernard Berteau recalled that the waves never exceeded a meter. He anchored till the worst of it passed.

Sailing conditions during our Thailand trip included a mix of light to moderate winds and only one squall in eight days. Write-ups advertise northeast winds during the driest months in Phuket, November to April, though during our March trip we had westerlies, southeasterlies, you name it.

Phangnga Bay poses no special challenges for experienced sailors, except that the enormous health of the southern waters means that your anchor can snag robustly growing coral at depths even greater than eight meters—a problem both for the environment and for you, trying to disengage your yacht's tangled anchor rode (line).

floated on a mooring in mid-channel off Laem Phrao, a marina consisting of a set of sheds and an open-air, palm-roofed, waterside restaurant. While snow buried Washington, we basked under hazy, hot skies in the 80s.

A dinghy ferried our supplies out to the yacht. Nickolas, Eleanora and Madeline stowed our gear and provisions while a member of the Sunsail staff debriefed Jim and me on *Sweet Robin's* operation, from the battery and bilge pump to the engine and stove. I dutifully made notes—"Engine 1,200-1,500 rpm while

using anchor windlass"—as my inner child shouted, "We're really going sailing in Thailand!!"

Poised on the brink of discovery, we loosed our mooring line and made way down the channel leading to Phangnga Bay. We would see how reliable our pre-trip research was, based on the scanty information available:

Snippets from travel books, such as a chapter in David Yeadon's *The Back of Beyond:* "a fantasy-shaped archipelago, full of soaring limestone cliffs, crystal-clear coral reefs."

The charter company's lavish brochure: "picture book tropical islands, crystal clear waters and superb sailing conditions."

And the exceptional scenery filmed here for the 1974 James Bond film *Man with the Golden Gun*. A lot could have changed, and not necessarily for the better, in 20 years. (After our trip, the same scenery would be the best thing about the 1995 film *Mortal Kombat*.)

Passing from the channel into the bay, *Sweet Robin* clipped smartly northward, toward jagged rows of islands marching like vine-clad icebergs. A perfect 12-knot westerly washed over her port rail. Eleanora, her Russian accent full of wonder, pronounced the first verdict. "It is like fairy tale," she said, standing at the helm.

"You're learning to sail in the world's finest cruising ground," I replied, thoroughly pleased with our adventure so far.

"We're roughing it in Thailand," said Jim, revising our "roughing it in Africa" maxim. This dated from our 1989 trip to Kenya's coast, which had focused on loafing, having lobster at least daily and reading novels by Ernest Hemingway and Beryl Markham.

Nickolas wore a grin that would not be chiseled off his face for the better part of eight days.

Off we went to anchor at Ko Roi, an empty fishing shack its only habitation. Nick and Eleanora immediately went over the side and swam to the beach, impressively at home in the water for two highly educated intellectuals originally from a massive, largely landlocked nation.

All the superlatives about the splendid waters of Phangnga Bay proved to be fully deserved. The bay lay still as glass, the sky and water a soft blue-gold, the limestone peaks rosy. Our first afternoon at Ko Roi marked the beginning of eight days of delirious swimming and snorkeling. We swam for hours, from the boat to mysterious shores, under stalactites and lime arches. Swallows darted from their nests in the cliffs as we floated by. We followed channels into the col-

lapsed centers of Ko Roi and other islands, where natural chimneys offered peepholes to the sky. We floated and backstroked Olympian stretches from boat to islet to shore and back, distances requiring a dinghy in the Virgin Islands or the Chesapeake or Greece. Here we preferred to swim because the water was so tranquil and warm.

We swam as though our DNA had forgotten the eons since we evolved from saltwater into amino acids and finally life on land. Maybe a week before we labeled ourselves *Homo washingtonianis*, rats in a race. But now we lived in bathing suits and bare feet, sleek otters in the water and, later as we sailed, clambering monkeys on the foredeck fiddling in a forest of sails and lines.

Our route around the bay traced clockwise. You could call its scenic northern half Islands from a Chinese Painting, and the vivid blue southern waters the Incandescent Caribbean.

The twisted karst of the Chinese Painting Islands—a feature found here and in Vietnam and South China—rose from water made green by three rivers emptying into the upper bay.

Islands in the southerly Incandescent Caribbean (where the Andaman Sea begins) rose less sheerly from crystal water. Snorkeling here rivaled anywhere in the world, with lilac- and cream-colored plate corals the size of Winnebagos, unmarred by fishing, diving and pollution.

Eleanora enjoys her first moments at the helm of a sailboat.

Thailand trip map

0 200
MILES

THAILAND

Bangkok

Andaman Islands

Andaman Sea

Nicobar Islands

Ko Samui
Gulf of Thailand

Phuket

7 Ko Na Khae

Phangnga Bay

Ko Roi 1

Laem Phrao

2 Ko Hong

Ao Nang 3

Krabi

Laem Nang

Ko Yao Yai

6 Muslim village

Phuket Town

Phi Phi Don

4

Andaman Sea

Phi Phi Le

5 Racha Yai

0   10
MILES

Madeline's forte lay in route planning: without her input, we never would have visited a Muslim fishing village on bamboo stilts, perched 20 feet above low tide, at the tip of Ko Yao Yai.

I had felt an instant rapport with Nickolas and Eleanora, whose home displayed roomfuls of Indonesian batik paintings, masks and carvings, a hundredfold increase to the five Javanese and Balinese paintings and masks in my home.

Eleanora had seemed shy at first. But once she decided that the rest of us qualified as friends, she began sharing her thoughts and observations fervently and warmly.

Eleanora sailed *Sweet Robin* straight and true from the first afternoon. She also had a perhaps Russian way of speaking English formally, adverbs appearing anywhere within a sentence, with either dry comedy or grand seriousness depending on the situation.

Jim watched how Nick sailed, eyes locked to the compass. "If this is Interstate 270, you've hit 10 cars," he said, getting Nick to think of the compass as a verification on his scanning of the horizon, like the speedometer and rear view, rather than something to study constantly. That was at the beginning. Nick became a polished navigator as the days continued.

A typical captain, I sailed the least and mostly taught the three newest sailors the drill. By our last evening, our team had jelled. Navigation and sail changes more resembled the America's Cup and less the Keystone Kops.

Crew dynamics, as critical as weather and the boat to a sailing trip's success, went well. Fortunately our group had only one heated argument, over missing sunblock—not bad for five people spending nearly 200 hours together, usually within 39 feet or less of each other.

FRIDAY, MARCH 20
A new definition of 'uninhabited'
Before we lifted anchor and sailed away from Ko Roi, I wrote in my diary:

> No photos can capture the immense chalky cliffs with echoes and birds (including a hornbill relative). We are alone in the anchorage except for longtails and fishing boats (painted bright red and gold like a Chinese temple) with arms of bright lights that start chugging by at 7 a.m.

We sailed southeast to Ko Hong and anchored off its northern shore. We swam toward the left side of a narrow beach, up a narrow channel with a strong out-

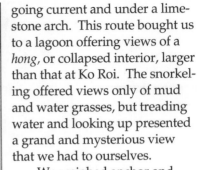
Sweet Robin lays at anchor at Ko Roi.

going current and under a limestone arch. This route bought us to a lagoon offering views of a *hong*, or collapsed interior, larger than that at Ko Roi. The snorkeling offered views only of mud and water grasses, but treading water and looking up presented a grand and mysterious view that we had to ourselves.

We weighed anchor and sailed around to the southern side of Ko Hong. As we continued to cruise the bay, our cruising guide, copyright 1991, offered a touch of suspense as we approached islands, such as Ko Hong, described as "uninhabited." We were about to learn that uninhabited either meant "uninhabited" (like the north of Ko Hong) or "swarming with New Agers and Japanese day-trippers from a massive Love Boat hovering offshore" (like the south of Ko Hong).

LESSON NUMBER 1: THE SAME HAPPENS IN BELIZE AND ELSEWHERE; THE TRAVEL BOOM IS FILLING IN ALL THE QUIET CORNERS OF THE PLANET.

We swam ashore to "uninhabited" Ko Hong. Five tents housed backpackers on the beach. About 30 Japanese tourists bearing sun umbrellas strolled around, looking confused about what they were supposed to do until they returned to their cruise ship.

We met "Mr. Man," a Thai entrepreneur we nicknamed based on the logo on his ball cap, who seemed quite happy to talk to us sailors. He was paying the Thai government $500,000 a year for the right to collect birds' nests from cliff sides for the Chinese soup market and to run the campground and some bungalows.

At Mr. Man's open-air bar, a staff of eight lolled around a cassette player run by a car battery. Their job description seemed to be to remain generally motionless in the shade. Only if a Madonna tape ran out, and with as great economy of motion as could possibly be achieved, would someone unhurriedly stick out a hand to insert more Madonna from a stack of pirated cassettes.

Nick, Jim and I quickly got into the swing of Ko Hong. We drank Cokes under the perfect palms and sat around, feet splayed in the sand, in solidarity with the cassette changers, doing not very much except displaying the satisfied expressions of lottery winners. We eventually stirred ourselves to return to the boat, sloshing through the low surf off Ko Hong.

Our euphoria and giddy high spirits continued as we flew to Ao Nang. *Sweet Robin* scampered along on

At Laem Nang, looking back toward Ao Nang, we swam for hours.

a close reach. We enjoyed a fine boat, views of the distant jagged peaks, perfect weather and plenty of Gatorade courtesy of Madeline's foresight. We wanted for nothing. For a fraction of our lives, everything felt simple and pleasant.

After anchoring in the wide sweep of Ao Nang (*ao* means bay in Thai), we took our orange Nomad dinghy ashore in shifts. A storm threatened from the north as I took in a nervous Eleanora and Nick.

We surfed on to shore but failed to move the dinghy up the sand swiftly. A following wave half filled the dinghy with water. My comprehension of what was involved in military amphibious landings grew manyfold. I imagined Marines and others train for years on how to shoot the surf without damaging their craft or crew.

All five of us ate at an open-front restaurant called Mama's, where fried whole fish, chicken, coconut soup and squid set us back $16, or a bit more than $3 each. Rain plowed in, and the wind swung from the southwest to a more seasonal northeast. We dinghied back in the dark to our yacht, one of three at anchor.

Rain over, we rigged the deck light for a leisurely post-dinner chat. Eleanora gave everyone neck massages. She sat on the topsides. Each of us in turn sat in the cockpit below her, chin on chest, while her fingers loosened our neck muscles and vertebrae and sought out any residual modern tensions. Fulfilling the role of boat mystic, she lulled us with her prettily accented voice.

"Imagine you are walking down a long corridor," she said in a low, hypnotic voice. "You enter a room, you know somehow if you continue, you will find your favorite thing, you will find a place of great happiness."

We all sat under the Thai stars. Eleanora returned to the here and now, noticing the so-French synchronicity of the make of our boat, a Jeanneau, the Belliveau surname, and my dog's name, Beau. Further,

she and Nick lived in a housing development called Beau Monde Estates, and Beau's full registered name is Lingard Beau Monde.

"Beautiful world," I explained to Madeline. Nick looked thoughtful. "Doesn't *beau monde* mean 'high society'?" he asked. From an educated Russian, I learned that I had misnamed my own dog in my own ancestral language; I bowed to Nick's learnedness.

SATURDAY, MARCH 21
Swimming the dreamlike distances

We hopped east one cove, to Laem Nang (*laem* means cape). The natural setting enthralled us. A crescent-shaped hill, looking like an eroded volcano rim, cupped the placid bay. Stalactites dropped from its emerald sides nearly to the water.

For hours we unhurriedly explored, taking the dinghy by pairs in turn to look around the cliff bases, or swimming hundreds of yards. I invented a new swim stroke, lying on my back and doing a sort of inverted butterfly while flutter-kicking. I found I could go many minutes with little effort, occasionally tilting my head far back to see if I held any sort of straight course toward my goals: small islands, shore outcroppings or back to *Sweet Robin*.

Our 1991 cruising guide extolled a "colorful coral reef" here, but by 1993 it had died, victim of either the constant traffic of longtail boats between Ao Nang and the nearest town, Krabi, or perhaps a storm.

As happens over a week, *Sweet Robin* devolved from sleek and shipshape to the Sampan Look. Tarps sagged from the boom to offer shade, and our damp T-shirts and towels swung below deck, drying as they hung from twine. Trashy novels, counterfeit Elvis cassettes, cameras, snorkeling fins and cookie tins were strewn hither and yon in the cockpit.

A giant jumble of squeeze bottles, tubes and applicators swung from the boom in a string bag Madeline had picked up on one of her boutique buying trips to Central America. We dubbed it the "products bag." Our supplies of sun lotion, sun block and after-sun moisturizer (a must for sailors) could stock a cosmetics store on one of these tropical isles. For a group that certainly saw itself as hardy, no-frills adventure travelers, we seemed to need as many accouterments as a group of Palm Beach matrons.

Looking like a floating yard sale, we made a grand entrance to the international sailing community lying at anchor at Phi Phi Don, the most popular island in the area. Most atypically for these islands, Phi Phi Don boasts nearly half a million visitors a year.

Upon our arrival in Ao Ton Sai, a big wind swept in. We anchored in the bay and waited for a storm to

The perils of being a beautiful people

Prior to flying to Thailand, a country with handsome people, a booming sex trade and at least 500,000 cases of HIV as of 1993, our sailing group received powerful lectures to be careful. The Johns Hopkins international travel clinic warned us that, given the HIV rates there, even a beach manicure might be risky if our cuticles got deeply nicked by infected scissors.

Thai people are known for physical beauty and openness to pleasure-seeking. The downside of this is prostitution (practiced by an estimated 250,000 Thai girls, women and lady boys, according a U.S. State Department report) and the spread of AIDS.

I first encountered Thai prostitution at the live sex shows on Patpong Road in Bangkok in 1985, on my first trip to Asia. Poor village girls engaged in sex with men on stage or negotiated to sell themselves to foreigners in the audience. My travel companions and I watched agog, but by the end of the show our fascination yielded to sadness at the tawdriness that robbed the spectacle of sensuality.

Quite unlike the prostitutes who periodically work in my neighborhood in East Baltimore, a haggard and homely bunch, many Thai women who sell sex possess an utterly natural loveliness: clear skin, balanced features and pretty hair and eyes.

The men of Thailand also may strike women as appealing. As an exercise, in Bangkok Madeline and I surveyed the men at a noodle shop and concluded that easily one in two rated as certifiably handsome.

We are not alone in our admiration, though it has taken a sinister turn with estimates that more than 50,000 Thai women engage in prostitution in Japan, and additional thousands in the Netherlands, Germany and Denmark, and concerns by health authorities that the women may spread HIV infections. A University of Amsterdam report notes that the number of postwar Thai "brides," some of whom who viewed marriage and prostitution as compatible states, began to rise in the Netherlands 20 years ago. By 1984, the German ambassador to Thailand felt compelled to decry German men who procured Thai women to sell for sex back home.

LESSON NUMBER 2: THAI PHYSICAL BEAUTY HAS BEEN MISAPPROPRIATED FOR CHILD AND ADULT PROSTITUTION.

In recent years, female art students in Germany and workers in South Korea have described humiliating encounters with men who insulted and groped them, viewing all Thai women as hookers.

In 1995, the U.N.-affiliated World Tourism Organization met in Italy to seek ways to curb sex tours to Thailand and other nations. Attendees reported that 12 German tour operators had signed a contract promising not to do business with hotels that permit child prostitution. Australia, New Zealand, Sweden and Germany passed laws making participating in child prostitution abroad a crime. And Japan Airlines and Northwest Airlines have agreed to show in-flight videos warning against sex tourism.

end, comfortable under the bimini, "riding out the raindrops," as Jim put it. We chatted about world population, segueing into relaxation techniques, President Clinton's budget, the media and other journeys we had taken.

LESSON NUMBER 3: THE CLOSE QUARTERS AND UNSCHEDULED TIME OF A SAILING TRIP INSPIRE WIDE-RANGING CONVERSATION.

We perused guidebooks to plan Nick and Eleanora's next segment in the mountains near Chiang Mai, in the part of northwestern Thailand near the border with Burma. Madeline went below decks to play my Thai language tapes on the cassette player and fell fast asleep. And finally, after dark we dinghied ashore to explore.

Shops and restaurants lined the single path running through the village, where we found copies of *USA Today* for sale. (Jim and I, ever predictable and provincial, checked to see if the Washington Redskins had signed Reggie White.)

Tall "lady boys" with glossy waist-length hair wore heavy makeup, black slit mini-shirts, Spandex halter tops, perfume, hose and pumps. They trolled the path, speaking to each other with resonant deep voices of James Earl Jones masculinity. Huge fake eyelashes gave them a walleyed look. The lady boys we saw on Phi Phi Don reflected Thai tolerance for transvestism and homosexuality, as manifested by transvestite beauty pageants held at village fairs and effeminate, heavily made-up men we saw perform at a dance review in Bangkok.

The lady boys made Nick's persistent reference to the country we were sailing as "Thigh-land" seem fairly appropriate. Sailor Tristan Jones noted another mispronunciation in *To Venture Further*. Tourist touts referred to Phi Phi Don as "Pee Pee," he wrote, signifying how "Thailand was considered to be not much more than one great brothel, instead of the beautiful land that it is."

We stopped in a restaurant, again named Mama's. We examined wooden market trays out front in the open air and selected 10 tiger prawns, a red snapper and a giant squid, perhaps 10 inches long not counting tentacles, for dinner. Our waitress sent our picks back to the kitchen to be prepared.

As we waited at our table, everyone demanded that I retell how I put an ad in *The Washington Post* to initiate this trip. Though all present were principals in the tale and knew the story inside and out, they still wanted to hear it again.

"I figured I'd need at least eight or so calls to get three or four people seriously interested enough to go," I said by rote to my crew mates, rapt like children at the 200th rereading of *Green Eggs and Ham*.

"I got only two calls," I continued, "and that gave

us three people: Nick, Eleanora and Madeline, none of whom had sailed extensively. Nick couldn't believe my ad. It had been his dream to sail in Thailand. Madeline called from Delaware, and she was serious about going too."

"Wow, you should go into sales," Jim said. "Three for two. What a close rate."

Tale retold, we could let the story rest briefly, but I'd be asked to tell it again a few days later. The story, however, slights the inspirational role of David Yeadon's book, *The Back of Beyond*.

Every trip I've taken has resulted from a distinct catalyst. Words by Henry Mitchell of *The Washington Post* inspired me to form a group to visit to Madagascar, and songs by Milton Nascimento set in motion a trip to Brazil. Asked to review Yeadon's book while I worked at the *Baltimore Sun*, I read his lyrical description of Phangnga Bay with the helpless feeling of a goner. *Sounds fabulous, gotta go*, I had thought.

He told of hiring a longtail—a wooden boat with a diesel engine attached to a steel propeller shaft that enters the water at a shallow angle—on Phangnga Bay. "The limestone karst pillars that had followed me most of the way south from Bangkok congregated here in the hundreds, rising like an abandoned city of eroded skyscrapers out of shallow waters," he wrote.

The largest, over 1,000 feet high, he described as

great gray monoliths, sheer-sided and topped by scrubby jungle and vines, showing yellowed scars where slices of eroded limestone had fallen off recently and tumbled into the coral beds at their bases. They receded into the heavy haze of the bay like solitary hooded monks on some strange and lonely pilgrimage.

After dinner at Mama's, we strolled around the village and discovered a less lovely aspect to these islands. We followed the general drift of the lady boys a block inland, past ugly dumps and work yards, to see what they were up to.

There stood the Casablanca Lounge, a high-ceilinged, warehouse-sized transvestite sex cabaret à la Bangkok. We peeked in to see if we wanted to pay for admission. The lady boys took to the stage to spin and pirouette to a Phil Collins song in front of three male couples and one female couple, lying back in an almost horizontal position on bed-length batik cushions.

A low table, about breakfast-tray height, appeared at every third place. We suspected what activities could be hidden by the tray table over the waist, but we declined to confirm our suspicions by watching any further.

As we watched the cabaret, Nickolas and Eleanora told us for the first time that their medical research focused on HIV, which one could imagine was not unknown hereabouts. Eleanora surveyed the lady boys, the Casablanca Lounge, the extraordinary juxtaposition of this strange scene with such lovely surroundings, and said in her her utterly Russian, gravely portentous way, "It is most interesting impressions."

To this day, whenever I see something highly unusual, I hear Eleanora's voice, with the gravity of Charlton Heston playing Moses, providing her all-purpose summation.

SUNDAY, MARCH 22
The highlight of a week of highlights

We donned snorkeling gear and hopped off the *Sweet Robin's* transom, heading along an arm of the cliffs sheltering the west side of Ao Ton Sai. The long reef seemed in stunningly good shape, given the heavy ship traffic and in comparison to Laem Nang. Under a bright sun and ebbing tide, we saw lilac corals that provided shelter for clown fish, of a chestnut color with white stripes.

In the afternoon we reprovisioned, weaving our dinghy around cargo ships and stevedores wading waist deep with plastic cartons to unload. A huge wind swept in, stranding Jim and Eleanora on shore. In the hours before I could safely collect our two crewies, Madeline, Nick and I talked about families, in general and specific terms, as *Sweet Robin* swayed.

Late that afternoon, we made an unorthodox move, leaving Phi Phi Don—the archipelago's most protected anchorage—a half-hour before dark. Sailors know that, by the book, you rarely move after mid-afternoon, especially in the tropics with their swift 6 p.m. sunsets. But the big wind, freakishly from the southeast and straight into the harbor's lone point of vulnerability, ripped into this usually superior shelter and turned *Sweet Robin* into a rocking horse.

Our decision to make a late move won us a reward. The strange wind nudged us on to the highlight of a week of highlights.

Junk and clutter swiftly stowed, the sampan a secure yacht again, we plowed through the heavy wind and raced the light to Maya Cove, a coral garden on the west side of Phi Phi Le, 45 minutes south of Phi Phi Don.

Uninhabited Phi Phi Le rose steeply ahead of us

We fought a noisy crosswind on the way to Phi Phi Le.

like the prow of a 20-story high Viking longboat. The sea calmed as soon as we passed west of the prow. Its chalk cliffs, sheer and bright like the White Cliffs of Dover, gleamed in the low, bright sun.

Then we neared Maya Cove to see—in such a remote place!—moorings. Five giant metal balls bobbed in place for now-departed dive boats. A lone catamaran was attached to one mooring. We snagged one of the four others and sat securely, riding a sighing wind that found a cleft in the hills. *Sweet Robin* swung to offer us a 180-degree panorama of the sun lowering over distant Phuket.

At 6:40 p.m. we turned to photograph the sun slipping below the horizon. At first, it only glowed reddish behind a silhouetted trawler. Then the left two-thirds of the sky became molten, and I called out the colors as they emerged: ivory, slate, crimson, aquamarine, indigo, coral. A deep wine-colored storm cloud appeared at the skyline. Eleanora said first it looked like Dumbo, then a brontosaurus. Fork and heat lightning played over Phuket, 20 miles away.

Enya's *Watermark* wafted from below decks. On Phuket, I had been surprised to find many cassettes of Celtic music, such as those of Enya and Clannad, for sale. As unlikely as it seemed at first, the haunting melodies of misty Ireland fit this Asian waterland's ethereal beauty. Songs such as "Orinoco Flow" referred to sailing half a world away—to waves carrying travelers to "lands I've never been."

Venus appeared on the horizon, and our anchor light atop the mast swayed due overhead, making a circuit through Orion. I wondered aloud, would we see for our first time the "green flash" of the tropics?

Sure enough, two celadon bars appeared on either side of the sun as it eased below the sea. Maroon troughs appeared in the indigo waves. We sat rapt for 45 minutes on *Sweet Robin's* westward rail, as the Celtic harp and singing wafted on the water.

Nature spared nothing that night, not one trick from her bag of visual phenomena. Fluorescent sea creatures danced alongside the boat. A shooting star zoomed overhead.

I forced myself to go below decks to fix dinner, dressed in bathing suit, puddles of water under my bare feet, thinking how lovely it was to be unburdened of house chores, job, commute, bill payments, laundry, telephone voice mail and appointment book. As I

A squid boat also enjoys the sun setting over distant Phuket island.

cooked I played David Byrne's *Rei Mo Mo*, his melodic Latin-based 1989 album that I inexplicably never got around to buying until it became another sensational find from a Thai cassette vendor.

Either I had experienced an amazing run of luck in discovering beautiful music here, or these perfect seas had me in a drugged-with-love mood that alters one's critical faculties and makes music sound especially gorgeous. As I served fried rice and succulent pineapple for dinner, seven squid boats ringed the cove, bright lights dangling on arms over the water so that they resembled UFOs.

We photographed each other's tanned faces. Instead of "cheese," we said, "think of the Washington blizzard."

LESSON NUMBER 4: SOMETIMES THE BEST THING TO DO, AS TINA TURNER ONCE NOTED, IS TO BREAK EVERY RULE. WE WOULD HAVE MISSED THE ANDAMAN SEA LIGHT SHOW IF WE HAD STAYED IN PHI PHI DON, WHERE CLIFFS BLOCK THE VIEW TO THE WEST.

MONDAY, MARCH 23
To an island pointing to the Andamans
We splashed over the side at 6 a.m. the next day, to snorkel before the dive boats with their noisy compressors arrived. Parrot fish, unlike the blue-green palette found in the Caribbean, here displayed a decorator's delight of mauve, magenta, violet and black. Flounder, grouper, rays, wrasse, barracuda, pipefish, snapper, butterflyfish and clown fish darted around. We could see them before we even left the boat, as they played around the anchor rode or flocked to the swim ladder, seeking stale bread. We snorkeled for three hours, then weighed anchor at 9:20. We saw no dive boats and preserved our impressions of Maya Cove as a private paradise.

We sailed next to Ko Racha Yai. I had to shield my eyes from the brilliance of its vivid green palms and dazzling beach sands as we rounded into its bay. It

At Phi Phi Le: Jim, Madeline, me, Nick, Eleanora.

Local fishing boats float off Racha Yai. *Racha*, like *raja*, means "king."

looked like St. Barts as rendered by an artist who did Jimi Hendrix album covers on the side. Here stood the pristine Caribbean of a century ago, with wooden buildings half the height of the palms, every color plugged in to a hot 1,000-volt intensifier.

Truly we were in the clear waters and little-developed islands of the Andaman Sea now. The coral grew as robustly as I'd ever seen. To my horror, our yacht's anchor chain snagged under a brain coral, where it could easily damage the delicate reef structure. Jim put on flippers and went overboard. I gently nudged the throttle forward to slacken the anchor rode, and he dove and gingerly shook it free. Mission accomplished, floating around on his back like the world's most carefree otter, he declared airily, "Al Gore would be proud of me."

Racha Yai's development consisted of a few bamboo bungalows down a jungle path, run by Gary, a colorful New Zealander. We hiked away from our anchorage over a steep hill to have dinner at his Jungle Bungalows, where two pet gibbons played and geckos walked upside down under the eaves.

Gary told tales of his Thai wife's brother, whom Burmese officials arrested and imprisoned when his boat strayed slightly over the invisible watery border. In his 10th month, during a political demonstration, he broke out of jail and made his way to Rangoon harbor. He stole a boat and got home, to the family's surprise and delight. As we listened to Gary's tale, we felt ourselves at one of the world's edges where pirates roam, clandestine deals are brokered and only your Indiana Jones wits can keep you from peril.

Gary put the gibbons to bed, carefully tucking them into blankets on large outdoor platforms. We ate our dinner as cicadas dive-bombed us.

After eating, Jim and I discovered a giant map of southern Thailand and its surrounding waters displayed on the wall. We studied the Nicobar and Andaman islands a few days' sailing to the west. Gary said *National Geographic* had recently visited these little-known islands, which could be visited only by permit granted by the Indian government. I had read of the islands in only one book, Gavin Powell's *A Slow Boat to China*, which led me to believe that they were little publicized, little known and quite little touristed.

Our imaginations run rampant thinking what it would be like to be among the first people to sail there from Thailand. We further imagined just how thrilled our yacht charter company would be for us to take their boat off to what is politically part of India.

The bright moon illuminated our way back to the boat. A thin white line of surf only inches high rolled in gently, as we quietly launched our dinghy into the mysterious night of dark water and sky to the refuge of *Sweet Robin*. The moment felt intensely romantic, impossibly exotic in retrospect—could anything be more different from our routine lives back home?

Racha Yai had hypnotized me with its dazzling brightness and frontier flavor. Still, Nickolas seemed to prefer where we had already been.

"Tell me, Jeannette, why do we spend so little time at Phi Phi Le when it was so beautiful?" he asked.

"Have you read *The Unbearable Lightness of Being?*" I asked rhetorically.

LESSON NUMBER 5, BASED ON MILAN KUNDERA'S BOOK: "YOU CAN NEVER GET YOUR LIFE RIGHT, BECAUSE YOU CAN NEVER REHEARSE EVENTS. YOU FACE SURPRISES AND MAKE THE WRONG DECISIONS."

"If we had two weeks here," I said, "we could sail for one week in rehearsal, and one week for real, and perfect the itinerary." But you would never want to rehearse a trip, because discovery is the very reason for going.

TUESDAY, MARCH 24-THURSDAY, MARCH 26
To the Muslim village
On our last days, we completed our clockwise circuit. We sailed to the southern tip of Ko Yao Yai, dinghied through placid waters to the shore, and walked a rocky path to a Muslim fishing village. Its stilted walkways and buildings stood 20 feet above the low tide. The religion of its inhabitants attested to how this stretch of Thailand had stronger links, in terms of families, culture and economics, to Singapore, Penang and Kuala Lumpur than to Bangkok.

I attempted the ask if we could buy fish, a word

sounding like *plar* or *plaa* in Thai. No one seemed to understand, perhaps indicating that I had not used the correct tones or inflection for this complex language, or maybe that the men had not returned yet with the catch of the day.

We snorkeled the next morning at a nearby islet called Ko Khai Nok. Bright coral studded a long shelf extending west and south of its dazzling white-sand beach. We desperately wanted not to harm this aquatic wonderland, yet again our anchor snagged on the healthy reef despite our attempts to stay in 50 feet of water away from the ledge. Nickolas gently eased the rode out of the tangle as I nudged *Sweet Robin* forward and back at his direction.

On our final afternoon, moderate breezes pushed us north. The scenic monoliths seemed perfectly shaped and placed to let wind pass yet flatten the waves. We anchored off Ko Na Khae and explored nearby Ko Hong, identically named to the island we'd visited earlier and likewise featuring a spectacular interior lagoon. Macaques played on Ko Yai, a third island in the scenic anchorage. Only a plugged-up head ("toilet" to landlubbers), which Nick nobly repaired, bought a touch of difficulty to a sublime day.

We woke the next morning at dawn to a fiery red sky and began to make our way back to Laem Phrao and our lives in the West.

APRIL 1993
A postscript

After we'd been back for a month, I received a birthday card.

> Dear Captain!
>
> On your birthday we wish you many happy sailings and trips to interesting places in coming years.
>
> If you find a way to do it full time, do not forget about one handyman, who would not mind to repair toilets every time, even every day.
>
> I know the way how to do it!
>
> All we need is a little bit … money. So let's rob a Bank! Happy birthday!
>
> Nick and Eleanora

Thailand and the big lesson: ultimate sailing

Sailing charters in Thailand, the Chesapeake, the Virgin Islands, Greece, Belize and other places display radically different characters and changeable features depending on season and weather. Most places, while not quite as stellar as Thailand, are perfectly delightful if you accept their limitations.

Sailors tend to start in local waters, so I learned on the Chesapeake. Its serenity may be its most striking feature. Soft orange-pink dusks fall as you drop anchor in little coves, and mallards come quacking up for handouts. In June, the Chesapeake feels like the faux tropics, with limpid waters, moist heavy air carrying the smell of farmland, and flowering trees on the hills silhouetted in late afternoon like palms. I've shared gunkhole anchorages with a few cruising sailboats. At dawn on freshwater creeks, whitetail deer would come down to the water for a drink.

The atmosphere summons childhood memories of commercials on the local weather newscasts for National Bohemian beer—"brewed in the Land of Pleasant Living," a corny but perfectly accurate summing up of the Chesapeake.

In late summer, jellyfish make swimming in the Chesapeake risky. Still, the bay promises easy, accessible fun, with good restaurants to lash up to in Solomon's and Deale, the scenery around the U.S. Naval Academy in Annapolis, an infinity of snug creeks and coves and the ease of day sailing. I give it high marks for culture based on, among many other features, the Chesapeake Bay Maritime Museum in St. Michael's, the 18th and 19th century homes of Chestertown, and the fascination of watching the watermen's boats ply the Choptank River and the area around Tilghman Island.

Many American sailors graduate to sailing in the Virgin Islands (the "VI" to boaters), with their steady wind, deep water and decent swimming. This is where in 1988 I learned the basics of cruising sailing: staying out for days at a time and completing a circuit. The Annapolis Sailing School assigned Captain Bill Lee to take a group of five of us out of St. Croix and then to St. John, Peter and Norman islands, Tortola, Virgin Gorda and Jost Van Dyke.

Bill patiently answered our questions about every tiny aspect of sailing. The bet-your-life-on-it wind, almost always at 15 to 18 knots out of the northeast, simplified our grasp of sail trim, anchoring and navigation. All the complex physics of sailing could be absorbed in relation to a single compass point, unlike the twirling whispers and roars from all quarters on the Chesapeake.

We saw bays full of turtles and sailed behind a breaching humpback whale off St. John for an entire morning. I also had the first taste of the communal feeling of dinner aboard ship, with assigned tasks, small miracles of tastiness produced from the galley and story-telling under the stars. The focus on wide-ranging conversations reminded me of a visit in 1976 to my Acadian aunts and uncles in Nova Scotia, who never turned on the TV at night and would instead talk after dinner for hours in accented English.

After the Virgin Islands, Greece or Turkey present a logical next step for sailors. Most sailors think the Aegean Sea has much less consistent weather than the VI and much more in the way of archeological sites and overall culture. The archipelago smells like a spice

Finding perfect seas

One of history's greatest sailors and writers was Captain Joshua Slocum, who became the first man to circumnavigate the globe single-handedly, during a voyage that lasted from 1895 to 1898.

Slocum was born in the Annapolis Valley of Nova Scotia. He noted on the first page of *Sailing Alone Around the World* that

> The people of this coast, hardy, robust, and strong, are disposed to compete in the world's commerce, and it is nothing against the master mariner if the birthplace mentioned on his certificate be Nova Scotia.

"We make astonishing landfalls"—Hilaire Belloc might have been describing Ko Na Khae.

Slocum learned to sail on St. Mary's Bay, adjacent to the Belliveau ancestral homestead in Nova Scotia, established when our ancestors left the Loire Valley in France in 1644. (Jim and I share our Nova Scotian relatives' love of the sea; would that we shared particularly Slocum's skill and knowledge.) As a seasoned captain years later, Slocum rebuilt the sloop *Spray* in Fairhaven, Massachusetts, for his record-setting voyage.

Slocum described feeling awe and introspection as he looked at the constellations and meditated during "those supreme hours on the sea." Swordfish and dolphin escorted him for hundreds of miles. He wept upon seeing the beauty of the palms of Christmas Island, south of Java.

He discovered his own "perfect seas" in the Indian Ocean. For 23 days, as he headed toward the Cocos islands southwest of Sumatra, *Spray* kept a true course though Slocum took the wheel for only three hours during that time. Simple straps attached to her helm kept *Spray* on course—a testament to fine design, given that modern yachts require self-steering gear to achieve the same end.

In *The Riddle of the Sands*, Erskine Childers ascribed the beauty of the *Dulcibella*, during a sail off the Netherlands, to "a perfect fitness for her functions." English author Hilaire Belloc, who primarily wrote historical works, described in *The Cruise of the "Nona"* how sailing "is alive with discovery, emotion, adventure, peril and repose."

> The cruising of a boat here and there is very much what happens to the soul of a man in a larger way. We set out for places which we do not reach, or reach too late; and on the way, there befall us all manner of things which we could never have awaited. We are granted great visions, we suffer intolerable tediums.

Slocum, Childers, Belloc and other writers demonstrate how sailing can delight both the engineer and the poet found in many mariners, who appreciate fine design in a boat, a dolphin and the stars.

The characters of John Barth sail the Chesapeake in his novel *Sabbatical: A Romance.* They enjoy the "preciousness of such an hour, such a morning, on such a planet" as they sail out of a Maryland cove:

> The air is as sensuous on the Chesapeake this Sunday forenoon as ever in Jamaica or Trinidad.

Explorer Tristan Jones, who has sailed more than 400,000 miles, described encountering perfect seas on a passage from Capetown in South Africa to Recife in Brazil. He let *Barbara* "rip away into the horizon," with no reefs or shipping lanes to worry about, he wrote in *The Incredible Voyage*:

> This is the best kind of ocean sailing, with a clear way ahead, plenty of food and water onboard, a sound vessel and gear, and moderate weather. Sailing like this, you feel as free as a bird on the winds of the wide ocean.

Sailors recognize these moments: when a yacht hums along smoothly, a self-contained universe surrounded by the immensity of nature. When these times are shared with others, conversation soars; solo sailors enjoy intense contemplation. Captain Slocum said at such times his mind felt open to the events of his life:

> My memory worked with startling power. The ominous, the insignificant, the great, the small, the wonderful, the commonplace—all appeared before my mental vision in magical succession.

On perfect seas, we feel what Tristan Jones called "the pure hymn of the oceans."

Selected sailing areas

The world's great cruising grounds feature indented coasts with necklaces of islands. Seven of them are compared below.

1 Sea of Cortés (Gulf of California)

Swimming	★★★★
Culture	★★
Food	★★
Snorkeling	★★★
Weather	★★★
Scenery	★★★★

2 Belize

Swimming	★★★
Culture	★★
Food	★★★
Snorkeling	★★★★
Weather	★★★
Scenery	★★★

3 Virgin Islands

Swimming	★★★
Culture	★
Food	★★
Snorkeling	★★★
Weather	★★★★
Scenery	★★★

4 Chesapeake Bay

Swimming	★
Culture	★★★
Food	★★★★
Snorkeling	
Weather	★★★
Scenery	★★★

5 Greece

Swimming	★★
Culture	★★★★
Food	★★★★
Snorkeling	★★
Weather	★
Scenery	★★★★

6 Thailand

Swimming	★★★★
Culture	★★★
Food	★★★★
Snorkeling	★★★★
Weather	★★★★
Scenery	★★★★

7 Tonga

Swimming	★★★★
Culture	★★★★
Food	★★★
Snorkeling	★★★★
Weather	★★★★
Scenery	★★★

Ratings of Belize, Virgin Islands, Chesapeake Bay, Greece and Thailand by Jeannette Belliveau; ratings of Sea of Cortés and Tonga by Tina Sverdrup.

Key

A	★★★★
B	★★★
C	★★
D	★
E	

shop leaning heavily to oregano and thyme, with unforgettable anchorages near temples and suitable breakfasts for the gods: sublime fresh bread, honey, yogurt and grapes.

Belize offers a far more rustic and challenging alternative to the Virgin Islands, feeling like the West Indies might have in 1700—a pirate hideyhole. Two boats comprised the entire national charter fleet at the time of a February 1991 charter including Jim, me, and our friend Steve from London. Belize, though trickier to sail in than the popular Virgin Islands, blessedly lacked crowds.

In Belize, we gained much experience in reef navigation, learning to negotiate a watery maze. Our route took us south out of Belize City along a string of cays (uncanny how the word resembles the Thai *ko* for island). We placed a lookout on the foredeck to point to blue-water highways winding through mangrove and yellow-brown patches indicating coral tops at the water line.

A book called *Best Sailing Spots Worldwide* also recommends the waters between Vancouver Island and the Canadian mainland, from Puget Sound to Desolation Sound; Norway; Newfoundland; Florida's Gulf Coast; and New Zealand's Bay of Islands.

I have yet to sail in two other superlative grounds noted for quality snorkeling: the starkly beautiful Sea of Cortés off Baja California, an area of red cliffs echoing the American Southwest, and Tonga, an archipelago kingdom in the South Pacific.

Cruising sailor Tina Sverdrup, who lives in Colorado Springs, Colorado, gave high marks to the marine life in the Sea of Cortés. "We heard over the radio that there were dolphins in the area," she recalled. "We saw what seemed to be a natural or wind-created wave. It was hundreds of dolphins. We turned on the motor to follow them, and they turned around as one dolphin and came back toward us. Then they broke up and played a bit around the boat."

Compared to the Sea of Cortés, with its "spellbinding" sunsets and red and gold rocks, she said that "Tonga was entirely opposite, so lush and fairly untouched, though a little greed had begun to creep into the children."

She recalled Tonga's "incredible" feasts. "All guests sit cross-legged on two sides of a very long 'table' along which are placed, beautifully presented in shells or leaves, bits of pork, fish, breadfruit, sweet potato or yam and shellfish."

Sverdrup indicated that Tonga resembled Belize with its challenging reefs: "You had to be really careful, with someone on the bow as a lookout. We would do a 90-degree turn followed by another 90-degree turn, in a zigzag."

Combine the best features of all the globe's sailing areas and you have Thailand: swimming, snorkeling, scenery, food, culture, a lack of crowds.

Before we soared off to meet *Sweet Robin*, I asked my globetrotting travel agent, Phyllis Benjamin, whether she enjoyed her own sailing trip in Thailand. "Oh, the water," she said, raving about how she had swum for hours.

What makes for "ultimate sailing," however, is more than just an area possessing beautiful qualities. One also needs excellent companions, a fine boat and clement weather. Little is perfect in life, but our week on Phangnga Bay came close.

THE ODYSSEY OF *SANDSTORM*

Greece … and lessons on national greatness and decline

Jim and Chris watch the sun set over the Aegean.

If Helen of Troy launched a thousand ships, Athena of Olympus inspired tens of millions of trips. Lavishly illustrated children's storybooks depicting the enduring myths of Greece have been the catalyst for many an adult's decision to visit the country marketed in advertisements as the birthplace of Western civilization.

Seeing the playground of the gods became my dream when I reached my mid-20s and began to travel in Europe. Getting there proved easier than expected. In 1981, I began 3 1/2 years of working in England, where I had six weeks of vacation a year. Inexpensive charter flights from London permitted quite a few of those weeks to be taken in Greece. Many charters flew directly to resort islands as well as to Athens, illustrating the appeal of Greece's beaches as well as its ruins.

In 1982, on my first trip, I visited the Parthenon in Athens and the temple of Delphi. Then I flew to spectacular Santorini, perhaps the most dazzling Greek island, which consists of half of a volcano rim remain-

A man on Santorini rides a donkey to a hilltop monastery.

ing from a cataclysmic explosion. There I photographed a man riding a donkey up a steep path to the Profitias Ilias Monastery. He looked thoughtful and expressive, as might be expected of a citizen of a nation known in ancient times for philosophy. Yet his mode of transport, dating to biblical days, attested to how Greece lagged behind the rest of Europe economically.

In 1984 I cycled around most of western Crete. In the White Mountains, a Cretan with a handlebar moustache and bandolier of cartridges strapped across his chest stood beside a primitive track, holding his rifle in one hand and a dead hawk in the other. Like the man on the donkey, he radiated ancient pride yet seemed centuries apart from the modern world.

LESSON NUMBER 1: THE SIGHT OF THAT FIERCELY DIGNIFIED MOUNTAINEER EXPLAINED RATHER SIMPLY WHY THE VENETIANS, TURKS AND NAZIS NEVER ERADICATED THE RESISTANCE FIGHTERS IN THE INTERIOR OF CRETE.

And in 1988, I led a group that sailed in the Cyclades, a cluster of islands in the middle of the Aegean. A desire to see Greece once in my lifetime had escalated to three trips in seven years. And each time, I wondered about two things:

These unassuming guys sipping coffee on the village square and riding donkeys in the hills, are they really the descendants of the great philosophers?

What will happen to the United States when its time too is past—when the Greatest Power slips to just a Power, and maybe even a Non-power?

The contrast between the gods and philosophers depicted in children's books, clad in their spotless togas, and today's underemployed villagers and simple goatherds, in dark garb head to toe, seemed impossible to ignore.

And in picture books, ancient Athens was depicted as an urban Utopia, of clean buildings and citizens who treasured a developed mind and body. The road from the airport into modern Athens, however, was my first exposure to the dilapidated, jumbled look typical of the cities of much of Eurasia, in a giant arc between Naples and southern China. Nondescript cement apartment complexes bore rust and fluttered laundry on lines.

The constrained circumstances of modern Greece are not news to anyone who studies the area. Robert D. Kaplan wrote in *Balkan Ghosts: A Journey Through History* that

> In the learning centers of the West … the most recent 2,000 years of Greek history were virtually ignored in favor of an idealized version of ancient Greece, a civilization that had already died before Jesus' birth. The West would not accept that Greece was more a child of Byzantium and Turkish despotism than of Periclean Athens.

Similarly, Emily Hiestand described in *The Very Rich Hours* a scholar of pre-Socratic literature who refused to visit Greece any more, bemoaning the dirtiness of its cities and sites overrun by tourists.

And a Maryland friend who lived as a child in Greece recalled asking his mother why these descendants of philosophers now herded goats. She urged him to not judge the Greeks harshly and to retain sight of Greek achievement.

Greeks themselves wrestle with their modern condition, which results not from cultural freefall but largely from political events. Greece made little progress during nearly four centuries of Turkish rule beginning in 1456. When Greece became independent in 1830, it was a destitute peasant country.

In the 20th century, Greece suffered greatly during the Nazi occupation, and later endured civil war and long stretches of political chaos.

And at the time of my visits in the 1980s, inflation and corruption beset the country. Because of Westerners' exalted and sentimental view of Greece, Kaplan wrote that few of us

> could understand what began happening in Greece in the 1980s, an era when Greece's former Prime Minister and President, Constantine Karamanlis, described the country as a "vast lunatic asylum."

Modern Greece gave an impression that it had given its all to the West and kept little for itself. Its people have been emigrés from ancient times to the modern day. Five million Greeks have emigrated in a 20th century diaspora to the United States, Germany and Australia, and only 10 million people remain in Greece itself.

Greece today lives outside of Greece, in children's imaginations, in scholars of Hellenic descent at Europe's and America's universities, in the *kafeneions* of

East Baltimore's Greektown and politicians with names like Dukakis and Sarbanes and Sfikas. *The conquered conquers the conqueror*, historians wrote of how Rome adopted the culture of subjugated Greece, a reference that could apply to much of the West.

The Greeks even bequeathed a tradition of individualism, seen today, for example, when NBA star Charles Barkley barks, "You can't guard me!" to Scottie Pippin.

In ancient times, the Athenians honored their patron Athena at her temple, the Parthenon, on the Acropolis. They could not foresee that in the future the symbol of Greece and even Western civilization would be dissolving in acid rain created by pollution, its best statuary on display 1,500 miles away in the British Museum. The loss of prestige by the nation held in esteem perhaps by almost every idealistic Western schoolchild unnerves the American visitor, who may wonder, *Can it be that here go I, eventually?*

MONDAY, OCT. 24, 1988
Down the coast of ancient Attica

My brother Jim motored us out of Kalamaki harbor, the profile of Athens' low skyline receding behind our stern. Our conveyance around the islands was the noble *Sandstorm*, a 38-foot Beneteau yacht with a price tag we estimated at around $130,000. A Maryland-based yacht broker helped us to charter Sandstorm for a week from an Athens-based company called Seafarer for about $1,400.

When you tell people you plan to go sailing in Greece, it sounds like a carefree exercise. But a fine yacht like *Sandstorm,* a comfortable white fiberglass cruising sailboat that handled well, carried weighty responsibilities. Whether our pooled experience would measure up to the task remained an open question.

LESSON NUMBER 2: MOST PEOPLE PROBABLY THINK OF SAILING AS A RELAXING ACTIVITY. YET THIS IMAGE CAN BE DECEPTIVE. SAILING REQUIRES CONSTANT VIGILANCE AND ADJUSTMENTS TO SAILS AND RUDDER TO MEET CHANGING SEA CONDITIONS.

Three of us had a few years of experience on the Chesapeake Bay: Jim, our friend Stephany, and I.

My brother and I, who would split leadership responsibilities, fortunately had complementary skills. Jim's résumé at the time focused on motorboats, mine on sailboats—"stinkpots" and "ragtops" in Chesapeake Bay parlance. I'd done day trips and captained a one-week jaunt on the Chesapeake. Most important, I had completed a week-long live-aboard sailing course in the Virgin Islands with an excellent instructor.

Still, the Greek voyage would be only my second experience as a captain. It was bit early in my career at the helm to go overseas, especially late in the Aegean

Navigating in popular cruising areas

Navigating in Greece: Look for a white town against a brown island, such as Tínos, above. Head for it.

Our home waters on the Chesapeake can be tricky. Numbered navigation aids mark the extensive shallows of the Chesapeake, more of a drowned river than a true bay. A navigator must identify a nun (red, with a pointed top and an even number) or a can (green, flat-topped and odd numbered) and match it to chart information to avoid going aground.

Belize requires nudging through a bewildering maze of reef and mangrove. More than once during a 1991 trip there, we threaded our way along only to watch nervously as what we thought were separate reefs met in a closed loop. We would retrace our route, sometimes only to dead-end again.

Few of Belize's perplexing conditions can be found either in the Aegean or the deep Caribbean water lying between the big, easy-to-recognize Virgin Islands. In either place, we could usually see the ridge lines of the next big island first thing in the morning. All we had to do was raise anchor and point the bow toward our unmissable target. Greece, simpler even than the Virgin Islands, did not have any reefs to avoid along the way.

LESSON NUMBER 3: IN TERMS OF NAV-IGATION, GREECE SEEMED TO BE THE EASIEST PLACE WE'D EVER SAILED.

season, when a vicious wind the Greeks call the *meltemi* can roar down from the north.

A fourth crew member also had some sailing experience. Ursula, a colleague from the *Baltimore Sun*, planned to rendezvous with us on Míkonos at the halfway point of the trip.

Two nautical rookies rounded out our group. Chris, an editor at the *Minneapolis Star-Tribune*, was Ursula's friend going back to when they worked together in Tokyo on the Pacific edition of the military tabloid *Stars and Stripes*.

We had never even met our final member, Steve, a software writer in London. A friend of a friend of mine, he got wind of the trip. Thinking it sounded fun, he signed on. We had snagged him the previous night at Athens' international airport by holding up his name lettered on a sign, as though we were package tour operators.

Our trip planning had required quite a bit of telephoning and faxing between Maryland and Minneapolis, London and Athens. And finally, we found ourselves actually sailing in the Greek Isles.

Undeveloped shoreline lay on our port side as *Sandstorm* pulled smartly southeast. After three uneventful hours we cleared Cape Soúnion—the last finger of mainland Greece, known as Attica in ancient times.

We pointed to the dramatic Cyclades (sih-CLA-deez), a cluster of 56 islands known for both white cubelike buildings and a role in Greek mythology as the homes of Apollo and Artemis.

A Maryland friend with extensive experience as a charter captain in Greece, Dick Allen, thought our planned route—Athens to Míkonos and back—might be overly ambitious. Usually people with a simple seven-day charter out of Athens stick to nearby Hydra, Póros and Aegina.

Yet our charter company in Athens did not think our itinerary out of the question and helped us to plot its details. So we left the Saronic Gulf and pointed east toward the first Cyclades island, Kéa, rather than south toward Aegina. We aimed for Vourkari, a protected harbor on Kéa's northwest side.

Vourkari would provide our first experience with Greek-style anchoring. We had been coached on the procedure by Captain Allen. He had described how we would have to drop anchor in open water, motor backwards several boat lengths to the dock and affix stern lines. A swim ladder on the transom would swing down to double as a gangplank.

All this maneuvering seemed a lot trickier than just swinging free on an anchor or docking in a marina. Yet Greek-style anchoring did offer two advantages:

It made good use of the limited harbor space.

It cost nothing, unlike the $1 per foot of sailboat length that many Chesapeake marinas charge.

We reached Kéa and threaded our way down Agios Nikolaos Bay, which narrowed to a protected inlet. When we reached the docks at the hamlet of Vourkari, Jim again took over motoring duties. We anchored correctly on our first try. Seeking dinner, we hiked an undulating path toward a town called Korissía, back near the mouth of the bay. A full moon shone on the footpath and reflected off the dark water below.

A large and busy taverna was open. Like the restaurants at which I'd eaten on previous trips, it seemed to offer a typical menu of a half-dozen items:

• *Tzatziki* (cucumber and yogurt salad) with pita bread.

• Greek salad. In Greece itself, this consisted simply of feta cheese, vine-ripened tomatoes and sliced cucumbers with a dusting of oregano and olive oil.

- *Moussaka* (eggplant and ground lamb casserole).
- *Souvlaki* (grilled lamb on a skewer).
- *Pastitsio* (baked macaroni with a topping of white sauce).
- *Dolmathes* (stuffed grape leaves).

LESSON NUMBER 4: EATING IN TAVERNAS INVOLVED LOOKING AROUND THE KITCHEN TO SEE IF BY SOME MIRACLE, ANY OF THE HUNDREDS OF ENTRÉES IN OUR PHRASEBOOK MIGHT BE AVAILABLE. THEN, UPON FINDING THE ANSWER TO BE NO, WE'D ORDER THE UNVARYING STANDARD SIX AND SHARE IT ALL, LIKE A CHINESE MEAL.

Back aboard the moonlit *Sandstorm*, we slept and set off the next day for Tínos.

TUESDAY, OCT. 25
Deeper into the Cyclades
When our vessel rounded the north end of Kéa, Andros lay straight ahead, with Tínos to its right. We steered toward the southern tip of Tínos.

We had two easy tasks: to avoid hitting either Yíaros, an uninhabited island roughly in the middle of the Andros-Tínos-Kéa triangle, or a lone freighter that we saw around noon. That left us plenty of time to cast stars to play roles in our imaginary movie, *Sandstorm Odyssey*.

Bjorn Borg would play Chris, with Connie Chung for Ursula, Jodie Foster for Stephany and Tom Selleck as Jim. The boyish-looking Steve would be played by Jerry Mathers (Beaver Cleaver). Steve either was so much like the Beave that he took the comparison in stride, or so British that it missed him completely. The group flattered me by picking Katharine Hepburn for my role.

The town dock appeared by afternoon: a white cluster at the waterline, stark against the brown hills. We made a sharp turn to port and then starboard to negotiate the breakwater protecting Tínos harbor.

The crews of two yachts already in port regarded our smooth anchoring in silence. These blond yachtsmen appeared to be Germans in their fifties and sixties. They wore matching foul-weather gear of a bright school-bus yellow and safety harnesses, which can be attached in wild weather to points on the yacht deck.

They seemed too surprised at our youthful and ragtag appearance to offer words of welcome. Their demeanor conveyed a clear message: *We are prepared, as you are not, to sail in Greece.* *Sandstorm*'s crew averaged about 27 years old. We modeled:
- A ballcap reading "Governor Schaefer welcomes you to Maryland" (Jim).
- A rugby sweater (Steve).
- A Day-Glo orange bike poncho and non-matching gray Orioles visor (me).
- An assortment of parkas, Irish wool sweaters and running shoes.

We sat down for another all-six-things-on-the-menu dinner at a dockside taverna. Murals ran along its upper walls depicting Greek maritime history. We sampled the fiery anise-flavored liqueur, ouzo and felt the promise ahead of a week of idyllic sailing in the historical wake of Odysseus.

As the wind gathered strength, we returned to our berths to sleep.

WEDNESDAY, OCT. 26
Feels like stormy weather
Stephany's diary recorded events of the next morning:

We wake in Tínos to unbelievable winds. A 44-foot Jeanneau attempted to leave, was blown into a fisherman's anchor line, and it took two hours and a scuba diver to unhook them.

Under gray skies, we watched the Jeanneau's troubles somberly, hoping that similar problems would not befall us. The diver maneuvered slowly in the protected harbor, sheltered from the worst of the norther, or *meltemi,* by the bulk of Tínos' steep hills. Even so, ripples raced across the harbor, and whitecaps blew in the Aegean beyond.

Jim and Stephany took advantage of the delay afforded by the blow and rented a motorcycle to explore hilltop villages. Chris and I walked partway up the hills above Tínos town, chatting and enjoying the view. Steve took it easy on the docks.

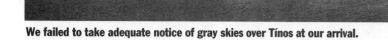
We failed to take adequate notice of gray skies over Tínos at our arrival.

Stephany wrote later:

The view of the ocean captivated me. I could not believe we had crossed that open area in a 38-foot sailboat to arrive where we were. It was beautifully mystifying.

We stopped by the boat to grab a bite and found Jeannette etc. preparing to shove off. The wind had slowed so much that it did not seem very strong, comparatively.

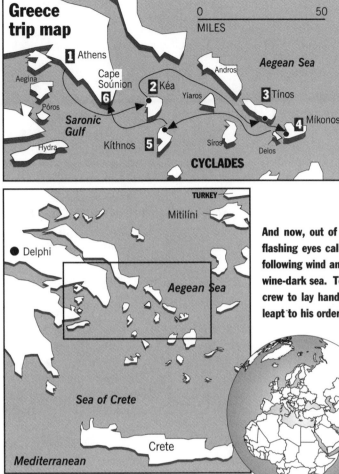

Before deciding what to do, I studied the sea for a long while. I looked at the the waves in the Aegean, which appeared to be about four feet high and steep yet tolerable.

I wondered, however, what would happen when we left the wind shadow of Tínos for the dash across an open strait to Míkonos. There we might face the full brunt of a wind roaring down from the Russian steppes.

I stood on *Sandstorm's* white foredeck and pondered this dilemma. The answer arrived out of the ether. Into my head came the voice of Peter Meredith, a long-time friend from *Baltimore Sun* days and my original sailing teacher. I recalled something he'd said on our day sails on the Chesapeake:

LESSON NUMBER 5 (FROM PETER): "WHEN IN DOUBT, ALWAYS CARRY LESS SAIL THAN YOU THINK YOU NEED."

Even using a handkerchief's worth of sail, Peter would not have been foolhardy enough to go out in the rising wind. But we had a planned rendezvous the next day with Ursula. It would be horribly confusing if after her dawn flight landed, *Sandstorm* was not waiting on schedule at the Míkonos dock.

We didn't want to get ourselves in trouble in a bad weather passage. Nor did we relish being stranded across a channel, 10 miles from our friend, who had proposed this trip in the first place.

Ursula had described a fantasy involving a cabin boy mixing margaritas and serving them on trays as we lolled in swimsuits on the foredeck. Alas, our imaginings would be more suited to the 375-foot

Onassis yacht *Christina* in July than *Sandstorm* in late October. Our trip occurred one week into the dubious weather season, and, as my husband the historian later pointed out, in seas *The Odyssey* portrays as treacherous rather than kindly.

And now, out of the West, Athene of the flashing eyes called up for them a steady following wind and sent it singing over the wine-dark sea. Telemachus shouted to the crew to lay hands on the tackle and they leapt to his orders. They hauled up the fir mast, stept it in its hollow box, made it fast with stays, and hoisted the white sail with plaited oxhide ropes. Struck full by the wind, the sail swelled out, and a dark wave hissed loudly round her stem as the vessel gathered way and sped through the choppy seas, forging ahead on her course.

Homer depicted Greek mastery of sailing in *The Odyssey*

LESSON NUMBER 6: IF WE WERE BETTER EDUCATED IN CLASSICAL LITERATURE, WE WOULD HAVE BEEN MORE PREPARED FOR THE RIGORS OF SAILING IN THE AEGEAN.

I thought that, for two hours, we might be able to handle a fair amount of bad weather, and the risk was acceptable to stay on schedule. So we reefed the main sail, sailor talk for furling and tying down its bottom two-thirds. We replaced the regular jib, the forward triangular sail, with a much tinier storm jib.

The two German crews looked on with justifiable amazement as we shoved off, probably expecting to next hear of us as a disaster story on the news. We headed southeast. A mammoth ferry bound for Míkonos soon followed, right on our stern. To get out of the way, we tacked right. They passed left, and all was well. The sight of a Greek ship on the otherwise lonely water gave us a scrap of reassurance that we were not loons to be out in this weather.

The wind stepped up, its whistle gradually getting

Chris gets us out of the way of a Greek ferry as we sail off the coast of Tínos on our attempt to cross to Míkonos.

louder. Slowly we could see the tip of Tínos passing off our port side, as an incipient gale gathered strength. *Sandstorm* raced along at a speed that felt like seven to eight knots. We passed the tip of Tínos, and Míkonos hove into view, directly in front of us.

In calmer weather, this would be a milk run, an hour and a half to barely get the sails raised and the topsides wet before making harbor. On that late October day, however, the waves rose a mountainous (to our eyes) 10 feet, pounding in from the northeast.

After one hour, at the midpoint of the run, the waves began to crest higher. If we kept to our true course, a southeasterly one, they would pound us directly on the port side and turn *Sandstorm* into a wallowing beast.

We had to cut a bit to the east or even northeast to ride up the waves at a more comfortable angle. The waves climbed to 10 to 13 feet high, indicating, according to the Beaufort wind scale, that a force 7 near-gale (at the least) would be part of our holiday memories.

Solid *Sandstorm* proved to be a trooper, climbing each wave like a mountaineer and skiing down each trough, without noise or groaning or misdirection. She felt sound. And that fact meant that we could probably survive any storm, as long as our keel did not touch a shore.

LESSON NUMBER 7: THE ONLY POTENTIAL DANGER TO A WELL-MADE YACHT, DESIGNED TO WITHSTAND ALL SEA CONDITIONS, ARISES FROM CONTACT WITH THE LAND.

Jim and Chris alternated on the helm during the storm. Gut survival techniques replaced our egalitarian plan to rotate duties, making sure that everyone got equal time on the helm. The storm dictated Darwinism on the tiller.

Stalwart Chris stood at the wheel, legs spread apart and balanced. Six foot three, blond and green-eyed, he resembled a Viking chieftain, if the Norse voyagers had possessed red rain slickers and stayed as calm as a midsummer day in Nebraska, Chris' native state.

During his turn, Jim squinted at Míkonos and made his calculations of wave, wind and distance. He took *Sandstorm* up and down the water mountains with

minor course adjustments, gripping the helm easily like just another set of weight equipment at the gym. He had begun to look like a Greek deck hand, with moustache, a three-day stubble and windburn.

Views on the seriousness of our predicament off Míkonos varied depending on where people sat on *Sandstorm*. Stephany occupied the most fearful vantage point, on the port side at the front of the cockpit, hanging on to the main sheet. Tons of water heaved and sunk just a few yards from her elbow. I sat directly across from her, on the starboard side, yet the heeling of the boat meant that my head was about three to four feet lower than hers. Thus the tilted port side of the yacht itself blocked much of the unpleasantness of the scene.

As Stephany wrote later:

> My heart pumped, my eyes were mesmerized as I watched a procession of two waves about 15 feet high. I was no longer mesmerized but praying for safety. I was the only one on the high side of the boat with a life-threatening job on the sheet to the mainsail, my only job being to let it fly if a gust caught the main. I could barely move and wondered if anyone else on the boat was half as frightened as I, because if they were, it did not show.
>
> I will never forget this two-hour period of my life and the intensity and flood of emotions, fear, anxiety, and faith which accompanied it.

But those of us on the low side of the cockpit, not grasping the full extent of the cauldron buffeting the high side, enjoyed pranks. When a series of giant waves came and struck the side of *Sandstorm*, Stephany and I anticipated them and ducked. Walls of water cascaded over the deck and our heads and caught Steve full in the face.

He sat as soaked as if someone had upended a bucket over his head. We laughed as though we were kids watching *The Three Stooges* rather than adults living *The Poseidon Adventure*.

As we drew closer, we could discern the first details of the harbor on Míkonos' west coast. Yet it appeared frozen in place after we first spotted it. We made no more progress. The sails could not convert enough of the wind's fury into forward motion to counter the wave's sideways pounding. Natural forces began to sweep us sideways, toward Crete.

Either I had underestimated this storm when we left Tínos, or more likely, guessed wrong that it would not strengthen. We could no longer hold *Sandstorm* to face the white cluster of buildings marking the mouth of the harbor. The bow pointed toward jagged rocks jutting south of the town.

Sandstorm was losing ground. Spray smacked Stephany more than ever, as we tried to cut more steeply into the waves. As captain, I began to realize how unfair it was to stick Stephany with the rotten task of hanging onto the mainsheet in a gale. I should have taken that job.

Stephany later wrote:

Fear had begun to set in when the following words were spoken. "Why don't we start the engine?" Jeannette said.

I was befuddled by the accolades from the crew that followed my suggestion to switch on *Sandstorm's* motor. Without the engine, we would either crunch on the rocks south of Míkonos harbor or spin on the breeze to say hello to Colonel Qaddafi in Libya. This seemed obvious to me. Yet they carried on as though it were the greatest example of high-seas brilliance since Admiral Nelson defeated the Spanish and French fleets at Trafalgar.

With the engine on, the yacht finally began to claw straight ahead. We bucked and surfed continuously on the stalwart back of *Sandstorm*, as if riding the Rebel Yell roller coaster at King's Dominion in Virginia.

After what felt like an eternity, we drew into the harbor of Míkonos. To my distress, the harbor barely protected us from the fierce winds. We had almost as much turbulence and racket from the wind and waves as on the open sea.

Our pilot book gave Míkonos harbor a "D" rating. It could not have been more opposite to snug Tínos, which had natural indentations and sheltering hills blocking wind from the north.

Míkonos' harbor lacked all natural protection, being just a low man-made stone wall that screened only the worst of the waves and let the north wind pass unchallenged.

I stood amidships to supervise our docking in this morass. From my vantage, I could talk (or in this case, yell) to Jim at the helm and Stephany on the anchor.

The international sailing community marooned by the gale—Polish, German, French and Japanese sailors—gathered on the dock to watch us. Nobody wanted to miss the entertainingly grim spectacle of neophytes in a grade "D" harbor anchoring Greek style in a gale.

Jim guided us in perfectly. Stephany dropped the anchor accurately at the optimal spot. *Sandstorm* reversed flawlessly against 40 mph winds, in what would be a remarkable feat even in dead calm given the way sailboat propellers tend to "walk," or pull the boat to one side, while reversing.

Four feet from completing our finest anchoring attempt of the week, despite the howling gale, the anchor chain snagged as it was being fed out of its foredeck locker into the water.

I felt sick with disappointment. We would have to go back into the roiling harbor and try again.

As we prepared for a second approach, I watched a sight so unwelcome that my mind still balks at registering it: Stephany pulling the anchor chain up, hand over hand, until reaching its final link. She discovered just one problem: no anchor. Its empty chain lay in Stephany's hands like a riddle.

Apparently the anchor had snagged on a tangle of modern and antiquated sea junk that lay at the bottom of the 5,000-year-old harbor, constructed during the Cyclades civilization that even predates the ancient Greeks.

At the instant Stephany discovered the missing anchor, Jim announced, "The throttle cable's broke." We had twin disasters underway, and I was the only one to realize it.

Sailors rely on six principal controls: throttle, engine, sails, sheets (ropes to control the sails), helm, and anchor. With sails furled, sheets irrelevant, no anchor and a broken throttle cable, *Sandstorm* was crippled in four areas. All we had to work with was the helm and the engine.

As I stared at Stephany, frozen in contemplation of the non-anchor, and processed Jim's little announcement, a huge gob of information arrived in a mental flash:

• The wind was pushing us into the rocky riprap of the eastern edge of Míkonos harbor.

• We were powerless to do much about it. Perhaps we could stick three fenders over the side to protect, at best, the cosmetics of a token bit of the fiberglass finish as the rest got destroyed.

• It would take five people many weeks of take-home wages to pay off a totaled $130,000 yacht.

Solutions to these predicaments eluded me. Fortunately, Jim came up with our second inspiration of the afternoon. He would control *Sandstorm* by turning on the engine. Without a throttle, it would run, but only at a sickening 5,000 rpm (3,000 is the usual maximum). Jim would race the sailboat, then hit the kill button. In this fashion we could lurch forward.

He experimented with the technique. *Sandstorm* twirled around the cramped harbor in a tight little circle. Unlike a sailboat engine's usual steady clip-clop, at this speed we could have dragged water-skiers.

The peanut gallery gathered at harborside offered words of wisdom.

"S L O O W W   D O W W N," they advised, a distant shout mixed with the howl of the wind.

"W E C A N ' T T T T," came our reply, stuffed back in our throats by the gale. Busy trying to survive, we had no time to provide details as to why we mishandled our noble yacht as though it were a Jetski.

Jim took aim at the dock. We approached it head on. Just when it appeared our Beneteau was going to score a bull's-eye and become a heap of fiberglass toothpicks, Jim hit the engine's kill button.

Sandstorm glided forward swiftly. Unnervingly close to the dock, she finally slowed, as the gale held her up.

Directly alongside the 65-foot Polish schooner *Zyawa* ("Spirit"), *Sandstorm's* momentum expended itself. She came to a perfect halt, balanced motionless for the merest second between forward progress and slipping away.

LESSON NUMBER 8: JIM, LIKE THE CREW OF APOLLO 13, HAD PERFECTLY COMPUTED THE PHYSICS INVOLVED IN GUIDING A CRIPPLED CRAFT TO SAFETY ON WHAT MIGHT BE A ONE-SHOT CHANCE.

Before the wind could bulldoze us back a second time to potential disaster, *Zyawa's* crew grabbed our lines.

We'd made it. *Sandstorm* would be the last private boat to arrive in Míkonos for three days.

Zyawa's crew tied *Sandstorm* alongside, with lots of fenders to protect our sides. In passable English, they invited us over for hot coffee. We changed into our last dry clothes and headed next door for a social.

"Welcome to Poland," said a rail-thin, bearded mate. He directed us down a long staircase of dark wood, along a labyrinthine corridor and into a captain's reception room. We sat in the near dark on narrow benches around a large square table that nearly filled the low-ceilinged room.

Zyawa's captain knew no English. He directed the others to give us coffee and shots of Polish vodka.

Our encounter in the near dark felt like an audience granted to explorers bought to the tent of an Arab prince. Apparently rituals attended the rescue of mariners. We had no means to thank these Polish seamen for their lifelines except to accept the additional kindness of their hospitality.

LESSON NUMBER 9: TRAVEL'S DANGERS MAY BRING REWARDS. THE GALE HAD CREATED A RELATIONSHIP THAT WOULD NOT HAVE EXISTED HAD WE MADE AN UNEVENTFUL ARRIVAL ON A PLEASANT AFTERNOON.

Rank needed to be sorted out. The two mates, full-time teachers back in Poland, spoke English well.

"Who is your captain?" they asked. Braced for disbelief or teasing, I raised my hand, knowing that I would be their last guess, after our three men and probably even Stephany.

They seemed a bit surprised, but at least they did not laugh out loud.

"And your first mate?"

In response, Jim raised his hand.

When Stephany, Steve and Chris said they were from Washington, London and Minneapolis, the sailors did not respond. They lit up when I said "Baltimore," a major port like their home, Gdansk.

They fairly erupted at Jim's one-word utterance, "Annapolis." "An-nah-PO-liss," they repeated with delight, reworking the syllable stress. Why, they were scheduled to go there in a year on a goodwill mission!

LESSON NUMBER 10: THE POLISH SAILORS, LIKE MANY PEOPLE WE MET ON THE WATERS OF GREECE, KNEW PORTS BEST AND WERE FAMILIAR WITH A U.S. GAZETTEER OF MORE THAN JUST LARGE CITIES.

Our emotional reactions to 15-foot waves might have seemed trivial to rugged Polish sailors of the stalwart wooden ship. They described having persevered in the face of 50-footers on the Bay of Biscay (off Bordeaux in France) on their way to Greece.

After one hour and one empty bottle of vodka, we left under the dark skies of a stormy late afternoon to get dinner. The wind continued to whistle. The storm showed no sign of ending when we later bunked down on the *Sandstorm*, beside our big buddy *Zyawa*.

I slept, or tried to, in the salon. Our vision of sailing around in swim suits as cabin boys serve us margaritas seemed like a cruel joke. Instead, the bitter cold had us sleeping unwashed and wearing everything we'd packed: coats, sweatshirts and sweat pants we'd planned to wear not a minute before our return to the wintry United States.

The noise followed a pattern all that night and the next. The wind would shove *Sandstorm* back, straining against the spare jib sheets we had run from her winches to the dock and *Zyawa*. A shuddering sound ran down the sides of the boat. *Sandstorm* would rock back, stretching the fibers in the sheets to the maximum, then rebound forward as far as a spring line attached diagonally to *Zyawa* would permit. The sheets emitted a screaming noise, and the winches groaned.

The wind vibrated the mast from its top, through where it passed into the salon and down to where it met the keel, shaking *Sandstorm* to her roots. And this was in a harbor! We were fortunate not to still be at sea, where only a profound ignorance of our ignorance had allowed us to remain calm through the day's events.

We had not expected to be bundled in winter clothes in Míkonos. From left: Chris, me, Jim, Stephany and Steve.

Captain's log

Tínos	1:50 p.m.
Míkonos	4 p.m.
	(Time of mid-anchor)
Distance	About 12-14 miles
Time elapsed	2 hours, 10 minutes
Attempted course	120 degrees
	East-southeast

THURSDAY, OCT. 27

Yacht baby-sitting on Míkonos

Heavy footsteps trod on the deck of *Sandstorm* at 6:30 a.m. Then voices called out in an unknown language.

Where was I? Oh yes, in Greece, in a gale, eyes swollen with fatigue and strain. Aha, these voices must be our saviors from the *Zyawa*.

"You have a friend here," they announced.

Ursula stood silently on the dock, at the bow of *Sandstorm*, in blue windbreaker, fanny pack, camera around her neck.

We had called her in the United States and left the name of our yacht on her answering machine. She made her way to Athens and transferred to the last flight into Míkonos before the ever-rising wind closed the airport. She headed for the dock, where huge white letters on her blue mainsail cover spelled out *Sandstorm's* presence as scheduled.

I staggered up to greet her in the wrinkled clothes I'd slept in. Ursula bore a silent air that said, *Okay, here we are, what are we gonna do?* She sized up the situation and decided to stay in a hotel until we left. The rest of us remained loyal by sleeping on the boat.

By the time I returned to the galley, the throttle cable, all eight feet of it, snaked across the cockpit. Before I could even start to boil water for coffee, Jim had found some tools and disassembled the wheel post and the paneling around the engine to remove the cable. I offered thanks to whichever Greek god handles vocational-technical education that Jim had taken auto mechanics at Richard Montgomery High School in Rockville, Maryland. The journalists and computer software designers of our crew would need many hours to begin to comprehend what was obviously a simple task for a mechanic.

When you're sixteen, everybody—adults, that is—urges you not to waste your time on motorhead pursuits, to concentrate on useful endeavors like algebra and Latin. Driving around Africa was gratifying if for no other reason than it proved all those people wrong. I constantly found myself trying to remember the offhand mechanical comments of my friends and cursed myself for dedicating even a moment to algebra and Latin when I could have been doing something productive, like taking apart transmissions.

Stuart Stevens in *Malaria Dreams: An African Adventure*

That day we had planned to visit Delos, the mythical birthplace of Apollo and Artemis, where ruins attest to a thriving trading center 2,000 years ago. With no choice in the matter, we accepted our mandated new itinerary. Delos: scratch. Added starter: a marine parts store.

It looked like we would spend more, maybe considerably more, than one day in Míkonos, and it wouldn't be a giddy round of beaches and discos either. We'd get a close off-season look at a shuttered town during a gale. The harborside seemed particularly melancholy, its cafe restaurant closed. Only a pair of German men, months past the summer hordes and probably lost and bored, strolled the dock.

Everyone felt a bit confused to be in a party town that had rolled up the sidewalks, as though we were so many robins blown by a hurricane from our Key West vacation back to Ohio.

As we strolled into the maze of Míkonos town, we waved the cable and stitched together a few words from my phrasebook, such as *mechanico* (mechanic) and *varka* (a word, eerily like ark, meaning boat, and somehow close to *vahka, waga* and *wa'a* in various Polynesian dialects). We obtained sufficient directions to march south through the town and then ascend a hill on its outskirts.

A local marine shop stood on the left, in a plain barn-like building. I was pleased to see that this island of just 4,500 people, catering to celebrities and to an extent the European gay party scene, had not become so touristic as to lack a decently stocked source of nautical equipment. We bought a regular plow anchor, not quite as valuable as the Danforth (a type with better holding capabilities) we'd lost, and a shackle to affix it

Zyawa breezes out into the gale, above. The other yachts, including *Sandstorm* (right, center), huddle at Míkonos harbor.

to the anchor rode (chain). The little shop also had throttle cables. Though the cable available was longer and of a slightly different design to our broken one, Jim thought it would work reasonably well.

LESSON NUMBER 12: THE AVAILABILITY OF A MARINE THROTTLE CABLE ON A TOURIST ISLAND SHOWED HOW DEEP GREECE'S MARITIME TRADITIONS RAN.

The unexpected bill came to the equivalent of $140, wiping out our kitty of Greek drachmas for taverna meals and on-board provisions. We passed the hat, and Chris handed over most of the last of the money he'd bought for the trip.

On the way back, we left our laundry to be done at the hotel Ursula had found. The staff also allowed us to take showers for only a few dollars. I stood for many minutes under the hot water.

It was a pleasure to [Odysseus] to see a hot bath again, for he had not been used to such comforts since leaving the home of the refined Calypso.

Homer in *The Odyssey*

We took turns going for showers. During the day, we left one person aboard the sailboat at all times, a duty that crimped our ability to relax and explore Míkonos. But we had to keep an eye on our tenuous attachment to *Zyawa* and the possibility of other yachts breaking loose and drifting around the harbor.

As I returned after my shower, the wind blew so

strongly that I could hardly pull breath into my lungs. I had to lean almost horizontally to fight my way back. On a little rise overlooking the harbor, I composed a photograph of *Sandstorm* and her five yacht companions huddled under the malevolent skies. The wind pushed my hands and the camera sideways. I had to lie on my stomach and prop my left (leeward) elbow against a rock.

The wind stepped up yet another notch as we returned to *Sandstorm* and began our repairs. Worse, our Polish saviors left us. Tough as an aircraft carrier, *Zyawa* breezed out into weather that we found fearsome even on land.

With *Zyawa* gone, at first we just tied up parallel to the dock. The water there was a nightmare of conflicting currents. The cement began to beat up *Sandstorm* as Jim affixed the replacement cable as best he could. He warned everyone that it could slip and that we would have to to baby the throttle from now on.

I stood on the heaving foredeck and cautiously attached the new anchor, not wanting it to fall and join its predecessor on the bottom of Míkonos harbor. I found a bit of wire as my *Chapman Piloting* manual suggested, tying the top of the anchor to the third link as a safety in case the shackle or first two links failed.

In the middle of the project, Stephany walked up wobbily to the dock, a used car tire in each hand. On her own volition, she had explored, found the town dump and retrieved the tires. These would serve as free fenders, to augment the four or so on board. *Good job!* I thought.

We had no time to savor the triumph of our repairs. The Eurosailors told us that as soon as the weather permitted, a ferry would arrive at our end of the dock. We would have to move.

We motored in, bow first, beside a boat occupied by a Frenchman and a Japanese woman. The move posed the question of how to position an anchor off the stern to stabilize *Sandstorm*.

The couple came over to help. After many suggestions, we finally decided on a plan. Via the dinghy, two of our number would lower the spare anchor in the middle of the harbor. As the rest of us reeled them back on a line, they would play out the anchor rode, then cleat it tightly to the stern of *Sandstorm*.

The procedure sounded straightforward. Yet the powerful wind added a degree of danger to going out in a dinghy, and its incessant howling struck a note of fear as well.

Both boats rounded up spare jib sheets to create a lifeline for the dinghy. The Japanese woman took infinite care in knotting the sheets into one long line. With the ritual of a traditional tea ceremony, she painstakingly took the line and stacked it in a coil, smoothing each segment until it was free of all kinks and snags. This took many minutes to accomplish properly. Her audience watched in silence.

Jim and the Frenchman, who oozed nautical competence, seemed to know without saying that they would be the designated team for the dinghy outing. Life jackets went on over their windbreakers, each strap fastened and tightened and scrutinized like NASA space suits being readied for a space walk. Nothing would be rushed. I double-checked the fit of Jim's life jacket, testing the straps.

Normally he would have protested that we were being ridiculously fussy. That day he remained silent.

"Okay," I finally said.

The guys stepped down into the dinghy. We played out its line, and the wind swept the small tender out to mid-harbor with sickening alacrity. Jim gingerly let the anchor over the side. As he did so, the dinghy wobbled ominously. I feared that, if the line failed, the dinghy would squirt backwards out of this D-grade harbor entrance and into the tossed Sea of Crete.

Everything went according to plan. After completing the slow process, we reeled the men back. Now *Sandstorm* hung suspended between anchor rode and dock lines. The rear anchor would prevent *Sandstorm* from swinging side to side and keep her bow several yards off the dock.

Our arrangement rated as only marginally adequate. All the other yachts, in harbor with

Poor in land, rich in sea lanes

***Eptanisos* docks alongside *Sandstorm* in Míkonos.**

For the Phaeacians have no use for the bow and quiver, but spend their energy on masts and oars and on the graceful craft they love to sail across the foam-flecked seas.

Homer in *The Odyssey* describing the people of Corfu

Greek ferries' ability to handle bad weather demonstrated how modern Greeks still display nautical prowess, a response to their environment that dates back thousands of years. British historian Arnold J. Toynbee wrote in his last work, *The Greeks and Their Heritages,* that Greece

was a poor country with a bare minimum of fertile soil and of accumulated capital. Yet she has held her own at sea. … The Greek grocer in Brooklyn, as well as the Greek ship-owner whose vessels circumnavigate the globe, is a living witness to the Modern Greeks' success in engaging in the economic life of the Modern World.

The only others to emulate the Greeks' modern maritime achievements, Toynbee wrote,

are the Norwegians, and the Norwegians have been spurred by similar conditions at home. Norway and Greece have longer coastlines and smaller rations of fertile soil than any other European countries.

Factors in maritime achievement

WORLD RANKS FOR …	GREECE	NORWAY
Shipping	4th	10th
Coastline	11th	8th
Population	64th	99th
Agriculture share, gross domestic product	51st	86th

Based on data from *The New Book of World Rankings*

Aristotle Onassis and Stavros Niarchos demonstrated an age-old talent for shipping. They built fortunes transporting oil and other commodities around the world. Later they used their wealth to bid for yachts the size of destroyers, as well as modern art and the favors of famous widows.

time to prepare for the gale, had set two anchors for better stability.

The one good thing about our haphazard hookup—bow first, facing into the wind, unlike the other yachts anchored in correct Greek style—involved the matter of fine red dirt that covered the boats and their crews, carried from somewhere—northern Míkonos? Turkey? Bulgaria?

This grit bounced harmlessly off the front of our mast. All the others had the grit driven deep into the slot on the back of the mast where the mainsail is raised, making the slides difficult to raise or lower.

Our various damage control activities left us dirty and disheveled. Yet the Franco-Japanese couple somehow looked not only clean but downright stylish, like models advertising Nautica outfits. They also displayed more bilingual ability than we did. They translated marine forecasting information, common knowledge among the five other boats. They told us we were experiencing force 9 winds—a strong gale, and at 50 mph, well beyond the 30 mph that would lead to a small craft advisory back home on the Chesapeake. The French man and the German sailors in port seemed to know, either from reading the skies or talking to the locals, that we would be here for a while.

The five-story structure of the *Eptanisos* (*epta* is "seven," *nisos* is "islands"), a ferry originating in Athens' port, Piraeus, chugged into the harbor that afternoon. *Eptanisos* skidded in, pointed its bow at the coffee shops lining the south harbor, stopped on a dime, turned its stern into us and wheeled backwards. The ferry stopped crisply, just off the dock and only a few yards from *Sandstorm*. The crew dropped the looped ends of two lines over the cleats on the docks, and pedestrians and scooter riders dashed off.

LESSON 13: THE PRECISE MANEUVERS OF *EPTANISOS* DEMONSTRATED THE OUTSTANDING SKILLS OF GREEK MARINERS. WE AMATEURS WATCHED HOW THE PROS DO IT.

The resumption of the Greek ferries signaled that the weather was beginning to improve. The second the European sailors left, we'd follow them out.

Our dwarfed vessel safe for the moment, we headed off to dinner, a task now more complicated than before. No longer could we clamber onto *Zyawa* and

Petros and a small pelican stroll the dock, and a *kafeneion* displays a Dukakis sticker.

hop from her bow to the dock. We rigged up the dinghy as a shuttle. We had to step down from the pitching pulpit of *Sandstorm* one at a time into the dinghy, lay on our backs, and pull ourselves along a guide rope to the dock, hand over hand like commandos. Then we scrambled from the jouncing trampoline of the dinghy to grab cleats on the dock.

We invited the helpful couple to dinner, by screaming at the closed companionway of their yacht. Huddled inside, they leaned out to decline, looking their usual handsome and self-sufficient selves yet a bit forlorn.

We explored the dockside *kafeneions*. Mustachioed men in berets drank small cups of *cafe hellenico*, a scene familiar from my earlier trips to Greece. Míkonos' famous mascot, a giant pink pelican named Petros II, strolled about.

With 12 days to go before the U.S. elections, Míkonos pinned its hopes on son of Greek soil Michael S. Dukakis to beat President Bush. We saw our first of several bumper stickers for the Democrat. When waiters learned we were *amerikanos*, they asked who we planned to vote for: "Bush? Dukakis?" A few kicks under the table spurred our group, despite various political leanings, to always give the waiters the answer they sought.

We walked up the tangled streets to Nico's, a large restaurant, crowded even on this godforsaken night. There we met Ursula's friends, Jane and Don, from the *Hartford Courant*. Finally our group had reached full strength, plus two. For our table of eight, a remarkable gathering that owed much to Ursula's organizing skills, I again ordered the entire six-item Greek menu.

ble gale from the north. He covered land and sea with a canopy of cloud; and darkness swept down on us from the sky. Our ships were driven sidelong by the wind, and the force of the gusts tore their sails to rags and tatters. With the fear of death upon us, we lowered these onto the decks, and rowed the bare ships landward with all our might. Thus we lay for two days and two nights on end, with exhaustion and anxiety gnawing at our hearts. But on the third morning, which a beautiful dawn had ushered in, we stepped the masts, hauled up the white sails.

Homer in *The Odyssey*

Ursula tried to persuade Jane and Don to accompany us on our return, sailing with us during the day and taking rooms on the islands at night. But they didn't like the look of the weather. Their evaluation, while utterly rational, struck me as staid and risk averse.

LESSON NUMBER 14: ADVENTURE TRAVELERS SUBSCRIBE TO THE PHILOSOPHY OF ALAN SHEPARD, AMERICA'S FIRST MAN IN SPACE. AS DEPICTED IN THE MOVIE *THE RIGHT STUFF*, WHEN ASKED TO JOIN THE FLEDGLING NASA SPACE PROGRAM, HE RESPONDED, "SOUNDS DANGEROUS! COUNT ME IN."

Over dinner, we sketched scenarios for the rest of our trip. We could leave as late as Saturday morning, a day and a half hence. If we sailed nonstop, we could cover the 100-odd miles back to Kalamaki harbor to return *Sandstorm* on time, by noon Sunday.

That plan meant that we would have to scratch plans to visit (in addition to Delos) Síros, Kíthnos and Cape Soúnion on the Attica peninsula. We would need to hot-rod back, keeping a wary eye for freighters at night. These crowded sea lanes recorded a fair number of ferry and freighter collisions.

We could only afford one more day of bad weather before making a tough decision. If the high wind did not settle by Saturday morning, we'd have to fly back to Athens and pay somebody to take *Sandstorm* home.

All that night on our yacht, the motion and racket continued, though at less upsetting levels. After the noise had kept her up for the previous night, Stephany finally slept, for 12 hours.

On a famed party island, we baby-sat a valuable Beneteau in a gale. Not that we begrudged *Sandstorm*, with whom we had entered a mutual protection pact.

FRIDAY, OCT. 28
A stately procession

Zeus who marshals the clouds, now sent my fleet a terri-

Sun washed the scene that greeted us the next morning, one of brisk activity on every yacht in Míkonos. The *meltemi* still roared out of the north, but some sort of Jungian collective resolve had taken hold. Everyone knew somehow that the gale was expending its final fury, and we could leave as soon as our boats were ready.

A sight I had never seen—an entire harbor completely emptying at once—unfolded as all the yachts flew out onto the Aegean. One, two, three, four, five, six. Ahead the others moved west in single file. *Sandstorm* brought up the rear. Our sails filled with wind, making a gratifying sight above our heads. Receding Míkonos lay behind our spreading wake.

We still wore heavy outdoor gear, but at least we weren't cold to boot. The break in the weather meant we could salvage some of our schedule, aiming for stops at Kíthnos and Cape Soúnion our final two nights.

Sandstorm ran on a beam reach (the wind perpendicular to the yacht), in a moderate breeze, one of the best courses for combined speed and comfort. As we sailed to Kíthnos, the wind dropped steadily.

LESSON NUMBER 15: SAILING ON THAT LATE OCTOBER DAY IN THE AEGEAN FELT LIKE PERFECT TRAVEL.

Steve and Stephany look ahead toward Kíthnos.

A boat like Sandstorm operated as a perpetual motion machine, a transport of delight that made up for the horrors of Chinese trains and Malagasy canoes. *Sandstorm* needed no refined petroleum, new tires, alignment or tune-up (barring the auxiliary engine). With moving air and a knowledge of the rules of physics—breeze direction, sail trim, water depth—we could traverse the seas on wind power alone.

Sandstorm sits at anchor among the fishing boats at Loutrá.

Sandstorm advanced continually west, in a landscape replete with drama. Islands sprouted more thickly from the sea here. The storm had washed the crystal air of late autumn and rendered the Aegean a vivid aquamarine. Síros to our south and Kíthnos ahead wore a shade of rust-red. We six watched, at turns jolly and quiet in our enjoyment of the gorgeousness of these waters. We might have found the day more precious because we nearly had it taken from us by the *meltemi*.

As dusk approached, we put on our running lights and grabbed cameras. The ebbing light rendered the Aegean a bejeweled gold, ruby and turquoise. A cluster of diamond-bright lights, indicating the tiny fishing port of Loutrá, glittered larger and brighter as night fell and rendered the bulk of northeast Kíthnos black.

At Loutrá, once more we anchored Greek style. On our first try, the anchor snagged. I knew technically I was not strong enough to free the anchor. This had

become one of powerful Chris's jobs, along with taking the helm in gales.

Yet instead of calling for Chris, I told myself with determination, *This anchor is coming up*. I had had enough of snags both literal and figurative on this trip. We were going to have some smooth sailing. And that all there was to it.

I exhaled, clamped my gloved hands on the anchor rode and straightened my knees. The bow dipped under my straining legs. I put my butt into the effort and hauled on the rode. I felt the debris of the centuries clutch at the anchor—and then yield. Up came the anchor, a testament to will rather than strength.

We lowered the anchor a second time. The procedure went smoothly. *Sandstorm* sat placidly between two fishing boats, swim ladder lowered to the dock, on water so calm you could do watch repair on the chart table. We could have used this snug harbor during our gale, so of course we arrived instead as the winds died to a breath. Still, we could enjoy its calmness for its own sake.

LESSON NUMBER 16: TO BORROW FROM THE ROLLING STONES, "YOU CAN'T ALWAYS GET WHAT YOU WANT," BUT YOU'LL GET WHAT YOU NEED.

Katerina fed our sailing crew at her taverna and then taught us how to dance to bouzouki music.

Chris relaxes on the trapeze as I take the helm on the way to Cape Soúnion.

Sailing in Greece gave a tremendous boost to our skills and confidence. We could hardly imagine how many islands we could have visited without our two-day layby for the gale. We felt reasonably unhurried even given the problems of the trip. And later squalls in other sailing areas held no terrors for us after the *meltemi*.

We lowered the gangplank and walked on to Loutrá. The air smelled of sage and oregano. Wild times on these dark seas receded in our memories. A new phase of our trip had begun, one of wonder and enjoyment.

We asked where to go to eat. Fishermen directed us up a hillside path to a modest establishment overlooking the harbor. In Katerina's taverna, a small building that looked like a private residence, Jim and I walked toward the kitchen and pointed at everything remaining in the display case after the peak dinner hour. Katerina made us an octopus appetizer and an omelet of potatoes and eggs. Lots of bread and Amstel beer rounded out the meal.

Then Katerina, a kerchief on her gray head, closed the kitchen, pushed the tables to the side and put a cassette into her tape player. She taught us to dance to bouzouki, traditional music played on an instrument like a mandolin. Like so many things Greek, bouzouki music seemed half Western and half Eastern, with the air of both North Africa and a French folk tune.

Stepping slowly and pausing, snapping fingers in the air, Katerina took each of us in turn and taught us the steps. She had apparently taken a shine to us.

So forward now, my champion dancers, and show us your steps, so that when he gets home our guest may be able to tell his friends how far we leave all other folk behind in seamanship, in speed of foot, in dancing, and in song.

Homer in *The Odyssey*

Ursula later called it "one of the perfect days of my life."

SATURDAY, OCT. 29

A Greek isle to ourselves

Without discussion we all scattered the next morn-

ing for private explorations. Each of us found ourselves encountering aspects of a fishing town going about its day. Chris and I watched the fishermen put the catch in boxes of ice.

Loutrá's fisherman did not seem sick of tourists, especially sailing ones. Ferries put in on the other side of Kíthnos, so we comprised the only non-residents in the town.

The lack of an airport on Kíthnos lowered the number of tourists. The people seemed less tired of tourists and more friendly, and the island had a more traditional feel.

I walked in the brown hills above Loutrá and looked out on the Aegean at a white freighter. A man rode a donkey up the hill (by now a familiar sight to me). "*Kalimera*" (good morning), I said, and he smiled and returned the greeting. The others were invited into local homes to look at family photographs, played with cats, and photographed dogs who seemed happy just to sit on the side of a sunny hill. The day seemed an exemplar of my Great Zero Theory: good follows bad, everything evens out.

Sandstorm had to be home the next day. So we reconvened and made an unhurried departure for Cape Soúnion, halfway back to Athens.

Blast the Greek wind: There was always either too much or none. In the days of Odysseus sailors would row at such times, but we switched on the engine and motored noisily across the glass lake that served that day as our Homeric "highway of fishes." Chris leaned against the swim ladder, surveying these legendary seas as I took the helm. Later we switched places. I ate a pomegranate, letting its juice fall in the Aegean behind *Sandstorm's* transom.

Meanwhile we were sailing in company over the sea from Troy, Menelaus and I, the best of friends. But when we were abreast of the sacred cape of Sunium, where Attica juts out into the sea, Phoebus Apollo let fly his gentle darts at Menelaus' helmsman and struck him dead, with the steering-oar of the running ship in his hands.

Nestor's tale in *The Odyssey*

At fabled Soúnion, we encountered a better fate than Menelaus's helmsman. At sunset, the vermilion of its exposed bluffs reflected on our faces. We glided in, silently gazing at the 20-story bluff graced by the gleaming white Temple of Poseidon. A lone fishing vessel shared the wide bay. For the first time that week, we anchored offshore instead of at a dock. Jim rowed us ashore in the dinghy one at a time, a process that felt like an algebra test question: "If you have six people on a yacht, and a dinghy only takes two people at a time, how many trips will it take to get everyone ashore?"

We found an expensive taverna and told the waiters we all supported Dukakis. Jim got his exercise rowing us all back to *Sandstorm*.

SUNDAY, OCT. 30
Rockin' round the temple

We walked around the Temple of Poseidon, praised for its visual drama in the 1823 epic "Don Juan" by Lord Byron. The Greeks dedicated only a handful of temples to the earthquake god, who was more feared than worshiped. The dazzling temple, with about a quarter of its columns still standing, resembled a more isolated Parthenon. From it we could see 360 degrees. Islands lay to our southeast, and to the west *Sandstorm* sat at anchor.

After three days in salt air without showers, we could run our fingers through our stiffened hair and make it stand straight up as though lacquered with hair spray. Chris especially could emulate the platinum punk look.

We accused him of looking like Lord Byron's countryman, Billy Idol. Chris began to growl the words to the catchy but distinctly anti-romantic rocker, "White Wedding."

After we returned to our yacht, for the first time we sailed, rather than powered, off anchor. Chris hauled up the anchor, the rest of us raised the sails, and without starting the engine, off we went. We left Soúnion peacefully, a safe option given the wide mouth of the bay and a favorable breeze.

Back at Kalamaki, the face of the charter company's mechanic lit up with relief. "We were so worried!" he said. "We knew about the storm." His eye took in the unblemished hull and the intact mast and rigging.

As we clambered off, Jim reached a hand down, followed by the rest of us, to thump the solid foredeck of our worthy craft. "Goodbye, *Sandstorm*," each said in turn.

Greece and the big lesson: on national greatness and decline

Modern Greece, to use a comparison of Hellenic origin, rests on the astounding laurels of ancient Greece. The list of contributions, at least in embryonic form, of ancient Greece to Western thought is remarkable:

Logic	Drama
Ethics	Medicine
Democracy	Psychology
Mathematics	Rhetoric
Philosophy	Musical harmony
Architecture	Politics
Sculpture	Metaphysics

Jim rows to *Sandstorm*, at anchor in the quiet waters of Cape Soúnion.

Ancient Greeks advanced a belief system based on logic that eventually set modern Western nations apart from the Asian acceptance of multiple, contradictory truths, a difference in outlook that reverberates in every U.S.-Japan trade argument. Yet the modern Greeks' contributions have slipped to:

Islands that cater to package tours
Invention of the modern oil tanker

The remaining Greek population consists disproportionately of the elderly who haven't emigrated. Twenty percent of the Greek population is above the age of 60, vs. 17 percent in the United States. These oldsters ride donkeys in the hills and sip tiny cups of *cafe hellenico* on the square. They may still debate, as did their classical forbears, the fine points of democracy, reality and truth. But I suspect that today they discuss village matters and complain about local and national politics.

Americans have certainly as of the mid-1990s mastered the knack for lingering at Starbucks, much like the Greek men in the *kafeneions*. But in its decline the United States may not be as picturesque as the Cyclades, with its pelicans by the quay and goats with tinkling bells in the hills. One fears it would more resemble the chaotic, smoggy jumble of Athens.

Today Greece has sagged to a place as one of Europe's poorer nations, behind Spain and slightly ahead of Portugal, akin to the United States sinking economically to the level of Venezuela. How so, the brilliant Greeks lagging Spain? If Greece can slip from catalyst for virtually every major tenet of modern Western thought to the low-middle tier of Europe, where might the United States end up in 2,500 years?

Much data suggests that since its 1945-65 heyday, the United States has fallen in its world share of oil production, automobile manufacture, monetary reserves, exports and patents, as Geir Lundestad, director of the

Mass tourism: The fate of the Once-Great Powers and islands alike

The tourists ogling Greece's ruins and Britain's palaces illustrate the indignity that former Great Powers suffer when relegated to the trivial status of tourist attraction.

Tom Wolfe wrote a memorable futuristic piece for *Esquire* called "2020 A.D.," in which Walt Disney Enterprises converted the entire British Isles into a theme park.

Yanks with videocams firmly pressed to their skulls flew over to record lifestyle packages depicting Eighteenth and Nineteenth Century Aristocratic, Nineteenth Century Cozy or Twentieth Century City. Three-quarters of the population lived in period costume. The British economy, despite producing nothing, became the "envy of all Europe," Wolfe wrote.

Wounded pride at the degree to which Wolfe's parody is accurate colors numerous encounters in modern Britain, evidenced in potshots taken at U.S. accents, clothes, television shows and presidents. Americans used for a century to being on top will probably be equally rankled if Japan or China wrests the No. 1 spot away—if we no longer make products others want to buy and only serve tourists braying in foreign tongues.

Most tourism today involves First World vacationers going to other First World areas: Japanese, Americans and Europeans visiting each others' Disney compounds and the Eurowide Theme Park that gauges the slipping prestige of France, Spain, Italy and Britain.

For sunny playground islands, on the other hand, the central economic role of tourism can indicate an issue more serious than reduced prestige: that a place earns little from making things, growing food or catching fish.

Mass tourism (vs. exploring or backpacking) in Greece, Spain, Hawaii, Polynesia and the Caribbean

Hundreds of tourists explore the Parthenon in Athens during my 1982 visit.

creates low-wage jobs where locals may end up serving fussbudgets from richer places.

LESSON NUMBER 17: SOME CRITICS ASSAIL MASS TOURISM (PARTICULARLY IN THE CARIBBEAN) AS PROMOTING A NEO-PLANTATION ECONOMY, WITH PROFITS HEADED BACK TO FIRST WORLD INVESTORS.

Other observers believe that tourism jobs may be a necessary way station on the road to skilled positions. In a discussion in 1991 with journalists, Hawaii Gov. John D. Waihee III defended the development of luxury hotels on Lanai, once a pineapple-growing island.

"The people voted for it," he said. He outlined a generational progression from agricultural to skilled jobs. "Pineapple harvesting is tough and uncomfortable work. The laborers would prefer air-conditioned jobs in a hotel. And the people who get those service jobs will want high-tech jobs for their own children."

Meanwhile the tour-bus drivers at Delphi and concierges in Athens descend from olive growers, sea captains—and great thinkers. Some indicators point to a disgruntlement among the proud Greeks with a switch from being a nation of philosophers to one of pension and taverna keepers.

Tourism levels have stagnated in Greece, and books on the hospitality industry blame this on antiquated facilities of little quality.

Tourism and travel jobs, selected countries, 1994

AS AN INVERSE MEASURE OF WORLD POWER

	JOBS IN TOURISM AS A PROPORTION OF ALL INDUSTRIES
Most Mediterranean and Caribbean islands	1 in 3
Spain	1 in 5
United Kingdom	1 in 7
Greece	1 in 9
United States	1 in 10
Japan	1 in 11

Based on data from *International Tourism: An Economic Perspective* and "Tourism and Travel Jobs, By Country" in *Gale Country & World Rankings Reporter*

Norwegian Nobel Institute, wrote in *The American "Empire"*. Two presidents, Richard M. Nixon and Jimmy Carter, even acknowledged America's reduced status. Ronald Reagan, however, revived the role of cheerleader displayed earlier by John F. Kennedy. Both projected confidence and refuted those who saw decline.

In his 1987 book, *The Rise and Fall of the Great Powers,* Yale University Professor Paul Kennedy shaped much of the debate about the future of the United States. He wrote that America is now shrinking to its "natural" possession of world output based on population, size and natural resources. Thus it declines in a relative, not absolute, sense to the entire world.

U.S. share of world production

1950	50%*
1960	33
1970	29
1980	27
1987	26
1992	23

* Believed to be the highest proportion ever achieved by a Great Power.

Based on data in *The American "Empire"*

Kennedy, conservative economist Thomas Sowell and many other scholars indicate that inevitably, the United States will decline, and Japan and China wait in the wings as the Great Powers of the future. As with Super Bowl champions attempting to repeat despite trades and injuries, Great Powers face built-in limits to their longevity. The reason: the relative strengths of Great Powers vary given uneven rates of growth and technological advances among nations.

Oswald Spengler, in *The Decline of the West,* compared the life-cycle of a civilization to that of living things, such as plants and animals, which are born, bloom, and die after exhausting their possibilities. Great Cultures, he wrote

appear suddenly, swell in splendid lines, flatten again and vanish, and the face of the waters is once more a sleeping waste.

Historians, economists, Buddhists and sports fans agree: The only constant is change. So indeed, the United States' time at the top may be quite long but not infinite.

Americans who have not seen real wage gains entertain doubts on the future of the United States, a problem addressed by Paul Krugman in *The Age of Diminished Expectations.* Krugman argues that Japan and an increasingly unified Europe will soon begin to move past the United States in many measures, including exports, foreign investment, and gross national product. These events, he wrote, "will be a blow to traditional views of America's place in the world."

The United States will most likely drift along economically in coming years, Krugman indicated. He also sketched two alternative scenarios: a productivity boom leading to a flourishing economy (likelihood: 20 percent) and a debt and dollar crisis leading to a hard landing (likelihood: 25 percent). He concluded

---

Rome's approach to minorities: sharing power and insisting on cultural assimilation

The length of time a Great Power gets to stay at the top may hinge upon how much it ensures that its diverse population shares a stake in national success.

My husband, artist and historian Lamont W. Harvey, notes that Great Powers such as the United States, China or the former Soviet Union cover large areas and comprise more than one ethnic group. (The exception is comparatively homogeneous Japan.)

Thus Great Powers need a policy to prevent instability among differing peoples. History reveals some widely divergent approaches taken by Great Powers toward minorities (defined in the sociological sense, as persons subjected to different treatment, rather than groups smaller in numbers).

In the Greek colonies and British Empire, for example, no one could hope to join the ruling classes except by birth. The Greeks in their cities and colonies simply considered themselves innately superior to barbarians outside and saw no purpose in trying to civilize their neighbors. Thus virtually all citizens of Athens came only from married Athenian parents.

The Romans looked at things quite differently. Non-Romans during the imperial era could exercise power, particularly in their home provinces. For Rome's subject peoples, who came to cherish the peace established under Roman rule, to become a Roman citizen was a high honor.

Stephen Neill, in *Colonialism and Christian Missions*, wrote that

Citizens in Spain who had never once seen the eternal city became more Roman than the Romans, and spoke and wrote the Latin tongue with an almost classical elegance. Rome seemed identical with the civilization and stability of the world.

Rome only permitted those who adopted its language and culture to become citizens. It tolerated but did not celebrate diversity, even as it absorbed elements of other cultures (especially Greece's). Rome allowed its subjects to continue to speak Celtic, Aramaic, Libyan and other languages. But officials, soldiers, traders and schoolchildren learned Latin, which became the official language of the Mediterranean. As John

that "history teaches us to be humble and to entertain a variety of possibilities."

Compared especially to earlier declines in history, the United States may be able to crash with a soft landing. We are not likely, Kennedy wrote,

> to shrink to the relative obscurity of former leading Powers such as Spain or the Netherlands, or to disintegrate like the Roman and Austro-Hungarian empires; [the United States] is simply too large to do the former, and presumably too homogeneous to do the latter.

LESSON NUMBER 18: WITH INCOMPARABLY MORE NATURAL RESOURCES THAN ANCIENT GREECE AND FOUR TIMES THE POPULATION OF THE MODERN UNITED KINGDOM, THE UNITED STATES MAY SIMPLY BE RICH ENOUGH AND LARGE ENOUGH TO AVERT A PRECIPITOUS WEAKENING.

After Kennedy wrote his 1987 book, the Soviet Union crumbled, further reversing or at least masking any U.S. degeneration.

Though none of the academics put it this way, the United States can be compared to a Michael Jordan, a superstar in a class of his own. Jordan competes against huge players with enormous potential (such as Shaquille O'Neal, metaphorically comparable to China) and smart, talented teams (such as the Indiana Pacers, standing in for Europe) that lack almost nothing—except the iron will and competitiveness of a Jordan, and his willingness to reinvent his game every off-season, working on new shots against invited competitors.

Although news reports focus on evidence of social collapse in the United States—single-parent families, cheating scandals, a million Americans in prison—many economic analysts paint a less pessimistic picture.

Some observers see the United States as possessing unusual demographic strengths that may keep abrupt economic decline at bay for a long period. For example, Asian immigrants to the United States form a potentially crucial economic bridge to the future.

Asian-American census figures

Chinese	1,645,472
Filipino	1,406,770
Japanese	847,562
Other Asian or Pacific Islander	821,692
Asian Indian	815,447
Korean	798,849
Vietnamese	614,547
Hawaiian	211,014
Samoan	62,964
Guamanian	49,345
TOTAL	**7.3 million**

Based on 1990 data from the U.S. Census Bureau

Joel Kotkin and Yoriko Kishimoto wrote in *The Third Century: America's Resurgence in the Asian Era* that, unlike the peoples of Europe,

> Americans are not prisoners of a national culture

Matthews wrote in "Roman Life and Society: Distances and Diversity":

> It was precisely the achievement of the Roman Empire to have assimilated in one political and administrative system the immense diversities of the Mediterranean, and much of the northern European, worlds.

Like modern U.S. conservatives, Rome also came to emphasize public safety and family values. People in the empire had to obey the law and allow free passage on the Roman roads. And Augustus Caesar introduced numerous social reforms designed to strengthen the family and the integrity of marriage. (Though his own family failed disastrously in this regard, as the BBC television series based on Robert Graves's book *I, Claudius* amply demonstrated.)

The United States has, like Rome, attempted to acculturate minorities and assign them civil jobs. This has two crucial ramifications: greater internal security and maintenance of territorial integrity.

Civil rights leaders in the 1960s tried to appeal to American beliefs in fairness. They also insisted that all Americans were entitled to certain rights. Yet the link between inclusiveness and long-lasting greatness of the Roman Empire seems a more persuasive argument for equality of opportunity, although for some reason the civil rights leaders did not seem to promote this historical lesson. The example of Rome's inclusion of minorities could have huge appeal to white Americans, based as it is on survival, a basic human instinct, rather than idealism.

LESSON NUMBER 19: WHITES, PERHAPS CONSERVATIVES ESPECIALLY, COULD BE RECEPTIVE TO THE IDEA OF POWER-SHARING IF IT WERE PRESENTED NOT IN THE RESENTED FORM OF AFFIRMATIVE ACTION OR CULTURAL RELATIVISM BUT AS AN ESSENTIAL COMPONENT OF U.S. GREATNESS.

dependent on a specific racial identity. From its earliest days, the United States always has been something of a "world nation."

The large influx of new immigrants from India, China and Southeast Asia provides the United States with unprecedented social, cultural and economic ties to most of the ascendant nations of Asia. The new Americans from Asia give the United States the energy, connections and know-how required to break down many of the barriers that long have stood in the way of profitable relations with the nonwhite world. … By synthesizing ideas bred in Japan, Hong Kong, Taiwan or Korea with the entrepreneurial spirit of the United States, American business can forge an effective economic response.

Having traveled more widely in Asia than almost anywhere and seen first hand the region's dynamism, I certainly hoped Kotkin and Kishimoto were right, for the sake of the United States.

Similarly, the authors of *American Renaissance: Our Life at the Turn of the 21st Century* feel that the United States will benefit as Japan feels greater internal Asian competition from Korea, Taiwan and Hong Kong.

And given U.S. free-trade agreements with Mexico and Canada, and standards adopted by the European Economic Community for electronics, aerospace, chemicals and pharmaceuticals based on those of the United States, authors Marvin Cetron and Owen Davies see the United States at the fulcrum of numerous beneficial economic alliances through the next century.

Meanwhile support for capitalism has grown in Eastern Europe, Russia, China, Burma and other states formerly under pure socialism. A U.S. economy committed to openness, Kotkin and Kishimoto noted, can take advantage of this ever-more capitalistic landscape.

LESSON NUMBER 20: WHEN ONE PUTS TOGETHER THE ARGUMENTS OF *AMERICAN RENAISSANCE*, *THE THIRD CENTURY* AND *THE RISE AND FALL OF THE GREAT POWERS*, ONE SEES AN OUTSIDE CHANCE FOR THE UNITED STATES, IF IT CAN CORRECT NUMEROUS SOCIAL PROBLEMS, TO BE A SECOND ROME, ON TOP FOR 1,000 YEARS.

Kotkin and Kishimoto point to the extraordinary power of the "fundamental ideas" that nations rest upon. China believed in Confucianism, Rome in social order, Britain in a "civilizing mission," and America in its role as a "land of liberty."

The idealistic principle at the root of the United States may pay off in purely material terms, as an Atlantic-oriented society evolves into a multiracial world nation with built-in ties to overseas markets.

Kishimoto wrote to me via the Internet:

I think of the U.S.'s strength lying not only in its pursuit of liberty, but its continuing attempts to develop ever more robust "open systems"—open economic and social systems. Robust open systems mean that we have to have our minds and hearts open to all players (all peoples as well as new physical factors), but still have a core value system.

With improvements in three key areas—educating the non-college bound, ensuring that as many children as possible grow up with two parents and protecting its environment for the next millennium or two—the United States may decline only slowly, a Rome or, more colloquially, a perpetually youthful Dick Clark on the international scene.

As for Greece, it tumbled ages ago from being the world's Great Power. As a tourist mecca today, it still sets off a staggering level of resonance for Western visitors.

Greece maintains much of its beauty and ability to excite the imagination. More than 2,500 years after its heyday, we saw the Homeric islands from the vantage of the sturdy deck of *Sandstorm*. The United States would be lucky to look so good 2,500 years hence, to the Asian or African package tourists of the year 4500 A.D.

Yoriko Kishimoto looked ahead:

The greatest challenge we face—as United States and as the human civilization—is to continue the tremendous progress we've made over the last century in technological and economic and process/governance terms, and to explore the riches of cultural, psychological, spiritual and natural development. Market and democratic systems are a major accomplishment, and a better-than-average base for human endeavors, but that's not all there is. There is still much work ahead of us, so I'm looking forward to the next 2,500 years myself.

And Americans can only hope that two millennia in the future, the visiting Japanese graduate students studying the contributions of the Classical Era of the United States do not wonder quietly to themselves how these people sipping cappuccino at the harborside mini-malls, their children all emigrated to Tokyo and Shanghai and Perth and Johannesburg, could ever have managed the derring-do to end world wars and send men to the Moon.

PYRAMIDS IN THE AMERICAS

The Yucatan … and lessons on parallel evolution

El Castillo at Chichen Itza echoes the look of Old World ziggurats.

One dreams of winning the lottery and traveling the world. The next best thing is to be handed a year's pay and to celebrate among the ruins of the Maya, history's most intriguing combo of monumental builders, astronomers and warriors fixated on blood rituals.

A windfall enabling our group tour to the Yucatan—the eastern thumb of Mexico—occurred as a result of events at the *Baltimore Sun,* where I worked as a financial editor. My colleagues and I had palm trees on the brain and worked toward our dreams of early retirement by chipping in to a kitty to buy Maryland lottery tickets. Our boss, who wrote columns on prudent bond investments, watched in horror as we did so.

We never bought the right combination of numbers, but fortune smiled in another way. On a Friday afternoon in November 1991, managers told us that to trim staff, they would offer a buyout.

I became one of 294 workers to sign up for the payment. With a few weeks off before starting a job at *The Washington Post,* I called my sister Sharon, a computer wizard at the Federal Reserve Board in Washington, D.C. "If I bought you an air ticket," I asked, "would you come to Mexico for a couple of weeks?"

It was an offer she couldn't refuse. And two friends also signed on: Marci, from the *Baltimore Sun's* sports desk, who had also taken the buyout; and Edward, a witty fellow who worked at a Maryland facility for mental health patients.

Our inexpensive air tickets read "Cancun," but we planned to leave the airport instantly and head south, not even setting foot in the tourist resort proper. Our interest in that computer-selected resort site, which doesn't even appear on any pre-1970 maps, was minuscule. We wanted to see places a thousand years older. In a way, however, Cancun was a wonderful place as far as we were concerned.

LESSON NUMBER 1: THE CREATION OF CANCUN IN 1974 OPENED MEXICO WIDE TO TRAVELERS FROM THE EAST COAST.

For us, the chapter order of many guidebooks, which assume you are driving from Mexico City to the Yucatan, had become backward and obsolete. Cancun would serve as an el cheapo gateway for our sketchy trip goals: to hit the beaches, explore the ruins—and toast our good fortune.

As with most of our trips, an original goal to relax on found money evolved into much more: cultural fascination. To this day Sharon and I continue to read books and the articles that appear like clockwork in *National Geographic* about the Maya. And for once, I would not be alone in my lingering bafflement at what we had seen on our trip. Aspects of the culture that flourished in the Yucatan continue to stymie researchers, who believe they have uncovered only 5 percent of the knowledge to be had about the Maya.

FRIDAY, FEB. 7, 1992
Philosophically opposite passengers

We headed for Cancun to begin our travel backward in the Maya time machine, from Tulum's peak of 1200 to 1500 A.D., west to Palenque, which flourished from 600 to 900 A.D.

Divisions exist among the Yucatan's visitors. Some are passionately interested in seeing the Maya ruins. Others prefer a beach or golf vacation. We tended to the first group. Our flight threw together the various camps. Passengers had as little in common as would a bus tour stopping first at a casino and then a cathedral.

Though our group consisted of backpackers sans fixed itinerary, amateur travelers of the lower ranks, by the standards of some of our flight companions we qualified as distinguished scholars of archaeology.

A woman already sporting her hot-pink "Cancun" visor in the air over the Carolinas airily dismissed our travel plans. "Oh the ruins? Waste of time. They're too far. They're not worth it."

"She likes the beaches," her husband said.

We nodded with feigned agreement. Later I would hear a variant of their point of view from a tourist on a golf package: "You've seen one ruin, you've seen 'em all," she said.

LESSON NUMBER 2: WE WOULD SOON EXPERI-ENCE THE UTTER UNIQUENESS OF EACH MAYA SITE, MANYFOLD MORE VARIED THAN MOST BEACHES OR GOLF COURSES.

Our airplane landed at Cancun, where we changed out of winter clothes into something more appropriate to the instant heat. The photo record showed that Sharon and I, with straw hats and worn backpacks, looked like smugglers. Marci projected an elusive Lauren Bacall look behind dark shades. Our slack jaws worked on lollipops, lending us an additional air of lawless mystery, or perhaps infantilism.

Edward had concocted a look halfway between a mercenary and G. Gordon Liddy: a "Yukon Big Game" ball cap, wheat-colored photojournalist vest over raspberry Wallace Beery T-shirt, and khaki pants with high-topped sneakers.

Edward, Sharon and Marci just after landing at Cancun airport.

After a half-hour cab ride south, our feet touched the ground in Playa del Carmen, a splendid place to our winter-weary eyes. The one-road backpacker resort featured restaurants and reasonable lodgings, with glimpses of the blue-green Caribbean through the palms. Sunburned hippies lounged bare chested in hammocks. The sounds of televised sports or Bryan Ferry, Roxy Music and Aretha Franklin wafted from palm-roofed restaurants. Sharon appropriately nick-named the town "Playa del Karma." The name reflect-ed Playa's New World variation of fairy-light-strewn places such as Lamu in Kenya and Kuta Beach in Bali.

Sharon knew the phrase "*¿Quando el baño?*" I knew so little Spanish that I didn't even get her joke, which asks, "When is the bathroom?"—an apt question given the pace some days as we flew through one pyra-mid complex to the next. She could manage a second simple sentence, "*¿Quando refrescos?*" ("When are the soft drinks?") as well.

Edward and Marci held title as translators, and Edward also served as our official Mexico expert, hav-ing traveled previously with his father in its northwest reaches. I was the closest thing we had to a Maya spe-cialist, having been in 1991 to Belize and Guatemala. And as the backpacker emeritus of the group, I had

blithely predicted we'd be able to find "clean, comfort-able" rooms for about $5 a night, as promised in our adventure guidebooks.

However, what I found to be relatively clean and comfortable compared to some other places I'd stayed in Asia and Africa struck the others as shabby. In Playa, for example, we stayed at a lodging house writ-ten up as "the Caribbean's own makeshift Taj Mahal." A mule wandered out front. Clusters of metal reinforc-ing bars sprouted from the roof, a sign of an intention, perhaps since abandoned, to add a second story. Bougainvillea grew up an abandoned wall.

The proprietor showed us a large room with four beds and a bathroom. The details revealed Mexico's happy-go-lucky approach to construction. The wiring to our bedside light tumbled out of an open switch box. More wires spaghettied out of arbitrary gaps in the stucco ceiling. A bare bulb lit the shower.

Our budget hotel featured a spider.

Still, by my lights, any place that didn't stink or have dirty sheets rated as acceptable. Sharon, not yet sub-scribing to the backpacker ethos, compared our room not to the Taj Mahal but rather to "the cell in *Midnight Express*" in a "condemned building."

We headed to dinner, dodging various wire har-nesses hanging at throat level on the patio. At a restau-rant called Dona del Carmen, the tabletop quickly grew covered with a forest of empty *refresco* bottles. We ate fried whole fish *(pescado frito)* and side dishes.

We decided this would be as good a time as any to plan our trip. In the spirit of effortless adventure, we had arrived without an itinerary. The time had come to open our guidebooks to the Yucatan. On a sheet of my notebook, I drew gridlines representing a calendar for the February.

I suggested we do a counterclockwise circuit of the Yucatan's snorkeling sites and major Maya temples and then continue west to Palenque in Chiapas, hitting places that various friends had recommended. That was fine with everyone. Our planning was complete. Time elapsed: perhaps five minutes.

We retired early to bed back at our lodging. Despite our fatigue, all of us awoke in the night, freez-ing under our thin, worn sheets.

LESSON NUMBER 3: COLD NIGHTS AND NO BLANKETS CAN BE A SURPRISINGLY COMMON PROBLEM IN THE TROPICS.

I got up groggily and dragged a University of Maryland hooded sweatshirt over my head, and the others must have done the same as the night pro-gressed. By morning, our tropical hideaway looked like a dorm full of passed-out joggers.

MONDAY, FEB. 10

Paddling around turquoise tidal pools

The bus south to Akumal ("place of the turtles" in Maya) took 35 minutes. From Akumal Bay, we walked about two miles along a minor coastal road running north past private villas with archways framing glorious Caribbean views. We managed to find an unmarked path leading to a scene of exquisite beauty: tidal pools of a startling aqua and lime-green hue, dotted by rocks and mangrove islands and palm trees.

We had arrived at Yal-ku lagoon, recommended as a hidden gem in the Lonely Planet guidebook. The sheltered snorkeling, perfect for beginners, revealed parrotfish, pipefish and sergeant majors. We could work our way around the highly indented margins of the lagoon or explore the area around an island in the middle. About 20 others also swam in the lagoon.

After snorkeling, we relaxed on the rocks, which bore the fossil outlines of trilobites, extinct marine invertebrates. We watched a great blue heron snag a parrotfish. Iguanas scurried out of their dens.

We walked back to Akumal, where two Indian children played on the beach. Instead of making a sand castle, they constructed a Maya pyramid.

LESSON NUMBER 4: DESPITE BURGEONING TOURISM IN THE YUCATAN, MAYA CULTURE SHOWS SIGNS OF GREAT RESILIENCY—EVEN IN LITTLE WAYS, SUCH AS THE CHILDREN BUILDING A SAND PYRAMID.

After another short bus ride, we arrived in Tulum town. At a hole-in-the-wall bus station on Route 307, we checked on the possibility of connections inland to

Sharon examines a sand pyramid.

Coba (at the time, buses mainly ran north and south along the coast). In the station, various groups waited for the bus to Chetumal, near the border with Belize.

Two lads from the North of England lazed on their packs. Wearing indolent grins, they proudly told us in working-class accents that they were "on the dole" (which they pronounced "doyle") back in England. They flew each winter to Miami and then bopped around Latin America on the Queen's treasury.

The class background of Caribbean explorers has fallen since the days of Christopher Columbus, Ponce de León and Hernán Cortés, when conquistadors were often second sons and minor gentry who became gentleman-adventurers.

World travel was once the province of explorers such as Marco Polo and Ibn Battuta, joined later by royalty and the religious pilgrim. Today areas such as the Yucatan witness a tidal wave of backpackers, retirees in guided educational groups, second homers and pack-

Update on Yal-ku

Four years after our first visit, I returned with Lamont to find new villas crowding the edge of Yal-ku. The lagoon had been designated as an ecological reserve. A guard instructed us not to wear sun lotion, yet the water was somewhat cloudy, as though others had ignored the warning. At the time of our visit, perhaps 60 people explored the lagoon, which had little remaining aura of discovery.

age tourists—and now, journalists on buyouts and welfare recipients.

The encounter with the U.K. dole boys reminded me of when I had lived in England in the early 1980s as the Thatcher revolution attacked handouts, linking them to an entitlement mentality. Yet I couldn't get too high and mighty. After all, Marci and I traveled on a buyout package rather than our own earnings. No doubt the corporate parent of our newspaper would take a hefty tax write-off for the money we had received.

The dole boys, our former employer and we American buyout recipients all worked the system to get cash without labor.

TUESDAY, FEB. 11

Just 'a pile of rocks'

Our quartet rose early to beat the Cancun swarms to Xel-ha lagoon. We backtracked north, hitchhiking up Route 307. We walked up to the ticket window at Xel-ha (pronounced shell-HA), one of a growing number of coastal areas requiring paid admission, and became the day's first visitors to test the water at this aquatic treasure house.

Schools of fish posed, silhouetted in coral arches like Gothic cathedrals, as though hamming it up for my disposable underwater camera. I saw grouper and a three-foot-long silvery game fish, perhaps a young tarpon, as well as midnight blue tangs and parrotfish. Sharon saw two rays, and Marci, tangs and blue-and-yellow grunts. Edward got a look at a huge ray and also a five-foot barracuda, which sent him airborne.

At 10 a.m., just as the tour groups began to arrive, we departed and crossed Route 307 to an area of minor ruins. Towering nests built by ants stood off from the path. The forest led to a well-hidden cenote. These sinkholes provide the only access to the subterranean waters of the riverless, arid limestone tabletop that is the Yucatan.

LESSON NUMBER 5: UNLIKE CHINA, EGYPT AND MESOPOTAMIA, THE YUCATECAN MAYA CIVILIZATION DEVELOPED IN MANY PLACES DISTANT FROM RIVERS.

Lianas and bromeliads surrounded the cenote and gave it a wild, Tarzan feel. Steep walls encircled the water of the sinkhole. I clambered down their sides and eased in to snorkel. Little fish called cyclids and danios hovered in tea-colored water around huge tree roots. The experience seemed a bit creepy. Just the knowledge that the murky waters plunged huge depths made the experience quite the opposite of paddling around the crystalline shallows of Yal-ku and Xel-ha.

The cenote across the road from Xel-ha.

Sharon played Smithsonian docent, offering her botanical and zoological expertise. "Those are houseplants," she said of the forest life forms, "and those"—the danios and cyclids—"are tropical fish."

Back on Route 307, a pickup truck of jolly Maya gave us a lift down to the ruins of Tulum for a quite modest gas payment, which we insisted upon.

At the ruins, local tour guides hovered by the entrance. "Without a guide, it's just a pile of rocks," they said earnestly.

These "piles of rocks" attracted swarms of tourists from Cancun. At Tulum—the most visited site in the Maya world—the smallish but gorgeously sited

Tulum, the most visited Maya site, overlooks turquoise waters.

Castillo, the Temple of the Frescoes and the Temple of the Diving God would be the only Maya structures most of the daytrippers would ever see.

LESSON NUMBER 6: TO ENJOY TULUM, ARRIVE EARLY IN THE MORNING, WHEN ONLY ITS GIANT IGUANAS AND A HANDFUL OF TOURISTS ARE LIKELY TO BE PRESENT.

The ruins stood on low cliffs overlooking turquoise seas and a powdery sand beach. Five hundred years ago, Maya in cargo canoes fought the northerly current up the Yucatan coast. After days of low shoreline, they would finally see a high bluff bearing temples—in those times most likely painted a fearfully intense

'Whatever country this is, it is not Mexico'

—Journalist John Kenneth Turner, upon visiting the Yucatan, circa 1900.

From the time of Cortés to today, the Maya have been in continual rebellion in various parts of the Yucatan, Chiapas and Guatemala. The eastern Yucatan peninsula, an area known today as Quintana Roo, in particular offered rebels plenty of scrubland to hide in until roads were built in the 1970s to ferry tourists about.

While Yucatan and Campeche were named separate states of Mexico in 1862, Quintana Roo was only made a territory in 1902 and a state in 1975.

We had no idea as we flew to Cancun that we would be entering a rump nation, like a piece of former Yugoslavia. Quintana Roo and the Yucatan possess the charm of a place in rebellion, fulfilling the same role that Texas, a former republic , does in the United States. (In fact, for a time the Yucatan paid the navy of Texas to

protect it from Mexican invasion, John L. Stephens wrote in *Incidents of Travel in Central America, Chiapas and Yucatan*.)

In modern times, women might be the first to notice the Yucatan's different and unthreatening atmosphere. Braced for whistles and aggravation from Mexican men, we encountered only friendly, well-behaved Mayans. An explanation appeared in one of our guidebooks, noting less machismo among the Maya compared to westerly Mexicans.

Perhaps one is less likely to

harass women in a culture where historically, law demanded "that the intestines of an adulterer should be drawn out through his navel," as the first bishop of Yucatan, Diego de Landa, wrote circa 1566 in *The Maya: Account of the Affairs of the Yucatán*.

In food as well as love, the Yucatan seemed apart from central Mexico. In Mérida, we visited the famed restaurant Los Almendros. Reviews from *Gourmet* magazine were framed in the entranceway.

We discovered why. One divine appetizer featured turkey on a bed of *frijoles* and cheese in a tortilla shell (*panuchos yucatecos con pavo*). Flavor exploded from our main courses as well: *cochinta pibil*, a pork dish, and *pollo ticuleno*, chicken with red peppers and peas.

Yucatecan cuisine, believed to be descended from Maya cooking, seemed of a higher order than Mexican food, with inventive yet harmonious combinations of ingredients.

Lamont stands beside a sign in Maya at the Coba ruins.

A must detour

Upon returning to Coba in 1996, Lamont and I met a letter carrier from Vancouver. He recommended that we take a tiny path, on the left if you are facing the front of Nohoch Mul, leading from a corner of the temple into the jungle.

We came upon a splendid hidden temple, with giant trees growing above arched chambers. We climbed around the underbrush and found the outlines of platforms, as romantically wild as anything depicted in a Catherwood engraving. The temple further sealed for us Coba's magic.

shade of scarlet with blue and yellow accents. Even today, anyone on an offshore pleasure or merchant ship must be stunned at Tulum's appearance.

We proceeded by taxi to Coba. (By 1996, as tourism in the Yucatan continued to boom, a half-dozen buses a day would bring tourists from Tulum to Coba, for $1 one way.)

Tulum seemed to offer the best ruins site (excluding the modest El Rey ruins on Cancun's peninsula) for beachophiles. Wild Coba, an hour away, indulged any amateur archaeologist fantasies.

Like Tikal in Guatemala, Coba seemed to attract the more serious visitors. At the site, we followed for a time two men with a video recorder making a solemn record of each artifact. In a breathy voice, one of the men intoned, "Stela … *Nine.*" He aimed the recorder at a pillar covered with glyphs, the carved images the Maya used to write words or dates. The pair lapsed into a reverent silence broken only by the soft buzz of their recording device.

Sharon and Edward, never adverse to recycling an old joke, took to exclaiming "Stell-LAAAAH!" at each of the carved pillars, in the manner of Marlon Brando in *A Streetcar Named Desire*.

We walked a mile into the quiet jungle to Nohoch Mul ("giant mound" in Maya). As Edward and Sharon clambered up its steps, I warned them, based on an earlier fright I'd received at a towering Maya pyramid at Tikal, "Don't go too high. It's steeper than it looks and it's freaky when you turn around and look out."

Marci kept my timid self company, and we perched less than halfway up the ruin. Sharon rolled her eyes dismissively. She and Edward scampered far higher, almost to the top of its 120 steps and 10 stories, turned around—and froze. They experienced a fraction of the panic I'd felt at Tikal. They hunched down and held firmly onto bits of rock.

The measure of Coba

A STORY MEASURES ABOUT 10 FEET

Nohoch Mul	10 stories
Tallest pyramid in the Yucatan	
Temple IV, Tikal	21 stories
Tallest Indian building, Western hemisphere	
Great Pyramid of Cheops	48 stories
Tallest pyramid, found in Egypt	

After Sharon and Edward slowly descended, sitting on each step, our foursome retraced our steps to look at one last temple near the entrance to the complex. On the way we saw pretty blue birds with black heads and stopped to watch a line of industrious ants working to carry plant bits across the trail.

Many people skip over Coba, a big complex with a mix of restored and unexcavated structures. Rough, wild, moody and evocative, Nohoch Mul and the other structures at Coba probably look to the literal minded like a rock slide covered with underbrush. Yet, of our 17 days in the Yucatan, it was during the one spent at Nohoch Mul that we felt most like discoverers.

In Coba, we could conjure up the time of the illustrator-explorers who depicted emerald-leaved trees growing out of the roofs of ocher temples and pyramids. Our imaginations filled in the gaps and returned us to the era of the engravings of Frederick Catherwood, an English architect who with archeologist John L. Stephens explored the Maya region in the 1830s. Our intrigue with things Maya had begun.

All of us climbed to various heights up Coba's Temple of the Churches. We looked at the placid, sil-

Edward and Sharon ascend steep Nohoch Mul.

Fear of climbing

My profound fear at climbing higher than the first 10 steps of the pyramids traced to 1991, when my brother Jim, our friend Steve and I took a three-day trip to Tikal.

We rented a dilapidated Grand Sierra in Belize City. Just past the border, a Guatemalan soldier on a motorbike stopped us. He attempted to shake us down, but our lack of Spanish came in handy. Frustrated at our bland smiles responding to his hints for a bribe, he eventually waved us on.

As Jim said later, "I was glad we hadn't read up on Guatemala." His remark summarized one component of our traveling philosophy, which also proved handy in a gale while sailing in Greece:

LESSON NUMBER 7: IGNORANCE OF THE GRAVITY OF A SITUATION CAN SOMETIMES KEEP ONE FROM PANICKING.

Once we got to Tikal, we breezily ascended the sheer steps of Temple II, an athletic endeavor made famous in an early 1990s Reebok commercial.

At the top of its 13 stories, we turned to gaze at the other pyramids and temples jutting through the top of the jungle. (This view appears at the 96-minute mark of *Star Wars,* when Han Solo and Luke Skywalker arrive at the rebel base.)

The exceptionally steep steps we had just ascended could not be seen. The platform felt as if it were hanging in air. We enjoyed an eagle's-eye view.

That view abruptly seemed horrifying to this wingless human. I looked at the empty space off the edge of the temple platform and felt an insane urge to step off, as though my human brain had the vestige of a bird's nervous system and wanted to fly or as though I were on a mind-altering drug.

My heart raced. The sense of fear, as real as if I were under attack, left me feeling unanchored. I was experiencing vertigo, a dizzy feeling sometimes manifested by an irrational impulse to jump into empty space.

This vertigo-inducing view of Tikal's Temple I greeted me from the top of Temple II.

I finally got a word out.
"Jim."
He looked over.
"I'm having a panic attack. I need a Valium and for you to charter a helicopter."

Bemused but knowing to take me seriously, Jim said, "Okay, come on." He acted like he talked down panicked climbers on Tikal's Temple II every day. "Turn around and back down the steps. Don't look out."

Ingloriously we made our descent, I lowering one knee at a time, one palm at a time. I counted aloud Temple II's 80 or so steps, my eyes almost shut.

I dared not keep track of our progress through the fearful air. So I ended up crawling rump first down the lowest three steps, as safe as baby's playpen, onto the grass.

A tour group from the Midwest stood on the Grand Plaza between Temples I and II. A man in a plaid shirt, who had observed the drama, noted, "We should have struck up a brass band for you."

Colleagues later reacted to stories of my Tikal panic. "Next thing you'll be scared to drive on the freeway," said Ursula, looking at me with either pity or contempt. Mike said with more forbearance, "The same thing happened to my wife when we went to Tikal." His observation, remark-ably, was echoed by a four male friends, all referencing their wives or girlfriends.

An acquaintance recalled a fellow medical school student who had fallen down all the steps of Temple I and had to spend a year in the hospital with broken bones and internal injuries.

You could slip and get badly hurt at Tikal—or worse. Lonely Planet's *La Ruta Maya* guidebook tells how two people have fallen to their deaths from Temple I, which was closed to climbers at the time of our visit.

So part of my fear had been based on reality. The panic may have also been an unusually dangerous manifestation of Stendhal syndrome, the physical effects—racing heart, weak knees—of being overcome with one's surroundings. It happened to Stendhal, a Jesuit-educated Frenchman (real name: Marie Henri Beyle) considered one of the first realists in 19th century literature, while viewing the art of Florence. Travelers have also experienced it in the Vatican, while driving Scottish glens, and in the Colorado Rockies. A darker variant affects visitors to Jerusalem and Washington's Holocaust Museum and Vietnam Veterans Memorial.

The Stendhal syndrome, a form of panic attack, "afflicts people who make themselves vulnerable to the stimulation that is unique to unique destinations," wrote Irene Schneider in *Condé Nast Traveler.* Both syndromes "only affect those lucky enough to be vulnerable to ravishment," she wrote.

Panic at Tikal may also reflect an openness to the unholy power of these ancient religious sites. Beheadings and heart removals once occurred at the Maya sites. Some archaeologists believe prisoners, tied into balls, were bounced down the steps of some temples to their deaths.

The Maya displayed a bloodthirstiness, seemingly incongruous with an intellect capable of great astronomical achievements, that leaves the modern mind shaken. Prisoners might be decapitated, have their living hearts cut out, or be taken to altars for ritual bloodletting over months or years. Rulers even used awls to draw blood from the foreskin of their own penises, and their wives drew ropes through their tongues, based on religious beliefs requiring blood offerings to the gods.

A company of about 50 Indians ... led us to some very large buildings of fine masonry which were the prayer-houses of their idols, the walls of which were painted with the figures of great serpents and evil-looking gods. In the middle was something like an altar, covered with clotted blood, and on the other side of the idols were symbols like crosses, and all were coloured. We stood astonished, never having seen or heard of such things before.

Bernal Díaz del Castillo, a soldier with the 1519 voyage of Hernán Cortés to the Yucatan, in *The Conquest of New Spain*

All blood reaches its place of rest, as all power reaches the throne.

The Book of Chilam Balam, an 18th century chronicle written in Yucatec Maya

And the stones of many pyramids act as astronomical predictors, lining up precisely with plaza buildings during solstices and equinoxes. Twice a year, a serpent created by a lighting effect at dawn and before sunset crawls up and down the steps on the north face of Chichen Itza's El Castillo. A remarkable photograph in the book *Pyramids* depicts an alignment of Jupiter and Venus over Temple I.

At the risk of sounding like a soup-for-brains New Ager, I felt that my Celtic corpuscles had detected mysterious forces at the site.

Though that is not the full picture. On some level, my panic at Tikal, at the age of 36, marked a turning point in adulthood, when the bold personality of youth begins to crumble, replaced with a more cautious identity. Through a chink in my armor sneaked retroactive fears for all the romantic risks and derelict means of transit I'd taken throughout my life, coming back to haunt me in a cumulative fashion.

LESSON NUMBER 8: YOU CAN'T SHORTCHANGE THE METAPHYSICAL REAPER OF REALITY-BASED FEAR WHEN HE COMES TO SQUARE ACCOUNTS.

very waters and completely undeveloped shoreline of shallow Lakes Macancox and Coba. After we emerged from the wilds, we stopped at a little open-air eatery, Restaurant Isabel, outside the complex's entrance, to wait for a rumored bus to Valladolid, a town near the famed pyramids of Chichen Itza.

Mauro, the restaurant's proprietor, told us he was Mayan. A barrel-chested man, perhaps five feet tall, he had the sloping forehead and prominent convex nose of the feathered royals depicted on the temple glyphs. Mauro held an extended conversation in Spanish with Edward and Marci, who translated for us. He rattled off common words in his Maya dialect and in Spanish, as Edward taught us both.

Before meeting Mauro, I hadn't thought much about whether such a thing as a living, breathing Maya existed in the modern world. I guess I had thought there were a handful of pure Maya hiding somewhere in the Lacandon jungle south of Palenque.

Yet it had proved rather easy to meet Mayans, both hitch-hiking to Tulum and later while buying *refrescos* at Coba. Their population totals an estimated 4 million to 6 million today. The Maya outnumber their European conquerors in at least part of their former realm: the highlands of Guatemala and Mexico's Chiapas state.

Mauro stood many minutes in a posture described by J. Eric S. Thompson in *Maya Archeologist:*

feet together with arms folded across the breasts and tips of the fingers under forearms. Exactly similar poses occur in ancient Maya sculpture and on painted vessels.

As the bus out of Coba remained a rumor, we whiled away the hours drinking beers and colas and modeling an assortment of headgear, Sharon a white cowboy hat and Edward a generic ball cap. "You have 'The Look,' " I said, taking a photo of their air of lassitude.

LESSON NUMBER 9: THE MODERN BACKPACKER IDLES IN GRAHAM GREENELAND SETTINGS SUCH AS BACKWOODS MEXICO DRESSED NOT IN MILITARY UNIFORM, CLERICAL GARB, TROPICAL SUITS OR CONSULAR ATTIRE, BUT CASUAL FOURTH OF JULY COOKOUT TOGS.

Our nonchalance regarding the non-existent bus proved warranted. A family of four pulled up to Restaurant Isabel in a Pinto, the rear shocks sagging so profoundly that we could notice its dip even in the dark from a distance.

Mauro negotiated a fee for a lift to the main road, Mexico

Edward and Sharon languorously await a nonexistent bus in Coba.

180, which runs from Cancun to Mérida. Then we experimented with ways to arrange six adults, two children, and a mountain of gringo backpacks in a subcompact.

As we jounced along in the dark, our sweat commingled wherever our sides mushed together. Yet the density of our packed selves failed to absorb the blast waves of mariachi music from the Pinto's rear speakers.

Our ad hoc chauffeurs deposited us at a bus shelter at the crossroads of Nuevo Xcan. There we boarded the bus to various towns along the way to Mérida, telling the driver our destination. Edward coached us to provide the correct, spitfire pronunciation, "Bye-ya-da-LEED." Sharon and I amused ourselves by calling it Valluh-DAW-lid.

In Valladolid we found a pleasant restaurant with a courtyard and arbor to have some regional specialties, *sopa da lima* (chicken broth with lime juice, spices and garnishes) and *pollo pibil* (chicken with red peppers and local onions).

As we ate, we reviewed our financial situation after six days in Mexico. This was not turning out to be a dirt-cheap jaunt akin to, say, India in the 1960s.

Three factors made Yucatan travel costs a wildly moving target: the peso's erratic moves, price rises related to the influx of U.S. and European tourist money, and signs of Mexican modernization, such as plush first-class buses. Many purchases cost almost as much as they would in the United States.

Admission fees for ruins were adding up to a big part of our daily costs, which we were trying to keep to $30 or so a day. This day alone had included a $5 fee for Xel-ha, $3.30 for Tulum and another $3.30 for Coba. I'm certain one of our guidebooks said that "entrance to the ruins is pennies." At least our money might support preservation of the fragile structures.

The only bargains we found were local buses and our room costs, once they were split four ways. The 1994 peso devaluation would later bring some relief from high prices.

WEDNESDAY, FEB. 12
Monuments built in wilting heat

We bought freshly baked bread and bottled water in Valladolid and hopped a bus for the short trip to Chichen Itza. Unlike Coba or any of the other sites, Chichen Itza had an air-conditioned gift shop, giant tour buses parked out front and busy drink stands with $3 *refrescos* (which would drop to 85 cents by the time of my return trip in 1996). Unhappy with the prices, we paid anyway, parched in the pounding sun as we explored the giant site.

At this complex of undeniable fascination, seem-

Belliveau's Top 10 tips for group travel

Sharon and I offer others in the amateur ranks our keys to a successful road trip:

1. **Never confuse the locals.** If you're in a group of four, and only three want tickets on the next train to Timbuktu, make sure only three faces appear in front of the ticket seller.

2. **Keep to the menu** in restaurants. It might be fine in U.S. establishments to heavily revise the listed specials. But in most of the rest of the world, you'll just bang your head against a brick wall:

• English pubs won't have many of the menu listings. ("We have shepherd's pie and sausage rolls, but we're out of shepherd's pie.")

• In Madagascar, dinner is that duck walking around back of the lean-to beside the tables.

• On Chinese riverboats and airplanes, choice may be limited to fish fins, tripe, pig stomach lining, a single hard candy or orange soda.

• In Greece, all restaurants will have the official government-issued menu with hundreds of delectable items, of which only mutton stew is actually available, which can be discovered by poking around in the kitchen, peering under the lids of the cookpots.

3. My sister, Carol, furnished an excellent tip learned on her honeymoon excursion to Cancun and Tulum: **Pack a bag of Chips Ahoy or Fig Newtons** for your American snack cravings after a few days.

4. **Take a mini-library** of paperback books. Pulp reading takes the sting out of trip delays.

5. **Avoid highly opinionated people,** especially when sharing the close confines of a sailboat. (The author waives this rule for herself only.)

6. **Pick safe topics** for group bull sessions. Our favorites: Computer software. The Washington Redskins. Past trips. Shetland sheepdogs. Sailing. Tactics for training your boss not to even try to give you work. Or along the same lines, shop talk.

7. **Puns, songs and jingles solid-**ify in-group relations. Mispronounce "Valladolid" and have fun with "Codz Poop" for laughs, or pick your own words.

8. **Learn the words** for "hello," "thank you," "soft drink," "bathroom" and 17 things you like to eat.

9. **Select appropriate adventure attire** for your trip. We recommend straw hats or ball caps, "Budweiser/-The Washington Redskins Decade of Champions" T-shirts and bright Guatemalan shorts woven of spirit cloth **(see above).**

10. And if you win the lottery or get a buyout, **spread the good luck around.**

ingly on a par with the wonders of the ancient world, we enjoyed reprising the words of our neighbors on the flight down.

Sharon: "The ruins—too far, not worth it."

Marci: "She likes the beaches."

Chichen Itza had the whole Maya package, and most of what it had was bigger than specimens at other sites: a gigacenote, the Sacred Well; the Castillo, or Temple to Kukulcan; the Temple of the Warriors; an astronomical observatory, the snail-shaped Caracol; and a Great Ball Court—the largest yet found, a Mesoamerican Superdome. Glyphs of players on the walls of the Great Ball Court made it easy to imagine a game being played there more than a thousand years ago.

Yet Chichen Itza's groomed jungle and well-restored temples lacked the atmosphere of discovery we had enjoyed at partly derelict Coba. Crowds of tourists and peddlers also robbed the site of mystery. Dozens of Maya women, with small children in traditional garb, sold trinkets under the trees and on every path. They offered to pose for photos for a small fee.

Borrowing from the Steve Martin movie *L.A. Story*, in which Martin's ditzy love interest, SanDeE, takes courses in "spokesmodeling," we photographed each other framing the Chichen Itza monuments with our arms arranged in the manner of bimbos gesturing toward the prizes on TV game shows.

Sharon "modeled" a bas-relief of skulls skewered on a rack at the Platform of the Skulls. These depict the decapitation of ball players, presumably those who lost.

Sharon strikes a cheerful pose at the Platform of the Skulls.

For many years, authorities believed that the violence of the imagery at Chichen Itza resulted from a heavy influence by the Toltecs, a militaristic people from an area northeast of modern Mexico City. Today however, scholars believe the imagery reflects internal change toward a more violent philosophy.

In blistering heat we worked our way along a *sacbe* (a straight, wide, sacred footpath made of limestone) toward the southernmost reaches of Chichen Itza. We learned that afternoon to scurry from one shady area to another and that, in the future, we should cart around bottled water at the Maya sites.

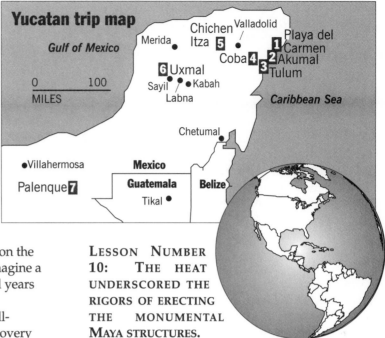

LESSON NUMBER 10: THE HEAT UNDERSCORED THE RIGORS OF ERECTING THE MONUMENTAL MAYA STRUCTURES.

Just walking to look at the ruins, we became sapped and sweaty. If walking was this punishing, how did the Maya lug massive limestone blocks up the eight stories of El Castillo at Chichen Itza, let alone the incredible 21 stories of Temple IV at Tikal?

Our thoughts lined up with the observations of archeologist J. Eric S. Thompson, who dismissed theories of water shortages, chronic warfare, and agricultural failures to explain the collapse, almost complete by the time of the conquistadors, of Maya society.

"Peasant uprising," Thompson said simply.

However, University of New Mexico Professor Flora Simmons Clancy challenges the image of abused slaves, forced to haul limestone blocks and groaning under the whip, as so much Hollywood fantasy.

In her book *Pyramids* she describes evidence suggesting that, in Egypt and perhaps other early civilizations, many of the men who built the pyramids actually might have been proud and cooperative folks, eager to lend their energy and skill to a monumental task that would be observable centuries later.

Our minds slowed by the heat, we regarded El Caracol, which looks exactly like what it is: an astronomical observatory. Its dome is shaped eerily like that of Palomar in California or the Mauna Kea Observatory in Hawaii.

With observations made at El Caracol and elsewhere, the Maya predicted solar and lunar eclipses. They even determined that the moon orbits the earth every 29.53020 days, remarkably close to the modern calculation of 29.53059.

The Maya achieved more than just the monumental architecture of these Babylonian-looking pyramids, as shown by the studies of the heavens conducted at El Caracol.

The shape of El Caracol at Chichen Itza resembles Mount Palomar.

A ruin with Athenian impact

That morning, Edward headed back to the United States, able to accompany us only for the first of our 2¹/₂ weeks. In parting he challenged our claim that we would continue to study ruins. He pretended to be convinced that as soon as he left, we would proceed directly to our true interest: the seamy underbellies of Mexican port cities.

"Now you ladies have a wonderful time in Villahermosa," he said jauntily. We had indeed been intrigued by passages, remarkably damning for a travel guidebook, on how Villahermosa was "bathed in heat and humidity" and enjoyed a "landscape marred by shantytowns and refineries reeking of sulphur."

Despite Edward's suspicions, Marci, Sharon and I stayed true to our newfound incarnation as cultural mavens. We found a tour bus to take us to ruins at four sites: Kabah, Sayil, Labna and Uxmal.

Our bus driver asked where we were from. "Baltimore," I said. He didn't recognize the name. Using my horizontal left hand as a map of the United States, I gave a geography lecture. My right index finger pointed to spots on the East Coast, near the fingertips of my hand map:

"New York. Philadelphia. Baltimore. Washington."

"Ah," his eyes lit up, "Waltimore! Waltimore *Or-ree-OH-les*. Very good baseball." Clearly this was one *yucateco* who knew his baseball dynasties, and it was better to be from the home town of the Orioles than, say, the Mets.

Each site that we saw that day featured a unique structure well worth a visit. Impressive palaces stood at Sayil and Kabah. The Codz Poop palace at Kabah featured with nearly 300 masks of the long-nosed Chacmool, the rain god. We came to recognize his mask at many ruins, reflecting the Maya pleas for rain and suggesting drought conditions. Labna is known for a vaulted arch, nearly 20 feet high, in a freestanding wall, perhaps at one time a ceremonial passageway between plazas.

Uxmal (pronounced oosh-MAHL), however, clearly stood as the grand-slam attraction of the region. Mysterious, brooding and uncrowded in the pummeling heat, Uxmal lived up to a recommendation by a friend, Audrey, that had bought us here.

The Temple of the Magician (*Piramide del Adivino*) seemed steeper, bulkier, and more bewitched than your standard *castillos* at other sites. Up close, it induced dizziness. Seen from the vantage of the House of the Governor, it erupted like a hallucination, architecture from a Nile civilization rising eerily from the bramble of an American jungle.

As for the House of the Governor itself, it seemed the most thought-provoking single thing we saw on our trip, even more so than Chichen Itza's astounding El Caracol observatory. Even today, I struggle to articulate exactly why I felt an overwhelming feeling of, *How on earth did this huge stone structure come to be built here?*

The building and its platforms sit like a soccer-field-sized conundrum. One senses that if it is much easier to borrow culture than to invent it, and if no proof exists of contact with other civilizations, that the Maya achievement represented by the House of the Governor displays a singular level of creativity and persistence in world history.

Many scholars consider the rectangular structure, built between 600 and 900 A.D., to be the masterpiece of Maya buildings. Though it doesn't really look like the Parthenon, it *felt* like the most splendid building of the golden age of Athens (500 to 400 B.C.). The House

Our tour bus driver poses at the Palace at Sayil, left. Sharon stands at the arch at Labna, center, and the Codz Poop palace, right.

Uxmal's Temple of the Magician erupts from the jungle, left. Right, climbers tackle its steep stairs.

of the Governor resembled the Parthenon not so much in its exact proportions as in its epic size, harmonious proportions and the extent of its formal decoration.

The very rectangular shape of the structure may be its most Athenian aspect. At Tulum, Coba and Chichen Itza, we had principally seen square-based, bulky pyramids. Clearly the Maya could switch hit, constructing both Babylonian-style pyramids and Greek-style rectangular monuments. And its square corners and giganticness set it apart from the various sorts of dwellings of the Great Plains and Eastern seaboard Indians.

The Maya, lacking a natural hilltop such as Athens' Acropolis, needed to raise the site of the House of the Governor. They made an artificial hill via three successive platforms, rising cumulatively more than 40 feet on a massive volume of piled-up earth and rubble. The top platform, 21 feet high, is as long as a football field and half as wide.

Two vaults divide the building itself into three portions. An intricate stone mosaic runs around the entire building above the doorway level, combining a giant frieze with remnants of human figures, canopies of masks and squares called step-frets, which feature a maze-like pattern.

Looking at the House of the Governor, you can feel in your bones the years of labor involved in constructing the filled platforms, designing and cutting the building's limestone blocks to specification and carving the exceptional finish of the mosaic.

Jeff Karl Kowalski, in *The House of the Governor*, also compared the structure to the Parthenon, and to Chartres Cathedral in Northern France. He wrote that that the structure demonstrated how "architecture played an important social role, serving to display the economic power and political authority of the ruler."

Remarkably for a building at such a remote site, the House of the Governor has inspired raves from travelers for more than a century, a detailed book (most books on the Maya ruins focus on one or more sites, rather than a single building) and virtual-reality software permitting a computer walk-through.

As we looked at the giant structure, Sharon jokingly suggested that UFOs had bought it and the other edifices to Mesoamerica.

Almost everyone who has ever seen the more dramatic Maya sites wonders the same thing. They raise profound questions—which I returned to after our trip—about whether, absent Maya contact with European, Asian or African civilizations, humankind inevitably feels an urge at a certain stage of development to construct pyramids and study the stars.

The doorways of the House of the Governor provided a blessedly cool retreat. We shared swigs of our bottled water. Though the heat outside seemed incompatible with human settlement, good soils in this area apparently attracted settlement and the attendant ritual monuments.

In Egypt, the pyramids were designed to protect the bodies of kings for eternity, and ever greater numbers of Maya pyramids are being demonstrated to fulfill the same function. Yet the swelter made me wonder if the Maya built pyramids, not only to bury

The House of the Governor at Uxmal features classical proportions.

their dead and to approach the gods on high but to also provide what nature forgot: artificial mountains offering clear views of the countryside and places with cool interiors.

Our trio had one more ruin to see. We boarded the overnight bus, with its sound system blasting "My Way," "Jailhouse Rock" and other songs the entire way to Palenque.

SUNDAY, FEB. 16
The most beautiful ruins

Moving slowly, still feeling the aftereffects of our long bus ride, we left the hotel at 11:30 a.m. for the Palenque ruins. We hoped that these ruins, the hardest ones to reach, would be "worth it."

At the entrance gate, we encountered a Mayan who handed out Indian liberation literature. I read his flier over in fascination and carefully held on to it. Later I passed it along to a journalist friend based in Mexico City, who chose not to investigate this and other signs of increasing unrest in the Maya lands. Two years later, the Maya in nearby Chiapas staged a revolt.

Guidebooks made much of the fact that the Palenque occupies a more dramatic, mountain-like setting than all the other Maya ruins. Four temples—of

A rare Maya tower rises at the Palace at Palenque.

the Inscriptions, the Sun, the Cross and the Foliated Cross—rise near the tops of pyramid-shaped hills. The Palace, one of a handful of Mesoamerican structures featuring a tower, lay below the temples in a flat plaza and looked oddly like a Spanish colonial building.

The structures bore numerous glyphs. At Palenque, the glyphs appeared to be in good condition with sharp edges and

The Temple of the Cross's hillside setting.

little wear. They depicted feathered serpents (to the Maya, the god Kukulkan; to the Aztecs, Quetzalcoatl) and human figures in headdresses holding sheaves of maize. The temples displayed some of the few surviving roof combs used to create taller and more impressive pinnacles at Palenque, Tikal, Edzna and other Maya pyramids.

Maya pyramids compared

Tikal	Peerless
Chichen Itza	Impressive
Uxmal	Magical or bewitched
Tulum	Stunning
Coba	Lost
Edzna	Majestic
Palenque	Jewel-like

A Eurotraveler at the Temple of the Cross told us the roof combs might last only a hundred or so more years. He may well be correct, given the construction techniques of Maya works. *Pyramids* author Clancy noted that

The ancient Mesoamerican pyramid was never constructed to withstand all time. Its heartings were not designed with carefully engineered stone coursings, but were made instead of rubble-fill, mud-mortar, or adobe (sun-dried) bricks. ... Clearly, [the Maya] counted on continual maintenance and/or rebuilding projects.

A visit to Agua Azul

We took a day off from visiting ruins to see Agua Azul, located an hour by bus from Palenque. Its 500 small waterfalls tumble layer upon layer, like an animated version of the limestone terraces at Mammoth Hot Springs in Yellowstone National Park in Wyoming.

Swimming in the tree-shaded pools of swift water created a refreshing contrast to trekking through the dry, hot ruins. But visitors beware: Many have died, swept down the falls between the pools, their fates marked by small white crosses beside the path.

The color of the water, as turquoise as the stones in a Navajo silver bracelet, stayed in our minds, as did the profiles of the local Indians on the bus, who revealed the broad lips and straight line of nose and forehead of the Maya gods on the ancient glyphs.

LESSON NUMBER 11: THE LIMESTONE EDIFICES OF THE MAYA—WITH MOST OF THEIR PAINT GONE, AND MOST OF THEIR ROOF COMBS GOING—SEEMED A PRIORITY FOR THE ADVENTURE TRAVELER: "SEE IT NOW BEFORE IT DISAPPEARS."

Palenque also has one of the Maya pyramids known to have functioned as a funeral tomb: the Temple of the Inscriptions, where the remains of a Lord Pacal, a large man wearing a jade mosaic funerary mask, were found in 1952.

Getting to Lord Pacal's tomb required climbing to the top of the temple and then descending an internal tunnel a considerable distance, to a chamber nearly level with the base of the exterior. Because I had suffered an attack of vertigo at Tikal, I was afraid I would experience more psychic turmoil descending into the bowels of the Temple of the Inscriptions. I left the exploration of the tomb to the others and sat in safety on the grass to wait.

Sharon and Marci managed the descent, saying a British woman in the tiny passageway nearly went nuts with claustrophobia. It was intriguing that many women lost their mental equilibrium exploring the heights and depths of the Maya sites. But statistics show twice as many U.S. women (7 percent vs. 3.5 percent for men) suffer from agoraphobia, an exaggerated fear of heights or open spaces.

After Palenque, our eighth Maya ruin in six days, we backtracked to the beaches of Playa del Carmen and Cozumel for six more days of snorkeling, lunching on guacamole, and beginning to look past our buyout vacations to new chapters in our lives.

The Yucatan and the big lesson: parallel evolution

Anthropologists have grappled for more than a century with attempts to explain similarities in geographically separated cultures. Diffusion—the spread of culture by contact—is one explanation. Parallel evolution, or independent discoveries, is another.

No direct evidence exists of contact between the Maya and others, despite recurring similarities with some aspects of East and Southeast Asian culture. That leaves parallel evolution (on a giant scale) as the most likely reason the Maya constructed pyramids similar to Babylon's, more cities than ancient Egypt, monumental rectangular temples like those of the Minoans, roads comparable to the Romans' and sea-trade routes on the order of the Phoenicians.

Further, one temple (Xpuhil, far to the south of Mérida) with three narrow, solid towers resembles a Burmese pointed-dome temple. The roof combs at Tikal echo the ornate towers at Cambodia's Angkor Wat, and a Norman-style moat surrounds a temple near Xpuhil called Becan.

Ziggurats—stepped pyramids with temples at the top—rose toward heaven in Babylon and the Yucatan. Pyramids served as burial chambers for Egyptian, Kushite and in some cases, Maya rulers. These may show a universal human proclivity for creating monuments as soon as a society advances enough to have

---

Trends in viewing the Maya

The Spanish conquerors observed Maya idolatry and concluded that they dealt with non-Christian savages. Archaeologist Eric Thompson focused on El Caracol, the observatory at Chichen Itza, and decided that the Maya were a gentle society led by pious priests.

The Maya continue to be all things to all people. New Agers still cling to Thompson's view of the Maya as primitives living Rousseau's simple life in idyllic preindustrial cities, while scholars now focus on their warlike aspects.

Interpretations of the Maya, Professor Clancy of the University of New Mexico noted in a letter to me, "change with generational regularity. During the 20th century, the noble-savage gave way to the philosopher/astronomer priest, who has now become the bloodthirsty dynast sacrificing his way to divinity. I figure we have about 10 to 15 more years of this latest paradigm.

"There is no denying the importance of warfare and sacrifice in the lives of the ancient Maya; each paradigm has served and serves a real and clarifying purpose. But to think that we now have, at last, 'discovered' the most truthful paradigm is to take a decidedly 19th century, positivist view of the way history works."

University of Pittsburgh Professor Jeremy A. Sabloff wrote in *The New Archaeology and the Ancient Maya* that new ways of looking at the Maya reflect changes in the social backgrounds of archaeologists themselves and changing U.S. political concerns. During the Vietnam War, Maya aggressiveness came under study; as the environmental movement gained momentum, scholars focused more on links between their farming techniques, possibly overintensive, and their population collapse. T. Patrick Cuthbert wrote in his 1993 book, *Maya Civilization* that

> the Maya had overpopulated and overexploited their environment, had fought each other viciously, and eventually had destroyed themselves.

LESSON NUMBER 12: THE MAYA NOW RIVAL THE ANCIENT ROMANS AS A PEOPLE STUDIED FOR THEIR RELEVANCE TO THE CONTEMPORARY UNITED STATES.

The inevitability of inventions

Parallel evolution, at which the Maya excelled, lives in the sphere of science. Though one would imagine scientists to be in close communication with each other, they frequently stumble upon things independently, as my father, Louis J. Belliveau, wrote to me in an Internet message:

> The example that comes to mind immediately is that of Newton's fight with Hooke over what is now called Hooke's law of elasticity, and Newton's parallel discovery of the calculus with Leibnitz. The claim as to who really invented the electronic digital computer is similarly clouded.

Independent scientific discoveries

Year	Discovery (number independent discoverers)
1558-1609	Telescope (9)
1592-1617	Decimal point (4)
1611	Sun spots (4)
1774	Oxygen (2)
1831-1837	Telegraph (4)
1839	Cellular basis of tissue (7)
1845	Planet Neptune (2)

Based on a list of 148 such discoveries in *Social Change*

Leslie A. White wrote in *The Science of Culture* that the right to manufacture the telephone rested on an interval of only hours between the recording of descriptions by Alexander Graham Bell and Elisha Gray:

> The simultaneity of multiple inventions or discoveries is sometimes striking and remarkable. Accusations of plagiarism are not infrequent; bitter rivalries are waged over priorities.

White suggested that creative individuals are born at steady rates in large populations but require a certain level of civilizational attainment to flourish. "There were brains as good as Newton's" among many comparatively primitive peoples, he wrote, "but the calculus was not invented in these other times and places because the requisite cultural elements were lacking." When a culture such as the Maya one reaches a given level, he indicates, it is not surprising that many people can make the same discovery independently:

> It goes without saying that a given synthesis cannot be achieved until the requisite elements for the synthesis are available: the steam engine could not have been invented in the Neolithic age. ... When certain factors and conditions are present and in conjunction an invention or discovery takes place; when they are not present, the invention or discovery does not occur.

food surpluses sufficient to support laborers, artisans, oversees and designers.

Many other developments provide examples of parallel evolution:

• Writing arose independently in five different parts of the world, most probably Sumeria, China, Egypt, the Indus Valley in Pakistan and the Yucatan.

• Farming arose independently in prehistoric Mexico, Mesopotamia, Thailand and along the Nile, Danube and Yellow rivers. Irrigation arose in China, Mesopotamia and Peru.

• Japan and England independently developed knights and castles.

• Separately, ancient Turkey and China came up with the idea of issuing the first coins.

Parallel evolution became less possible in Europe, Asia and Africa when Marco Polo, Magellan and other explorers set out on their travels. The isolation of ideas slowly became a thing of the past. Global communications satellites, beginning in 1960 with Echo 1, accelerated cultural diffusion, as did the emergence of the WorldWide Web in the 1990s.

Some of the earliest chroniclers of the Maya recognized overwhelming evidence that they had developed monumental architecture independently. The first bishop of Yucatan, Diego de Landa, wrote circa 1566 in *The Maya: Account of the Affairs of the Yucatán*, that the figures in the temple glyphs displayed long girdles and other clothes still worn by the Maya of his day.

> It is untrue to say that these buildings were built by other nations to whom the Indians were subject; for there is evidence that they must have been built by native Indian people.

Yet hypotheses persisted, as with the African ruins at Great Zimbabwe, that European or Asian civilizations lent help. The idea that culture had to be spread by contact with a superior group reflected a viewpoint that most people, particularly non-whites, are uninventive.

Stephens and Catherwood, the archeologist and illustrator team of the 1830s, demolished the view that other civilizations helped construct the Maya monuments.

Stephens addressed the controversy in a passage called "Who Built These Ruined Cities?" in *Incidents of Travel in Central America, Chiapas and Yucatan*. He noted that giant terraces underlay Maya, but not Egyptian, pyramids. Maya sculptures rendered the human form radically differently from Hindu art. These dissimilarities, and the early accounts by de Landa and others of Indians still living among splendid stone buildings, led Stephens to

Maya parallels to Asia

Anthropology professor Michael D. Coe acknowledges in *The Maya* the speculation that

the previously undistinguished Maya came under the influence of travelers from shores as distant as the China coast.

While "no objects manufactured in any part of the Old World have been identified in any Maya site," Coe cited recent, scholarly works that ponder whether an Asian-Pacific group, perhaps Indonesians, somehow bought an influence.

A matching sequence of animal names appears in the 20 days of the Mesoamerican calendar and the lunar zodiacs of many East and Southeast Asian groups. And the Han Chinese and ancient Maya used the same calculations to predict lunar and solar eclipses.

Further, a few screen-fold books of bark paper, used for several Maya codexes (records of ritual, calendar, and astronomical information), have survived to the modern day despite the Spanish penchant for obliterating most of those they found. This type of book was also used in ancient China and Southeast Asia—and even in present-day Indonesia, by the Batak people of Sumatra.

If any of these theories holds water, Indonesia would serve as cultural parent of not only Madagascar and Polynesia, but also Mesoamerica. The connection sounds far-fetched to me, for it seems the Polynesians would have certainly received intervening exposure to any Sumatran invention that got as far as the Yucatan. On the other hand, the Viking landings in Newfoundland suggest that there may have been

An Indonesian *wayang kulit* puppet, left, and an item found at the Maya site of Copan in Honduras, right.
Based on sketches in *Indonesia Handbook* and *Maya Civilization*

more long-distance ocean contacts than modern minds realize.

LESSON NUMBER 13: PEOPLE THROUGHOUT HISTORY HAVE GOTTEN LOST, AND THAT COULD INCLUDE ASIAN FISHERMEN IN STORMS.

A photograph in *Maya Civilization*, for example, depicts the head and headdress of a figure on a stone silhouette found at the Honduran ruins of Copan. The figure uncannily resembles the look of Javanese shadow puppets (*wayang kulit*), flat leather figures with quite similar straight nose-forehead combinations, open lips and ornate headgear.

And Maya musical tastes, which seemed a thing apart from either the gloppy Mexican mainstream or the vibrant Caribbean-Brazilian salsa style, made me wonder about an Asian connection.

In 1996, Lamont and I stumbled upon a political rally in Cancun featuring entertainment by a band

called Montalvo. A high-stepping singer, a classic example of Latin handsomeness, led a band of tight horns and driving percussion. The smattering of gringo tourists danced (Lamont doing a Rio-quality samba). The Maya, munchkin-like and with bowl haircuts, made up a majority of the crowd in the plaza. They stared with interest but did not move a muscle.

A soundman explained to us that Montalvo hailed from Veracruz, Mexico's giant Gulf port. That Montalvo's Cuban-influenced music seemed to bypass much of the crowd made me wonder if in fact the Maya connected in some fashion, as their ancient calendars and bark-paper books indicated, with the flute-and-gong-loving Indonesians?

Professor Clancy wrote in a letter to me that

Most scholars, while not rejecting out of hand theories of contact between the ancient Amerindians and Old World cultures, are definitely skeptical, and this includes myself. Nonetheless the parallelisms are patently obvious and ought not to be ignored. My interests and speculations run toward the question of why these similarities exist (given the total lack of archaeological evidence for actual contact) rather than to what or which are the best (or closest) comparisons.

conclude that a native people had independently arrived at original forms of architecture, sculpture, writing and astronomy.

The simple act of planting and harvesting, a Maya activity readily seen from the windows of tour buses in the Yucatan to this day, holds the key to their extraordinary level of parallel evolution.

Clearly creative individuals among the early Maya did a terrific job of domesticating maize and later

developed intensive methods of agriculture to increase yields. Their agricultural revolution from the intensive farming of corn, as well as pumpkins, squash, chili peppers and other grains and vegetables, helped support a Maya population in the Yucatan of perhaps as many as 10 million, more than double the number today. Some scholars believe the Maya, at the height of their population, created continuous permanent settlements from one end of the Yucatan to the other.

V. Gordon Childe, a professor of prehistoric archaeology at the University of Edinburgh, wrote in *Social Evolution* that

> Obviously the cultivation of edible plants, the breeding of animals for food, or the combination of both pursuits in mixed farming, did represent a revolutionary advance in human economy. It permitted a substantial expansion of population. It made possible and even necessary the production of a social surplus. … If stages of economic and social evolution are to be defined on technological bases, food production should surely mark the beginning of a major stage.

Anthropological theorist Leslie A. White came up with a formula for this in *The Science of Culture:*

> We can now formulate the basic law of cultural evolution: Other factors remaining constant, *culture evolves as the amount of energy harnessed per capita per year is increased, or as the efficiency of the instrumental means of putting the energy to work is increased.*

In fact, Maya architectural achievements are all the more remarkable because they lagged in "instrumental means," or tools, to multiply the surplus energy unleashed by their agricultural talents.

They developed many aspects of civilization despite operating with a number of handicaps, notably a lack of ploughs, metal implements, the wheel and draft animals.

Civilizations arise from surplus food and then begin to address human needs other than sustenance: social organization, law and order, knowledge and self-expression. Anthropologists call this the "universal culture pattern." So perhaps it is no great surprise that the Maya resemble the Minoans, Greeks, Romans, Babylonians and others. The pyramids and temples of all the groups responded to an additional human need: religious expression.

Food surpluses eventually led to a need for writing to record trading and the exploits of leaders. Writing, Childe wrote,

> was the necessary instrument of exact science, the applications of which have revolutionized technology. Its use led to calendrical astronomy, predictive arithmetic, and geometry—tools demonstrably used by the first civilized societies in the Old and New Worlds, by the Egyptians, the Sumerians, and the Mayas. At the same time a consideration of these earliest literate societies reveals that writing is a convenient and easily recognizable index of a quite revolutionary change in the scale of the community's size, economy, and social organization.

So perhaps the way in which the Maya most truly parallel patterns of civilization on other continents is

Palenque's Temple of the Inscriptions served as a burial chamber, as did the Egyptian pyramids.

not in their obvious pyramids but the glyphs that adorn them.

And perhaps that defines why buildings such as the House of the Governor at Uxmal and the Parthenon on Athens' Acropolis maintain their power to move us so. They are symbols writ large of how our barbarian ancestors departed the woods and became civilized, learning to write and figure numbers, two developments that link the modern man or woman at a computer to the pyramid builder.

English writer Hilaire Belloc wrote in *The Cruise of the "Nona"* that the "chief lesson" of the past was "that the developments of society follow no mechanical process; that their way is not the way of an arrow, but of a serpent."

But German philosopher Oswald Spengler disagreed, writing in The *Decline of the West* that

> Every Culture, every adolescent and maturing and decay of a culture, every one of its intrinsically necessary stages and periods, has a definite duration, always the same, always recurring with the emphasis of a symbol.

Probability theory would predict that extra tortillas would lead to pyramids, even absent contact with external influences. Except for the Celts, most preindustrial civilizations with agricultural surpluses eventually created cities and then monuments. Anthropologist Edward B. Tylor wrote in 1878 that parallel evolution "strikingly illustrates the extent of mental uniformity among mankind."

The Maya seem to prove that many people are creative, that they share with others an extraordinary underlying psychic unity, and that there is a fixedness to the pattern of human development.

Pyramids pointed to heaven wherever clever humans developed unusually productive grains—even in the isolated Americas.

SHIMMERING HEAT AND RADIANT BUDDHISTS

Burma … and lessons on the nature of poverty

Little girls in Pegu attend to their prayers.

During a World War II visit to Rangoon, journalist Martha Gellhorn noted her overriding impression: "The heat was indescribable."

In her book *Travels with Myself and Another*, she recalled,

> You felt you could cut the heat and hold it like chunks of wet blotting paper. … The only way to sleep or in fact live was to lie naked on the marble floor under the paddle fan in the hotel bedroom.

She had arrived, as I did later, during "the dog days just before the monsoon rains." The passage of 40 years had done little to improve the availability of air-conditioning. I learned the unchanged wisdom of lying still indoors, sweating quietly on a mattress or a plywood bunk.

In April, before the arrival of the annual monsoon in May, eyeball-smashing heat bakes Burma. (In June 1989, military dictators renamed the country Myanmar, an unpleasant-sounding name. Democracy advocates stick with the original.) In Rangoon or Pagan, 110 degrees sledgehammers the human body in a way that an equivalent temperature in a place such as Phoenix, for example, could not begin to compare.

Heat in Arizona can be a brief, almost sensual tickle on the skin between machine-cooled vehicles and buildings.

LESSON NUMBER 1: HEAT IN BURMA, LIKE THE SENSATION OF FOREIGNNESS IN CHINA, SURROUNDS THE TRAVELER 24 HOURS A DAY, WITH FEW OASES.

Only the early morning and late afternoon provide safe times to explore. Green tea, served in tiny cups the size of a dollhouse play set's, may be the only safe thing to drink. Slaking one's thirst was a losing battle. With each passing day, the heat sweated out more fluid. The blood and organs feel drawn down, like those of an unwatered camel fading in the desert. The one good thing about Burma's old visa limit, which permitted only seven days, was you returned to places with drinkable liquids before you collapsed of dehydration.

Out of this incredible heat comes light. In one of the world's poorest nations, the only non-African country to crack the bottom 20, the visitor discovers a national character worth more than rubies or gold.

LESSON NUMBER 2: THE BURMESE REVERENCE FOR KNOWLEDGE AND KINDNESS CHALLENGES NOTIONS THAT A LACK OF MONEY INEXORABLY LEADS TO SOCIAL PATHOLOGIES. BURMA MAY SERVE AS THE WORLD NATION MOST OPPOSITE TO THE UNITED STATES.

Burma's learned and honorable may possess only a worn shirt, a cloth wrap and their books. The American poor have more possessions—VCRs, home appliances and often automobiles—and less in the way of strong educations and families.

Encountering a nation where millions live like St. Francis of Assisi, following the Biblical prescription to possess nothing but do good everywhere, recasts many daily encounters once a traveler is back in the West. Westerners often find Burma to be the single place that most alters their outlook. For with a gentle wave of the hand, most Burmese dismiss all our cherished notions of an inevitable desire for goods or pleasures.

A young monk such as this one in Pagan may have few possessions: perhaps a robe, begging bowl and a needle.

Burma conveyed an impression as one of the world's less commercial holy places. Even the more jaded backpackers' guidebooks use terms like "fascinating" and "unforgettable" to describe the temples, the monks and the Burmese laity. Without aggressively advertising itself as Insights for Westerners Inc., as India, Nepal and the New Age outposts of Brazil sometimes do, Burma seemed to be a place that might quietly transform its visitors.

My opportunity to visit Burma came during a 100-day swing through Asia and the South Pacific in 1985. Most of my itinerary, ambitious though it was, represented a fairly straightforward loop for a Far East trip. I added Burma to my route, wanting to see one of Southeast Asia's more remote destinations.

Writers dwell on Burma's lost-world aspects: its ancient cars, its lack of things Western and the ramshackle domestic airline. Passages in *The Great Railway Bazaar* in particular piqued my interest in Burma. Author Paul Theroux wandered from one magical-sounding city to the next: Rangoon to Mandalay, Maymyo to Goktiek. I had read the book during a 1980 cycling trip through the Netherlands, Belgium and France. In particular, its description of an anachronistic hotel in the hills above Mandalay stayed in my mind.

And guidebooks invariably raved about Pagan, Burma's ancient capital with thousands of temples, as one of the three greatest Buddhist monuments, along with Angkor Wat in Cambodia and Borobudur in Java.

That's not to say Burma presents a particularly sharp image to the West. Go to a major reference library, and wallfuls of recent books will address East Asia's giants, Japan and China, and because of the war there, Vietnam. Meanwhile, a handful of books at best deal with Burma. Burma, with 45 million people and the largest land area in Southeast Asia, seemed to also have the lowest profile in the region.

Books dealing with selected Asian nations

AS MEASURED BY LIBRARY OF CONGRESS SUBJECT HEADINGS, 1968-96

India	54,744
Japan	18,014
China	17,610
Indonesia	15,428
Thailand	6,686
Vietnam	4,383
Burma	**1,386**
for comparison:	
United States	*302,692*

Burma's isolation further positions it outside the orbit of world attention, relegating it to the genre of hidden worlds such as Bhutan, Sikkim and Andorra, far smaller places. But if the traveler wants to go there, Burma can be visited as a side journey from Bangkok, Singapore, Jakarta, Dhaka, Kunming, Moscow or Vientiane, according to tourist information posted on the Myanmar government's Internet page. (This constitutes a mindbogglingly modern touch for the country. Fortunately, for balance, Free Burma, BurmaWeb,

the Burma Project home page at the Soros website and Amnesty International also provide cyberinformation on the fight for democracy in Burma.)

In the 1980s, the visitor could look around the country for just seven days. At the time, Burmese officials, horrified by overdevelopment in clogged Honolulu and Bangkok, rejected both the tawdriness and the contact with Western ideas implicit in modern mass tourism. Burma then held title as the world's biggest nation with a deliberately non-Western outlook.

Much has changed since those days, of which more later. In my brief encounter with Burma, however, the sense of great gentleness in the essential national character shone through. I flew on my own from Bangkok to Rangoon, expecting to enjoy glittering temples by the score. Burma also offered far more: an encounter with a poor people of noble temperament.

THURSDAY, MARCH 28, 1985
A travel group forged of necessity

A blast of heat greeted our flight as soon as our airplane's door opened. We left behind the air-conditioning, purple sarongs, complimentary corsages and general competence of Thai Airways for antimodern Burma.

Britain left Burma with a civil service bureaucracy and railways as the two principal legacies of its colonial rule, which began in stages over the 1800s and ended in 1948. Once independent, Burma overlaid the reams of paperwork of the raj with its own homegrown and spectacular inefficiency. Thus a tourist's first precious hour in Burma involves completing numbing paperwork involving customs, health, immigration and currency declaration. With only seven days and every minute precious, the delay especially rankled.

Finally I was cleared to set foot in Burma proper. The first order of business involved selling duty-free goods bought at Bangkok's airport—a bottle of Johnny Walker Red and 555s brand cigarettes—to the cab driver who would take me into Rangoon. The deal netted me a free ride and $50 from the driver for goods that had cost me $18. That profit would go a long way in Burma.

I made my way to the tourist bureau, where I met three English people. David, a London lawyer, resembled the actor Peter O'Toole in his looks and wittiness. James, a computer specialist, and his friend, Elizabeth, worked in Hong Kong. We formed an instant tour group.

LESSON NUMBER 3: ENGLISH SPEAKERS FORM GROUPS FOR MUTUAL SUPPORT WHEN ATTEMPTING TO NAVIGATE IN A LITTLE-VISITED FOREIGN LAND.

Together we booked a flight the next morning to

Pagan, which at its peak (1056-1200 A.D.) had more than 10,000 temples. With so little time, we would follow our guidebook's advice to get out of Rangoon and upcountry as swiftly as possible.

En masse we headed for the Strand, in better days one of a trio of famed Southeast Asian hotels. Raffles in Singapore and the Eastern & Oriental in Penang continue to operate as diamonds spun off from the tiara of the former Eastern & Oriental Hotels chain. But at the time of our visit, the Strand had fallen on the stony soil of the Burmese Way to Socialism, making it simultaneously the most derelict of the three in its physical appearance, the most hilariously *Fawlty Towers*-like in its service and the most redolent of the faded splendor of the raj.

David and I went to dinner in the Strand restaurant and ordered its famous $3 lobster—really even less considering the black market rate for kyats we had received for our duty-frees. It was not only cheap but quite delicious.

Afterward, we walked around town. Rangoon gave a striking first impression, equal parts heat, rats, temples, palm trees and physically beautiful people who smiled a lot. Little lights resembling Christmas decorations decked out the public buildings.

For $5, a shopkeeper sold us Burmese leather sandals, with velvet straps fashioned from from theater curtains. The leather conformed to the shape of our feet, and the sandals could easily slip off at temple entrances.

Back in my stifling room, ceiling fans chopped uselessly at the still air. The temperature prevented rest, as did anticipation over how interesting Pagan might be, if unlauded Rangoon had been so exotic.

FRIDAY, MARCH 29
Temples by the thousands
Two gecko lizards hung like suction-cup toys from the interior of the little 6:45 a.m. airplane for Pagan. The rubber gaskets on the interior of the windows bore the telltale crisscross pattern of advanced dry rot. By

A pony trap ferries tourists around Pagan.

some good fortune, the plane, which looked this side of abandoned property, did not crash and kill us all, and we landed safely at 8:15 a.m.

Once we landed, Pagan offered a safer, low-tech mode of transport: traps harnessed to a single pony, with a bench for the driver and two or three passengers. The ponies seemed small and delicate.

We booked into the Si Thi Guesthouse. Mosquito nets extended down to plywood beds. Its rattan walls stopped short of the ceiling, allowing the sultry air a small chance to circulate.

The four of us rented two pony carts to go around the temples with Odile and Jean-Paul, a French couple worthy of Central Casting—très chic, naturellement. Jean-Paul, about 5 foot 7, looked classically Parisian: dark eyed, dark haired and stylish. Odile, taller and more theatrical, clutched their guidebook to *La Birmanie*.

The pony carts carried us along often-deserted roads between dozens of temples—the 2,000 or more that remain in 16 square miles, an area roughly one-quarter the size of Washington, D.C.

We arrived first at Htilominlo, or the "Blessings of

Ramshackle transportation and post-traumatic syndromes

Two years after my trip, an airplane flying from Rangoon to Pagan experienced a fatal accident. A 1987 news item reported how 14 Americans were among those killed when the plane caught fire and crashed.

News accounts of airplane, boat and train accidents on many of the Asian routes I'd taken held a grim fascination for me for a decade after my trip. A 1995 headline, for example, reported the deaths of 102 Burmese in a train wreck north of Mandalay. Other Asia crash reports would mention "four foreign tourists" or "two Americans" among the victims.

The loss of lives attested to the major risk involved in the age of adventure travel: Third World transportation, particularly airplanes and buses.

As I got older, I could work up quite a retroactive fear over Third World travel—twinges of anxiety felt not in the slightest as a younger backpacker actually boarding these rattletraps.

One side note: When Burma extended its visa to 28 days, making visiting less of a pell-mell rush, guidebooks strenuously recommended avoiding the unsafe internal airline.

Three Worlds" temple. We made sure to slip out of shoes or sandals, and the women wore skirts or *longyis*—long clothes that could be wrapped around the waist to create a skirt—out of respect for local tradition.

Ornate carvings and decorations

Pagan features spectacular tall structures , above, and hundreds of smaller temples, right.

covered the exterior wedding-cake tiers of Htilominlo, a massive structure of a dark brick hue identical to the dusty pony trails.

Its top terrace offered a fabulous view of the Irrawaddy River and glinting temples in all directions. Giant white and gold temples rose above the dusty plain, and smaller brown stupas, many five to 20 feet tall, rose between the larger structures. Htilominlo, at 15 stories, stood a shade taller than the 13 stories of Temple II at Tikal in Guatemala.

I took a photograph on Htilominlo of a new 12-year-old friend, a smiling girl wearing on her face the local *thanaka* makeup of sandalwood-colored bark.

Myamya Wen, small for her age, appeared like many Burmese people to be of incredibly slim hips and torso. Given the national slimness, I looked at blouses in street markets but, being wider, could never dream of buying them. My only purchases would be *longyis*.

Myamya Wen poses at temple.

LESSON NUMBER 4: LATER, THE UNITED NATIONS WOULD PROVIDE A SINISTER EXPLANATION FOR THE SMALLNESS OF BURMESE CHILDREN, ESTIMATING THAT ONE-THIRD UNDER THE AGE OF 5 SUFFER FROM MALNOURISHMENT.

Our group went along to Shwezigon, a circular pagoda of glittering gold, where three novice monks agreeably posed for a picture.

Their essence, probably an uncapturable quality like that of a ghost, did not appear on my developed film. There, they seem pleasantly featured but no

more. In my memory, possibly more accurate in recording Burma than a photographic record of surfaces, they drifted gracefully like spirits through the heat of the temple interior, only slightly less broiling than that outside. They recalled Paul Theroux's observations in *The Great Railway Bazaar* that the Burmese in Rangoon looked

like a royal breed, strikingly handsome in this collapsing city, a race of dispossessed princes.

After waving off two young men who offered me dope for my watch, we visited huge Ananda ("divine love" in Sanskrit), a 17-story temple containing four 31-foot-high golden Buddhas with their hands in different positions, representing the attainment of nirvana. They glowed brightly despite the half-light of the temple interior. Their gaze appeared to look right down at the worshippers lighting joss sticks and candles.

Fast forward: hunger and relocations

A 1995 article by Joel L. Swerdlow in *National Geographic* reported that food prices had risen fourfold since 1988, and starvation now affects even adults in urban centers such as Mandalay.

And a tourist named Hnin Hlaing Oo wrote of a return visit to Pagan in the bulletin *Dawn*, published in Bangkok by the All Burma Students Democratic Front.

Hnin had loved a first trip to Burma in the 1980s. But she discovered on her return in 1995 that 5,000 residents of Pagan town, who had been living around the temples, had been cleared out after backing reformers in the 1990 elections. The military believed too much contact with tourists had filled the heads of Pagan residents with visions of democracy.

Pagan's people drifted serenely through the temples, where the heat seemed only the merest bit less than elsewhere.

We repaired to the veranda of the Thiripyitsaya Hotel, a pleasant place, to watch the sun set over the Irrawaddy. Because of the dry season, the river sat back at a phenomenal distance from the hotel terrace, with flowering trees on the hotel grounds and a vast mud flat in between. Behind the distance river rose the Chin Hills, handsome mountains that could have been from the American Southwest.

All six of us decided to leave the next day for Mandalay. We had only scratched the surface of Pagan, but the seven-day visa weighed heavily on our minds. We hailed another pony cart to get back to the guest house. After a dinner of sweet and sour chicken at the adjacent restaurant, we retired at 10:30 p.m. to our plywood beds. Our bus to Mandalay was scheduled to leave at the frightful hour of 3:30 a.m.

Our day had seemed remarkable to me, as a first-time visitor to Southeast Asia. Guidebooks generally refer to Pagan as the most impressive sight of Burma and perhaps of the region. I would be tempted to go further and nominate it as one of the world's wonders.

We had seen the temples by pony cart, a gentle means of transport, perfect for an anachronistic nation with a simple, unadorned daily life. We took our shoes off to display humility as we explored temples at a slow-motion pace prudent for the season. We had explored only in the early morning and the late afternoon, so that we and the ponies could avoid the 100-degrees plus of midday. At night we lay hot as in a fever dream in our un-air-conditioned bungalows.

Asia had begun to sort itself out. I cannot ever recall a minute of formally studying the area in high school or college, so my American notions arose from news coverage of Vietnam and a few literary travel books.

Now I could encounter the realities of Burma and learn by looking around. My image of holy Asia, of contemplative monks and golden temple spires, mate-

rialized in Pagan, first with the three boys with wise eyes and gentle smiles at Shwezigon pagoda.

The names of various Asian capitals offered a clue to Burma's different outlook. Beijing means "northern capital" and Tokyo means "eastern capital." Bangkok's Thai name, Krung Thep, means "city of angels" (Los Angeles!). And Burma's Rangoon, or more lately Yangon, means "End of Strife"—referring to the Buddhist concept of nirvana: the end of desire, attachment and suffering.

SATURDAY, MARCH 30
A day more like a week

We awoke in the brief cool of the predawn. A few steps down a path running in front of the guest house was a small bench, where we waited in the dark with some trepidation for the "bus" to Mandalay. The locals were not completely certain if our transport would be in working order.

Fortunately for us, with our limited time, a vehicle showed up. We six sat in a long line down one bench of a Toyota pickup with roof cover. Soon we were experiencing an unforeseen problem for Burma in April: freezing in a motion-created breeze as we raced along dark roads.

The pickup stopped to take on more passengers and then to pick up black-market gasoline. This process departed substantially from pulling up to a Western service station, inserting a credit card into a pump and filling 'er up. Our driver drew up to a firmly shut gate at a compound somewhere along the dark and unknown stretch of road between Pagan and Meiktila, and honked the horn for quite some time. Eventually a couple of men emerged from the night and began to fuel the pickup from various cans in a long row.

This completed, they arbitrarily switched the remaining gasoline among three different cans, back and forth and back again. We watched in a stupor of ignorance born of the early hour, our location in the middle of nowhere and the inexplicable nature of whatever was going on. "It's a ritual," said David, to punchy laughs.

The packed pickup headed along with 28 passengers, including two children, one covered with white sores. They sat at our feet, throwing up. Are they going to a hospital? I wondered. A white-haired, bearded man in a turban, apparently their grandfather, placed his hands gently on their backs as they suffered wordlessly. Our bumpy road to Mandalay, with its extremes of temperature, must have been doubly miserable for the children.

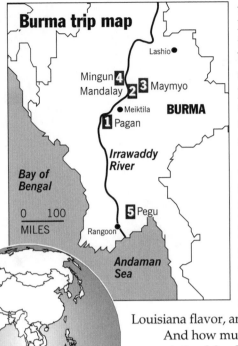

LESSON NUMBER 5: THOUGH AMERICAN CHILDREN CRY READILY AT EVEN MILD FRUSTRATIONS OR IN FATIGUE, FEW OF THE CHILDREN OF ASIA DO.

Chinese children in particular have been closely studied by U.S. researchers to find the source of their poise and good behavior. Their reports noted an almost smothering level of closeness between parents and their children, combined with careful restraint of independent activity. Also, children cannot help but be aware that a tantrum cannot get them goods or activities that their parents simply cannot afford.

These stoic little Burmese seemed admirable. I wondered if they were more readily soothed by their grandfather's hand because their nervous systems were not tightly wound from U.S. television cartoons, sugar highs and video arcades.

We pulled up to a roadside shack at the crossroads town of Meiktila for a breakfast of chapatis, a fried bread that indicated India's influence on Burma. Sunrise revealed a gently rolling landscape with scrubland and palm trees, giving way to rice paddies nearer the Irrawaddy. Water buffaloes pulled carts along the road.

During our 10-hour ride, the heat built up. I put on my personal stereo's headphones and blasted the Pretenders' *Learning to Crawl*. The cassette's first song, "The Middle of the Road," noted how in the Third World, the babies "just come with the scenery," an apt soundtrack for two sick children displaying everyday bravery.

Elizabeth sat next to me on the Toyota bench, her strained facial expression emitting distinct vibes that I

was playing the music too loud, irritating her with that awful high-frequency buzz that is the sound of someone else's headphones. I felt past caring, compelled to spend 50 minutes self-medicating my discomfort with music.

We discovered when we arrived in Mandalay that while it might sound fantastic in name (as do Jakarta and Bangkok), it was not especially magical in reality. Mandalay's wide boulevards, jacaranda-type trees and blistering sun seemed to possess a Louisiana flavor, and little else.

And how much we were even capable of appreciating Mandalay, Burma's historic capital throughout most of the 1800s before the British moved it to Rangoon, was an open question. Stupefied with fatigue, the six of us piled into a minuscule pony cart to go to Tourist Burma in the Mandalay Hotel. All our sweaty legs stuck together. James, the biggest, looked distinctly hot and jammed in.

We ate duck and roast beef in the hotel restaurant. Feeling a bit recovered despite our sore backsides, we decided to hop another pickup, departing at 3 p.m., to move directly along to Maymyo, a hill station 30 miles east on the edge of the large Shan plateau.

During the 2½-hour ride, we climbed out of the stifling cauldron of the plains. Every minute bought us higher and into cooler air. Behind us, the vast Irrawaddy glinted silvery and ever lower and farther away.

With this quick flip up to Maymyo (the military government has since renamed the place Pyin U Lwin), we were flying through an itinerary more ambitious than even the zip-around suggested by our guidebooks. This pace piled Burma-induced exhaustion on top of my China fatigue—two tough destinations in a row. Yet the goal to see a lot during my brief week seemed worthwhile.

And few Westerners reached Maymyo. I had suggested we visit it based on Theroux's descriptions of the anachronistic Candacraig Hotel and the former homes of British civil servants. The houses, half-timbered with red brick, slate roofs and leaded windows, echoed London's Home Counties architecture. "Surrey in the Sun," I said to Elizabeth, David and James, who appreciated the reference to the stockbroker belt county I'd departed a month previously.

The Candacraig itself was booked but would take

us the following night. So we checked into the Nann Myaing Hotel, had dinner and went wearily to bed at 9 p.m.

Rolling on Stagecoach 99

Meeting just one person can make some travel days memorable. Mohammed Sawley, operator of Rolling Stone Stagecoach 99, would do the honors in Maymyo. He stood in front of the Candacraig, where we'd repositioned ourselves.

Mohammed said that his original fare had just told him that he wasn't needed after all, a cancellation that worked to our gain. An ebullient Pakistani with fine English, Mohammed suggested a little trip to take in the sights around Maymyo. He loaded us into his tiny, bright purple stagecoach. The pony, named John, clipped along when Mohammed flicked the reins.

In our Cinderella's carriage, driven by an exotic driver out of the Arabian nights, we headed along to the market. Jean-Paul, Odile and I viewed a collection of silks and *thanaka* makeup. I traded my Washington Redskins sweatshirt and a U.S. $5 bill for a silk *longyi*, a gorgeous blend of blue, white and silver threads, made by the Shan ethnic group.

Mohammed then took us to see a lovely glade with a waterfall, five miles to the east toward Lashio. Non-Burmese couldn't go farther than the falls.

The ride possessed a forbidden thrill, for beyond lay rebel fighting and the anarchy of the Golden Triangle where Burma, Thailand and Laos meet. Our waterfall visit would be the closest we could get to the fabled Burma Road. In 1937-38 the Chinese connected Kunming in south China to Lashio, creating a military supply route. The Allies used the road during the early months of World War II until April 1942, when the Japanese captured Lashio.

Mohammed and I prepare to roll out in Stagecoach 99.

We turned around to visit the botanical garden in Maymyo. On the way we stopped at Mohammed's house to meet his blind father and his sisters, all of whom he supported. He showed us photos of himself sent back from tourists around the world. Then he changed horses, taking John away, hitching up Mary, and introducing their colt (11 months old). Mohammed grinned at his own joke of giving his horses the simplest English names.

After a stir-fried lunch at a Chinese restaurant in town (tastier than the indifferent rice dishes of Burma itself), we walked back to our hotel, meeting a little Burmese boy on the way. He winsomely stuck out his hand to be shaken. A Burmese man we had met earlier in the market joined the encounter and translated.

He told the boy where we were from and then prattled on. The smile left the child's face, replaced by a look of deep worry. The boy had been told that I would take him back to America in my rucksack. Whereas this proposal would fill the typical Chinese college student with delight, this boy wanted to stay right at home.

At the Candacraig, one hint that we were not in Surrey was the slight brown-purple cast to the dark maroon bricks, a shade close to the memorable color of Htilominlo, the massive temple in Pagan.

Eight rooms set around a second-floor landing overlooked the vast open lounge and fireplace on the ground floor. A glass lost-and-found case by the fireplace contained blankets and miscellany, each with a carefully filled-in card with the guest's name, country, date and which staff member had found the item.

The case seemed an almost too-obvious metaphor for Burma itself, sitting in the modern world's lost and found. Here was a country rich in oil, rice and ruby treasures, all at the time as disused as an umbrella in the Candacraig's lobby gathering more dust with each passing year. (By 1996, however, Burma's military would begin to profit from the nation's riches, selling rice to China and oil to U.S. companies, as its people slipped into greater hunger.)

The nature of borders

The itinerary we followed on our stagecoach day trip—a bit east of Maymyo and no farther—provided a textbook case of the problems of unstable borders.

Burma allows visitors only on its central plains and deltas. Its mountainous border regions, full of smugglers and warring tribes, lack stability. Around the world, the very geography of mountain environments with their different climates and languages and few roads makes their people seem "strange and often hostile to the lowlands," as C.B. Fawcett wrote in *Frontiers: A Study in Political Geography*.

The same pattern prevails in China, the former Soviet Union, Iraq, Brazil, India, Nigeria and many other nations with long borders and cantankerous minorities on the periphery.

It seemed that I had committed the bulk of Paul Theroux's descriptions of the Candacraig to memory, and early in the day I suggested that we put in an order for the rather incredible dinner option, more than 5,000 miles from York, of roast beef and Yorkshire pudding.

We drank tea and beer on the veranda, awaiting the evening meal. James began to emit the distress signal of the Englishman abroad who's had a little too much heat, humidity and unfamiliarity. He began to talk about train spotting. This obsessive hobby of some Britons involves standing on an overpass or siding, identifying any locomotive that passes by its exact model, year and specifications, and checking off the model spotted in a workbook.

It's hard to think of an American hobby sufficiently dotty to be comparable. Train spotting, which reflects a British male admiration for engineering, does not really resemble a more typical hobby like stamp collecting or bird watching. Perhaps the U.S. equivalent is collecting refrigerator magnets, something distinctly American and instantly funny to non-believers.

Elizabeth snorted something about "train spotters." I couldn't tell where her affection for the tradition of British eccentricity ended and derision began. She talked to James and David in low tones, and their conversation became private.

The improbable Candacraig Hotel looks like it belongs in Surrey.

Funny, I thought, how the British could close ranks. Like musk oxen drawn into a circle, they conducted an Anglo bonding session, probably sparked by the idea of being physically in a former piece of the Empire. Jean-Paul and Odile, for all their overwhelming Parisianness, readily spoke to me in English all day, a kind gesture that I know can be exhausting. We three seemed to be on a closer wavelength during the second half of our Burma week, eager to prowl around the edges of this unusual nation and not experience any Last Days of the Raj sentimentality or Death of the Empire regrets.

Jean-Paul and the henna-haired Odile plunged into the night markets in various Burmese cities, seeming as at home as they would be buying Le Creuset cookware at Galeries Lafayette near Boulevard Haussmann in Paris.

The pair would pinch the fabrics (almost certainly smuggled goods), discuss prices, frown and put a forefinger to their eyebrow. They launched into spitfire dialogues. At the Mandalay market, they struck a deal for material that their tailor back home could make into Bermuda shorts. All parties seemed well satisfied at the conclusion of business.

MONDAY, APRIL 1
First day of the hottest month

Our jeep wound down the switchbacks and eased into the ever more fevered air of the Mandalay inferno. At 2:30 p.m., we boarded a riverboat for a journey to Mingun, an ancient and partly abandoned city seven miles up the vast, glassy and gentle Irrawaddy. The character of the river appeared to be perfectly in tune with everything else in Burma.

Mingun's attractions numbered three: the world's biggest bell at 90 tons, built in 1790; the world's biggest brick building (the incomplete Mingun Pagoda); and Burma's prettiest pagoda, Hsinbyume, built in 1816 by King Bagyidaw in memory of his senior wife.

A playful boy named Pottos approached us as we strolled around. It seemed we met many of Burma's open and friendly children, particularly around their national patrimony, the temples.

Hill stations: keeping cool in colonial times

Many Asian towns at elevations between 1,200 and 10,000 feet above sea level became sanitaria for ill colonists during the British raj (the French and Dutch also created a few). Later, these towns evolved into recreation centers. Colonial administrators departed the sweltering plains and coasts to enjoy cool evenings of cricket.

Some hill stations, including Maymyo, also became summer capitals and hubs of administration and commerce. Often found in tea-growing areas, many now offer lakeside tourist accommodations and golf courses.

INDIA
More than 125, including Simla, Leh, Srinagar, Darjeeling, Dharmsala

MALAYSIA
Fraser's Hill, Tanah Rata (Cameron Highlands), Maxwell Hill

VIETNAM
Dalat

PAKISTAN
Ziarat

BURMA
Taunggyi, Maymyo

JAVA
Sukabumi

Pottos borrows a boat to play on the Irrawaddy and shows the slingshot he used to get me a mango.

Pottos' shirt hung from his thin shoulders in tatters, so I gave him a kyat (12 cents then) to replace it.

LESSON NUMBER 6: I WOULD NOT HAND OUT MONEY TODAY, GIVEN THE WAY HANDOUTS DISTORT RELATIONS BETWEEN THE TOURIST AND THE LOCAL PEOPLE, WHO MAY BECOME BEGGARS.

Pottos took the money with grace, however, allowing me to gibber in my non-Burmese language and point at the shoulder of his shirt. Then he seemed to promptly forget the matter and to turn his thoughts to play.

Pottos shot a mango out of a tree with his slingshot and gave it to me. He then rowed a boat that had a painted eye in the prow, designed to bring luck and protection. In an un-Asian manner, he enjoyed being the center of attention as I photographed his antics.

On our return boat ride, we silently contemplated the Irrawaddy, flat and a silvery-violet in the lowering sun, seemingly lending a bit of coolness to its ribbon of Burma. Unlike Mandalay, the 1,300-mile Irrawaddy did live up to its magical name. (Our little journey might not be possible today, given a Burmese government edict that foreigners should not be on boats.)

Back in Mandalay that night, we found a little hole-in-the-wall noodle eatery, which distinguished itself by offering a glimpse of one of the little but significant anthropological indices of world travel: the availability of Coca-Cola.

The delicately pretty Hsinbyume pagoda.

By 1985, Coca-Cola could be bought even at the Great Wall of China. In 1991, we bought it by the case in the wilds of Kenya's Masai Mara park. Meanwhile, at the time of my visit, Coca-Cola could not be imported in Burma, in keeping with a general doctrine at the time of keeping out soft drinks, Madonna, Rambo movies and everything else that was the rage in trendy Thailand and all the rest of Southeast Asia.

Nonetheless I could readily buy the soft drink in Mandalay. A waiter peered around the back of the shop and finally found a cobwebbed and battle-scarred can, its scratches and the appellation "product of Hong Kong" attesting to the soft drink's exciting ride across Burma's porous borders via opium smugglers' mules and trucks. (I later found another can from Singapore.)

LESSON NUMBER 7: THE SCRATCHED, SMUGGLED CAN OF COKE ATTESTED TO BURMA'S INNOCENCE COMPARED WITH BANGKOK, WITH ITS DUNKIN' DONUTS, PIZZA HUTS, SHOPPING MALLS AND TRAFFIC-CHOKED STREETS.

In Burma, the scalding "shwwwwwww" of the wind, a sound close to the Burmese word for gold *(shwe)*, was the only noise in the temples of Pegu, Pagan, Mingun and Rangoon. Meanwhile Madonna and George Michael boomed from every lean-to eatery and ferry pier I visited elsewhere in Southeast Asia in 1985. And China was a nightmare of 100 million loudspeakers.

Active opposition by Burma's leaders kept soft drinks and rock music out for more than a genera-

Yin and yang, Burma and Thailand

Like two skewed halves of a Rorschach inkblot test, the irregular shapes of Burma and Thailand share the Indochinese and Malay peninsulas. Thailand appears to be as modern, earthy and pleasure oriented as anywhere on Earth. Burma seems reclusive, spiritual and nonmaterialistic.

In Burma, a man commits a grave offense if he touches a woman other than his wife. Guidebooks warn Western men against even casually resting a hand on the shoulder of a Burmese woman.

On Bangkok's Patpong Road, girls from poor Thai villages sold themselves and created a spectacle in the process, shooting Ping-Pong balls out of their vaginas into beer mugs and engaging in live sex shows on stage. Thailand, though nominally with Burma and Sri Lanka one of the world's most Buddhist nations, has managed to coexist with a sex trade that catered originally to Viet Nam soldiers on R&R and more recently to Germans and Japanese on sex tours. (Distinctions regarding respect for women have become muddied with the arrival of poor Burmese girls in Thai brothels.)

On the right side of Indochina, Thailand sits underneath China, original home of Bangkok's merchant class. The Chinese immigrants lent their skills to the Siamese economy and their daughters to enriching the handsomeness of the Thai royal line. China exported its culture to Thailand. To Burma, unfortunately, China lent its socialist revolution.

The Burmese half of Indochina looks to the west, not toward the mercantilism of South China and its emigrant traders, but to India, birthplace of great religions. Peoples from India have had "an obvious and profound influence on Burma's law codes, med-

icine, royal traditions, nationalist movements, education system, and economy," wrote John P. Ferguson in *Burma: A Country Study*.

Asia's poorest nation (Burma) sits right beside the world's fastest-growing economy from 1985 to 1994 (Thailand). Can Burma continue to be an island in an Asia becoming consistently more prosperous from Japan to Indonesia? And if its poverty creates the essence of its spirituality, as with St. Francis of Assisi, will Burma become as sleazy as parts of Thailand if its wealth increases?

Maureen Aung-Thwin of the Burma Project at the Open Society in New York believes that

even the devout Buddhists in Burma, over time, would get more materialistic, but nothing like the rate or extent of what has happened in Thailand. For one thing, the Burmese were always more spiritual and less materialistic (precisely because they are "practising" Buddhists).

Unlike Thailand, she wrote to me in an Internet message, Burma did not, until recent moves by the military government to increase links to China,

have a big entrepreneurial class, even if you count the colonial days when the Chinese and Indian populations "ran" the Burmese economy.

She pointed out that the Chinese,

as we can see in Southern China and overseas Chinese networks all over, are brilliant entrepreneurs. I would bet a very large portion of "Thais" are partly Chinese, or full, with Thai names. This could also account for their distance from the daily, "practising" Buddhism prevalent in Burma, where the layman takes his Buddhism really seriously.

Burmese Buddhism "means shunning materialism, at least publicly," she wrote, "which means money will be spent on 'good deeds' such as building pagodas."

During the short decade or so when Burma was democratic and open to the world, "the Burmese never aped the West or flashed riches," she said.

Of course, this was just after the war and no one was really rich, but it indicated strong cultural, religious roots. I'm sure some of these strong ties will have been destroyed perversely because they were kept isolated and repressed. In other words, they might just choose the worse of Western ways just because they've been kept without choices for so long.

tion after they became popular in the West. General Ne Win, Burma's strongman in the 1960s and 1970s, once personally put a stop to a rock dance in Rangoon. He believed that with Western music, much more enters a country than just decibels.

However, by 1995, reporters noted that the sound of Guns 'n' Roses, as well as faxes, karaoke bars and

satellite dishes, had arrived in Burma. Perhaps these presaged the end of both innocence and tyranny?

TUESDAY, APRIL 2
Dusty views from a train

At 5:30 a.m., a trishaw driver named Maung Nyo awaited outside my hotel. The preceding day, I had run into him and asked him to get me to the station for the 6 a.m. train to Rangoon.

I thanked Maung Nyo profusely. Now I wouldn't have to scrounge around Mandalay's wide and at times empty boulevards for another means of transport. Deeply impressed that he was there, I asked how he managed to be on time. Burma no doubt lags the United States considerably in numbers of clock radios.

"I slept here," Maung Nyo said.

I felt perhaps as pensive as I had ever felt in my travels. To earn 10 kyats, $1.18 at the then-official rate, Maung Nyo slept the night outside the Mandalay Hotel as I slept inside.

Though my records show that I paid him the 10 kyats, I hope that he had asked only for seven or eight. If so, that would mean I had tipped him well but not condescendingly.

Vendors sell food to train passengers on the Mandalay-to-Rangoon run.

Our train for the 14-hour (on a good day) trip to Mandalay had spacious wooden carriages. The green-and-red padded seats featured huge wooden-loop arms, like 1950s dentist office furniture. Unlike on my most recent train journey in China, I could look directly observe the landscape without 40 intervening heads. In the distance chains of pagodas marched up mountain ridges. Nearer to the tracks peasants plowed rice paddies, and a water buffalo cart wobbled with one wheel fallen off.

Pleasant clacking noises rose from the rails. As in Indonesian and Madagascan rail stations, vendors sold decent curry (wrapped in banana leaves) and tea, handed in through the windows.

Out the window appeared a sight both commonplace in Asia and marked different. A man, in worn T-shirt and *longyi,* drew water from a well and loaded the bucket into a cart drawn by a water buffalo. I looked at his clothes, his pack animal, his cart and his water bucket. That's probably about all he owns, I realized.

On the surface the sight resembled the lives of hundreds of millions in rural China, India or Indonesia. But what set this Burmese man apart was his demeanor. Even at a distance, a pleasant expression, something just under a permanent smile, could be discerned.

By the standards of the world's developing countries, Burma was a marvel. Its central motif did not appear to be want. In its temples and pagodas, smiling children managed an easy rapport with the few Westerners making their barefoot explorations. Hushed novice monks glided by in the heat, offering a

ready smile. Virtually every boy and man and a fair number of girls served as religious novitiates. During this period they owned only a robe, mending needles, an alms bowl and a few personal necessities. A Burmese adult who had only worn clothes and a water buffalo still possessed more than when he was a novitiate.

Burma started to set off mental earthquakes. In the poorest country I'd visited lived the most radiant people. Was it possible their lack of goods was in some way necessary to their spirituality, in the same way the Bible warns that it is easier for a camel to pass through the eye of a needle than for a rich man to go to heaven?

A station stop interrupted my musings. During these, the hottest days of the year, Burmese cooled each other with the "water festival." We got soaked at every station by gleeful youngsters hurling buckets of water into our open window. The prank actually achieved its purpose, making us feel cooler for a time.

No one had thermometers and no one knew the weather report. And why would they want to?

> "Today we have a 100 percent chance of the timeless searing tropical valley heat that brutalizes lowland India, Bangladesh and Burma prior to the spring monsoon."

So the smashing heat goes unmeasured, and we could only gauge it by examining the extent to which we felt ourselves drained. I surmised about 105 degrees, which is probably correct, according to texts on Burma.

I sat on the train facing backwards. David sat across from me, downwind of the open window. Halfway to Rangoon I looked at him and laughed out loud.

"You look like the locals," I said, pointing to the crowd on a station platform. The red dust of many a foreign trip had covered me—in Kenya, Madagascar and

The dust and the heat take a toll on David.

Míkonos. Now it thickly coated David's face. Like a chimney sweep's, the whites of his eyes gleamed against his blackened skin. In the half-light of the carriage, he presented an effect like that of a desperate unshaven explorer, perhaps someone in the tragic last days of a doomed expedition.

James sat across the aisle with Elizabeth. He did not look as dirty as David. With his sweat-drenched hair, flushed face and stricken expression, he merely looked near death.

Elizabeth and I decide to have fun with the guys.

"This train is a snap," I said. "Compared to Chinese trains, this is first class at the Ritz."

"Oh quite," Elizabeth agreed. We droned on like members of the Royal Geographical Society about how

Flash forward: the political deterioration since 1988

By 1996, Burma had begun to allow PepsiCo to sell soft drinks. Pro-freedom groups, such as the Boston-based Coalition for Corporate Withdrawal from Burma, objected, noting that trade with Burma provides the military with hard currency and props up its cruel regime.

Eddie Bauer, the Maine-based wilderness outfitter, ended its use of Burmese factories in 1995, citing "the political climate." Levi-Strauss left in 1992, stating that "under present conditions, it is not possible to do business in Myanmar without directly supporting the military government and its pervasive violations of human rights."

Oil giants Texaco, Total and Unocal, as well as other companies, continue to operate in Burma. Travelers as well as corporate titans grapple with the ethics of dealing with Burma at this time. Both groups benefit from infrastructure such as roads and railroads built by forced labor.

The U.S. State Department noted its 1995 report, *Burma Human Rights Practices*, that

> Out of sight of most visitors, citizens continued to live subject at any time and without appeal to the arbitrary and sometimes brutal dictates of the military. There continued to be credible reports, particularly from ethnic minority dominated areas, that soldiers committed serious human rights abuses, including extra-judicial killings and rape. Disappearances continued, and members of the security forces beat and otherwise abused detainees.

The use of porters by the army—with attendant mistreatment, illness, and even death for those compelled to serve—remained a standard practice. The military continued to force ordinary Burmese on a massive scale (including women and children) to "contribute" their labor, often under harsh working conditions, on construction projects throughout the country.

Illustrating the gravity of Burma's condition, the U.N. Development Programme now lists it as one of the world's eight "countries in crisis," a wretched club that includes Iraq and Sudan. Burma spends a disproportionate amount on its military budget, much of which goes to fights with ethnic groups that live in a horseshoe-shaped arc along the borders with China, Laos, India, Bangladesh and Thailand. The government has entered into cease-fires with most ethnic groups, but "these are fragile peaces," according to Maureen Aung-Thwin, Burma Project director at the Open Society in New York.

Opposition leader Daw Aung San Suu Kyi (pronounced awng sahn soo chee), the daughter of Burma's independence leader, is the best-known target of suppression. Held under house arrest from July 1989 until July 11, 1995, her supporters refer to her as simply "the Lady." (The role of the serenely beautiful leader in the 1995 film *Beyond Rangoon*, which described Burma's political turmoil, was played by lookalike Adelle Lutz, rock singer David Byrne's wife.)

In 1991, Aung San Suu Kyi won the Nobel Peace Prize, later creating a connection in my mind between my visits to Burma and to the Maya lands, whose own female advocate of human rights, Rigoberta Menchu, won the Peace Prize in 1992 for her work in combating the Guatemalan military's abuses.

The Burmese government firmly brushes reports of civilian abuse under a rug, the way China officially shuts off access to knowledge of genocide in Tibet. And while China keeps records on many of its executions, as they occur quite publicly in stadiums, Burma can camouflage its offstage slayings, more along the lines of a soldier deciding impulsively to plug a civilian on a quiet road.

In 1988, a newer group of more brutal generals took control, and 3,000 people were gunned down in Burma, tenfold the final numbers linked to the Beijing massacres outside Tiananmen in 1989. As *Beyond Rangoon* pointed out, Tiananmen-type massacres occurred in Burma, but no one saw them on CNN.

In 1993, Burma began to expand tourism facilities and privatize hotels. Amazingly, by 1996 a room at the renovated Strand would cost $260 to $350 a night. Aided by longer, 28-day visas, tourism rose from about 38,000 in 1984 to 65,000 in 1994.

The irony of upgraded visitor facilities is that travelers end up supporting the dictators. Officials now demand $300 in hard currency from travelers. (My records show I spent just $135 there in 1985, money that tended to end up directly in the hands of small business people.) And reports indicate that the tourism upgrades are designed not only to bring in cash but to launder drug profits.

Many advocate skipping Burma for now, feeling that, unlike in China, where contact with Westerners helped spur a call for democracy, the Burmese are fully aware of the horrors of their regime.

---

this Burmese rattletrap—comfortable, spacious and bright—compared to the netherworld of third class on a Chinese train. Elizabeth especially had mastered the vocal affectation of boredom, the world weariness of the British expat.

Because I'd played tennis and ridden bikes in sweltering Maryland summers since childhood, I knew how to turn off my mind and sweat quietly as the hours passed.

The four of us luxuriated in space that would equate to 30 Chinese people in hard seat. Elizabeth and I appreciated this fact, so we enjoyed the view and the conversation. David and James rejected the assertion that we were, in fact, basking in luxury. They looked at us with as much skepticism as could be mustered by two doomed Englishmen on a dusty train on what could be the hottest day of the tropical lowland year, except you'd never know for sure in thermometer-less Burma.

WEDNESDAY, APRIL 3
Come-on from a Buddha statue
We shared a taxi to Pegu and doffed our sandals for some temple visits. In one temple, called Shwethalyaung, a famous statue depicted a reclining Buddha on his side with an expression of bliss that almost resembled a "come hither" look. A big fellow at 180 feet long by 53 feet high, the statue with the teasing smile dated from 994 A.D.

The icons of Buddhism in Burma gave off an aura of peace and contentedness. Such benign images, with a calmness that verged on sensual bliss, came as a shock to someone raised with the more harsh images of Roman Catholicism. The Pegu Buddha set a much different tone than the icon of Christianity, Christ bleeding on a cross. Padding around barefoot on the cool stones of the temple also seemed comparatively sensual compared to a Christian service. Perhaps the typical Roman Catholic church altar could appear pagan and barbaric to an Asian Buddhist, like an Aztec temple of sacrifice in its emphasis on blood. Both religions share, however, a message of family above materialism.

In Burma, the wandering monks, the sunniness of the smile and the alms that constructed reclining statues all attested to the way Buddhism was woven into the daily fabric of life.

A family poses in front of the reclining Buddha at Pegu.

THURSDAY, APRIL 4
A last look at Rangoon
Back at the Strand, at its *Fawlty Towers* worst at breakfast, I couldn't get coffee. The waiter said there "weren't any pots left," whatever that meant.

Odile found her toast less than hot, her tea too strong, and her 50-cent glass of pineapple juice positively tiny.

A religion that appeals to reason

The approximately 300 million adherents of Buddhism worldwide follow the teachings of Siddhartha Guatama, an Indian prince born in 563 B.C. who left his gilded life to pursue the basic questions of living.

Buddhism holds that our desires and attachments to people, pets, possessions and states of mind cause suffering when inevitable change occurs. The religion also teaches that if we inject our egos into a situation, we may fail to see it clearly.

These ideas, which I first encountered in a Lonely Planet guidebook description of Asian religions, clanged into my head. I had never heard a bit about Buddhism, and suddenly I thought, *That's right. This is my belief.*

At first Buddhism sounds like a dour religion, perfectly suited to an Asian continent that throughout history has known epic natural and political disasters. *All life is suffering.*

Yet even Westerners, whose self-absorption may tend to put personal angst on a par with a faraway flood in Bangladesh, encounter genuine setbacks.

LESSON NUMBER 8: ALMOST EVERYONE HAS A WATERSHED IN LIFE, A MOMENT WHEN YOUTHFUL OPTIMISM AND UNEXAMINED CONFIDENCE DISAPPEARS, WHEN TEMPORAL WORRIES ABOUT LOSS BEGIN.

It's a change that seems to happen to many people by age 30, when a husband gets cancer or a father heart disease, when an assailant rapes a friend, when a marriage ends, even when a childhood pet dies.

Buddhism seemed to be a good religion for societies encountering the famine and disasters of Asia, and also for Westerners who have encountered loss—in other words, eventually everyone.

The Swiss theologian Hans Küng acknowledged the appeal of Buddhism to introspective Westerners. He wrote in *Christianity and the World Religions*:

There is power in Buddhism's great concentration on the "Four Noble Truths," in its rejection of superfluous metaphysical "speculation," in its appeal to human reason and cognitive faculties. It is a religion without an "afterworld" in Nietzsche's sense; it demands no sacrifice of the intellect and imposes no moral casuistry—ideally designed, or so it would seem, for the critical Western intelligensia.

In his best haughty Parisian manner, Jean-Paul told the waiter, "My wife's toast is cold." Odile seemed to bask almost theatrically in her husband's chivalrous defense of her right to decent, hot, quality toast.

"We are not pleased," Jean-Paul said, with a weighty seriousness as though he were de Gaulle ordering U.S. bomber bases out of France.

Jean-Paul worked himself into the proper level of agitation for the waiter's misdeeds. Eyes flashing, he turned to me. He repeated the curious phrase, "It's a chain! A CHAIN!"

After a few seconds' reflection, I smiled. A "shame" indeed.

At 10 a.m., I squeezed in a trip to Shwedagon Pagoda, in the middle of Rangoon. Pagan had more overwhelming vistas. Yet Shwedagon appeared to be the most impressive single pagoda in Burma. Its great dome rises 33 stories.

Wondrous materials sheath Shwedagon: gold leaf, gold plates, silver bells and plates, and 5,452 diamonds. The Burmese seemed to flaunt their wealth only in the spiritual realm.

In *The Travels*, Marco Polo described a trip to "Mien," the capital of Burma, reached by traversing "vast jungles teaming with elephants, unicorns, and other wild beasts" for 15 days. In Mien, he saw a tower ordered built by the king, almost as bejeweled as Shwedagon:

> One tower was built of fine stones and then covered with gold, a full finger's breadth in thickness, so completely that it appeared as if made of gold only. It was fully ten paces high and of a width appropriate to its height. In form it was circular, and round the whole circuit were set little gilded bells which tinkled every time the wind blew through them.

Six centuries later, Shwedagon's bare marble pavement and huge number of minor pagodas, temples and shrines, 14 acres in all, resembled a summer fairground riot of primary colors. A shrine to the northeast of the main pagoda, surrounded by flowers, statues, temple columns, masks of fantastic creatures and offering bowls,

I pour water over a Buddha for those born on Sundays.

was devoted to those born on a Sunday. At the shrine, I poured water over a Buddha to bring me good luck.

In my memory, I can still picture Shwedagon as an uncomplicated place, where my biggest concern was shading my eyes from the dazzling light reflecting off its precious metals. A decade later, pro-democracy advocates sneaked banners onto the pagoda, and I read with a bit of an ache of soldiers combing the sacred ground to find the culprits.

Burma and the big lesson: the nature of poverty

Westerners who see how others live in places such as Guatemala, China and East Africa learn that what America calls "poverty" would be a great comfort to many a poor person elsewhere. In fact, American "poverty" can look more comfortable than life in middle-class Japan, let alone threadbare Burma.

A rehabbed low-rise housing project in East Baltimore near where I live compares favorably to the dreary high-rise apartments outside Tokyo. One day as we drove past the Johnstown Homes on Pratt Street, my friend Ted, who had worked as a foreign correspondent in China, pointed to the project's clean brick and new window moldings and doors.

"This is better than almost all the housing in China," he said. He waved his hand across the street to Lombard Middle School, a bit worn by American standards. "And forget this! You'd never have a fully equipped school right across the street."

We looked at the Johnstown Homes parking lot, full of cars, many late model. The lot attested to the fact that two-thirds of America's "poor" own cars (an expensive durable that I personally have not owned since 1981, putting the money that would go for monthly payments and insurance into travel instead). For the typical Chinese or Burmese, a car of any description is an unheard-of luxury.

"Every American should be forced to travel abroad," Ted said. "Then they'd know how much we have."

An American poor family may drive an old car and wear worn clothes. Yet more than likely they enjoy a color television set and a wide variety of modern appliances. Before demolition teams blew up the Lafayette Courts housing project in East Baltimore in August 1995, city officials noted that the buildings' 40-year-old electrical systems couldn't handle all the air conditioners, washing machines and microwave ovens of the "poor" residents.

One can point to the U.S. homeless as being perhaps as badly off as foreign poor people. Yet their hunger and discomfort seem tied tightly to different factors: untreated mental illness, or drug and alcohol abuse, with urban renewal's destruction of ultra-cheap flophouses also part of their difficulty.

For the U.S. poor overall, census data shows that

essentially what's missing in their lives are personal computers or dishwashers. At least half of U.S. poor families, in surreal contrast to the poor abroad, have VCRs and clothes driers.

Possession of home appliances by income

POOR PEOPLE TYPICALLY LACK ITEMS AT THE TOP OF THE CHART, SUCH AS PCs, AND OWN ITEMS AT THE BOTTOM OF THE CHART, SUCH AS REFRIGERATORS

	MIDDLE INCOME AND UPPER INCOME (A)	POOR (B)	RATIO (A) to (B)
Personal computer	28%	7%	3.8
Dishwasher	58	20	3.0
Clothes drier	87	50	1.7
Freezer	46	29	1.6
Microwave oven	90	60	1.5
Air conditioner	72	50	1.4
VCR	86	60	1.4
Washing machine	93	72	1.3
Telephone	97	77	1.3
Color television set	99	93	1.1
Stove	100	98	1.0
Refrigerator	100	98	1.0

Data taken from 1992 Census Bureau report P70-#50, "Beyond Poverty: Extended Measures of Well-Being"

A poor family in the United States is more likely to have a dishwasher (20 percent) than a typical household in either Italy (18 percent) or the Netherlands, the United Kingdom or Spain (11 percent). A poor American is twice as likely as a Dane to have a microwave oven, twice as likely as an Italian to have a VCR, and four times as likely as a French person to have a clothes drier.

VCR ownership

United Kingdom	69%
Denmark	63
U.S. poor	**60**
The Netherlands	50
Sweden	48
Belgium	42
Germany	42
Switzerland	41
Spain	40
France	35
Italy	25

Based on "Percent of Households Owning Selected Appliances, by Country: 1991" in the *Statistical Abstract of the United States*

What the U.S. poor don't have, in many cases, is intact families. Americans who return from trips to developing nations cannot help but note how remarkably well-off "poor" Americans are in the world context—except for their family structure. Developing countries may not have money, but children have plenty of direction from parents and grandparents, and cultural values are transmitted.

LESSON NUMBER 9: THE PROBLEM FOR MANY POOR AMERICAN CHILDREN LIES IN HAVING A VIDEOCASSETTE RECORDER BUT NOT A FATHER PRESENT.

Not only is the machine no substitute for a human guide to adulthood, but playing the wrong videos teaches violence as a means of obtaining property, a distressing phenomenon seen not only in the United States but in the world's most remote hamlets.

While middle-class Americans who benefit from the poverty industry (social workers, farmers, grocery executives, corner-store operators and slum landlords) might disagree, many historians, economists, ethicists and social observers consider it self-evident that America's "poor" are well off, compared both to the rest of the world and to historical levels of comfort in the United States.

To be poor in America is to be comfortable in Portugal or Indonesia, to be unthinkably opulent in the Congo. Anyone who thinks otherwise hasn't been paying attention to the nearly 10 million immigrants heading each decade for the United States.

In 1992, the 75th anniversary issue of *Forbes* magazine showcased numerous writers who focused on how America's poor fare today comparatively. *Forbes* editor James W. Michaels noted that

> Unless they blow their money and energy on booze or drugs, the American poor have more physical comforts today than the average American did 75 years ago.

UCLA professor James Q. Wilson urged Americans grumpy over America's imperfections to "cheer up," because no better system had evolved for governing a large, complex society. He wrote, "If you don't believe it, travel." Novelist John Updike stated, "Few residents of our worst ghettos would swap their assets for a one-way ticket back to Africa, Mexico, Eastern Europe or Vietnam."

Well-traveled friends elaborated on Updike's point. "I have no doubt," said Chris, a neighbor with perspective on living conditions both abroad and in East Baltimore's Johnstown Homes, "that if India annexed some of America's slums, the slums would have some of the highest living standards in India."

So how is it that we talk of "poverty" in America and poverty in Burma in the same breath?

In the West, poverty receives a far broader definition, describing those who do not fully participate in the middle-class lifestyle. Many European nations say the poor are those whose earnings fall in the bottom quarter of the national range.

Meanwhile, the U.S. government for 30 years has defined the poverty line as three times the dollar amount needed to buy a nutritious but low-cost diet.

In 1994, for a family of four with two children, the poverty line was $15,536 (coincidentally close to the bottom quarter of income), a figure that translated into 38 million people.

Measures of poverty

1994 FIGURES

U.S. poverty line, family of 4	$15,536
U.S. median income, all households	$32,264
Number of world nations with lower per capita product than U.S. poverty line	152
Percentage of 172 nations below U.S. poverty line	88%

Based on data from the U.S. Census Bureau, 1994 *United Nations Human Development Report*

British social thinker and researcher Charles Booth devised the term "the poverty line." In 1886, he calculated the minimum costs for adequate food, rent, clothing and utilities. He analyzed and mapped where London's paupers lived and defined four classes below the poverty line and four above.

Booth defined the "poor" as "living under a struggle to obtain the necessaries of life and make both ends meet, while the 'very poor' live in a state of chronic want."

In the modern era, European nations have switched to "relative" definitions of poverty. This approach has troubled me since I first heard of the concept in the mid-1970s while attending a class on poverty at the University of Maryland. The concept divorced poverty from any baseline measures of modern human comfort—that is, shelter, food and health care. Poverty became tied to a mathematical proportion of the glories of the middle class in Western nations.

Economists also note that the relative standard is a moving target. No matter how high the median income is, 50 percent of it would be the poverty line. Carried to its logical extreme, if the United States were a nation of millionaires, each citizen living on his or her own Southfork ranch, then using relative measures someone earning $500,000 would be "poor."

Dictionaries define poverty as either a state where someone lacks an acceptable amount of money or material possessions, or the lack of sufficient income to obtain minimal levels of health services, food, housing, clothing and education. A report by the International Bank for Reconstruction and Development further noted that "the perception of poverty has evolved historically and varies tremendously from culture to culture."

Some social scientists want to stretch our definition of Western "poverty" to include people, as Suzanne Coil wrote in *The Poor in America*, who "can't afford a good education, legal services or vacations," who "can't eat out in restaurants or take their children to the movies," and who "may be treated as less important than those with a higher social and economic status."

Compare Coil's definition to the United Nations' definition of absolute poverty, a far more wretched state suffered by perhaps 600 million of the world's 5.7 billion people in 1995. Absolute poverty exists if a person does not have the means to purchase sufficient food to ensure 2,250 calories per day.

The absolute poor, most of whom are illiterate and live in the tropics, lack more crucial things than vacations, movies and restaurants. About half of the absolute poor live in India, Pakistan and Bangladesh. If you were absolutely poor, wrote Elizabeth Morgan in *Global Poverty and Personal Responsibility*:

> You would most likely be a landless laborer in a rural area, unreachable by decent roads. You might well spend six hours a day simply obtaining water clean enough to wash and prepare food. Your life expectancy would be at least twenty-four years less than someone living in an industrial nation.

Professor Peter Singer wrote in *Practical Ethics* that

> people living in relative poverty in Australia might be quite comfortably off by comparison with old-age pensioners in Britain, and British old-age pensioners are not poor in comparison with the poverty that exists in Mali or Ethiopia.

While all affluent nations have some relatively poor people, he wrote that "absolute poverty is limited largely to the poor nations. Those living on the streets of Calcutta, or in a drought-stricken region of the Sahel, are experiencing poverty unknown in the West."

Singer noted that a condition of "absolute affluence" exists in Western Europe, North America, Japan, Australia, New Zealand and the oil-rich Middle Eastern states, with Eastern Europe close to this level of affluence. In these areas, most people buy "food to please the palate, not to assuage hunger"; purchase clothes to look good, not to keep warm; and select houses to be in a better neighborhood, "not to keep out the rain."

So the world presents at least three wildly different experiences, all characterized as poverty:

• Grinding poverty, as evidenced by disease, hunger and slow starvation, found in places such as parts of India and Bangladesh.

• Genteel shabbiness, as found in Burma, whose nonmaterialistic, literate people appear to long more for relief from their awful government than for modern symbols of affluence.

• An inability to fully participate in the middle-class lifestyle, as found in the United States.

My father, Louis J. Belliveau, a retired nuclear physicist and Jesuit-educated polymath, pinpointed why the issue of U.S. "poverty" seems to lack the troublesome ethical dimension of world poverty. The poverty line in America, he said, really indicates a dividing line between "those people who pose a drag on the economy and those who contribute. In the United States, poverty is an issue for theoretical economists."

Welfare in the United States, he indicated, provides a means to continue efficient delivery of goods and services. Grocery chains, farmers, housing contractors, lawyers and social workers can offer their services more affordably to all, middle class included, if welfare gives "poor" Americans some money to spend as well.

"I get it," I replied. "Safeway and Giant Food and little Korean markets can operate their distribution systems more efficiently if they have welfare customers in the city than if they only serve bands where the middle class live."

"Correct," he said. "Welfare exists just to maintain the system for everybody."

My father's remarks offered a plausible explanation for what $15,536 for an American family of four (1994) meant when it was called the "poverty line." It really defines an "economic drag point."

Most poor people in the United States don't live a half-step from malnutrition. They have access to some form of health care, even if it is a clinic or hospital emergency room. They differ from the middle class in lacking access to top-quality health care and educations.

That's not to say the weak education received by poorer U.S. children, not bound for college, is a trivial matter. The prospect of "tens of millions of unskilled, nonprofessional workers in the developed world, whose prospects are poor, and in many cases getting worse," augurs for social unrest, noted Paul Kennedy in *Preparing for the Twenty-first Century*.

The most serious problems linked to U.S. poverty involve health and longevity. From 1960 to 1986, although death rates declined for the U.S. poor and the poorly educated, the rate fell far more rapidly for those with higher education levels.

Broad indexes of health

	LIFE EXPECTANCY, YEARS	INFANT MORTALITY/ 1,000 LIVE BIRTHS
Japan *(highest)*	79	4
U.S. whites	**76**	**7**
United Kingdom	76	7
Developed world, average	74	10
U.S. blacks	**72**	**14**
Chile	72	15
Developing world, average	64	67
Central African Republic *(lowest)*	41	122

Based on 1995 World Population Data Sheet and the *Statistical Abstract of the United States*, 1995 (1992-93 data)

And U.S. blacks, who make up a disproportionate share of what the Census Bureau defines as the poor, lag U.S. whites by four years in life expectancy. They live 12 years longer than the developing world's average and 30 years longer than than the absolute poor in the Central African Republic.

One can broadly surmise from these figures that the U.S. poor have access to health care comparable in quality to Chile and that those with more money have access to care comparable to that in the United Kingdom. Drives to lower U.S. health costs and ration care may reduce the gap between rich and poor longevity; behavioral factors such as drug, alcohol and cigarette use may keep the gap in place.

In the United States, some people at the bottom of the scale, particularly the homeless, drink themselves to death or die of exposure. The vast majority of the U.S. poor, however, do not starve, fry in the heat or do without their favorite television programs. Their frustration is one of a poverty of opportunity—their ill-preparedness to participate in the U.S. economy. This is a real problem, but one that is not helped by exaggerated pieties about U.S. hunger either not backed up by data or preposterous in the world context. The Malagasy peasant or Calcutta street person faces the ultimate poverty of opportunity, with no immediate choice but to slash and burn the land or pick through trash for food.

Western attitudes toward the primacy of possessing consumer goods creep into many definitions of poverty, even for developing nations. A magazine article on Burma noted:

> Poverty is apparent at every turn, from the faded, threadbare lungis—skirtlike garments worn by male workers—to mothers bathing children at pumps on the street because running water is a rarity at home.

At this point in my travels I would be reluctant to automatically categorize this as poverty. Western eyes can take time to recognize that plank or thatch housing or street pumps may not indicate a problem absent additional evidence of hunger, sickness or neoslavery.

I recall a conversation on Bora Bora with a local Westerner, who warned me not to be fooled by the shacklike houses of the Tahitians, tin-roofed and decorated with tattered posters. Many islanders owned land and had adequate money, which might go into a small boat and outboard motor. Money would not be invested in anything more than a basic house in the humid area.

Groceries, particularly healthful, unprocessed foods, are quite cheap in global terms in the United States; shelter is not. The expense of installing plumbing to code in a Western dwelling wildly distorts shelter costs and makes Americans "poor" who might be able to get by quite well given affordable lodgings.

Philip K. Howard wrote in *The Death of Common Sense* that

the law, aspiring to the perfect housing abode, has accumulated so many good ideas that the only type of new housing that is permitted must satisfy middle-class standards A law that dictates either a model home or no home is probably fine for some, but what about those trying to provide housing for the poor?

"Essentially we don't have a free market for housing for the poor," said Patrick F. Fagan, William H.G. FitzGerald senior fellow in family and cultural issues at the Heritage Foundation in Washington, D.C., in a telephone conversation with me. "To live, you

Burma's people display delight despite few possessions, as these scenes in Mingun show.

need a roof, heat, cleanliness, running water, a structure to keep out the rain and the cold. Housing for the poor isn't commensurate with their income. We have Cadillac housing for people with poor incomes."

And bathing at a standpipe is not such a stunning sight in the developing world. In fact, on the island of Nosy Komba off Madagascar, I viewed a girl bathing her little brother.

The scene seemed tender and simple, a chance for a public display of family values, and not automatically an example of deprivation.

Is poverty worn clothes and a standpipe? If so, what do we call life in upcountry Borneo, with its intact families and resourceful children, where there are not even standpipes?

Is it worrisome that so many of Borneo's older women seem to have clouded eyes or goiters and that a cut can become a fatal infection?

Yes. A lack of basic health care and education, signals of human distress or misery, might be the true bedrock definers of poverty—not one's clothing, movie attendance, ability to afford a good lawyer or fend off social snobbery.

For an American visitor, Japan redefines cleanliness. China gives "crowding" a whole new meaning. And Burma gives a new perspective to our concepts of "poverty." The conditions that the poverty industry advocates in the United States wring their hands over

seem like a cosmic joke to someone returning from the developing world.

LESSON NUMBER 10: BURMA DEMONSTRATED A LESSON CENTRAL TO BOTH BUDDHISM AND ROMAN CATHOLICISM: THAT LOW INCOME DOES NOT NECESSARILY TRANSLATE INTO A HOST OF OTHER ILLS. IN FACT, INDICATORS SHOW AN EXTRAORDINARY DISCONNECT FOR MANY BUDDHIST NATIONS BETWEEN INCOME, OFTEN QUITE LOW, AND MEASURES OF THE QUALITY OF HUMAN LIFE, OFTEN ROBUST.

"Many countries have a high GNP per capita, but low human development indicators—and vice versa," noted the U.N.'s *Human Development Report 1994* in a passage called "Opulence and Human Development."

The report noted that "individuals and societies make many choices that require no wealth at all."

For example, a family does not need money to treat each member with respect. A nation does not require wealth to treat women equally. A culture can maintain its traditions at almost all levels of income.

"National wealth might expand people's choices. But it might not," the report noted. In many societies, the "definite correlation between material wealth and human well-being" breaks down.

The Buddhist dimension

Quality of life data for various Buddhist and non-Buddhist nations with similar per capita incomes. Each Buddhist nation shows lower infant mortality and higher female literacy. Burma and Sri Lanka also show improved life expectancy.

	ADJUSTED GDP PER CAPITA	FEMALE LIFE EXPECTANCY	INFANT MORTALITY RATE PER 1,000	ADULT FEMALES WHO CAN READ PER 100 MALES
Least developed countries				
Burma	**$659**	**60 yrs**	**72**	**85**
Gambia	$763	56 yrs	138	35
Developing countries (medium income)				
Sri Lanka	**$2,650**	**73 yrs**	**19**	**91**
Algeria	$2,870	67 yrs	61	60
Developing countries (relatively high income)				
Thailand	**$5,270**	**69 yrs**	**39**	**95**
Turkey	$4,840	69 yrs	59	77

Based on data from *Human Development Report 1994* (1991 data), *1992 World Population Data Sheet*, and U.N. report, *The State of the World's Children 1996*, table 7 (1994 data)

"The Buddha considered economic welfare a prerequisite for human happiness," Walpola Rahula wrote in *What the Buddha Taught*. Yet

> he did not recognize progress as real and true if it was only material, devoid of a spiritual and moral foundation. While encouraging material progress, Buddhism always lays great stress on the development of the moral and spiritual character for a happy, peaceful and contented society.

Buddhism certainly should increase one's compassion. Yet for me seeing the nonmaterialism of Burma up close had precisely the opposite effect. Burma and other poor countries ironically created a severe case of compassion fatigue in me.

Travel if anything provides support for those who think the poverty in America is one of values rather than material goods. In a society with strong values, both parents of a child realize that they must attempt to stay together, offer a role model and keep their job skills up to date.

The expense of such things as housing and car insurance in the West dictates two wage-earning parents, preferably with advanced skills and earning ability, to give children a big advantage in ultimately becoming economic contributors.

A Heritage Foundation memorandum by Fagan, based on U.S. 1994 poverty figures, noted that about 53 percent "of all children in female-headed families are in poverty," a rate that drops to 11 percent among children in intact married families. Fagan wrote that

> Married family life is the best protection against

poverty for children. Single parenthood—the "feminization" of poverty—results from the father and his paycheck being absent.

U.S. measures of monetary, cultural poverty

MEDIAN FAMILY INCOMES, 1991

Two parents	$40,137
Divorced mother	16,156
Never-married mother	**8,758**

FAMILY STRUCTURES
MILLIONS

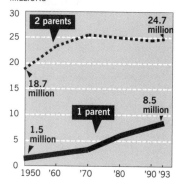

ANNUAL DIVORCE RATES PER 1,000 MARRIED WOMEN, AGES 15-64, 1991

United States	**21**
United Kingdom	13
Denmark	12
Sweden	12
Canada	11
France	9
The Netherlands	8
Germany	7
Japan	6
Italy	2

Based on data from the U.S. Census Bureau and the *Statistical Abstract of the United States*

Fagan related in conversation how a colleague attended a Pan-American conference in 1994 in Mexico City. A South American told the colleague, "You're a First World nation in terms of money. But in terms of family, we're the First World and you're the Third World."

"America's a Third World country, let's face it," Fagan said. "There's a breakdown of the family and community richness. Poverty in the West is not due to a lack of resources or lack of distribution. It's the alienation of the homeless, classic alienation as described by Camus, that progress cannot reach."

Paul L. Wachtel, in *The Poverty of Affluence*, states that

> the misery of those at the bottom of society is not due simply to a lack of goods. ... It is the invidious quality in their lives that particularly constitutes their poverty; it is having less than everyone else.

Though Buddhism calls for compassion, it also calls for clear thinking. To a Buddhist, "having less" per se does not create "misery." Having less could be a good thing. Buddhism holds that attachments to people, goods or transitory sources of happiness create suffering. True happiness can be achieved only if desire can be overcome. *The Buddhist Proverbs* note that "Without any possessive desire, a man does not worry that 'This is mine, that is others.' "

Burma's Buddhists "see themselves as spiritually blessed and, in that sense, regard themselves as incomparably wealthier than Western societies," wrote Frederica M. Bunge in the introduction to *Burma: A Country Study*.

Material poverty in Burma comes not from lack of values, but only a lack of freedom. As in Madagascar, dictatorship has introduced its handmaidens, hardship and poverty. Once again, Margaret Thatcher's observation comes into play: Free societies encourage economic progress, scientific advance and public debate, and offer the means to protect individuals and the environment.

For all their current woes, many of Burma's people still appear to be living examples of the link between a spiritual character and a literate and long-lived populace. The Burmese prize books and consider it offensive to put anything written on the floor. They honor authors and respect teachers and students (resembling the Irish in their reverence for literature and academia). They hold physicians in awe.

Burmese women—in a key departure from most of the world's poorest nations—may hold formidable status, running businesses, inheriting land, forming their own scriptural study groups, and even leading the battle for human rights, as has Aung San Suu Kyi.

For a nation seeking a direction, "much depends on how the fruits of economic growth are shared—particularly primary health care and basic education," noted the U.N.'s report on "Opulence and Human Development." "What is decisive is not the process of wealth maximization but the choices that individuals and societies make—a simple truth often forgotten."

Most of Burma's people seem to cling to this simple truth, even if their military rulers do not.

EARTHLY PARADISES

Java and Bali ... and how we view Heaven

Two Javanese boys make music at a train station west of Yogyakarta.

After arduous travel in China and Burma, at the time barely in the modern era with regard to tourist comforts, I drifted down the Malay peninsula and across the Strait of Malacca and the Java Sea. There I would learn if Java and Bali could supply the antidote to weary weeks spent in the heat, dust, smoke and crowding of other parts of Asia.

Even the most intrepid adventurer wants to balance hard travel in difficult areas with easy times in beautiful places. I had reason to hope for respite in Indonesia. My travel guide, *South-East Asia on a Shoestring*, raved about Indonesia, especially Java and above all Bali. Author Tony Wheeler was far from alone in his rapture. In 1936, Mexican painter and ethnologist Miguel Covarrubias wrote in *Island of Bali* that

> Because of its peculiar and fantastic nature, its complex variety of peoples, and its fabulous richness, the [Indonesian] archipelago is one of the most fascinating regions of the earth.

A half-century later, the nation of islands had maintained much of its original cultural richness. Westerners could watch ethereal dance and listen to hypnotic music. Masseuses would soothe the muscles with gentle hour-long rubdowns.

And Bali proved to be so impossibly lovely that our band of travelers discussed whether we had discovered an Earthly mirror for heaven. Our discussion would prove memorable for two reasons: subsequent developments in some of our lives, and how mass tourism would tarnish some of the island's luster a decade later. To these events in due course.

To visit Indonesia, I had signed on—for the first time in my life—with a package tour. Trailfinders, a West London agency catering to adventure travelers, offered a Bangkok-to-Bali Rover costing the equivalent of $300. Our group would go to Thailand, Malaysia, Singapore, Java and Bali, traveling mostly overland, for 21 days.

APRIL 1985
Our roving band assembles

At the Swan Hotel in Bangkok, we all met each other and our guide, John Horne, a mustachioed Englishman with a receding hairline. He told our group of a dozen English, Canadian and American travelers, accurately as it turned out, that our itinerary would progress in an orderly way: "Thailand's interesting," John said, "Malaysia is more exotic than Thailand, and Indonesia is the most exotic of all."

Among the dozen who had signed up for the Bangkok-to-Bali trip was a married couple from Vancouver, British Columbia. Michael Kaye, a businessman, and Diane Mason, a lawyer, joined the group in the middle of their own 18-month world tour. They had already spent months in Africa, India and China. After Southeast Asia, they would explore Australia by van and finally continue to French Polynesia.

They became my favorites of the group: amiable, intelligent and perceptive at drawing comparisons between the many places they'd been. Seven years after our trip, illness lay in wait for Diane, making poignantly apt the couple's decision to see the world, particularly the paradise of Bali.

We got to know each other as we explored Bangkok, Penang in Malaysia, and Singapore. En route to Jakarta, our airplane crossed the equator. We sailed by bright pink clouds shaped like ice-cream cones in a streaky sky of blue and violet, descending east of Krakatoa, the volcano famous for its catastrophic past.

The island had exploded in 1883, destroying two-thirds of its mass with one of the loudest noises in history and coloring the world's sunsets brilliantly for three years. Plenty of other Indonesian islands remain, however—between 12,000 and 18,000, with recent satellite surveys indicating the higher figure. Indonesians have named 6,000 of the islands but live on only 900 of them.

LESSON NUMBER 1: THOUGH IT LANGUISHES WELL OUTSIDE THE WORLD SPOTLIGHT, INDONESIA RANKS FOURTH IN THE WORLD IN POPULATION. ITS SIZE ALONE MUST EVENTUALLY DICTATE AN END TO WESTERN IGNORANCE OF THE ARCHIPELAGO.

Nations above 100 million population

	MILLIONS
China	1,219
India	931
United States	263
Indonesia	**198**
Brazil	157
Russia	148
Pakistan	130
Japan	125
Bangladesh	119
Nigeria	101

Based on mid-1995 data from the World Population Data Sheet

'You can bargain'

At the Tangkuban Prahu volcano, north of Bandung in west Java, a young vendor offered Mike and Diane 10 postcards for $3. When they refused, he said earnestly, "You can bargain." He reminded his amused Western visitors to follow the Indonesian practice of negotiating a price for most purchases.

While the typical Westerner probably knows little about Indonesia, adventure travelers have discovered the nation's variety of attractions: palm-fringed beaches, towering live volcanoes, temples with playful monkeys, cheap and delicious shrimp, and simple rooms set amid beautiful gardens. Most of all, its refined and friendly people—musicians, dancers and artisans for whom art is a part of daily life—stay in the memory.

SUNDAY, APRIL 21
The 5:20 a.m. to Yogyakarta

John Horne wasted no time getting us out of Jakarta's airport and on to our first night's stop, a large city called Bandung. The next day before dawn, we boarded a train to Yogyakarta, Java's primary cultural capital. We saw hundreds of possible character portraits in each station—a beggar, a woman selling rice,

A woman sells food at a train station, above. A shoeshine man, right, entertains in our compartment.

two boys with a guitar. Many of those we passed waved to us. A man came into our car, twirling a shoeshine brush. He made bird-whistling noises while pretending to swallow a cigarette, which he then retrieved and puffed—no hands.

Then he sang a haunting melody a cappella. The moment seemed magically anachronous. In the Middle Ages, jesters and conjurers performed at the markets. In Shakespeare's plays at London's Globe Theatre, clowns named Pompey, Trinculo and Touchstone served as sidekicks to the principal characters of the bard's dramas.

LESSON NUMBER 2: THE JAVANESE SHOESHINE MAGICIAN HARKED BACK TO THE DAYS OF STREET ENTERTAINERS WHO DID NOT RELY UPON THE GIMMICKRY OF 20TH CENTURY ENTERTAINMENT.

At 2:30 p.m., we arrived at Yogyakarta (we were taught to pronounce it "yogya-" rather than "jogja-," though one hears both) and checked into the Rose Guesthouse. Dinner was at Hanoman's Forest Garden Restaurant. The name refers to the monkey god Hanoman, who reunites Prince Rama with his kidnapped wife Sita in the Hindu epic, the *Ramayana*. As we ate tasty chicken satay (grilled meat on skewers with peanut sauce), the restaurant sound system provided our first exposure to an enchanting sound. Diane, Mike and I stopped eating to ask John excitedly what the music was.

John told us we were listening to Javanese gamelan (other types include Balinese, Sundanese and Maduran gamelan). Colin McPhee in *A House in Bali* compared the sound to

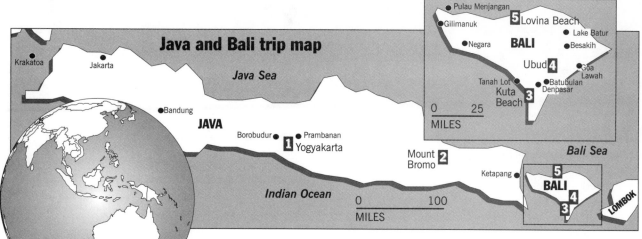

Java and Bali trip map

Pulau Menjangan
Gilimanuk
Negara
5 Lovina Beach
BALI
Lake Batur
Besakih
Ubud **4**
Goa Lawah
Tanah Lot
Kuta Beach **3**
Batubulan
Denpasar

0   25
MILES

Krakatoa
Jakarta
Java Sea
Bandung
JAVA
Borobudur **1** Prambanan
Yogyakarta
Mount Bromo **2**
Bali Sea
Ketapang
5
BALI
4
3
LOMBOK

Indian Ocean
0   100
MILES

the stirring of a thousand bells, delicate, confused, with a sensuous charm, a mystery that was quite overpowering. ... The melody unrolled like some ancient chant, grave and metallic, while around it wove an endless counterpoint of tones from the little gongs in front. From time to time, above the drums there floated the soft, reverberating tone of a great gong, deep, penetrating, seeming to fill the temple with a faintly echoing sound.

It seemed incredible that the world could possess such a multi-layered sound, as McPhee had described perfectly, and none of us had ever heard it before actually setting foot on Java. The rhythm orchestra of gongs repeated a trance-inducing motif that subtly modulated and evolved. The airy, simple music conveyed a serenity and deepness on a par to that of the rumbling pipe organ at High Mass at Notre Dame in Paris. We got the name of the cassette that had been playing, *Sangkala*, by Degung Instrumental, and bought it the next day.

MONDAY, APRIL 22
To dance as you walk

A delightful guide showed us around the Kraton

Our guide wore traditional Javanese garb.

(sultan's palace). He was an older man with few teeth, wearing traditional Javanese court dress: a *kris* (dagger) stuck in his embroidered belt, a sarong and head cloth. We could barely understand his English, except for the odd phrase, such as "1938" or "Dutch." We smiled bravely through his lecture.

What did he think of the Japanese, the main winter tourists? I asked. He replied that he didn't like them. He

had been a prisoner of war, escaping just before the bombing of Nagasaki. He returned home, where he had been assumed dead.

"My mother was glad to see me," he said with understatement.

LESSON NUMBER 3: OUR GUIDE SAID HE DRANK IN MODERATION. HIS REMARKS INDICATED THAT ISLAM IN INDONESIA TOOK A RELAXED FORM COMPARED TO MORE CONSERVATIVE SECTS ELSEWHERE.

We next visited the Agastya Arts Foundation to see the daily performance of the shadow puppets, or *wayang kulit*. The flat puppets are cut from leather and have hinged joints. A puppeteer manipulates them with attached sticks so that their backlit shadows appear on a cloth screen.

A gamelan orchestra accompanied the puppets with gongs, a xylophone and inverted metal pots that emitted the sound of bells when struck. While we

A mask at the Kraton.

were not able to follow the plot well, the music captivated us. And the arts foundation provided a useful

A gamelan musician accompanies a performance of shadow puppets.

Classical Javanese dancers perform a selection from the *Ramayana*. **The figure at the far right represents Hanoman the monkey.**

legal-sized paper in English describing clearly how Javanese arts and crafts rely upon the *Ramayana* and a second Hindu epic, a poem called the *Mahabharata*. (Though Java became Islamic in the 16th and 17th centuries, it preserved Hindu artistic influences from India.)

In the evening we viewed a classical dance troupe called the Grhadika Yogya Pariwisata. The dancers performed a tale from the *Ramayana* called "Sita's Trial of Purity."

Four singers bent haunting quarter notes. Dancers in gilded costumes balanced on one leg, flashing sharp looks. They twirled double-jointed hands, slowly curled their toes, pushed their hands in the air and swiveled their heads. Muscles popped out of calves as they subtly moved and froze, in motions like Michael Jackson's early robotic dances. A trickle of sweat ran down a girl's face, the only sign that these iron-willed dancers could be as human as the rest of us.

Their subtle motions portrayed magic arrows, spells, attempted suicides, giants, a big army battle and trial by fire, according to our English-language program. We were a bit lost in matching the program descriptions to the action but that proved to be no bar to enjoying the dance for its own sake.

Clove cigarettes called *kreteks* scented the soft night as we returned to our lodging in Yogyakarta. Later in the United States, whenever I detected this smell, I whirled around to see if I could spot an Indonesian, instead of a trendy college student, puffing away.

The driver of our *becak* (bicycle rickshaw), a part-time dance student, twirled his hands in the motions of the classical dance as he accompanied us to the galleries or arts performances. In Yogya, home of the high Javanese dance, beat one of many cultural hearts of these islands. There was a feeling that the arts were paramount, unlike in Bangkok, Hong Kong, Tokyo or any of East Asia's more mercantilist cities. A nation of enchanting artists and dancers seemed to walk the streets of Java.

TUESDAY, APRIL 23
One of Asia's wonders
That morning, our expectations may have been that we would be trundled to just another temple, not so different from the many we'd seen in Bangkok.

Without the fanfare merited by the occasion, John quietly took us to the astonishing sight of Borobudur, 26 miles northwest of Yogyakarta.

Borobudur belongs to a trio of the most magnificent Buddhist temples, the others being the Pagan complex in Burma and Angkor Wat in Cambodia. An English colonel found the vine-clad ruins in 1814. The structure dates from the 8th century, making it contemporaneous with the delicate Palenque ruin in Chiapas, Mexico. The temple attests to a lost era of Javanese history, when Buddhism prevailed before a conversion to Islam in the 16th and 17th centuries.

Unlike Pagan, set in acres of red dust with the New Mexico-style Chin Mountains in the distance, Borobudur faces across to two big volcanoes and craggy but green hills. I did not realize until later, upon reading the book *Pyramids*, that Borobudur could be classified as a stepped pyramid, of the same broad type as the Maya structures. To my eye it seemed far more intricate in its overall design and panel details, a reflec-

A Buddha statue at Borobudur appears to contemplate a far-off volcano.

tion of the ornate style of an Indian stupa, the type of temple topped by a cone.

At 11 stories, Borobudur stands between the heights of two Maya temples, Nohoch Mul at Coba in the Yucatan and Temple II at Tikal. The Javanese temple lacked the queasy open-air feel of steep Tikal in Guatemala. The gentleness of its slope and the way its stonework ornamentation, as elaborate as a wedding cake, screened off lower levels made the view from its top levels less vertigo-inducing.

Today observers describe Borobudur as one of the seven wonders of the world, a cosmic mountain of huge bulk and great religious significance. Borobudur's six square platforms plus three round ones total nine, a magic number matching the levels at El Castillo at Chichen Itza in the Yucatan. Its circle-within-a-square design represents a mandala, a prayer symbol found in Buddhism. The round platforms at the top support 72 individual bell-shaped stupas, each with a seated Buddha, and a single giant stupa. With the lighter circles on top of the solid square base, the architects of Borobudur set out to achieve an overall effect like that of a lotus floating on a lake.

Borobudur is designed as a walkthrough religion lesson. Pilgrims can walk three miles clockwise, first past lower levels with reliefs depicting earthly pleasures then upward to the circular terraces with Buddhas representing enlightenment.

We galloped directly to the top, much of the significance of the temple flying right by our heads. All the members of our group strained to reach into the individual small stupas, placing our hands and arms into small diamond-shaped cutouts that barely permit the fingers to graze the Buddha.

Simplified plan of Borobudur.

We laughed and teased each other as we stretched to touch the statues inside, said to bring good luck—always welcome when traveling thousands of miles using at times sub-par transportation.

THURSDAY, APRIL 25
A Hindu temple complex

After spending Wednesday browsing in Yogyakarta's art galleries, we began to move east toward another of Java's great sights: Bromo, one of 27 volcanoes on the island, 11 of which are active.

But soon, our bus broke down. This may not sound like good fortune, yet that was precisely what it turned out to be. During a three-hour wait for repairs, John Horne found a backup bus and admirably filled

our time with a visit to the Prambanan temples, 10 miles from Yogyakarta. The timeless site appeared, incongruously, as the "Temple of Light" in the 1995 film *Mortal Kombat*.

At the largest temple, dedicated to Shiva, the destroyer in Hindu belief, we studied the bas-reliefs of other dieties: Brahma the creator, Ganesh the elephant-headed son of Shiva, and Vishnu the preserver. For a moment we felt ourselves to be in India, a logical impression given that the temple is considered one of the finest examples of Hindu art. Our brief visit did not permit us to do justice to its hundreds of ruins.

LESSON NUMBER 4: OUR VISITS TO PRAMBANAN (HINDU), BOROBUDUR (BUDDHIST) AND THE KRATON (MUSLIM) UNDERLINED THE SUCCESSIVE WAVES OF RELIGION IN JAVANESE HISTORY.

Indian traders exposed the Javanese to Hinduism by the 2nd century, and Indian missionaries bought Buddhism by the 8th century. Islam became predominant in the 16th century. Prambanan was built during a Hindu renaissance in the 8th to 10th centuries, a little after the construction of Borobudur. The complex, overgrown by vegetation, was rediscovered by Westerners in 1733.

Our bus repaired, we made our way to a dormitory near the crater rim of Tengger, a giant caldera containing Mount Bromo and three other volcanoes.

FRIDAY, APRIL 26
Bromo, without coffee

We arose at 4 a.m. to ascend Mount Bromo and view the sunrise there. In the dark we trudged from the caldera rim down a path leading across the Sea of Sand, a black lava field within ancient Tengger. On our right stood a mini-volcano with perfect ridges, looking like Jell-O from a mold or a sand castle raked by giants. Steam rose out of cracks in the dimly visible surrounding mountains.

We clambered up 250 steps on the slope of Bromo to its rim. I climbed steadily behind Diane. Her foot dislodged a giant boulder of lava the size of two basketballs, which crashed onto the front of my foot. Like a Flintstones cartoon boulder, it weighed less than it looked, but it still packed enough wallop to sting my big toe. Over the next months the toenail gradually died.

Once on the southern rim of Bromo, we could see why the volcano lent its name to Bromo Seltzer, a remedy for upset stomachs, which in turn lent its name to the Bromo Tower in Baltimore. A yellowish fog rose from a cauldron of hissing steam and swirled against the yellow-green streaked sides of the pit. Sulfurous acid stung our eyes and skin. I could even taste it if I opened my mouth.

Jane, a young woman from Norwich in England who had taught language in Japan before this trip, and I walked to the right of an observation platform to see the beginning of a one-mile path around the rim of volcano. I had no intention of taking it.

"Go on, let's give it a try," Jane said. The path looked a mess: six inches wide, with steep drops and crumbling ash on each side, plunging and twisting and even disappearing completely.

"No," I replied. "One, it's too dark. Two, I haven't had any sleep. Three, I haven't had coffee …"

On my backside, I began to slide down the steep path.

"Four, I'm too tired to keep my footing. Five, it's dangerous …"

At first, the path resembled the rim of a bowl pared by a giant knife, to create a small, undulating yet adequate walkway. Then it narrowed and disappeared. We had to walk on the steeply angled outside slope, clinging to the rim with our fingertips. Twice our way became frightening, and we nearly quit.

In the subdarkness, the cauldron glowed and seethed a fearful, venomous pale green. Afraid to look directly down at the molten pit and too scared to retrace our steps, we continued on. The path reappeared, and though it continued to be steep, it got wider and easier.

A red bar, the rising sun hidden by a cloud, appeared over the eastern rim, silhouetting a faraway, massive volcano. The atmosphere also seemed to play tricks on our eyes. A pink splotch appeared in the western sky, opposite to where the sun rose.

Jane and I caught up with three of the men in our group at the halfway point, where we could see another volcano to the north, which erupted every 15 minutes. It had a coat of cloud at its summit like a mushroom cap, and a dirty gray ball of ash formed slowly above its peak. All around stretched the vast blackness of the Sea of Sand. The scene appeared, more than any other place in my travels, to have the fantasy look of another planet. Quiet hung in the cool air, broken only by the noise of the crackling in Bromo's crater.

We finished our circuit of the rim easily, as the final portion was all downhill. We descended the outer slope of Bromo to recross the Sea of Sand, able to see the area clearly for the first time. Thirty-foot-deep ravines around Bromo reflected pinkish in the sun, and clouds streaked above the far edge of Tengger. All was still, except for a Javanese boy with a shoulder pole and two wicker baskets, picking his way down into the caldera. He broke the morning silence by greeting us in English: "Hello."

Jane and I shook hands afterward, proud of our achievement. So far, I thought, climbing Mount Bromo counted as one of the highlights of my months-long trip through Asia, right up there with cycling around Yangshuo in southern China.

At 8:15 a.m., we departed for Kuta Beach on Bali. We had yet another bus breakdown, this one on a rise looking down on the ferry dock that connects the last stop in Java, a little place called Ketapang, to Gilimanuk, across the glittering Bali Strait.

To torture everyone, Bruce Tupper, a red-bearded Yorkshireman in our group, opened his battered copy of the "yellow bible," Lonely Planet's *South-East Asia on a Shoestring*. He read aloud:

> Bali is a tropical island so picturesque and immaculate, it could easily be a painted back drop.

Cut it out, Bruce, we replied en masse. Ignoring us, he continued in a tone of great significance:

> Bali is a shatteringly beautiful country, gleaming white beaches, warm blue waters and a friendly people who don't just have a culture but actually live it.

He paused meaningfully. "Shatteringly. Beautiful," he repeated, with great weight on each word.

Bruce, stop, we ordered.

The heat climbed in our stalled bus. We pondered the pain of missing the ferry and being stuck on Java for a few hours more than would be optimum. Java had been marvelous, but now Bali beckoned.

Our driver effected the repairs. We sped down the hill just in time to catch the ferry, waved on frantically by the attendants.

We drove to Kuta Beach, a resort aimed at budget travelers near the southern tip of Bali's rough diamond, along 50 of perhaps the most beautiful miles in the world. Green rice paddies, red flowering trees and deerlike, delicate cattle lined either side of the road. Carved archways decorated each bridge. Distant volcanoes loomed on our left. On our right, perfect tube surf rolled in on the Indian Ocean. Even the sky appeared big and colorful.

Some of our group thought the setting to be merely fantastic. The rest of us—a couple from London named the Finches, Mike and Diane, and myself—never wanted to leave. In particular, Mike, Diane and I quickly realized that given the proper investments, expatriates could live cheaply on Bali on interest alone. I confirmed this by interviewing American expat artists who lived on the island. One said that a family would place him in a spare room, asking only that he provide them with an inexpensive sack of rice each month. His main expense was bribing immigration officials for visa extensions.

We understood why many in a group of the first Dutch sailors who arrived in Bali in 1597 refused to leave until months of cajolery by the captain. Already we could see the way in which Bali offered "the contemporary substitute for the nineteenth-century

An island paradise copes with crushing popularity

As with Adam and Eve in the Garden of Eden, the lushness of Bali historically has made life there unusually simple and easy. "In general the Balinese have little need of cash to procure the daily necessities of life," Covarrubias noted in 1936. "Normally the cost of living is extremely low and food and the requirements for shelter are produced by the Balinese themselves."

A Balinese then could grow and raise his or her own rice, fruit, vegetables, pigs, chickens and ducks, and collect fuel from fallen dry leaves and coconut stems.

Housing, as well as food, could be provided without difficulty. Families generally shared walled ancestral compounds looking out on common areas, as at a house in Negara where I stayed toward the end of my trip. A relative in need of a room could move in and share the kitchen. Cash was needed mainly for transport on *bemos* (minibuses), medicine, salt and spices.

Today cash, especially a constant flow of tourism dollars, fuels Bali's economy, growing at about 9 percent a year. Agricultural output has fallen, and a 10-fold increase in tourism over the past decade has bought water shortages, pollution, a decline in craft standards, and the mining of reef coral for hotel wall construction.

During my 1985 visit, Bali could be divided into several tourist sectors: higher-spenders at Sanur and Nusa Dua, the wild party set at Kuta, and backpackers split between Kuta and Ubud. In 1988 the governor of Bali authorized a master plan for 14 centers of tourism. The plan raised concerns over whether it would redirect crowds from noisy Kuta into unspoiled mountain villages.

In 1983, Bali received 160,000 visitors. By the early 1990s, the island was receiving 1 million foreign visitors and 500,000 Indonesian tourists annually, remarkable figures for an Asian island of just under 3 million residents. For a time, a fence enclosed Kuta Beach, and gatekeepers charged a fee for access. As Jeff Wise wrote in 1994 in the *New York Times Magazine*:

Four Balinese enjoy Kuta Beach in less crowded times.

> The fringe eventually becomes mainstream; Bali becomes Fort Lauderdale. The wonder isn't that it's happening, but that it's taken so long.

Backpackers, British royals and other visitors in search of the "old Bali" moved east along the Indonesian archipelago to Lombok, Flores and lesser known islets.

It seemed a shame that people felt compelled to bypass Bali, given its people's high artistic sophistication, with only Java comparable.

Backpackers on Bali may abandon Kuta altogether for Lovina Beach, Ubud, Candi Dasa and remote points, given 1996 reports on the Internet that at Kuta Beach, "you get hassled and hassled" and that "the vendors are in the thousands." Some authors have noted that 1960s visitors to Bali would be heartbroken to see its packed state today, and I wonder if that would be true of 1980s visitors as well.

Optimists hope that the historical resiliency of the Balinese, already tested during sharp increases in tourism during the 1930s, 1960s and 1980s, will allow the island to survive. They point to the continuance of religious observances by the Balinese, even when surrounded by Kuta Beach revelry, and the surviving innocence of most mountain villages.

Fred B. Eiseman Jr. wrote in the 1993 book *Bali and Lombok* that

> the economy is robust enough for people to satisfy their basic needs without undue strain and still have plenty of time for relaxation and family activities.

Positive thinkers also see the tourist spending as funding a cultural renaissance. I wonder about this, given that during my 1985 trip, only two of our group sought out original, quality batik paintings by top artists. The 10 others, to the amusement of our tour leader, John Horne, gravitated toward the Balinese equivalent of Elvis on black velvet: foot-square batiks showing garish purple butterflies and orange stilt villages.

romantic conception of primitive Utopia," as Covarrubias noted in *Island of Bali*.

The author also wrote that the Balinese were puzzled by tourism:

> They would never willingly leave their island, and once a woman remarked that surely the foreigners must have done something at home that forced them to leave their own lands.

What an exalted mental picture of the outside world the Balinese must have held at one time, touching in its innocence—to think everyone came from a place as alluring as Bali.

SATURDAY, APRIL 27

An encounter with Aussies on holidays

We spent our first day bicycling along some of the island's southern roads and at dusk went to dinner at TJ's, a well-known Mexican restaurant in Kuta Beach.

The food scene in Bali resembled what you read of Kathmandu in Nepal: endless pseudo-Western specialties, from pizza to apple pie. We took care to ask for our drinks without ice to avoid stomach upsets.

Then we headed to Peanuts, Kuta Beach's barn-sized disco. Australian surfer boys wore Casablanca Pub headbands, tank tops and short shorts. Tan, blond and of vacant expression, they danced like pogo sticks. Big Aussie girls wore the awful-colored shorts and blouses, with shocking pink and electric yellow splotches, sold locally for the equivalent of $1 an item.

On either side of Mike and Diane, two couples petted and groped away. One girl had her hand publicly pressing on her man's trouser zipper, and his hand was clamped to her breast. He stopped for a few seconds to sip his beer, indicating what I took to be the general drift of the priorities of the Australian male.

Diane took it all in. "Wonder if we can change our air tickets to skip Australia and go straight to Polynesia?" she mused. I had been wondering the same thing.

A row of Kuta Cowboys lined the far wall of the disco. Indonesian trendies with long gleaming black hair, they constituted a male equivalent of the Brazilian *morena*, a darkly beautiful and sexy woman. These men, some of the world's most exotic-looking gigolos, looked for Western girls. A certain hardness to these calculating men, most unlike other Balinese, repelled me, at least.

The third line of our ticket, right, reads "Cremation." Above, mourners begin by carrying the deceased around the clearing. Below, an Australian makes a video recording of the corpse as it burns on a stack of logs.

MONDAY, APRIL 29
An enjoyable funeral

After spending Sunday snorkeling off Sanur, back at Kuta Beach on Monday, we bought tickets to a cremation. That may sound strange, but tourists quickly learn that these ceremonies are one of Bali's colorful traditions. Covarrubias wrote that at cremations, "the Balinese have their greatest fun."

We headed at 8 a.m. to the ceremony, held in a village northwest of Denpasar past Tanah Lot. About 20 men marched around a clearing carrying a platform, bedecked with ribbons and streamers, bearing the coffin. Under the trees, dozens of women sang while men beat gongs.

The pallbearers removed the deceased, an elderly man, from the bier. They took off his shroud and placed his remains on metal rods between two rows of thick logs. Mourners laid clothes and sashes on him. A big crowd around the week-old corpse blocked an easy view. But I could smell the mild, almost sweet, decay of the body.

A pipe connected to a gas canister emitted flames to aid the burning of the body. First the hair melted. Then the body took on the look of a charred log, a gray-black silhouette in burst of orange flame. The grimly fascinating scene resembled photographs of the Buddhist monks who immolated themselves in Saigon in the early 1960s to protest the Diem government in South Vietnam.

Diane, Mike and I clucked a bit at an Australian who not only wore shorts to the cremation (considered disrespectful by the Balinese at temples and religious ceremonies) but who videotaped the ceremony in a rather obtrusive way. Perhaps we couldn't talk—after all, we had also bought tickets and took photographs of the event. Still, one had to wonder if the local people, despite near-legendary cultural resiliency, did not at some point have to notice and on some level resent all of us tourists at their funerary events.

After 90 minutes, the corpse had been reduced to a skeleton. The deceased's distraught wife was led away from the pyre at one stage, showing that all is not fun and games even at a Balinese cremation. We left before all the bones were thoroughly burnt—a long business.

At 6 p.m., we attended a *kecak* dance, the only Balinese dance not accompanied by a gamelan orchestra but rather by a choir of 70 men sitting in concentric circles. (The wordless 1992 movie *Baraka* contains a segment depicting a *kecak* performance.)

The men chanted and emitted low shouts of incredible depth …

chak a chak a chak

… that created tingles at the nape of the neck. A sea of brown arms erupted, the skin of the bare-chested men handsome against their red-and-white sarongs. They fluttered their arms in unison and then swooped low, bent at the waist, and lowered the volume. Some dancers, a secondary part of the performance, enacted a 50-minute *Ramayana*.

Our program notes, typed and dittoed on inexpensive tan paper, described monkey kings, golden deer, various battles and magic arrows turning into dragons. As in the classical Javanese dance we had viewed earlier in Yogyakarta, the *kecak* dance concluded with the lovers, Rama and Sita, along with Rama's younger brother Laksmana, returning home happily.

TUESDAY, APRIL 30
On to Ubud

At a village called Batubulan, near the southeast coast of Bali, we watched a Barong dance, one of our favorites. Barong, a lionlike creature, and Rangda, more witchlike, engaged in an epic struggle of good vs. evil.

We had a ditto in charming English to follow the musical "overtone" (overture) and the five acts. The attempted synopsis bore an impossible burden. Imagine if you had to translate the plot, the characters and the radically different culture of five seasons' worth of *Dallas* into Indonesian. We found the Javanese epics reciprocal in their complexity.

Performers portray Ranga.

The plot included monkeys helping tigers to fight three men, and a witch influencing the prime minister who then refused to have pity on the son of a character named Dewi Kunti, whose relationship to the other characters was rather sketchily presented. Rangda unsuccessfully attempted to cast a spell so that Barong's supporters would stab themselves suicidally.

Still, we had a vague idea of what we were supposed to be seeing. Monkey and wild boar characters clowned, as they might in Shakespearean comedy. And as in the bard's tragedies or *I, Claudius*, lots of people lay around dead at the end.

We continued to Ubud, Bali's artsy, peaceful alternative to the bacchanalia of Kuta Beach. For the equivalent of $3 a night, we stayed in cottages surrounded by tropical gardens at Pura Muwa (Little Palace). Huge verandahs featured cane chairs, two tables, cut flowers and potted plants, and pitchers of fresh tea.

In the afternoon we visited an art gallery. Then at Peliatan village, we watched the pretty Legong dance, less martial than the *kecak* or Barong dance.

What struck me as almost more memorable than the Legong dance itself was the ease of seeing the arts in Bali. So many villages offered dances or shadow puppets that it seemed one only had to stand in the road and wave down a *bemo* and arrive shortly thereafter at a performance. Or one could visit, just as effortlessly, a village where artisans carved masks or cast gongs.

A man carves wood in Mas.

WEDNESDAY, MAY 1
Exploring Bali's highlands

After breakfast we walked to Ubud's Monkey Forest and bought peanuts to feed the 14 little simians.

Above, a traditional house sign depicting a family's boys and girls in the village of Pujung. Left, impatient monkeys at Ubud's Monkey Forest grab for peanuts. (I'm wearing a sarong, required at Balinese temples.)

Scenes in upland Bali: Above left, a repairman fixes my bicycle's handlebars. Above right, I ride between villages on my birthday. Right, terraces constructed by the Balinese to grow rice retain water and secondarily act as beautiful "mosaics of mirrors that reflect the clouds," as Covarrubias noted.

cent green shade found in Van Gogh. The terraced fields formed giant steps down the hillsides. Women threshed rice, each helping to get a few more grains out by bashing the stalks against a board the size of a door. We spoke to the threshers and they to us, without either side really understanding, or needing to.

Most of the route was flat or consisted of gentle grades. With loads of places to stop for Coke or *es teh* (ice tea), we found it easy to see the potential for cycling around the whole island. The most tiring part was saying hello and explaining where we were from to virtually every single person we passed. "I love you—you're beautiful!" shouted one young man playing pool.

Creaking noises came from my handlebars after I stood on the pedals to climb a grade. A few minutes later the handlebars broke in two—right in front of Sayan's bike repair shop. Twenty minutes and 1,500 rupiah ($1.36) put it right. Instead of a receipt to hand to the rental shop owner, the mechanic gave me the broken part.

LESSON NUMBER 5: ON THE RIDE BACK, DIANE AND I DECIDED THAT IF THERE WAS A HEAVEN IT MUST BE JUST LIKE BALI, THOUGH JUST A BIT COOLER AND WITH ICE THAT WAS SAFE FOR DRINKS.

And in the heaven modeled on Bali, one's bike would break down only in front of a repair shop.

The Balinese agree that Heaven would be like home. Between incarnations, they believe, the soul goes to a heavenly reservoir where "life is just as in Bali, but devoid of all trouble and illness," Covarrubias wrote.

My lunch at a restaurant called Murdi's was perhaps only appropriate for a heaven where neither calories nor nutritional balance mattered: cashew nut pie, two ice teas and a Coke. Later we enjoyed a Balinese dinner of smoked duck, *lawah* (spicy vegetables) and

Three crawled up my legs, and another peered directly into the camera lens and tried the shutter. A baby tried to climb up an adult's erect tail. The juveniles wrestled, and adults studiously picked each other's fleas.

At noon we cycled to a wood-carving village, Pujung, climbing continuously for $2^1/_4$ hours. We passed beautiful terraced hillsides of rice paddies. In the village, we found a traditional sign on the side of a family complex, an example of the charming Balinese practice of listing the number of one's children: *laki* meaning boys, *perempuan* meaning girls, and *jumlah* for total. On our 50-minute freewheeling descent, we passed a baby pig, keeping cool while tied in a drainage ditch.

In the afternoon we watched trance and fire dances, then ate dinner at Uli Watis— tuna steak for $2.20, seasoned with garlic, onion, salt and hot pepper.

THURSDAY, MAY 2
Viewing the mirrorlike paddies

We cycled to Sayan village, a ride even prettier than that to Pujung. This is the upland Bali that, even today, one hears has not yet been ruined by the explosion of tourism.

Palm trees fringed paddies of an irides-

A duckherd tends his quackers near Sayan village.

red rice, followed by apple pie. The food was fit for a birthday celebration—my 31st, in fact. Without any deliberate intention, I had celebrated May 2 in Bali, as I have in other years in Italy, France and China.

FRIDAY, MAY 3
To the north coast
Many tourists did not stray from Kuta Beach and its deservedly famous sunsets and party scene, so the rest of the island, equally gorgeous, could be surprisingly uncrowded.

> **LESSON NUMBER 6: AS HAPPENS AT RESORT ISLANDS SUCH AS BALI, CROWDS PREFER TO SEEK OUT EXISTING CROWDS.**

In search of additional manifestations of paradise and fewer manifestations of fellow tourists, we departed Ubud to establish a new base on Bali's north coast.

First we toured the central island, beginning with the bat cave at Goa Lawah, which made a more lasting impression for its stench than for its hundreds of bats. Then we visited the Mother Temple at Besaki, overlooking miles and miles of rice terraces, and scenic Lake Batur, which occupies a caldera.

At 1 p.m., we arrived at Lovina Beach, at the time a little-touristed collection of *losmen* (family-run lodgings) on the north coast. Its volcanic black sand beaches could become considerably hotter than white sand. This ostensible drawback deterred the sunbather swarms, so our tiny group could enjoy the colorful reefs without crowds of other snorkelers.

Prahus, small outrigger canoes with pastel-striped sails suggesting beach umbrellas, sat on the beach. We hired one for a snorkeling trip on the Bali Sea. A brief sail took us to an idyllic reef, where we splashed around for 90 minutes. Yellow and magenta coral lay in about 12 feet of crystal water, populated by azure starfish, huge sea slugs, blue neons, angelfish and catfish. Schools of small lime-green fish swam in red coral. Dehydrated by our lengthy stay in the water, we drank everything in sight when we got back to the al fresco restaurant at our lodgings, Nirwana Cottages.

The sunset behind the silvery water featured rain clouds of a vivid color—electric lavender?—against wide streaks of red and chalky blue.

At dinner at the Badai Restaurant, we split a big fish for four in garlic butter, $1 each. I noticed a faded flier on the wall describing snorkeling at Terok Terima Marine Park to the west. Even allowing for possible hyperbole, it sounded exceptional, and I decided to try to get there in a day or two.

SUNDAY, MAY 5
Snorkeling in the Bali Sea
At 7 a.m., we woke our boatman, Mah, to go snorkeling again, as we had the previous two days. The

Prahus rest on the dark volcanic sands of Lovina Beach.

water lay smooth as glass, and visibility seemed perfect. We saw more marvels: pipefish, seersucker-patterned fish, sea cucumbers (looking like exploded truck tires) and electric-blue neons on coral resembling a tree.

An Aussie named Keith taught us how to duck dive. We jackknifed and kicked strongly to descend, picking up starfish and shells.

The equivalent of one dollar allowed us two hours, or more time if we desired, of snorkeling off Lovina Beach. One dollar seemed to be the price of almost everything in Indonesia: a snorkel, an hour massage, a fish dinner, a bemo ride or a pirated cassette.

We sunbathed later, then ate lunch and enjoyed a lazy afternoon. For dinner, we had "Fish in Union Sauce" (onion sauce) with "guakomole" at a local restaurant.

Mike and Diane entertained us with travel tales, including how they fought altitude sickness when climbing Mount Kilimanjaro in Tanzania. They recalled traveling in India and having to brush flies off cold food kept in shop windows.

We all felt that cuisines we'd loved at home, such as Indian and Chinese, could be spectacularly awful in their home territories, where the best cooking might be found only in homes or at banquets rather than in restaurants.

In Java and Bali, we'd seen dances, gamelan performances, temples, monkeys and bats. Our Bangkok-to-Bali trip began to wind down. We could now devote successive days to increasing inertness, resting on the beach, reading, napping, eating and watching one fine sunset after another.

On Monday, for example, we idled except for in the evening. Then a woman from London named Vivienne and I went on a "night snorkel" with some men hunting octopus. They caught nothing but sang a haunting Arabic-sounding melody as we sailed back under the stars.

Lovina Beach seemed to be my definition of heaven: a place with pleasant breezes, unscheduled time permitting reading, fine nearby snorkeling—and it was cheap!

A hidden gem

A dozen Balinese and I rode in a *bemo* winding along a little road on Bali's northwest coast. I had left the rest of our group back at Lovina Beach, as they did not share my interest in exploring a new snorkeling spot.

The *bemo* passed under an archway of trees and in front of the long-tailed macaques at Pulaki Temple. At Terok Terima, a ranger directed me to get a 1,000-rupiah (90-cent) permit at a national park office in Cekik, a village to the west, and then return to go snorkeling at Bali Barat Marine Reserve.

Back at the landing at Terok Terima, I met a group planning to go out to the reserve, encompassing Pulau Menjangan, an island offshore. Four Aussie exchange students and I would snorkel. Two Canadian supervisors of a hydrology aid project would dive, along with a Japanese film crew making a diving documentary. The Japanese toted massive amounts of camera equipment and lights and even waterproof personal stereos designed for underwater use.

We shared a boat to Pulau Menjangan (Deer Island). Its steep coral drop-off looked like an Alpine mountainside with wind-tumbled wildflowers. Thousands of green, orange, purple and yellow-and-blue three-inch fish blanketed the edge. Shoals of cornflower-blue fish with black-tipped tails swam calmly about, as did garfish and angelfish. Octopuses and starfish lay in the coral. Beyond a ledge, studded with small clams, were midnight-blue depths.

Tiny orange clown fish with white and black stripes, my favorites, came out from their home corals to play with my fingers.

It was the best snorkeling I'd experienced so far, better than Malaysia even, and there was more to come.

Reef life and a family compound

We snorkelers and divers spent the night at a *losmen* about a mile west of the pier, on the north side of the coast road. At 10 a.m. we returned to Pulau Menjangan, motoring by boat to the west side of the island, having visited its southern edge the previous day. An Indonesian diver and I worked our way south on the coral. We observed even more fish, corals and clams than on the day before.

As we snorkeled, a medium-sized gray reef shark, perhaps $4^1/_2$ feet long, swam in about six feet of water between us and the island, heading slowly in the opposite direction. We clasped hands, turned around and slowly followed the shark from about 10 yards behind, fascinated with its powerful swimming. He moved slowly on the coral shelf and then over the edge into the indigo depths.

This personal first—sharing the water with a shark—stopped my heart at Pulau Menjangan, as would a later experience on Rangiroa in Tahiti's outer islands. Over time, the sight would become a bit more commonplace, though always thrilling.

The Canadians, Gary and Matthew, headed out to dive. They found a baby sea turtle hiding in the coral and then a massive one, which Gary got very close to before it banked and disappeared.

Jane enjoys the banter of Canadian and Japanese divers on our boat returning from Pulau Menjangan.

As we motored back, Jane, an Australian exchange student, invited me to stay with her host Balinese family in Negara in southwestern Bali. This invitation proved to be a godsend, offering insight into how local people lived.

A couple of *bemo* rides brought us to Negara by the middle of the afternoon. I got to see the classic arrangement of a Balinese home. An arched entrance with folding chairs lined up on either side led to a central courtyard featuring an open-air kitchen and dining table. A television set had been placed on a table under a tree.

Reasonably spacious bedrooms, a *kamar mandi* (room with a cistern of water for washing) and a pantry surrounded the courtyard. Many Indonesians, even on crowded Bali, appeared to enjoy more living space than the jammed Chinese.

Several toddlers played with male relatives, both teenagers and adults, who seemed to be home without work.

LESSON NUMBER 7: THE UNDEREMPLOYMENT OF MEN IN PARTS OF INDONESIA SEEMED TO BE A BOON FOR THE CHILDREN, WHO WERE REMARKABLY EVEN-TEMPERED, AS CHINESE AND BURMESE CHILDREN HAD BEEN. THEY HAD A SOLICITOUS BLOOD RELATIVE TO PLAY WITH 24 HOURS A DAY, AND IT FOLLOWED THAT THEY HAD NO COMPLAINTS.

I wonder if Asia's economic boom of the past decade may have provided work for more of these men yet altered their closeness to the children.

In Negara, the family served gourmet fare for dinner: tiger prawns (giant shrimp), rice and grilled coconut with banana for dessert. I contributed a cake bought hastily at a nearby market as a hostess gift.

Jane told me she hailed from a 50,000-acre station (ranch) in Katherine in Australia's exotic-sounding Northern Territory, where she had a pet wallaby and a pig. Her family raised water buffalo and sold them in Java. (It seems noteworthy that Australia and Indonesia can actually be adjacent nations, given the gulf in culture, terrain and standard of living.)

Jane told me in her high twang that she lived in a trailer with her boyfriend Duane, details so archetypically Aussie I could hardly keep a straight face.

We shared a bed, a less racy proposition than it sounds. Jane placed something called a Dutch wife, a long sausage-shaped canvas pillow, down the middle. I thought it was designed to allow two people to share a bed without touching, but I learned later that it also draws away sweat in the night.

THURSDAY, MAY 9
Visiting a local school

The whole family rose quite early. Someone played a tape by the rock band AC/DC at 5:20 a.m right outside the bedroom. So much for the exalted artistic taste and gentle grace of Bali.

After a breakfast too exotic to contemplate back home—more tiger prawns—we visited the high school Jane attended as an exchange student, located amid rice paddies. The teenage students, in two long buildings, sat at long desks in classrooms with huge windows. They could see us as we walked up. Shouts of "Hi, Jane" greeted us from 100 yards away, followed by questions about who I was.

LESSON NUMBER 8: INDONESIANS ARE AMONG THE WORLD'S MOST UNABASHEDLY OPEN AND CURIOUS PEOPLE.

Later I returned to Denpasar and then Kuta by *bemo*, promptly running into Mike and Diane. We enjoyed what could only be summed up as more lounging around on the beach at Kuta.

We mastered the slang replies to the casual Balinese query of where we were headed as we loafed. "*Jalan jalan*," we'd say. "Walking around." Or "*makan angin*"—eating the air.

FRIDAY, MAY 10
Massages on the beach

My days began to follow a pattern:
• Explore parts of Bali by bicycle.
• Return to Kuta Beach by 4 p.m.
• Say hello to all the masseuses: Putu, Maria, Made and Ketut.

LESSON NUMBER 9: THE NAMES REFLECTED BALINESE CULTURE, IN WHICH CHILDREN ARE OFTEN NAMED ACCORDING TO THEIR BIRTH ORDER: WAYAN FOR THE FIRSTBORN, FOLLOWED BY MADE, NYOMAN AND KETUT, WITH THE NAMES REPEATED IF THERE ARE CHILDREN FIVE THROUGH EIGHT.

• And finally, enjoy a divine one-hour massage for $1 from Maria.

Maria, who had a softer touch than the rough Putu, spread a big batik cloth on part of the beach nearest some bushes and worked on my topless self, with all the other women gathered around to provide privacy.

Even though Maria used coconut oil during the massage, her hands felt warm and dry. She said I had a Balinese (stub) nose and Balinese (small) breasts, to shrieks of laughter from all the other masseuses, so used to heavy-breasted Western women.

Toward sunset, locals arrived on Kuta Beach to play soccer and toss Frisbees. The Balinese, like the Cariocas of Rio de Janeiro, see no reason to leave the beach to the tourists.

The next day, Saturday, my notekeeping became as lazy as the days themselves. The two-word entry in my trip diary reads, "To beach."

SUNDAY, MAY 12
Back to the First World

After 23 days in Java and Bali, I said goodbye to Mike and Diane. I would not see Mike for another eight years.

That evening I flew to Sydney. Because it was the Australian winter, I had to force my feet, accustomed to sandals, into shoes for the first time since landing in Burma on March 28, six weeks previously. The open shop fronts of Southeast Asia gave way in Sydney to doors of metal and glass. Air conditioning set at teeth-chattering levels replaced Bali's lulling heat.

I must have gone troppo (tropical), as the Australians say. I missed Indonesia dearly.

Java and Bali and the big lesson: how we view Heaven

I'm sometimes asked, what's your favorite country? Indonesia, I answer with certainty. Java rang with chimes, and its rickshaw drivers danced as they walked. And Bali felt like heaven made tangible on Earth. Imagine living in a place so lovely that your religion holds that heaven would be no different, except that there would be no illness.

Covarrubias described Bali as an Eden:

a land of steep mountains, with such abundant rains, crossed in all directions by streams and great rivers, on a soil impregnated with volcanic ash,

where the earth attained "great richness and fertility." At the time of my 1985 visit to the island (during the dry season, so I recall rain during only a single thunderstorm), life there still seemed so easy.

Bali came close to epitomizing how Westerners have historically conceived of paradise. The Greek word *paradeisos* literally means garden or orchard. Paradise, according to the dictionary, can mean the Garden of Eden, Heaven or any place of ideal beauty or loveliness.

The "theme of the garden has been at the very heart of dreams of paradise, first in the Middle East and then in the West," wrote Collège de France Professor Jean Delumeau in *History of Paradise*. "The reason is that paradise was first imagined in lands in which water was rare and the countryside easily turned into desert."

The Koran (76:11-21) reflects the longing of the desert dwellers for an oasis. It describes Heaven as a sensuous place of silken robes, low-hanging clusters of grapes, drinks from silver flagons and "garments of the finest green silk and brocade."

In Ubud on Bali, a vision of such an Eden greeted us on waking. The window of our *losmen* looked out on to a tropical garden. The red-and-yellow leaf of a croton in the courtyard could be seen each morning set against a perfect blue sky.

Eden (a term that may refer to Edinn, the plain of Babylon) also connotes a garden or a particularly fertile area—such as Bali, one of the easiest places in the world to grow rice.

Genesis 2:8 refers with great specificity to a river flowing out of Eden onto the verdant landscape of Mesopotamia, where it became four rivers, including the Tigris and the Euphrates:

> And the Lord God planted a garden in Eden, in the east; and there he put the man whom he had formed. And out of the ground the Lord God made to grow every tree that is pleasant to the sight and good for food.

Numerous writers from before the time of Christ through the 13th century took the Creation story as literal truth. They attempted to locate the earthly paradise of Adam and Eve in the East, perhaps in Asia. Medieval cartographers even drew the earthly paradise on their maps, located variously as an island at the mouth of the Ganges or as a round island encircled by gated walls.

They envisioned the earthly paradise as a peaceful, well-watered place with a springtime climate. They also described fanciful locales just outside the gates of earthly paradise—including Ceylon, Egypt and Madagascar—where noble and wealthy people reputedly dwelled.

In the 13th and 14th centuries, some writers described Brazil (a legendary name later applied to the real place) and Ireland as paradises, as well as the mythic St. Brendan's Island, Avalon and Arcadia. The Happy Isles, another mythical paradise, were thought to lie beyond Morocco in the seas off Mauritania. All these mythic places shared certain characteristics: perfumed breezes, fruit trees and long-lived inhabitants with no need to work.

Delumeau noted that the vision of blessed countries "had haunted the Western imagination since

Javanese children, like those of Bali, seem to regard the here and now as Heaven.

antiquity." For example, Christopher Columbus believed that the New Indies lay near the earthly paradise. Only the voyages of exploration in the 16th century forced dreamers to set aside the goal of actually finding the Biblical Eden.

LESSON NUMBER 10: MODERN TRAVELERS TO PLACES SUCH AS BALI FOLLOW ANCIENT HUMAN LONGINGS TO DISCOVER LEGENDARY PARADISES, MUCH LIKE ESCAPEES TO ANYWHERE THAT REMAINS SPRING-LIKE DURING THE NORTHERN WINTER, SUCH AS THE CARIBBEAN, MEXICO AND FLORIDA.

Heaven itself was originally conceived of as a place where mortals might continue to enjoy the pleasures of earthly life, as in the Valhalla of the Germans and Scandinavians and the happy hunting ground of the American Indians.

In the Revelation to John 4:5-6 (the Apocalypse), Heaven appears as a Steven Spielberg spectacular. God sits on a throne surrounded by a rainbow that looks like an emerald:

> From the throne issue flashes of lightning, and voices and peals of thunder, and before the throne burn seven torches of fire … and before the throne there is as it were a sea of glass, like crystal.

Fantastic animal spirits and chants of praise complete the celestial picture.

Christians portray Heaven as the abode of God, the angels and the souls of those who are granted salvation. Within this view, however, the concrete depiction of Heaven has evolved enormously over time, as a book by Colleen McDannell and Bernhard Lang called *Heaven: A History* describes.

By the 4th century, the North African-born St. Augustine had composed his *City of God*. The work envisioned Heaven as a place of perfect bodies removed of earthly blemishes, with erotic appeal yet not inspiring desire or possessiveness. His view showed considerable restraint for a former good-time Charlie who had written in his *Confessions,* "Give me chastity and continence, but not just now."

In medieval times, as European populations began to shift from the countryside to the cities, religious writers started to describe Heaven as a city, perhaps resembling walled Jerusalem or a Gothic cathedral. In this enclosed haven, which came to replace the vision of a garden or Eden, the saved would eternally contemplate the divine.

A view of Heaven centered on people rather than God began to emerge in 1745 in the writings of Swedish scientist and philosopher Emanuel Swedenborg. The idea of Heaven as merely an opportunity to meet God no longer seemed to excite people. In fact, Alfred North Whitehead dismissed the idea of arriving in Heaven to sing the praises of God as "idiotic." Christians came to view Heaven instead as a state that provided the sensations of love, domestic contentment or sex itself.

The Romantic poets and painters vigorously adopted this view. *Heaven: A History* analyzes an example: an 1808 engraving by William Blake called "The Meeting of a Family in Heaven," showing a couple in a rapturous embrace alongside their hugging children.

McDannell and Lang note that in the 19th century, the clergy saw Heaven as a place for the continuation of married love, and poets saw it as a place for romance to flourish unrestrained by Earthly conventions. Victorians, the authors wrote, agreed that "the main purpose of heaven was to cultivate human love." Heaven would be a perfected Earth (as the Balinese thought), where "love, marriage, children, family, friends, social relations" would survive in a sanctified state.

Boston College theologian Peter J. Kreeft, in *Everything You Ever Wanted to Know About Heaven,* reflected the view of Heaven that emerged after the time of Swedenborg. He noted that human beings have sexual souls, because biological sexuality is innate and pervasive to every cell in the body, including the brain. Therefore he posits that we will definitely enjoy spiritual intercourse in Heaven and the possibility of physical love as well. Perhaps there will be no physical sex, he wrote, but only "for the same reason earthly lovers do not eat candy during intercourse: there is something much better to do."

What happens in Heaven for the divorced where one partner remarries and the other does not? Or when a much-loved spouse dies and the survivor marries happily again? Kreeft wrote that a sexual relationship "need not be confined to one in Heaven. Monogamy is for earth. … In the Communion of Saints, promiscuity of spirit is a virtue." Still, this sounds like Heaven's potentially most awkward social aspect.

Friends of mine have expressed a longing for reunion with departed family members. On a July evening some years ago, my housemate, Rose, her friend, Joan, and I all sat on the roof deck of my home in Baltimore. Joan had recently lost her brother prematurely to illness. She said she believed in Heaven and would eagerly look forward to seeing her brother again there. Rose, a nurse, told me of a patient who told her of a near-death experience. He described a place of overwhelming joy, love and peace. Other survivors tell of a bright white light beckoning them for a time, a description oddly similar how heroin addicts describe their rush.

In Buddhism, a religion that never seems to pander to human longings, including the desire to be reunited after death with loved ones, Heaven is nirvana: a state of extinction of all desire. Obviously this could not be more distant from the Romantic poets' vision of a highly sensual heaven, or the view of a male friend that Heaven would be a continuous sensation like that of "getting laid."

As unsatisfactory as it may seem emotionally, I suspect intellectually that Buddhism may hold the truth on the nature of Heaven.

Lesson Number 11: A number of social activists and modern non-Catholic theologians share the broad emphasis of Buddhism, believing that one's focus should be not on Heaven, but on conducting a proper life on Earth.

The *Catechism of the Catholic Church* published in 1994 portrays Heaven as delightful yet unimaginable, a mystery that

> is beyond all understanding and description. Scripture speaks of it in images: life, light, peace, wedding feast, wine of the kingdom, the Father's house, the heavenly Jerusalem, paradise.

The *Catechism* cites St. Paul in 1 Corinthians 2:9: "No eye has seen, nor ear heard, nor the heart of man conceived, what God has prepared for those who love him."

In 1995, a Gallup poll reported that nine in 10 Americans (near-unanimity for such a diverse culture) believe that there is a Heaven. Surveys also show that most Americans expect Heaven to be a continuation of earthly life without wars, disease, pain and fatigue.

A 1983 article in *U.S. Catholic* presented readers' views on the afterlife. One respondent said that "to picture Heaven as a sort of super vacation resort is childish." Many described Heaven prosaically. Most of those polled felt that Heaven would involve being reunited with loved ones in a place resembling a region that pleased individual tastes.

Heaven as a place to resolve premature passings

My relationship with the couple I traveled with in Indonesia, Mike and Diane, continued longer than those with many others whom I had casually encountered on trips. Yet this may be more a function of how unusually conscientious they were about corresponding. I first wrote to them from French Polynesia, providing my impressions of the place in a letter sent care of the American Express office in Sydney. When they finished touring Australia, I thought, they could possibly use my notes as a guide during their own trip to Tahiti.

When they returned to Vancouver, they began to have a family: First Amanda came along, then Lauren. Even with two toddlers, Mike and Diane found time to continue to write. The family sent letters every Christmas, recalling their continued travels as they visited London and Hawaii.

Seven years after we visited Bali, a letter arrived from Mike. Diane had died Aug. 7, 1992, of a heart infection, after only a few days of feeling poorly.

How Mike must have felt after all they had shared, including the exceptional experience of traveling the world together, I could only imagine. I was disturbed that someone about my age had died in such cir-

Diane enjoys our day cycling in Bali's heavenly uplands.

cumstances, and talked to my sisters about Diane's premature death. They suggested writing to Mike with as many memories of our travels together as I could summon. I did so, enclosing some photographs.

Eventually a business trip bought Michael to Baltimore, and we went for dinner to the Phillips seafood restaurant at Harborplace in September 1993, a bit more than a year after Diane's passing.

With offhand courage Michael described how well their two daughters were doing. He kept busy by taking them to after-school activities. He continued to assiduously stay in contact via letters and visits with many of the people he and Diane had met on their travels.

We talked about sports and other lighter topics, such as the rivalry

between the Baltimore Orioles and the Toronto Blue Jays, and how U.S. basketball was also expanding to Vancouver.

Only in passing did he reveal an incident with Diane. "The night before she died," he said evenly, "she told me she wished she had written a travel book." Diane's one regret registered with me. I resolved to finish my own book.

And maybe Diane can contentedly await reunion with her loved ones. Kreeft described Heaven as a place that would "deal with the injustice of premature deaths." He envisioned a Heaven that would permit children and parents to complete their unfinished business, a great consolation to children whose parents die too soon—be they 8 years old or 28, as my husband was when he lost his hero, his father, of whom he still often dreams.

Diane didn't get to write about her adventures. Yet she was blessed to realize that life is short and to travel widely while she could. If there is a heavenly paradise, maybe it resembles the earthly one of the paddies around Ubud, where we decided Heaven would be Bali with water safe to drink.

So the Balinese, the Polynesians and to an extent even Americans regard their homelands as a stage set for Heaven. Certainly I would not immediately regard Baltimore or Washington as paradise—although with the right boat and good company, perhaps the Chesapeake qualifies on a perfect spring or autumn evening.

LESSON NUMBER 12: IN SURVEYS AND ESSAYS, HEAVEN IS SURPRISINGLY FREQUENTLY DEPICTED AS A PLACE WHERE LOTS OF BASEBALL IS PLAYED.

The 1989 movie *Field of Dreams* explored this theme. So did a conversation I had at an Orioles preseason game in 1996 in St. Petersburg, Fla., with the Elwoods, a friendly couple from Hancock, N.Y.

We looked out from seats in Al Lang Stadium, right on the waterfront. We had all left unseasonably

cold home towns behind. Sailboats raced on Tampa Bay on an 80-degree day. Seagulls swooped around the outfielders. The smell of grilled hamburgers wafted from below our section. George Elwood, a retired attorney, surveyed it all and concluded, "This is Heaven."

My Heaven would combine that day in Florida with family and pets, and in the evening the Redskins would win the Super Bowl. Theologian Kreeft described Heaven as a place where we will enjoy love and reunions, where music may be our language, and where we will have our pets because, why not?

Kreeft wrote that we will attain a state known on Earth only in part by artists, who foreshadow the creativity of Heaven.

Java and Bali certainly had many of the ingredients for Heaven: artists everywhere, a spring-like climate, music of the spheres and an atmosphere of joy to be shared in a community of many friends.

A CRESCENT CALLED NEW AFRICA

Brazil ... and lessons on racial democracy

A boy takes his birds for a walk in the restored colonial city of Alcântara.

After hours bearing southeast on an overnight flight from New York City, our American Airlines flight slowly descended in sunlight over bare pinkish hills. Below stretched an empty expanse, an Outback-style middleland with no sign of settlement.

Then—boom!—São Paulo rose from the bareness. The hills yielded to the pale concrete of a city of 16 million, the same size as greater New York. After a brief stopover, a handful of remaining passengers roared off for a final leg to Rio de Janeiro.

Over the next 19 days, I would visit what I thought of as the Four Corners of Brazil:

• The Pantanal, one of the world's premier wildlife areas.

• The moody and grand Amazon, as seen through the eyes and heard through the ears of an Indian guide.

• Alcântara, a largely abandoned coastal city resembling a de Chirico painting made tangible.

• Salvador, the African heart of the Americas, home of many of Brazil's 70 million blacks, most descended from 3.7 million slaves.

As with most of my other trips, I'd originally set forth because of curiosity about one thing (in Brazil's case, the ethereally beautiful music of a singer named Milton Nascimento) and stumbled into a much bigger lesson relevant to the United States. The unplanned insight of this journey would be experiencing the southern end of the African diaspora in the Americas.

Growing up white in Maryland, a state now nearly one-quarter black, I'd lived in a state that, unknown to me, was toward the northern end of the dispersion. From Maryland south to Rio de Janeiro live the heaviest concentrations of the descendants of Africans in the New World.

In 1853, German naturalist and New World scholar Alexander von Humboldt first described a "colored empire" around the Caribbean and eastern Atlantic, consisting of nearly 1.5 million free and enslaved blacks. In 1947, Latin American historian Frank Tannenbaum pinpointed the geography of this pivotal area in *Slave and Citizen: The Negro in the Americas:*

Humboldt spoke of a possible colored empire in the Caribbean. If Humboldt's reference is taken in a demographic rather than a political sense, the colonization of the Western Hemisphere has involved the settlement of many thousands of square miles by peoples come from Africa rather than from Europe, and if we draw an arc from Rio de Janeiro to Washington, D.C., and include the West Indian islands in it, we shall have, in outline, the empire Humboldt talked about.

I have replaced Humboldt's term of a "colored empire" with my own phrase, a more modern one: the

A crescent called New Africa

Historians describe how an arc drawn approximately from Rio de Janeiro to Washington, D.C., would encompass a New World region profoundly affected by the importation of slaves from Africa. This map depicts the distribution of the descendants of Africans in the modern day.

In both Brazil and the United States, descendants of Africans in search of work have migrated away from agriculturally depressed regions bordering the Atlantic Ocean and Gulf of Mexico.

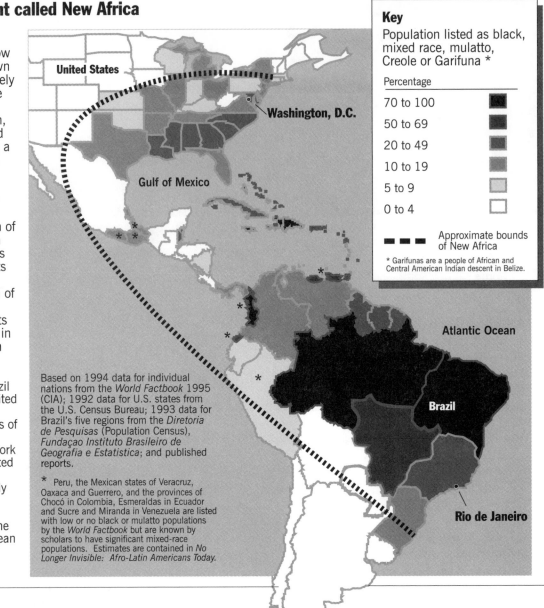

United States

Washington, D.C.

Gulf of Mexico

Atlantic Ocean

Brazil

Rio de Janeiro

Key

Population listed as black, mixed race, mulatto, Creole or Garifuna *

Percentage

70 to 100	■
50 to 69	■
20 to 49	■
10 to 19	■
5 to 9	■
0 to 4	□

- - - Approximate bounds of New Africa

* Garifunas are a people of African and Central American Indian descent in Belize.

Based on 1994 data for individual nations from the *World Factbook* 1995 (CIA); 1992 data for U.S. states from the U.S. Census Bureau; 1993 data for Brazil's five regions from the *Diretoria de Pesquisas* (Population Census), *Fundaçao Instituto Brasileiro de Geografia e Estatistica*; and published reports.

* Peru, the Mexican states of Veracruz, Oaxaca and Guerrero, and the provinces of Chocó in Colombia, Esmeraldas in Ecuador and Sucre and Miranda in Venezuela are listed with low or no black or mulatto populations by the *World Factbook* but are known by scholars to have significant mixed-race populations. Estimates are contained in *No Longer Invisible: Afro-Latin Americans Today.*

Crescent of New Africa. Brazil and the United States, the two endpoints of the crescent, became the places where Europeans and Africans from wildly different places mixed their blood, creating people in many shades of brown.

Saturday, July 30, 1994
Why prices seemed steep

I was fortunate to begin my visit to the biggest nation in South America under the wing of two friends. Waiting at Rio's airport was Luis Macedo, whose son Renato is a good friend of my nephew Matt. Luis, who now lives in Maryland, was spending the month of August in his homeland.

And Jerry Davila, a former *Washington Post* editorial aide, was in Rio that summer conducting postgraduate research.

Jerry and a fellow graduate student, his roommate Zach, took a break from their studies to show me the weekend social whirl around Leblon and Ipanema beaches.

Rio de Janeiro's appearance vaguely resembled Honolulu's. Both cities feature steep mountains rising behind a strip of mid-rise buildings.

Yet more than Honolulu or even Sydney, Rio also felt like the world's "beachiest" city. Ten million water-loving residents gave the place the feel of a New York plunked down at Ocean City, Maryland.

After swimming briefly in waters polluted, according to warning signs, by *E. coli* bacteria, we sat on the sand. I became the only student in the Jerry 'n' Zach Economics Tutorial.

They explained that on July 1, just four weeks before my visit, the Brazilian government had introduced a new currency, called the real (and pronounced something like *hay-yow* or *hi-yaum*). To fight inflation, the real had been tied to a basket of currencies, including the U.S. dollar. The plan succeeded, but the U.S. tourist faced high prices as a result. Food, in particular, cost more than at home and seemed of lower quality. And street vendors, loath to charge less than a whole currency unit, now asked for the equivalent of $1 for a lone ear of roasted corn or a canned soft drink.

LESSON NUMBER 1: MY THEORY THAT "IF MEXICO IS CHEAP, GUATEMALA IS CHEAPER, AND BRAZIL CHEAPEST" IS NOT NECESSARILY SO. PRICES DO NOT ALWAYS DECLINE AS ONE MOVES AWAY FROM THE UNITED STATES.

We walked along to numbered signposts beside the beach that *Cariocas* (residents of Rio) use as rendezvous points. Zach and Jerry made the rounds of their giant circle of Brazilian and expatriate American friends. I made another "Rockville connection," as I had before in Madagascar's airport. One Brazilian woman on the beach, a friend of Jerry and Zach and a premed student, had lived for a time in my Maryland home town, while studying computer science at Montgomery College.

LESSON NUMBER 2: PEOPLE IN THE MODERN WORLD ARE IN PERPETUAL MOTION. TEN MILLION AMERICANS TRAVEL TO EXOTIC FOREIGN NATIONS A YEAR, AND 45 MILLION FOREIGNERS VISIT THE UNITED STATES ANNUALLY, INCLUDING 700,000 FROM BRAZIL.

MONDAY, AUG. 1
First discussions on racial democracy
The domestic Brazilian airlines, Varig, VASP and Transbrasil, make giant circuits of the country as though they were a fleet of shuttle buses. Each plane lands and takes off again on one of various loops connecting a half-dozen or more cities.

Two cute little girls sat beside me as we flew to Belo Horizonte and points north of Rio. They chattered away at me in Portuguese. Fortunately they issued continuous declarative sentences about their stuffed toys and no interrogative ones. As long as I smiled genially, the one-sided conversation proceeded well.

After Belo Horizonte we hopped along to Brasília, the planned capital dedicated in 1960 and now home to 1.6 million people. Reddish scrubland surrounded the grid of its streets. The orderly yet reputedly sterile city looked like Orlando without the Disney World. Jerry told me later that at 5 p.m. each Friday, many of Brasília's residents fly immediately to Rio to party.

Our Varig flight puddle-jumped along, finally arriving at my destination, Cuiabá. The city serves as one of three major entry points to the Pantanal. My Brazilian friends, Luis Macedo and his wife, Vittoria, had recommended visiting the vast floodplain, home to panthers, otters and millions of birds. Though the area

is little known to foreigners, many Brazilians have become aware of it because of a soap opera called *The Pantanal*.

LESSON NUMBER 3: TOURISTS UNDESERVEDLY NEGLECT THE PANTANAL, WHERE IT IS FAR EASIER TO SEE WILDLIFE, IN FAVOR OF THE MORE FAMOUS AMAZON.

The Amazon seems to hold an exaggerated attraction, not only for ecotourists but for writers and publishers. The Library of Congress subject catalog lists 512 books on the subject of the Amazon region and 22 on the Pantanal. Even Hollywood seems to be mesmerized by the famed jungle.

Selected movies set in Brazil

	SETTING
Medicine Man (1992)	Amazon
At Play in the Fields of the Lord (1991)	Amazon
The Emerald Forest (1985)	Amazon
Fitzcarraldo (1982)	Amazon, Manaus
Pixote (1981)	São Paulo
Bye Bye Brazil (1980)	Northeast, Amazon, Brasília
Dona Flor and Her Two Husbands (1978)	Salvador
Black Orpheus (1959)	Rio de Janeiro
A MOVIE NOT SET IN BRAZIL	
Brazil (1985)	The paranoid future

A guide arrived in Cuiabá to fetch me. Edson dressed in the same style as an African safari guide: camouflage vest over olive-green T-shirt and frayed khakis. We took a road west out of straggling Cuiabá and through scrubland, and after more than an hour drove through a town called Poconé. A few minutes later, buildings disappeared and the road became unpaved. We had reached the Transpantaneira, a dirt road built in 1973 that enters the Pantanal from the north. The construction of its surface, raised about 10 feet above the surrounding land, created side ditches that filled with water. Birds loved the miles upon miles of incidental canals, and thus inadvertently a nature park was born—much like that adjoining the Tamiami Trail in the Everglades.

Edson pointed out five toco toucans, the largest of numerous varieties of the bird with the giant golden-orange beak, in distant trees. Closer to the road, kingfishers and herons in flight appeared to keep pace with our Toyota cruiser. We drove by a giant jabiru stork, an ibis, five howler monkeys and a savannah hawk.

Edson named the vivid trees blossoming all around. Ones covered with vivid yellow blossoms he called *combera*, and others of a brilliant magenta shade were *ipê* (known as the trumpet tree in the United States).

Two of the Pantanal's signature creatures appeared. The capybara, essentially a 100-pound guinea pig, holds title as the world's largest rodent. And we spotted our first caiman, an alligator-like reptile.

Edson spotted the slithering trail of an anaconda in the road's dust. In his unmuted enthusiasm and sharp eyes, he reminded me of my African safari guides. He drove slowly, always scanning each side of the road. A boyish, gap-toothed smile wreathed his face whenever he saw a bird or other animal.

We arrived at Pousa Alegre, a small farm and ranch whose name meant "the happy place," and met a Belgian tourist family. The parents and their two sons had visited Kenya the year before. In all, family members spoke four languages. If one met an erudite family like this in the United States, one would assume the parents taught at a major university. Yet they ran a photocopying center.

The Belgian family had a guide named Roberto, a gravelly voiced, quite solidly built man, with a large head and shoulders. His swarthy skin indicated that he was a *caboclo*, of Portuguese-South American Indian descent.

We sat down to eat at the ranch house's long kitchen table. I asked what the population of Cuiabá was. The Belgian paterfamilias answered with confidence that it was 140,000. But his guidebook, though barely out of date, had long been overtaken by events.

"Cuiabá has 1 million people," Roberto corrected. I nodded. The figure sounded more in line with the vast sprawl of buildings Edson and I had driven through.

LESSON NUMBER 4: CUIABÁ'S EXPLOSIVE GROWTH REFLECTED THE HIGH LEVELS OF INTERNAL MIGRATION WITHIN BRAZIL.

Poor people from the *sertão* of the Northeast, a desert that millions of years ago was contiguous with the Sahara, seek work in the boom towns of Brazil's interior. An estimated 25,000 to 80,000 uneducated poor people have moved to two states in the interior, Para and Mato Grosso do Sul. They have been trapped into paying inflated debts for food, lodging and transportation and cannot leave arduous jobs, such as making charcoal. Neoslavery, the form of peonage, continues—in the 1990s.

TUESDAY, AUG. 2
In the realm of the world's largest parrot

At 5:30 a.m., a noise like that of deafening roosters woke me. I arose and met my guide for the day,

---

If not Brazil, where?

Roberto, a guide working for a Belgian family, gave the first indication that the level of racism in Brazil had been wildly underestimated by many outsiders.

The Belgian mother mentioned that they had been assured on their transatlantic flight by white Brazilians that "racism was not a problem in Brazil."

Roberto, of mixed race, shook his head and aptly summed up the racial situation in Brazil. "If there is a job open, the white man gets the first chance. After, it could go to me. A black man would be last in line."

If Brazil could not fill its self-proclaimed role as a racial democracy, what place could?

In most of the world, through most of history, people harbored suspicions of any others who looked different, especially if they arrived in significant numbers. In my own travels, I'd seen examples of the extent to which this phenomenon could vary.

As measured by interracial offspring, Brazil indeed indicates a sort of tolerance. Hawaii does as well, with many children having bloodlines from two to a dozen different ethnic groups. In my home state, Maryland, several cities—including Baltimore, Takoma Park and Columbia—seem reasonably accepting of interracial couples. Young Americans in varied parts of the United States, as well as in Paris, seem to date interracially in significant numbers.

LESSON NUMBER 5: SOME PLACES SEEM RELATIVELY MORE TOLERANT, OR AT LEAST LESS XENOPHOBIC, THAN OTHERS. YET TOLERANCE CANNOT REALLY BE READILY PINNED DOWN TO SPECIFIC AREAS. IT MAY VARY FROM STREET TO STREET, PERSON TO PERSON AND MOMENT TO MOMENT.

As measured by friendliness to outsiders, Indonesia, especially Borneo, and Kenya seemed to be highly tolerant. College-age students in China also appear willing to approach travelers, as will the children of Brazil, Burma and France.

As measured by black educational achievement, the data show that the United States is far ahead of Brazil and somewhat ahead of the black-majority island nations of Barbados, Trinidad and Tobago, and the Bahamas. The Belliveau Pilot Index also supported a conclusion that Brazil lagged other places. In only two places—the Bahamas and Kenya—had I ever flown with black pilots.

While the United States probably exhibits less tolerance on the surface than Brazil, much of Brazil's easygoing attitude toward skin color relies on blacks "knowing their place" and accepting shockingly inferior educational and job opportunities, as will be shown later.

LESSON NUMBER 6: ROBERTO'S REMARKS ILLUSTRATED HOW TOLERANCE AND EQUAL OPPORTUNITY ARE TWO VASTLY DIFFERENT CONCEPTS.

Hyacinth macaws challenge a camera-toting visitor, above left, while a toco toucan hides shyly.

Marcus Kiamm. He explained that the dawn chorus was actually the screaming of rare hyacinth macaws. They lived right by the ranch house, where they felt safe from poaching.

Marcus, who was half Austrian and half German, had an accent like Arnold Schwarzenegger's. He was handsome in the straightforward way of Harrison Ford. He strolled along with a walking stick, taking me on a trail from the ranch house into the countryside for a nature walk.

A bush with white flowers gave out a powerful odor like bubble gum. Parakeet feathers lay on the ground. A ranch dog, big and dun, paced in a grove of trees. A jaguar and baby had been sighted on the ranch recently, Marcus said, speculating that the dog smelled either them or an ocelot.

Marcus read the dust of the trail as others would read a book and issued crisp reports. "Anteater." "A man and his dog." He pointed out a giant iguana and then, accent rising, a herd of "kettles"—oxlike zebu.

On our walk, we saw dozens of pretty birds, a sampling of the 600 species of the Pantanal. Marcus named them:

hyacinth macaw, yellow-billed cardinal, white-necked heron, wood stork, jabiru stork, troupial, savannah hawk, kingfisher, snail kite, limpkin, chopi blackbird, ratfaced ibis, spot-crested woodpecker, caracara, great antshrike, rufous hornero or ovenbird and grassland yellow finch.

The vermilion flycatcher, a finger-sized flash of color, may have been the prettiest. Some migrate from as far as Texas. The tiny slip of a creature flies as far on its own as I had with the assistance of a 747.

A chance to see the hyacinth macaw, the world's largest parrot at more than three feet from head to tail feathers, probably draws most of the Pantanal's visitors. In *The Pantanal: Brazil's Forgotten Wilderness*, Vic Banks described the birds' "iridescent color—blue with hints of deep purple on the tail, cobalt on the breast,

and turquoise on the head." He estimated in his 1991 book that perhaps 3,500 still lived in the wild and perhaps an equal number in captivity, most in the United States.

Marcus put the figure in the wild at about 2,500, including nine breeding pairs at Pousa Alegre. Poachers target the designer-shaded birds, taking them via Paraguay to Europe and then the United States. The limited number of birds that survive the journey sell for $9,000. Each live macaw in an exotic restaurant or pet store probably represents five or so birds that died on the roundabout route.

We had to rest in the ranch house through the middle of the day. Even in August, the Southern Hemisphere's winter, temperatures could range up to 113 degrees.

At 3 p.m., the day had cooled enough for a horseback ride. At the barn, Marcus and I met one of the gauchos, who adjusted the tack for our small horses. We all mounted our steeds and rode through an area resembling pastureland in the eastern United States, yet wilder and almost African. Termite mounds dotted the dusty ground, and big cats lurked unseen under an immense sky.

The gloriously hued red ipê made almost as much of an impression as the fact that we might see jaguars. The trees bloomed as far as the eye could see, with an unearthly magenta color that reminded me of the alien worlds depicted on the covers of my father's science fiction magazines.

A stand of trees concealed a watering hole, where the raw Australian Outback look of the red ipê gave way to a luminescent scene reminiscent of the Venetian painter Canaletto. Vaporous greens and golds glowed warmly in the slanting light of the Southern Hemisphere.

Roseate spoonbills and wood storks filled the trees around the water hole. One capybara and four caiman, heads up and alert, remained so motionless that at first I didn't notice their presence. The breeze carried the blossoms' smell of bubblegum.

The Pantanal's beauty did not overwhelm like Africa's nor appear as fraught with peril as Madagascar's. The first corner of Brazil appeared as peaceful and delicate as a bird's song.

Our horses picked their way over the ground. In the dry season, the Pantanal resembles a drained pond-bottom, with clods of drying mud and the remains of aquatic vegetation.

In vain, Marcus scanned a wide grassy clearing for

a resident jaguar. He found something else, however: four rheas, resembling small ostriches, trotting away into the trees.

The Pantanal's birds and flowers displayed a delicate beauty mingled with tropical exuberance. The trail wound through a cluster of trees, and a red cardinal flew above us into the branches of an ipê. A red-orange and black troupial, colored similarly to the Baltimore oriole, zipped around a combera, which looked like it had feather dusters, of an electric yellow found in Peter Max's pop art, grafted to the tips of its branches.

My poky horse, whom I had silently named Secretariat, lagged behind Marcus and the gaucho. The barefoot black cowboy wrapped his legs around his pony's belly. He wore a straw hat with a fat brim, and a western cowboy shirt with a scalloped, double-top-stitched yoke across his broad shoulders. He had shoved two large sheaved knives into the back waistband of his jeans. He struck me as a frontier exotic, with a wonderfully piratical air.

LESSON NUMBER 7: THE PRESENCE OF THIS BLACK COWBOY IN SOUTHWESTERN BRAZIL DEMONSTRATED THE EXTENT OF THE AFRICAN DIASPORA.

The cowboy and Marcus spoke Portuguese in an easy, laconic way. Marcus told me a few hours later, "Everyone, white, niggah, gets along in Brazil." The phrase spoke volumes. Marcus may have merely been modifying the German word for Negro, *neger*. Semantics authority S.I. Hayakawa had written of people who use the word "nigger" who simply had never learned another word for black people—but that was 30 years ago.

LESSON NUMBER 8: AS MY HUSBAND LAMONT W. HARVEY POINTED OUT LATER, IT IS DIFFICULT TO IMAGINE ANYONE TODAY REALLY HAVING NO CLUE THAT THE "N-WORD" CAUSES OFFENSE.

After our ride, we left our steeds in the care of the gaucho. In the lowering light, we tiptoed back toward a massive tree beside the ranch house. Fourteen hyacinth macaws roosting there screeched as we approached. They appeared to stare us down—unlike Africa's lions or cheetahs, which would ignore people, or zebra or hyenas, which would just mosey off.

The macaws fled our arrival by dashing, a pair at a time, to a slightly more distant tree. The length of their tails made them sizable flying machines. A red sky silhouetted their curved heads and long tails.

At dinner, two petite, vivacious Spanish teachers from Madrid, Carmen Montero Arroyo and Theresa Ramírez Ruiz, arrived at Pousa Alegre. Carmen could

speak serviceable English, and she exhibited a dry wit emphasized by a toney Madrid lisp. "Emmmm," she began, sharing a piece of a candy bar. "*Como se dice*," she said, "… a moment on the lips, a lifetime on the hips."

Edson and Marcus took us out on a 10 p.m. safari. They said they saw a jaguar in the shadows. I spotted marsh deer and capybara. Edson strolled outside the cruiser among a group of caiman and grabbed a five-footer by the tail. It tensed into a semi-circle. Fortunately for Edson, he did not lose his leg in a provoked attack.

WEDNESDAY, AUG. 3
Bello. Bellissimo!

In the morning, Carmen, Theresa and I joined a pair of Milanese families, elegant even in casual clothes. We rode in the back of a large open-top truck down the Transpantaneira and turned left on a side road. Two parrots heaved themselves out of a treetop, their flight ungainly like that of pigeons. A black-collared hawk, muscovy duck, and white-necked and blue-capped heron could be spotted in the roadside ditches.

The ride felt like an Ecotourism 400 class merged with Romance Languages 100. "*Bello*," declared one of the Milanese husbands, a balding fellow.

The second husband, taller and with the profile and rippling silver hair of Julius Caesar, upped the ante. "*Bel-LIS-simo*," he corrected, in flowery tones: *very* beautiful.

"*Exquisito*," Carmen and Theresa declared. Or sometimes, "*Maravilloso*."

A flood of adjectives with flowing vowels ecstatically greeted each *falcone* and *pappagallo* (parrot), sounding much more refined than the U.S. standbys, "wow," "cooo-el" and "neat."

In the afternoon, Marcus and I drove farther down the Transpantaneira in the Toyota cruiser. In a nest high in a tree, a mother fed a baby jabiru stork; the offspring's head was intermittently visible. Marcus said the huge baby was just four days old.

Slat-sided cattle trucks passed us in the opposite direction, heading north. Marcus said the livestock were going not to slaughter, but to less dry grazing areas. They would be killed in February when fat.

The Transpantaneira was built in 1973, according to Marcus. It features 127 bridges and is 151 kilometers (94 miles) long. Each bridge, its planking milled from the wood of the ipê, constituted a wildlife observatory in miniature. Near one bridge, an anhinga, a cormorant-like creature, looked for fish. It and the snail kite, another widely dispersed bird, also live in Florida's Everglades.

Five types of kingfisher live in the Pantanal: the ringed, green, Amazon, brown breasted and pygmy. A resident kingfisher seemed to preside at each bridge as though elected mayor of the surrounding water. At

A caiman stares from a ditch beside the Transpantaneira.

one bridge, a kingfisher madly flew upright in place, its neck craned to stare straight down, and then dived for fish.

The ubiquitous caimans (locally called *jacaré*), after feasting on Pantanal fish, looked as well fed as fat earthworms after a rain. The sun provided energy for a protein factory—the food chain of plants, fish, birds and mammals—as it does on the Chesapeake Bay, the Everglades and Lake Nakuru.

We stopped for lunch at a rough building that served as a restaurant. Along came a truck, Roberto at the wheel, bearing the friendly Belgian family. They'd hit the wildlife jackpot, seeing river otters near Porto Joffre and a jaguar on the road at night. We discovered that we would all be staying at Pousada Araras ("lodge of the hyacinth macaws"), toward the northern end of the Transpantaneira.

As we made our separate ways, a savannah hawk slammed against the Toyota's windshield and then bounced off the bumper. Marcus stopped our cruiser.

The bird lay back on the road pathetically. Marcus kneaded its neck. "Not broken, so it's good," he said.

I watched in silence, worried at the prospect of killing a bit of Pantanal wildlife. The hawk spread its wings and opened its beak angrily as Marcus poured water down its throat.

He laid the bird on the ground and poured more water on it. It finally sat upright, resting on its wingtips, its mouth gaping. The hawk panted for a while and then abruptly took flight. It

Marcus watches the stunned savannah hawk after he gave it water.

climbed in tight circles, higher and higher, to our great relief.

Later that night, on the grounds of Pousada Araras, Marcus and Edson led 15 Italians and Carmen, Theresa and I on a *jacaré*-spotting walk. Carmen pretended to count the nigh-infinite caiman. "*Dos millones, tres millones,*" she said idly, by then bored with their abundance.

"Did the savannah hawk bite you?" I asked Marcus.

"Yes, but I did not mind, I was so unhappy to see it hurt. I was so sad."

"Do you hit birds sometimes?"

"No. One time I found a white heron, it was shot and had a hole. It was alive, but only … I …"

"What happened?"

"I killed it. I cried. That's why I was so happy to see the hawk leave. He was just …." He searched for the word in English. "… in shock, saying, 'What happened?' "

Marcus related his own shock the previous night when Edson had grabbed the big caiman. "Its mouth was open," Marcus said, indicating Edson put himself in some danger, and only "to impress the women." I began to see a maturity and restraint in Marcus.

The stars shone. The Milky Way appeared as a luminous band, as bright as a cloud in daytime. Carmen and Theresa called it the *Via Latte*. The Southern Cross they dubbed the *Croz du Sul*. I recalled the lilting melody of a song called "Only a Dream in Rio," a duet with Milton Nascimento and James Taylor on the compact disc *Angelus*. The lyrics extolled the romantic Portuguese language and the beauty of the "holy" Southern Cross, and the melody seemed to reflect the sweet softness of a night like this in Brazil.

THURSDAY, AUG. 4

The cool southwesterlies

We drove to a nearby ranch, Estancia São Sebastian on the Rio Clarinho, and the truck let us off on a dirt path in a wood. On our walk we saw a tiger heron, two American rheas, parrots and a $2^1/_2$-foot-high bird called a curassow, which resembled a turkey. Small capuchin monkeys and a dingo-looking creature called the crab-eating fox also appeared.

At a stretch of the Rio Clarinho below the ranch outbuildings, we boarded canoes. An azure sky set off the profound magenta of a giant ipê on the shore. The guides, one wearing a shirt the precise shade of an ipê, paddled our four canoes downstream. "*Tocano è bellissimo,*" the Milanese observed, as was the *falcone*.

A cool breeze blew out of the southwest, usually a direction for warm zephyrs in the United States. The sensation felt odd to me.

LESSON NUMBER 9: IN THE SOUTHERN HEMISPHERE IN AUGUST, THE COMPASS OF COLD REVERSES. ONE FEELS THE BREATH OF THE ANTARCTIC.

At lunchtime, we returned for a repast of piranha, rice and vegetables. Eighteen people from Italy, Spain, Belgium and the United States sat outside at two long picnic tables. The younger Belgian son played with a family of three tame, green-and-yellow parrots.

The Milanese seemed to have an intrinsic elegance as though all were Fiat heirs and heiresses and just weren't telling any of us. A couple from Rome joined our lunch group. Though fellow Italians, they looked nothing like the aristocratic Milanese and more like Rolling Stones roadies gone AWOL. The woman, in a tight halter top, sat on the lap of her chain-smoking man, a disheveled and laid-back Mediterranean version of Keith Richards with several days' worth of facial stubble.

The pair had skipped the mild exertion of the canoe trip to sit under the trees. Though it was only noon, they steadily drank *caipirinhas*, a mix of a sugarcane alcohol called *cachaça* with lime, sugar and ice. They laughed easily and virtually ignored their compatriots, demonstrating that an invisible boundary separates Northern and Southern Italy.

All week, except for the grad students in Rio, I had seen no other Americans, though 120,000 per year visit Brazil, of a total of 1.5 million foreign visitors. In the Pantanal, for example, most visitors were Germans, Japanese or Swiss, according to Marcus.

LESSON NUMBER 10: ONLY 1 PERCENT OF THE 10 MILLION AMERICANS WHO GO OVERSEAS EACH YEAR TO NON-EUROPEAN DESTINATIONS VISIT BRAZIL, AUGURING POORLY FOR U.S. UNDERSTANDING OF SOUTH AMERICA.

On our last night in the Pantanal, Marcus took us out for yet another caiman drive. Our enthusiasm for seeing more reptiles had been dimmed by massive overexposure, and the caimans had become like so many pigeons in the park to us. Even we ecologically motivated travelers could almost see how their apparent abundance led poachers to kill them for the small strip of the skin taken from their side to make shoes.

With so many around, and with their uncuddly appearance, caimans probably had a difficult time mustering the sympathy that comes the way of endangered lemurs or elephants.

"Here's something different, a caiman," said Marcus with mock sincerity. "It's fantastic. A caiman," he intoned as he shone a portable lamp on their inert forms. "Look, Carmen, another caiman."

"*Dos millones, tres millones*," she replied out of habit.

A family of parrots entertained us at the Estancia São Sebastian (above). Our lunch (right) I thought of as a Brazilian still life: *Piranha with Beer and World Cup Can.*

FRIDAY, AUG. 5

Six continents, six children

I got up early and grabbed my camera for a walk behind the Pousada Araras. A catwalk led over a tangle of streams and marsh to a China-blue pond, where caimans cut wakes in the water.

There golden light bathed a mother capybara, two suckling babies and white wading birds in various shapes and sizes.

Later Carmen, Theresa and I headed out with Edson for a final wildlife walk. We began to mutiny when he pointed out a caiman. Carmen spotted a ditch of weeds by the road and threatened to photograph it. "A caiman-free zone," she declared, defiantly.

During our walk, out of nowhere a thought occurred to me. At age 40, I had visited six continents. My mother at that age had six children. Our different experiences seemed to testify to the changed priorities and choices of two generations of women—and to how a mother's provision of a secure family base permits her children to confidently seek adventure.

I pondered another matter: What to conclude of the Pantanal? I marveled at its prodigious bird population. Viewing Brazil's toucans, macaws and flycatchers, a birdwatcher would be in rapture. Surely the Pantanal must be one of the best places in the world for watching creatures that fly, the equivalent of visiting Africa for mammals and the Western Pacific for marine life.

The relative health of the Pantanal, despite threats from nearby gold mining and potential giant hydropower projects, starkly contrasted with the troubling dryness besetting the Everglades, induced by massive diversion of its water for agriculture. Though

Carmen (left) insists on a group shot of her and Theresa to send to Edson.

kingfishers and cormorants line stretches of South Florida's Tamiami Trail, they make not a hundredth of the roadside display found along the Transpantaneira. Surely the Everglades once resembled this part of Brazil.

Edson drove us back to Cuiabá airport. Carmen said, with straying verbs but perfect nostalgia, "In Spain, in Madrid, I will be walking the car by a big avenue and I will think of the *jacarés* and I will feel sad."

Deciphering the Amazon

I first encountered my guide to the secrets of the rainforest in a Manaus shantytown in the dead of night.

Christão emerged from an anonymous one-story dwelling. He stood only a bit taller than my 5 feet 4 inches. His high cheekbones and glittering brown eyes evidenced the pan-Indian appearance shared by Apache and Peruvian alike. A small hair tie gathered his gleaming inky hair in a tiny ponytail.

Christão sat in the second cab in our two-vehicle convoy. His boss, a heavyset Indian named Soares Pereira da Silva, and I shared another taxi. Soares ran an Amazon adventure camp. That morning, his job entailed scurrying around Manaus, a city of 600,000, gathering tourists and guides in time for an early bus heading east into the jungle.

After picking me up at the Manaus airport at 3:30 a.m., and Christão about 90 minutes later, Soares directed the taxis to a budget hotel. After a delay, a handsome couple emerged.

Melissa, a 31-year-old New Yorker, flashed a friendly smile. Unlike the Milanese families touring the Pantanal in flimsy canvas shoes and gold foil hairbands, she toted a rugged black Eddie Bauer backpack and a giant telephoto lens for capturing wildlife on film—both nearly identical to my own.

Her dark-haired fiance, Mario, 28, originally came from a São Paulo family with roots in Italy, and now also lived in New York. Both Jewish, they planned to get married later in the year and were traveling around Mario's homeland on a "pre-honeymoon." They exchanged endearments constantly, calling each other

"sweets" and *"pushka"* (a Polish word sometimes used with the connotation of "doll," I learned later).

Soares shepherded us to the bus station for our 112-mile ride east. After a couple of hours, the bus left us at a roadside collection of a half-dozen dilapidated stores selling tea, soft drinks and cakes.

We could see that seven others, a collection of eco-tourists from Central Casting, would be heading onward with us to the Indian camp. A pair of Australian girls on a yearlong tour appeared friendly. Melissa and I tried to talk a bit to the others. An Austrian hippie journalist chain-smoked and scribbled in a spiralbound notebook, and four young Germans wore tie-dyed shirts, purple boots and other Haight Ashbury-style regalia. But the Europeans did not seem responsive, and from then on we went our separate ways.

A riverboat, a bigger version of the *African Queen* with a flat tin roof, sat moored on an arm of the Amazon a minute's walk from the collection of stores. We boarded for the 12-mile final leg to the camp.

Dolphins arced out of the tea-colored water, under a big sky dotted with clouds. We passed a pair of ranch houses. The Indians played tunes by Foreigner on the boat's sound system. The sounds of "I Want to Know What Love Is" blasted out over the Amazon waters, followed by "I've Been Waitin' for a Girl Like You." The Indians not only bypassed their homeland's sublime music, they did so in favor of a late 1970s rock group from the exact middle of the road. At least the remote inhabitants of Borneo and Thailand had the savvy, when ignoring their own folklore, of playing Bryan Ferry, David Byrne or hip hop.

LESSON NUMBER 11: TRAVELERS HAVE AN EVER-TOUGHER TIME FINDING AUTHENTIC FOLKLORIC TRADITIONS OVERSEAS. AND SOME CULTURES SEEM HIPPER THAN OTHERS WHEN ADOPTING THE UBIQUITOUS INFLUENCE OF THE WEST.

The jungle camp appeared, a collection of thatched buildings with partial, shoulder-high walls. Eurohippies lounged around, including a woman with pinkish-maroon hair, a tint favored by Parisian matrons. We hopped down to a damp-earth bank. Mario, Melissa and I tied our hammocks to the main building's support posts and found a rudimentary shelf for our backpacks.

Christão soon took us on a canoe trip, paddling in the front with Mario in the back. A minute or two of canoeing west of the camp bought us to the *igapó*, a drowned forest feeling a bit like a cypress swamp. As our canoe glided forward under the woody canopy, the emerald water rippled in an almost syrupy way. Its deep green seemed to almost echo black, a look even darker than the brown, particle-laden waters of the Everglades.

Our canoe exited the *igapó* and crossed open water, heading toward a little clump of trees. There we fished quietly. The serene spot felt far from modern cares. I felt sleepy from my dead-of-night Varig flight. Yet even for someone in a zombie state, the rich mood of the Amazon was apparent: the bird song, the sky dramas and clear, clean air in the birthplace of perhaps one-fifth of Earth's oxygen.

We ate dinner back at the camp. Afterward, by lantern light, Christão told legends of the Amazon. Most involved fantastic creatures of the forest and

Trees hit by lightning rise out of the *igapó*.

adventures with *botos* (dolphins). One tale concerned a *boto* that could anthropomorphize into a handsome man, who seduced women yet always wore a hat to hide his blowhole. Melissa, who had translated at the 1992 Olympics in Barcelona, and Mario provided running English versions of Christão's chronicles.

Above the jungle to our south, sheet lightning, white and silent behind towering storm clouds, fired up the sky. More distant lightning was of greater intensity, brighter and spookier than any I had seen, almost looking like a spacecraft from *Close Encounters of the Third Kind* was cruising east and south to terrorize Rio.

Frogs and bugs created a stupendous racket. Later another noise made itself heard. The cook, a disfigured woman, got into a stash of *cachaça* and screamed horribly for an hour.

"*Os turistas dormem*," she hollered with sarcasm to the Indian guides as they attempted to settle her down. We could do no more for her than to lie awake. In her alcoholic misery, "tourists sleeping" mattered not.

SUNDAY, AUG. 7
Waking up to bird song
Melissa, Mario and I rose at dawn and again clambered into the canoe behind Christão. He planned to show us Indian ways on a $2^1/_2$-mile walk through a stretch of nearby jungle.

We cruised along the *igapó*. Leafless trees, singed by the lightning of frequent thunderstorms, rose from the water, which at first light

was pewter-colored rather than black-green as the day before. Mario paddled along, his blade creating perfect whirlpools.

Unusual noises carried through the air. A bird called the japu seemed to mimic a xylophone. A parrot chattered like an electric generator. A monkey sounded as if it were mooing, and the wind whispered in the distance. We saw one kingfisher and one falcon, a fraction of the sightings possible in the Pantanal.

We beached the canoe, which would be returned to the camp by other guides, and filed into the jungle, I behind Christão, followed by Melissa and Mario. Our Indian guide wore not beads and a loincloth, but a ballcap, brown tank top, puce jeans and high-tops.

As we walked, Christão partly snapped branches along the trail at shoulder height and pointed the tips down, creating markers. His work was as neat as turned-down page corners indicating one's place in a book. Despite the markers, Christão warned Mario that "if there is no sun, now we are lost."

Christão used the flat of a well-sharpened machete to swat at flies nearly three-quarters of an inch long that lit on the back of his calves. The machete also came in handy in creating a bird caller. He trimmed a branch and rubbed the butt end along the flat of the blade. An unseen toucan, somewhere ahead and to the right of the trail, obligingly responded with a high squeak.

Given the difficulty in actually seeing any birds on our walk, I felt glad to have already visited the Pantanal. Otherwise, hearing and not viewing the tou-

Christão makes a sound to call a toucan, left, and cuts a vine to give Mario a drink of water, above.

cans of the Amazon would have been frustrating. The main wildlife we saw were *tucanderas,* or killer ants. We stepped carefully around them.

In the jungle, Christão made it evident that listening would often be more important than seeing. He heard five macaques straight ahead and more toucans off to the right.

Melissa quizzed him: "Do you hear the monkey first or see it?"

"Hear it," he replied.

Melissa asked for more details and then translated his reply: "He says they pee and he can smell it, it has a strong smell. And he smelled it back there," she said, pointing behind us on the path.

With great economy of motion, Christão waved his hand to tell us to go forward toward the monkeys. The gesture reminded me of a statement in a book on Indians I had read in childhood, noting that they analyze how to perform tasks without wasted effort.

Christão peered around at small noises and interpreted them for us. Walking with Christão in the jungle, I felt like a person wearing earplugs at a symphony. I could hear crickets and bird song but only in a general way. Christão knew the location and type of birds and monkeys.

LESSON NUMBER 12: OUR INDIAN GUIDE INHABITED A THREE-DIMENSIONAL AUDITORY UNIVERSE. OTHERS PASSING THROUGH THE JUNGLE COULD MISS A GOOD PORTION OF THE INFORMATION TO BE HAD.

We deliberately took no water, no canteen, no food, no compass, and just a bit of insect repellent, for Christão intended to demonstrate how Indians could fend for themselves in the jungle. He showed us a water vine, called the *sepo d'agua* in Portuguese, perhaps six inches thick and 50 yards long. He sliced it with his machete and held a section up. Water streamed out, more than enough for all of us.

The forest canopy, which had never been logged, rose 15 stories above us. Christão gave us a shaman's guide to the secrets of these trees and plants. The bark of one tree could be brewed to make tea for stomachache. Resin from a particular pine could treat headache and repair boats. He cut into another tree. Gleaming red juice, an oil for muscle aches, dripped down the trunk. Another tree, with yellow wood giving off a pungent smell, possessed roots that could stun fish.

Christão showed us more: plants that acted as antibiotics, or smelled like menthol heating rub, or whose bark could make tea for sore throats.

The sorva tree, perhaps the most fascinating plant, could provide emergency milk for babies. Christão chopped into the trunk, and we drank its liquid, which had a chalky but pleasant milk of magnesia taste. I

would think the "tree milk" would have commercial possibilities as an exotic drink.

Christão told us he earned the equivalent of $10 per day, probably half the typical Brazilian wage. We thought the figure low and told him so. Soares was collecting about $50 a day from each of us, and the camp overhead, aside perhaps from the boat, seemed negligible. But Christão's goal was grander than a higher salary: He eventually wanted to be in business for himself as a guide.

Our walk eventually returned us to the camp, whose two tame scarlet macaws offered as much viewable bird life than the jungle itself.

In the afternoon, we sat around talking. "The Amazon is not what I expected," said Karen, one of the Australian girls. "It's more like the Australian

Two tame scarlet macaws lived at the jungle camp.

bush. I thought it'd be anacondas every few feet and orchids. There are better rainforests within two hours of Sydney." I agreed. To me, the longhouses and plant life of Borneo had seemed more dramatic. Yet the Amazon did have one uniquely fascinating aspect: Christão's interaction with the jungle.

Like upcountry Borneo, the Amazon lacked residents. One average, less than three people per square mile lived in the jungles inland of the giant river.

LESSON NUMBER 13: THE AMAZON IS ONE OF THE WORLD'S EMPTY PLACES, ALONG WITH THE YUKON, SIBERIA, TIBET, THE SAHARA AND MUCH OF NEVADA.

That night, Christão took us to sleep in the jungle, forsaking even the limited shelter of our rudimentary camp. At dusk, we paddled east across an arm of water. We took nothing but hammocks, the fixings for *caipirinhas* and a single communal drinking glass.

Christão tied up the canoe and led us up a hill, stepping carefully around a tarantula on the trail. We all cleared underbrush, hung the hammocks, collected twigs and branches and started a bonfire.

Christão squatted on his haunches, making a *caipirinha* and handing it around. Our drinking served as a ritual. We felt no thirst or appetite. Nothing in our surroundings fanned a desire to eat: no watches or clocks, no growling stomachs, no tension, no frying and animal-fat smell of a McDonald's, and no food of any kind readily apparent. We had adequate paddings of First World fat, so our bodies sent no signals of genuine hunger. I thought I understood why Indians were so lean, how Christão could go a day or two without eating, as he said he could.

LESSON NUMBER 14: AS THE SEX DRIVE DISAPPEARS DUE TO LACK OF STIMULI WHEN ONE TRAVELS IN CHINA, HUNGER SHRIVELS IN THE JUNGLE.

We reclined and swung gently in our hammocks. To the accompaniment of an orchestra of insects, we discussed our personal goals and philosophies, as people seem wont to do outdoors with new companions.

Christão explained that he been separated for four years from his wife, who had run off to Belém with what he described as a group of party girls. The engaged couple sat on one side of the clearing, the separated and divorced ones, Christão and I, on the other.

Christão was 28 years old, the same age as Mario, and one of 16 children. Because his wife had moved to Belém while pregnant, Christão had never seen his youngest child. He told us that he used to sleep with their two eldest children, then 6 and 9 years old, one under each arm. He did not love his wife anymore, he said, but missed the kids.

From relationships, we moved along to the subject of whether God exists and eventually to the obvious topic for Amazon travelers: the fate of the environment. "This is the lungs of the world," Mario said with great animation.

I wondered, would the Amazon region be opened like the western United States, or remain vast and empty, like Australia and Tibet? Would leaving the Brazilian frontier alone be the best course, to ensure that the forests that create oxygen survive?

Much of Brazil's population, like those of Australia, China and to an extent the United States, clusters along the eastern third of the nation. With 158 million people and almost as much land as the United States, Brazil seems to have the potential to be a future superpower.

World's six biggest nations in land area

	LAND AREA MILLIONS OF SQUARE MILES	1995 POPULATION MILLIONS	1994 GNP PER CAPITA
Russia	6.6	148	$4,820
Canada	3.8	30	22,760
China	3.7	1,219	2,500
United States	3.7	263	25,850
Brazil	**3.3**	**158**	**5,580**
Australia	3.0	18	20,720

Based on data from 1995 World Population Data Sheet and the 1995 *World Factbook*

Yet inland Brazil had the look of a frontier. An unusual statistic presented in the *World Factbook* stands out: Only 7 percent of Brazil's roads are paved. Even Australia, with its frontier Outback, paved half its roads.

Eventually I fell asleep. Despite the novelty of

being in a hammock suspended in an immensity of jungle, my sleep remained free of dreams. I felt I could have slept through a jaguar attack, given the aftereffects of flying on Varig's dead-of-night schedules.

MONDAY, AUG. 8
Strange food combinations

My scant two days at the camp ended, and I had to return to Manaus. Mel and Mario also came along for part of the ride, via a motorized canoe this time. With Christão controlling the outboard, we lounged and looked at the bright sky and fluffy clouds.

The conversation ranged from attitudes about romance and sex to the rude behavior of the German youth at the jungle camp. They seemed to have months to go around Brazil. They used this heaven-sent opportunity not to study the culture, but to brusquely order Christão and the other Indians to run out for more *cachaça* and *cervezas*.

The canoe pulled into the landing near the bus stop. We shared warm goodbyes and, well aware of his pay scale, I tipped Christão. With grave sincerity, he thanked me: "*Muito obrigado.*"

Back in Manaus, I checked into the Hotel Amazonas. I had a few hours to shower, nap and explore before yet another 3 a.m. flight, this one to São Luís.

As I strolled around Manaus just before sunset, strange twilight cloudscapes arranged themselves to the west. In the jungle the night before, the same huge pink thunderheads had seemed appropriately striking and vivid. Their wild look, juxtaposed now against a city skyline, reminded me that all around Manaus, more than 800 miles from the Atlantic Ocean, the next stop in every direction was wilderness.

The famed Teatro Amazonas opera house rated as Manaus's only bona fide attraction. I walked by for a quick look and was not distressed that it was shut. For an incredible sight presented itself: street vendors who sold popcorn covered in ketchup! The sight offended my vestigial French refinement.

LESSON NUMBER 15: A COUNTRY THAT ENCOURAGES KETCHUP ON POPCORN HAS LITTLE CHANCE OF JOINING THE RANKS OF GASTRONOMICALLY ADVANCED NATIONS.

Seeking a place to exchange traveler's checks, I next walked and took buses to the famed Shopping Amazonas. Somehow in the middle of a jungle as sweeping as the entire U.S. Eastern Seaboard, a glitzy, duty-free retail complex had sprouted, complete with a multiplex cinema and familiar chain stores, such as Benetton. I bought a slice of pizza at a stand at the eatery, declining with a shudder an offer of the ubiquitous ketchup.

I decided to call my parents. A pay phone with a

blue metal hood permitted international calls. After many tries I got through to a U.S. operator.

"How's Brazil?" my parents asked in a perfunctory tone.

"It's interesting. I spent last night in the jungle," I replied.

They moved on briskly to more pressing topics. "We're watching the Redskins vs. Buffalo, and it doesn't look good," my mother said. "Buffalo is so polished. The Redskins have a ways to go."

That was Mary Belliveau-speak for "the team is terrible." The Redskins, like her own blood children, receive only tactfully worded criticism. Our chat resembled how, also via long-distance telephone, we lauded or deplored Redskins plays during the regular season.

"They signed Heath Shuler," my father added. I doubled over, trying not to guffaw. Word of a quarterback signing could flash across 3,000 miles, even to a fan one bus trip and one canoe ride away from the pleasant vacuum of jungle newslessness.

Shopping Amazonas employs a macaw motif modeled on the jungle that surrounds Manaus.

TUESDAY, AUG. 9
Do you know the way to São Luís?

More than one Brazilian had clucked in concern at my plan to visit a little-known northeastern city called São Luís, a decision inspired by a conversation that had occurred as I planned my trip.

At the offices of the Brazilian airline Varig, on K Street in Washington, D.C., an agent named Louisa had sold me an air pass permitting visits to five Brazilian cities. She listened gravely as I listed the cities I wanted: Cuiabá, Manaus, Fortaleza, Salvador and a return to Rio de Janeiro.

She folded her arms, tilted her head and stared directly at me. What had I said wrong?

"This route is rather standard. Tell me," she asked, "what are looking for on your trip?"

"Photography and adventure," I said instantly.

"I think," Louisa said, "that you should go to São Luís instead of Fortaleza." She hadn't been there herself, but based her recommendation on reports that state officials in Maranhão, to lure more visitors, had spent millions to restore the old district of São Luís and nearby Alcântara, an even more obscure destination.

I vaguely recalled the description of São Luís in my guidebook: a humid place, population 200,000, at the intersection of two zones, the Amazon rainforest and the Atlantic coast. São Luís had been the only

Brazilian capital founded by the French. They arrived in 1612 and were expelled two years later by the Portuguese.

I noted a favorable omen: My dad's name is Louis. His Acadian mother pronounced it *Lou-ee*, the same as Luís.

"Yeah, I'll take that," I told Louisa.

The choice horrified Luis and Vittoria Macedo, my trip advisers. Telling these chic former *Cariocas* that I planned to visit a Maranhão backwater apparently compared to telling a New Yorker, "I'm going to Mississippi."

"It's poor," said Vittoria, her face creased in a frown. "Nobody goes there. We make jokes about Maranhão."

More derision awaited me my first day on the beach of Ipanema. Jerry and Zach's Brazilian friends could barely disguise their feelings. Jerry translated their mutterings: "They think São Luís is pretty lame."

"Fine," I shrugged. I wondered if *Cariocas* and *Paulistas*, residents of Brazil's two largest cities, ever got out and explored their own country.

I allotted three days for exploring São Luís and Alcântara, a nearly abandoned colonial city an hour's boatride away. If São Luís turned out to be a dud, all the *Cariocas* would feel entitled to say, "I told you so." Only the airline agent and I seemed to think the city rated a roll of the dice.

I looked out the window of the bus bringing me from the São Luís airport to the center of town. These Brazilians came in all the shades of human skin color, "charcoal and rose," as Brazilian singer Marisa Monte noted on her album of that title. The tide of humanity on the streets looked somehow Baltimorean, unpolished people of open expressions moving along to basic jobs. Simple clothes showed a lack of Rio-style money and glitz.

At a tourist office 15 minutes' walk from the bus stop, a young staffer, tellingly, could speak French. She said that I'd missed the 7 a.m. boat to Alcântara but another would leave soon, at 9:15.

I walked downhill quickly, past the intact colonial buildings of São Luís to the waterfront along the Baía de São Marcos. I noted the brightly painted buildings on the small streets. São Luís displayed a faded port atmosphere, comparable to that of Mombasa in Kenya, Cádiz in Spain or Campeche in Mexico's Yucatan.

I sat on a bench near the berthed ferry, near a closed ticket window. A couple from Paris, Denis and Sylvia, also waited. He worked for a French arm of the

Kellogg Co., the cereal maker; she for *Médecins Sans Frontières* (Doctors Without Borders). Handsome and dark-haired, Denis seemed like a more chic and less saccharine version of Alan Alda, with a similar bright smile and cozy sweater. Sylvia's honey-blond hair and heart-shaped face gave her a sweet, serene air, a beauty perhaps both physical and spiritual, given her line of work with volunteer physicians on the front lines of many famines and other disasters.

Their striking Western European attractiveness made me realize that, apart from Marcus, Melissa and Mario, for the past 12 days I had mainly seen dark beauty norms harking to Portugal, Africa, indigenous people or all three. Sylvia's fair hair color seemed as extraordinary to me as it might to a Chinese in a remote village.

Eventually a ticket seller, a tall young man named Toquino, showed up. He spoke no English. Now I was truly in Brazil and would have to sink or swim without the translation assistance of Jerry, Zach, Mario or Melissa.

Toquino asked me something that sounded like the obvious: Did I need a ticket? *"Sim,"* I replied in the affirmative, "Alcântara." He wrote out a ticket and then asked: *"A volta?"*

I pondered. In French, *volte-face* means about-face. So Toquino must be asking me if I wanted a return ticket.

"Sim, a volta," I said.

On the ferry over, Toquino latched on to me. He proved to be an implacable language teacher. We had to discuss the 1994 World Cup match between the United States and Brazil, he decided with great intensity. I understood parts of his Portuguese sentences, and all of his meaning. Toquino grabbed the hair at the back of his head, obviously praising the play of Tony Meola, the ponytailed U.S. goalie.

After an hour, the flaking pastel colors of a row of shops flanking Porto do Jacaré, the landing for Alcântara, hove into view on the right side of a channel. On the left, over an expanse of mangrove, was a vivid sight: an impossibly red bird, as electrically pigmented as the trees of the Pantanal. I whooped out loud at its startling color, which instantly surpassed that of the birds, all four of them, that I'd seen in the Amazon. Toquino said the locals called the bird a *guara*. In English, it is called the scarlet ibis.

A steep street led up from the landing past attached dwellings to a wide grassy square, the Praça da Matriz, surrounded by colonial buildings. I checked into the Pousada Pelourinho, at the north end of the *praça*. In midafternoon, the ferry returned Toquino and a handful of day trippers to São Luís. I seemed to be the only overnight tourist in Alcântara, which the locals pronounced "al-CAN-tra."

At the *pousada*, I tidied up my backpack in my gigantic room, a cube 25 feet in length, width and height, which felt as spacious as a converted barn. My room contained a bed, a table and two chairs, all rattling around in a huge realm. Planks a full foot wide made up the floor.

Massive French doors stretching from the floor almost to the ceiling opened to a balcony. The doors framed a view of the praça. Often no people could be seen, only cows ambling home untended. The emptiness and an ocher tinge to the light lent the square the deserted quality of a painting by Giorgio de Chirico, the Italian artist, yet without his slight hint of menace.

The pousada had formerly served as a bordello. It was much nicer and more atmospheric than the whorehouse/hotel where I had stayed in Diego, Madagascar. With breakfast, the room cost seven reals (about $7) a night.

My comparison meter started to gauge Alcântara. It seemed to me to echo Pompeii, the ghostly, excavated Italian city below Vesuvius, and Albufeira, a seaside resort along the Algarve, the southerly coast of Portugal. Various corners of Brazil reminded me of Australia, East Africa, West Africa, Portugal and other places.

LESSON NUMBER 16: EXTENSIVE TRAVEL CAN BE A BLESSING AND A CURSE. ONE MAY NOT BE ABLE TO TELL IF A COUNTRY IS EXCEPTIONALLY DERIVATIVE—OR IF ONE HAS SEEN TOO MUCH, SUCH THAT LITTLE IN THE WORLD APPEARS MARVELOUS AND ORIGINAL ANY MORE.

About 90 minutes before sunset, I walked out the northeast corner of the praça and through the town to take photographs in the golden light. No one stirred along the Rua Grande, a street lacking not only vehicles but people, displaying only its beautifully dilapidated low façades. To get even one person in my photos, which might make the place seem merely desolate as opposed to utterly abandoned, I often had to wait a while.

Macondo! I thought. It's certainly a cliché to compare the legion of Latin American towns bypassed by politics or economics to the celebrated Colombian city of Gabriel García Márquez's *One Hundred Years of Solitude*. But Alcântara seemed to qualify admirably. Money had been poured into rehabbing the place, yet so far only a handful of tourists had visited. The town still felt like a living museum.

Music drifted out of some of the homes. Brazilian pop displayed the melodic quality of the early Beatles and felt like an integral soundtrack composed for this exact spot in the universe. For such a worn-out part of the world, the home stereo systems sounded of high quality.

At intervals I saw at four soccer games, each involving such deflated balls that they might as well have been wadded bits of cardboard. To break the ice,

I pointed to the young players. "Bebeto! Leonardo! Romario!" I tried to pronounce the last star player's name as Brazilians seemed to: "ho-MAH-hrio."

The boys beamed at being compared to the national team's one-named aces. I asked *"permiso"* to shoot pictures, and they became the first children I could ever recall saying *"obrigado"* (thank you) after I snapped the shutter.

Perhaps Brazilians enjoyed having an American visitor in the year the World Cup had been held in the States. A woman sitting on her front steps inquired, *"Suiço? Alamão?"* She looked quite happy when I replied, *"Estados Unidos."*

Many locals asked me questions. As this was my first day immersed in Portuguese, I often could not understand them. I would provide a relaxed statement anyway, hoping I had guessed the question. I probably carried my half of the conversation on a quite separate topic, resembling the Monty Python tobacconists' sketch. Everyone had the exquisite charity, however, not to act puzzled.

I looked into small homes made of a type of cinder block. Past an open door, a boy in a front room snapped a towel at his brother, as Grandma, in a hammock, watched with a toothless grin. We exchanged smiles.

Women on the narrow side streets sorted rice and laughed and told stories, scenes to delight an artist or photographer. A woman watered the plants in her side-yard container garden.

As I explored, at 6 p.m. drummers and trumpeters marched unseen but clearly heard around the nearby hills—a trick worthy of Márquez's magical realism.

I eventually returned to the pousada. Three boys clustered shyly outside the entrance, staring at me. Luis, 13, Fernando, 12, and Ivan, also 12, all looked closer to 8 years old.

I opened my Lonely Planet guide to Brazil and showed them some color photographs of Alcântara and other parts of their homeland.

They crowded around and then told me the history of their town. They pointing to the *pelourinho,* a whipping post standing across the square from the pousada.

Remarkably for children partly African blooded, in eerily perfect mime they re-enacted the punishment of a slave. One boy slumped dejectedly as though slipping down the whipping post, pantomiming his hands tied behind his back.

Another wielded an air whip. "Toooshh, toooosh," he said, the

A whipping post stands in the praça at Alcântara. Background, the Pousada Pelourinho appears.

noise a bit unnerving even in a reenactment. I watched silently as these doe-eyed children dealt unsentimentally with slavery.

I introduced myself, giving the Brazilian pronunciation, "Jah-NET-jeh." *"Escola?"* I asked, a one-word question as I didn't know all the words for, "What school do you go to?"

"Jawwnn Ken-NEJZ-huh," said Luis, the rolling pronunciation rendering the name of his school into a mini-samba. The only reason I comprehended what he said was that I'd taken pictures of John F. Kennedy School during my afternoon photo safari. A number of Brazilians told me that Kennedy, three decades after his death, continued to be held in high esteem.

Before bed, I examined the inn's guestbook, a giant ledger with browning pages. It revealed that I was the first American to stay overnight in 18 months, and maybe the second in a long, long while, perhaps two decades.

Ten days into this trip, I had met only one fellow American tourist, Melissa, in the entire nation outside of Rio de Janeiro. Certainly the exchange rate was atrocious. Yet I had a sneaking feeling that Americans had a troubling incuriosity about this entire region, a blind spot that may hamper the United States should Brazil gather political and economic strength.

WEDNESDAY, AUG. 10
Zinha's love and language lessons

As I ate breakfast on the praça, at a round table with a Cinzano umbrella, a loud radio could be heard from the hotel bar, playing "Magic" by Olivia Newton-John, followed by a jingle for Coca-Cola in Portuguese. I wondered again, as with the Amazonian Indians who played Foreigner, why local people turned their backs on their own music.

An elderly woman shuffled across the square, leaning on her walking stick. She looked like she hailed directly from Ghana, with her angular Picasso cheekbones, weathered face of dark ebony, and scarlet headwrap and matching dress with silver vertical stripes on its bodice.

She spoke at length, fixing a direct gaze upon me, as though she were a priestess trying to divine the essence of my self. She used the word *agradavel.* Later I looked up the term, which means pleasant or nice. I wanted to believe she was a seer and had complimented me, a complete stranger, accurately. But who knows, maybe she was only discussing the weather.

I walked out of the main town of Alcântara and down a cliff-side path to the local beach, the Praia de Baronessa. Two scarlet ibises rooted in the exposed mud flats of low tide, their color even more attention-getting than the hue of the hyacinth macaw.

That evening in Alcântara, I joined a woman named Zinha, the proprietress of the Pousada Pelourinho, on the praça for a drink.

Zinha, 38 years old and a Susan Sarandon looka-like, owned the pousada, a pizza stand and sundry other properties around the square. She expounded on her well-developed *philosophie d'amour*.

Without hesitation she divulged her life story, most notably her acquisition of seven husbands. The first, a pilot resembling Tom Cruise, she married when she was 15. *"Tupp Gawn!"* she exclaimed. He was a handsome man, she said, who died in an airplane crash when she was 18. Zinha's subsequent husbands had included Swiss and Spanish men. If I followed her correctly, more than one had been named Marcos.

As we talked, a remarkable phenomenon occurred. I began to speak Portuguese. Zinha's clear, slow pronunciation and contextual clues made her a fine teacher.

"Vôce gosta de homens lindos," I said, to my own great surprise. In Portuguese, Zinha confirmed my observation. "I am not beautiful," she said, with excessive modesty. "But yes, I like handsome men."

Zinha had been at the pousada 15 years and said that I was only the second American tourist to stay overnight in Alcântara. She had been occupied with so many of her own weddings, though, I wondered if she might have missed the arrival of others.

Suddenly, six Americans, plainly not tourists, entered the praça. They were part of a group of 65 or more NASA scientists and other staff helping a Brazilian team launch rockets at a modern facility four miles from sleepy Alcântara.

The NASA fellows were in Brazil either to measure a dip in the strength of gravity at the equator or, as the story evolved over Antarctica beer, to make certain that the Brazilians didn't put any warheads atop their Titan boosters.

They joined us to participate in Zinha's love and philosophy discussion group under the stars.

"I've heard the AIDS rate is 10 percent in Alcântara," said one of the scientists, a Marylander named Dean, "and 20 percent in São Luís."

Zinha wrinkled her nose in disgust. "Men in Brazil, sexsexsexsexsex," she said in Portuguese, and no translation was required.

The pousada's stereo stayed tuned to a São Luís radio station, playing all the hits of yesteryear: Bobby Goldsboro, Pink Floyd, Bronski Beat and Boz Scaggs.

Mark, a broad-shouldered ex-Marine from the NASA Wallops Flight Facility on Virginia's Eastern

Shore, began to tease Zinha fondly. "Zinha, how's my Portuguese? Zinha! We're here to teach you English. *Fala inglês!*" Speak English, he told her, in acceptable Portuguese.

"Fala Port-inglês," Zinha shot back. Speak a mixture!

A guided tour of Alcântara

Tomais, 24, a local guide, took me around for the day. He provided his version of local history. Alcântara was founded in 1648, he said. What now were ruins in the praça had at various times been a prison, a prefecture and a church. Tomais claimed a population of 13,000 in Alcântara, 12,800 of whom I saw no sign of.

He showed me the ruins of the slave market. Goats cropped the grass between its roofless walls of brown stone. In the background, the sun washed over a brilliantly white church. I thought as I watched the

Goats crop the grass outside the former slave market.

goats how time simply didn't register in Alcântara. The women sorted rice, the boys played soccer, and not much else seemed to happen. The natural world showed the greatest activity. Huge tides in the Baía de São Marcos set a rhythm, rolling out to expose mud flats where the supernaturally red *guara* fed.

I was seeing an arrested version of the decline of Macondo at the end of *One Hundred Years of Solitude*, "a plain of wild grass," where the "lizards and rats fought over the inheritance of the nearby church." Whereas quasi-fictional Macondo fell when a banana company departed, Alcântara's fortunes had been tied to sugar and cotton.

Now the region may liven up again, given the presence of the rocket-launching facility. Similarly, São Luís appeared to be on an upswing, with iron ore and oil recently discovered in the region. The twin cities also benefited from the 1985-88 presidency of José Sarney, originally from Maranhão, who helped obtain more than $25 million in restoration funds.

In the afternoon, I boarded the return ferry to São Luís. That day the water seemed shockingly turbid, the filthiest I'd seen, perhaps due to oil drilling in the area. Waves looked more like sewage than water. A smell similar to that of cat food hung over the bay. I guessed it might be the odor of dead shrimp.

After the ferry docked, I checked into the Hotel Lord and then wandered around São Luís. I stopped to eat at a pizza place. Hundreds of people down the street were listening to a band playing a type of reggae with a Brazilian tinge. When my food arrived, a little boy walked in and tapped my elbow.

"What do you want?" I asked.

"Pizza," he said simply.

I nodded and indicated with my raised index finger, *one moment*. The request struck me as remarkable: In the Yucatan and Madagascar, cynical children had asked me for money, never food. The boy retreated to the street, where a little girl also waited. I cut up a huge slice I had planned to cart around for lunch the next day, making four pieces, two for each child. I wrapped the food in napkins and handed it over. The girl smiled angelically. They would be less hungry, and I had less to carry.

At the end of the evening, I walked back to my hotel. Rua de Nazaré, as steep as any street in San Francisco, connected the upper and lower parts of São Luís. Brass carriage lights shone on buttercup-yellow house façades.

At the foot of a wide terrace of worn steps, on the side street of Rua do Giz, a dozen teenagers and small children conducted a jam session.

A black youth, about 15 years old and wearing a pink T-shirt, coaxed a symphony of rhythm from his tambourine:

BANG BANG BANG BANG.
BANG BANG BANG BANG.

He danced the samba hip to hip with a young coffee-colored girl. A white boy added an acoustic guitar. Their sound was *forró*, the music of Brazil's Northeast. The music resembles Louisiana's zydeco and serves the same cultural niche as country & western in the United States, with songs about lovin' and cheatin' and hardscrabble lives.

A Salvador vendor prepares *acarajé*, a ball of dried shrimp, beans, onions and pepper fried in dendê (palm) oil.

Then the players gave their music a harder edge. The other children danced like M.C. Hammer. A trio of locals leaned out from a wrought-iron balcony on a second story to watch as a tiny girl wearing a frilly white dress danced with the others.

This pure and delicate moment demonstrated how music defines Brazil. It showed how the closing scene of the 1959 movie *Black Orpheus,* of exuberant children dancing and singing in the slums high above Rio, was utterly faithful to reality.

A cool breeze rattled the palms. I sat on a terrace, half-hidden by a palm tree, not wishing to distract the juvenile musicians. For once, I kept my camera stowed. The spontaneous harmony of Brazil's children seemed too sacred for intrusion by outsiders.

That night in São Luís, I fell asleep with my ear glued to the radio of my personal stereo. São Luís had stations that played much more interesting fare than Bobby Goldsboro. I listened for an hour in thrall to captivating tunes.

Knowing that I would probably hear these songs but once in my life made listening bittersweet. These artists were not the familiar ones whose recordings one could readily buy in the States—Milton Nascimento, Margarethe Menezes, Caetano Veloso—but they seemed equally lovely. Single hearings on late-night radio almost qualified as torture, as though the stations were playing fabulous found music, the popular equivalent to Mozart, only once in all eternity. Listening to the radio that night felt like a dream or being in a drugged state, where music possesses an otherworldly beauty. If only I could tape this stuff and put out a compact disc entitled *Late-Night Radio, São Luís, 1994,* to capture and share these sounds now being lost in the ether.

FRIDAY, AUG. 12
Exploring America's Africa

Much as black Americans are most likely to visit the western nations if they go to Africa, when they go to Brazil they tend to visit Salvador.

The reason became apparent after my airplane landed in Salvador and I made my way by two buses to the Praça Pelourinho, "whipping post square." The praça serves as the equivalent of Kingston in Jamaica or Dakar in Senegal, an New African whirl of dreadlocks swinging and snare-drums cracking. African-Americans who had visited both Africa and Salvador told a *Los Angeles Times* reporter in 1994 that they felt closer to Afro-Brazilians, who shared the history of being slaves in the New World.

At 9 p.m., I walked along the narrow streets lined with bars and coffee shops just north of the praça. A slender black man, with an open and gentle face like Sugar Ray Leonard's, sang lyrically and played an amplified acoustic guitar in front of one bar. Four percussionists, with skin colors ranging from coal to café, accompanied him. Couples danced in the street, and then a conga line formed.

I wandered up the Rua João de Deus, past the Dida Escola de Musica. An impromptu concert was about to begin in the tiny street. Two young women wearing head mikes stood in the door of the music school. They started off a cappella with much note bending and repetition, like Algerian *rai* or Arabic music.

Filling the street were about 60 women arrayed in

10 rows possessing every size of drum. As the women sang, a conductress cued the drummers. The bass drum repeated five deep soft notes:

BumbumbumbumBUM.
[Pause.] BumbumbumbumBUM.

Over and over, on top of the bass drum came the cantering toms and snares:

Tap, tapatapa tap, tapatapa tap.

Drums of other sizes joined the aural assault. The sound gathered force until it seemed to equal that of a symphony orchestra. The drums felt all encompassing, like the animal and insect drone of the Amazon.

Two drummer girls in the second row threw their heads back, shoved their padded drumsticks to the sky and abandoned themselves to ancient dances. Flinging their arms back, they shouted, "*Axé!*" The expression, pronounced ah-SHAY in Yoruba, refers to God's cosmic force on Earth, and to the drum-based music of Bahia.

A crowd gathered to dance. Three street urchins, sporting the cloth wristbands worn by Brazilians for good luck, danced Hammer style, flinging out limbs with enormous energy. I began to dance, standing in the broad sill of a large shuttered window overlooking the street. Others gyrated on the second-story balcony of a nearby restaurant.

A skinny dark man, his back to the drummers, directed an ad hoc dance troupe. Line dancers threw both hands left and then right, and then raised their arms as though caressing the moon. They bowed and stepped back like the Temptations, performing perhaps a combination of harvest symbolism and *Soul Train*.

A boy with thick black hair, glasses and a blue windbreaker aped the skinny man's fluid moves quite well. The boy was white and nerdy looking. But he was, after all, Brazilian. He whipped his torso back and forth and kicked back one bent leg, then another, with rhythm and grace.

The drummers' song began a decrescendo, as the smaller and then the medium-sized drums fell silent. The music faded to the bass drums and then nothing, as the white boy, still dancing, slowly descended the street and disappeared into the crowds on the square.

SATURDAY, AUG. 13
A candomblé feast day

At the tourist office, a woman provided me with an address in Mussurrunga, a neighborhood perhaps 20 miles east of the city center, practically as distant as the airport. A *candomblé* ceremony in the neighborhood that night would mark the annual feast day of Iemanjá, the goddess of the ocean.

A travel video on Brazil that my parents had given me showed participants in the African-based religion, a cousin to voodoo, shaking and shimmying, leaning back with their arms raised. Their eyes rolled into their heads as they entered trances. Participants believe that they act as mediums to particular gods. Sometimes first-time observers are shocked to find themselves in trances, too.

Salvador leads Brazil in the practice of candomblé, with 4,000 *terreiros* or centers for worship.

African religions in the New World

CANDOMBLÉ IS ONE OF MANY NEW WORLD MANIFESTATIONS OF AFRICAN RELIGIONS BLENDED WITH CHRISTIANITY.

Candomblé	Brazil
Voodoo	Haiti
Santeria	Cuba and Puerto Rico
Shango	Trinidad and Tobago, Venezuela and Brazil
Kumina	Jamaica

Getting to the ceremony first required taking several buses that passed along perhaps 15 miles of beaches east of Salvador. Every 50 yards of beach seemed to be hosting a separate soccer game.

LESSON NUMBER 17: NO WONDER BRAZILIANS DOMINATED SOCCER: THEY PLAYED CONSTANTLY AND OFTEN HAD TO WORK HARD TO COUNTER THE INCLINE OF A BEACH AND THE RESISTANCE OF THE SAND.

After $2^1/_2$ hours, I finally arrived at a suburb called Itapão. A cabbie took me inland to find the Terreiro Guineara Koongo, an unadorned, low white building along a thinly developed neighborhood street. The name apparently referred to two West African nations.

Four participants who had arrived early for the 8 p.m. celebration welcomed me. They offered me fruit juice and indicated that I should wait for a moment. They fetched a man named Emile, who said he could understand my English if I spoke slowly.

With his glasses, thin face, dark short hair and trimmed moustache, he resembled Jean-Bertrand Aristide, Haiti's sober-looking but revolutionary cleric. We shared big smiles and an instant rapport after I noted that my grandfather had also been named Emile.

Emile, originally from Rio, said he had two children but was *separado* from his wife. He had visited Spain and Portugal and worked as a chemical engineer. I wondered, why did a learned man practice voodoo? The question may sound insulting, as it implies that florid religiosity is only for the ignorant. Yet scholars have begun to find that trance-based and evangelical religions are not necessarily lower-class phenomena.

LESSON NUMBER 18: THE WIDE APPEAL OF CANDOMBLÉ TO BRAZIL'S MIDDLE CLASS MAY REST UPON SEVERAL FACTORS:

• **BRAZIL HAS ALWAYS HAD A SHORTAGE OF CATHOLIC PRIESTS, SO AFRICAN RELIGIONS OFTEN TAKE THE PLACE OF THE ROMAN CHURCH FOR EVERYDAY PRACTICES. FORMAL CHRISTIANITY WAS SAVED FOR FORMAL RITUALS SUCH AS BAPTISMS.**

• **THE SAINTS WORSHIPPED IN CANDOMBLÉ HAVE SUBSTANTIAL RESEMBLANCE TO CATHOLIC SAINTS, MAKING WORSHIP ACCESSIBLE TO THE DESCENDANTS OF EUROPEANS.**

• **BRAZILIANS, LIKE THE IRISH AND BALINESE, ARE A GENUINELY SPIRITUAL PEOPLE, AND MAGIC AND MYSTICISM COLOR DAILY LIFE.**

"What do you think of Brazil?" Emile asked.

I thought to myself how Brazil seemed to suffer a bit in comparison to Africa or Asia, continents stupendously blessed with peerless people and scenery. (However, this critical perception may have resulted from moodiness linked to Lariam, the powerful malarial drug I was taking.) Brazil offered lighter and airier attractions: birds, music, the lightning of the Amazon. In Brazil, bright scarlet and hyacinth macaws chattered, whereas in Tanzania, lionesses sighed with majestic fatigue after killing their prey.

This intricate line of thought defied expression in simple English and would be too disappointing for Emile, who regarded me with hopeful expectation. He seemed proud of his homeland. I stayed on the safe topic of sports. "I think *futt-gee-bawl* is number 1," I said.

Emile smiled. He led me into the terreiro for a tour. The large squarish room, perhaps 50 feet on each side, featured an alcove in a corner to the right. In it stood a colorfully decorated shrine crisscrossed with paper streamers of green and yellow—Brazil's colors, much in evidence during this World Cup victory year.

The shrine contained a three-foot-high cowboy mannequin with a vaguely Howdy Doodyish grin and a cobra skin draped on his shoulders. Vases of flowers surrounded his image. The mahogany-skinned mannequin represented a minor god, a *caboclo* (Portuguese-Indian) cowboy named Pedra Preta, or black stones. He served as a messenger to major gods.

The room itself looked like a high school auditorium decorated for the prom. Silver stars and hundreds of small white paper strips hung from the ceiling. Animal horns hung from the wall. Two leaping fish made of glitter paper decorated the latticework marking off a little stand for the drummers. Laurel leaves lay scattered on an otherwise spotless floor.

The congregants entered the terreiro, women standing left of the door, men on the right. Just as the ceremony was to begin, my hopes of being one of a handful of tourists disappeared. Vans had zipped directly over from hotels near the Praça Pelourinho. Only a minute before the ceremony, 30 tourists, who had arrived by far simpler means than I, entered the room with great rustle and commotion. More women, mostly Europeans, joined me on the left side of the room. My view partly blocked by the late arrivals, I had to crane my neck to see the ceremony.

A circle dance of 11 women and one young man began to shuffle clockwise, calmly at first and then with more agitation. The man wore a bandolier of beads over a white shirt and trousers. The women wore beads, hoop skirts and head wraps of brightly printed cloth, and white cotton blouses and white lace cummerbunds. The clothes, which set off their dark skin tones, resembled those seen in old etchings of Haiti and the early American South.

A woman representing Iemanjá, the goddess of the ocean, wore a visor of gold strings that almost covered her face. A second woman portrayed another of the 100 or so *orixás* (gods), Oxúm, the goddess of fresh water and a symbol of feminine power. She wielded a gold sword.

The woman portraying Oxúm was heavyset, and a layer of fat covered her back. Her broad face was coarse featured, and she bent over in an unflattering way to show her bloomers. Yet the fabrics, styled on African patterns, flattered her. And somehow she radiated an acceptance of herself and a belief in her attractiveness and magnetism.

On a stage, the main drummer and a singer chanted. Two other drummers also kept rhythm on *atabaque* drums, about 3 feet tall. The chants appeared to be in a non-European, singsong language with a texture quite reminiscent of the sound of Nigerian *juju* artist King Sunny Adé—Yoruba, as Emile and my guidebook confirmed after the ceremony.

Remarkably, at the close of the 20th century, Brazilians could chant in a language spoken daily by 20 million people in Nigeria and Benin, whose sound is mimicked in the talking drums used by *juju* musicians.

During the first hour, the women continued their shuffling dance, bending double to grasp laurel leaves off the floor. They made restrained hand motions, gently pushing the palm forward, that suggested cleaning and primping.

The American tourists, two women from New York whom I spoke with later, displayed respect for the ceremony. The Euros spanned the spectrum from intrigued to bored to rude. A blond woman resembling Madonna chattered away in Italian at my left. I shushed her. She kept right on talking to a boyfriend who stood outside the window. As at the Indian camp in the Amazon, with its overbearing young Germans, it seemed the torch of the "Ugly American" was now widely shared with other nationalities.

White interest in African culture

After the candomblé ceremony, a white woman from Brooklyn, her light brown hair crew cut except for a single long braid, asked me to describe São Luís, and I recommended that she visit there.

She seemed quite interested in São Luís and Salvador, two of Brazil's most African places. I wondered later why some white people, myself and others, hold such an interest in places linked to the African diaspora?

Maybe whites view Africans, as well as Asians and American Indians, as more mystical, sensual or spiritual. Once upon a time, our European pagan ancestors—especially the Celts, found from the Black Sea to Ireland—knew

A woman wears traditional dress on Salvador's Praça Pelourinho. Female candomblé worshippers wear similar headwraps, blouses and skirts.

lives of sorcery, magic, feasting, drinking and fighting. But this exotic, wild facet of Europe has been submerged for more than a thousand years.

Perhaps some whites admire the African capacity for rapture and release, the way the young drummers could throw their arms in the air and shout passionately, "*Axé!*"

For me, the interest probably began the way it did for many white kids of the 1960s: with the music of Aretha Franklin, Wilson Pickett, Junior Walker, James Brown and others. Given the great appeal today of rap music to white suburbanites, and the immense popularity of Michael Jordan and other sports figures, white fascination with African-American culture is not at all rare.

The authors of *The Altruistic Personality*, Samuel P. and Pearl M. Oliner, describe a simple explanation for those who take an interest in other cultures. Children of secure families, they indicated,

> often extend trust to others more readily. Persuaded that attachment rather than status is the source of basic life gratifications, as they mature they choose friends on the basis of affection rather than social class, religion or ethnicity. … They feel more comfortable dealing with people different from themselves and are readier to emphasize the likenesses that bind them to others than the distinctions that separate them.

A white Brazilian couple joined in singing an "*ayé ayé*" response. For the Yoruba tribe, *ayé* is the visible, tangible world of the living, while *orun* is the world of spirits and ancestors—who visit *ayé* when worshippers enter trances.

A black man in tie-dye and dashiki, who resembled Marion Barry circa 1968, had warmly welcomed their arrival. The white man looked almost exactly like Richard Nixon, a seemingly odd resemblance for someone at an African-derived religious ritual. The woman had a tossed blond mane of Mae West hair on a tiny body. They, along with most of the other worshippers, were dressed head to foot in white. My guidebook had noted that visitors should try to wear white and not brown, purple or black.

The second half of the ceremony started with two of the 75 or so congregants throwing scented blossoms over us. The drums picked up. The dancers twisted their torsos left and right as they continued the overall clockwise movement. Finally, the awaited moment arrived: They entered trances. A man's eyes snapped shut in his upturned face. Other women entered appeared to enter spells, establishing contact with Iemanjá. They bobbed at the waist, eyes shut, with their faces toward the floor.

A woman with straightened hair and glasses placed her hands on the shoulders of a woman in a trance to lend her support. The gesture uncannily resembled the finale of a James Brown concert in the 1960s, when the drained singer would begin to move offstage, and an aide would gently place a cape over his shoulders. Brown would theatrically fling the cape off and summon enough energy for one last song.

LESSON NUMBER 19: THE CANDOMBLÉ PERFORMANCE IN MUSSURRUNGA ILLUSTRATED THAT ASPECTS OF JAMES BROWN'S PERFORMANCES GO BACK NOT JUST TO MACON, GEORGIA, BUT ALL THE WAY TO NIGERIA AND BENIN.

One goddess held out her skirt for money, and I tossed in a few coins. Then the service ended, and a man offered us plates with little samples of food.

I spoke with a dance student from New York, a young, attractive black woman, who had studied African dance in particular. "I've been to East Africa," I said, "and it's got nothing to do with this."

She nodded. "Country by country, within West African even, there are variations," she said. She explained that the gestures we'd observed represented women grooming themselves, for their own appreciation rather than that of a suitor.

"Are you too young for James Brown?" I asked her.

"No," she said, smiling instantly and nodding.

SUNDAY, AUG. 14

Beaches and a drum show

I took the ferry to Itaparica, an island south of Salvador. Its beaches, such as the Barra Grande, had an empty peacefulness that I preferred to the jammed ocean-side of Rio. Three riders on two horses cantered by. A boy of African darkness was teaching a darkly beautiful *morena* girl how to ride the trailing horse. He tapped their mount with a thin cane.

A couple rides along the Itaparica.

The image of the couple, like that of the children playing street music in São Luís, summed up Brazil. When I later read John Updike's novel *Brazil*, an update of the Tristan and Isolt myth, the couple in my mind's eye looked like the boy and girl I saw on Itaparica.

That evening, I returned to the Praça Pelourinho to watch Olodum, a Bahian drumming and vocal ensemble of international renown. Olodum, whose name means God in Yoruba, had backed Paul Simon on his song "The Curious Child."

Each song began with a cappella singing. An audience of thousands in the praça began to twitch and dance and swoop as the rat-a-tat-tat of axé began. The Praça Pelourinho had to be the most steeply inclined and most African-feeling dance floor in the Americas. Everyone really began to gyrate at the deeper tom-tom attack:

bum-bum-bum da-da-da-da bum-bum-bum.

Olodum's singer sang over and over of "Af-ree-kah, Af-ree-kah." Most in the crowd knew the words of the songs, repetitive like Islamic prayers. Olodum's lyrics cited Ethiopia, Atlantis, Brixton (a West Indian neighborhood in South London) and Jamaica. The singers extolled the dark queen of Madagascar, Ranavalona, and the rebel slave Zumbi.

"Duas Histórias" com-

pared the Sahara and Brazil's Northeast, united in ancient geography and modern suffering. More than 100 million years ago, when the continents of South America and Africa were still joined, Nigeria and Brazil also touched each other. Continental drift created an ocean, crossed by Africans sorrowfully during the Middle Passage and later optimistically as Afro-Brazilians maintained cultural links to their racial mother.

At the high end of the steeply sloping square, big, blond, crewcut guys towered above the rest of the crowd. The frigate USS *Samuel B. Roberts*, repaired after almost breaking in two in 1988 when it struck an Iranian mine in the Persian Gulf, had arrived in port.

"I'm from Ohio. Where you from?" a sailor asked me. Others hailed from Delaware and New York, and wove drunkenly on their feet, beers in hand.

More interested in the music than drunken sailors, I returned to the body of the crowd. I took up at the side of the praça, behind a little wooden stand selling beer and soft drinks. A fellow there passed me a Coke for a quick swig.

Everyone dancing near the beer stand laughed as a sailor, prostitute in hand, raced down the praça to board a waiting taxi. One onlooker mimicked the sailor's uneasy gait. Other sailors, looking unnerved by the scene, walked swiftly to the bottom of the praça for taxies that would whisk them back to port.

A handsome couple observed these goings-on from a post near the taxies. The dark-haired man resembled Alec Baldwin or Chris Isaak. His girlfriend had long blond hair. They acted cool yet seemed a bit … perhaps not fearful exactly, but weighing, weighing, weighing: *Are we safe because we are beautiful, or are we unsafe because we are white?* At least they appeared more self-possessed than the sailors, who looked either

Olodum's ranks of drummers energize a huge crowd in Salvador.

stricken or oblivious to the fact they had stumbled onto a musicalized black nationalist address.

It seemed from their behavior that some of the whites present felt a little overwhelmed by the otherness of black people en masse. I felt this otherness in Olodum's cries of "Af-ree-kah" and "Etiop" and their wailing about the slave ships, all set to angry-sounding drums. I felt the otherness, as I had in Kenya upon hearing the *whummhhhh* accompanying the Masai dances—the chesty Darth Vader bass that few whites have. And Salvador's singers and dancers could let go of the conscious self and readily experience release.

But I was not uncomfortable. I was treated like a guest by a group near the beer stand, who offered drinks from time to time, much as the congregants had been welcoming the night before at the candomblé ceremony.

MONDAY, AUG. 15
Children who assist travelers

The fame of Cachoiera, a city of 28,000 located 75 miles west of Salvador, rests upon an annual celebration of black liberation from slavery, the Festa da Nossa Senhora de Boa Morte. I arrived four days too early for the celebration. So for me, Cachoiera's appeal came from the way its children, like those at Alcântara, would talk to you.

On my last full day in Brazil, I descended from the bus from Salvador and promptly ran into little Antonio. The small, bright-eyed boy showed me the market and an art museum devoted to Hansen Bahia, a German-born artist who dedicated himself to making lithographs of the Middle Passage. For $5, I purchased a print depicting a slave who had hanged himself in the hold of a ship. The scene reminds me of a story recounted in the 1991 film *Daughters of the Dust*, which described how some slaves arriving at the Sea Islands off Georgia and South Carolina looked at America and, seeing their future, walked back into the surf and drowned themselves.

Antonio led me down the main street and into the Praça da Aclamaçao. As we peered at the ruins of an old prison, the Casa da Câmara e Cadeia, a fellow tourist strolled up.

Lode—blond, thin and about 5 feet 10 inches tall—

Understanding clues in foreign languages

Lode and I talked about the patterns and vocabulary of Portuguese, and the Belgian appliance distributor made a point about how its participles and infinitives compared with English. A similar conversation was impossible to imagine with the average product of U.S. schools working in a comparable blue-collar job. A non-professional American would be unlikely to possess Lode's grammar, language and geographic skills or to be traveling solo in Brazil. For that matter, few American families speak four languages, as did Lode's fellow Belgians, the family I met in the Pantanal who ran a photocopying center back home.

Else Hamayan wrote in *The Need for Foreign Language Competence in the United States* that

> The geographic isolation of the United States and the growing importance of English in the world have contributed to giving Americans a false sense of security vis à vis their need for foreign language competence.

U.S. students in foreign language courses

	GRADES 9-12	COLLEGE	OBTAINING DEGREE
1970-71	28%	13%	2.4%
1980-82	23	8	1.3
1990	38	9	1.1

Based on data in *Digest of Educational Statistics 1994* and the *Statistical Abstract of the United States 1995*

Despite the dominance of English worldwide, understanding other languages is crucial to divining the clues to culture and thinking patterns essential for conducting business effectively. With better language skills, General Motors staff would not have tried to market the Chevrolet Nova ("it doesn't go" in Spanish) in Latin America. And Asian languages often point to differences with Western thought. Frances FitzGerald wrote in *The Fire in the Lake* of how the Vietnamese language conveys its people's intellectual framework. "Struggle," "peace" and many other words convey vastly different meanings than in English, contributing to profound U.S. misunderstanding and political and military blundering in Southeast Asia.

The Clinton administration and various business schools have recog-

nized the need for U.S. competency in foreign languages. The good news is that more high school students are taking foreign languages. The bad news is that fewer college students are, and only 14,000 bachelor's degrees in foreign languages were awarded in 1992. Further, only 6 percent of elementary students—at the best age to study foreign languages—are enrolled in these classes.

In all subjects, not just foreign languages, we poorly educate our workers not bound for college. MIT Professor Lester Thurow noted in 1992 in *Head to Head: The Coming Economic Battle Among Japan, Europe, and America* that K-12 education for the "bottom half" of the U.S. population lags far behind that for comparable Western Europeans and Japanese. He wrote that "the United States is unique among industrial countries in that it does not have an organized post-secondary system for the non-college-bound." Meeting Lode and other Belgians in Brazil lent support to Thurow's observations.

had three months' vacation available from his job in Belgium handling distribution for a chain of appliance stores. He had originally planned to go to China but couldn't get a visa. So instead he decided to swing through much of Brazil, Bolivia and Peru and rendezvous with his wife in La Paz.

Lode hailed from Bruges, a beautiful canal city that I had visited during a 1980 cycling trip through the Low Countries. I could never pronounce his name quite correctly—it was something like LO-gee.

We all walked to have soft drinks at a nearby bar, which featured walls covered by intricate, high-quality wood carvings of various *orixás*.

There we met a raft of other kids: a most engaging 11-year-old named Andre, his brother, Luis, 14, and a girl named Yvett. They borrowed my guidebook to Brazil and read it, fascinated. They possessed loads of charm and a fearless approach to English, which they had begun to learn in school.

We spoke with Andre, a child with melting eyes and smile, in what Zinha would have termed *Port-inglês*. "Do you know what occupation you want to follow?"

Andre: "*A guia!*" (A guide.)

Me: "But you are *in-tell-ih-hent-je* (intelligent)."

Lode: "What about something professional? *Médico?*"

Me: "*Universidade?*"

Andre agreed amiably and perhaps half-seriously. We tried to plant a seed for him to aim high with his intelligence.

At around 9 p.m., our youthful guides heard firecrackers. "*Candomblé!*" they exclaimed, a command to follow them. We trotted down the street to the steps of a landing on the Rio Paraguaçu. Two canoes prepared to push off, bearing women dressed in white for a curtainraiser for the Boa Morte festival. Two of the women quarreled over who was going to wear a giant white headdress, detracting from the solemnity of the occasion.

Unfortunately, I could get only one quick photograph of the women, as Antonio had used up almost all my film taking dozens of unauthorized, out-of-focus pictures of us at the bar.

We all returned for a last round of drinks. Lode talked about the ignorance of Americans on group tours of Europe. "They almost don't know if London is in France or England," he said. "Independent travelers are better."

"Oh yeah," I said with a shrug. "We're a continental nation. What do we know about anybody else?"

We played a map game. Drawing on memories of my 1980 bicycle tour through Lode's home town, I drew the Netherlands and Belgium. I plotted the places I could remember: Rotterdam, Texel, Den Helder, Vlissingen, Bruges and Zeebrugge.

Lode evaluated my work. I'd given lots of

Northern France to Belgium and had no accurate idea of where Antwerp or Ghent were. Lode neatly rebordered the map and finished it.

"Can you do U.S. cities?" I asked.

He shook his head. "No."

"C'mon," I said, outlining the United States. Lode drew on request Seattle, San Francisco, Los Angeles, New York, Baltimore and Miami, all close to perfectly located. Chicago he placed near Oklahoma City, and Minneapolis was too far south. Yet overall, his knowledge was excellent, especially considering he had not visited the United States.

Lode, a Belgian with a job as an appliance distributor, could analyze Portuguese grammar and could locate major U.S. cities—knowledge that many Americans of higher professional standing could not demonstrate with regard to language or geography.

Brazil and the big lesson: racial democracy

For obvious reasons, race relations in the United States and Brazil, the two biggest nations to experience modern slavery, are often compared.

In Brazil, a national mythos evolved beginning in the 1920s, when observers such as Gilberto Freyre espoused the notion of "racial democracy." This theory held that Brazil was a less racist society than the United States, as evidenced by a lack of formal segregation and negrophobia and a notion that upward mobility was available to skilled blacks. Social observers also cited the cult of *mulatta* beauty, a preference by Brazilian males for dark-eyed, mixed-race women.

A 1967 travel guide to Brazil, for example, noted cheerily that

> The populace ranges from blondes with blue eyes to dark-skinned Negroes and many strains between, yet racial discrimination is virtually unknown.

A college textbook used in my 1974 class on "The Sociology of Racism" at the University of Maryland similarly cited the "relative lack of prejudice in Brazil."

Brazil has the heaviest concentration of blacks and their descendants outside Africa and also the largest concentration of Japanese and their descendants outside Japan. Many authorities believe that persons of European descent have made the greatest contribution to the physical formation of Brazilians, but extensive miscegenation over the years has created a population so genetically complex that some authors consider Brazilians a new and distinct people.

Area Handbook for Brazil

Brazil even enjoyed a reputation as a nation

"developing a new amalgam of the human species uniquely suited for tropical civilization," as Rollie E. Poppino wrote in 1973 in *Brazil: The Land and People*. Academicians do conclude that Brazil, with a population at least 38 percent of mixed race, has created a new sort of human being. Yet underlying this phenomenon is a philosophy of "bleaching," or trying to have light-skinned children, a peculiarly Latin American sexual and social answer to racism.

From the 1950s to the present, however, numerous research projects have uncovered high levels of inequality in Brazil and subtle forms of discrimination. By 1988, the century mark of the abolition of Brazilian slavery, fresh census data became available. Statistics strongly indicated that dark skin could be linked to greater infant mortality, lower life expectancy, higher rates of illiteracy, fewer opportunities in education, lower income, and limited job and housing choices.

Racial measures, Brazil and U.S.

MEDIAN EARNINGS COMPARED
AS A PERCENTAGE OF WHITE EARNINGS (1987)

United States

Black women	.98
Black men	.63

Brazil

Mulatto men	.58
Mulatto women	.58
Black men	.56
Black women	.52

PERCENTAGE OF PEOPLE OVER 25
WHO HAVE COMPLETED COLLEGE (1987)

U.S. whites	20.5%
U.S. blacks	10.7
Brazilian whites	9.2
Brazilian mulattos	2.0
Brazilian blacks	1.0

Based on data from "Racial Inequality in Brazil and the United States: A Statistical Comparison"

Social scientists and historians conclude that Afro-Brazilians lagged both white Brazilians and Afro-Americans on most measures of well-being. But there was one notable exception. "Nonwhite families in Brazil were much more likely to be headed by couples than were nonwhite families in the United States," wrote George Reid Andrews of the University of Pittsburgh, in a comprehensive report entitled "Racial Inequality in Brazil and the United States: A Statistical Comparison."

LESSON NUMBER 20: **TODAY HISTORIANS BELIEVE THAT BETWEEN 1950 AND 1980, MANY MEASURES OF RACIAL EQUALITY IMPROVED MARKEDLY IN THE UNITED STATES, WHILE THE SAME MEASURES EITHER REMAINED STABLE IN BRAZIL OR DECREASED.**

Demands for greater opportunity by Afro-Brazilians, according to Andrews, met resistance based on "the official ideology of racial democracy, and Brazilian elites' deep-seated resistance to redistributive policies of any sort."

The United States had a stronger postwar economy than Brazil's, producing a much bigger pie to share. And the contentiousness of its black and white people drags racial matters into the open to a greater extent. This may lead eventually to solutions to racial inequality. Kelli Moore, a black American studying in Brazil who was quoted in a June 1994 *New York Times* article, noted that "in terms of racial democracy, the United States has a much better chance than Brazil does. We confront things, we discuss things. Here, race is taboo."

Andrews concurs. Until Brazil reforms education and employment for blacks, he wrote that "the United States will provide more convincing evidence of racial democracy than will Brazil."

LESSON NUMBER 21: **THE VERY STRENGTH OF AFRICAN CULTURAL SURVIVAL THAT MAKES BRAZIL FASCINATING TO VISIT MAY HINDER ITS BLACK AND MIXED-RACE CITIZENS FROM PARTICIPATING FULLY IN THE NATIONAL ECONOMY.**

Thomas Sowell wrote in *The Economics and Politics of Race* that

historic head starts in acculturation seem as highly correlated with economic advancement in comparing people of African ancestry in Brazil and the United States as in making internal comparisons among the Negro populations of both countries.

Sowell implied that blacks in the United States, though encountering a more openly bigoted society, achieve more precisely because they belong more fully to the predominant American culture:

Even mixed-blood Negro individuals have risen less in class in Brazil than in the U.S.A. This suggests that racism may be less of a factor in economic advancement than is commonly supposed.

Findings of shockingly high illiteracy among Afro-Brazilians support Sowell's observation of poor acculturation. University of Pittsburgh historian Andrews found that

Brazil's 1987 literacy figures were roughly comparable to those for the United States in 1910, when 95 percent of whites were literate, and 70 percent of blacks.

He also noted that while most adult Americans, black and white, have completed high school, the average nonwhite Brazilian has only completed second grade or less, compared with fourth grade for white Brazilians.

Some commentators believe racism in Brazil affects blacks as a group rather than as individuals, and that the reverse applies in the United States, which has done more to define racism as a problem and create remedies. Yet a debate among Afro-Brazilians on the merits of adopting U.S.-style remedies such as affirmative action founders on two levels: "the political difficulties of enacting such measures in Brazil," as Joseph A. Page wrote in *The Brazilians*, and the fact that "given the racial mix in Brazil, who would qualify for benefits under affirmative action?"

Categories in 1990 U.S. census

		NUMBER (MILLIONS)
1	White	199.7
2	Black	30.0
3	Other race	9.8
4	American Indian	1.9
5	Chinese	1.6
6	Filipino	1.4
7	Japanese	0.8
8	Other Asian or Pacific Islander	0.8
9	Asian Indian	0.8
10	Korean	0.8
11	Vietnamese	0.6
12	Hawaiian	0.2
13	Samoan	0.1
14	Eskimo	0.1
15	Guamanian	0.05
16	Aleut	0.02
	1990 total:	248.7 million

Note: Hispanics can be of any race; many describe themselves as in the "other" category.

Data from U.S. Census Bureau

Some historians see indications that the United States has moved away from a two-tone, black-white society into a multiracial one closer to the rainbow-hued Brazilian model. In 1993, Thomas E. Skidmore, a professor of Latin American studies at Brown University, noted several indicators of this, including:

• The 16 categories that appeared on the 1990 census. (And with more mixed-race children being born the United States— about 124,000 in 1992, the latest count—biracial families and civil rights groups are now locking horns over whether to add a "multiracial" category in the year 2000 census.)

• The rapid growth of the Hispanic population (22 million in 1990), a category neither black nor white, but including both.

• The sensitivity within the U.S. black community itself to color gradations.

The U.S. population, in the extent of its race mix-ing, resembles Brazil's more than many people realize. In the United States, an estimated three out of every four blacks have some white blood. And millions of whites have some black blood.

Many social observers have debated whether racial mixing will be the ultimate solution to racism. British historian Arnold J. Toynbee was quoted in a 1969 interview as saying, "I think the only radical cure for racism is fusion, and the only radical way of fusing is to inter-marry." Professor Joseph R. Washington Jr. countered in *Marriage in Black and White* that

> We cannot, and we need not, create conditions whereby blacks and whites marry en masse. We can and we must create conditions whereby every American home anticipates with high expectation the possibility of welcoming in to the family a black or white sister, brother, daughter, or son, though this may be a reality for only a precious few.

Richard L. Jackson concluded in "The Color Crisis in Latin America" that "racial amalgamation is not necessarily a sign of racial harmony."

My husband Lamont says that the answer to bigotry may lie not so much in intermarriage as in the "progress possible in democratic nations."

And family friend Dr. Winston C. Murray, a lecturer in world history at Morgan State University in Baltimore and writer on the African diaspora, says what is needed is simply "the moral acceptance of equality." After millennia of writings from Aristotle to the Scottish philosopher David Hume supporting black inferiority, he says, whites must find a way to look at the descendants of slaves as their equal.

The experience of Brazil suggests that, while intermarriage can play a role in reduced bigotry, it is no panacea. Social pressures to marry lighter-skinned partners quash potential unity among blacks and mulattos. Carl N. Degler wrote in *Neither Black Nor White*, a landmark study of race relations in Brazil that appeared in 1971, that a mixed population tends to become a lighter, whiter population:

> Indeed, it has been argued that a national policy of Brazil is to have everyone eventually white, through the mixing of blood. This expectation has been called "the progressive Aryanization of Brazil."

Mulattos in Brazil, according to many scholars, lack a racial consciousness and unity with blacks, diluting nonwhite political power. Mulattos in the United States have provided many charismatic civil rights activists—a phenomenon that has not occurred in Brazil.

The United States received a hard push toward becoming a racial democracy from the 1960s civil rights movement. In the 1990s, a soft nudge continues as

Slavery and cultural survival

The fact that some black Brazilians in the waning years of the 20th century still worship in Yoruba, an African language, demonstrates that language is the cardinal indicator of culture and that language survives when a people maintain their numbers. Yoruba remains alive 150 years after the last new African slave stepped onto Brazilian soil because of the continuing black majority in northern Brazil. In the U.S. melting pot, few blacks other than Haitian, Puerto Rican or African immigrants know any language except English.

In Brazil, where an estimated 44 percent to 75 percent of the people have some African ancestors, Afro-Brazilians seemed more knowing of their heritage and original language and customs.

LESSON NUMBER 22: DIFFERENCES IN BRAZILIAN AND U.S. SLAVERY ACCOUNT FOR THE GREATER CULTURAL SURVIVAL AMONG AFRICAN DESCENDANTS IN BRAZIL.

• Nearly 10 times as many African slaves went to Brazil as to the United States. Blacks formed a majority of Brazil's population from 1817 (or

perhaps even earlier) to circa 1905, according to my calculations. An influx of 5 million Europeans that lasted from 1870 to 1970 made Brazil a white-majority country sometime after 1905.

Of U.S. states, South Carolina provides an intriguing parallel to Brazil demographically. Blacks constituted a majority of South Carolina's population from 1820 to 1920.

LESSON NUMBER 23: NUMBERS ALLOWED AFRICAN LANGUAGE AND CULTURE TO SURVIVE IN THE FORM OF THE GULLAH SPEECH OF THE SEA ISLANDS IN SOUTH CAROLINA.

• In Brazil, slaves from West Africa and Sudan often shared the bond of Islam. These Muslim slaves often proved more intractable than those from areas farther south who practiced animist religions. And people from some tribes, such as the Yorubas and the Kongo, arrived in enough numbers to preserve their cultures despite attempts at dispersal by

Black, mixed-raced populations
PERCENTAGE

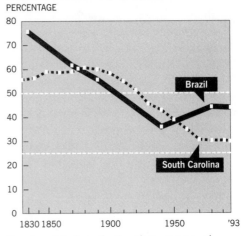

Based on data from the Brazilian censuses of 1835, 1872, 1890, 1940, 1980 and 1993, and "South Carolina" in the *Encyclopedia of African-American Culture and History*

NOTE: The post-1940 upswing in blacks in the Brazilian census reflects lessening white immigration, lower birthrates among middle-class whites and higher infant survival rates among blacks.

Brazilian overseers. Slaves also maintained greater contact with one another in the urban environment of Salvador de Bahia than in the rural American South.

• Slaves continued to arrive in Brazil from Africa for nearly a half-century after such arrivals in the United States ended.

Slave arrivals in the New World

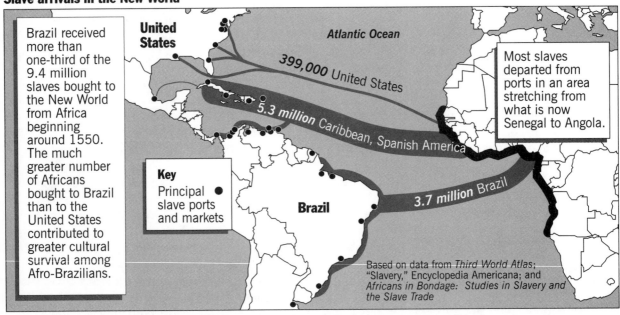

Brazil received more than one-third of the 9.4 million slaves bought to the New World from Africa beginning around 1550. The much greater number of Africans bought to Brazil than to the United States contributed to greater cultural survival among Afro-Brazilians.

United States

Atlantic Ocean

399,000 United States

5.3 million Caribbean, Spanish America

3.7 million Brazil

Most slaves departed from ports in an area stretching from what is now Senegal to Angola.

Brazil

Key
Principal ● slave ports and markets

Based on data from *Third World Atlas*; "Slavery," Encyclopedia Americana; and *Africans in Bondage: Studies in Slavery and the Slave Trade*

• By the late 1800s, Brazil enjoyed diplomatic and commercial ties with West Africa to a greater extent than did the United States. Ships from Salvador repatriated some black Brazilians to Lagos. These ties reflect at least in part Brazil's greater proximity to Africa. Monrovia in Liberia lies 2,320 miles from Salvador de Bahia in Brazil and 4,670 miles from Washington, D.C.

LESSON NUMBER 24: DISTANCE FROM AFRICA MEANT LESS AFRICAN CULTURE FOR AMERICAN SLAVES—BUT GREATER LIKELIHOOD OF HAVING SURVIVING DESCENDANTS.

Historians provide various reasons for the greater survival rates of blacks in the United States. Thomas Sowell, in *Race and Culture: A World View,* points to the relatively high costs of a slave in the United States vs. in Brazil or on the coast of Africa. Professor George Reid Andrews of the University of Pittsburgh wrote to me that

Once the slave trade was abolished, the U.S. slave population then became self-reproducing, in part because slaves were more valuable in the United States once imports had been cut off, and owners therefore had greater incentive to keep them healthy.

And, he wrote, the slave trade had brought two males for every female. The slave population gradually became balanced after the trade stopped.

The end of the slave trade in the United States cut off the stream of new arrivals from Africa. African-Americans ultimately evolved a new culture "neither African nor European, neither white nor black, but rather both," as Joel Williamson wrote in *New People.*

In the United States, the descendants of 399,000 Africans imported as slaves accounted for most of the 33 million blacks, an 80-fold increase, counted in 1995 in the United States. In Brazil, 3.7 million slaves left a legacy of between 70 million and 118 million people, a 20- to 30-fold increase.

Populations compared, 1995

	UNITED STATES	BRAZIL
Total	264 million	158 million
Black, mixed race	33 million	70 million
As percentage	12%	44% *

* Brazil is officially 6 percent black and at least 38 percent mixed race. Some scholars estimate a higher Afro-Brazilian proportion: up to 75 percent, or 118 million.

Based on data from the 1995 World Population Data Sheet, 1994 *CIA World Factbook,* 1996 U.S. Census Bureau, and Brazil's *Diretoria de Pesquisas,* Population Census 1993, *Fundaçao Instituto Brasileiro de Geografia e Estatistica (IBGE).*

young people adopt darker norms of beauty and flexible dating patterns. *People* magazine's 1995 listing of "The 50 Most Beautiful People in the World" included 12 nonwhites. Of these, the text described at least five as being of mixed race. These handsome people featured lovely blends of Scandinavian cheekbones, rich brown skin tones, and eye colors ranging from green or hazel to onyx.

And in 1991, pollsters found that, for the first time, more Americans approved (48 percent) than disapproved (42 percent) of interracial dating. The survey also found that among persons age 18 to 29, 64 percent approved of interracial dating, a figure that dropped to 27 percent for those above 50. The researchers noted "the widest age divergence of any Gallup trend question" on the point.

LESSON NUMBER 25: THE ISSUE THAT *MOST DEFINES* WHETHER YOU THINK AS AN OLDER OR YOUNGER AMERICAN IS YOUR VIEW OF INTERRACIAL DATING.

Views on interracial dating, all Americans

	APPROVE
1968	20%
1973	36
1983	43
1991	48

Based on a poll reported in August 1991 by *The Gallup Poll Monthly*

This shift on dating may translate into something hopeful. While intermarriage almost always seems to be an affair of the heart rather than a political gesture, greater tolerance at least allows couples to act on an attraction with less disapproval.

In mostly black U.S. cities such as Baltimore, some whites may find a medium or dark brown skin tone attractive. Lamont cites as an example a white acquaintance who attended Baltimore's predominantly black Southwestern High School. Because blacks set the norm, she came to like the way they looked, talked and moved.

In some areas, blacks may additionally be the most prestigious dating partners available. In our own Baltimore neighborhood, for example, some whites are Appalachian migrants with low education and few prospects, and some blacks hold advanced degrees and professional and technical jobs.

These straws in the wind support the idea of the United States, despite its sometimes uneasy and occasionally cantankerous race relations, as the New World nation closest to a true racial democracy.

Even the murder trial of O.J. Simpson may have done little to damage this perception. Many whites feared that the Simpson acquittal pointed to a tit-for-tat attitude toward justice, with a majority-black jury paying back Los Angeles for the Rodney King beating and subsequent police trial. The United States, they believed, had reached a nadir where blacks and whites could not agree on right and wrong, evidence and fabrication, reality or paranoia.

Yet a Gallup poll published in October 1995 suggested that racial attitudes remained largely unaffected by the trial.

Views on race relations
DO YOU THINK THAT RACE RELATIONS BETWEEN BLACKS AND WHITES

	BLACKS	WHITES
... WILL ALWAYS BE A PROBLEM		
1963	26%	44%
1993	55	53
1995	55	55
... THAT A SOLUTION WILL BE FOUND		
1963	70%	53%
1993	44	44
1995	41	40

Based on data from the October 1995 *Gallup Poll Newsletter*

My husband Lamont believes this is because black pessimism on solutions to problems in race relations long predated the Simpson trial. Black veterans from World War I to the present, he noted, have been well aware that blacks had served in all U.S. military engagements in the 20th century yet continued to face discriminatory laws.

Other cultural indicators show, if not progress, at least the blurring of racial boundaries. Madonna dating Dennis Rodman illustrated that the races meet at the level of the wacko celebrity. And *The Ricki Lake Show* demonstrates the melding that occurs at the screaming, stomping low end of American culture. The color-blindness of low-income people also evidences itself on my block in Baltimore. Black, Hispanic and white boys alike dress in baggy jeans and backwards ballcaps, engage in petty and grand mischief and dance to silent music.

Many point to controversies involving Rodney King and O.J. Simpson, and the disparate treatment of Mike Tyson and William Kennedy Smith when charged with rape, as evidence of a giant and widening gulf between black and white perceptions and experiences of justice.

Yet sometimes progress is measured in quiet everyday encounters more than via big news events. I can point to least one personal example.

In 1995, I married a mixed-race man. My husband Lamont notes, for example, that his parents were not crusaders, just two people who insisted on their right to a normal family life. His white father, a Westinghouse engineer named Arthur Harvey who was originally from Hammond, Indiana, married a fellow designer of rockets, Cynthia Camper, a black

woman with roots in St. Michaels, Maryland. Lamont's parents could not wed in Maryland in 1960 because interracial marriage was illegal. So they drove to Howard University in Washington, D.C. His father was ostracized by blood relatives for decades.

Interracial marriages in the United States
INCLUDES ALL CATEGORIES, NOT ONLY BLACK/WHITE

	NUMBER OF COUPLES	PERCENTAGE OF ALL MARRIAGES
1960	149,000	0.4%
1970	310,000	0.7
1980	651,000	1.3
1990	964,000	1.8
1993	1,195,000	2.2

Based on data from the U.S. Census Bureau

Our wedding 35 years later was not only legal, it was far more common, as statistics show. We were able to have our ceremony in Maryland, on an oyster boat in Fells Point, Baltimore's maritime district. Both families attended. They not only lent strong support, but seemed to hit it off in a genuine way and even enjoy great areas of common interest. Our siblings discussed the martial arts, computer software and youth soccer leagues.

Lamont's mother and my parents even discovered that they had all worked at the same naval testing laboratory in Carderock, Maryland, in the 1950s.

On that same day, Sept. 9, 1995, four other people who worked at *The Washington Post* also got married. One of the other couples consisted of a white man and black woman. A few weeks earlier, yet another couple—a black man who also worked at the *Post* and an Asian woman—were married in a ceremony attended by nearly 600.

A study published a year later in *New Democrat* magazine confirmed the trend, noting that despite fears of an increasingly polarized America, blacks and white were falling in love with each other—and that class was superseding race in social matters. Douglas J. Besherov, an author of the study, said that as blacks achieve higher education levels and middle-class status, their attractiveness to white middle-class suitors increased.

During the season of our wedding, America's eyes might have been on the ongoing O.J. Simpson trial in Los Angeles. In Maryland, however, the eyes of a number of newlyweds were fixed to a hopeful future.

LESSON NUMBER 26: A QUIET REVOLUTION CONTINUED ON ITS STEADY WAY, MAKING THE MYTHOS OF BRAZIL MORE TANGIBLE AT THE NORTHERN END OF THE CRESCENT OF NEW AFRICA.

OVERALL LESSONS

Classroom Earth teaches us history, economics, language, politics and culture

Abandoned Maya cities such as Uxmal caution us regarding over-intensive agriculture.

My travels, and the writing of this book to order my impressions, have led to seven overall observations.

Travel's keys to history: Our eyes take in living history and economics in action as we travel—when Chinese people won't talk to foreigners after Tiananmen; when Afro-Brazilians worship in a Nigerian language; when our airplane to Kenya goes through Europe instead of direct; when it is easier to stay with Polynesians on Tahiti's outer islands than in Hawaii; and when Burma and Madagascar demand cash from Western tourists to prop up dictatorships. Mundane aspects of a trip can shed great light on fundamental forces of history and ignite an interest in reading to learn more.

Travel's keys to learning: Some learners seem better able to absorb facts about a place best *after* their feet have walked on its soil. For example, my brother Jim and I read a brief popular article about lemurs, flew to Madagascar to see them and only later attempted weightier books on primate behavior.

My approach to independent travel generally parallels the constructivist approach to teaching science and other subjects, in which students are first allowed an exploratory period of handling materials, with concepts introduced later. Constructivist education focuses on tackling big concepts and on recognizing that people construct their own meaning from experience and are not blank slates to be provided with ready answers.

Package tours seem closer to basic skills education, where information is presented directly. Learning takes place, yet perhaps without the feverish excitement and pride linked to one's own discovery of principles. Booms in both types of travel may serve as a powerful corrective to the insularity of U.S. education and media coverage. More states may end up with well-traveled populations approaching that of Utah, with thousands of former missionaries whose multilingualism and foreign contacts led to booming exports.

Travel's key to culture: Cultural memory seems powerful among Afro-Brazilians and Tahitians and weaker among their respective U.S. cousins, African-Americans and Polynesian Hawaiians. Yet the latter groups seem generations ahead in politics, with representation from local levels up to the U.S. Senate. The

United States, like ancient Rome, has performed a balancing act in uniting disparate cultures. Even so, we play a price in being what Philip M. Hauser termed a "chaotic society," with enormous riptides created when the powerful perpetual memory of one group clashes with those of others. As Thomas Sowell pointed out in *Race and Culture: A World View*, all groups have evolved unique priorities and values that tend to last over time and geographical relocation. These differences make travel fascinating, trade necessary, quota programs dubious and U.S. society contentious.

The most valuable traveling strategy: traveling independently without a fixed itinerary, using local transportation (when safe) and exploring areas outside of big cities. Americans have begun to emulate most Europeans, Australians and New Zealanders, who travel confidently in this manner.

The most valuable traveling tactic: seeking simple connections with people. The fact that my grandfather was christened Emile broke the ice with a like-named missionary pilot in Borneo and a religious worshipper in Brazil. Family photos go a long way in places such as China and Indonesia. Staying with local families or being led by local guides reveals day-to-day life in Polynesia, Bali and Brazil. Children in many nations offer first-rate language tutoring.

The most valuable preparation in school: French taken in high school paid off in ways I never anticipated. Travelers will find English widely spoken worldwide—except in Francophone regions. Without French, I would have struggled mightily in Madagascar and at times in French Polynesia. Though Spanish is the other invaluable travelers' tongue, I suspect that it is easier to learn French first and then Spanish rather than the other way around.

And finally, **the admirable dedication of professional travelers:** Scholars and foreign correspondents, who study and travel more methodically, provided me with swift, thoughtful and insightful assistance, making clear how deeply they felt a responsibility to ensure that even a book designed for popular readership contained informed impressions. Independent travelers would do well to consult their work, whether in the daily press, periodicals or books.

BIBLIOGRAPHY

Senior and junior hippos swim in Kenya's Mara River.

Note: Internet addresses are given for documents where available.

General

Historical Statistics of the United States, Colonial Times to 1970. Bicentennial edition, Washington, D.C.: U.S. Bureau of the Census, 1975.

Hammond Citation World Atlas. Maplewood, N.J.: Hammond Inc., 1990.

Statistical Abstract of the United States. 115th ed., Washington, D.C.: U.S. Bureau of the Census, 1995.

Barraclough, Geoffrey, ed. *The Times Atlas of World History*. 3rd ed., Maplewood, N.J.: Hammond, 1988.

Central Intelligence Agency. *The World Factbook*. Washington, D.C.: Superintendent of Documents, 1994 (available at http://www.odci.gov).

Famighetti, Robert, ed. *The World Almanac and Book of Facts 1996*. Mahwah, N.J.: World Almanac Books, 1995.

Haub, Carl, et al. *World Population Data Sheet*. Washington, D.C.: Population Reference Bureau Inc., 1995.

Kurian, George Thomas. *The New Book of World Rankings*. 3rd ed., New York, Oxford: Facts on File, 1991.

Microsoft. *Cinemania 96*. Seattle, Wash.: 1992-95.

Microsoft. *Encarta: CD-Rom Multimedia Encyclopedia for the Macintosh*. Seattle, Wash.: 1994.

Wallbank, T. Walter, et al. *Civilization Past and Present*. 4th ed., Glenview, Ill.: Scott, Foresman and Co., 1971.

Madagascar

WTO Yearbook of Tourism Statistics. 47th ed., vol. I. 1995.

Adams, Douglas, et al. *Last Chance to See*. New York: Harmony Books, 1990.

Bradt, Hilary. *Guide to Madagascar*. Chalfont St. Peter, Buckinghamshire, England: Bradt Publications, 1988.

Bradt, Hilary, et al. *Madagascar Wildlife: A Visitor's Guide*. Old Saybrook, Conn.: Globe Pequot Press, 1996.

Brown, J.D. "Lemurs to Flying Squirrels, Unique Wildlife Puts Isle of Madagascar in a Class by Itself." *Newsday*, Jan. 29, 1989, Travel p. 8.

Central Intelligence Agency. "Madagascar." In *Indian Ocean Atlas*, Washington, D.C.: Superintendent of Documents, 1976.

Chadwick, Douglas H. "Epilogue." In *The Fate of the Elephant*, 465-476. San Francisco: Sierra Club, 1992.

Cincotta, Richard P. "Population Does Not Mean Progress." *The Washington Post*, Oct. 1, 1993, A17.

Durrell, Gerald. *The Aye-Aye and I*. New York: Touchstone, 1992.

Ember, Carol R., et al. *Cultural Anthropology*. 4th ed., Englewood Cliffs, N.J.: Prentice Hall, 1985.

Farhi, Paul. "Abroad, a Market for Mayhem; Overseas Sales Keep TV Violence Profitable." *The Washington Post*, Feb. 3, 1995, A1.

Fricke, Hans. "Coelacanths: The Fish That Time Forgot." *National Geographic*, June 1988, 824-838.

Grzimek, Dr. Bernhard. *Grzimek's Animal Encyclopedia*. Van Nostrand Reinhold Co., 1974.

Hammond, Allen L. "Wildlife and Habitat." In *World Resources 1996-97*, New York: Oxford University Press, 1994.

Hoeltgen, Dominique. "Where the Hills Catch Fire; Caught in a vicious circle of destruction, drought and desperation, Madagascar struggles to turn in a new direction." *Ceres* (publication of the U.N. Food and Agriculture Organization), January-February 1994, 42-45.

Iyer, Pico. *Video Night in Kathmandu*. New York: Alfred E. Knopf, 1988.

Jolly, Alison. *A World Like Our Own; Man and Nature in Madagascar*. New Haven, Conn., and London: Yale University Press, 1980.

Jolly, Alison. "Madagascar: A World Apart." *National Geographic*, February 1987, 149-183.

Jolly, Alison. "Madagascar's Lemurs: On the Edge of Survival." *National Geographic*, August 1988, 132-161.

Keenan, Edward Louis, et al. "Becoming a Competent Speaker of Malagasy." In *Languages and Their Speakers*, ed. Timothy

Shopen. 113-157. Cambridge, Mass.: Winthrop Publishers Inc., 1979.

Kenworthy, Tom. "Senate acts to protect desert land" [California Desert Protection Act]. *The Washington Post*, April 14, 1994, A1.

Knox, Margaret L. "No Nation An Island: The world has much to lose in Madagascar, where human poverty grinds away at nature's plenty." *Sierra*, May/June 1989, 78-84.

Lamb, David. *The Africans*. New York: Random House, 1983.

Linklater, Andro. *Wild People; Travels with Borneo's Head-Hunters*. New York: Atlantic Monthly Press, 1990.

Lovejoy, Thomas J. "Biodiversity: The Most Fundamental Issue." Speech to Australian Academy of Science, March 1, 1994 (available at ftp://keck.tamu.edu-/pub/bene/bene_texts/tl_3194_aas.txt).

Marsh, Jeffrey. "From Malthus to Al Gore." *The Washington Post*, Aug. 28, 1994, Book World p. 4.

Miss Manners. "Getting Through Foreign Customs." *The Washington Post*, Jan. 29, 1989, F1.

Mitchell, Henry. "180 Million Years Not Enough For Madagascar." *The Washington Post*, Nov. 28, 1986, A1.

Mitchell, Henry. "On Madagascar, Friends & Lemurs; Wildlife Watching and Other Pleasures." *The Washington Post*, Jan. 25, 1987, H1.

Mitchell, Henry. "Around the World for Love of Lemurs." *The Washington Post*, Aug. 4, 1989, B2.

Murphy, Dervla. *Muddling Through in Madagascar*. Woodstock, N.Y.: The Overlook Press, 1989.

Nowak, Ronald M. *Walker's Mammals of the World*. 5th ed., Vol. 1. Baltimore: The Johns Hopkins University Press, 1991.

O'Rourke, P.J. *Holidays in Hell*. New York: Atlantic Monthly Press, 1988.

Okie, Susan. "Planet of the Lemurs: In Search of the Curious Primates of Madagascar." *The Washington Post*, Sept. 4, 1994, E1, E5.

Parfit, Michael. "The Growth of Antarctic Tourism." *The Washington Post*, Jan. 24, 1988, E8.

Payer, Lynn. "The Land of the Lemurs;

Madagascar is Home to Exotic Species of Plants and Animals Found Nowhere Else." *The New York Times*, Oct. 29, 1989, Travel p. 8.

Pereira, Michael E. "Agonistic Interaction, Dominance Relation, and Ontogenetic Trajectories in Ringtailed Lemurs." In *Juvenile primates: Life History, Development and Behavior*, ed. Michael Pereira and Lynn Fairbanks. 428. New York: Oxford University Press, 1993.

Polo, Marco. *The Travels*.

Protzman, Ferdinand. "Effort to Capture 'Fossil Fish' Draws Fire; Japanese aquarium hopes to be first with a live coelacanth." *The New York Times*, Sept. 12, 1989, C4.

Quammen, David. *The Song of the Dodo*. New York: Charles Scribner's Sons, 1996.

Raymo, Chet. "Dr. Seuss and Dr. Einstein: Children's Books and Scientific Imagination." *The Horn Book Magazine*, September 1992, 560.

Richman, Sheldon. "Population Means Progress, Not Poverty." *The Washington Post*, Sept. 1, 1993, A23.

Russell, Robert J. *The Lemur's Legacy: The Evolution of Power, Sex and Love*. New York: Jeremy P. Tarcher, Putnam, 1993.

Shoumatoff, Alex. "The Last of the Dog-Headed Men." In *African Madness*, 43-89. New York: Alfred A. Knopf, 1988.

Sowell, Thomas. *The Economics and Politics of Race*. New York: Quill, 1983.

Sparks, John. "Islands Exploited." In *Island Life*, 114-139. Madrid: The Danbury Press, 1976.

Stalcup, Brenda, ed. *Endangered Species*. Opposing Viewpoints. San Diego, Calif.: Greenhaven Press Inc., 1996.

Stephenson, Peter J. "The Impacts of Tourism on Nature Reserves in Madagascar; Perinet, a Case Study." *Environmental Conservation* 20 (3 [Fall] 1993): 262-265.

Sun, Lena H. "Tourists Allowed, but Brake for Yaks: China Choosy About Who Climbs Mountain to See Tibet's Splendors." *The Washington Post*, Sept. 21, 1994, A35.

Tattersall, Ian. "Madagascar's Lemurs." *Scientific American*, January 1993, 110-117.

Thatcher, Margaret. *The Downing Street Years*. New York: HarperCollins, 1993.

Trueheart, Charles. "Canada saves wild area." *The Washington Post*, June 24, 1993, A1.

Ward, Peter. "Lost Islands." In *The End of Evolution: A Journey In Search Of Clues To The Third Mass Extinction Facing Planet Earth*, 213-244. New York: Bantam, 1994.

Wright, Patricia C. "Primate Ecology, Rainforest Conservation, and Economic Development: Building a National Park in Madagascar." *Evolutionary Anthropology* 1 (1 1992): 25-33.

Wright, Robert. "Infidelity: It May Be In Our Genes." *Time*, Aug. 15, 1994, 45-52.

China

Chinese for Travelers. Oxford, United Kingdom: Berlitz Publishing Co. Ltd., 1980 (revised edition, 1994, and now titled *Berlitz Chinese Phrase Book and Dictionary*).

Policies and Regulations of Shanghai Pudong New Area. People's Bank of China, 1990. English translation for reference only

"Britannica World Data." In *Britannica Book of the Year*, ed. William A. Cleveland. Chicago: Encyclopædia Britannica, 1995.

Immigration by Country of Last Residence, 1820-1991. Immigration and Naturalization Service, Department of Justice, 1996.

Belliveau, Jeannette. "Chinese Byways: By Water: Slow Boats and Glimpses of Everyday Life." *The Washington Post*, April 13, 1986, E1, E7.

Belliveau, Jeannette. "Riding the Rails: Chinese 3rd Class: No, It Wasn't Fun." *The Baltimore Sun*, Nov. 1, 1987, N1, N9.

Browning, Graeme. *If Everybody Bought One Shoe: American Capitalism in Communist China*. New York: Hill and Wang, 1989.

Butterfield, Fox. *China: Alive in the Bitter Sea*. New York: Times Books, 1990.

Campbell, Jeremy. *Winston Churchill's Afternoon Nap*. New York: Simon and Schuster, 1986.

Domes, Jurgen. "China's Internal Dynamics in the 1990s: Political, Economic and Social Trends." In *After Tiananmen Square: Challenges for the Chinese-American Relationship*. Cambridge, Massachusetts: Brassey's Inc. for the Institute for Foreign Policy Analysis, 1990.

Foster, R.P. *Modern Ireland, 1600-1972*. London: Allen Lane, 1988.

Garvin, James Louis. "English-Speaking World, Section V: Ireland's increase, disaster and exodus overseas." In *Encyclopædia Britannica*, 606-607. Vol. 8. Chicago: University of Chicago Press, 1948.

Gellhorn, Martha. *Travels with Myself and Another*. New York: Hippocrene Books, 1978.

Greeley, Andrew M. *The Irish Americans: The Rise to Money & Power*. New York: Harper & Row, 1981.

Holley, David. "13 Injured as Chinese, African Students Clash." *The Los Angeles Times*, Dec. 27, 1988, I-7, I-10.

Holley, David. "Africans Press China on Student Dispute." *The Los Angeles Times*, Jan. 5, 1989, I-13.

Holley, David. "200 African Students Protest Racism in China." *The Los Angeles Times*, Jan. 9, 1989, I-6.

Hsieh, Chiao-min. *The Atlas of China*. New York: McGraw Hill, 1973.

Iyer, Pico. *Video Night in Kathmandu*. New York: Alfred A. Knopf, 1988.

Johnson, Ian. "Tiananmen Massacre Marked Despite Police Patrols; Authorities Clamp Down, but Dead Are Not Forgotten." *The Baltimore Sun*, June 5, 1995, A3.

Kalogerakis, George, et al. "The Disorient Express; Our rail journey through China proved one thing: The People's Republic, while eager to take Western-style tourism out for a spin, remains charmingly at the learner's-permit stage." *GQ*, November 1994, 242-248.

Kaplan, Fredric M., et al. *The China Guidebook*. 13th ed., Houghton Mifflin, 1993.

Knecht, G. Bruce. "The Chinese Diaspora; Wealth Hazards. Overseas Chinese Have Made Crucial Contributions to South Asia, But Their Success Has A Price." *National Review*, Nov. 21, 1994, 56-59.

Kraar, Louis. "Overseas Chinese: Lessons from the World's Most Dynamic Capitalists." *Fortune*, Oct. 31, 1994, p. 91.

Lamberg, Lynne. "The Value of Naps." In *Bodyrhythms: Chronobiology and Peak Performance*, 75-76. New York: William Morrow and Co., 1994.

Mahoney, Rosemary. *The Early Arrival of Dreams; A Year in China*. New York: Fawcett Columbine, 1990.

Mathews, Jay and Linda. *One Billion: A Chinese Chronicle*. New York: Random House, 1983.

Mathews, Jay. "Political turmoil hurts China's tourist industry; some travelers having a good time anyway." *The Washington Post*, May 27, 1989, A21.

Mathews, Jay. "First Poll of China Finds Materialism Alive; Gallup Survey Shows Populace Has Big Appetite for Wealth, Goods—But Few Have Hot Water." *The Washington Post*, Feb. 16, 1995, A13, 15.

O'Rourke, P.J. "Famine." In *All the Trouble in the World*. New York: Atlantic Monthly Press, 1994.

Perrottet, Tony. "Deep Cover in Belize." *Escape*, October 1995, 54.

Reid, T.R. "Confucius Says: Go East, Young Man; Many Asians Now Think Their Lives and Values are Better Than 'The American Way'." *The Washington Post*, Nov. 19, 1995, C2.

Samagalski, Alan, et al. *China: A Travel Survival Kit*. 1st ed., Berkeley, Calif.: Lonely Planet, 1984.

Shoumatoff, Alex. "The Silent Killing of Tibet; Why does the U.S. refuse to recognize the Dalai Lama's pacifist resistance in Tibet, where more than one million have died under Chinese tyranny?" *Vanity Fair*, May 1991, 76-104.

Simmie, Scott, et al. *Tiananmen Square: An Eyewitness Account of the Chinese People's Passionate Quest for Democracy*. Seattle: University of Washington Press, 1989.

Sowell, Thomas. *The Economics and Politics of Race*. New York: Quill, 1983.

Sowell, Thomas. *Ethnic America*. New York: BasicBooks, 1981.

Strauss, Valerie, et al. "How Many Died? New Evidence Suggests Far Higher Numbers for the Victims of Mao Zedong's Era." *The Washington Post*, July 17, 1994, A22.

Swaine, Michael D. *China: Domestic Change and Foreign Policy*. RAND's National Defense Research Institute, 1995.

Theroux, Paul. *Riding the Iron Rooster: By Train through China*. New York: Putnam's, 1988.

Toops, Stanley W. "Tourism in China and the Impact of June 4, 1989." *Focus: The American Geographical Society* (Spring 1992): 3-6.

Tyler, Patrick E. "Deng's Economic Drive Leaves Vast Areas of China Behind." *The New York Times*, Dec. 27, 1995, A1, A6.

Tyler, Patrick E. "Crime (and Punishment) Rages Anew in China." *The New York Times*, July 11, 1996, A1, A8.

Wilson, John. *Chinese Americans. American Voices*, Vero Beach, Fla.: Rourke Corp., 1991.

Winchester, Simon. "Coming: The Great Flood of China." *Condé Nast Traveler*, May 1996, 152-219.

Woodham-Smith, Cecil. *The Great Hunger*. New York: Harper & Row, 1962.

Borneo

"John Paul II on Evangelism." *The Christian Century*, Feb. 6-13, 1991, 138.

Belliveau, Jeannette. "The Wilds of Borneo; The headhunting days are over, but there are leeches to cope with." *The Baltimore Sun*, Oct. 27, 1991, 1N, 4N.

Benthall, Jonathan. "Missionaries and human rights." *Anthropology Today* 11 (February 1995): 2-4.

Berger, Joseph. "Spreading their Faith Wherever It Leads: Catholic Laity Is Increasingly Replacing Priests and Nuns as Missionaries." *The New York Times*, Jan. 4, 1996, B1, B5.

Bevis, William W. *Borneo Log: The Struggle for Sarawak's Forests*. Seattle, Wash.: University of Washington Press, 1995.

Brook, James. "What's Doing in: Manaus" [description of missionaries' Indian museum]. *The New York Times*, Feb. 21, 1993, Travel, p. 10.

Coote, Robert T. "Good News, Bad News: North American Protestant Overseas Personnel Statistics in Twenty-Five-Year Perspective." *International Bulletin of Missionary Research* 19 (January 1995): 6-8, 10-13.

Dalton, Bill. *Indonesia Handbook*. 4th ed., Chico, Calif.: Moon Publications, 1989.

Elshout, J.M. *De Kenja-Dajaks uit hep Apo-Kajangebied*. 's-Gravenhagem: Martinus Nijhoff, 1926.

Ember, Carol R., et al. *Cultural Anthropology*. Englewood Cliffs, N.J.: Prentice-Hall, 1985.

Escobar, Samuel. "Missions' New World Order." *Christianity Today*, Nov. 14, 1994, 48-52.

Fanning, David. "Cannibals on Main Street" [role of Roman Catholic missionaries in Papua New Guinea]. *Condé Nast Traveler*, August 1996, 68-77, 106-09.

Fox, Michael W. "In Praise of the Natural Dog." *HSUS News: Humane Society of the United States*, Fall 1993, 27-29.

Hansen, Eric. *Stranger in the Forest: On Foot Across Borneo*. Boston: Houghton Mifflin Co., 1988.

Johnston, Tracy. *Shooting the Boh: A Woman's Voyage Down the Wildest River in Borneo*. New York: Vintage Departures, 1992.

King, Ben, et al. *The Collins Field Guide to the Birds of South-East Asia*. Lexington, Mass.: The Stephen Greene Press, 1975.

Kinnaird, Margaret F. "Indonesia's Hornbill Haven; On the slopes of a volcano, wild fig trees support a threatened bird." *Natural History*, January 1996, 40.

Lees, Shirley. *Drunk Before Dawn* [account of missionary work in Sarawak]. London: OMF Books, 1979.

Linklater, Andro. *Wild People: Travels with Borneo's Head-Hunters*. New York: Atlantic Monthly Press, 1990.

Mortimer, Wm. James, publisher. *Deseret News 1993-94 Church Almanac of the Church of Jesus Christ of Latter-Day Saints*. Salt Lake City, Utah: Deseret News, 1992.

Muller, Kal, et al. *Borneo: Adventures in East Kalimantan*. Singapore: Times Editions, 1988.

Muller, Kal. *Borneo: Journey into Tropical Rainforest*. Passport's Regional Guides of Indonesia, ed. David Pickell. Lincolnwood, Ill.: Passport Books, 1990.

Neill, Stephen. *Colonialism and Christian Missions*. New York: McGraw-Hill, 1966.

Nieuwenhuis, Anton Willem. *Quer Durch Borneo*. Leiden, the Netherlands: E.J. Brill, 1904.

North, David M. "Flying Missionaries Rely on Fleet to Spread the Word." *Aviation Week*, Jan. 3, 1994, 49-51.

O'Hanlon, Redmond. *Into the Heart of Borneo*. New York: Random House, 1985.

Oey, Eric, ed. *Indonesia*. 2nd ed., Insight Guides. Singapore: Apa Productions, 1986.

Ostling, Richard N. "The New Missionary: Proclaiming Christ's message in daring and disputed ways." *Time*, Dec. 27, 1982, 50-56.

Perrins, Christopher M., et al., ed. "Hornbills in Human Cultures," in *The Encyclopedia of Birds*. New York: Equinox for Facts on File, 1985.

Rapoport, Robert N. "Anthropologists and Missionaries." *Man* 26:4 (December 1991): 740-743.

Rivenburg, Roy. "Modern Missionaries." *The Los Angeles Times*, Sept. 2, 1992, E1.

Rousseau, Jérôme. *Central Borneo: Ethnic Identity and Social Life in a Stratified Society*. New York: Oxford University Press, 1990.

Sellato, Bernard. *Nomads of the Borneo Rainforest: The Economics, Politics, and Ideology of Settling Down*. Honolulu: University of Hawaii Press, 1994.

Smith, Brad L. "John Testrake: A Remembrance." *Flight Log: The Monthly Information Newsletter of MAF* X:3 (March 1996): 1, 2.

Stahel, Thomas H. "A Missionary Encyclical" [report on Pope John Paul II]. *America*, Feb. 9, 1991, 115-116.

Tapia, Andrés. "New look for missionaries: Third World finds the West ripe for harvest." *Christianity Today*, Oct. 4, 1993, 64.

United Press International. "Fire Reported to Ravage Huge Tract in Indonesia." *The New York Times*, Oct. 30, 1984, A7.

Van der Geest, Sjaak. "Anthropologists and Missionaries: Brothers Under the Skin." *Man* 25:4 (December 1990): 588-601.

Weiss, Lowell. "Speaking in tongues; A vast missionary effort is under way to translate the Bible into languages spoken by the world's most remote tribes and ethnic groups." *The Atlantic Monthly*, June 1995, 36-42.

Wooding, Dan, et al. "Mayday! After this landing, missionary pilot Terry Wohlgemuth vowed to return to America." *Moody* (Moody Bible Institute, Chicago), February 1989, 48-49.

Wysocki, Bernard. "Utah's economy goes global, thanks in part to role of missionaries; Mormon's overseas stints lead to linguistic skills and network of contacts." *The Wall Street Journal*, March 28, 1996, A1.

East Africa

"Kenya: Murder in the Game Reserve; Roving poachers bring down the man who helped lions live free." *Time*, Sept. 4, 1989, 21.

"Poachers shot." *The Guardian* [London], July 4, 1989, 10.

"French tourists shot dead." *The Guardian* [London], July 8, 1989, 8.

"Poachers link." *The Times* [London], July 12, 1989, 9.

Achebe, Chinua. *Things Fall Apart*. Nairobi: Heinemann Kenya, 1958.

Agence France Press. "Experts end count of Tsavo elephants." *Daily Nation* [Nairobi, Kenya], June 20, 1989, 3.

Barr, Ann, et al. *The Official Sloane Ranger Handbook*. London: Ebury Press, 1982.

Bentsen, Cheryl. *Maasai Days*. New York: Summit Books, 1989.

Blum, Deborah. *The Monkey Wars*. New York: Oxford University Press, 1994.

Boyles, Denis. *Man Eaters Motel: And Other Stops on the Railway to Nowhere: An East African Traveler's Nightbook*. New York: Ticknor & Fields, 1991.

Boynton, Graham. "Slaughter of the Herds: At the current rate of killing, the African elephant and black rhino will barely survive another decade." *Condé Nast Traveler*, September 1989, 140-170.

Bull, Milan. Personal communication. Dec. 11, 1995.

Campbell, Andrew. "In their decades watching the baboons of Kenya, Jeanne and Stuart Altmann have discovered a rich social world where behavior and biology meet." *University of Chicago Magazine* 87:6 (1995): 31-35.

Carey, Susan. "Tracking travel: Travelers book safaris despite unrest in Africa." *The Wall Street Journal*, May 31, 1994, B1.

Carey, Susan. "Tourism Blooms in 'New' South Africa, Now That Political Skies Are Clearing." *The Wall Street Journal*, Nov. 11, 1994, A10.

Chadwick, Douglas H. "Elephants: Out of Time, Out of Space." *National Geographic*, May 1991, 2-49.

Crowther, Geoff. *East Africa: A Travel Survival Kit*. 1st ed., Victoria, Australia: Lonely Planet, 1987.

Davidson, Basil. *Africa in History*. New York: Macmillan, 1968.

Davidson, Basil. *African Kingdoms*. Great Ages of Man: A History of the World's Cultures. Alexandria, Va.: Time-Life Books, 1971.

Degler, Carl N. *Neither Black Nor White: Slavery and Race Relations in Brazil and the United States*. New York: Macmillan, 1971.

Dieke, Peter U.C. "Cross-National Comparison of Tourism Development; Lessons from Kenya and The Gambia." *The Journal of Tourism Studies* 4:1 (1993): 2-18.

Douglas-Hamilton, Oria. "Africa's Elephants: Can They Survive." *National Geographic*, November 1980, 568-603.

Entwhistle, Jim. ""An African Primer" [Letter to Book World: Recommended Reading on *Things Fall Apart*]. *The Washington Post*, April 2, 1989, Book World page 15.

French, Mary Ann. "Hunger pangs: For the troops, the famine is hard to bear. And maybe a little harder if you are black." *The Washington Post*, Jan. 3, 1993, F1.

Gellhorn, Martha. *Travels With Myself and Another*. London: Allen Lane, 1978.

Haltenorth, Theodor, et al. *A Field Guide to the Mammals of Africa including Madagascar*. London: Collins, 1980.

Harris, Eddy. *Native Stranger: A Black American's Journey into the Heart of Africa*. New York: Simon & Schuster, 1992.

Henry, Neil. "Kenya Burns Tusks to Dramatize Effort to Wipe Out Ivory Trade." *The Washington Post*, July 19, 1989, A19.

Henry, Neil. "Nyerere Bows Out With Tanzania In Deep Decline." *The Washington Post*, Sept. 26, 1990, A27.

Henry, Neil. "Distant War Brings Hard Times to Lamu; On Kenyan Island, Charlie Green Eyes Returns to Sea as Fear of Terrorism Keeps Tourists Home." *The Washington Post*, Feb. 24, 1991, A17.

Henry, Neil. "A Stranger in Africa: In the Continent of My Ancestors, Was I a Returned Son or Just Another Westerner?" *The Washington Post*, Aug. 18, 1991, C1.

Hevesi, Dennis. "19 Connecticut Residents Return After Theft and Slaying in Kenya." *The New York Times*, July 31, 1989, B3.

Hevrdejs, Judy. "Safaris survive big problems in a big continent." *Chicago Tribune*, July 10, 1994, 12-1.

Hiltzik, Michael A. "For Africa's Hunters, It's a New Battle; Beast is Bureaucracy." *The Los Angeles Times*, June 24, 1988, I-1, I-8.

Hiltzik, Michael. *A Death in Kenya: The Murder of Julie Ward*. New York: Delacorte Press, 1991.

Hitchings, Thomas E., ed. *Facts on File Yearbook 1989*. New York: Facts on File, 1990.

Johnson, Adrienne M. "A heritage reclaimed" [Report on visit to Ghana, including Elmina Fort where captive slaves were loaded]. *The Los Angeles Times*, Oct. 23, 1994, L16.

Kelley, Kitty. *Jackie Oh!* New York: Ballantine Books, 1984.

Lamb, David. *The Africans*. New York: Vintage Books, 1987.

Lee, Mary. Personal communication, Voyagers International, Ithaca, N.Y. Dec. 13, 1995.

Markham, Beryl. *West with the Night*. San Francisco: North Point Press, 1942, 1983.

McCarthy, Colman. "A Perfect Match-Up: Mark Gearan and the Peace Corps of the '90s." *The Washington Post*, Aug. 10, 1995, C5.

McEvedy, Colin. *The Penguin Atlas of African History*. London: Penguin Book, 1980.

McKinley Jr., James C. "Warily, the Masai Embrace the Animal Kingdom." *The New York Times*, March 13, 1996, A4.

Mochi, Ugo, et al. *A Natural History of Giraffes*. New York: Charles Scribner's Sons, 1973.

Moss, Cynthia. *Elephant Memories: Thirteen Years in the Life of an Elephant Family*. New York: William Morrow and Co. Inc., 1988.

Murray, Jocelyn, ed. *Cultural Atlas of Africa*. New York: Equinox for Facts on File, 1993.

Noble, Ron. "U.S. Blacks and Africans Seek Stronger Ties." *The New York Times*, May 27, 1993, A10.

Omari, Emman. "Minister condemns malicious US Press; Reports on tourist murders in Kenya 'alarmist'." *Daily Nation* [Nairobi, Kenya], Aug. 2, 1989, 1, 12.

Packer, Craig. "Captives in the Wild; They seem the picture of health, these lionesses hunting in an extinct volcano. But cut off within its walls, they are threatened by an unseen foe—inbreeding." *National Geographic*, April 1992, 122-136.

Padgett, Bill. "The African Elephant, Africa, and CITES: The Next Step." *Indiana Journal of Global Legal Studies* 2 (2 Spring 1995) (available at http://www.law.indiana.edu/glsj/vol2-/no2/padgett.html).

Payne, Katharine. "Elephant Talk." *National Geographic*, August 1989, 264-277.

PBS Home Video. "A World of Ideas with Bill Moyers: Chinua Achebe." Beverly Hills, Calif.: Pacific Arts Video Publishing, 1990.

Reuter. "Conservationist George Adamson killed in Kenya." *The Baltimore Sun*, Aug. 22, 1989, 1A, 4A.

Reynolds, Christopher. "The African-American Connection; Finding 'links to the souls of our ancestors' on a cultural pilgrimage to West Africa." *The Los Angeles Times*, Sept. 20, 1992, L1.

Reynolds, Christopher. "Opening Travelers' Eyes to Africa's Big Picture." *The Los Angeles Times*, May 31, 1992, L2.

Richburg, Keith B. "Swahili's Mixed Blessing for Tanzania; English Abilities in Decline as Language Conversion Effort Succeeds." *The Washington Post*, March 22, 1992, A25.

Richburg, Keith B. "Continental Divide." *The Washington Post Magazine*, March 26, 1995, 30.

Schaller, George B. *The Serengeti Lion; A Study of Predator-Prey Relations*. Chicago, Ill.: The University of Chicago Press, 1972.

Sindiga, Isaac. "Employment and Training in Tourism in Kenya." *The Journal of Tourism Studies* 5:2 (December 1994): 45-52.

Sowell, Thomas. *The Economics and Politics of Race*. New York: Quill, 1983.

Sowell, Thomas. *Race and Culture: A World View*. New York: BasicBooks, 1994.

Thomas, Elizabeth Marshall. "Of Ivory and the Survival of Elephants." *The New York Review of Books*, March 24, 1994, 3.

Wiebers, D.O., et al. "Animal Protection and Medical Science." *Lancet* 343 (April 9, 1994): 902-904.

Yenckel, James T. "The Prevailing Winds of Africa; Update: Hot Spots to Watch and Rules to Remember." *The Washington Post*, Oct. 28, 1990, E1.

Japan

The Outline of Atomic Bomb Damage in Hiroshima. Hiroshima Peace Memorial Museum, 1978.

The Making of James Clavell's Shogun. New York: Dell, 1980.

Learning from Shogun: Japanese history and western fantasy. Santa Barbara, Calif.: Program of Asian Studies, University of California, Santa Barbara, 1980.

An English Dictionary of Japanese Ways of Thinking. Japan: Yuhikaku, 1989.

A Brief Summary of the Atomic Bombing and Its Effects. Hiroshima Peace Memorial Museum, 1989.

Japan: A Pocket Guide. Japan Foreign Press Center. 1990.

Hiroshima. Hiroshima Peace Culture Foundation, 1991. 3rd edition.

Associated Press. "Bush: No Apology to Japan for A-Bombs." *The Washington Post*, Dec. 2, 1991, A18.

Associated Press. "Japanese Issues Apology

in S. Korea." *The Washington Post*, Jan. 17, 1992, A28.

Baldrige, Letitia. *Letitia Baldrige's Complete Guide to Executive Manners*. New York: Rawson Associates, 1985.

Barry, Dave. *Dave Barry Does Japan*. New York: Random House, 1992.

Belliveau, Jeannette. "A Tale of Two Cultures; Japanese, Americans Wonder, What's Life All About?" *The Baltimore Sun*, Nov. 24, 1991, 4N.

Blustein, Paul. "Japan Issues Apology for War Actions; Kaifu Statement Bespeaks New Japanese World Role." *The Washington Post*, May 3, 1991, A18.

Blustein, Paul. "Japan Sets New Plan to Aid WWII Victims; $1 Billion Pledged to Benefit Asian Neighbors." *The Washington Post*, Sept. 1, 1994, A31.

Chamberlin, William Henry. "Japan." In *Encyclopædia Britannica*, 893-954. 12. Chicago: University of Chicago Press, 1948.

Chambers, Kevin, et al. *Japanese Phrasebook*. Language Survival Kit, Hawthorn, Australia: Lonely Planet, 1989.

Clavell, James. *Shogun*. New York: Dell Publishing, 1975.

Dale, Peter N. *The Myth of Japanese Uniqueness*. New York: St. Martin's Press, 1986.

De Hoog, John. "Shelties in other countries" in *Shetland sheepdogs FAQ* (available at http://www.magicnet.net/~michon-/ssfaq.html and other sites). 1995.

East, W. Gordon. *The Geography Behind History: How physical environment affects historical events*. New York: W.W. Norton and Company, Inc., 1965.

Editors of Army Times, ed. *Pearl Harbor and Hawaii: A Military History*. New York: Walker and Co., 1971.

Goldberg, Carey. "The honors come late for a Japanese Schindler; A month of tribute to savior of thousands." *The New York Times*, Nov. 8, 1995, B1.

Gup, Ted. "Up from Ground Zero: Hiroshima." *National Geographic*, August 1995, 78-101.

Halloran, Fumiko Mori. "War's Memory; Battle of Souls: Who was responsible? And who will be?" *Japan Update*, April 1993, 14-15.

Halloran, Fumiko Mori. "Flash of Darkness: Hiroshima's shadow." *Japan Update*, November 1993, 16-17.

Halloran, Fumiko Mori. "A Legacy of Democracy: The deaths of war were not in vain." *Japan Update*, May 1995, 14-15.

Hershey, John. *Hiroshima*. New York: Bantam, 1946.

Hiatt, Fred. "Japan Offers Apology for Colonizing Korea; Emperor Expresses 'Deepest Regret' to Roh." *The Washington Post*, May 25, 1990, A31.

Iyer, Pico. *The Lady and the Monk*. New York: Alfred A. Knopf, 1991.

Iyer, Pico. *Video Night in Kathmandu*. New York: Alfred E. Knopf, 1988.

Katzenstein, Gary J. *Funny Business: An Outsider's Year in Japan*. New York: Soho Press, 1989.

Kennedy, Paul. *The Rise and Fall of the Great Powers: Economic Change and Military Conflict from 1500 to 2000*. New York: Random House, 1987.

Kristof, Nicholas D. "Tokyo Journal; Why a Nation of Apologizers Makes One Large Exception." *The New York Times*, June 12, 1995, A1.

Kristof, Nicholas D. "Tokyo Journal; Today's History Lesson: What Rape of Nanjing?" *The New York Times*, July 4, 1996, A4.

Levine, Hillel. "Sugihara's List." *The New York Times*, Sept. 20, 1994, A23.

Martin, Judith. *Miss Manners' Guide for the Turn-of-the-Millennium*. New York: Pharos Books, 1989.

McQueen, Ian L. *Japan: A Travel Survival Kit*. 3rd ed. Hawthorn, Australia: Lonely Planet, 1989.

Moore, David W., et al. "People Throughout the World Largely Satisfied with Their Lives." *The Gallup Poll Monthly* 357 (June 1995): 2 (available at http://-www.gallup.com/international/6-95.html).

Morita, Masayoshi, ed. *Japan 1995: An International Comparison*. Tokyo, Japan: Keizai Koho Center, 1994.

Newport, Frank. "Majority Still Approve Use of Atom Bombs on Japan in World War II." *The Gallup Poll Monthly* 359 (August 1995): 2 (available at http://www.gallup-.com/newsletter/aug95/3atombom.html).

News Services. "Japan's Apology to Pyongyang." *The Washington Post*, Jan. 31, 1991, A20.

Nobile, Philip, ed. *Judgment at the Smithsonian: The Bombing of Hiroshima and Nagasaki*. New York: Marlowe, 1995.

O'Rourke, P.J. "Seoul Brothers." In *Holidays in Hell*, 257. New York: Atlantic Monthly Press, 1988.

Oliner, Samuel P., et al. *The Altruistic Personality: Rescuers of Jews in Nazi Europe*. New York: The Free Press, 1988.

Reid, T.R. "Miyazawa Expresses 'Remorse'; Japanese Premier Calls Pearl Harbor 'Unbearable Blow'." *The Washington Post*, Dec. 7, 1991, A1.

Reid, T.R. "Official Voices Japan's 'Remorse' Over War." *The Washington Post*, Dec. 4, 1991, A1.

Reid, T.R. "Doves Fill Sky Over Hiroshima; For 47 Years, City Serves as Conscience of World." *The Washington Post*, Aug. 7, 1992, A14.

Reid, T.R. "New Japanese Leader Begins Policy Changes; Prime Minister Apologizes for World War, Vows to Open Markets to Foreign Exports." *The Washington Post*, Aug. 24, 1993, A12.

Reid, T.R. "Openly Apologetic, Japan Recalls War's End." *The Washington Post*, Aug. 16, 1993, A12.

Reid, T.R. "Japan Apologizes to Sex Slaves; Premier Cites WWII Abuse of Captive Women." *The Washington Post*, Aug. 5, 1993, A1.

Reid, T.R. "Japan Apologizes to Itself for Pearl Harbor; 'Deeply Regrettable' Lapse by Diplomats Said to Have Bought Shame to Country." *The Washington Post*, Nov. 22, 1994, A23.

Reid, T.R. "50 Years After the Bomb, Japan Agonizes Over Its Role in the War." *The Washington Post*, Aug. 6, 1995, A22.

Reid, T.R. "Once Again, Life Stops in Hiroshima: 50 Years From Moment the A-Bomb Struck, City Stands Still." *The Washington Post*, Aug. 6, 1995, A1, A22.

Reid, T.R. "Asia Underwhelmed by Japan's Apology: Statement on WWII Gets Tepid Reaction Elsewhere, but Could Play Well Politically at Home." *The Washington Post*, Aug. 16, 1995, A21, A22.

Reid, T.R. "Nagasaki Voters Oust Mayor Who Called A-Bomb War Crime." *The Washington Post*, April 25, 1995, A13.

Reid, T.R. "Mayor of Nagasaki Equates A-Bombs With the Holocaust." *The Washington Post*, March 16, 1995, A29, A35.

Reinhold, Robert. "Recalling Pearl Harbor, Bush Urges an End to Rancor." *The New York Times*, Dec. 8, 1991, A1.

Reischauer, Edwin O. *The Japanese Today*. Rutland, Vt.; Tokyo, Japan: Charles A. Tuttle Co., 1988.

Ringle, Ken. "At Ground Zero; 2 Views of History Collide over Smithsonian A-Bomb Exhibit." *The Washington Post*, Sept. 26, 1994, A1.

Ringle, Ken. "A-Bomb Exhibit Plan Revamped; Smithsonian Acts to Defuse Criticism." *The Washington Post*, Aug. 30, 1994, C1.

Ringle, Ken. "Still Waiting for an Apology: Historian Gavan Daws, Calling Japan on War Crimes." *The Washington Post*, March 16, 1995, D1, D2.

Seward, Jack. *The Japanese*. Tokyo, Japan: Yohan Publications, 1988.

Silverstone, Paul H. *Directory of the World's Capital Ships*. New York: Hippocrene Books, 1984.

Sun, Lena H. "Emperor Regrets War Acts in China; Japan's Akihito Stops Short of an Apology." *The Washington Post*, Oct. 24, 1992, A13.

Tannen, Deborah. *Gender and Discourse*. New York: Oxford University Press, 1994.

Tanzer, Andrew. "Techie heaven; Part electronics bazaar, part product showcase and test market, Tokyo's Akihabara district has become a prime tourist destination." *Forbes*, Sept. 16, 1991, 184-185.

Theroux, Paul. *The Kingdom by the Sea: A Journey Around Great Britain*. Boston: Houghton Mifflin Co., 1983.

Ukers, William H. "Tea." In *Encyclopædia*

Britannica, 857-861. 21. Chicago: University of Chicago Press, 1948.

United Nations Development Program. *Human Development Report 1994*. New York, London: Oxford Press, 1994.

Walmsley, Jane. *Brit-Think, Ameri-Think: A Transatlantic Survival Guide*. New York: Penguin Books, 1987.

Weinraub, Bernard. "Islamic nations move to keep out 'Schindler's List'." *The New York Times*, April 7, 1994, C15.

White, Leslie A. *The Concept of Cultural Systems: A Key to Understanding Tribes and Nations*. New York: Columbia University Press, 1975.

Wicker, Tom. *On Press: A Top Reporter's Life in, and Reflections on, American Journalism*. New York: The Viking Press, 1975.

Wolferen, Karel van. *The Enigma of Japanese Power*. New York: Knopf, 1989.

Zich, Arthur. *The Rising Sun*. World War II • Time-Life Books, ed. William K. Goolrick. Alexandria, Va.: Time-Life Books, 1977.

Polynesia

"Protests hurt wine's sales." *The New York Times*, Dec. 25, 1995, A58.

Housing Vacancy Survey, Annual Statistics. U.S. Census Bureau, 1995. Table 13: Homeownership Rates by State: 1984 to 1995 (available at http://www.census-.gov/hhes-/housing/hvs/annual95-/ann95t13.html).

NAEP (National Assessment of Educational Progress) 1994 U.S. History Assessment and *1994 U.S. Geography Assessment*. Office of Educational Research and Improvement, U.S. Department of Education, 1994 (available at http://www.ed.gov/NCES-/naep/y25flk/hbro.shtml and at http://-www.ed.gov/NCES/NAEP/y25flk/-gbro.shtml).

Population of states on July 1, 1992 by race. Administrative Records and Methodology Research Branch, U.S. Census Bureau, Sept. 20, 1995. PPL-3 (available at http://www.census.gov/ftp/pub/population/estimate-extract/state/intnttbl1.tbl).

Polynesian Voyaging Society Information Service, 1996, web site available at http://leahi.kcc.hawaii.edu/org/pvs-/pvs.html). 1996.

Attributed by some authorities to Captain James Cook. *A Journal of a Voyage Around the World in H.M.S. Endeavour 1768-1771*. Reprint of the London, 1771 edition. New York: Da Capo Press, 1967.

"NTSB urges increase in frequency of fatigue testing of transports." *Aviation Week and Space Technology* 131 (20 1989): 83.

Baldridge, H. David. *Shark Attack*. Anderson, S.C.: Droke House/Hallux Inc., 1974.

Banks, Joseph. *The Endeavour Journal of Joseph Banks 1768-1771*. Vol. I. ed. J.C. Beaglehole. Sydney, Australia: Trustees of the Public Library of New South Wales in association with Angus & Robertson Ltd., 1962.

Barclay, Glen. *A History of the Pacific*. New York: Taplinger, 1978.

Belliveau, Jeannette. "Beyond Tahiti: Of Sharks & Sand on Restful Rangiroa." *The Washington Post*, Jan. 12, 1986, E2.

Belliveau, Jeannette. "Molokai's Aloha Spirit: On the island of Molokai, Hawaii is as it used to be." *The Baltimore Sun*, Feb. 9, 1992, K1, K5.

Belliveau, Louis J. Personal communication. Sept. 27, 1995.

Bellwood, Peter. *The Polynesians: Prehistory of an Island People*. Revised paperback ed., New York: Thames and Hudson, 1987.

Bendure, Glenda, et al. *Hawaii: A Travel Survival Kit*. Victoria, Australia: Lonely Planet, 1990.

Bisignani, J.D. *Maui Handbook: Including Molokai and Lanai*. 2nd ed., Chico, Calif.: Moon Publications, 1989.

Bisignani, J.D. *Big Island of Hawaii Handbook*. Chico, Calif.: Moon Publications, 1990.

Bunge, Frederica M. et al., ed. *Oceania: A Regional Study*. 2nd ed., Foreign Area Studies, The American University. Washington, D.C.: Department of the Army, 1984.

Burgess, George H., director, International Shark Attack File (available at http://www.flmnh.ufl.edu/natsci/ichthyology/shark.html). Personal communication. Jan. 4, 1996.

Bushnell, O.A. "Seafarers Find the Islands." In *Hawaii Volcanos National Park* [descriptive brochure]. National Park Service, U.S. Department of the Interior.

Cannon, Lou. "Waving (and Lowering) Flag in Hawaii; Pride, anger result as governor pushes native people's cause on coup's centennial." *The Washington Post*, Jan. 17, 1993, A33.

Clark, Eugenie. *The Lady and the Sharks*. New York: Harper & Row, 1969.

Clarke, Thurston. "The Wayfinders; A revival of ancient seafaring techniques launches a Polynesian renaissance." *Travel Holiday*, October 1995, 42.

Courbet, Yves. Personal communication. June 3, 1996.

Curtsinger, Bill. "Close Encounters with the Gray Reef Shark." [Describes conditions at Bikini Atoll.] *National Geographic*, January 1995, 45.

D'Souza, Dinesh. *The End of Racism*. New York: The Free Press, 1995.

Dingerkus, Guido. *The Shark Watchers' Guide*. A Messner Guide, New York: Julian Messner, 1985.

Fernandez-Armesto, Felipe, ed. *The Times Atlas of World Exploration*. New York: HarperCollins, 1991.

Finlay, Iain, et al. *Across the South Pacific: Island-hopping from Santiago to Sydney*. London: Angus & Robertson, 1981.

FitzGerald, Frances. *Fire in the Lake: The Vietnamese and the Americans in Vietnam*. Boston: Little, Brown and Company, 1972.

Hakewill, Peter, et al. "Health consequences of nuclear tests in French Polynesia." *The Lancet* 346 (Aug. 26, 1995): 576.

Hall, Ron. "Passage through paradise; Undertraveled, underpopulated, and definitively idyllic, Polynesia's islands awaited only the assiduous guide." *Condé Nast Traveler*, April 1991, 102-174.

Helm, Thomas. *Shark! Unpredictable Killer of the Sea*. New York: Dodd, Mead, 1961.

Hough, Richard. *The Last Voyage of Captain James Cook*. New York: William Morrow, 1979.

Hough, Richard. *Captain James Cook: A Biography*. New York: W.W. Norton, 1994.

Johnson, Donald D. "American Impact on the Pacific Islands Since World War II." In *Oceania and Beyond: Essays on the Pacific Since 1945*, ed. F. P. King. 232-243. Westport, Conn.: Greenwood Press, 1976.

Kami, Taholo. Personal communication. Jan. 5, 1996.

Kay, Robert F. *Tahiti and French Polynesia: A Travel Survival Kit*. 2nd ed., Victoria, Australia: Lonely Planet, 1988.

Linden, Eugene. "Reimagining Polynesia." *Condé Nast Traveler*, June 1996, 110-119, 160-165.

Lintner, Bertil. "Not Neighbourly: Australia bristles at France's presence in its backyard." *Far Eastern Economic Review*, Nov. 30, 1995, 20-22.

McGarvey, Stephen T. "Obesity of Samoans and a perspective on its etiology in Polynesians." *The American Journal of Clinical Nutrition* 53 (6 June 1991): 1586S-1594S.

McMahon, Bucky. "Lord Long Arms I Presume? Just when you thought it was safe to go back into the water, shark attacks are on the rise. A report from the impact zone." *Outside*, July 1993, 62-67, 131-135.

Michener, James A. "From the Inland Sea." In *Hawaii*. New York: Random House, 1959, 752-761.

Moorehead, Alan. *The Fatal Impact: An Account of the Invasion of the South Pacific, 1767-1840*. New York: Harper & Row, 1966.

Murphy, Geri. "Rangiroa: Sharks On Parade in a South Seas Paradise." *Skin Diver*, April 1993, 74-107.

Osborn, Annie Marion. *Rousseau and Burke*. New York: Russell & Russell, 1940 (reissued in 1964).

Patrick, John J. *Achievement of Knowledge by High School Students in Core Subjects of the Social Studies*. ERIC Clearinghouse for Social Studies/Social Science Education, 1991. ED329486 (available by searching for "social studies" at gopher://gopher.-ed.gov/11/programs/ERIC/searchs).

Perrine, Doug. "Reef shark attack! New clues raise new questions about why sharks bite people." *Sea Frontiers*, Jan. 1, 1989, 31-41.

Philip, Maurice. "A Visit to Kia Ora Village [Rangiroa]." *Tahiti Magazine*, March 1985, 25-27.

Prince, Al, et al. "Trouble in Paradise: France's nuclear test causes Tahitian riots and brings global condemnation." *Time*, Sept. 18, 1995, 85-87.

Raeder, Kit. "Paradise on the Horizon: Tahiti, Bora-Bora, Moorea. Are the South Pacific islands really the Garden of Eden or simply a tired cliché?" *European Travel & Life*, March 1991, 103-108.

Royte, Elizabeth. "On the brink: Hawaii's vanishing species." *National Geographic*, January 1995, 2-37.

Saavedra, Rodolfo. Personal communication. Jan. 5, 1996.

Shapiro, Walter. "'The Plane Was Disintegrating:' A jet with its roof blown off makes a miracle landing." *Time*, May 9, 1988, 38.

Shenon, Philip. "Nuclear Test Tarnishes France's Image in Pacific." *The New York Times*, Sept. 1, 1995, A3.

Sinoto, Yosihiko. "The Marquesas." In *The Prehistory of Polynesia*, ed. Jesse D. Jennings. 130-132. Cambridge, Mass., and London: Harvard University Press, 1979.

Stanley, David. *Tahiti-Polynesia Handbook*. Chico, Calif.: Moon Publications, 1996.

Suggs, Robert C. *Marquesan Sexual Behavior*. New York: Harcourt, Brace and World, 1966.

Tagupa, William E. "France, French Polynesia and the South Pacific in the Nuclear Age." In *Oceania and Beyond: Essays on the Pacific Since 1945*, ed. F. P. King. 200-215. Westport, Conn.: Greenwood Press, 1976.

Theroux, Paul. *The Happy Isles of Oceania: Paddling the Pacific*. New York: G.P. Putnam's Sons, 1992.

Toynbee, Arnold J. *A Study of History*. Abridgement of volumes I-VI by D.C. Somervell. New York and London: Oxford University Press, 1947.

Trask, Haunani-Kay. *From a Native Daughter: Colonialism and Sovereignty in Hawaii*. Monroe, Maine: Common Courage Press, 1993.

Trask, Haunani-Kay. "Comment: Hawaiian sovereignty drive signals trouble in paradise; professor says the islands' native Hawaiians are among the poorest in the nation." *USA Today*, Nov. 3, 1993, Op-Ed.

Veeken, Hans. "French Polynesia: a nuclear paradise in the Pacific." *BMJ* [British Medical Journal] 311 (7003 Aug. 19, 1995): 497-99.

Walker, Bryce S. "Molokai: This island off the beaten track lets you luxuriate in Hawaii's natural beauty and sensuous tropical atmosphere without encountering droves of fellow tourists." *National Geographic Traveler*, July 1990, 34-46.

Ward, Peter. "Lost Islands" [Description of extinctions on Hawaiian and Tahitian islands]. In *The End of Evolution*, 213-44. New York: Bantam, 1994.

Whitney, Craig R. "Paris Defends Seizing Ship in Atom Test Zone." *The New York Times*, July 11, 1995, A12.

Whitney, Craig R. "France Ending Nuclear Tests That Caused Broad Protests." *The New York Times*, Jan. 30, 1996, A1, A4.

Withey, Lynne. *Voyages of Discovery: Captain Cook and the Exploration of the Pacific*. New York: William Morrow, 1987.

Thailand

Travel Industry Targets Sex Tourism. World Tourism Organization, 1995 (available at http://www.world-tourism.org/travind-.html).

Thailand. Nagel's Encyclopedia-Guide, Geneva: Nagel, 1973.

Thailand Human Rights Practices, 1995. U.S. State Department, March 1996 (available at http://dosfan.lib.uic.edu/0F-1%3A23308%3-AThailand).

Sail Thailand. ed. Collin Piprell. Bangkok: Artasia Press, 1991.

Barth, John. *Sabbatical: A Romance*. New York: G.P. Putnam's Sons, 1982.

Belliveau, Jeannette. "Thai Tack: Escaping Washington's Woes for a Week of Perfect Sailing Amid the Islands off Phuket." *The Washington Post*, March 6, 1994, E1, E7.

Belloc, Hilaire. *The Cruise of the "Nona."* Westminster, Md.: The Newman Press, 1956 (originally published in 1925).

Brummelhuis, Han ten. *Mobility, Marriage and Sex Work: Thai in the Netherlands*. Faculty of Socio-Political Sciences, University of Amsterdam, April 1996.

Childers, Erskine. *The Riddle of the Sands*. The Mariners Library, London: Rupert Hart-Davis Limited, 1955 (first published 1903).

Donner, Wolf. "The South (Peninsular Thailand): Topography." In *The Five Faces of Thailand: An Economic Geography*, 406-410. New York: St. Martin's Press, 1978.

Gray, John C. *Sea Canoes and Their Importance to Thailand* [contains explanation of *hong* formation]. Available at http://www.inet.-co.th/cybermall/seacanoe.tei.html.

Higsborg, Marianne, et al. *Prostitution and Its Context in Denmark*. Commission of the European Community, Europe against AIDS, 1994.

Jones, Tristan. *The Incredible Voyage*. London: Grafton Books, 1977.

Jones, Tristan. "The Bay of Phangnga." In *To Venture Further: An Incredible Sea-Voyage — An Inspiring Challenge*, 103-107. London: Grafton Books, 1991.

Kundera, Milan. *The Unbearable Lightness of Being*. New York: Harper & Row, 1984.

Lambert, David. *The Field Guide to Geology*. New York: Facts on File, 1988.

Moore, Frank J., ed. *Thailand*. New Haven, Conn.: Hraf Press, 1974.

Ohse, Ulla. *Forced Prostitution and Traffic in Women in West Germany*. Edinburgh, Scotland: Human Rights Group, 1984.

Robinson, Bill. *Best Sailing Spots Worldwide*. New York: Hearst Marine Books, 1991.

Robinson, Daniel, et al. "The North: Halong Bay." In *Vietnam: A Travel Survival Kit*, 431-435. Berkeley, Calif.: Lonely Planet, 1993.

Slocum, Captain Joshua. *Sailing Alone Around the World*. New York: Dover Publications, 1956 (originally published in 1900).

Strahler, Arthur N. *Physical Geography*. 2nd ed., New York: John Wiley & Sons, 1960.

Sverdrup, Tina. Comparative evaluation of sailing areas worldwide (personal communication). Jan. 28, 1996.

Yeadon, David. "Southern Thailand: Sea Drifting and Other Serendipities." In *The Back of Beyond: Travels to the Wild Places of the Earth*, 379-404. New York: HarperCollins, 1991.

Yeung, Linda. "Trafficking in women is becoming a growth industry." *South China Morning Post*, Sept. 4, 1995, reprinted in Migration News 2 (October 1995): 10 (available at http://128.120.36.171/By-Month/MN-Vol-2-95/MN_Oct_1995.html).

Young, Gavin. *Slow Boats to China*. London: Hutchinson, 1981.

Greece

Staff and wire reports. "Names and Faces: Not-So-Hot Yacht" [difficulty in auctioning *Christina*]. *The Washington Post*, June 1, 1993, C3.

"Roman History," "Roman Law." In *Encyclopædia Britannica*, 505-544; 544-553. Vol. 19. Chicago: University of Chicago Press, 1967.

Atkinson, Rick. "Why Ted Kennedy Can't Stand Still" [analysis of stress of sailing]. *The Washington Post Magazine*, April 29, 1990, 11.

Boardman, John, et al., ed. *The Oxford History of the Classical World*. Oxford, England: Oxford University Press, 1986.

Bull, Adrian. *The Economics of Travel and Tourism*. New York: Wiley, 1991.

Cetron, Marvin, and Owen Davies. *American Renaissance; Our life at the turn of the 21st century*. New York: St. Martin's Press, 1989.

Durgan, Charity A. "Tourism and Travel Jobs, By Country: 1994." In *Gale Country & World Rankings Reporter*, 559. New York: Gale Research Inc., 1995.

Hall, Rosemary. *Greece: Travel Survival Kit*. 1st ed., Lonely Planet, 1994.

Harrington, Spencer P.M. "Shoring Up the Temple of Athena." *Archaeology* 45 (1 January 1992): 30-43.

Hiestand, Emily. "Following Hermes." In *The Very Rich Hours: Travels in Orkney,*

Belize, the Everglades and Greece, 57-110. Boston, Mass.: Beacon Press, 1992.

Homer. *The Odyssey.*

Howe, Marvine. "Now It's Official: Athens Smog is Europe's Worst." *The New York Times,* May 12, 1983, A2.

Jenkins, Loren. "Lesbos Declares Dukakis a Winner; Greek Isle Loves the Candidate, Who Visited Once 12 Years Ago." *The Washington Post,* June 26, 1988, A22.

Kaplan, Robert D. "Greece: Western Mistress, Eastern Bride." In *Balkan Ghosts: A Journey Through History,* 233-281. New York: Vintage Departures, 1993.

Kennedy, Paul. *The Rise and Fall of the Great Powers: Economic Change and Military Conflict from 1500 to 2000.* New York: Random House, 1987.

Kennedy, Paul. *Preparing for the Twenty-first Century.* New York: Random House, 1993.

Kotkin, Joel, and Yoriko Kishimoto. *The Third Century: America's Resurgence in the Asian Era.* New York: Crown, 1988.

Krugman, Paul. *The Age of Diminished Expectations: U.S. Economic Policy in the 1990s.* Revised and updated ed., Cambridge, Mass.: The MIT Press, 1994.

Liversidge, Joan. *Everyday Life in the Roman Empire.* New York: G.P. Putnam's Sons, 1976.

Lundestad, Geir. *The American "Empire;" and other studies of US foreign policy in a comparative perspective.* Oxford, England: Oxford University Press, 1990.

Lundestad, Geir. "The End of the Cold War, the New Role for Europe, and the Decline of the United States." *Diplomatic History* 16 (2 Spring 1992): 247.

Maloney, Elbert S. *Chapman Piloting: Seamanship & Small Boat Handling.* 57th ed., New York: Hearst Marine Books, 1985.

Matthews, Harry G. *International Tourism: A Political and Social Analysis.* Cambridge, Mass.: Schenkman Publishing Co., 1978.

Matthews, John. "Roman Life and Society: Distances and Diversity." In *The Oxford History of the Classical World,* ed. John Boardman, et al. 748-754. Oxford, England: Oxford University Press, 1986.

Mehling, Marianne, ed. *Athens and Attica. A Phaidon Cultural Guide.* New York: Prentice Hall Press, 1986.

Mouzeli, Nicos P. "Cultural Underdevelopment and the Ancient Greek Heritage." In *Modern Greece: Facets of Underdevelopment,* 145-147. New York: Holmes & Meier Publishers, 1979.

Neill, Stephen. *Colonialism and Christian Missions.* New York: McGraw-Hill, 1966.

Rousmaniere, John. *The Annapolis Book of Seamanship.* 2nd ed., New York: Simon and Schuster, 1989.

Shapiro, Andrew L. *We're Number One: Where America stands—and falls—in the New World Order.* New York: Vintage Books, 1992.

Spengler, Oswald. *The Decline of the West.* Vol. I. New York: Alfred A. Knopf, 1926.

Stevens, Stuart. *Malaria Dreams: An African Adventure.* New York: The Atlantic Monthly Press, 1989.

Thomas, Robert McG. Jr. "Stavros Niarchos, Greek Shipping Magnate and the Archrival of Onassis, Is Dead at 86." *The New York Times,* April 18, 1996, B9.

Toynbee, Arnold J. *The Greeks and Their Heritages.* Oxford: Oxford University Press, 1981.

Vellas, François, et al. *International Tourism: An Economic Perspective.* New York: St. Martin's Press, 1995.

Wolfe, Tom. "2020 A.D." *Esquire,* January 1985, 88-97.

Yeadon, David. "Kea: Looking for Zorba." In *The Back of Beyond: Travels to the Wild Places of the Earth,* 226-240. New York: HarperCollins, 1991.

The Yucatan

"The Cutting Edge; Vital Statistics—Prevalence of Mental Disorders." *The Washington Post,* Feb. 15, 1994, Health section, p. 5.

Abercrombie, Thomas J. "Ibn Battuta: Prince of Travelers." *National Geographic,* December 1991, 2-49.

Barnouw, Victor. *An Introduction to Anthropology: Ethnology.* 3rd ed., Vol. 2. The Dorsey Series in Anthropology, Homewood, Ill.: The Dorsey Press, 1978.

Baudez, Claude, et al. *Lost Cities of the Maya.* New York: Henry N. Adams, 1992.

Belloc, Hilaire. *The Cruise of the "Nona."* Westminster, Md.: The Newman Press, 1956 (originally published in 1925).

Brosnahan, Tom. *La Ruta Maya: Yucatan, Guatemala & Belize.* Berkeley, Calif.: Lonely Planet, 1991.

Bruns, Rebecca, ed. *Hidden Mexico: Adventurer's Guide to the Beaches and Coasts.* Berkeley, Calif.: Ulysses Press, 1987.

Charney, Désiré. "The Two Discoverers of Yaxchilan." In *They Found the Buried Cities,* ed. Robert Wauchope. 184. Chicago: University of Chicago Press, 1965.

Childe, V. Gordon. *Social Evolution.* Cleveland and New York: Meridian Books, 1951.

Clancy, Flora Simmons. *Pyramids.* Smithsonian Exploring the Ancient World, Montreal and Washington, D.C.: St. Remy Press and Smithsonian Institution, 1994.

Coe, Michael D. *The Maya.* New York: Thames and Hudson, 1993.

Coe, William R. *Tikal: A Handbook of the Ancient Maya Ruins.* Philadelphia, Pa.: The University Museum, University of Pennsylvania, 1988.

Craine, Eugene R., et al., ed. *The Codex Pérez and The Book of Chilam Balam of Maní.* Norman, Okla.: University of Oklahoma Press, 1979.

Cuthbert, T. Patrick. *Maya Civilization.*

Smithsonian Exploring the Ancient World, Montreal and Washington, D.C.: St. Remy Press and Smithsonian Institution, 1993.

De Landa, Diego. *The Maya: Diego de Landa's Account of the Affairs of Yucatán.* Translated by A.R. Pagden. Chicago: J. Philip O'Hara, 1975.

Dalton, Bill. *Indonesia Handbook.* 4th ed., Chico, Calif.: Moon Publications, 1989.

Demarest, Arthur A. "Violent Saga of a Maya Kingdom." *National Geographic,* February 1993, 95-111.

Díaz del Castillo, Bernal. *The Conquest of New Spain.* Translated by J.M. Cohen. Harmondsworth, Middlesex, England: Penguin Books, 1963.

Garrett, Wilbur E. "La Ruta Maya." *National Geographic,* October 1989, 424-478.

Greene, Graham. *The Power and the Glory.* New York: The Viking Press, 1953.

Ferguson, William M. *Maya Ruins of Mexico in Color.* Norman, Okla.: University of Oklahoma Press, 1977.

Haviland, William A. *Cultural Anthropology.* 5th ed., New York: Holt, Rinehart and Winston Inc., 1987.

Kowalski, Jeff Karl. *The House of the Governor: A Maya Palace at Uxmal.* Norman, Okla.: University of Oklahoma Press, 1987.

Matheny, Ray T. "El Mirador: An Early Maya Metropolis Uncovered." *National Geographic,* September 1987, 317-339.

Maudslay, Alfred P. "In the Village of Savage Dogs." In *They Found the Buried Cities,* ed. Robert Wauchope. 185-189. Chicago: University of Chicago Press, 1965.

Miller, Mary. "Maya Masterpiece Revealed." *National Geographic,* February 1995, 50-69.

Morales, Demetrio Sodi. *The Maya World.* Mexico City, Mexico: Minutiae Mexicana, 1989.

Ogburn, William Fielding. "Inventions, Mental Ability and Culture" [List of independent inventions taken from "Are Inventions Inevitable? A Note on Social Evolution," by Dorothy Thomas, *Political Science Quarterly,* 27:1.] In *Social Change with Respect to Culture and Original Nature,* 80-102. Gloucester, Mass.: Peter Smith, 1922 (reprinted 1950, 1964).

Sabloff, Jeremy A. *The New Archaeology and the Ancient Maya.* New York: The Scientific American Library, 1990.

Schneider, Irene. "Dangerous Rapture." *Condé Nast Traveler,* May 1995, 122-124.

Somerlott, Robert. "Mayan Mexico: The Yucatan Peninsula and Chiapas." In *The Penguin Guide to Mexico,* ed. Alan Tucker. 632. New York: Penguin Group, 1991.

Spengler, Oswald. *The Decline of the West.* Vol. I. New York: Alfred A. Knopf, 1926.

Stephens, John L. *Incidents of Travel in Central America, Chiapas and Yucatan.* Vol. II. New York: Dover Publications, 1969 (originally published in 1841).

Stuart, George E., et al. *The Mysterious*

Maya. Washington, D.C.: The National Geographic Society, 1983.

Theroux, Alexander. "The Stendhal Syndrome." *Art & antiques*, April 1993, 72-77.

Thompson, J. Eric S. *Maya Archeologist*. Norman, Okla.: University of Oklahoma Press, 1963.

Turner, John Kenneth. *Barbarous Mexico*. Austin: University of Texas Press, 1969 (originally published in 1910).

Tylor, Sir Edward Burnett. *Researches into the Early History of Mankind and the Development of Civilization*. New York: Henry Holt, 1878.

White, Leslie A. *The Science of Culture*. New York: Grove Press, 1949.

White, Leslie A. "The Agricultural Revolution." In *The Evolution of Culture; the Development of Civilization to the Fall of Rome*, 281-302. New York: McGraw Hill, 1959.

White, Leslie A. *The Concept of Cultural Systems: A Key to Understanding Tribes and Nations*. New York: Columbia University Press, 1975.

Burma

Beyond Poverty: Extended Measures of Well-Being. U.S. Census Bureau, 1992. P70-No. 50. (available at http://www.census.gov/ftp-/pub/hhes/poverty/beyond/index.html).

Current Population Reports, Series P2, *Household and Family Characteristics*, table 1. U.S. Census Bureau, 1993 (available at http://www.census.gov/households and families/families by presence of own children).

Gross National Product, by Country: 1985 to 1993 (Table 1373); *Percent of Households Owning Selected Appliances, by Country: 1991* (Table 1376); and *Marriage and Divorce Rates, by Country: 1970 to 1992* (Table 1366). In *Statistical Abstract of the United States*, 115th ed., Washington, D.C.: U.S. Census Bureau, 1995.

1996 The State of the World's Children. United Nations, Dec. 11, 1995. Table 7: Women (includes statistics on adult female literacy; available at http://www.unicef.org-/sowc96-/swc96t7x.html).

Associated Press. "Burma air crash kills 49; toll of Americans 14; Tourism plane catches fire after warning of terrorism." *The Washington Post*, Oct. 12, 1987, A21.

Aung-Thwin, Maureen, et al. "Add Sanctions to the Pressure on Burma." *The Washington Post*, July 21, 1994, A31.

Bennett, William J. *The Index of Leading Cultural Indicators: Facts and Figures on the State of American Society*. New York: Touchstone, 1994.

Bunge, Frederica M., et al. *Burma: A Country Study*. 3rd ed., Washington, D.C.: Department of the Army, 1983.

Butterfield, Fox. "Growing Up Guai [Well Behaved]: The Chinese Passages." In *China:*

Alive in the Bitter Sea, 203-220. New York: Times Books, 1990.

Cockburn, Andrew. "Dilemma on the Irrawaddy." *Condé Nast Traveler*, June 1996, 130-141, 166-173.

Coil, Suzanne. *The Poor in America: Issues for the '90s*. Englewood Cliffs, N.J.: Julian Messner, 1989.

Cox, James. "Thailand grows as auto hub." *USA Today*, March 5, 1996, 1B, 2B.

Critser, Greg. "Way Beyond Rangoon." *Escape*, July 1996, 64-71.

De Koster, Katie, ed. *Poverty: Opposing Viewpoints*. Opposing Viewpoints. San Diego, Calif.: Greenhaven Press, 1994.

Fagan, Patrick F. "Behind the Census Bureau's Good News on Poverty." The Heritage Foundation, 1995. Executive Memorandum No. 431 (available at http://www.heritage.org/heritage/library/categories/healthwel/em431.html).

Fawcett, C.B. *Frontiers: A Study in Political Geography*. Oxford, England: Clarendon Press, 1918.

Gellhorn, Martha. *Travels with Myself and Another*. New York: Hippocrene Books, 1983.

Gugliotta, Guy. "Drawing the Poverty Line: A Calculation of Necessity." *The Washington Post*, May 10, 1993, A3.

Hodgson, Bryan. "Time and Again in Burma." *National Geographic*, July 1984, 90-121.

Howard, Philip K. *The Death of Common Sense: How Law is Suffocating America*. New York: Random House, 1994.

International Bank for Reconstruction and Development. *Poverty: World Development Report 1990*. Oxford: Oxford University Press, 1990.

Iyer, Pico. *Video Night in Kathmandu*. New York: Alfred A. Knopf, 1988.

James, Michael. "Lafayette Courts: 40 years from high hopes to oblivion." *The Baltimore Sun*, Aug. 16, 1995, 1A, 10A.

Kaylor, Robert. "Burma: A Hermit Nation Edging Into the Modern World." *U.S. News & World Report*, March 19, 1984, 64-65.

Kennedy, Paul. *Preparing for the Twenty-first Century*. New York: Random House, 1993.

Küng, Hans. *Christianity and the World Religions: Paths of Dialogue with Islam, Hinduism, and Buddhism*. Garden City, N.Y.: Doubleday & Co. Inc., 1986.

Lavelle, Robert, ed. *America's New War on Poverty*. San Francisco: KQED Books, 1995.

Mathews, Jay and Linda. "Children." In *One Billion: A China Chronicle*, 121-137. New York: Random House, 1983.

Michaels, James W. "Oh, Our Aching Angst." *Forbes*, Sept. 14, 1992, 47.

Morgan, Elizabeth. *Global Poverty and Personal Responsibility*. New York: Paulist Press, 1989.

Oo, Hnin Hlaing. "A few observations on a brief tourist trip to Burma." *Dawn* (monthly

news bulletin of the All Burma Students Democratic Front, Bangkok) 4 (2 1995): April/May 1995.

Pappas, Gregory, et al. "The increasing disparity in mortality between socioeconomic groups in the United States, 1960 and 1986." *The New England Journal of Medicine* 329 (2 1993): 103-109.

Polo, Marco. *The Travels*.

Rahula, Walpola. *What the Buddha Taught*. New York: Grove Press, 1974.

Reuters. "Burma Assailed on Human Rights." *The Washington Post*, Nov. 23, 1994, A16.

Reuters. "Despite Arrests, Burmese Democrats Meet and Vow to Press On." *The New York Times*, May 27, 1996, 5.

Reuters. "Train Crash in Burma Leaves 102 Dead." *The Washington Post*, Jan. 1, 1995, A30.

Rowntree, B. Seebohm. "Poverty Line." In *Encyclopædia Britannica*, 383-385. 18. Chicago: University of Chicago Press, 1948.

Samagalski, Alan, et al. "Buddhism," in *China: A Travel Survival Kit*. 2nd ed., Berkeley, Calif.: Lonely Planet, 1988, 50-52.

Shenon, Philip. "Head of Democratic Opposition is Released by Burmese Military; 6 Years' House Arrest Comes to an End as Junta Courts West." *The New York Times*, July 11, 1995, A1, A8.

Singer, Peter. *Practical Ethics*. Fakenham, Norfolk: Cambridge University Press, 1979.

Sowell, Thomas. *The Economics and Politics of Race*. New York: Quill, 1983.

Sun, Lena H. "In China, Flying Is a Test of Valor." *The Washington Post*, Dec. 8, 1993, A25.

Swerdlow, Joel L. "Burma, the Richest of Poor Countries." *National Geographic*, July 1995, 70-97.

Theroux, Paul. *The Great Railway Bazaar: By Train Through Asia*. New York: Washington Square Press, 1975.

U.S. State Department. *Burma Human Rights Practices, 1995*. March 1996.

United Nations Development Programme team. "Opulence and Human Development." In *Human Development Report 1994*, 14-17. New York, Oxford: Oxford University Press, 1994.

Updike, John. "The Space to Chase Rainbows." *Forbes*, Sept. 14, 1992, 72.

Weymouth, Lally. "SmackLand; It's Time to Attack the Drug Lords in Burma." *The Washington Post*, March 24, 1995, A23.

Wilson, James Q. "The contradictions of an advanced capitalist state." *Forbes*, Sept. 14, 1992, 110-118.

Zinsmeister, Karl, ed. "Incredible Shrinking Incomes." *The American Enterprise*, January/February 1995, 17.

Java and Bali

The Bible: Revised Standard Version.

Al-Qur'an.

Catechism of the Catholic Church. Liguori, Missouri: Liguori Publications, 1994.

Blamires, Harry, et al. "Heaven & Hell: Who will go where and why." *Christianity Today*, May 27, 1991, 29-39.

Breig, James. "Beyond the afterlife: What U.S. Catholic readers believe about the afterlife." *U.S. Catholic*, May 1983, 6-18.

Bryan, C.D.B. "Bali: Island of Dieties and Dance." *National Geographic Traveler*, March/April 1990, 91-106.

Clancy, Flora Simmons. *Pyramids*. Montreal and Washington, D.C.: St. Remy Press and Smithsonian Institution, 1994.

Clapp, Rodney. "Rumors of heaven; A new book fuels our perennial interest in life after death." *Christianity Today*, Oct. 7, 1988, 16-20.

Costello, Father Andy. "Eternal life is on the line." *U.S. Catholic*, August 1992, 40-2.

Covarrubias, Miguel. *Island of Bali*. New York: Alfred A. Knopf, 1937.

Cummings, Joe, et al. *Indonesia: Travel Survival Kit*. 2nd ed., Berkeley, Calif.: Lonely Planet, 1990.

Dalton, Bill. *Indonesia Handbook*. 4th ed., Chico, Calif.: Moon Publications, 1989.

Delumeau, Jean. *History of Paradise; the Garden of Eden in myth and tradition*. New York: Continuum, 1995.

Doyle, Brian. "Winging it: What Catholics believe about Heaven." *U.S. Catholic*, June 1990, 6-13.

Eiseman, Fred B. Jr. *Bali and Lombok*. New York: Prentice Hall Travel, 1993.

Funke, Phyllis. "Island of the Gods." *Travel/Holiday*, May 1981, 64-84.

Holmquist, David. "Will There Be Baseball in Heaven?" *Christianity Today*, Jan. 10, 1994, 30-33.

Kaylor, Robert. "Bali: No Longer Undiscovered but 'Still Paradise'." *U.S. News & World Report*, Jan. 16, 1984, 66-67.

Kreeft, Peter J. *Everything You Ever Wanted to Know About Heaven, but Never Dreamed of Asking*. New York: Harper & Row, 1982.

McAneny, Leslie. "It Was a Very Bad Year: Belief in Hell and the Devil on the Rise." *The Gallup Poll Monthly*, January 1995, 14-15 (available at http://www.gallup.com/newsletter/jan95/beliefs_poll.html).

McDannell, Colleen, et al. *Heaven: A History*. New Haven and London: Yale University Press, 1988.

McPhee, Colin. *A House in Bali*. Oxford: Oxford University Press, 1944.

Oey, Eric, ed. *Bali: Island of the Gods*. Lincolnwood, Ill.: Passport Books, 1995.

Schaefer, John. "Indonesia" [describes gamelan music]. In *New Sounds: A Listener's Guide to New Music*, 143-146. New York: Harper & Row, 1987.

Wheeler, Tony. *South-East Asia on a Shoestring*. 4th ed., Victoria, Australia: Lonely Planet, 1982.

Wise, Jeff. "Is the Hippie Circuit Washed Up?" *The New York Times Magazine*, Nov. 13, 1994, 58.

Woodward, Kenneth L. "Heaven; This is the season to search for new meaning in old familiar places." *Newsweek,* March 27, 1989, 52-55.

Brazil

"The 50 Most Beautiful People in the World." *People*, May 3, 1993, 54-149.

"The 50 Most Beautiful People in the World." *People*, May 8, 1995, 66-182.

Enrollment in Foreign Language Courses, grades 9-12 (Table 57). In *Digest of Education Statistics 1994*, Washington, D.C.: U.S. Department of Education, Office of Educational Research and Improvement, 1994.

Higher Education Registration in Foreign Language (Table 293); *Bachelor's Degrees Earned, by Field* (Table 300). In *Statistical Abstract of the United States 1995*, 115th ed., Washington, D.C.: U.S. Bureau of the Census, 1995.

Population Census 1993 (Diretoria de Pesquisas), IBGE (Fundaçao Instituto Brasileiro de Geografia e Estatistica) (available at http://www.ibge.gov.br; racial statistics available in Portuguese only).

Population of States on July 1, 1992 by race. Administrative Records and Methodology Research Branch, U.S. Census Bureau, Sept. 20, 1995. PPL-3 (available at http://www.census.gov/ftp/pub/population/estimate-extract/state/intnttbl1.tbl).

Minority Rights Group, ed. *No Longer Invisible: Afro-Latin Americans Today*. London: Minority Rights Publications, 1995.

Andrews, George Reid. "Racial Inequality in Brazil and the United States: A Statistical Comparison." *Journal of Social History* 26:2 (1992): 229-263.

Andrews, George Reid. (1980). *The Afro-Argentines of Buenos Aires, 1800-1900*. Madison, Wis.: University of Wisconsin Press.

Banks, Vic. *The Pantanal: Brazil's Forgotten Wilderness*. San Francisco: Sierra Club Books, 1991.

Bernard, Hans-Ulrich, ed. *Amazon Wildlife*. Insight Guides. Singapore: APA Houghton Mifflin, 1993.

Besharov, Douglas J., et al. "One Flesh: America is experiencing an unprecedented increase in black-white intermarriage." *The New Democrat*, July/August 1996, 19-21.

Bloom, Pamela. *Fielding's Brazil 1993*. New York: William Morrow, 1993.

Bradbury, Alex. *Backcountry Brazil: The Pantanal, Amazon and North-East Coast*. Chalfont St. Peter, Bucks, England: Bradt Publications, 1990.

Brooke, James. "U.S. Blacks Find Study in Brazil a Bittersweet Experience." *The New York Times*, June 12, 1994, A17.

Brooke, James. "Long Neglected, Colombia's Blacks Win Changes." *The New York Times*, March 29, 1994, A3.

Brown, Diana. "Umbanda and Class Relations in Brazil." In *Brazil: Anthropological Perspectives*, ed. Maxine L. Margolis and William E. Carter. 270-304. New York: Columbia University Press, 1979.

Burns, E. Bradford. *A History of Brazil*. 2nd ed., New York: Columbia University Press, 1980.

Crow, Ben, et al. *Third World Atlas*. Milton Keynes, England, and Philadelphia: Open University Press, 1983.

D'Souza, Dinesh. *The End of Racism*. New York: The Free Press, 1995.

Dawood, Dr. Richard. "Are these pills safe? Controversy over antimalarial drug [Lariam]." *Condé Nast Traveler*, April 1996, 37-42.

Degler, Carl N. *Neither Black Nor White: Slavery and Race Relations in Brazil and the United States*. New York: Macmillan, 1971.

Draffen, Andrew, et al. *Brazil: Travel Survival Kit*. 2nd ed., Hawthorn, Australia: Lonely Planet, 1992.

Dunning, John S. *South American Birds: A Photographic Aid to Identification*. Newton Square, Pa.: Harrowood Books, 1987.

Dutcher, Nadine. *Overview of Foreign Language Education in the United States*. Center for Applied Linguistics, Washington, D.C., Spring 1996. NCBE Resource Collection Series, No. 6 (available at http://www.ncbe.gwu.edu/ncbepubs/resource/foreign.html).

Ember, Carol R., et al. *Cultural Anthropology*. Englewood Cliffs, N.J.: Prentice-Hall, 1985.

Escobar, Gabriel. "Economist Winning Brazilian Election; Cardoso's Margin Appears to Preclude Runoff." *The Washington Post*, Oct. 4, 1994, A11.

FitzGerald, Frances. "States of Mind." In *Fire in the Lake: The Vietnamese and the Americans in Vietnam*, 3-31. Boston: Little, Brown and Company, 1972.

Fleming, Mali Michelle. "African Legacy" [description of photographic exhibit, "Africa's Legacy in Mexico: Photographs by Tony Gleaton"]. *Hispanic*, Feb. 28, 1994, 86.

Freyre, Gilberto. *New World in the Tropics: The Culture of Modern Brazil*. New York: Vintage Books, 1945.

Gallup, George Jr., et al. "For First Time, More Americans Approve of Interracial Marriage Than Disapprove." *The Gallup Poll Monthly* 311 (August 1991): 60.

Goslin, Priscilla Ann. *How to Be a Carioca*. Rio de Janeiro: Twocan Press, 1991.

Hamayan, Else. *The Need for Foreign Language Competence in the United States*. ERIC Clearinghouse on Languages and Linguistics, Washington, D.C., 1986. ED276304 (available by searching for "language competence" at gopher://gopher.ed.gov/11/programs/ERIC/searchs)

Harris, Ron. "U.S. Blacks Seek a Part of

Their History in Brazil." *The Los Angeles Times,* Sept. 5, 1994, A1, A12, 13.

Harris, Marvin, et al. "Who Are the Whites? Imposed Census Categories and the Racial Demography of Brazil." *Social Forces* 72:2 (December 1993): 451-462.

Haviland, William A. *Cultural Anthropology.* 5th ed., New York: Holt, Rinehart and Winston, 1987.

Hellwig, David J. "Racial Paradise or Run-Around? Afro-North American Views of Race Relations in Brazil." *American Studies* 31:2 (Fall 1990): 43-60.

Hayakawa, S.I. *Language in Thought and Action.* New York: Harcourt Brace Jovanovich, 1972.

Holmes, Steven A. "Number of Black-White Couples is Rising Sharply, Study Says." *The New York Times,* July 4, 1996, A16.

Humboldt, Alexander von and Aimé Bonpland. "Cuba and the Slave Trade." In *Personal narrative of travels to the equinoctial regions of America during the years 1799-1804,* 228-284. III. London: Henry G. Bohn, 1853.

Jackson, Richard L. "The Color Crisis in Latin America." *Black World* 24 (July 1975): 4-21.

Kane, Joe. *Running the Amazon.* New York: Vintage Books, 1989.

Knight, Franklin W. "Slavery." In *Encyclopedia Americana,* 19-24, vol. 25. Danbury, Conn.: Grolier Inc., 1991.

Krich, John. *Why Is This Country Dancing?* New York: Simon & Schuster, 1993.

Lovejoy, Paul E., ed. *Africans in Bondage: Studies in Slavery and the Slave Trade.* Madison, Wis.: African Studies Program, University of Wisconsin-Madison, 1986.

Moore, David W., et al. "No Immediate Signs Simpson Trial Intensified Racial Animosity." *The Gallup Poll Monthly* 361 (October 1995): 2 (available at http://www.gallup.com/newsletter/oct95/5post-oj.html).

Nyrop, Richard F. *Brazil: A Country Study.* 4th ed., Washington, D.C.: Superintendent of Documents, 1982.

Oliner, Samuel P. and Pearl M. *The Altruistic Personality: Rescuers of Jews in Nazi Europe.* New York: The Free Press, 1988.

Page, Joseph A. *The Brazilians.* Reading, Mass.: Addison-Wesley, 1995.

Palmer, Colin A. "From Africa to the Americas: Ethnicity in the Early Black Communities of the Americas." *Journal of World History* 6:2 (Fall 1995): 223-236.

Paset, Pamela S., et al. "Black and White Women's Attitudes Toward Interracial Marriage." *Psychological Reports* 69 (December 1991) 3: 753.

Pierson, Donald. *Negroes in Brazil: A Study of Race Contact at Bahia.* Carbondale, Ill.: Southern Illinois University Press, 1942, 1967.

Poppino, Rollie E. *Brazil: The Land and People.* New York: Oxford University Press, 1973.

Preston, Julia. "Brazil Through the Back Door; The Wild Harmony of the Pantanal." *The Washington Post,* July 21, 1991, E1.

Puente, Maria. "Multiracial families want identity respected." *USA Today,* Jan. 2, 1996, 1A, 2A.

Puente, Maria. "Census 2000: Countdown to the millennium." *USA Today,* Jan. 2, 1996, 1A.

Rodman, Dennis. "Madonna: An Old-Fashioned Tale of Romance." In *Bad as I Wanna Be,* written with Tim Keown. 181-206. New York: Delacorte Press, 1996.

Rodrigues, Jose Honorio. *The Brazilians: Their Character and Aspirations.* Austin, Texas: University of Texas Press, 1967.

Salzman, Jack, et al., ed. "South Carolina," *Encyclopedia of African-American Culture and History.* Vol. 5. New York: Macmillan Library Reference USA, 1996.

Schemo, Diana Jean. "Brazilians Chained to Jobs, and Desperate." *The New York Times,* Aug. 10, 1995, A1, A6.

Schemo, Diana Jean. "São Paolo Journal; The Elevator Doesn't Lie: Intolerance in Brazil." *The New York Times,* Aug. 30, 1995, A4.

Shoumatoff, Alex. *The Capital of Hope* [examines construction of Brasilia]. New York: Coward, McCann & Geoghegan, 1980.

Simpson, George Eaton. *Racial and Cultural Minorities; An Analysis of Prejudice and Discrimination.* 4th ed., New York: Harper & Row, 1972.

Skidmore, Thomas E. "Bi-Racial U.S.A. vs. Multi-Racial Brazil: Is the Contrast Still Valid?" *Journal of Latin American Studies* 25 (May 1993): 373-386.

Sowell, Thomas. *The Economics and Politics of Race.* New York: Quill, 1983.

Sowell, Thomas. *Race and Culture: A World View.* New York: BasicBooks, 1994.

Spickard, Paul R. *Mixed Blood: Intermarriage and Ethnic Identity in Twentieth-Century America.* Madison, Wis.: University of Wisconsin Press, 1989.

Stone, Norman, ed. *The Times Atlas of World History.* 3rd ed., Maplewood, N.J.: Hammond, 1989.

Tannenbaum, Frank. *Slave and Citizen: The Negro in the Americas.* New York: Knopf, 1947.

Thompson, Vincent Bakpetu. *The Making of the African Diaspora in the Americas, 1441-1900.* Essex, England: Longman Group UK Limited, 1987.

Thurow, Lester. *Head to Head: The Coming Economic Battle among Japan, Europe, and America.* New York: William Morrow and Company, 1992.

Updike, John. *Brazil.* New York: Alfred A. Knopf, 1994.

Washington, Joseph R. Jr. *Marriage in Black and White.* Boston: Beacon Press, 1970.

Weil, Thomas E., et al. *Area Handbook for Brazil.* 3rd ed., Washington, D.C.: Foreign Area Studies Division of American University, 1975.

Whitney, Hunter. Review: "In the Cities and Jungles of Brazil," by Paul Rambali. *Escape,* Summer 1995, 83.

Wilbanks, T.J. "Geography Education in National Context." *Journal of Geography* 93 (1 January 1994): 43-45.

Williams, Eric. *Capitalism and Slavery.* London: Andre Deutsch Limited, 1964.

Williamson, Joel. *New People: Miscegenation and Mulattoes in the United States.* New York: The Free Press, 1980.

Overall lessons

Brooks, Jacqueline Grennon, et al. *The Case for Constructivist Classrooms.* Alexandria, Va: Association for Supervision and Curriculum Development, 1993.

Chaudhuri, K.N. "Perpetual memory." In *Asia Before Europe: Economy and Civilisation of the Indian Ocean from the Rise of Islam to 1750,* 375-377. Cambridge, England: Cambridge University Press, 1990.

Hauser, Philip M. "The Chaotic Society: Product of the Social Morphological Revolution." In *Social Change: Sources, Patterns and Consequences,* ed. Amitai Etzioni and Eva Etzioni-Halevy. 428-442. 2nd ed. New York: BasicBooks, 1973.

Ryan, Kevin, et al. *Those Who Can, Teach.* Boston: Houghton Mifflin, 1995.

Sowell, Thomas. *Race and Culture: A World View.* New York: BasicBooks, 1994.

INDEX

The Similan Islands in Thailand shelter coral reefs, habitats of great biological diversity.

MORE ADVANCE PRAISE

This is just wonderful, a joy to read. The China train trip and the Irish analysis are worth the price of admission.

Jay Mathews, author with his wife, Linda, of One Billion: A China Chronicle;
first Washington Post bureau chief in Beijing

An Amateur's Guide to the Planet describes every experience I had in East Africa. Enjoyable, sobering, thoughtful and thought-provoking, it captures the essence of the wildlife viewing and the harsh contrast of African politics and ever-present danger of adventure travel.

Jane Burtnett of Scottsdale, Ariz., who visited all seven continents before her 40th birthday

I found myself torn between laughter and understanding the seriousness of the situation Madagascar faces. I like the fact the chapter ends with a positive outlook and gives credit to the organizations that are trying to help.

World traveler Stephany Porter of Pasadena, Maryland

An Amateur's Guide to the Planet looks like it was fun to write, and will be fun to read. The write-up drawing parallels between the United States and Greece is quite good and thought-provoking.

Yoriko Kishimoto, author of The Third Century: America's Resurgence in the Asian Era

The Borneo chapter conveys a great deal of what it is like to BE in the interior very well. The information on what it takes to be a good bush pilot is particularly good.

Professor Allen R. Maxwell, University of Alabama

About the author

Jeannette Belliveau was born in 1954 in Washington, D.C., and grew up in Rockville, Maryland. She graduated in 1976 as a journalism major from the University of Maryland at College Park.

Belliveau worked at newspapers in Maryland (1976-1981, 1986) and England (1981-1985) before becoming a Metro copy editor and an assistant financial editor at the *Baltimore Sun* (1987-92) and a graphics editor on the National Desk of *The Washington Post* (1992-95).

From 1985 through 1994, she traveled in six continents, mostly during vacations. In 1991, she revisited parts of Asia as a Jefferson Fellow, sponsored by the East-West Center in Honolulu, Hawaii.

She lives in the maritime district of Fells Point in East Baltimore with her husband, artist and historian Lamont W. Harvey, and their singing Shetland sheepdog.